Mental Health, Neurodiversity, and Criminal Justice

Melanie Clark Mogavero

Mental Health, Neurodiversity, and Criminal Justice

A Guide for Students and Practitioners

palgrave
macmillan

Melanie Clark Mogavero
Criminal Justice
Georgian Court University
Lakewood, NJ, USA

ISBN 978-3-031-88815-1 ISBN 978-3-031-88816-8 (eBook)
https://doi.org/10.1007/978-3-031-88816-8

Cover credit: It was created by eStudio.

This Palgrave Macmillan imprint is published by the registered company Springer Nature Switzerland AG
The registered company address is: Gewerbestrasse 11, 6330 Cham, Switzerland

Preface

Mental health and its connection to criminal behavior has been a topic of intense debate, particularly in recent years after multiple school shootings. On December 14, 2012, 20-year-old Adam Lanza shot and killed his mother, Nancy Lanza, in their home in Newtown, Connecticut. Shortly after, he walked into Sandy Hook Elementary School and shot and killed 20 first-graders and six staff members. Lanza then turned the gun on himself before police arrived. Investigations into the shootings focused on Lanza's mental health. Lanza was diagnosed with autism at age 13, and media reports described him as a "mentally ill recluse" (Smith, 2013). The link between autism and violence sparked a controversial debate, particularly after the May 21, 2014, Washington Post headline, *Study: Significant' Statistical Link Between Mass Murder and Autism, Brain Injury.* Other researchers disputed the findings, calling them "anecdotal and speculative" (McCoy, 2014).

On November 30, 2021, 15-year-old Ethan Crumbley, a sophomore at Oxford High School in Oxford, Michigan, shot and killed four students, and wounded six other students and one teacher. Crumbley was charged as an adult, and prosecutors sought a prison sentence of life without the possibility of parole. Again, an investigation into the shootings focused on Crumbley's mental health, especially when his defense attorney entered an insanity defense plea (Burke, 2022). His mental health was a primary focus in the media, who described him as a "feral child" and "mentally ill" (Sanchez et al., 2023). Psychologist Dr. King conducted his mental health evaluation and diagnosed Crumbley with several mental illnesses. At trial, Dr. King testified for his defense team and claimed he was experiencing "psychosis, a break from reality" (White, 2023). Crumbley eventually pleaded guilty to terrorism causing death, first-degree murder, and 19 other charges. In December 2023, he was sentenced to life in prison without parole, the most severe punishment allowed for a juvenile in the United States (US) (Sanchez et al., 2023).

Misconceptions linking autism or mental illness with violence were propagated by media portrayals of notorious murder cases (Allely & Faccini, 2017; Palermo & Bogaerts, 2015). High-profile cases that link mental health to violence lead to assumptions that people with mental illnesses are more prone to commit acts of violence. On the contrary, most people with mental illnesses are not more dangerous or violent than those in the general population (Elbogen & Johnson, 2009) and are more likely to be victims of crime (Desmarais et al., 2014; Van Dorn et al., 2012). Insanity defense pleas are also extremely rare and comprise less than 2% of cases (Cirincione et al., 1995). Although the insanity defense is covered in Chapter 12, this book focuses on the more common justice system interactions among those with mental illnesses and disabilities as defendants, victims, and witnesses.

This book aims to provide current and future practitioners with the knowledge and tools to support the unique needs of those with mental illnesses, substance use disorders (SUDs), juveniles, and those with neurodevelopmental disabilities (NDDs). Although not all practitioners are unfamiliar with the needs of these populations, the many nuances of crime and behavior create confusion when handling such individuals as they navigate through the complex justice system. Unfamiliarity can lead to subsequent actions that can worsen one's mental or physical well-being, legal situation, and even miscarriages of justice. This book addresses these challenges by providing details of current and past policies, their effectiveness, and recommendations to become effective and confident practitioners.

Special Features of This Book

This book contains standard and unique features to provide readers with the most comprehensive information and maximum learning experience.

1. **Abstract and Learning Objectives**—Each chapter contains an abstract—a brief summary to allow readers to gather the essence of the chapter's content. The learning objectives listed under each abstract provide readers with valuable, clear learning expectations of what is covered.
2. **Legal Case Briefs**—This book contains 32 legal case briefs of State, Federal, and US Supreme Court cases, with Facts, Issues, and Outcomes with decisions, to give readers detailed context of **case law** practices. Typically, with the formation of case law, a previous law or current practice is challenged in court to violate one more of the constitutional amendments. Much of the policy and practice in the criminal justice and mental health systems have been determined by case law based on judicial decisions rather than statutes or regulations.
3. **Practitioner Spotlights**—Nine chapters spotlight various justice system practitioners to provide readers with first-hand knowledge and experience of their profession. All nine practitioners provide guidance on what is most important to know and how they successfully work with persons with mental illnesses or disabilities.
4. **Real Case Examples**—Twelve chapters provide real-life case examples to provide context and allow readers to observe how the concepts presented in the chapter are applied. This book contains eight anonymous cases and six high-profile cases of predominantly violent or sexual offenses. The cases also provide a "human context" in the application of law and policy with the intersection of mental health.
5. **Key Terms and Chapter Questions**—Each chapter concludes with a list of terms and chapter review questions. The terms are in boldface font and have precise and technical meanings to help readers understand the chapter's content. Some terms are defined in the chapter text, and all have definitions provided in the glossary. The questions at the end of each chapter focus on the main topics and allow readers to review or apply their newfound knowledge.
6. **Scholarly References and Suggested Readings**—The sources used throughout each chapter include peer-reviewed scholarly journals, government reports, historical documents, and books by academic publishers to provide the most credible, relevant, accurate, and authoritative information. Readers will find a comprehensive list of scholarly references and suggested reading to enhance their knowledge or follow up on particular topics.

7. **Glossary and Index**—The glossary at the end of the book provides a clear and concise definition of each key term mentioned in the book. The index at the end also includes a list of terms, names of significant people, legislation, and court cases, identifying the pages in which these are presented.

Lakewood, USA Melanie Clark Mogavero

References

Allely, C.S., & Faccini, L. (2017). "Path to intended violence" model to understand mass violence in the case of Elliot Rodger. *Aggression and Violent Behavior, 37*, 201–209. http://dx.doi.org/10.1016/j.avb.2017.09.005

Burke, M. (2022, January 27). Oxford High School shooting suspect to pursue insanity defense. *NBC News.* https://www.nbcnews.com/news/us-news/oxford-high-school-shooting-suspect-pursue-insanity-defense-rcna13821

Cirincione, C., Steadman, H. J., & McGreevy, M. A. (1995). Rates of insanity acquittals and the factors associated with successful insanity pleas. *The Bulletin of the American Academy of Psychiatry and the Law, 23*(3), 399–409.

Desmarais, S. L., Van Dorn, R. A., Johnson, K. L., Grimm, K. J., Douglas, K. S., & Swartz, M. S. (2014). Community violence perpetration and victimization among adults with mental illnesses. *American Journal of Public Health, 104*(12), 2342–2349. https://doi.org/10.2105/AJPH.2013.301680

Elbogen, E., & Johnson, S. C. (2009). The intricate link between violence and mental disorder. Results from the National Epidemiologic Survey on Alcohol and Related Conditions. *Archives of General Psychiatry, 66*(2),152–161. https://doi.org/10.1001/archgenpsychiatry.2008.537

McCoy, T. (2014, May 21). Study: 'Significant' statistical link between mass murder and autism, brain injury. *Washington Post.* https://www.washingtonpost.com/news/morning-mix/wp/2014/05/21/study-finds-significant-portion-of-mass-murderers-and-serial-killers-had-neurological-disorders-including-autism/

Palermo, M. T., & Bogaerts, S. (2015). The dangers of posthumous diagnoses and the unintended consequences of facile associations: Jeffrey Dahmer and autism spectrum disorders. *International Journal of Offender Therapy and Comparative Criminology, 59*(14), 1564–1579. https://doi.org/10.1177/0306624X14550642

Sanchez, R., Brown, N., & Sangal, A. (2023, December 8). Ethan Crumbley sentenced to life in prison without parole for killing 4 students in Michigan school shooting. *CNN*. https://www.cnn.com/2023/12/08/us/oxford-shooting-ethan-crumbley-sentencing/index.html

Smith, M. (2013, November 26). Sandy Hook killer took motive to his grave. *CNN*. https://www.cnn.com/2013/11/25/justice/sandy-hook-shooting-report/index.html

Van Dorn, R., Volavka, J., & Johnson, N. (2012). Mental disorder and violence: Is there a relationship beyond substance use? *Social Psychiatry and Psychiatric Epidemiology: The International Journal for Research in Social and Genetic Epidemiology and Mental Health Services, 47*(3), 487–503. https://doi.org/10.1007/s00127-011-0356-x

White, E. (2023, August 1). Oxford school shooter was 'feral child' abandoned by parents, defense psychologist says. *Associated Press*. https://apnews.com/article/oxford-school-shooting-ethan-crumbley-sentencing-620f26e9fc28919e5a5d48fb0b71fa3e

Acknowledgments I would first like to thank and acknowledge all those who work in and with the criminal justice system, juvenile justice system, and mental health system. No words can adequately describe the importance of your work, as it ensures the safety, protection, and well-being of the community and the pursuit of justice. I would also like to thank the dedicated practitioners who shared their wisdom and their occupational success with me: Chief Mitch Little, Lieutenant Dr. Robert Louden, Corporal John Burke, Mark Mahoney, Elizabeth Kelley, Cristina Russo, Joshua Wolarik, Samantha Etzi, and Major Luis Soto.

I also acknowledge many others who assisted me in making this project possible. I thank my colleagues at Georgian Court University for their endless support and encouragement, including the members of the Department of Crime and Justice Studies, Dr. Anna King, Dr. Cynthia Ninivaggi, Marny Requa, JD, with a special acknowledgment to Dr. Matthew Sheridan for his guidance on my book proposal. I thank the members of the Sabbatical Committee (Dr. Scott Bennett, Dr. Lili Bruess, and Dr. Louise Wootton), Dr. Mary Chinery, Dr. Janice Warner, and Dr. Joseph Marbach for supporting my sabbatical application, and the Board of Trustees for granting me a sabbatical to make this project possible.

I acknowledge my colleagues at the Drexel University Autism Institute at the Policy and Analytics Center. A special thank you to Dr. Lindsay Shea for selecting me to work on the autism and criminal justice system project and Kaitlin Koffer Miller and Dylan Cooper for all your efforts and coordination on the project. Working with you on this project led me to develop a deeper understanding of the needs and resources those with mental health and disabilities require when encountering and navigating the complexities of the criminal justice system. I thank INSAR for recognizing this important topic and awarding Drexel University Autism Institute at the Policy and Analytics Center the grant to make these efforts possible.

I also acknowledge the strength and bravery of the individuals and their families in the cases presented in this book. A special thank you to the anonymous individuals and their families for sharing their stories with me. All the cases in this book remind me why the justice and mental health systems require more resources and the best and most dedicated people working in them.

I thank my students for inspiring me to write this book and motivating me to be a better educator and fight for social justice for oppressed groups in our criminal justice system. Finally, I thank my family for all their patience, support, and encouragement, including my husband, parents, stepparents, and siblings, with a special acknowledgment to my brother, Garret, who inspires me every day to fight and advocate for justice.

Competing Interests The author has no competing interests to declare that are relevant to the content of this manuscript.

Contents

List of Figures

Part I

Understanding Mental Health, Neurodiversity, and Cognitive Development

1

Introduction to Mental Health, Neurodiversity, and Criminal Justice

Learning Objectives

After this chapter, readers should be able to understand the:

(1) Overview and objectives of this book.
(2) The difference between person-first and identify-first language and their importance
(3) Steps and processes of the criminal justice system and appellate court system
(4) The role of the mental health system in the criminal justice system
(5) Development and application of the Sequential Intercept Model.

Introduction

The prologue highlighted high-profile cases and the consequential misconceptions about those with mental illnesses and disabilities. Unfortunately, those with mental illnesses, substance use disorders (SUDs), and disabilities have increasingly been involved in the criminal justice system for various matters. Misconceptions from criminal justice practitioners could lead to negative interactions, experiences, and outcomes. Because those with mental illnesses, substance use disorders, and disabilities are often marginalized and experience stigma and discrimination, justice system practitioners failing to

M. C. Mogavero, *Mental Health, Neurodiversity, and Criminal Justice*,
https://doi.org/10.1007/978-3-031-88816-8_1

address these populations respectfully, including using humanizing language and avoiding outdated terms, could negatively impact the interaction and erode trust. In this introductory chapter, these topics are presented to assist readers in becoming knowledgeable consumers of this book's content. A brief overview of the criminal justice system (CJS) is included to familiarize readers with standard legal terms used throughout the rest of the book. To ensure the best outcomes for all, the criminal justice system should collaborate with the mental health system (MHS) and other service providers.

A Note About Evolving Language and Terms: Words Matter

Many terms have been used to describe people with mental illnesses and disabilities over time. These terms were used to identify those needing specialized care or treatment but often were used to stigmatize or isolate individuals. This topic is addressed in Chapters 2, 3, and 7, but any terms used in this book deemed offensive by today's standards are used from a historical perspective, as they were deemed appropriate at the time. When using other terms, they are placed in quotation marks to indicate that these were the appropriate terms at the time yet would be offensive if used today. When CJS practitioners encounter people with mental illnesses and disabilities, it is of the utmost importance to demonstrate respect and compassion. The use of respectful and unbiased language is an essential first step.

Intellectual Disability

Significant changes have been made to describe and diagnose people with intellectual developmental disorder or intellectual disabilities. Before any formal diagnostic terms, "feeble-minded" was commonly used in the United States (US) and Europe to broadly describe those with reduced mental capacity. The first standardized **IQ** (intelligence quotient) **test** in 1905 used the terms "idiot" and "imbecile" to describe one's age-functioning level (Huey, 1912). The first edition of the Diagnostic and Statistical Manual of Mental Disorders (DSM-I), published by the American Psychiatric Association (APA) in 1952, used the diagnostic term, "mental deficiency" and coded levels of severity by IQ scores: "Moron" (IQ < 50), "Imbecility" (IQ < 20), and "Idiocy" (when familial or hereditary) (*see* Chapter 3 of this book for details). The term "retard," meaning slow or delayed, was used to describe one's cognitive functioning, and in the DSM-II, "mental retardation" became the official diagnosis and replaced "mental deficiency" (APA, 1968). The revised third and fourth editions of the DSM also used this diagnostic term (APA, 1987, 2000). When the APA published the fifth edition of the DSM in 2013 (DSM-5), the diagnosis changed to intellectual developmental disorder (IDD) or ID (APA, 2013).

Terms initially intended to describe medical conditions or identify those needing specialized care, over time, morphed into non-medical, stigmatizing, and derogatory words (Wehmeyer et al., 2000). Terms such as "retard," "retardation," and "retarded" have become offensive and disrespectful to the disability community. The Arc, a national organization that has served the disability community since 1953, has acknowledged on its website: "We...strongly believe the only 'r-word' that should be used when referring to people with intellectual and developmental disabilities is respect" (The Arc, 2024a). Following these changing social views, intellectual disability became the preferred term by various professionals, the lay public, and advocacy groups (APA, 2013). In 2010, President Barak Obama signed Rosa's Law, which amended several Federal Acts and required the removal of the terms "mental retardation" and "mentally retarded" from federal use. In this book, the term intellectual disability (abbreviated to ID) is used to refer to individuals diagnosed with intellectual developmental disorder or a similar diagnosis from previous versions of the DSM, except Chapter 7, when using other terms from a historical perspective.

Mental Health Terminology

There are also many stigmatizing and dehumanizing terms to describe people with mental illnesses. Rose et al. (2007) identified 250 offensive labels, and some of the more frequently used terms identified were "nuts," "psycho," "crazy," and "loony" (short for lunatic). The term "lunatic" was also used as a term for insanity, where one was determined not legally responsible for their actions (*see* Queen v. M'Naghten, 1843 in Chapter 12). More recent use of the term "lunatic" was used to stigmatize and describe someone as "crazy" or "foolish" (Riva et al., 2011). When used as a historical reference, such terms will be in quotation marks, even in direct quotes from historical figures, to demonstrate that the term is being used historically and not in a disrespectful or stigmatizing manner. The term, insane can be considered disrespectful when describing someone as having a mental illness (Rose et al., 2007); however, in this book, insane is used as a legal term, not a psychological term.

Disability Versus Disorder Versus Illness

As renowned psychologist Dr. Simon Baron-Cohen explained, the terms "disability" and "disorder" are not synonymous. Disability necessitates acceptance of one's differences, where one requires societal support and accommodations. Disorder, however, assumes one has an illness or condition that requires treatment or a cure (Baron-Cohen, 2017). Although the DSM uses the term "mental disorder" broadly, both ID and autism are under the category of NDDs. In this book, both conditions are referred to as a disability that denotes acceptance, support, and necessary accommodations in the CJS. However, mental illness and substance use disorder are referred to as disorders that require treatment to manage symptoms, in addition to support and accommodations in the CJS. The terms "mental disorder" and "mental illness" are both widely accepted terms. The Centers for Disease Control and Prevention (CDC) and the National Institutes of Health refer to mental disorders as illnesses and use the terms interchangeably (CDC, 2024; NIH, 2024a, 2024b). According to the National Institutes of Health,

> A disorder is a disturbance of normal functioning of the mind or body. ... In mental health, the terms mental disorder, mental illness, and psychiatric disorder are used interchangeably. Mental disorders are defined as "conditions that affect your thinking, feeling, mood, and behavior...They can affect your ability to relate to others and function each day. (NIH, 2024b)

The DSM-5-TR (APA, 2022) uses the term mental disorder broadly and includes disorders consistent with the above definition of mental illness, but also other conditions that are not considered "illnesses," such as learning disabilities and developmental disorders. According to the DSM-5-TR, a mental disorder is defined as,

> a syndrome characterized by clinically significant disturbance in an individual's cognition, emotion regulation, or behavior that reflects a dysfunction in the psychological, biological, or developmental processes underlying mental functioning. Mental disorders are usually associated with significant distress or disability in social, occupational, or other important activities. (APA, 2022, p. 14)

The DSM-5-TR lists and defines hundreds of different mental disorders, which are heterogeneous and present a range of symptoms, severity, and experiences. To avoid confusion, throughout this book, the term mental illness is used when referring to psychiatric disorders such as bipolar disorder or schizophrenia, disability when referring to developmental disabilities such as autism, or the general term "condition" when referring to any or all diagnoses.

Person-First Versus Identity-First language

The origin of person-first language began in 1968 with a Swedish parent's organization for children with developmental disabilities. The self-advocacy "People First" movement began during a conference, advocating for the word "people" or "person" to be placed before their disability (e.g., person with a disability vs. disabled person). Self-advocacy meetings were held in the United Kingdom and Canada over the next several years, and the first meeting held in the United States took place on January 8, 1974, in Salem, Oregon (The Arc, 2024b). Person-first language was documented in the Americans with Disabilities Act (1990) and the Individuals with Disabilities Education Act (1997) (Wooldridge, 2023). The person-first language has become more widespread and includes people with mental illnesses and is preferred by the medical and research community over the identity-first language (Bagatell, 2010; Orsini & Smith, 2010; Ortega, 2009; Ortega & Choudhury, 2011).

The person-first language is also preferred when referring to individuals with SUDs. Using one's condition to describe a person or persons (e.g., "a schizophrenic," "an addict," or "the disabled") also became offensive (Wooldridge, 2023). The use of diagnostic terms out of context or to describe someone's behavior (e.g., "he's acting schizophrenic") when one displays various emotions or odd behaviors, is also offensive and stigmatizing. The use of the person-first language for those with mental illnesses and SUDs is humanizing, as it recognizes individuals as "people first."

Autism and the Neurodiverse Community

Person-first language is not a "one-size-fits-all" approach. Language, societal views, and values are constantly evolving, leading to confusion for many as to what terms and language are appropriate. Within the autism community, there is disagreement as to whether one should use the person-first (e.g., person with autism) or identity-first language (e.g., autistic person) (*see* Botha et al., 2023; Vivanti, 2020). In the 1990s, self-advocates led many to embrace their neurodiversity, rejecting the idea of identifying as a "person first," and preferring the identity-first language (Sinclair, 1993). Using the person-first or identity-first language is a personal choice, often depending on how much one identifies with one's diagnosis. A survey of 198 individuals diagnosed with autism rated the person-first "person on the autism spectrum," and identity-first "autistic person" as the most preferred and the least offensive terms (Bury et al., 2023). To insist on or mandate one over the other can be demeaning, so it is important to be receptive to both options (Kenny et al., 2016). The person-first and identity-first language is used throughout this book to respect both preferences, but "autistic individual" is used more often to respect this preference.

The (Mis)Use of Functioning Labels

Common but outdated terms used to further describe neurodiverse individuals, mainly autistic individuals, are functioning labels (e.g., low functioning or high functioning). Such labels were often used to describe one with or without with co-occurring ID. Such labels have since been found to be inaccurate clinical descriptors and are not used in research or clinical practice (Alvares et al., 2020). Further, autism is a spectrum, and assigning an arbitrary binary label can diminish one's struggles and downplay one's strengths (Gillette et al., 2023). To describe a person as "low functioning" or "high functioning" is offensive, hurtful, and demeaning and should no longer be used when referring to neurodiverse individuals. Another important acknowledgment is that people live with, or experience symptoms related to their disabilities or illnesses. Using language such as "suffers from" should be avoided because whether one is suffering is subjective. One may or may not identify or feel they are suffering, and such terms should be used by the individual experiencing the condition and not placed upon them by others.

Criminal Justice System Terminology

Some terms used to describe people involved in the CJS can also be offensive, stigmatizing, and dehumanizing. Often, labels such as "criminal," "convict," or "inmate" stereotype and marginalize people rather than support them to no longer engage in the behavior that led them to be assigned the label in the first place (Bryant & Jefferson, 2021; Tran et al., 2018). To continue to refer to someone by a label that we would no longer wish to have them identify and behave as (e.g., "criminal" or "sex offender") is contradictory and, therefore, not used in this book. How we refer to and speak about individuals is often related to how we treat them. This is particularly important for those in correctional institutions such as jails and prisons (Tran et al., 2018), which are dehumanizing environments. To avoid dehumanizing views and subsequent treatment, it is essential to refer to human beings as people or individuals, not by a condition or their prior actions. In this book, the term "criminal" is used to refer to a system, set of laws, or behaviors, not an individual. The main objective of this book is to provide information and knowledge to guide students and practitioners to become more self-reflective and improve their professional capacity to be more effective in their professional careers.

Overview of Book's Content

The following 15 chapters in this book are divided into five parts: Part 1, *Understanding Mental Health, Neurodiversity, and Cognitive Development*, provides comprehensive information on neurodiversity, neurodevelopment disabilities (specifically autism and intellectual developmental disorder), mental illnesses, and adolescent cognition. The mental illnesses detailed in Chapter 3 include schizophrenia, delusional disorder, bipolar disorder, post-traumatic stress disorder (PTSD), and SUDs. These three chapters provide essential knowledge for CJS practitioners to better understand brain development, mental health symptoms, and to familiarize them with these various mental health conditions and disabilities to reduce stigma and misconceptions.

Part 2, *The History and Progression of the Justice and Mental Health Systems*, provides a historical background to better understand Parts 3, 4, and 5, which describe how the three components of the CJS (Police, Court System, and Correctional System) operate today. This section provides a historical overview of significant developments in the CJS, juvenile justice system (JJS), and MHS, including advances in mental health diagnosis and treatment. There have also been various political movements and policies that shaped the current practices and provide context for how CJS, JJS, and MHS came to overlap.

The following three parts of this book address the needs and resources of juveniles, those with mental illnesses, SUDs, and NDDs in the three components of the CJS: police (Part 3), courts (Part 4), and corrections (Part 5). These chapters highlight the struggle to balance one's individual needs with the safety of society while protecting one's constitutional rights. Without addressing individuals' specific needs, they may fall further into or have repetitive contact with the CJS. As a result, they may experience deterioration or worsening of their mental health conditions, which not only impedes the effectiveness of treatment or rehabilitation programs but places additional strains on the CJS. Each chapter presents empirical research on current practices and their effectiveness. Such research is necessary to understand the CJS's current state and "what works," bridging the gap between research and practice. At the end of each chapter, considerations and recommendations from experts in the field are presented to enable readers to contemplate specific practices that may assist in managing these diverse populations.

Part 3, *Mental Healthand Neurodiversity—Implications for Police*, covers the different police encounters when working with people with mental illnesses, SUDs, juveniles, and NDDs. Police face unique challenges when working with populations with cognitive, social, or communication barriers. Situations include interactions in the community as first responders, interviewing suspects, and gathering witness/victim statements and identifications during investigations. This section seeks to provide police with knowledge and tools to increase their confidence and communicate more effectively while protecting individuals' civil rights.

Part 4, *Mental Healthand Neurodiversity—Implications for the Court System*, covers the unique challenges of judicial system practitioners when working with juveniles and people with mental illnesses and NDDs. Defense attorneys, prosecutors, and judges work directly with mental health professionals, as they conduct evaluations for the court and present opinions as expert testimony. Defendants and witnesses with mental illnesses, NDDs, and children can also present communication challenges or experience additional stress that requires accommodations in court. Mental health professionals also assist in identifying and making these accommodations. These chapters provide legal professionals with knowledge and tools to work more effectively and confidently while protecting one's due process and constitutional rights. This section also overlaps with the police and correctional systems and can guide practitioners on handling particular cases or diverting individuals from the CJS when appropriate.

Part 5, *Mental Healthand Neurodiversity—Implications for the Correctional and Mental Health Systems*, covers the intersection of community corrections, institutional correctional facilities, and the MHS. This section covers the challenges that practitioners who work in corrections face to balance the safety of society with one's treatment needs while protecting one's constitutional and human rights. These chapters highlight the challenges for practitioners when supervising, rehabilitating, and managing those with mental illnesses, SUDs, and disabilities while also addressing the successful integration or reintegration into the community.

Race and Ethnicity in the Criminal Justice System

Black people and other ethnic minorities are overrepresented in the CJS. Their overrepresentation and other factors showed they have an increased risk of use of force by police (Gilbert & Ray, 2016; Hetey & Eberhardt, 2018; Owusu-Bempah, 2016). Research has also shown that Black people have higher rates of mistaken eyewitness identification, leading to false accusations and wrongful convictions (Mogavero et al., 2022; National Registry of Exonerations, 2017). Disparities in access to community services for racial and ethnic minorities can lead to adverse outcomes when involved in the CJS. These are further compounded when those individuals also have a disability such as autism, as confirmed in the research review by Cooper et al. (2022). Issues of race in the CJS are addressed in Chapters 5, 6, and 10. Some individuals with mental illnesses, SUDs and/or disabilities may experience multiple forms of discrimination related to, for example, race, ethnicity, social class, and gender, referred to as **intersectionality**. Although it is crucial for practitioners to consider the complexity of identity during interactions, the central focus of this book is the experiences of those with mental illnesses, cognitive, social, and communication challenges, and those with SUDs in the CJS. These conditions occur across racial and ethnic groups (APA, 2022) and may be directly or indirectly related to criminal behavior.

Overview of the US Criminal Justice System Process

The contemporary CJS comprises political agencies that function in the three branches of government: legislative, judicial, and executive. These political agencies can be divided into three groups: Police, Court System, and Correctional System. Police are generally tasked with maintaining order, responding to emergencies, investigating crimes, detaining those suspected of and apprehending those who have allegedly committed crimes. The court system is generally tasked with charging those who allegedly committed crimes, conducting hearings and trials, and determining sentences (i.e., punishments). The correctional system is generally tasked with supervising, monitoring, treating, and rehabilitating those convicted of crimes. Those who encounter the CJS go through a formal process of a series of steps before they are convicted and sentenced, although not all individuals go through each step.

Steps of Criminal Justice System Involvement

1. **Initial contact**—In most cases, an individual has contact with the CJS as a result of police action, whether it be a traffic stop, if they observe a suspicious person, or if someone reports a crime, and the police will detain the accused individual.
2. **Investigation**—The purpose of an investigation is to identify a suspect for an arrest and/or to gather evidence for an arrest.
3. **Arrest**—Once police have sufficient evidence that a crime is being or has been committed, and a suspect has been identified, the suspect is placed under arrest and is now in the custody of police.
4. **Custody**—After an arrest and while the suspect is being detained, police may search for evidence and conduct an interrogation. Witnesses may be brought in to view and identify the suspect.
5. **Charged**—If the police believe there is sufficient evidence to charge the individual with a crime, the evidence will be turned over to the prosecutor, who then decides whether to file charges.
6. **Preliminary hearing/grand jury**—A preliminary hearing or grand jury hearing is held to determine whether there is enough evidence to charge the accused.
7. **Arraignment**—Before the trial begins, the defendant must be arranged and brought before the court that will hear the case. The defendant is read the formal charges, and they enter an initial plea (e.g., guilty or not guilty).
8. **Bail or detention**—**Bail** is a money bond collected to ensure defendants return to court. This allows defendants to remain in the community to prepare for their defense while continuing to work and support themselves and their families. Those who cannot afford or are denied bail will remain in custody, usually in **jail**.
9. **Plea bargaining**—After the arraignment, the prosecutor, defense attorney, and the defendant often discuss options for a plea bargain, a guilty plea in exchange for dropping or reducing the charges, usually for a more lenient sentence.
10. **Trial/adjudication**—The case will go to trial if a plea bargain cannot be reached or if one is not offered. Defendants have the right to a **jury** trial

but can opt for a **bench trial**, where the case will be heard before a judge instead.

11. **Sentencing**—If the defendant pleads guilty or a trial renders a guilty verdict, the defendant is convicted and sentenced. The sentence can be a fine, probation, another form of community-based sentencing, incarceration in a jail or prison, or, in some cases, the death penalty. After sentencing, the defendant can appeal the conviction or the sentence to an **appellate court**. The appellate court reviews the case and can grant the defendant a new trial or order their release (Seigel & Worrall, 2019, pp. 10–12) (Fig. 1.1).

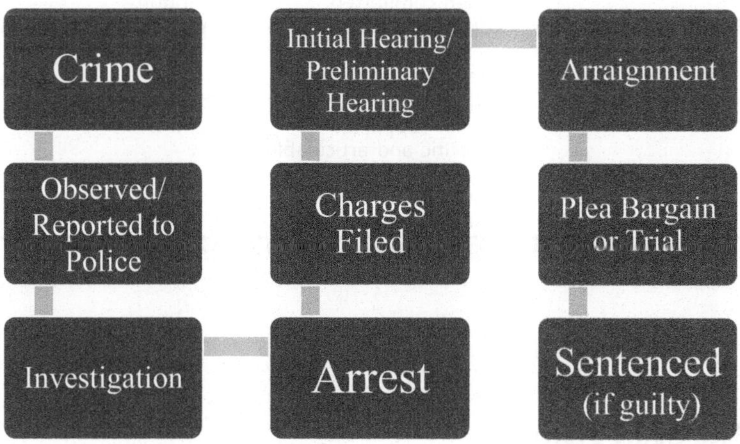

Fig. 1.1 Criminal justice system process

The various steps in the criminal justice system process require various evidentiary standards, depending on the degree of civil liberties at stake. Beyond a reasonable doubt is the highest burden of proof used in the CJS, which is different from absolute certainly, with no percentage chance of error. Box 1.1 lists and defines these standards in descending order.

Box 1.1 Degrees of Certainly for Evidentiary Standards of Proof in the Criminal Justice System

Standard	Definition	Use
Absolute Certainty	100% certain with no chance of error	Not Used
Beyond a Reasonable Doubt	Conclusive and complete evidence with no reasonable doubt the defendant is innocent	Trials for guilty verdict
Clear and Convincing	Prevailing and persuasive evidence	Insanity defense evidence and civil commitments
Probable Cause	Sufficient facts to warrant a crime has been committed	Arrests, search warrants, preliminary hearings, motions
Sufficient Evidence	Adequate evidence to reverse a trial court decision	Appellate court hearings
Reasonable Suspicion	Rational, reasonable belief supported by specific and articulable facts that warrant an investigation into a crime	Police Investigations, stop and frisks

Source Garner (2019) and Seigel and Worrall (2019, p. 210)

Appellate Court System

When defendants believe that the criminal court procedures were in violation of their constitutional rights or if errors were made, they can file a **writ of certiorari** (petition) for an appellate court to review their case. All states have an appellate court system; some have multiple appellate courts, but all have a State Supreme Court or a court of last resort. Appellate courts do not retry cases; they review the trial process and procedures to determine if errors have been made. The losing party can then appeal to the federal court system. The federal court system also has a hierarchy: US District Courts, US Court of Appeals, and the US Supreme Court. The Federal Courts can decline to hear the case, to which the lower court decision stands, or the losing party can appeal to a higher appellate court. The US Supreme Court is the highest appellate court in the United States and can hear cases tried before various federal and state courts. About 5,000 cases are appealed to the US Supreme Court each year, which the justices only decide to hear and make decisions on about 100 cases (about 2%). If the US Supreme Court declines to hear a case, the lower court decision stands. When the US Supreme Court rules on a case, and the majority of the judges agree, the rule or decision becomes precedent and is considered a **landmark decision** that must now be followed in all lower courts (state and federal). That decision also becomes precedent, referred to as **stare decisis** (Latin for "let the decision stand"), where courts will adhere to precedent in future cases making their decisions (Seigel & Worrall, 2019).

Mental Health in the Criminal Justice System

When the MHS and CJS work together, the term **forensic** is often used. Forensic comes from the Latin word "forensis," meaning "of the forum," where the law courts of ancient Rome were held. Today, forensic refers to applying scientific principles and practices to the judicial process (American Board of Forensic Psychology, 2024). The MHS typically becomes involved in the CJS during court processes or the judicial system, a field referred to as **forensic psychology**. Forensic psychology is "the application of the science and profession of psychology to questions and issues relating to law and the legal system" (American Board of Forensic Psychology, 2024).

Various MHS, CJS, and education system policies and practices led to significant changes in how juveniles, individuals with mental illnesses, SUDs, and disabilities are treated by society and social institutions. In the latter part of the twentieth century, specific CJS policies, including a shift to "get tough" on crime, led to expanding jail and prison populations. As a direct consequence of these policies and changing societal attitudes, those with mental illnesses, SUDS, and disabilities were increasingly encountering the CJS, creating new challenges for police and practitioners in the court and correctional systems.

As detailed in Parts 1–5 of this book, people with mental illnesses, SUDs, and disabilities have high rates of contact with the CJS. Due to this increase, researchers and stakeholders developed a plan to use the MHS and community services to intervene and address their individualized needs to prevent them from going through the entire CJS process. The Sequential Intercept Model (SIM) was developed in the early 2000s by researchers at the Policy Research Associates, Inc., located in Troy, New York (Abreu et al., 2017; Munetz & Griffin, 2006). The SIM was designed to develop interventions to address, limit, and, when possible, divert those with mental illnesses from the CJS. The revised model includes 988, an emergency line for mental health and suicide prevention support. The SIM is a practical model that maps out six points (i.e., intercepts) in the CJS to highlight gaps and

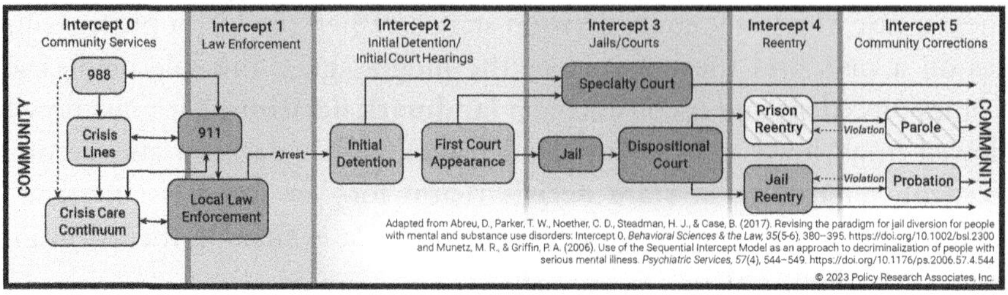

Fig. 1.2 The Sequential Intercept Model (*Source* Policy Research Associates, Inc., https://www.prainc.com/sim/)

resources (*see* Fig. 1.2). The intercepts are different points of contact where one may progress through the system. By identifying these potential points of interception, interventions and supports can divert individuals back into community-based services. As a strategic tool for policymakers and CJS practitioners, the SIM model can identify and link individuals with treatment needs to the necessary programs and services and potentially prevent further involvement in the CJS (Abreu et al., 2017; Bonfine et al., 2020; Munetz & Griffin, 2006). The SIM model is versatile and has been adapted successfully for other populations, including those with SUDs (Bonfine et al., 2018).

Autistic Individuals in the Criminal Justice System: The Revised Sequential Intercept Model

Researchers have also demonstrated high rates of contact among autistic individuals with the CJS (Rava et al., 2017; Tint et al., 2017) as both perpetrators and victims of crime (Cooper et al., 2024). In 2019, the International Society for Autism Research (INSAR) selected interactions between autistic individuals and the CJS as the theme for its third funded policy brief (*see* INSAR, 2022; Shea et al., 2021). The A. J. Drexel Autism Institute at Drexel University's Policy and Analytics Center in Philadelphia, PA, was selected to receive the grant, creating a Global Autism and Criminal Justice System Consortium. The Consortium formed a work group consisting of researchers, academics, clinicians, and parents of autistic children, who met virtually monthly to guide the revisions of the original SIM model. The work group sought to ensure the framework was organized to include autistic individuals' experiences with the CJS from the perspectives of victims to include their voices and differing needs for support. The Consortium also held a virtual two-day Summit in October 2020 with multiple sessions allowing participation across time zones to assist in developing the revised SIM and policy brief.[2]

Figure 1.3 shows an adapted version of the revised SIM,[3] which was amended from the linear model of the original to a cyclical one that begins and ends in the community. Like the original SIM, the community is conceptualized as the main intercept and the central point of contact for the range of services supporting victims and defendants in the CJS process. Exit ramps are aspirational and detail potential pathways for individuals to exit the CJS without traversing through each intercept. Exit ramps are also symbolic and may represent a co-response team where a trained MHS professional responds with police during a crisis or a diversionary program that directs individuals to community services and supports, instead of incarceration.

The intercepts were also reorganized to align with the policy and programmatic needs of autistic individuals. For example, in the original SIM, Intercept 3 is identified as courts/jails; however, in the revised SIM, there are two separate Intercepts: (3) Courts and (4) Prisons/Jails/Confinement. Intercepts 3 and 4 account for the distinction between the court system processes and the correctional system's use of jails versus prisons or other institutions of confinement. Different policy and programmatic responses are required to

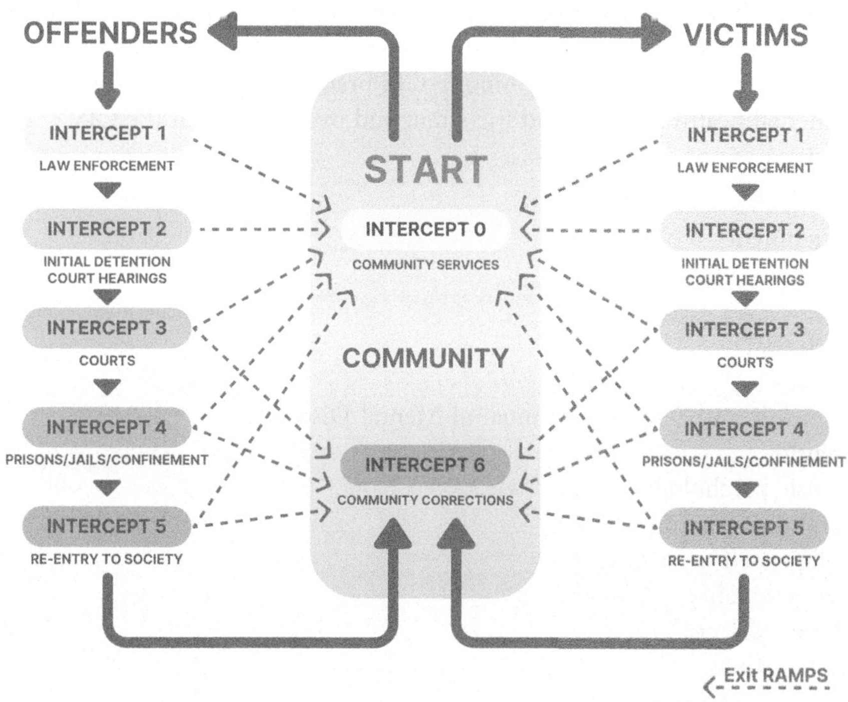

Fig. 1.3 Revised Sequential Intercept Model (*Source* Adapted from Drexel University www.drexel.edu/autism/criminaljustice)

address the needs of autistic individuals in court (e.g., communication aids). The revised SIM seeks to address the specific needs of autistic individuals but also recognizes the model's ability to support those with mental illnesses, SUDs, and other disabilities, such as ID.

Conclusion

The CJS is a complex web of procedures and standards that are challenging for the average person to navigate. Thus, these challenges are compounded for those with mental illnesses, SUDs, or disabilities. Practitioners who work in or with the CJS must also address the needs and challenges of these diverse populations, adding to the stress and complexity of their professional duties. Failing to address the specific needs of these populations is a notable strain on the CJS, including the overreliance on jails and prisons. Without practitioners' awareness of these conditions, addressing stigma, and collaborating with other systems to prevent or divert can lead to deeper involvement in the CJS. Deeper involvement can magnify the risk of reoffending, reincarceration, and deteriorating mental health, further complicating the overall system of care. Consistent themes and issues presented in this book are a need for greater awareness and training among CJS practitioners, the lack of funding for mental health services, and the strain and overreliance on the CJS.

Key Terms

Arraignment
Appellate court
Bail
Bench trial
Case law
Diagnostic and Statistical Manual of Mental Disorders
Forensic
Forensic psychology
Grand jury hearing
Intelligence Quotient (IQ)
Intersectionality
Landmark decision
Plea bargaining
Preliminary hearing
Sequential Intercept Model
Stare decisis
Writ of certiorari

Chapter Questions

(1) Provide a summary of the objective of this book. In this summary, which do you believe or anticipate being the greatest problem for the CJS? Explain your response.
(2) List and describe the steps that someone encounters when going through the criminal justice system process. Of these steps, which do you believe requires mental health intervention the most? Explain your response.
(3) What is the rationale behind the use of person-first language?
(4) Compare and contrast the use of person-first and identity-first language. When is it deemed appropriate to use one over the other?
(5) What is the rationale behind developing the Sequential Intercept Model?
(6) Compare and contrast the original Sequential Intercept Model to the Revised Sequential Intercept Model.

Suggested Readings

Brewer, N., Zoanetti, J., & Young, R. L. (2017). The influence of media suggestions about links between criminality and autism spectrum disorder. *Autism, 21*(1), 117–121. https://doi.org/10.1177/1362361316632097

Christoffersen, M. N. (2019). Violent crime against children with disabilities: A nationwide prospective birth cohort-study. *Child Abuse & Neglect, 98*, Article 104150. https://doi.org/10.1016/j.chiabu.2019.104150

Weiss, J. A., & Fardella, M. A. (2018). Victimization and perpetration experiences of adults with autism. *Frontiers in Psychiatry, 9*, Article 203. https://doi.org/10.3389/fpsyt.2018.00203

Notes

1. Author was a member of this Consortium as a revised SIM work group participant and as an attendee and co-moderator at the Fall 2020 Summit.
2. This adapted revised SIM was developed by Dr. Vincent Chen, Associate Professor and Graphic Designer, Georgian Court University.

References

Abreu, D., Parker, T. W., Noether, C. D., Steadman, H. J., & Case, B. (2017). Revising the paradigm for jail diversion for people with mental and substance use disorders: Intercept 0. *Behavioral Sciences & the Law, 35*(5–6), 380–395. https://doi.org/10.1002/bsl.2300

Alvares, G. A., Bebbington, K., Cleary, D., Evans, K., Glasson, E. J., Maybery, M. T., Pillar, S., Uljarević, M., Varcin, K., Wray, J., & Whitehouse, A. J. (2020). The misnomer of 'high functioning autism': Intelligence is an imprecise predictor of functional abilities at diagnosis. *Autism, 24*(1), 221–232. https://doi.org/10.1177/1362361319852831

American Board of Forensic Psychology. (2024). *What is forensic psychology*? https://abfp.com/

American Psychiatric Association. (1952). *Diagnostic and statistical manual of mental disorders* (1st ed.).

American Psychiatric Association. (1968). *Diagnostic and statistical manual of mental disorders* (2nd ed).

American Psychiatric Association. (1987). *Diagnostic and statistical manual of mental disorders* (3rd ed. Revised).

American Psychiatric Association. (2000). *Diagnostic and statistical manual of mental disorders* (4th ed. Text Revision).

American Psychiatric Association. (2013). *Diagnostic and statistical manual of mental disorders* (5th ed.). https://doi.org/10.1176/appibooks.9780890425596

American Psychiatric Association. (2022). *Diagnostic and statistical manual of mental disorders* (5th ed. Text Revision). https://doi.org/10.1176/appi.books.9780890425787

Americans with Disabilities Act of 1990, 42 U.S.C. § 12101 et seq. (1990).

Baron-Cohen, S. (2017). Editorial perspective: Neurodiversity—A revolutionary concept for autism and psychiatry. *Journal of Child Psychology and Psychiatry, and Allied Disciplines, 58*(6), 744–747. https://doi.org/10.1111/jcpp.12703

Bagatell, N. (2010). From cure to community: Transforming notions of autism. *Ethos, 38*, 34–58. https://doi.org/10.1111/j.1548-1352.2009.01080.x

Bonfine, N., Munetz, M. R., & Simera, R. H. (2018). Sequential Intercept Mapping: Developing systems-level solutions for the opioid epidemic. *Psychiatric Services, 69*(11), 1124–1126. https://doi.org/10.1176/appi.ps.201800192

Bonfine, N., Wilson, A. B., & Munetz, M. R. (2020). Meeting the needs of justice-involved people with serious mental illness within community behavioral health systems. *Psychiatric Services, 71*(4), 355–363. https://doi.org/10.1176/appi.ps.201900453

Botha, M., Hanlon, J., & Williams, G. L. (2023). Does language matter? Identity-first versus person-first language use in autism research: A response to Vivanti. *Journal of Autism and Developmental Disorders, 53*(2), 870–878. https://doi.org/10.1007/s10803-020-04858-w

Bryant, E., & Jefferson, R. (2021, August 16). Words matter: Don't call people felons, prisoners, or inmates. *Forbes*. https://www.forbes.com/sites/forbeseq/2021/08/16/words-matter-dont-call-people-felons-prisoners-or-inmates/

Bury, S. M., Jellett, R., Spoor, J. R., & Hedley, D. (2023). "It defines who I am" or "it's something I have": What language do [autistic] Australian adults [on the autism spectrum] prefer? *Journal of Autism and Developmental Disorders, 53*(2), 677–687. https://doi.org/10.1007/s10803-020-04425-3

Centers for Disease Control and Prevention (CDC). (2024). *About mental health*. https://www.cdc.gov/mentalhealth/learn/index.htm

Cooper, D., Frisbie, S., Wang, S., Jonas, V., Gibbs, V., Love, A. M. A., Mogavero, M., Benevides, T. W., Hyatt, J. M., Hooven, K., Basketbill, I., & Shea, L. (2024). What do we know about autism and policing globally? Preliminary findings from an international effort to examine autism and the criminal justice system. *Autism Research*, https://doi.org/10.1002/aur.3203

Cooper, D. S., Uppal, D., Railey, K. S., Blank Wilson, A., Maras, K., Zimmerman, E., Bornman, J., & Shea, L. (2022). Policy gaps and opportunities: A systematic review of autism spectrum disorder and criminal justice intersections. *Autism, 26*(5), 1014–1031. https://doi.org/10.1177/13623613211070341

Garner, B. A. (2019). *Black's law dictionary* (11th edn). Thomson Reuters.

Gilbert, K. L., & Ray, R. (2016). Why police kill Black males with impunity: Applying public health critical race praxis (PHCRP) to address the determinants of policing behaviors and "justifiable" homicides in the USA. *Journal of Urban Health, 93*(1), 122–140. https://doi.org/10.1007/s11524-015-0005-x

Gillette, H., Howard, A., Washington, N., & Wigley, S. (2023, December 12). Why we no longer say high or low functioning for autism. *Healthline*. https://www.healthline.com/health/autism/functioning-labels-autism#summary

Hetey, R. C., & Eberhardt, J. L. (2018). The numbers don't speak for themselves: Racial disparities and the persistence of inequality in the criminal justice system. *Current Directions in Psychological Science, 27*(3), 183–187. https://doi.org/10.1177/0963721418763931

Huey, E. B. (1912). *Backward and feeble-minded children*. Warwick and York.

Individuals with Disabilities Education Act, Pub. L. No. 105-17, 111 Stat. 37. (1997).

INSAR. (2022). *Autism and the criminal justice system: Policy opportunities and challenges*. https://cdn.ymaws.com/www.autism-insar.org/resource/resmgr/docs/2022_CJ_INSAR_Policy_Brief.pdf

Kenny, L., Hattersley, C., Molins, B., Buckley, C., Povey, C., & Pellicano, E. (2016). Which terms should be used to describe autism? Perspectives from the UK autism community. *Autism, 20*(4), 442–462. https://doi.org/10.1177/1362361315588200

Mogavero, M. C., Hsu, K.-H., & Bolger, P. C. (2022). A conjunctive analysis of false accusations, official misconduct, and race in violent and sexual exoneration cases. *Behavioral Sciences and the Law, 40*(6), 756–786. https://doi.org/10.1002/bsl.2587

Munetz, M. R., & Griffin, P. A. (2006). Use of the Sequential Intercept Model as an approach to decriminalization of people with serious mental illness. *Psychiatric Services, 57*(4), 544–549. https://doi.org/10.1176/ps.2006.57.4.544 and https://www.prainc.com/wp-content/uploads/2018/06/PRA-SIM-Letter-Paper-2018.pdf

National Institutes of Health. (2024a). *Appendix: Biomedical definitions.* https://www.nih.gov/nih-style-guide/appendix-biomedical-definitions

National Institutes of Health. (2024b). *Mental disorders.* https://medlineplus.gov/mentaldisorders.html

National Registry of Exonerations. (2017). *Race and wrongful convictions.* https://www.law.umich.edu/special/exoneration/Pages/Race.aspx

Orsini, M., & Smith, M. (2010). Social movements, knowledge, and public policy: The case of autism activism in Canada and the US. *Critical Policy Studies, 4*(1), 38–57.

Ortega, F. (2009). The cerebral subject and the challenge of neurodiversity. *BioSocieties, 4*, 425–445. https://doi.org/10.1017/S1745855209990287

Ortega, F., & Choudhury, S. (2011). 'Wired up differently': Autism, adolescence, and the politics of neurological identities. *Subjectivity, 4*(3), 323–345.

Owusu-Bempah, A. (2016). Race and policing in historical context: Dehumanization and the policing of Black people in the 21st century. *Theoretical Criminology, 21*(1), 23–34. https://doi.org/10.1177/1362480616677493

Queen v. M'Naghten, 10 Cl. & Fin. 200, 8 Eng. Rep. 718 (H.L., 1843).

Rava, J., Shattuck, P., Rast, J., & Roux, A. (2017). The prevalence and correlates of involvement in the criminal justice system among youth on the autism spectrum. *Journal of Autism and Developmental Disorders, 47*(2), 340–346. https://doi.org/10.1007/s10803-016-2958-3

Riva, M. A., Tremolizzo, L., Spicci, M., Ferrarese, C., De Vito, G., Cesana, G. C., & Sironi, V. A. (2011). The disease of the moon: The linguistic and pathological evolution of the English term "lunatic." *Journal of the History of the Neurosciences, 20*(1), 65–73. https://doi.org/10.1080/0964704X.2010.481101

Rosa's Law. 111-256 S. 2781, (2010).

Rose, D., Thornicroft, G., Pinfold, V., & Kassam, A. (2007). 250 labels used to stigmatise people with mental illness. *BMC Health Service Research, 7*(97), 107. https://doi.org/10.1186/1472-6963-7-97

Seigel, L. J., & Worrall, J. L. (2019). *Essentials of criminal justice*(11th ed.). Cengage.

Shea, L., Cooper, D., & Wilson, A. (2021). Preventing and improving interactions between autistic individuals and the criminal justice system: A roadmap for research. *Autism Research*, 1–8. https://doi.org/10.1002/aur.2594

Sinclair, J. (1993, November 3). Don't mourn for us. *Voice, 1*(3). https://www.autreat.com/dont_mourn.html

The Arc. (2024a). *About us. Our history.* https://thearc.org/about-us/history/

The Arc. (2024b). *History of People First.* https://thearcmov.org/history-of-people-first/#:~:text=People%20First%20is%20part%20of%20the%20self-advocacy%20movement.,for%20them%2C%E2%80%9D%20meaning%20parents%20speaking%20for%20their%20children.

Tint, A., Palucka, A. M., Bradley, E., Weiss, J. A., & Lunsky, Y. (2017). Correlates of police involvement among adolescents and adults with autism spectrum disorder. *Journal of Autism and Developmental Disorders, 47*(9), 2639–2647.

Tran, N. T., Baggio, S., Dawson, A., O'Moore, É., Williams, B., Bedell, P., Simon, O., Scholten, W., Getaz, L., & Wolff, H. (2018). Words matter: A call for humanizing and respectful language to describe people who experience incarceration. *BMC International Health and Human Rights, 18*(1), 41. https://doi.org/10.1186/s12914-018-0180-4

Vivanti, G. (2020). Ask the editor: What is the most appropriate way to talk about individuals with a diagnosis of autism? *Journal of Autism and Developmental Disorders, 50*(2), 691–693. https://doi.org/10.1007/s10803-019-04280-x

Wehmeyer, M., Bersani, H., & Gagne, R. (2000). Riding the third wave: Self-determination and self-advocacy in the 21st century. *Focus on Autism and Other Developmental Disabilities, 15*(2), 106–115. https://doi.org/10.1177/108835760001500206

Wooldridge, S. (2023, April 12). *Writing respectfully: Person-first and identity-first language.* US Department of Health and Human Services. National Institutes of Health. Retrieved from https://www.nih.gov/about-nih/what-we-do/science-health-public-trust/perspectives/writing-respectfully-person-first-identity-first-language

2

Understanding Neurodiversity—Overview and Implications for the Criminal Justice System

Learning Objectives

After this chapter, readers will understand the:

(1) Concept of neurodiversity.
(2) Characteristics and diagnostic criteria of autism spectrum disorder.
(3) Characteristics and diagnostic criteria of intellectual developmental disorder.
(4) Prevalence Rates of autism spectrum disorder and intellectual developmental disorder.
(5) Common misconceptions about people with autism and intellectual disability.

Introduction

Neurodiverse individuals interact with the criminal justice system (CJS) at high rates (Rava et al., 2017; Tint et al., 2017, 2019) for both criminal matters (e.g., suspect, victim), noncriminal matters (e.g., traffic incidents, lost or missing persons), or behaviors that could be interpreted as suspicious (e.g., repetitive body movements, loud noises) (Cooper et al., 2024). A lack of knowledge or misconceptions about people with such conditions may lead to inappropriate communications or interactions. Many autistic individuals[1]

M. C. Mogavero, *Mental Health, Neurodiversity, and Criminal Justice*, https://doi.org/10.1007/978-3-031-88816-8_2

and parents/caregivers reported dissatisfaction with their CJS experience and many of the complaints were related to communication (Haas & Gibbs, 2021; Koffer Miller et al., 2021). Possessing more knowledge can help to improve the experiences of neurodiverse individuals interacting with CJS practitioners, including having more patience with communication responses and making necessary accommodations when appropriate.

Neurodiversity

The origin of the term neurodiversity was developed collectively among autistic activists, mostly dating back to the 1990s; however, American journalist Harvey Blume (1997) and Australian sociologist Judy Singer (1998) are often credited as the first (Botha et al., 2024). Neurodiversity is a concept in which certain developmental disabilities are normal variations in the brain. Neurodiversity reimagined a "disability" as a "difference," which denotes more acceptance of people who are different. Neurodevelopmental disorders (NDDs) such as autism are "hidden" differences, and many may mask or deny them to avoid stigma due to **ableism** (Ortega & Choudhury, 2011; Portway & Johnson, 2005; Shtayermman, 2009). According to Dunn (2021) of the American Psychological Association, ableism refers to

> the prejudice and discrimination aimed at disabled people, often with a patronizing desire to "cure" their disability and make them "normal." Ableism, either subtly or directly, defines individuals by their disabilities and views them as inherently inferior.

Support and general agreement for neurodiversity erupted into a political self-advocacy movement known as the neurodiversity movement (Jaarsma & Welin, 2012; Ortega, 2009; Ortega & Choudhury, 2011). Self-advocates encouraged people to embrace their neurodiverse identity to improve their attitude and self-image and to combat the stigma commonly associated with having a disability (Kapp et al., 2013).

Neurological Differences of the Brain

The notion that there are differences in the brains and neurological functions among autistic individuals has been studied and supported by advanced brain imaging since the development of **functional magnetic resonance imaging (fMRI)** in 1991. The fMRI is a radiology tool that can detect changes in magnetic properties associated with blood flow in the brain, brain activity, or the degree of functional connectivity between brain regions, usually while performing tasks (Dow-Edwards et al., 2019). Scientists have compared the brains of autistic individuals and typically developed individuals without autism and noticed differences in the size of the brain structures. For example, Hardan et al. (2000) compared seven subregions in the cerebral cortex of 22 autistic and 22 typically developed individuals and noted that some subregions were smaller in the autistic individuals. Courchesne et al. (2001) compared fMRI images among 60 autistic and 52 typically developed individuals and revealed that 90% of autistic individuals had larger brains, and 37% met the criteria for developmental macrencephaly, a congenital malformation where the brain is abnormally large.

Scientists have also noted differences in the brain's **medial prefrontal cortex (mPFC)**. The mPFC is responsible for **executive functions** such as planning, decision-making, and impulse control. An analysis of 52 studies comparing fMRI images of 891 autistic to 967 typically developed individuals revealed that typically developed individuals had greater activity in the prefrontal cortex while performing perception tasks, while autistic individuals had greater activity in the visual cortex while performing visual tasks (Jassim et al., 2021). Recent research has been conducted to determine if fMRI imaging can improve diagnostic methods (Elakkiya & Dejey, 2023; Qiu & Zhai, 2024).

Neurodevelopmental Disorders

NDDs are a group of conditions that affect brain and nervous system development and typically affect an individual's ability to reason, learn, and communicate. The conditions within this category include (1) intellectual developmental disorder (IDD or ID); (2) autism spectrum disorder; (3) communication disorders (e.g., childhood-onset fluency disorder, i.e., stuttering); (4) attention-deficit/hyperactivity disorder (ADHD); (5) specific learning disorder (e.g., dyslexia-difficulties with reading); (6) motor disorders (e.g., developmental coordination disorder); and (7) tic disorders (e.g., Tourette's disorder). The criteria for each of these conditions are different; however, they all involve impairments in social communication and interaction, academic performance, occupational functioning, and are present in multiple settings (e.g., home and school). NDDs are not diagnosed by one method but by both clinical assessments and standardized tests. A multidisciplinary team of medical and mental health professionals identifies an NDD by gathering information from multiple sources and settings, including medical history, developmental milestones, and educational and psychological evaluations (APA, 2022).

The **Diagnostic and Statistical Manual of Mental Disorders** (DSM-5-TR), published by the American Psychiatric Association (APA), and the **International Classification of Diseases and Related Health Problems (ICD-11),** published by the World Health Organization (WHO, 2018), are the respected diagnostic guides for professionals. Unlike the ICD, the DSM is specific to cognitive or mental health-related conditions. Clinicians in the United States (US) and North America use the DSM, and most countries outside these regions use the ICD to diagnose various mental and cognitive disabilities. However, some countries (e.g., the United Kingdom (UK), Australia, and New Zealand) sometimes use the DSM.

Intellectual Disability: History and Progression of Diagnosis and Terminology

Prior to any formal classification system, the terms "idiot" and "feeble-minded" were commonly used in various and contradictory ways to describe one's intelligence or mental capacity. In 1904, the English Royal Commission recommended that the term "feeble-minded" be applied to all children needing institutional care (Huey, 1912, p. 6). The term was later used to describe the highest level of "mental deficiency," and the upper limit was placed at having a mental age of 12 years. Albert Binet (1857–1911) and Théodore Simon (1873–1961) created the first standardized **IQ (intelligence quotient)** test in 1905. The IQ test measures intellectual ability and cognitive functioning, mainly in children, to determine their educational needs. One's IQ score was determined by dividing the mental age score by one's chronological age, and the quotient was multiplied by 100. The term "feeble-minded" was then classified into three categories. Although offensive by today's standards, Binet and Simon did not use these classification terms to insult individuals (Huey, 1912).

- **"Idiots"**: Those so defective that the mental development never exceeds that of a normal child of about two years.
- **"Imbeciles"**: Those whose development is higher than that of an "idiot," but whose intelligence does not exceed that of a normal child of about seven years.
- **"Morons"**: Those whose mental development is above that of an "imbecile" but does not exceed that of a normal child of about twelve years (Huey, 1912, pp. 5–6).

The APA published the first DSM in 1952 (DSM-I) and included the diagnosis, "mental deficiency." The diagnosis included severity levels according to IQ scores: mild (70–85), moderate (50–69), and severe (under 50), with additional labels for those with scores under 50, using Binet's classifications: "Moron" (IQ < 50), "Imbecility" (IQ < 20), and "Idiocy" (when deficiency is familial or hereditary) (APA, 1952).

Since these early publications, there have been several progressions in the terminology and defining diagnostic characteristics. When the DSM-II was published in 1968, the APA replaced the diagnosis "mental deficiency" with "mental retardation" and revised the severity levels according to slightly broader IQ score ranges: Borderline (68–85), Mild (52–67), Moderate (36–51), Severe (20–35), Profound (under 20), and Unspecified (APA, 1968). The revised third and fourth editions of the DSM used these same severity levels (APA, 1987, 2000).

Diagnostic Criteria for Intellectual Developmental Disorder

When the APA published the fifth edition of the DSM in 2013 (DSM-5), the diagnostic term changed to intellectual developmental disorder (IDD or ID) (APA, 2013). The DSM-5 removed IQ scores as the sole form of criteria, and clinicians now use clinical assessments with standardized tests (APA, 2013). For a diagnosis of ID, the following three criteria must be met:

(1) Deficits in intellectual functions, such as reasoning, problem-solving, planning, abstract thinking, judgment, academic learning, and learning from experience, confirmed by both clinical assessment and individualized, standardized intelligence testing.
(2) Deficits in adaptive functioning that result in failure to meet developmental and sociocultural standards for personal independence and social responsibility. Without ongoing support, the adaptive deficits limit functioning in one or more activities of daily life, such as communication, social participation, and independent living, across multiple environments, such as home, school, work, and community.
(3) Onset of intellectual and adaptive deficits during the developmental period (i.e., childhood) (APA, 2022, pp. 37–38).

Autism: History and Progression of Diagnosis and Terminology

Swiss physician Paul Eugen Bleuler (1857–1939) conducted extensive research on schizophrenia and described those with autistic traits as a severe form of schizophrenia. His 1911 book, *Dementia Praecox; oder, Die Gruppe der Schizophrenien,* was translated into English and published in 1950 (*Dementia Praecox or the Group of Schizophrenias*). Bleuler used the term "autism" to describe individuals who had a detachment from reality and "have no more contact with the outside world, live in a world of their own" (Bleuler, 1911, p. 63). In 1926, Russian physician Grunya Efimovna Sukhareva (surname transliterated as "Ssucharewa") (1891–1981) published a clinical description of six boys with autistic traits (Sher & Gibson, 2021). In her paper titled *Die Schizoid Psychopathien im Kindesalter* (translated as *Childhood Schizoid Psychopathies*), Sukhareva used the term "*autistische*" (autistic) to describe a type of introverted child "*Intra Vertierter Typu*" (Ssucharewa, 1926, p. 249). Their publications influenced the work of Austrian physicians Leo Kanner (1894–1981) and Hans Asperger (1906–1980). Kanner published a paper titled *Early Infantile Autism* in 1943, describing 11 children as unable to relate to themselves, others, or situations. Kanner also referred to autism as a subset of schizophrenia (Kanner, 1943). In 1944, Asperger published *Die Autistischen Psychopathen im Kindesalter* (translated as *Autistic Psychopathy in Childhood*), describing four boys with focal preoccupations and poor interpersonal skills (Asperger, 1944). Although Bleuler and Sukhareva published accounts of children with autism traits decades earlier, Kanner and Asperger are often credited as being the first (Manouilenko & Bejerot, 2015; Resnick, 2017; Sher & Gibson, 2021).

In 1952, autism was added to the second edition of the DSM (DSM-II) as a psychiatric condition termed childhood schizophrenia (APA, 1952). When the APA published the third edition of the DSM in 1980, a new category was added: Pervasive Developmental Disorders (PDD), and the diagnosis of infantile autism was a separate condition in this category (APA, 1980). The revised third edition (DSM-III-R) in 1987 replaced the diagnosis of infantile autism with autism disorder (APA, 1987). The APA also broadened the concept of autism by adding a milder condition of pervasive developmental disorder-not otherwise specified (PDD-NOS). Individuals were identified as having PDD-NOS if they presented characteristics of autism and showed significant impairments but did not present enough characteristics to meet the full diagnostic criteria of autism disorder (APA, 1987).

British psychiatrist Lorna Wing (1928–2014) studied Asperger's work and, in 1981, published *Asperger's Syndrome: A Clinical Account*, bringing greater awareness, as little was known about Asperger's 1944 publication outside German literature (Wing, 1981). In 1991, German psychologist Dame Uta Frith translated Asperger's 1944 paper into English, which led to additional awareness and research. In 1994, the APA added Asperger's Syndrome to the PDD category in the fourth edition of the DSM (DSM-IV) (APA, 1994). **Asperger's syndrome** shared many features with autism disorder, but one of the significant differences between them was the typical development of language. Those diagnosed with Asperger's syndrome did not display significant delays in language or delays in cognitive development, although some may exhibit inappropriate use of speech and respond inappropriately in conversations. They also tended to have adequate grammar and vocabulary, age-appropriate self-help skills, and often had average or above-average IQ scores (APA, 2000).

Diagnostic Criteria for Autism Spectrum Disorder

In 2013, with the fifth edition of the DSM (DSM-5), the APA reclassified PDD as autism spectrum disorder. Due to this reclassification, Asperger's syndrome and PDD-NOS were removed from the DSM.[2] According to the DSM-5 criteria; autism spectrum disorder is characterized by two groups of features present in early childhood: (1) persistent impairment in reciprocal social communication and social interaction and (2) restricted, repetitive patterns of behavior. Both areas are further described by one of three severity levels indicated by required support: (1) Requiring support, (2) Requiring substantial support, and 3) Requiring very substantial support (APA, 2013, 2022). For a diagnosis of autism spectrum disorder, one must present the following characteristics, either currently or in the past:

Social Communication and Social Interaction Deficits:

(a) Lack of social-emotional reciprocity (e.g., abnormal social approach, failure to initiate or respond to social interactions),
(b) Nonverbal communication (e.g., abnormalities in eye contact and body language, lack of facial expressions and nonverbal communication), and
(c) Developing, maintaining, and understanding relationships (e.g., difficulty adjusting behavior to various social contexts; sharing, absence of interest in peers).

Restricted, Repetitive Patterns of Behavior, Interests, or Activities

(a) Insistence on sameness, inflexible adherence to routines, or ritualized patterns of verbal or nonverbal behavior (e.g., greeting rituals, need to take the same route every day),
(b) Highly restricted, fixated interests that are abnormal in intensity or focus (e.g., strong attachment to or preoccupation with unusual objects; excessive interest in topics),
(c) Hyper or hypo-reactivity to sensory input or unusual interests in sensory aspects of the environment (e.g., indifference to pain/temperature, excessive smelling or touching of objects, adverse reaction to sounds) (APA, 2022, pp. 56–57).

A common behavior among autistic individuals is **stimming** or self-stimulation. Stimming may include a wide range of behaviors such as rocking, hand-flapping, moving objects, or repetitive noises. Stimming gives autistic individuals a sense of calmness and helps them cope with sensory overstimulation in their environment or surroundings (Deweerdt, 2020). A common communication difficulty associated with autism is a decreased or lack of ability to interpret the meaning of one's communication, a concept referred to as the **Theory of Mind** (ToM). ToM refers to the "ability to recognize and understand the thoughts, beliefs, desires, and intentions of others" (Attwood, 2007, p. 112). A diminished ToM often makes communication and interaction with others challenging, as they have difficulty with indirect language such as "figures of speech," slang/jargon, and rhetorical questions. Individuals may also take a more literal meaning to language or words. For example, in a routine traffic stop, if police ask, "Have you had anything to drink?" an autistic individual may respond, "Yes," not understanding the officer was referring to alcohol and not if they had *anything* to drink, such as water.

Prevalence Rates of ID and Autism

The exact percentage of the population with ID is unknown; however, Maulik et al. (2011) and Wittchen et al. (2011) estimated 10 per 1,000 (1%) in the general population. The global prevalence varies by country's average income level, with rates of approximately 16 per 1,000 (1.6%) in middle-income countries and 9 per 1,000 (0.9%) in high-income countries (Bourke et al., 2016; Wittchen et al., 2011).

The exact percentage of the population with an autism diagnosis is also unknown; however, Christensen et al. (2019) and Maenner et al. (2023)

estimated between 1 and 2% of the population. Autism is more commonly diagnosed in males, at about a 4-to-1 ratio (APA, 2022). According to the latest prevalence study by Maenner et al. (2023), one in 36 children has an autism diagnosis. The Centers for Disease Control and Prevention (CDC) has documented an increasing prevalence rate. In 2000, the rate was one out of every 150 children, increasing to one in 69 in 2012 and one in 44 in 2018. The reasons for the rate increase are unknown but likely due to increased awareness, changes to DSM criteria, increased assistance for children in local communities, improved diagnostic skills among clinicians, and increased social acceptance (CDC; Haskins & Silva, 2006). However, these numbers are only estimates. Due to inequalities in accessing behavioral health services (Bishop-Fitzpatrick & Kind, 2017), not everyone is able to receive a formal diagnosis.

Prevalence Rates in the Criminal Justice System

The estimated prevalence of ID in correctional institutions has been shown to vary with population, methodological approaches, and has yet to be reliably established in the US and other countries. However, persons with various cognitive disabilities are overrepresented in the US correctional system compared with prevalence rates in the general population. According to the most recent report published by the US Department of Justice (DOJ), cognitive disability[3] was the most common disability category reported. Approximately 20% of those incarcerated in state and federal prisons and 31% of those incarcerated in jails reported having a cognitive disability compared to an estimated prevalence of only 5% in the general population (Bronson et al., 2015). Estimates of incarcerated individuals with ID in Canada and Europe suggest an overrepresentation. Matheson et al. (2022) estimated a 2% prevalence of ID and other developmental disabilities among those incarcerated in federal correctional facilities in Ontario, Canada. Murphy et al. (2017) estimated that about 7% of those incarcerated in prisons in England, and Young et al. (2018) estimated that 9% of incarcerated individuals in the UK have ID. These estimates outside the US suggest a possible overrepresentation in US correctional institutions, considering their 1% prevalence in the general population.

Neither recent nor comprehensive research has been published on the prevalence of individuals with autism incarcerated who have contact with the CJS or in correctional facilities. Fazio et al. (2012) estimated that the prevalence of autism in a one state prison in the United States was about 4%. Young et al. (2018) estimated that 9% of incarcerated individuals in the UK have autism. Several studies published in the last decade or so have examined the prevalence of individuals with autism in Europe in forensic mental health settings, where percentages varied widely. Søndenaa et al. (2014) reviewed 3,382 Norwegian forensic examination reports and found that 1.4% of patients had autism. Others found much higher percentages; for example, Lindsay et al. (2014) showed that more than 9% of individuals referred to forensic services in England and Scotland had a diagnosis of autism, and 13% of those in three forensic psychiatry and youth centers in Sweden met the criteria of autism (Anckarsäter et al., 2008). Although research findings vary, autistic individuals may be overrepresented in forensic populations, considering their 1–2% prevalence in the general population.

Offending Behavior Among Those with ID and Autism

Although most individuals with ID or autism who encounter the CJS are not perpetrators of crime (Cooper et al., 2024; Salekin et al., 2010), the social and communication challenges associated with their condition may result in some engaging in inappropriate or illegal behavior. There is no direct link between autism or ID and sexual offending, although they may be overrepresented among those who engage in sexual-related offenses (Hart-Kerkhoffs et al., 2009; Lindsay, 2011). Those with developmental disabilities often have delayed social maturity than their typically developed peers, which can delay and impede their social and emotional well-being. As a result, they may experience more social rejection and isolation, thus having reduced opportunities to learn sexual knowledge and appropriate sexual behavior from similar-aged peers (Brown-Lavoie et al., 2014; Loftin, 2021). In a research review, Mogavero (2016) explained how the characteristics and life experiences of autistic individuals can increase their risk of engaging in deviant sexual behavior and sexual offending, often without malicious intent. Autistic individuals implicated in sexually related offenses often do so unwittingly, particularly those involving indecent images of minors (Mahoney, 2009). The case of Anthony below describes an autistic man who, at the time, was experiencing social isolation and major depressive disorder (*see* Chapter 3 of this book for details), and his restricted and repetitive patterns of behavior related to his autism led him to unknowingly download indecent images of minors.

Case of Anthony[4]

Background: Anthony was 50 years old when he was convicted of possessing indecent images of minors. Although experiencing social and communication challenges since childhood, he was not diagnosed with autism until the age of 35. He has no prior criminal history, no history of substance use disorder, and no history of childhood abuse. About two years before his arrest, he began experiencing major depressive disorder symptoms, began isolating himself, and spent most of his time on his computer. He developed a compulsive behavior of downloading pirated material from the internet and hoarding (i.e., saving) the files on his computer. He first began downloading music, TV shows, and movies. Over time, he began downloading images of famous musicians and actors. His repetitive and compulsive behavior resulted in him downloading files simultaneously, often unaware of the specific content. The searching and downloading of such images eventually led him to sexually explicit websites, some of which contained indecent images of minors.

Instant Offense: Police arrived at Anthony's apartment, responding to an unrelated complaint. While speaking with Anthony, the police noticed an image on his laptop computer that looked "suspicious" and asked him if they could look at his laptop. Not believing there was anything alarming on there, Anthony agreed and handed the laptop to the officers, who searched through it for several minutes. The police returned early the next morning with a search warrant and seized his laptop. The inspection of his laptop later revealed dozens of explicit images of underage girls.

Police immediately took Anthony into custody, where he sat alone in a room for several hours with wrists and ankles handcuffed, anxious and confused as to why he was there. His anxiety was compounded by his inability to take his prescribed medication that morning. He was also denied anything to eat or drink the entire time. When officers arrived, he was interrogated for several hours, and police repeatedly accused him of being a "pedophile" (attracted to underage minors) and that he was going "rape children," which Anthony repeatedly denied. He pleaded that he did not know the images were on his computer. He was arrested and taken to jail and later charged with possessing indecent images of minors.

Evaluation: Anthony received a court-ordered evaluation. The evaluator assessed Anthony's sexual attraction and sexual recidivism (i.e., reoffending) risk using several validated instruments. From the results of the tests and clinical judgment, the evaluator concluded Anthony's sexual interests were consistent with "normal adult heterosexual men"[5] with no evidence of pedophilia (sexual attraction to prepubescent minors) or any paraphilic disorders (deviant sexual interests).[6] The evaluator concluded that downloading the images was the result of repetitive and compulsive behavior, characteristic of autism. Anthony's intent was to complete the action of downloading the image and not motivated by sexual gratification. The risk assessment instrument result placed him in the low-risk[7] category for reoffending.

Outcome: Anthony's defense attorney knew little about autism and did not effectively advocate for his autism as a mitigating factor in his culpability. Fearing the outcome of a trial, which would require a prison sentence, Anthony's attorney encouraged him to accept a plea bargain and plead guilty. He was sentenced to a probation term of ten years and was required to register on the state's "sexual offender" registry for 20 years (*see* Chapter 14 of this book for details). His probation included 12 general rules (e.g., comply with treatment, meet with his probation officer), but also included 34 special conditions that appear to be "standard" rules for those convicted of contact sexual offenses against children. For example, he was required to avoid schools, parks, and public pools and have no contact with minors. Others appeared inapplicable, such as "have no contact with your victim" and do not possess any "children's toys or books." The strict and extensive conditions, coupled with having to register and being labeled a "sex offender," negatively impacted his self-esteem and led to feelings of hopelessness. At his age, the ten-year probation and 20-year registry felt like a "life sentence." He sought additional treatment to handle these self-defeating thoughts, but they persisted. Anthony explored having his conditions reassessed, but the legal fees to bring his case to court were nearly $40,000, which he was unable to afford.

Misconceptions About ID and Autism

ID and autism are conditions where individuals can present a wide variety of characteristics and abilities. Misconceptions, stigma, and ableism related to these disabilities lead to mistreatment in inappropriate interventions in the criminal justice system. Below is a list of some common misconceptions and stereotypes about ID or autism, refuted or rebutted by research.

(1) All autistic individuals are alike.

Reality: While many autistic individuals share common features, every autistic person is unique, which is why autism is referred to as a "spectrum" (Autism Association of Western Australia, n.d.; Galiatsos et al., 2019). As Dr. Stephen Shore famously said, "If you've met one person with autism, you've met one person with autism" (Magro, n.d.).

(2) Individuals with ID or autism are unable to learn, graduate from high school, or go to college.

Reality: Most individuals with ID and autism can learn but often learn differently. Some may need different environments or process information differently than a typically developed student. Many do graduate high school and go on to attend college (Autism Association of Western Australia, n.d.; Think College, n.d.)

(3) Most with autism have co-occurring intellectual disability.

Reality: Some individuals with autism can also have ID, while others have an intelligence level with IQ scores within the average range or higher (APA, 2022; Autism Association of Western Australia, n.d.).

(4) Autism and other NDDs are mental illnesses.

Reality: A developmental disability is neurological, so it differs from a mental illness. While mental illnesses can co-occur, autism and other NDDs are not mental illnesses (APA, 2022; Autism Association of Western Australia, n.d.).

(5) Autistic people are violent or dangerous.

Reality: Most individuals with autism are law-abiding and not violent or dangerous (Mouridsen, 2012; Scragg & Shah, 1994; Woodbury-Smith et al., 2006). This myth is perpetuated by media portrayals of **posthumous** (occurring after death) autism diagnoses of notorious cases of people who committed murder (Allely & Faccini, 2017; Palermo & Bogaerts, 2015).

(6) People eventually outgrow their autism.

Reality: Developmental disabilities are chronic, lifelong conditions with no "cure." Although lifelong, therapies and interventions can improve a person's abilities, skills, and quality of life (The ACC Institute of Human Services, 2018).

(7) Individuals with autism do not feel empathy.

Reality: Autistic individuals do have the capacity to feel empathy, though they may not always express their empathy in a typical manner (Baron-Cohen, 2009; Brett et al., 2024; The ACC Institute of Human Services, 2018).

(8) Autistic individuals do not feel or express emotions.

Reality: Individuals with autism have a full range of feelings and emotions. Many autistic individuals can feel and express love, but sometimes in idiosyncratic or unique ways (Autism Association of Western Australia, n.d.; The ACC Institute of Human Services, 2018).

(9) Individuals with autism do not form bonds or relationships with others, even their families.

Reality: Autistic individuals often have strong bonds with important people in their lives. They can and do have fulfilling relationships with family, friends, partners, and children. Some may demonstrate attachments or affection on one's terms or express in a manner that is different from what society would typically expect (Autism Association of Western Australia, n.d.; Kahane & El-Tahir, 2015).

(10) Autistic individuals cannot live independently.

Reality: Many do live independently. A diagnosis of autism does not mean that someone is unable to live independently (Pearlma-avnion et al., 2017).

(11) Autistic individuals have special abilities.

Reality: Individuals with autism often have strengths and weaknesses across academic and functional areas (John et al., 2017). However, only a small percentage of individuals with autism have savant abilities (Jarrett, 2014; Treffert, 2009). This myth is likely due to media portrayals of autistic persons (Draaisma, 2009).

(12) Autism is caused by reactions to vaccinations such as the MMR.

Reality: This myth was based on the flawed and fraudulent study of 12 children by Wakefield et al. (1998)—(RETRACTED). Four decades of research found no reliable scientific evidence that childhood vaccinations cause autism. For example, a study of 95,727 children found that the MMR vaccine was not associated with an increased risk of autism at any age (Jain et al., 2015). The causes are still being studied, but experts believe genetic factors exist (National Autistic Society, n.d.). Gini et al. (2021) found that autism is more common in the first degree of biological relatives (i.e., mother, father, siblings) of children with autism than in the general population.

Conclusion

The information about neurodiversity provided in this chapter explains what NDDs are, what they are not, and how different neurodiverse individuals may present. CJS practitioners may unknowingly encounter an autistic individual or someone with ID who may have communication or comprehension difficulties. Therefore, initial communication should be clear and direct. Asking vague questions such as "Do you have anything on you?" may be confusing and result in no response. If someone is not making eye contact, not responding to questions, or delaying their responses, it does not necessarily mean they are under the influence of substances, being evasive, uncooperative, or dishonest (*see* Chapter 8 of this book for a case example). Instead, they may not understand the questions or still may be processing them. Comprehensive neurodiversity-specific training for CJS practitioners is an essential step in improving the communication and experiences of neurodiverse individuals. Some states (e.g., New Jersey, Indiana, Illinois, California, Massachusetts, and Florida)[8] have taken steps to improve awareness through mandated training for police and first responders.

More importantly, the impaired executive functioning in the pre-frontal cortex can lead those with autism and ID to unwittingly engage in inappropriate or illegal acts that appear to be obvious transgressions to individuals without any developmental disabilities. Such cases require additional communication and specific strategies from defense attorneys (Kelley, 2020; Mahoney, 2009). In the case of Anthony, he unwittingly committed an offense that stemmed from his autism and mental health (i.e., compulsive, repetitive behavior and depression). His attorney's lack of autism knowledge impeded his ability to establish an effective defense strategy. Despite Anthony's diagnoses, low-risk status, and no evidence of sexually inappropriate behavior with minors, his probation officer assigned strict conditions and restrictions that were consistent with someone at high risk of committing a sexual offense. This negatively impacted his self-esteem, exacerbated his depression and feelings of hopelessness, and deteriorated his mental health. Therefore, neurodiversity-specific training should include other practitioners in the CJS, including attorneys, judges, and corrections staff, to ensure they better handle neurodiverse individuals properly and justly. Understanding neurodiversity and one's unique needs is an important first step to improving communication and having more positive interactions.

Key Terms

Ableism
Autism Spectrum Disorder
Asperger's Disorder
Diagnostic and Statistical Manual of Mental Disorders
Executive Functions
Functional magnetic resonance imaging or fMRI
Intellectual Disability Disorder
Intelligence Quotient (IQ)
The International Classification of Diseases
Jurisdiction

Medial prefrontal cortex
Neurodevelopmental Disability Disorder
Posthumous
Stimming
Theory of Mind

Chapter Questions

(1) Define neurodiversity and how this term relates to those with neurodevelopmental disorders.
(2) What are the major diagnostic features of autism spectrum disorder (ASD)?
(3) What are the major diagnostic features of Intellectual Disability Disorder (ID)?
(4) What was the role of IQ scores in diagnosing ID? How are they used now?
(5) Why is it important for criminal justice practitioners to know about autism and ID?
(6) Consider the case of Anthony: The "sexual offender" registry was intended to alert community members of people who are at risk of offending. Describe your position as to whether low-risk individuals with no evidence of sexual deviant interest should be required to register or if it should only contain those who are at medium to high risk. Explain your response.

Suggested Readings

Copenhaver, A., & Tewksbury, R. (2019). Interactions between autistic individuals and law enforcement: A mixed-methods exploratory study. *American Journal of Criminal Justice, 44*(2), 309–333. https://doi.org/10.1007/s12103-018-9452-8

Jones, J. (2007). Persons with intellectual disabilities in the criminal justice system: Review of issues. *International Journal of Offender Therapy and Comparative Criminology, 51*(6), 723–733. https://doi.org/10.1177/0306624X07299343

Taylor, K., Mesibov, G., & Debbaudt, D. (2009). Autism in the criminal justice system. *North Carolina Bar Journal, 14*(4), 32–36.

Yarnell-Mac Grory, S., Mahoney, M., & Westphal, A. (2021). Neuroscience of autism in the legal context. In F. R. Volkmar, R. Loftin, A. Westphal, &

M. Woodbury-Smith (Eds.), *Handbook of autism spectrum disorder and the law* (pp. 71–96). Springer. https://doi.org/10.1007/978-3-030-70913-6_4

Notes

1. See *A Note About Evolving Language and Term* in Chapter 1 for information on identity-first language.
2. Those diagnosed with a PDD from an earlier version of the DSM sometimes maintain their diagnosis.
3. Measured with the question: "Because of a physical, mental, or emotional problem, do you have serious difficulty concentrating, remembering, or making decisions?" (Bronson et al., 2015, p. 2).
4. Name and some details have been changed for anonymity.
5. Direct wording from the assessment report.
6. A thorough investigation that included interviews of all minors Anthony had regular contact with found no evidence of sexual offending behavior.
7. "Low risk" is the lowest risk category, as there is no "no risk" category (e.g., a score of 0 = low risk).
8. California Senate Bill 1531, Florida Senate Bill 1352, Illinois House Bill 3454, Indiana House Bill 1242, Massachusetts House Bill 2098 and Senate Bill 1264, New Jersey Assembly Bill 1908.

References

Allely, C. S., & Faccini, L. (2017). "Path to intended violence" model to understand mass violence in the case of Elliot Rodger. *Aggression and Violent Behavior, 37*, 201–209. https://doi.org/10.1016/j.avb.2017.09.005

Anckarsäter, H., Nilsson, T., Saury, J. M., Råstam, M., & Gillberg, C. (2008). Autism spectrum disorders in institutionalized subjects. *Nordic Journal of Psychiatry, 62*(2), 60–167. https://doi.org/10.1080/08039480801957269

American Psychiatric Association. (1952). *Diagnostic and statistical manual of mental disorders* (1st ed.).

American Psychiatric Association. (1968). *Diagnostic and statistical manual of mental disorders* (2nd ed.).

American Psychiatric Association. (1980). *Diagnostic and statistical manual of mental disorders* (3rd ed.).

American Psychiatric Association. (1987). *Diagnostic and statistical manual of mental disorders* (3rd ed. Revised).

American Psychiatric Association. (1994). *Diagnostic and statistical manual of mental disorders* (4th ed.).

American Psychiatric Association. (2000). *Diagnostic and statistical manual of mental disorders* (4th ed. Text Revision).

American Psychiatric Association. (2013). *Diagnostic and statistical manual of mental disorders* (5th ed.). https://doi.org/10.1176/appibooks.9780890425596

American Psychiatric Association. (2022). *Diagnostic and statistical manual of mental disorders* (5th ed. Text Revision). https://doi.org/10.1176/appi.books.9780890425787

Asperger, H. (1944). Die 'Autistischen Psychopathen' im Kindesalter. *Archiv Für Psychiatrie und Nervenkrankenheiten, 117*, 76–136.

Asperger, H. (1991). 'Autistic psychopathy' in childhood (U. Frith, Trans.). In U. Frith (Ed.), *Autism and Asperger syndrome* (pp. 37–92).

Attwood, T. (2007). *The complete guide to Asperger's Syndrome.* Jessica Kingsley Publishers.

Autism Association of Western Australia. (n.d.). *Autism myth busters.* https://www.autism.org.au/what-is-autism/common-misconceptions/

Baron-Cohen, S. (2009). The empathising-systemising theory of autism: Implications for education. *Tizard Learning Disability Review, 14*(3), 5–13.

Bishop-Fitzpatrick, L., & Kind, A. J. H. (2017). A scoping review of health disparities in autism spectrum disorder. *Journal of Autism and Developmental Disorders, 47*(11), 3380–3391. https://doi.org/10.1007/s10803-017-3251-9

Bleuler, E. (1950 [1911]). *Dementia praecox or the group of schizophrenias.* International Universities. https://archive.org/details/dementiapraecoxo0000bleu/mode/2up

Blume, H. (1997, July 1). 'Autism & the internet' or 'it's the wiring, stupid.' *Media in Transition.* http://web.mit.edu/m-i-t/articles/index_blume.html?fbclid=IwAR3vkHBJc8GiommvlZcGN2MPZMCZuV6XQuvGzMhq9LAq8CSzg4nod0GfAPU

Botha, M., Chapman, R., Giwa Onaiwu, M., Kapp, S. K., Stannard Ashley, A., & Walker, N. (2024). The neurodiversity concept was developed collectively: An overdue correction on the origins of neurodiversity theory. *Autism, 28*(6), 1591–1594. https://doi.org/10.1177/13623613241237871

Bourke, J., de Klerk, N., Smith, T., & Leonard, H. (2016). Population-based prevalence of intellectual disability and autism spectrum disorders in Western Australia: A comparison with previous estimates. *Medicine, 95*(21), e3737. https://doi.org/10.1097/MD.0000000000003737

Brett, J. D., Preece, D. A., Becerra, R., Whitehouse, A., & Maybery, M. T. (2024). Empathy and autism: Establishing the structure and different manifestations of empathy in autistic individuals using the Perth Empathy Scale. *Journal of Autism and Developmental Disorders.* https://doi.org/10.1007/s10803-024-06491-3

Bronson, J., Maruschak, L. M., & Berzofsky, L. M. (2015). *Disabilities among prison and jail inmates, 2011–12*. US Department of Justice, Office of Justice Programs, Bureau of Justice Statistics.

Brown-Lavoie, S. M., Viecili, M. A., & Weiss, J. A. (2014). Sexual knowledge and victimization in adults with autism spectrum disorders. *Journal of Autism and Developmental Disorders, 44*(9), 2185–2196. https://doi.org/10.1007/s10803-014-2093y

Christensen, D. L., Maenner, M. J., Bilder, D., Constantino, J. N., Daniels, J., Durkin, M. S., Fitzgerald, R. T., Kurzius-Spencer, M., Pettygrove, S. D., Robinson, C., Shenouda, J., White, T., Zahorodny, W., Pazol, K., & Dietz, P. (2019). Prevalence of autism spectrum disorder among children aged 4 years—Autism and developmental disabilities monitoring network seven sites, United States, 2010, 2012, and 2014. *Morbidity and Mortality Weekly Report. Surveillance Summaries, 68*(2), 1–19. https://doi.org/10.15585/mmwr.ss6802a1

Cooper, D., Frisbie, S., Wang, S., Jonas, V., Gibbs, V. Love, Abigail M. A., Mogavero, M, Benevides, T. W., Hyatt, J. M., Hooven, K., Basketbill, I., & Shea, L. (2024). What do we know about autism and policing globally? Preliminary findings from an international effort to examine autism and the criminal justice system. *Autism Research,* https://doi.org/10.1002/aur.3203

Courchesne, E., Karns, C. M., Davis, H. R., Ziccardi, R., Carper, R. A., Tigue, Z. D., Chisum, H. J., Moses, P., Pierce, K., Lord, C., Lincoln, A. J., Pizzo, S., Schreibman, L., Haas, R. H., Akshoomoff, N. A., & Courchesne, R. Y. (2001). Unusual brain growth patterns in early life in patients with autistic disorder: An MRI study. *Neurology, 57*(2), 245–254.

DeWeerdt, S. (2020, January 1). Repetitive behaviors and 'stimming' in autism, explained. *Spectrum*. https://doi.org/10.53053/ERTG7729

Dow-Edwards, D., MacMaster, F. P., Peterson, B. S., Niesink, R., Andersen, S., & Braams, B. R. (2019). Experience during adolescence shapes brain development: From synapses and networks to normal and pathological behavior. *Neurotoxicology and Teratology, 76*, 106834. https://doi.org/10.1016/j.ntt.2019.106834

Draaisma, D. (2009). Stereotypes of autism. *Philosophical Transactions of the Royal London Biological Sciences, 364*, 1475–1480.

Dunn, D. S. (2021, December 15). Understanding ableism and negative reactions to disability. *American Psychological Association*. https://www.apa.org/ed/precollege/psychology-teacher-network/introductory-psychology/ableism-negative-reactions-disability.

Elakkiya, M. K., & Dejey, D. (2023). Stacked autoencoder with novel integrated activation functions for the diagnosis of autism spectrum disorder. *Neural Computing and Applications, 35*, 1–33. https://doi.org/10.1007/s00521-023-08565-2

Fazio, R. L., Pietz, C. A., & Denney, R. L. (2012). An estimate of the prevalence of autism-spectrum disorders in an incarcerated population. *Open Access Journal of Forensic Psychology, 4*, 69–80.

Galiatsos, S., Kruse, L., & Whittaker, M. (2019). Forward together: Helping educators unlock the power of students who learn differently. *National Center for Learning Disabilities.* https://www.ncld.org/wp-content/uploads/2019/05/Forward-Together_NCLD-report.pdf

Gini, S., Knowland, V., Thomas, M. S., & Van Herwegen, J. (2021). Neuromyths about neurodevelopmental disorders: Misconceptions by educators and the general public. *Mind, Brain, and Education, 15*(4), 289–298. https://doi.org/10.1111/mbe.12303

Haas, K., & Gibbs, V. (2021). Does a person's autism play a role in their interactions with police: The perceptions of autistic adults and parent/carers. *Journal of Autism and Developmental Disorders, 51,* 1628–1640. https://doi.org/10.1007/s10803-020-04663-5

Haskins, B. G. & Silva, J. A. (2006). Asperger's disorder and criminal behavior: Forensic-psychiatric considerations. *Journal of American Academy of Psychiatry & Law, 34,* 374–84. http://jaapl.org/content/34/3/374

Hardan, A. Y., Minshew, N. J., & Keshavan, M. S. (2000). Corpus callosum size in autism. *Neurology, 55*(7), 1033–1036.

Hart-Kerkhoffs, L. A., Jansen, L. M., Doreleijers, T. A., Vermeiren, R., & Minderaa, R. B. (2009). Autism spectrum disorder symptoms in juvenile suspects of sex offenses. *Journal of Clinical Psychiatry, 70*(2), 266–272. https://doi.org/10.4088/jcp.08m04635

Huey, E. B. (1912). *Backward and feeble-minded children.* Warwick and York.

Jaarsma, P., & Welin, S. (2012). Autism as a natural human variation: Reflections on the claims of the neurodiversity movement. *Health Care Analysis, 20,* 20–30.

Jain, A., Marshall, J., Buikema, A., Bancroft, T., Kelly, J. P., & Newschaffer, C. J. (2015). Autism occurrence by MMR vaccine status among US children with older siblings with and without autism. *Journal of the American Medical Association, 313*(15), 1534–1540. https://doi.org/10.1001/jama.2015.3077

Jarrett, C. (2014). Autism myth and reality. *The Psychologist, 27,* 746–749.

Jassim, N., Baron-Cohen, S., & Suckling, J. (2021). Meta-analytic evidence of differential prefrontal and early sensory cortex activity during non-social sensory perception in autism. *Neuroscience and Biobehavioral Reviews, 127,* 146–157. https://doi.org/10.1016/j.neubiorev.2021.04.014

John, R. P. S., Knott, F. J., & Harvey, K. N. (2017). Myths about autism: An exploratory study using focus groups. *Autism, 22*(7), 845–854. https://doi.org/10.1177/1362361317714990

Kahane, L., & El-Tahir, M. (2015). Attachment behavior in children with autistic spectrum disorders. *Advances in Mental Health and Intellectual Disabilities, 9*(2), 79–89. https://doi.org/10.1108/AMHID-06-2014-0026

Kanner, L. (1943). Autistic disturbances of affective contact. *Nervous Child: Quarterly Journal of Psychopathology, Psychotherapy, Mental Hygiene, and Guidance of the Child, 2,* 217–250.

Kapp, S. K., Gillespie-Lynch, L. E. S., & Hutman, T. (2013). Deficit, difference, or both? Autism and neurodiversity. *Developmental Psychology, 49*(1), 59–71.

Kelley, E. (2020). The intersection of ASD and the criminal justice system. In E. Kelley (Ed.), *Representing people with autism spectrum disorders: A practical guide for criminal defense attorneys* (pp. 1–6). ABA Publishing.

Koffer Miller, K. H., Becker, A., Cooper, D., & Shea, L. (2021). Justice system interactions among autistic individuals: A multiple methods analysis. *Crime & Delinquency, 68*(9), 1579–1603. https://doi.org/10.1177/00111287211054733

Lindsay, W. R. (2011). People with intellectual disability who offend or are involved with the criminal justice system. *Current Opinion in Psychiatry, 24*(5), 377–381. https://doi.org/10.1097/YCO.0b013e3283479dc9

Lindsay, W. R., Carson, D., O'Brian, G., Holland, A., Taylor, J. L., Wheeler, J. R., & Steptoe, L. (2014). A comparison of referrals with and without autism spectrum disorder to forensic intellectual disability services. *Psychiatry, Psychology & Law, 21*(6), 947–954. https://doi.org/10.1080/13218719.2014.918081

Loftin, R. (2021). Sexual offending and ASD. In F. R. Volkmar, R. Loftin, A. Westphal, & M. Woodbury-Smith (Eds.), *Handbook of autism spectrum disorder and the law* (pp. 257–267). Springer. https://doi.org/10.1007/978-3-030-70913-6_6

Maenner, M. J., Warren, Z., Williams, A. R., Amoakohene, E., Bakian, A. V., Bilder, D. A., Durkin, M. S., Fitzgerald, R. T., Furnier, S. M., Hughes, M. M., Ladd-Acosta, C. M., McArthur, D., Pas, E. T., Salinas, A., Vehorn, A., Williams, S., Esler, A., Grzybowski, A., Hall-Lande, J., Nguyen, R. H. N., & Shaw, K. A. (2023). Prevalence and characteristics of autism spectrum disorder among children aged 8 years—Autism and Developmental Disabilities Monitoring Network, 11 Sites, United States, 2020. *Morbidity and Mortality Weekly Report. Surveillance Summaries, 72*(2), 1–14. https://doi.org/10.15585/mmwr.ss7202a1

Magro, K. (n.d.). 10 inspiring quotes from people with autism. *Autism Speaks.* https://www.autismspeaks.org/life-spectrum/autism-quotes

Mahoney, M. J. (2009). *Asperger's syndrome and the criminal law: The special case of child pornography.* www.harringtonmahoney.com/documents/Aspergers%20Syndrome%20and%20the%20Criminal%20Law%20v26.pdf

Manouilenko, I., & Bejerot, S. (2015). Sukhareva—Prior to Asperger and Kanner. *Nordic Journal of Psychiatry., 69*(6), 479–482. https://doi.org/10.3109/08039488.2015.1005022

Matheson, F. I., Dastoori, P., Whittingham, L., Calzavara, A., Keown, L. A., Durbin, A., Kouyoumdjian, F. G., Lin, E., Volpe, T., & Lunsky, Y. (2022). Intellectual/developmental disabilities among people incarcerated in federal correctional facilities in Ontario, Canada: Examining prevalence, health and correctional characteristics. *Journal of Applied Research in Intellectual Disabilities, 35*(3), 900–909. https://doi.org/10.1111/jar.12995

Maulik, P. K., Mascarenhas, M. N., Mathers, C. D., Dua, T., & Saxena, S. (2011). Prevalence of intellectual disability: A meta-analysis of population-based studies. *Research in Developmental Disabilities, 32*(2), 419–436. https://doi.org/10.1016/j.ridd.2010.12.018

Mogavero, M. C. (2016). Autism, sexual offending, and the criminal justice system. *Journal of Intellectual Disabilities and Offending Behavior, 7*(3), 116–126. https://doi.org/10.1108/JIDOB-02-2016-0004

Mouridsen, S. E. (2012). Current status of research on autism spectrum disorders and offending. *Research in Autism Spectrum Disorders, 6*(1), 79–86. https://doi.org/10.1016/j.rasd.2011.09.003

Murphy, G. H., Gardner, J., & Freeman, M. J. (2017). Screening prisoners for intellectual disabilities in three English prisons. *Journal of Applied Research in Intellectual Disabilities, 30*(1), 198–204. https://doi.org/10.1111/jar.12224

National Autistic Society. *What is autism?* https://www.autism.org.uk/advice-and-guidance/what-is-autism/the-causes-of-autism

Ortega, F. (2009). The cerebral subject and the challenge of neurodiversity. *BioSocieties, 4*, 425–445. https://doi.org/10.1017/S1745855209990287

Ortega, F., & Choudhury, S. (2011). 'Wired up differently': Autism, adolescence, and the politics of neurological identities. *Subjectivity, 4*(3), 323–345. https://doi.org/10.1057/sub.2011.9

Pearlma-avnion, S., Cohen, N., & Eldan, A. (2017). Sexual well-being and quality of life among high-functioning adults with autism. *Sexuality and Disability, 35*(3), 279–293. https://doi.org/10.1007/s11195-017-9490-z

Palermo, M. T., & Bogaerts, S. (2015). The dangers of posthumous diagnoses and the unintended consequences of facile associations: Jeffrey Dahmer and autism spectrum disorders. *International Journal of Offender Therapy and Comparative Criminology, 59*(14), 1564–1579. https://doi.org/10.1177/0306624X14550642

Portway, S. M., & Johnson, B. (2005). Do you know I have Asperger's syndrome? Risks of a non-obvious disability. *Health, Risk & Society, 7*(1), 73–83. https://doi.org/10.1080/09500830500042086

Qiu, L., & Zhai, J. (2024). A hybrid CNN-SVM model for enhanced autism diagnosis. *PLoS ONE, 19*(5), 70302236. https://doi.org/10.1371/journal.pone.0302236

Rava, J., Shattuck, P., Rast, J., & Roux, A. (2017). The prevalence and correlates of involvement in the criminal justice system among youth on the autism spectrum. *Journal of Autism and Developmental Disorders, 47*(2), 340–346. https://doi.org/10.1007/s10803-016-2958-3

Resnick, J. (2017, April 6). Paul Eugen Bleuler (1857–1939). *Embryo Project Encyclopedia*. http://embryo.asu.edu/handle/10776/11464

Salekin, K. L., Olley, J. G., & Hedge, K. A. (2010). Offenders with intellectual disability: Characteristics, prevalence, and issues in forensic assessment. *Journal of Mental Health Research in Intellectual Disabilities, 3*(2), 97–116. https://doi.org/10.1080/19315861003695769

Scragg, P., & Shah, A. (1994). Prevalence of Asperger's syndrome in a secure hospital. *British Journal of Psychiatry, 165*, 679–682. https://doi.org/10.1192/bjp.165.5.679

Sher, D. A., & Gibson, J. L. (2021). Pioneering, prodigious and perspicacious: Grunya Efimovna Sukhareva's life and contribution to conceptualising autism and schizophrenia. *European Child and Adolescent Psychiatry*. https://doi.org/10.1007/s00787-021-01875-7

Shtayermman, O. (2009). An exploratory study of the stigma associated with a diagnosis of Asperger's Syndrome: The mental health impact on the adolescents and young adults diagnosed with a disability with a social nature. *Journal of Human Behavior in the Social Environment, 19*(3), 298–313. https://doi.org/10.1080/10911350902790720

Singer, J. (1998). *Odd people in: The birth of community amongst people on the "autistic spectrum:" A personal exploration of a new social movement based on neurological diversity.* A thesis presented to the faculty of Humanities and Social Sciences in partial fulfillment of the requirements for the degree of Bachelor of Arts Social Science (Honours), University of Technology, Sydney.

Søndenaa, E., Rasmussen, K., Helverschou, S. B., Steindal, K., Nilson, B., & Nøttestad, J. A. (2014). Violence and sexual offending behavior in people with autism spectrum disorder who have undergone a psychiatric forensic examination. *Psychological Reports: Disability & Trauma, 115*(1), 32–43. https://doi.org/10.2466/16.15.PR0.115c16z5

Ssucharewa, G. E. (1926). Die Besonderheiten der schizoiden Psychopathien bei den Mädchen. *Monatsschrift Für Psychiatrie und Neurologie, 60*(3–4), 235–261. https://doi.org/10.1159/000190478

The ACC Institute of Human Services. (2018, December 7). *Developmental disabilities—Myths vs. Facts.* https://acc.edu.sg/en/developmental-disabilities-myths-vs-facts/

The Center for Disease Control and Prevention. *Autism spectrum disorder.* US Department of Health and Human Services. https://www.cdc.gov/ncbddd/autism/index.html

Think College Institute for Community Inclusion. *Home*. https://thinkcollege.net/.

Tint, A., Palucka, A. M., Bradley, E., Weiss, J. A., & Lunsky, Y. (2017). Correlates of police involvement among adolescents and adults with autism spectrum disorder. *Journal of Autism and Developmental Disorders, 47*(9), 2639–2647. https://doi.org/10.1007/s10803-017-3182-5

Tint, A., Palucka, A. M., Bradley, E., Weiss, J. A., & Lunsky, Y. (2019). Emergency service experiences of adults with autism spectrum disorder without intellectual disability. *Autism, 23*(3), 792–795. https://doi.org/10.1177/1362361318760294

Treffert, D. A. (2009). The savant syndrome: An extraordinary condition. A synopsis: Past, present, future. *Philosophical Transactions of the Royal London Biological Sciences., 364*, 1351–1357. https://doi.org/10.1098/rstb.2008.0326

Wakefield, A. J., Murch, S. H., Anthony, A., Linnell, J., Casson, D. M., Malik, M., Berelowitz, M., Dhillon, A. P., Thomson, M. A., Harvey, P., Valentine, A., Davies, S. E., & Walker-Smith, J. A. (1998). Ileal-lymphoid-nodular hyperplasia, non-specific colitis, and pervasive developmental disorder in children. *Lancet, 351*(9103), 637–641. https://doi.org/10.1016/s0140-6736(97)11096-0. Retraction published (2004, March 6). *Lancet, 363*(9411), 750. https://doi.org/10.1016/S0140-6736(04)15715-2. (2010 February 6). *Lancet, 375*(9713), 445. https://doi.org/10.1016/S0140-6736(10)60175-4

Wing, L. (1981). Asperger's syndrome: A clinical account. *Psychological Medicine, 11*(1), 115–129. https://doi.org/10.1017/S0033291700053332

Wittchen, H. U., Jacobi, F., Rehm, J., Gustavsson, A., Svensson, M., Jönsson, B., Olesen, J., Allgulander, C., Alonso, J., Faravelli, C., Fratiglioni, L., Jennum, P., Lieb, R., Maercker, A., van Os, J., Preisig, M., Salvador-Carulla, L., Simon, R., & Steinhausen, H. C. (2011). The size and burden of mental disorders and other disorders of the brain in Europe 2010. *European Neuropsychopharmacology, 21*(9), 655–679. https://doi.org/10.1016/j.euroneuro.2011.07.018

Woodbury-Smith, M. R., Clare, I. C. H., Holland, A. J., & Kearns, A. (2006). High functioning autistic spectrum disorders, offending and other law-breaking: Findings from a community sample. *The Journal of Forensic Psychiatry & Psychology, 17*(1), 108–120. https://doi.org/10.1080/14789940600589464

World Health Organization. (2018). *International classification of diseases and related health problems* (11th ed.). https://idc.who.int/

Young, S., González, R. A., Mullens, H., Mutch, L., Malet-Lambert, I., & Gudjonsson, G. H. (2018). Neurodevelopmental disorders in prison inmates: Comorbidity and combined associations with psychiatric symptoms and behavioural disturbance. *Psychiatry Research, 261*, 109–115. https://doi.org/10.1016/j.psychres.2017.12.036

3

Understanding Mental Illnesses and Substance Use Disorders—Overview and Implications for the Criminal Justice System

Learning Objectives

After this chapter, readers should be able to understand the:

1) Characteristics and diagnostic criteria of schizophrenia and delusional disorder
2) Difference between delusions and hallucinations
3) Characteristics and diagnostic criteria of bipolar disorder, mania, and major depressive disorder
4) Characteristics and diagnostic criteria of post-traumatic stress disorder
5) Characteristics and diagnostic criteria of substance use disorder
6) The physiological sources of use and dependence
7) Prevalence rates of mental illness and substance use disorder in the general population and the correctional system

Introduction

Research has shown that those with mental illnesses and substance use disorders (SUDs) are overrepresented in the criminal justice system (CJS) (Bronson & Berzofsky, 2017; Maruschak et al., 2021). CJS practitioners interact with people with various mental health conditions at high rates, with approximately 5–10% of police encounters involving individuals with mental

M. C. Mogavero, *Mental Health, Neurodiversity, and Criminal Justice*, https://doi.org/10.1007/978-3-031-88816-8_3

illnesses (Fuller et al., 2015; Livingston, 2016), many of whom also have co-occurring SUDs (Cordner, 2006; Zhang et al., 2022). Surveys of police and correctional officers have shown that many felt ill-prepared to handle those with mental illnesses (Lavoie et al., 2006; Tartaro et al., 2021). Officers may give commands to which the individual may be unable to comply, which can be misinterpreted as noncompliance. Unfortunately, the use of force or violence to control situations involving those with mental illnesses is more common than those with no evidence of mental illness (Jun et al., 2020; Rossler & Terril, 2017).

Although there here are hundreds of diagnoses of mental disorders in the Diagnostic and Statistical Manual of Mental Disorders, Fifth Edition, Text Revision (DSM-5-TR), this chapter will describe just a few severe mental illnesses, including schizophrenia, delusional disorder, bipolar disorders, post-traumatic stress disorder (PTSD), and SUDs (APA, 2022). Some of the symptoms or characteristics may overlap, so awareness of the various conditions can help CJS practitioners from making assumptions that someone is under the influence of substances when, in fact, it may be a symptom of a mental illness and require additional care and treatment when involved in CJS. Greater knowledge and understanding of mental illnesses can improve the skills and confidence of CJS practitioners to work more effectively with those with mental health conditions and implement strategies to de-escalate situations or render aid when necessary.

Schizophrenia Spectrum and Other Psychotic Disorders

Schizophrenia spectrum and other psychotic disorders are defined by abnormalities of one's thoughts, sensory perceptions, behaviors, and movements where symptoms fall within one or more of the following five domains: (1) delusions, (2) hallucinations, (3) disorganized thoughts or speech), (4) grossly disorganized or abnormal motor behavior), and (5) negative symptoms (APA, 2022). **Delusions** are false beliefs that are firm and not amenable to change, even when presented with conflicting evidence. Some delusions are consistent with the individual's cultural or socioeconomic background (e.g., someone with a prior criminal record believes they are under police surveillance). Others may be considered bizarre and inconsistent with cultural background (e.g., someone believes they have superpowers). Other delusions may involve situations that could occur in real life, such as having a disease or believing their significant other is being unfaithful. For a diagnosis of

delusional disorder, one must present (1) one (or more) delusions for one month or longer, (2) the delusions must cause significant distress or impair one's social, occupational, or other areas of functioning, and (3) the delusions cannot be explained by the effects of a substance or another medical condition (APA, 2022).

Types or Categories of Delusions:

- **Persecutory**—that one is going to be harmed in some way such as being harassed, conspired against, cheated on, spied on, followed, poisoned, drugged, maliciously defamed, or obstructed in their pursuit of long-term goals by an individual, organization, or other groups.
- **Erotomania**—that another person is in love with them.
- **Grandiose**—they have some great (but unrecognized) talent, exceptional abilities, insight, wealth, fame, or having made some important discovery.
- **Referential**—that certain gestures, comments, and environmental cues are directed at oneself.
- **Nihilistic**—that a major catastrophe will occur.
- **Somatic**—has a preoccupation regarding one's health and organ function. These can occur in several forms, including believing one emits a foul odor, an infestation of insects on or under the skin, an internal parasite, certain parts of the body are misshapen or ugly, or that parts of the body are not functioning (APA, 2022, p. 105).

Delusions are a common symptom of **schizophrenia,** and another common symptom is **hallucinations**, which are false involuntary experiences that involve one's sensory perceptions. Unlike delusions, which are thoughts or beliefs, hallucinations are experiences that occur without an external stimulus (e.g., seeing a person when no one else is in the room). Hallucinations tend to be as prominent and clear as any other everyday perception (e.g., someone in the room speaking to them). They may occur in any sensory modality, auditory, visual, olfactory, tactile, and gustatory (see below), but auditory hallucinations are the most common in schizophrenia and related disorders. Auditory hallucinations are usually voices and are distinct from the individual's thoughts. Voices can be positive/friendly, negative/mean (e.g., command you to do something that may cause harm to yourself or others), or neutral (APA, 2022).

Types or categories of hallucinations:

- **Auditory**—hearing sounds that are not present, such as voices, music, footsteps, or doors banging.
- **Visual**—seeing objects that are not present, such as seeing people, shapes, animals, or lights.
- **Olfactory**—experiencing smells or odors that are not present or that no one else can smell.
- **Tactile**—feelings or sensations on or inside the body that are not present (e.g., bugs are crawling on their skin, or their internal organs are moving around inside them).
- **Gustatory**—experiencing tastes that are not present, often strange or unpleasant (e.g., metallic taste, poison). (Chaudhury, 2010)

Some with schizophrenia may display **disorganized thinking or speech**, where an individual may switch from one topic to another or answer questions with responses that are somewhat or completely unrelated. Below is an example of a response when the psychologist met a newly admitted patient for a psychological evaluation and asked a general rapport question:

> Psychologist: "How are you feeling this morning?"
>
> Patient: "My parents were into cults. They were disgusting people who would sit in feces."

Sometimes, speech is so severely disorganized that it is nearly incomprehensible, resembling a language disorder called **aphasia**. Incomprehensible speech is sometimes referred to as a **word salad,** where sentences contain an incoherent string of unrelated words or phrases (APA, 2022).

Some with schizophrenia may display grossly disorganized or abnormal motor behavior that manifests in various ways, including silliness, agitation, or **catatonia**. **Catatonic** behavior refers to having a noticeable decrease in responding to one's environment, such as refusing to follow instructions, a complete lack of verbal responses (**mutism**), or a complete lack of motor responses (**stupor**). Some may maintain rigid, inappropriate, or bizarre bodily postures or positions. Catatonic behavior can also include purposeless and excessive motor activity (catatonic excitement), such as staring, grimacing, and echoing of speech (APA, 2022).

Other symptoms, called negative symptoms, include diminished emotional expressions that generally emphasize speech, including facial expressions, movements of the eyes, tone of speech, and movements of the hands or head. Negative symptoms are common among schizophrenia but are less prominent in other psychotic disorders (APA, 2022). Below are four types of negative symptoms:

- **Avolition:** decreased motivation of self-initiated purposeful activities (e.g., may sit for extended periods or show little interest in participating in work or social activities)
- **Alogia**: using few words when speaking or giving short responses (poverty of speech)
- **Anhedonia:** the inability or decreased ability to enjoy pleasure or recall pleasure from previously positive experiences
- **Asociality**: a lack of interest in social interactions. (APA, 2022, pp. 102–103)

The five domains of symptoms listed above (delusions, hallucinations, disorganized speech, negative symptoms) are further classified into three categories: (1) positive (excessive or increased thoughts, emotions, and behaviors), (2) negative (lack of or decreased thoughts, emotions, and behaviors), and (3) psychomotor (unusual movements or gestures). Although most tend to experience positive and negative symptoms, some experience symptoms dominated by one type or the other (APA, 2022).

Diagnostic Criteria for Schizophrenia and Other Psychotic Disorders

Diagnosing schizophrenia or another psychotic disorder depends on the length of time individuals present symptoms. One must first experience one (or more) of the five domains of symptoms: (1) delusions, (2) hallucinations, (3) disorganized thoughts or speech), 4) grossly disorganized or abnormal motor behavior), (5) negative symptoms. Similar to delusional disorder, one must experience symptoms that:

1) cause significant distress or impair one social, occupational, or other areas of functioning and
2) the symptoms cannot be explained by the effects of a substance or another medical condition.

When the symptoms are present for at least one day but less than one month, a **brief psychotic disorder** diagnosis is confirmed. When the symptoms persist for at least one month but less than six months, one is diagnosed with **schizophreniform disorder.** A diagnosis of schizophrenia is confirmed when an individual's symptoms persist beyond six months or longer, and at least one of the symptoms is present most of the time. **Substance-medication-induced psychotic disorder** is a type of psychotic disorder caused by a substance or medication. The disorder is characterized by the experiencing of one (or more) of the above symptoms related to substance or medication use (APA, 2022).

Bipolar Disorder

Bipolar disorder is a condition where one presents two distinct behavioral moods: (1) **mania** or **manic episode**, which is characterized by intense and unrealistic feelings of excitement and euphoria, and (2) **depression or depressive episodes,** which usually involve feelings of extraordinary sadness and hopelessness. Bipolar disorder was formerly known as manic depressive disorder, but the APA replaced the diagnosis in 1980 in the third edition of DSM (DSM-III) (APA, 1980). The diagnostic criteria for major depressive episodes coincide with the diagnostic criteria for **major depressive disorder** (i.e., depression). When one presents only those symptoms (without mania), they meet the criteria for a diagnosis of major depressive disorder, which is classified under a separate category of disorders in the DSM-5-TR called Depressive Disorders.

For a diagnosis of bipolar disorder, one must alternate between mania and depression episodes. The DSM-5-TR distinguishes two types of bipolar disorders: bipolar 1 and bipolar 2. The difference between the two types is how long one presents mania symptoms. In bipolar 1, a person experiences a manic episode for one week or longer. With bipolar 2, the mania is not as prominent, and the person experiences a manic episode for at least four consecutive days but less than one week, referred to as hypomania. In both bipolar 1 and 2, the individual's major depressive episodes usually are more frequent and last longer than the manic episodes.

Diagnostic Criteria for Bipolar Disorder

Manic Episode

Must meet at least three of the following criteria (four if the mood is only irritable) for one week or longer for bipolar 1 or four days for bipolar 2.

- Inflated self-esteem or grandiosity (e.g., sense of superiority).
- Decreased need for sleep (e.g., feels rested after only 3 hours of sleep).
- More talkative than usual or feel pressured to keep talking.
- Flight of ideas or subjective experience that thoughts are racing.
- Distractibility (i.e., attention is too easily drawn to unimportant or irrelevant objects or events (i.e., external stimuli).
- Increase in goal-directed activity (either socially, at work or school, or sexually) or psychomotor agitation (i.e., purposeless non-goal-directed activity, e.g., pacing).
- Excessive involvement in activities that have a high potential for painful consequences (e.g., buying sprees, sexual indiscretions, or careless business investments). (APA, 2022, pp. 150–151)

Major Depressive Episode

Five (or more) of the following symptoms have been present during the same two-week period and represent a change from previous functioning; at least one of the symptoms is either (1) depressed mood or (2) loss of interest or pleasure.

- Depressed mood most of the day, nearly every day, as indicated by either subjective report (e.g., feels sad, empty, or hopeless) or observation made by others (e.g., appears tearful). In children and adolescents, it can present as irritability.
- Diminished interest or pleasure in all, or almost all, activities most of the day, nearly every day (either by subjective account or observation by others).
- Significant weight loss when not dieting or weight gain (e.g., change of more than 5% of body weight in a month), or decrease or increase in appetite nearly every day.
- Insomnia or hypersomnia nearly every day (i.e., too little or too much sleep).
- Agitated or diminished psychomotor activity nearly every day (observable by others; not merely subjective feelings of restlessness or being slowed down).
- Fatigue or loss of energy nearly every day.
- Feelings of worthlessness or excessive or inappropriate guilt (may be delusional) nearly every day (not merely self-reproach or guilt about being sick).

- Diminished ability to think or concentrate, or indecisiveness, nearly every day (by subjective account or as observed by others).
- Recurrent thoughts of death (not just fear of dying), recurrent suicidal ideation without a specific plan, specific plan suicide, or suicide attempt. (APA, 2022, p. 151)

3. The mood disturbance is sufficiently severe to cause marked impairment in social or occupational functioning or to require hospitalization to prevent harm to self or others, or there are psychotic features.
4. The mood disturbance is not attributable to the physiological effects of a substance, medication, or other treatment) or another medical condition. (APA, 2022, p. 152).

Post-Traumatic Stress Disorder

Experiencing some level of stress when faced with life's demands is a common and normal physiological response. Stress has two components: the **stressor** or the event that produces the demands and the **response**, which is the physiological reaction to the demands. A stressor can be a common everyday annoyance (e.g., waiting in heavy traffic), a life-altering event (e.g., marriage, divorce), a long-term problem (e.g., poor health or illness), or a major traumatic event (e.g., serious auto accident, violent or sexual assault, military combat). Arousal responses to stress demands begin in a structure of the brain called the hypothalamic–pituitary–adrenal (HPA), which includes the hypothalamus, pituitary gland, and adrenal glands. The HPA axis is connected to the central nervous and endocrine systems, which work together to activate the stress response. The hypothalamus activates the autonomic nervous system (ANS). The ANS is a network of nerve fibers that connect the brain and spinal cord to the body's other organs to control involuntary activities such as breathing, heartbeat, perspiration, and the endocrine system. The endocrine system is a network of glands throughout the body that releases hormones into the bloodstream. The sympathetic nervous system releases hormones, referred to as neurotransmitters, to communicate a response to stress. The sympathetic nervous system and the HPA axis are collectively called the "fight-or-flight response" because they arouse the body and prepare it to respond to danger or a threat. For most, the reactions subside soon after the stress or danger passes, but for others, these reactive responses of the body persist long after. Experiencing major stressors contributes to certain psychological disorders, where one's reactions become debilitating, long-lasting, and affect one's ability to function in daily activities (Lopez-Duran et al., 2020; Tresca, 2022). When symptoms persist, one may be diagnosed with **post-traumatic stress disorder (PTSD).**

Diagnostic Criteria for Post-Traumatic Stress Disorder[1]

PTSD presents with a range of symptoms triggered by extreme stress. The symptoms may begin soon after the traumatic event or any time after, but one is diagnosed when the symptoms persist for more than one month. Below are the diagnostic criteria for PTSD in the DSM-5-TR.

1) Exposure to actual or threatened death, serious injury, or sexual violation in one (or more) of the following ways:
    - Directly experiencing the traumatic event(s).
    - Witnessing, in person, the event(s) as it occurred to others.
    - Learning that the event(s) (violent or accidental) occurred to a close family member or close friend.
    - Experiencing repeated or extreme exposure to aversive details of the traumatic event. (p. 301)
2) Presence of one (or more) intrusion symptoms:
    - Recurrent, involuntary, and intrusive distressing memories of the traumatic event.
    - Recurrent distressing dreams (i.e., nightmares) in which the content and/or effect of the dream are related to the event.
    - Dissociative reactions (i.e., **flashbacks**) in which the individual feels or acts as if the traumatic event(s) were recurring.
    - Intense or prolonged psychological distress when exposed to cues that symbolize or resemble the traumatic event.
    - Physiological reactions when exposed to cues that symbolize or resemble the traumatic event.
3) Presence of one or both avoidance symptoms:
    - Efforts to avoid distressing memories, thoughts, or feelings about or closely associated with the traumatic event(s).
    - Efforts to avoid external reminders (people, places, conversations, activities, objects, situations) that arouse distressing memories, thoughts, or feelings about or are closely associated with the traumatic event(s).

4) Presence of two or more of the alterations of cognition and mood:
   - Inability to remember aspects of the traumatic event.
   - Persistent and exaggerated negative beliefs or expectations (e.g., I'm bad, no one can be trusted).
   - Distorted cognitions about the cause of traumatic event (i.e., blame self or others).
   - Persistent negative emotional state (e.g., fear, horror, anger, guilt, shame).
   - Diminished interest in significant activities.
   - Feeling detached or estranged from others.
   - Persistent inability to experience positive emotions (e.g., happiness, satisfaction, love).
5) Presence of two or more of the arousal symptoms:
   - Irritable behavior and angry outbursts (with little or no provocation), typically expressed as verbal or physical aggression toward people or objects.
   - Reckless self-destructive behavior.
   - Hypervigilance (i.e., increased alertness).
   - Exaggerated startle response (e.g., spastic jerking movement).
   - Problems with concentration.
   - Sleep disturbance (e.g., difficulty falling or staying asleep, restless sleep).
6) The disturbance causes clinically significant distress or impairment in social, occupational, or other important areas of functioning. (APA, 2022, p. 302)
7) The disturbance is not attributable to the physiological effects of a substance (e.g., medication or alcohol) or another medical condition. (APA, 2022, p. 303)

Prevalence Rates of Mental Illnesses

The prevalence of the abovementioned mental illnesses in the general population is relatively small. The estimated prevalence of delusional disorder is about 0.2% (Perälä et al., 2007), with no major gender differences (de Portugal et al., 2010). The typical age at onset is early adulthood, although the onset can occur anywhere from adolescence to late in life. The estimated prevalence of schizophrenia is between 0.3%–0.7% (McGrath et al., 2008;

Moreno-Küstner et al., 2018) and appears to be higher among men. The peak age at onset for the first psychotic episode is the early to mid-20s for men and in the late 20s for women, and onset prior to adolescence is rare (APA, 2013). The prevalence of substance/medication-induced psychotic disorder in the general population is unknown. However, between 7%–25% of individuals presenting a first episode of psychosis are reported to have substance/medication-induced psychotic disorder (Crebbin et al., 2009).

The estimated prevalence rate of bipolar 1 disorder in the general population disorder is between 1%–1.5% (Rowland & Marwaha, 2018), with no significant gender differences (Blanco et al., 2017). The estimated prevalence rate of bipolar 2 is slightly higher, with estimates between 1.6%–1.8%, and is more common in women, but these differences may reflect disparities in seeking treatment (APA, 2022; Rowland & Marwaha, 2018). The average age at the onset is 22 years and is slightly earlier for women (21.5 years) than men (23 years) (Blanco et al., 2017). Although the peak age at the onset of bipolar I and II is typically in the 20s, onset can occur at any age (Rowland & Marwaha, 2018).

Although many people experience traumatic events, most do not develop PTSD or receive a diagnosis. The estimated lifetime prevalence of PTSD is about 7% of the population (Kessler et al., 2005), and the 12-month prevalence is 3.6% and is higher among women than men (5% vs. 2%) (Harvard Medical School, 2007). About 25% of people diagnosed with PTSD do not develop the full diagnostic criteria until six months or more after their trauma. The onset of symptoms can occur in children and adults of any age, although there may be a delay of months or even years before the diagnostic criteria are met (Sareen, 2020).

Prevalence in Correctional Populations

The overall percentage of incarcerated individuals with mental illnesses is high, with prevalence rates significantly greater than the general population. According to the most recent reports by the United States (US) Department of Justice (DOJ), about 23% of those in federal prison, 43% of those in state prison, and 44% of those in jail have mental illnesses (Bronson & Berzofsky, 2017; Maruschak et al., 2021). Gender differences within incarcerated populations were also noted. About 66% of all women in jail and prison report a history of mental health problems, compared to rates of 35% among men in prison and 41% of men in jail (Bronson & Berzofsky, 2017). The rates of specific disorders also vary by type of institution and were slightly higher among those in jail. Reports published by the DOJ estimated that the prevalence of schizophrenia/other psychotic disorders is 9% in state prisons, 3% in federal prisons (Maruschak et al., 2021), and 12% in jails (Bronson & Berzofsky, 2017). The prevalence of bipolar disorder among those incarcerated in state prisons was 23%, 9% in federal prisons (Maruschak et al., 2021), and 25% in jails (Bronson & Berzofsky, 2017). The prevalence of PTSD in state prisons is 14%, 7% in federal prisons (Maruschak et al., 2021), and 16% in jails (Bronson & Berzofsky, 2017). PTSD can also develop after experiencing or witnessing an assault while incarcerated or due to the ongoing stress from the prison environment (Schappell et al., 2016) (*see* Chapter 16 of this book for details).

Substance Use Disorders

People consume a variety of substances for both their medicinal and pleasurable effects, including the widely used substances: alcohol, tobacco, and caffeine. Some substances require a physician's prescription for legal use, while others, such as alcohol and marijuana (in some jurisdictions), are legally available to adults. Others, such as heroin and cocaine, are illegal under all circumstances. The term, **addiction,** to describe compulsive or habitual use or "drug addict" to refer to those who use drugs are not diagnostic terms in the DSM, are not clearly defined, and can have negative connotations. The proper term is substance use disorder (SUD), although some clinicians choose to use the term addiction when referring to those with severe presentations of SUD. A **drug** is defined as any substance (other than food) that affects the body or mind, although the term, substance, is the preferred term. SUD is characterized by a problematic pattern of using a substance that leads to clinically significant distress or impairment in social, occupational, or other areas of functioning (APA, 2022). The substances included in the DSM are separated into ten classes, shown below.

1) Alcohol (e.g., Beer, Wine, Liquor)
2) Caffeine (e.g., Coffee, Tea)
3) Cannabis (e.g., Marijuana, Hash)
4) Hallucinogens (e.g., Lysergic acid diethylamide- LSD, Methylenedioxymethamphetamine-MDMA, Phencyclidine- PCP, Ketamine)
5) Inhalants (e.g., Nitrous Oxide, Chloroform)
6) Opioids (e.g., Heroin, Morphine, Codeine, Hydrocodone, Methadone)

7) Sedatives/Hypnotics/Anxiolytics (e.g., Barbiturates, Benzodiazepines)
8) Stimulants (e.g., Cocaine, Methamphetamine)
9) Tobacco (e.g., Cigarettes, Cigars)
10) Other or Unknown Substances (e.g., other substances such as synthetic or lab-created, not included above) (APA, 2022, p. 545)

In addition to physiological changes, substances may cause temporary changes in behaviors, emotions, or thoughts, referred to as substance **intoxication**. For instance, an excessive amount of alcohol may lead to alcohol intoxication, a temporary state of poor judgment, mood changes, irritability, slurred speech, and poor motor coordination. Similarly, substances such as LSD may lead to hallucinogen intoxication or hallucinosis, which primarily involves experiencing hallucinations and other perceptual distortions (APA, 2022).

Physiological Origins of Dependence

Even though some substances are commonly used and legally sold, virtually all substances, particularly when taken in excess, directly activate the brain's **pleasure center** or **reward center** of the **medial forebrain bundle**. The medial forebrain bundle is a structure in the pleasure center of the brain comprised of the ventral segmental area, nucleus accumbens, ventral segmental area, locus coeruleus, and amygdala. This pleasure center contributes to the reinforcement (i.e., repeating) of behaviors that provide pleasure. The brain also produces pleasurable memories, which are activated when an individual engages in pleasurable activities, such as using substances. Despite the pleasurable effects of many substances, some can be misused, cause harm, or disrupt one's behavior or mood (Coenen et al., 2018).

The characteristics of an SUD are a cluster of cognitive, behavioral, and physiological symptoms. The individual also continues using the substance despite experiencing significant substance-related problems. An important characteristic of SUD is an underlying change in brain circuits that may persist even when the substance is no longer present in the body. The behavioral effects of these brain changes may be exhibited by repeated relapses and intense cravings when exposed to the substance itself or something that reminds them of the substance (APA, 2022). Two key features of SUD are **tolerance** and **withdrawal.** Tolerance occurs when one requires an increased dose of the substance to achieve the same or desired effect or experiences a reduced effect when the usual dose is consumed. Tolerance involves a variety of central nervous system effects, and the degree to which tolerance develops varies among substances and among individuals. Withdrawal is a set of symptoms (e.g., nausea or vomiting, agitation, sleep difficulties such as insomnia) that occur when individuals who had maintained prolonged heavy use of the substance cease or decrease use. The symptoms of withdrawal vary significantly across the substances, and separate criteria sets are provided for the different classes. Physiological signs of withdrawal are common with alcohol and opioids, and after developing symptoms, individuals may consume the substance to relieve the symptoms (APA, 2022).

Diagnostic Criteria for Substance Use Disorders

The DSM-5-TR includes 11 criteria for each SUD by type, which are grouped into four categories: impaired control, social impairment, risky use, and pharmacological criteria. The diagnostic criteria can be applied to all classes of substances except for caffeine. To meet the criteria for SUD, an individual must (1) display a maladaptive pattern of substance use leading to significant impairment or distress and (2) meet two or more criteria (see below) in the same category for a year or more. The severity of the disorder is based on the number of criteria met: Mild: the presence of 2–3 symptoms; Moderate: the presence of 4–5 symptoms; and Severe: the presence of 6 or more symptoms (APA, 2022).

1) **Impaired Control**
    - Taking the substance in larger amounts than intended or for longer than intended.
    - Persistent desire or unsuccessful efforts to cut down or control use of the substance.
    - A great deal of time is spent on activities necessary to obtain or use the substance or recover from its effects.
    - A craving, or a powerful desire or urge to use the substance.
2) S**ocial Impairment**
    - Recurrent substance use resulting in a failure to fulfill major role obligations at work, school, or home.
    - Continued substance use despite having persistent or recurrent social or interpersonal problems caused or exacerbated by the effects.
    - Important social, occupational, or recreational activities are given up or reduced because of the substance use.

3) **Risky Use**
   - Recurrent substance use in situations in which it is physically hazardous.
   - The substance use is continued despite knowledge of having a persistent or recurrent physical or psychological problem that is likely to have been caused or exacerbated by the substance.
4) **Pharmacological**
   - Tolerance—a need for increased amounts or a diminished effect with continued use.
   - Withdrawal—experiencing symptoms or using the substance to relieve or avoid symptoms (APA, 2022, pp. 553–554).

Prevalence Rates of Substance Use Disorders in the General Population

The prevalence of SUD in the general population varies by substance and age. Alcohol is the most widely used substance in the US, with 47.5% of the population reported using alcohol within the last month, and more than 10% developed alcohol use disorder. Initial incidents of alcohol intoxication tend to occur when one is in their mid-teens, but the onset of an alcohol use disorder tends to occur in one's late teens through mid-20s (Schuckit, 2009; Trim et al., 2009). The estimated prevalence of alcohol use disorder is highest among adults between 18–25 years (15%), with lower rates among those 26 and older (10.7%) and adolescents between 12–17 years (3.4%) (SAMHSA, 2022).

Cannabis/marijuana is the most widely used illicit substance in the US, with a prevalence rate of almost 19%. Cannabis can be used in many forms, but smoking or **vaping** is the most common. Young people have the highest use rates, with over 35% of those between 18–25 years reported using marijuana within the last year (SAMHSA, 2022). The onset of cannabis use disorder can occur at any age but is most common during adolescence or young adulthood (Farmer et al., 2015; Hasin et al., 2015). The highest rates of cannabis use disorder are among those between 18–25 years (14%), with lower rates among adolescents aged 12–17 (4.8%) and adults aged 26 and over (4.6%) (SAMHSA, 2022).

Opioids, sometimes referred to as **narcotics**, are a group of chemically similar substances derived from the poppy plant and include heroin and prescription medications, such as morphine, hydrocodone, i.e., Vicodin®, and oxycodone, i.e., OxyContin®. Some synthetic versions can be made in a laboratory. Prescription **opioid misuse** is relatively common, with an estimated prevalence rate between 4%–5% (Han et al., 2017; Saha et al., 2016; SAMHSA, 2022) and use rates within the last year were similar among young adults aged 18 to 25 and adults aged 26 or older (3.1 vs. 3.5%). The estimated prevalence of heroin use is about 0.4% and is slightly higher among adults 26 or older (0.5%) compared to younger adults 18 to 25 (0.2%) (SAMHSA, 2022). The estimated prevalence of those who develop heroin use disorder is 0.4% and highest among adults 26 or older (0.4%) compared to those between 18 to 25 (0.2%) and adolescents aged 12 to 17 (<0.1%). The estimated prevalence of those who develop opioid use disorder is 2%, with higher rates among those 26 or older (2.2%) compared to those aged 18 to 25 (1.3%) and adolescents 12 to 17 (1%) (SAMHSA, 2022). The problems associated with opioid use tend to occur in one's late teens or early 20 s, but opioid use disorder can begin at any age (Wu et al., 2011).

An estimated 7% of the population used prescription stimulants within the last year, with 0.2% developing a stimulant use disorder (Compton et al., 2018). About 0.9% of the population use methamphetamine, with 0.6% developing methamphetamine use disorder. The overall prevalence rate of methamphetamine use disorder is highest among adults aged 26 or older (0.7%) compared to adults between 18 to 25 (0.3%) and adolescents aged 12 to 17 (0.1%). The estimated prevalence rate of cocaine use is 1.7%, with 0.4% of whom use crack cocaine (SAMHSA, 2022). Cocaine use is highest among those 18–25 years old (3.5%) compared to those 26 or older (1.6%) and adolescents aged 12 to 17 (0.2%). The estimated prevalence of cocaine use disorder is 0.5% and is highest among those between 18–25 years (0.8%), compared to adults 26 and older (0.5%) or adolescents between 12–17 years (>0.1%) (SAMHSA, 2022).

Prevalence in Correctional Populations

The rate of incarcerated individuals with SUDs is alarmingly higher than the general population. The most recent report by the DOJ estimated that 58% of those incarcerated in state prison and 63% of sentenced individuals in jail met the criteria for substance dependence or SUD (Bronson et al., 2017). According to Maruschak et al.'s (2021) report, 21% of those incarcerated in state prison and 15% of those in federal prison had alcohol use disorder, while 40% of those in state prison and 23% in federal prison had SUDs other than alcohol.

Reported substance use was high among individuals prior to being incarcerated. Among those in jail, marijuana was most common, with 64%

who reported regular use, followed by cocaine (39%), heroin or opiates (39%), stimulants (24%), and hallucinogens (23%). Similar percentages were noted among those in prison, except for heroin or opiates, which were much higher in jails. Marijuana was most commonly reported (63%), followed by cocaine (34%), stimulants (23%), and hallucinogens (22%), and heroin or opiate use (17%) (Bronson et al., 2017). Often, individuals are diagnosed with co-occurring mental illness and SUD. Below is a case of an individual with co-occurring mental illness and SUD who engaged in criminal acts that led to contact with the CJS and mental health system (MHS).

Case of Alex[2]

Background: Alex was 35 years old when he was arrested for criminal mischief. Alex had a long history of alcohol and substance use since his late teens. He grew up in a middle-class family with both parents and is the oldest of four siblings. All three of his younger siblings have completed college and have successful careers; however, Alex did not complete college and has never held a job for longer than six months. He spent most of his adult life living with his parents where and spent most of his time in his room listening to music or playing video games. Three years prior to his arrest, his parents asked him to leave, and he has not seen or spoken with them since. His prior criminal record consists of three misdemeanor assaults.

Instant Offense: At around 5 am, Alex stood outside on the front lawn of his childhood home and began shouting and throwing rocks at the vehicle parked in the driveway, breaking a window and causing damage to the body. Alex's parents moved from the home two years earlier, and another family resided there. When police arrived, Alex stated that he was throwing rocks because he was angry at his parents for kidnapping him from his biological parents, famous Hollywood actor Harrison Ford, and his first wife, Mary Marquardt. He also told police that he was a famous Hollywood actor, currently starring in a movie with Gwyneth Paltrow. Alex was arrested, but because of the bizarre statements to police, and was transported to the emergency room and eventually transported to the state psychiatric hospital nearby for an evaluation.

Outcome: An initial psychological evaluation was conducted, and due to his current mental state of experiencing delusions, Alex was found incompetent to stand trial (e.g., unable to understand the charges and assist in his own defense—*see* Chapter 11 of this book for details) and was admitted to the psychiatric hospital for treatment. Once admitted, his delusions persisted, as he continued to tell staff that his parents were not his "real parents" and that he was actually the son of Harrison Ford. He continued to elaborate on how he was the current Hollywood actor and had a mansion in Los Angeles, California. Alex refused any medications and threatened to kill anyone who forced medications on him. After further hospital evaluations, including information provided by his parents, Alex was diagnosed with schizophreniform disorder (because symptoms were present less than six months) with grandiose delusions, alcohol use disorder, and cannabis use disorder. Alex sought release from the hospital a few weeks after his arrival, and a hearing was scheduled. At the hearing, the presiding judge denied Alex's release, and he was remanded to the hospital due to a lack of capacity, his persistent delusions, and his perceived dangerousness due to the threats toward the staff. He was also court-ordered to take psychotropic medications to treat his delusions. Approximately one month later, he approached his assigned social worker in his office and denied all the delusions he once had. He also agreed to finally meet with his estranged parents. Once stabilized, he was released from the hospital and eventually pled guilty to the criminal mischief charges in exchange for a $500 fine.

Misconceptions About Mental Illnesses and Substance Use Disorders

There are many myths and misconceptions about mental illnesses that result in stigma, discrimination, and dismissal of the symptoms as "attention-seeking." Similarly, those with SUDs incur stigma and discrimination, mainly due to incorrect information about the disorder. Although many with a mental illness or SUD engage in reprehensible and sometimes criminal behavior, to which the CJS responds, societal reaction is often exacerbated by additional stigma and discrimination, which can impede treatment (Sack, 2013). Below is a list of incorrect assumptions about SUD and mental illnesses that have been refuted or rebutted by research.

1) Substance use disorder (i.e., addiction) is not a disease

Reality: Many argue that SUD/addiction is not a disease because it is not transmissible, contagious, or autoimmune but because it is self-acquired (Saitz et al., 2008). SUDs are chronic diseases because the brain incurs changes over time, often leading to withdrawal symptoms that interfere with a person's ability to resist intense urges to use substances. Indeed, substance use often begins with a decision, but in some cases, one uses a substance prescribed by a doctor for a medical problem or injury that evolved into abuse (Centers for Disease Control and Prevention; The National Institute on Drug Abuse; SAMHSA,2024).

2) Substance use disorder is a lack of willpower

Reality: The ability to stop using is a function of many factors, but not a lack of willpower. In a longitudinal study of 69 individuals, researchers found that a lack of willpower was not associated with controlling one's substance use (Snoek et al., 2016).

3) Only "hard" drugs like cocaine and heroin are addictive

Reality: Some substances, such as cocaine and heroin, can lead to dependence more so than others; however, all substances taken in excess have direct activation of the brain's pleasure center or reward system and could lead to SUD (APA, 2022).

4) Forcing someone into SUD treatment is not effective

Reality: Treatment does not have to be voluntary to be successful. People who are pressured into treatment by their family, employer, or the legal system can still benefit; however, non-compulsorily treatment is best to reduce potential drug-related harms (Werb et al., 2016).

5) People with mental illnesses are dangerous or violent

Reality: In the absence of an SUD, most people with mental illnesses are not dangerous and do not commit acts of violence (Elbogen & Johnson, 2009). A study of 18,112 incarcerated individuals convicted of violent offenses revealed that 53% had an SUD, but only 4% had a mental illness (Baillargeon et al., 2010). The media and the entertainment business perpetuate such myths. Violence not only attracts media attention, but the mental illness tends to be sensationalized, which only strengthens this myth and stigmatizes people (Desmarais et al., 2014).

6) People with mental illnesses cannot work

Reality: Some, particularly those with severe mental illnesses, might be unable to secure stable employment and may require government assistance. However, most people can and do work and can be as productive as individuals without mental illnesses (Luciano & Meara, 2014).

7) People with schizophrenia have a "split personality."

Reality: In 1908, Swiss physician Paul Eugen Bleuler (1857–1939) (*see* Chapter 1 of this book for details) originated the term schizophrenia when attempting to explain the disintegration of the mind (Park & Thakkar, 2010). The term schizophrenia is Greek for "split mind," which most likely explains this misconception. Schizophrenia should not be confused with dissociative identity disorder, which was termed multiple personality disorder in earlier editions of the DSM, which is characterized, in part, by a sense of being detached from oneself and one's emotions, a blurred sense of identity, and memory loss (APA, 2022).

8) Mental illnesses are not legitimate "illnesses."

Reality: Mental illnesses are genuine and legitimate medical conditions. According to the National Institutes of Health, genetic and environmental causes exist, and like other medical conditions, they can be treated effectively (National Institutes of Health, 2013).

9) Children cannot develop mental illnesses.

Reality: Some mental illnesses can occur at any age, and unfortunately, children can develop them, including major depressive disorder, PTSD, and other anxiety disorders. According to the National Alliance on Mental Illness, about 13% of children between the ages of eight and 15 years will develop or experience a mental illness. Mental illnesses in children tend to manifest differently than in adults, and therefore, their mental health may be dismissed or attributed to behavioral problems (Centers for Disease Control and Prevention, 2023).

Conclusion

People with mental illnesses and SUDs experience stigma, discrimination, and social exclusion, all of which can be exacerbated when they have additional involvement in the CJS. The higher percentages of those with mental illnesses and SUDs in correctional facilities demonstrate that the CJS has assumed responsibility for providing housing and treatment. Each of these incarcerated individuals had prior contact with police, who are often relied upon to assist when individuals are in crisis (Fuller et al., 2017; Tartaro et al., 2021). Uneducated and untrained CJS practitioners may confuse or misinterpret the symptoms of mental illnesses and may respond inappropriately, which may lead to violent encounters (Jun et al., 2020; Rossler & Terril, 2017), increasing injury risk to both parties. Individuals may be experiencing hallucinations or delusions, which are firm and non-amendable, and CJS practitioners denying or dismissing them can lead to frustration and escalation. Common tactics to control situations, such as restraints, may be contraindicated and could also escalate encounters. In Alex's case, police remained calm, did not react to his bizarre statements, spoke with him respectfully, and were able to transport him without issue.

Behaviors associated with one's condition can be misinterpreted as noncompliance, to which CJS practitioners may resort to force or violence to gain control. Those with mental illnesses have the added stigma related to fears that they may be violent or dangerous, which may also be present among CJS practitioners (Tartaro et al., 2021; Watson et al., 2004). The comprehensive knowledge about diverse types of mental illnesses provided in this chapter assists practitioners in better understanding what such conditions are, what they are not, and how different people with mental illnesses and SUDs may present to allow them to make more humane and equitable decisions during encounters.

Key Terms

Addiction
Alcohol
Aphasia
Bipolar disorder
Catatonic
Cocaine
Delusions
Delusional disorder
Dependance

Flashbacks
Hallucinations
Intoxication.
Major depressive disorder
Mania
Marijuana
Medial forebrain bundle
Methamphetamine
Narcotics
Opioids
Opioid use disorder
Pleasure center
Post-traumatic stress disorder
Schizophrenia
Substance/Drug
Substance use disorder
Substance-medication-induced psychotic disorder
Schizophrenia
Stressor
Tolerance
Vaping
Withdrawal
Word salad

Chapter Questions

1) Describe the differences between delusions and hallucinations.
2) What are the main features of PTSD?
3) Describe the stressful or traumatic events that could lead to PTSD.
4) What are the major diagnostic features of bipolar disorder?
5) What are the major diagnostic features of an SUD?
6) Compare and contrast tolerance and withdrawal symptoms.
7) Explain why it is so difficult to "just quit" when one has an SUD?

Suggested Readings

Fischer, B. A., & Buchanan, R. W. (2020). Schizophrenia in adults: Clinical manifestations, course, assessment, and diagnosis. *UpToDate*. Retrieved from https://www.uptodate.com

Holze, F., Vizeli, P., Müller, F., Ley, L., Duerig, R., Varghese, N., & Liechti, M. E. (2020). Distinct acute effects of LSD, MDMA, and d-amphetamine in healthy subjects. *Neuropsychopharmacology, 45*(3), 462–471.

Osher, F., & Thompson, M. (2019). Adults with serious mental illnesses who are arrested and incarcerated. In H. H. Goldman, R. G. Frank, & J. P. Morrissey (Eds.), *The Palgrave handbook of American mental health policy* (1st ed., pp. 471–508). Palgrave Macmillan.

Sevarino, K. A. (2019, July 1). Opioid withdrawal in adults: Clinical manifestations, course, assessment, and diagnosis. *UpToDate*. https://www.uptodate.com

Notes

1. Symptom for those age 7 and older.
2. Name and some details have been changed for anonymity.

References

American Psychiatric Association. (1980). *Diagnostic and Statistical Manual of Mental Disorders* (3rd ed.).

American Psychiatric Association. (2013). *Diagnostic and statistical manual of mental disorders* (5th ed.). https://doi.org/10.1176/appibooks.9780890425596

American Psychiatric Association. (2022). *Diagnostic and statistical manual of mental disorders* (5th ed. Text Revision). https://doi.org/10.1176/appi.books.9780890425787

Baillargeon, J., Penn, J. V., Knight, K., Harzke, A. J., Baillargeon, G., & Becker, E. A. (2010). Risk of reincarceration among prisoners with co-occurring severe mental illness and substance use disorders. *Administration and Policy in Mental Health, 37*(4), 367–374. https://doi.org/10.1007/s10488-009-0252-9

Blanco, C., Compton, W. M., Saha, T. D., Goldstein, B. I., Ruan, W. J., Huang, B., & Grant, B. F. (2017). Epidemiology of DSM-5 bipolar I disorder: Results from the National Epidemiologic Survey on Alcohol and Related Conditions-III. *Journal of Psychiatric Research, 84*, 310–317. https://doi.org/10.1016/j.jpsychires.2016.10.003

Bronson, J., & Berzofsky, M. (2017). *Indicators of mental health problems reported by prisoners and jail inmates, 2011–12.* US Department of Justice, Office of Justice Programs, Bureau of Justice Statistics.

Bronson, J., Stroop, J., Zimmer, S., & Berzofsky, M. (2017). *Drug use, dependence, and abuse among state prisoners and jail inmates, 2007–2009.* U.S. Department of Justice, Office of Justice Programs, Bureau of Justice Statistics.

Center for Disease Control and Prevention. (2023). *Children's mental disorders.* Retrieved from https://www.cdc.gov/childrensmentalhealth/symptoms.html

Chaudhury, S. (2010). Hallucinations: Clinical aspects and management. *Industrial Psychiatry Journal, 9*(1), 5–12. https://doi.org/10.4103/0972-6748.77625

Coenen, V. A., Schumacher, L. V., Kaller, C., Schlaepfer, T. E., Reinacher, P. C., Egger, K., Urbach, H., & Reisert, M. (2018). The anatomy of the human medial forebrain bundle: Ventral tegmental area connections to reward-associated subcortical and frontal lobe regions. *NeuroImage Clinical, 18*, 770–783. https://doi.org/10.1016/j.nicl.2018.03.019

Compton, W. M., Han, B., Blanco, C., Johnson, K., & Jones, C. M. (2018). Prevalence and correlates of prescription stimulant use, misuse, use disorders, and motivations for misuse among adults in the United States. *The American Journal of Psychiatry, 175*(8), 741–755. https://doi.org/10.1176/appi.ajp.2018.17091048

Cordner, G. (2006). *People with mental illness. Problem-oriented guides for police problem-specific guides series.* U.S. Department of Justice. Office of Community Oriented Policing Services

Crebbin, K., Mitford, E., Paxton, R., & Turkington, D. (2009). First-episode drug-induced psychosis: A medium term follow up study reveals a high-risk group. *Social Psychiatry and Psychiatric Epidemiology, 44*(9), 710–715. https://doi.org/10.1007/s00127-008-0490-2

de Portugal, E., González, N., Miriam, V., Haro, J. M., Usall, J., & Cervilla, J. A. (2010). Gender differences in delusional disorder: Evidence from an outpatient sample. *Psychiatry Research, 177*(1–2), 235–239. https://doi.org/10.1016/j.psychres.2010.02.017

Desmarais, S. L., Van Dorn, R. A., Johnson, K. L., Grimm, K. J., Douglas, K. S., & Swartz, M. S. (2014). Community violence perpetration and victimization among adults with mental illnesses. *American Journal of Public Health, 104*(12), 2342–2349. https://doi.org/10.2105/AJPH.2013.301680

Elbogen, E., & Johnson, S. C. (2009). The intricate link between violence and mental disorder. Results from the National Epidemiologic Survey on Alcohol and Related Conditions. *Archives of General Psychiatry, 66*(2), 152–161. https://doi.org/10.1001/archgenpsychiatry.2008.537

Farmer, R. F., Kosty, D. B., Seeley, J. R., Duncan, S. C., Lynskey, M. T., Rohde, P., Klein, D. N., & Lewinsohn, P. M. (2015). Natural course of cannabis use disorders. *Psychological Medicine, 45*(1), 63–72. https://doi.org/10.1017/S003329171400107X

Fuller, D. A., Lamb, H. R., Biasotti, M., & Snook, J. (2015). *Overlooked in the undercounted: The role of mental illness in fatal law enforcement encounters.* Treatment Advocacy Center. www.treatmentadvocacycenter.org/storage/documents/overlooked-in-the-undercounted.pdf

Fuller, D. A., Sinclair, E., Lamb, H. R., Cayce, J. D., & Snook, J. (2017). *Emptying the 'new asylums:' A beds capacity model to reduce mental illness behind bars.* Treatment Advocacy Center. https://www.treatmentadvocacycenter.org/new-asylums

Han, B., Compton, W. M., Blanco, C., Crane, E., Lee, J., & Jones, C. M. (2017). Prescription opioid use, misuse, and use disorders in U.S. adults: 2015 National Survey on Drug Use and Health. *Annals of Internal Medicine, 167*(5), 293–301. https://doi.org/10.7326/M17-0865

Hasin, D. S., Kerridge, B. T., Saha, T. D., Huang, B., Pickering, R., Smith, S. M., Jung, J., Zhang, H., & Grant, B. F. (2016). Prevalence and correlates of DSM-5 cannabis use disorder, 2012–2013: Findings from the National Epidemiologic Survey on Alcohol and Related Conditions-III. *The American Journal of Psychiatry, 173*(6), 588–599. https://doi.org/10.1176/appi.ajp.2015.15070907

Hasin, D. S., Saha, T. D., Kerridge, B. T., Goldstein, R. B., Chou, S. P., Zhang, H., Jung, J., Pickering, R. P., Ruan, W. J., Smith, S. M., Huang, B., & Grant, B. F. (2015). Prevalence of marijuana use disorders in the United States Between 2001–2002 and 2012–2013. *JAMA Psychiatry, 72*(12), 1235–1242. https://doi.org/10.1001/jamapsychiatry.2015.1858

Harvard Medical School. (2007). *National Comorbidity Survey (NCS).* https://www.hcp.med.harvard.edu/ncs/index.php

Jun, H. J., DeVylder, J. E., & Fedina, L. (2020). Police violence among adults diagnosed with mental disorders. *Health & Social Work, 45*(2), 81–89. https://doi.org/10.1093/hsw/hlaa003

Kessler, R. C., Berglund, P., Demler, O., Jin, R., Merikangas, K. R., & Walters, E. E. (2005). Lifetime prevalence and age-of-onset distributions of DSM-IV disorders in the National Comorbidity Survey Replication. *Archives of General Psychiatry, 62*, 593–602. https://doi.org/10.1001/archpsyc.62.6.593

Lavoie, J. A., Connolly, D. A., & Roesch, R. (2006). Correctional officers' perceptions of inmates with mental illness: The role of training and burnout syndrome. *International Journal of Forensic Mental Health, 5*(2), 151–166. https://doi.org/10.1080/14999013.2006.10471239

Livingston, J. D. (2016). Contact between police and people with mental disorders: A review of rates. *Psychiatric Services, 67*(8), 850–857. https://doi.org/10.1176/appi.ps.201500312

Lopez-Duran, N. L., Micol, V. J., &. Roberts, A. (2020). Neuroendocrinological models of stress and psychopathology. In K. L. Harkness & E. P. Hayden (Eds.), *The Oxford handbook of stress and mental health,* (pp. 463–486). Oxford University Press.

Luciano, A., & Meara, E. (2014). Employment status of people with mental illness: National survey data from 2009 and 2010. *Psychiatric Services, 65*(10), 1201–1209. https://doi.org/10.1176/appi.ps.201300335

Maruschak, L. M., Bronson, J., & Alper, M. (2021). *Survey of prison inmates, 2016 alcohol and drug use and treatment reported by prisoners.* US Department of Justice, Office of Justice Programs, Bureau of Justice Statistics.

McGrath, J., Saha, S., Chant, D., & Welham, J. (2008). Schizophrenia: A concise overview of incidence, prevalence, and mortality. *Epidemiologic Reviews, 30*, 67–76. https://doi.org/10.1093/epirev/mxn001

Moreno-Küstner, B., Martín, C., & Pastor, L. (2018). Prevalence of psychotic disorders and its association with methodological issues. A systematic review and meta-analyses. *PloS one, 13*(4), e0195687. https://doi.org/10.1371/journal.pone.0195687

National Institute of Health. *Mental illness.* U.S. Department of Health and Human Services. https://www.nimh.nih.gov/health/statistics/mental-illness

National Institutes of Health. (2013). *Common genetic factors found in 5 mental disorders.* US Department of Health and Human Services. https://www.nih.gov/news-events/nih-research-matters/common-genetic-factors-found-5-mental-disorders

Park, S., & Thakkar, K. N. (2010). "Splitting of the mind" revisited: Recent neuroimaging evidence for functional dysconnection in schizophrenia and its relation to symptoms. *The American Journal of Psychiatry, 167*(4), 366–368. https://doi.org/10.1176/appi.ajp.2010.10010089

Perälä, J., Suvisaari, J., Saarni, S. I., Kuoppasalmi, K., Isometsä, E., Pirkola, S., Partonen, T., Tuulio-Henriksson, A., Hintikka, J., Kieseppä, T., Härkänen, T., Koskinen, S., & Lönnqvist, J. (2007). Lifetime prevalence of psychotic and bipolar I disorder in a general population. *Archives of General Psychiatry, 64*(1), 19–28. https://doi.org/10.1001/archpsyc.64.1.19

Rossler, M., & Terril, W. (2017). Mental illness, police use of force and citizen injury. *Police Quarterly, 20*(2), 189–212.

Rowland, T. A., & Marwaha, S. (2018). Epidemiology and risk factors for bipolar disorder. *Therapeutic Advances in Psychopharmacology, 8*(9), 251–269. https://doi.org/10.1177/2045125318769235

Sack, D. (2013). 5 myths about addiction that undermine recovery. *Psychology Today*. https://www.psychologytoday.com/us/blog/where-science-meets-the-steps/201305/5-myths-about-addiction-undermine-recovery

Saha, T. D., Kerridge, B. T., Goldstein, R. B., Chou, S. P., Zhang, H., Jung, J., Pickering, R. P., Ruan, W. J., Smith, S. M., Huang, B., Hasin, D. S., & Grant, B. F. (2016). Nonmedical prescription opioid use and DSM-5 nonmedical prescription opioid use disorder in the United States. *The Journal of Clinical Psychiatry, 77*(6), 772–780. https://doi.org/10.4088/JCP.15m10386

Saitz, R., Larson, M. J., Labelle, C., Richardson, J., & Samet, J. H. (2008). The case for chronic disease management for addiction. *Journal of Addiction Medicine, 2*(2), 55–65. https://doi.org/10.1097/ADM.0b013e318166af74

Sareen, J. (2020, January 10). Posttraumatic stress disorder in adults: Epidemiology, pathophysiology, clinical manifestations, course, assessment, and diagnosis. *UpToDate.* http://www.uptodate.com.

Schappell, A., Docherty, M., & Boxer, P. (2016). Violence and victimization during incarceration: Relations to psychosocial adjustment during reentry to the community. *Violence and Victims, 31*(2), 361–378. https://doi.org/10.1891/0886-6708.VV-D-13-00188

Schuckit, M. A. (2009). Alcohol-use disorders. *Lancet, 373*(9662), 492–501. https://doi.org/10.1016/S0140-6736(09)60009-X

Snoek, A., Levy, N., & Kennett, J. (2016). Strong willed but not successful: The importance of strategies in recovery from addiction. *Addiction Behavioral Reports, 4*, 102–107. https://doi.org/10.1016/j.abrep.2016.09.002

Substance Abuse and Mental Health Services Administration. (2024). *Mental health myths and facts.* US Department of Health and Human Services. https://www.samhsa.gov/mental-health/myths-and-facts

Substance Abuse and Mental Health Services Administration. (2018). *Public online data analysis system (PDAS), using National Survey on Drug Use and Health.* US Department of Health and Human Services. https://pdas.samhsa.gov/#/survey/NSDUH-2018-DS0001.

Substance Abuse and Mental Health Services Administration. (2022). *Key substance use and mental health indicators in the United States: Results from the 2021 National Survey on Drug Use and Health.* Center for Behavioral Health Statistics and Quality, Substance Abuse and Mental Health Services Administration. https://www.samhsa.gov/data/report/2021-nsduh-annual-national-report

Tartaro, C., Bonnan-White, J., Mastrangelo, M., & Mulvihill, R. (2021). Police officers' attitudes toward mental health and crisis intervention: Understanding preparedness to respond to community members in crisis. *Journal of Police and Criminal Psychology, 36*(3), 579–591. https://doi.org/10.1007/s11896-021-09459-6

Tresca, A. J. (2022). *What is the hypothalamic-pituitary-adrenal (HPA) axis?* Retrieved from https://www.verywellhealth.com/hypothalamic-pituitary-adrenal-hpa-axis-5222557

Trim, R. S., Schuckit, M. A., & Smith, T. L. (2009). The relationships of the level of response to alcohol and additional characteristics to alcohol use disorders across adulthood: A discrete-time survival analysis. *Alcoholism, Clinical and Experimental Research, 33*(9), 1562–1570. https://doi.org/10.1111/j.1530-0277.2009.00984.x

Watson, A. C., Corrigan, P. W., & Ottati, V. (2004). Police officers' attitudes toward and decisions about persons with mental illness. *Psychiatric Services, 55*(1), 49–53. https://doi.org/10.1176/appi.ps.55.1.49

Werb, D., Kamarulzaman, A., Meacham, M. C., Rafful, C., Fischer, B., Strathdee, S. A., & Wood, E. (2016). The effectiveness of compulsory drug treatment: A systematic review. *International Journal of Drug Policy, 28*, 1–9. https://doi.org/10.1016/j.drugpo.2015.12.005

Wu, L. T., Woody, G. E., Yang, C., Mannelli, P., & Blazer, D. G. (2011). Differences in onset and abuse/dependence episodes between prescription opioids and heroin: Results from the National Epidemiologic Survey on alcohol and related conditions. *Substance Abuse and Rehabilitation, 2*(1), 77–88. https://doi.org/10.2147/SAR.S18969

Zhang, A., Balles, J. A., Nyland, J. E., Nguyen, T. H., White, V. M., & Zgierska, A. E. (2022). The relationship between police contacts for drug use-related crime and future arrests, incarceration, and overdoses: A retrospective observational study highlighting the need to break the vicious cycle. *Harm Reduction Journal, 19*(1), 67–77. https://doi.org/10.1186/s12954-022-00652-2

4

Understanding Adolescent Cognition and Decision-Making—Overview and Diversion from the Justice Systems

Learning Objectives

After this chapter, readers should be able to understand the:

1. Major theories explaining decision-making and delinquent behavior
2. Differences in maturity and development among adolescents
3. Explanations as to why delinquency decreases with age
4. Components of psychosocial maturity
5. Components of integrated maturation theory

Introduction

Crime and delinquency committed by juveniles are concerning phenomena for criminal justice system (CJS) practitioners and society. Adolescents under 18 comprise about 22% of the United States (US) population but a significant minority of crime arrests (Puzzanchera et al., 2022). According to the most recent report by the US Department of Justice (DOJ), juveniles 17 and under accounted for about 10% of all arrests for violent crimes and about 8% of all arrests for property crimes in 2022 (Tapp et al., 2024). However, these percentages likely underestimate the actual prevalence, as most crimes committed by juveniles do not come to the attention of authorities and, therefore, are not arrested (Puzzanchera et al., 2022). Whether adolescents

M. C. Mogavero, *Mental Health, Neurodiversity, and Criminal Justice*, https://doi.org/10.1007/978-3-031-88816-8_4

arrested for crimes are handled as adults or juveniles largely depends on their age and the statutory jurisdictional age limit of the juvenile court. In most states, the juvenile court has jurisdiction over those who commit crimes under 18. Depending on the nature of the offense, juveniles of a certain age can be waived to adult court (Puzzanchera et al., 2022) (*see* Chapter 6 of this book for more details).

Treating juveniles like their adult counterparts is a controversial matter due to the developmental differences between them. Adolescence is a developmental period characterized by biological, psychological, and social changes that begin at puberty (approximately age 9–10) and extend into early adulthood through about age 24 (Andrews et al., 2021; Sawyer et al., 2018). During this developmental period, adolescents and young adults have a diminished capacity for problem-solving, learning from past experiences, and decision-making across various domains and contexts due to the brain's underdeveloped **medial prefrontal cortex (mPFC)**. The **mPFC** is responsible for executive functions such as planning, decision-making, and impulse control. Scientists who have used functional magnetic resonance imaging (**fMRI**) (*see* Chapter 2 of this book for details) to compare the brains of adolescents and adults during mentalizing tasks (e.g., the ability to interpret mental states, feelings, and the actions of others) have consistently found differences in mPFC cortex activity. Specifically, the PFC cortex activity decreases between adolescence and adulthood (Blakemore, 2012), suggesting that the executive functions in this area of the brain are still developing in adolescence, and this process is not complete until one reaches adulthood.

Because adolescents lack the decision-making abilities or skills of adults, they are considered less blameworthy and culpable for their actions and receive different treatment by the CJS. This changed in the 1980s through the 1990s after a policy shift to "get tough on crime" swept the nation (*see* Chapters 5 and 6 of this book for details). Favorable attitudes toward treating justice-involved juveniles similarly to their adult counterparts by waiving them to the adult justice system increased, partly due to beliefs that they are morally on par (e.g., knowing right from wrong) with adults. The support for harsh penalties for juveniles still exists today, and laws to treat juveniles as adults are still on the books (Zimring, 2019). However, such attitudes fail to acknowledge the differences in cognitive maturity between juveniles and adults. Scientific advances in brain imaging and neuropsychology have demonstrated differences in human development and decision-making, demonstrating that laws that treat juveniles similarly to adults using the arbitrary measure of age are outdated.

Criminological Theories: Decision-Making and Juvenile Delinquency

Crime and delinquency are nuanced, complex, and multifaceted behaviors influenced by many factors, including legal, social, cultural, environmental, geographical, psychological, genetic, and biological. Dozens of theories explain crime and delinquency, including those that explain decision-making and the ability to control one's behavior. Views surrounding decision-making and criminal behavior began over 250 years ago with the ideas from classical criminology.

The Classical School of Thought

The **Classical School** of thought, sometimes called classical criminology, began with the work of Italian philosopher and social reformer **Cesare Beccaria** (1738–1794). Classical criminology follows the assumption that those who commit crimes do so by **free will**, calculating the risks and benefits of their actions. Beccaria became dismayed by the unfairness in the legal system and the use of torturous punishments. In his work, *An Essay on Crime and Punishment* (1963) (orginally published in 1764), Beccaria listed his rationale for profound changes in the legal system, which included clearly defined laws, removing judicial discretion, and applying laws and punishment equally to all those who violate laws. He asserted that individuals' behavior is due to one's free will, and thus, criminal behavior is a choice aimed at bringing "pleasure" and reducing "pain." In his work, he proclaimed that crime can be prevented by instilling a fear of punishment, known as **deterrence**. Beccaria called for the abolishment of the death penalty and torture and that punishments should *only* be severe enough to deter. For deterrence to be effective, they must also be certain (consistently applied to all) and occur swiftly or soon after the crime.

English philosopher and social reformer **Jeremy Bentham** (1748–1832) agreed with Beccaria and believed punishment should be a deterrent. Bentham is known for his principle of **utilitarianism**, where individuals evaluate their actions based on their consequences to bring "pleasure" and reduce "pain." The primary justification for implementing punishments should be to deter crime and not simply as a response once it occurs. The concepts of deterrence for punishment (certainty, severity, and swiftness, i.e., processing time) were tested by Jordan and Myers (2011) by comparing the outcomes of 345 juveniles handled in either the juvenile court or adult court system (i.e., treating juveniles harshly). Although there was greater punishment severity in adult court, there was greater swiftness (court processing occurred more quickly) in juvenile court. There was little difference in certainty between the adult and juvenile court systems, as conviction rates were similar. If deterrence is the goal of "get tough" policies of waiving juveniles to the adult court system, it will unlikely have an effect if the severity is the only deterrent element achieved.

Rational Choice Theory

Derek Cornish and Ronald Clarke (1941–2025) are pioneers in explaining the decision-making processes of committing crimes. Their Rational Choice Theory (RCT) is rooted in classical criminology, and their 1986 publication, *The Reasoning Criminal,* explains the foundation theory of decision-making. RCT supports the principles of Beccaria and Bentham in that decisions, including crime, are based on maximizing pleasure and minimizing pain. Cornish and Clarke (1986) added that individuals' decision to follow through with the crime depends on several personal and situational factors: (1) previous learning and experience with the crime, (2) immediate needs/wants, (3) evaluation of other options to meet those needs, (4) perceived solutions to meet those needs, (5) legal consequences of the crime (if caught), (6) reactions of others (if caught), and (7) readiness to commit the crime. The risks or consequences of committing criminal acts are social (i.e., adverse reactions of others such as disappointment or rejection) or legal (e.g., fines, jail). Each of these factors also considers one's decision-making ability, including age, cognitive ability, or being under the influence of alcohol or other substances. If an individual perceives the consequences as minor or lenient, their risk–benefit calculation will likely favor committing the crime. Cornish and Clarke argued that a low risk of being caught and lenient punishments are leading factors in the decision to commit crimes. RCT is one of the most researched and supported theories for explaining decision-making. RCT was supported by Ray et al. (2020) after measuring perceptions of risk, rewards, and offending behavior among 1,307 juveniles. Those who perceived greater risks (likelihood of being caught) reported engaging in less crime, while those who perceived greater rewards (gains received) engaged in more crime (Ray et al., 2020).

Social Control Theory

With crime and delinquency providing rewards and immediate gratification, Travis Hirschi (1935–2017) questioned why juveniles follow the rules, laws, and other social norms. Hirschi (1969) explained with Social Control Theory that various **social controls** prevent individuals from engaging in crime and delinquency. Social controls take the form of social bonds or attachments to people and social institutions that promote conformity. Hirschi described four social bonds: attachment, commitment, involvement, and belief, to explain conformity (*see* Fig. 4.1). Juveniles follow rules, laws, and other social norms because, for example, they fear disappointment from parents, rejection from peers, the guilt they would experience for violating their moral beliefs, or they are too busy with extra-curricular activities to engage in delinquency Thus, juveniles conform because they do not want to jeopardize their relationships or future goals and aspirations. The strength of these bonds depends on the quality of the relationships and the amount of time and energy invested in them. Hirschi posited that delinquency can develop and flourish when one or more social bonds or attachments are weak or absent.

Few studies evaluated the effects of all four bonds and gender on preventing delinquency behavior among juveniles. Hart and Mueller (2013) examined the role of all four social bonds on school delinquency (e.g., skipping class, breaking school rules, suspensions) among a nationally representative sample of 11,758 tenth graders. The bonds included (1a) Bond to parents (parent involvement in school, e.g., discuss school with their parents, parents check grades); (1b) Bond to school (e.g., attitudes toward school, relationship with teachers); (2a) Commitment to school-related sports (e.g., baseball, softball); (2b) Commitment to school-related non-sport activities (band, yearbook); (3) Involvement (i.e., amount of time spent on school-related activities); and (4) Belief (how critical social norms were to them, e.g., to education, career, family). For boys, all bonds had a significant relationship with reducing delinquency, with the school bond having the most substantial influence. For girls, the school bond also had the most decisive influence on reducing delinquency, followed by a commitment to non-sport activities. Beliefs and commitment to sports activities did not significantly affect girls' school delinquency (Hart & Mueller, 2013). These results suggest that boys require more social controls to prevent delinquent behavior than girls.

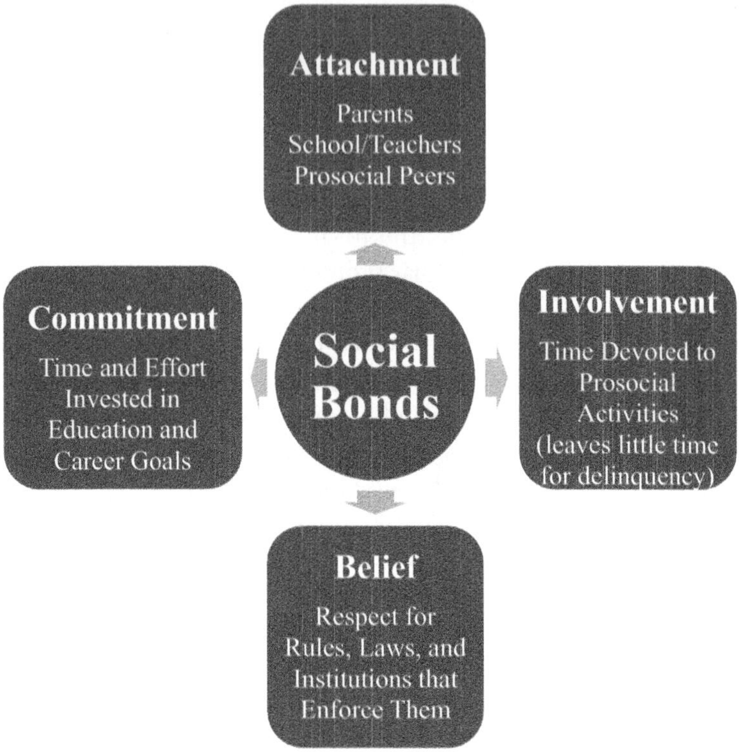

Fig. 4.1 Hirschi's four bonds of social control

General Theory of Crime

Researchers also explored the social factors that affect decision-making. Hirschi later developed the General Theory of Crime (1990) with Michael Gottfredson, who claimed that delinquency is determined by one's ability to exercise **self-control.** Self-control is defined as one's ability to use self-restraint and resist the temptation for short-term gratification. One's propensity to engage in crime, delinquency, and other **antisocial** behaviors results from having low self-control and an inability to delay gratification. Individuals with low levels of self-control often perform poorly in other life realms that require planning, effort, and delayed gratification, such as school, employment, and long-term relationships or marriage. Gottfredson and Hirschi (1990) mention numerous factors that are consistent with the trait of low self-control as they relate to crime:

1. **Impulsive**—crime results in immediate gratification.
2. **Insensitive**—crime results in pain and discomfort to victims- physically, economically, emotionally.
3. **Physical**—tolerant to physical discomfort, as crime increases the risk of experiencing physical violence.
4. **Risk-taking**—crime comes with a risk of arrest and penalties.
5. **Short-sighted**—crime provides short-term benefits and interferes with long-term commitments.
6. **Lack of verbal skills**—resolve conflict physically rather than verbally due to minimal tolerance for frustration.

According to Gottfredson and Hirschi, the development of self-control is influenced by child-rearing practices during early childhood and adolescence, as children are not born with self-control; it must be taught. Ineffective child-rearing practices, such as neglect, improper supervision, abuse, and failure to implement age-appropriate or socially appropriate consequences, do not allow children to develop self-control or become sensitive to the needs of others. Because crime and delinquency provide immediate gratification, those with low self-control or an inability to delay gratification will be more likely to engage in such behaviors. Gottfredson and Hirschi also recognize that self-control varies across genders, as parents tend to monitor girls' behavior more than boys; thus, girls develop higher levels of self-control. Having strong attachments and positive relationships with one's parents is an essential component of effective parenting and the development of self-control. Hirtenlehner and Blackwell (2015) measured self-control as it relates to parenting quality among 2,911 students in seventh and eighth grade. They surveyed students' level of self-control, the strength of their relationship with their mother and father, and the number of crimes they have committed (e.g., graffiti, fighting, vandalism, robbery, theft). Their findings indicated that low levels of self-control significantly increased engaging in criminal behavior, and boys demonstrated less self-control, more delinquency, and weaker attachments to their mothers than girls. For both boys and girls, a strong relationship with one's mother increased self-control and had a more significant effect than the attachment to one's father (Hirtenlehner & Blackwell, 2015).

Age-graded Theory of Informal Social Control

Robert Sampson (1925–2006) and John Laub expanded upon one's bonds to social institutions into adulthood. Sampson and Laub (1993) used a life-course framework to explain their age-graded theory of informal social control, emphasizing family, school, and career bonds to explain criminal behavior. These informal social controls are essential to prevent delinquent behavior and mediate the pathway to either violate or obey laws. This framework focuses on transitioning to adulthood and one's desire to conform to social norms or the institutions that encourage social norms (e.g., going to college, obtaining one's first professional job, getting married). The relationships individuals develop with others (e.g., family, friends, co-workers, and community members) across their lifespan are referred to as **social capital**. Social capital is generally measured by one's social network or the total value that individuals acquire from the people in their lives (Lin, 2001; Portes, 1998). In adolescence, one's social capital or informal controls are typically one's parents, peers, and school. Social capital can be negatively impacted by family disruptions, such as having an incarcerated parent and residential mobility (moving frequently). A decreased social capital and informal controls are associated with delinquency.

As people age into adulthood, informal social controls shift to focus on family, spouse, employment, neighbors, and one's reputation in the community. As social capital increases, individuals exercise more restraint, fearing the long-term negative consequences of losing their social capital. A strong emotional attachment to a spouse and a close tie to their community creates social capital to decrease the risk of deviant or criminal behavior. Sampson et al. (2006) followed 500 juveniles who committed acts of delinquency for 25 years until about the age of 32 and reviewed arrest records and marriage. They found that marriage decreased the odds of committing a crime by 35% and concluded that marriage can inhibit criminal behavior in adulthood among those most at risk (Sampson et al., 2006).

Adolescence-Limited and Life-course-Persistent

Terrie Moffitt pioneered long-term studies to explain the development of criminal behavior throughout one's life and has contributed substantially to understanding the pathways from juveniles committing delinquent acts to adults committing crimes (Moffitt, 1993, 2006). Moffitt also addressed age and crime to explain why some juveniles persist or desist (i.e., continue or stop) delinquent or criminal behavior. Moffitt identified two groups of individuals involved in the justice system: **adolescence-limited** and **life-course-persistent.** The life-course-persistent type accounts for only 10% of all justice-involved individuals. They tend to exhibit antisocial behavior in early childhood, including bullying others, and have difficulties with peer relationships. In contrast, those who are adolescent-limited, which is the most common type, typically do not exhibit antisocial and behavioral problems in childhood and usually do not begin offending until their teens. Moffitt and Caspi (2001) noted that delinquency among adolescent-limited individuals emerges around the same time they are entering puberty, where fluctuation in hormones and discomfort with body changes can lead to depression and anxiety. During this same time, they experience more privileges and responsibilities as they mature, referred to as the **maturity gap**. Delinquent behavior can be a relatively common way for adolescents to establish autonomy and independence from parents and gain acceptance from peers. Adolescents are heavily influenced by peers but "age out" of delinquency, return to conventional behavior, and desist as they enter adulthood. Figure 4.2 displays data from a 2024 report by the National Institute of Justice (NIJ), showing age-specific rates for violent crime arrests increasing from ages 10 to 22, stabilizing from ages 23 to 29, and declining thereafter.

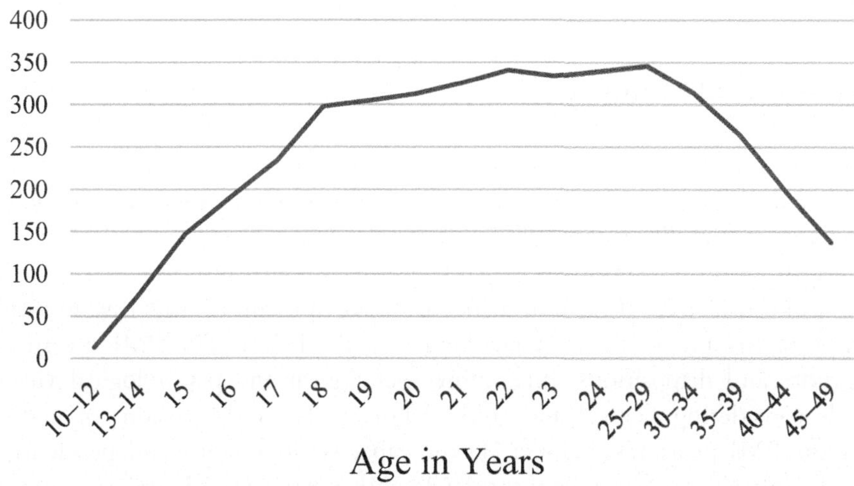

Fig. 4.2 Age and violent crime arrests per 100,000 population in 2020 (Adapted from National Institute of Justice, 2024)

Maturity Development

The definition and concept of maturity varies by scientific field, but more importantly, there is no agreed-upon definition in the law or the justice system. However, several psychologists and legal scholars have studied this concept and developed a definition and framework that helps explain risk-taking behavior, including delinquency and crime. Greenberger et al. (1975) defined maturity as "the capacity to function adequately on one's own, to contribute to social cohesion, and to interact adequately with others" (p. 128). Cauffman and Steinberg (2000) argued that this broad definition is not feasible for the law, as in early adolescence, there are substantial changes in sensation-seeking, risk-taking, and reward perceptions. Maturation of one's cognitive control system and its development is ongoing and continues into early adulthood, when risk-taking behavior decreases (Steinberg & Monahan, 2009). Monahan et al. (2013) examined factors related to maturity and decision-making among 1088 adolescents and young adults aged 14 to 25. They found that factors such as possessing impulse control, being considerate of others, taking personal responsibility, suppressing aggression, and resisting peer influences were still developing, even in one's mid-20s. These results were consistent with prior research that the maturation of brain systems responsible for self-regulation develops well into early adulthood.

Psychosocial Maturity

Psychosocial maturity is a multidimensional term used to describe individuals' general level of adaptive functioning and **socioemotional competence**, which is one's ability to recognize and manage one's emotions (Galambos & Costigan, 2003; Galambos et al., 2005). Greenberger and Sørensen (1974) first conceptualized this term with the development of the Psychosocial Maturity Inventory (PMI) (Greenberger et al., 1975). The PMI measures attitudes and dispositions, integrating sociological and psychological views while considering societal and cultural norms. Three dimensions of maturity the PMI measures include: (1) the capacity to function independently, (2) the capacity to interact appropriately with others, and (3) the capacity to contribute to social cohesion (e.g., work together with others). Scott et al. (1995) expanded upon the PMI and developed psychosocial maturity into a theory framework. Scott et al. argued that adolescents make decisions differently than adults due to three judgment factors: (1) conformity and compliance concerning peers and parents, (2) attitude toward and perception of risk, and (3) temporal perspective (i.e., the ability to consider both long-term and short-term benefits, risks, and consequences).

Steinberg and Cauffman (1996) and Cauffman and Steinberg (2000) further expanded Scott et al.'s psychosocial maturity framework, focusing on psychosocial factors regarding one's specific maturity of judgment. Although there are numerous factors, most of them fall into one of three categories:

1. **Responsibility** (i.e., healthy autonomy, self-reliance, and clarity of identity)—involves the development of a coherent sense of identity. This includes the adolescent's **capacity** (i.e., mental ability) to make autonomous choices independent of external influences, including peers and parents. As adolescents mature, they become less responsive to peer influences and more independent from parental influences.
2. **Temperance** (i.e., the ability to limit impulsivity and evaluate situations before acting)—refers to the understanding that risk-taking is higher among adolescents. Adolescents tend to be more sensation-seeking (which increases during puberty) and impulsive. Temperance also includes adolescents' ability to understand the long-term consequences of their behavior and cognitive ability to weigh risks and benefits (long-term and short-term), forgo immediate gratification to control one's impulses, and exercise self-restraint. Risk-taking behavior is unlikely to be changed by educational interventions and suggests, instead, interventions focus on reducing the harm associated with risk-taking behavior. Lastly, temperance includes the ability to evaluate a situation thoroughly before acting, including seeking the advice of others when appropriate, which occurs later in adolescence.
3. **Perspective** (i.e., the ability to acknowledge the complexity of a situation and frame a specific decision within a larger context)—involves seeing both short-term and long-term consequences (time perspective), understanding how one's actions might affect others (perspective taking), and weighing the costs and benefits of a decision. Borum and Grisso (2007) note that adolescents give more "weight" to potential benefits than potential costs and focus on the short-term rather than the long-term consequences.

Cauffman and Steinberg (2000) examined these three dimensions among 1,015 eighth, tenth, and twelfth graders and college students (under 21 and over 21) and measured their decision to engage in deviant or criminal behavior. They revealed that all age groups differed significantly across all three dimensions of psychosocial maturity, and those with higher psychosocial maturity, regardless of age, were less likely to support decisions to engage in deviant or criminal behavior. For instance, psychosocially mature 13-year-olds demonstrated less deviant or criminal decision-making than psychosocially immature adults. They also found that the development of perspective and temperance appears to increase from ages 16–19 but then tends to level off, as college students under 21 performed similarly to those over 21 (Cauffman & Steinberg, 2000). These findings were supported by Ozkan and Worrall (2017), who compared 4,530 students in grades 7–12 to 294 adults 18 and older and found that those with higher levels of psychosocial maturity (temperance, perspective, and responsibility) engage in less crime and delinquency. Specifically, those with more problem-solving skills, increased attention in school, strong relationships with others, and more focus on future goals reported fewer major offenses (e.g., serious assaults, burglary, selling drugs), minor crimes (e.g., vandalism, petty theft), and less delinquency and substance use (Ozkan & Worrall, 2017).

Integrated Maturation Theory

According to the above maturation theories, as individuals mature, they have an increased ability to make long-term decisions, problem-solve, and evaluate their interests and those of others. Rocque et al. (2015) expanded upon the concept of maturation, noting that it is not a function of age but a product of various domains that are a continuum of biological, psychological, and social changes. Rocque's (2015) Integrated Maturation Theory (IMT) provides a more comprehensive explanation of growth and maturation and applies this theory to explain desistance from crime with five domains:

1. **Adult Social Roles**—Drawn from Sampson and Laub's (1993) age-graded theory of informal social control and Hirschi's (1969) social control theory. Abstaining or desisting from offending is explained by one's social bonds, social capital, and involvement in social institutions such as marriage and employment.
2. **Identity/Cognitive**—A more subjective transformative view of maturity and draws from the work of Maruna (2001). Those who desist from crime and make life changes begin to reinterpret their past criminal behavior to be consistent with a prosocial view of themselves.
3. **Psychological/Psychosocial**—Drawn from Cauffman and Steinberg (2000) and Steinberg and Cauffman (1996), the factors of responsibility, temperance, and perspective.

4. **Civic/Communal**—Drawn from the work of Balsano (2005) and Flanagan and Levine (2010), who note that civic engagement, political engagement, and ties to one's community tend to increase in adulthood. One develops civic/communal maturation when one shifts the focus of one's own needs to what one can do for others and what one can do to become a better citizen.
5. **Neurocognitive**—Drawn from neurological research that suggests the brain's prefrontal cortex is fully developed once individuals are in their early to mid-20s.

Having ties to one's community has been shown to positively affect maturity development, and the role of education and one's relationship with teachers are essential community ties for adolescents. Abeling-Judge (2021) tested Rocque's (2015) IMT by comparing different education settings and whether attending school in one's community versus the education provided in institutional settings (e.g., juvenile detention facilities). Abeling-Judge examined data that followed 1,354 adolescents from 14–18 years of age to determine whether bonds to education/teachers improved maturational growth in the psychosocial, adult role, and identity domains. The results showed that although both psychosocial and identity maturity increased with age, adult role maturity was higher among those reporting strong bonds with teachers. Further, both adult role and psychosocial maturity were higher among those who were enrolled in schools in their community versus those in institutions, demonstrating that school is an important social environment for developing psychosocial maturity (Abeling-Judge, 2021).

Pathways to Desistance Study

Delinquency and the concepts related to Cauffman and Steinberg's (2000) psychosocial maturation theory and Rocque's (2015) IMT were examined using data collected from the *Pathways to Desistance Study* (PDS) (Mulvey et al., 2004). To date, the PDS is the most extensive long-term study of adolescents who have committed acts of delinquency and serious offenses that has been conducted. Mulvey et al. compared 1,354 adjudicated adolescents (1,170 males and 184 females; 654 in Phoenix, AZ, and 700 in Philadelphia, PA) between 14 and 17 years of age at the time of their offense from juvenile and adult court systems. The adolescents were followed for seven years, and the first (baseline) interviews took place between November 2000 and March 2003. The adolescents participated in six follow-up interviews occurring every six months and four additional interviews occurring every

12 months, with the last one occurring seven years after their first interview. To measure crime and delinquency, Mulvey et al. accessed records from the Federal Bureau of Investigation (FBI) and from juvenile and adult courts. According to PDS, the follow-up interview questions covered six maturity domains:

1. Individual functioning (e.g., work and school status and performance, substance use, mental health, antisocial behavior).
2. Psychosocial development and attitudes (e.g., impulse control, susceptibility to peer influence, perceptions of opportunity, perceptions of procedural justice, moral disengagement).
3. Family context (e.g., household composition, quality of family relationships).
4. Personal relationships (e.g., quality of romantic relationships and friendships, peer delinquency, contacts with caring adults).
5. Community context (e.g., neighborhood conditions, personal capital, social ties, and community involvement).
6. Monthly account of changes across multiple domains (e.g., education, income activities, romantic relationships).[1]

Several researchers used data from the PDS to explain the factors related to maturity dimensions and decisions to engage in crime and delinquency. McCuish et al. (2020) examined data from all adolescents from the PDS to evaluate IMT (Rocque, 2015) and adolescents' propensity to engage in or abstain from crime and delinquency. To measure psychosocial maturation, they examined *Adult Role Maturation* (using survey items measuring work/task orientation, consideration of others, and expectations of social institutions) and *Identity Maturation* (using survey items measuring self-identity and attitudes toward deviance). McCuish et al. found that these domains were interrelated and associated with offending and responsibility (psychosocial domain), work orientation (adult role domain), and self-identity (identity domain), which were most important in the development of maturation. When examining these domains simultaneously, consideration of others (adult role domain) and moral disengagement (identity domain) were related to lower levels of offending (McCuish et al., 2020). Monahan et al. (2013) examined data from only the adolescents who engaged in severe delinquency (1,088) from the PDS and compared levels of psychosocial maturity (temperance, perspective, and responsibility) and crime records to 25 years of age. Monahan et al. noted that by age 16, those who continued to engage in criminal behavior had significantly lower levels of psychosocial maturity than those who decreased or stopped engaging in crime.

Adolescents' level of maturity can influence their perceptions of the risks and benefits of crime and delinquency. However, this perception can also be influenced by individuals' experiences with crime and delinquency and their association with delinquency-involved peers. Lee et al. (2018) examined data from all adolescents from the PDS to evaluate whether variation in Cauffman and Steinberg's (2000) three domains of maturity of judgment (responsibility, perspective, and temperance) influenced adolescents' perception of risks, costs, and rewards associated with offending. They found that those who demonstrated more mature judgment were able to perceive the risks and costs of punishment and recognize fewer rewards from crime and delinquency. Perceptions of certainty of punishment were also significantly influenced by offending experience and associating with delinquency-involved peers. When individuals and/or their peers engage in crime and delinquency and get away with it, this decreases their perceptions of certainty of punishment, lowering their perceptions of risk. Those who perceive lower costs do not fear the costs associated with crime and delinquency and are, therefore, not deterred. Below is a case of a young adolescent who engaged in criminally destructive behavior due to its perceived benefits, low self-control, weak social bonds, low social capital, and psychosocial immaturity.

Case of Camile[2]

Background: Camile was 13 years old when she was summoned for burglary, larceny, and vandalism. Camile was the oldest of three children from her mother's second marriage. She has four older half-siblings aged 19 to 27 and two younger brothers. Her mother also had legal custody of her two granddaughters, ages two and four, by her oldest daughter, who was incarcerated for credit card fraud. They lived in a rented 200-year-old farmhouse in a rural area. Her mother was unemployed and received public assistance for herself and all five children. Camile's mother was estranged from her father due to repeated physical abuse. Camile's father has alcohol use disorder, an extensive criminal history, and has been "in and out" of her life since she was five. Her father was physically abusive toward her mother, and on many occasions, she and her siblings had intervened to try to stop the assaults. At the time of her arrest, Camile had not seen or spoken with her father in over two years.

For most of her childhood, Camile has exhibited behavioral problems at home and school. Her mother was verbally and physically abusive, usually when disciplining her problematic behavior. Around age 11, she began drinking alcohol, staying out past curfew, and skipping school. At school, her behavior issues included cursing at teachers and physical altercations with other students, and she has been suspended several times. Academically, she was performing below grade level. At the time of the summons, Camile's mother had an open case with the county's office of Child Protective Services (CPS) for confounded physical abuse and neglect and had regular meetings with their CPS caseworker.

Instant Offense: A mobile home park was adjacent to the house where they were residing. Camile, with two friends who reside in the park, a 13-year-old boy and a 14-year-old girl, entered a neighbor's mobile home when the owners were not home (a couple in their late 40s) and vandalized the inside. The damage was extensive; there were large holes in the walls, tears and holes in the sofa and mattress, the TV was smashed, the refrigerator contents were emptied on the couch and mattress, among other damage. They also stole cash, cigarettes, and alcohol. The owners called the police when they returned and saw the condition of their home. Police interviewed neighbors nearby, who positively identified Camile and her two friends outside the home earlier that day. Camile and her two friends were taken into custody, transported to the police station for booking, and then released into the custody of their parents.

Outcome: Because of her age, Camile's case was handled in family court, which had jurisdiction over juveniles. Camile was assigned an attorney through the public defender's office and a case manager to assess the best disposition for her. Because of the open CPS case, the CPS caseworker was also involved and attended several meetings. In conversations with her mother and attorney, Camile drank alcohol regularly because it was fun, and she was easily bored. She admitted she felt pressure from her friends to vandalize the home and feared they would reject her if she did not go along. The judge had to consider whether she required community supervision and placement through the county Department of Social Services (DSS).

Because of her behavior in school, her defense attorney and case workers requested a psychoeducational evaluation through the district school psychologist. The results of the evaluation revealed Camile had a learning disability, attention-deficit hyperactive disorder (ADHD), and post-traumatic stress disorder (PTSD) due to her witnessing her father physically abusing her mother. Her defense attorney and case workers advocated a treatment approach, not a disposition involving institutional placement, intensive probation, or excessive community service. Camile met with a psychiatrist who prescribed her medications to treat her ADHD and PTSD symptoms. She was given an education and behavior plan at school that required quarterly meetings. Camile was also ordered to participate in individual counseling and family counseling. She was ordered to provide **restitution** to the mobile homeowners and owners of the mobile home park by performing lawn care and other maintenance tasks on the property. Camile was also assigned a respite worker through the County Department of Social Services. The respite worker would arrive at her home every week and attend outings of various prosocial activities (e.g., bowling). She was also assigned a case manager to arrange the services, monitor her compliance, and assist with transportation. Camile responded well to the medications and other interventions, improving her behavior and school performance. Over time, she learned more positive ways to gain peer acceptance and build self-esteem.

Conclusion

Adolescents who engage in crime and delinquency are arguably concerning, but how society and the legal system responds to such behavior can have dire consequences. Viewing adolescents as "pseudo adults" and placing adult moral and cognitive expectations is inconsistent with research on maturation and brain development. Research has demonstrated that the medial prefrontal cortex of the brain, the part responsible for the higher executive functions such as planning, decision making, and impulse control, is not fully developed, and therefore, adolescents lack the capacity to understand the long-term consequences of their actions, how their actions affect others, and the ability to resist peer pressure. Adolescents are more influenced by immediate gratification than long-term consequences (Borum & Grisso, 2007).

According to the rational choice perspective, people, including adolescents, are indeed making a "rational" choice, even though the decision seems reckless or irrational to others. An adolescent's perceived benefits (immediate gratification, peer acceptance, enjoyment) outweigh the perceived costs of not engaging in delinquency, which may include peer disapproval. Further, as Moffit noted, delinquency in adolescence is a relatively common way for young people to exercise autonomy from their parents and gain peer acceptance. Most adolescents who engage in crime and delinquency do not persist into adulthood. Harsh treatment and punishment can be counterintuitive, as it may delay the development of maturation, particularly if they are removed from their community, family, school, and other social ties, leading to poorer long-term outcomes. As with Camile, a harsher sentence that included juvenile probation and community service would be difficult for her to comply with due to her remote location. This could have resulted in probation violations and stricter conditions, which could negatively impact her self-perception and drive her further down the path of delinquency and crime.

One's maturity and psychosocial maturity are multifaceted, and various biological, psychological, and social factors influence one's development. The justice system must recognize adolescents' cognitive limitations and assess each on a case-by-case basis. If the goal is for the adolescent to desist from further crime and delinquency, interventions should focus on risk-reduction strategies to address factors affecting impulse control, aggression, substance use, and building social bonds, particularly with school. Such interventions would allow for the development of maturity, improve one's self-concept, and increase one's social capital, all of which decrease the likelihood of future crime and delinquency.

Key Terms

Adolescent-limited
Capacity
Delayed gratification
Deterrence
Free will
Functional magnetic resonance imaging or fMRI
Informal social controls
Life-course persistent
Maturity gap
Medial prefrontal cortex
Perspective
Psychosocial maturity
Responsibility
Restitution
Socioemotional competence
Self-control
Social capital
Social control
Temperance
Utilitarianism

Chapter Questions

1. Discuss the main principles of classical criminology, referring to the ideas of Cesare Beccaria and Jeremy Bentham.
2. Select one of the control theories (Social Control, Self-Control, Age-graded) that resonates with you most. List and describe the aspects of the chosen theory to explain why you would avoid criminal behavior.

3. Compare and contrast Moffit's adolescent-limited and life-course-persistent individuals. What implications does this have for society and the criminal justice system if we were to treat all adolescents who commit delinquent acts harshly?
4. List and describe all three factors of Cauffman and Steinberg's psychosocial maturity and provide an example of each.
5. Explain how Rocque expanded upon Cauffman and Steinberg by detailing the four other aspects of maturity detailed in Integrated Maturation Theory.

Suggested Readings

Berk, C. (2019). Children, development, and the troubled foundations of Miller v Alabama. *Law & Social Inquiry, 44*(3), 752–770. https://doi.org/10.1017/lsi.2018.18

Brink, D. O. (2019). The moral asymmetry of juvenile and adult offenders. *Criminal Law and Philosophy, 14*, 223–239. https://doi.org/10.1007/s11572-019-09518-4

Morse, S. J. (2020). Against the received wisdom: Why should the criminal justice system give kids a break? *Criminal Law & Philosophy, 14*, 257–271. https://doi.org/10.1007/s11572-020-09524-x

Rocque, M., Beckley, A. L., & Piquero, A. R. (2019). Psychosocial maturation, race, and desistance from crime. *Journal of Youth and Adolescence, 48*(7), 1403–1417. https://doi.org/10.1007/s10964-019-01029-8

Notes

1. Additional details of the study and methods are detailed on the *Pathways to Desistance Study* website, https://www.pathwaysstudy.pitt.edu/context.html
2. Name and some details have been changed for anonymity.

References

Abeling-Judge, D. (2021). The value of school: Educational experiences and maturational growth among delinquent youth. *Journal of Developmental and Life-Course Criminology, 7*, 385–419. https://doi.org/10.1007/s40865-021-00171-x

Andrews, J. L., Ahmed, S. P., & Blakemore, S.-J. (2021). Navigating the social environment in adolescence: The role of social brain development. *Biological Psychiatry, 89*(2), 109–118. https://doi.org/10.1016/j.biopsych.2020.09.012

Balsano, A. B. (2005). Youth civic engagement in the United States: Understanding and addressing the impact of social impediments on positive youth and community development. *Applied Developmental Science, 94*(4), 188–201. https://doi.org/10.1207/s1532480xads0904_2

Beccaria, C. (1963). *On crimes and punishments*. In Bobbs-Merrill (Original work published 1764).

Blakemore, S. J. (2012). Development of the social brain in adolescence. *Journal of the Royal Society of Medicine, 105*(3), 111–116. https://doi.org/10.1258/jrsm.2011.110221

Borum, R., & Grisso, T. (2007). Developmental considerations for forensic assessments in delinquency cases. In A. L. Goldstein (Ed.), *Forensic psychology: Emerging topics and expanding roles* (pp. 553–570). Wiley.

Cauffman, E., & Steinberg, L. (2000). (Im)Maturity of judgment in adolescence: Why adolescents may be less culpable than adults. *Behavioral Sciences & the Law, 18*(6), 741–760. https://doi.org/10.1002/bsl.416

Cornish, D., & Clarke, R. V. (1986). *The reasoning criminal: Rational choice perspectives on offending*. Springer-Verlag.

Flanagan, C., & Levine, P. (2010). Civic engagement and the transition to adulthood. *The Future of Children, 20*(1), 159–179. https://doi.org/10.1353/foc.0.0043

Galambos, N. L., & Costigan, C. L. (2003). Emotional and personality development in adolescence. In R. M. Lerner, M. A. Easterbrooks, & J. Mistry (Eds.), *Handbook of psychology: Vol. 6. Developmental psychology* (pp. 351–372). Wiley.

Galambos, N. L., Turner, P. K., & Tilton-Weaver, L. C. (2005). Chronological and subjective age in emerging adulthood: The crossover effect. *Journal of Adolescent Research, 20*(5), 538–556. https://doi.org/10.1177/0743558405274876

Gottfredson, M. R., & Hirschi, T. (1990). *A general theory of crime*. Stanford University Press.

Greenberger, E., & Sørensen, A. B. (1974). Toward a concept of psychosocial maturity. *Journal of Youth and Adolescence, 3*(4), 329–358. https://doi.org/10.1007/BF02214746

Greenberger, E., Josselson, R., Knerr, C., & Knerr, B. (1975). The measurement and structure of psychosocial maturity. *Journal of Youth and Adolescence, 4*(2), 127–143. https://doi.org/10.1007/BF01537437

Hart, C. O., & Mueller, C. (2013). School delinquency and social bond factors: Exploring gendered differences among a national sample of 10th graders. *Psychology in the Schools, 50*, 116–133. https://doi.org/10.1002/pits.21662

Hirtenlehner, H., & Blackwell, B. S. (2015). Can differences in attachment to parents and level of self-control explain the gender gap in juvenile delinquency? Testing a gendered attachment-self-control theory. *Journal of Current Issues in Crime, Law, and Law Enforcement, 8*(3), 405–424.

Hirschi, T. (1969). *Causes of delinquency*. University of California Press.

Jordan, K. L., & Myers, D. L. (2011). Juvenile transfer and deterrence: Reexamining the effectiveness of a "get-tough" policy. *Crime & Delinquency, 57*(2), 247–270. https://doi.org/10.1177/0011128708319111

Lee, H., Sullivan, C. J., & Barnes, J. C. (2018). Maturity of judgment and perceptual deterrence. *Criminal Justice and Behavior, 45*(11), 1762–1781. https://doi.org/10.1177/0093854818789723

Lin, N. (2001). *Social capital: A theory of social structure and action.* Cambridge University Press.

Maruna, S. (2001). *Making good: How ex-convicts reform and rebuild their lives.* American Psychological Association.

McCuish, E., Lussier, P., & Rocque, M. (2020). Maturation beyond age: Interrelationships among psychosocial, adult role, and identity maturation and their implications for desistance from crime. *Journal of Youth and Adolescence, 49*(2), 479–493. https://doi.org/10.1007/s10964-019-01178-w

Moffitt, T. E. (1993). Adolescence-limited and life-course-persistent antisocial behavior: A developmental taxonomy. *Psychological Review, 100*(4), 674–701. https://doi.org/10.1037/0033-295X.100.4.674

Moffitt, T. E. (2006). Life-course-persistent versus adolescence-limited antisocial behavior. In D. Cicchetti & D. J. Cohen (Eds.), *Developmental psychopathology: Risk, disorder, and adaptation* (pp. 570–598). John Wiley & Sons.

Moffitt, T. E., & Caspi, A. (2001). Childhood predictors differentiate life-course persistent and adolescence-limited antisocial pathways among males and females. *Development and Psychopathology, 13*(2), 355–375. https://doi.org/10.1017/S0954579401002097

Monahan, K. C., Steinberg, L., Cauffman, E., & Mulvey, E. P. (2013). Psychosocial (im)maturity from adolescence to early adulthood: Distinguishing between adolescence-limited and persisting antisocial behavior. *Development and Psychopathology, 25*(4Pt1), 1093–1105. https://doi.org/10.1017/S0954579413000394

Mulvey, E. P., Steinberg, L., Fagan, J., Cauffman, E., Piquero, A. R., Chassin, L., Knight, G. P., Brame, R., Schubert, C. A., Hecker, T., & Losoya, S. H. (2004). Theory and research on desistance from antisocial activity among serious adolescent offenders. *Youth Violence and Juvenile Justice, 2*(3), 213–236. https://doi.org/10.1177/1541204004265864

National Institute of Justice. (2024). *Five things about youth and delinquency*. U.S. Department of Justice, Office of Justice Programs.

Ozkan, T., & Worrall, J. L. (2017). A psychosocial test of the maturity gap thesis. *Criminal Justice and Behavior, 44*(6), 815–842. https://doi.org/10.1177/009385481769492

Pathways to Desistance. A study of serious adolescent offenders as they transition to adulthood and out of crime. https://www.pathwaysstudy.pitt.edu/index.html

Portes, A. (1998). Social capital: Its origins and application in modern sociology. *Annual Review of Sociology, 24*(1), 1–24. https://doi.org/10.1146/annurev.soc.24.1.1

Puzzanchera, C., Hockenberry, S., & Sickmund, M. (2022). *Youth and the juvenile justice system: 2022 National Report.* National Center for Juvenile Justice.

Ray, J. V., Baker, T., & Caudy, M. S. (2020). Revisiting the generality of rational choice theory: Evidence for general patterns but differential effects across varying levels of psychopathy. *Journal of Criminal Justice, 66*, Article 101654. https://doi.org/10.1016/j.jcrimjus.2019.101654

Rocque, M. (2015). The lost concept: The (re)emerging link between maturation and desistance from crime. *Criminology and Criminal Justice, 15*(3), 340–360. https://doi.org/10.1177/1748895814547710

Rocque, M., Posick, C., & White, H. R. (2015). Growing up is hard to do: An empirical evaluation of maturation and desistance. *Journal of Developmental and Life-Course Criminology, 1*(4), 350–384. https://doi.org/10.1007/s40865-015-0018-x

Sampson, R. J., & Laub, J. H. (1993). *Crime in the making: Pathways and turning points through life.* Harvard University Press.

Sampson, R. J., Laub, J. H., & Wimer, C. (2006). Does marriage reduce crime? A counterfactual approach to within-individual causal effects. *Criminology: An Interdisciplinary Journal, 44*(3), 465–508. https://doi.org/10.1111/j.1745-9125.2006.00055.x

Sawyer, S. M., Azzopardi, P. S., Wickremarathne, D., & Patton, G. C. (2018). The age of adolescence. *The Lancet. Child & Adolescent Health, 2*(3), 223–228. https://doi.org/10.1016/S2352-4642(18)30022-1

Scott, E. S., Reppucci, N. D., & Woolard, J. L. (1995). Evaluating adolescent decision-making in legal contexts. *Law and Human Behavior, 19*, 221–244. https://doi.org/10.1007/BF01501658

Steinberg, L., & Cauffman, E. (1996). Maturity of judgment in adolescence: Psychosocial factors in adolescent decision making. *Law and Human Behavior, 20*(3), 249–272. https://doi.org/10.1007/BF01499023

Steinberg, L., & Monahan, K. C. (2009). Age differences in resistance to peer influence. *Developmental Psychology, 43*(6), 1531–1543. https://doi.org/10.1037/0012-1649.43.6.1531

Tapp, S. N., Thompson, A., Smith, E. L., & Remrey, L. (2024). *Crimes involving juveniles, 1993–2022.* U.S. Department of Justice, Office of Justice Programs, Bureau of Justice Statistics.

Zimring, F. E. (2019). *American juvenile justice* (2nd illustrated ed.). Oxford University Press.

Part II

The History and Progression of the Justice and Mental Health Systems

5

History of the Criminal Justice System—From Colonial Roots to Modern Reforms

Learning Objectives

After this chapter, readers should be able to understand the:

1. Role of the Puritans and Quakers in the shaping of laws and legal procedures in early America
2. Auburn and Pennsylvania systems and their influence on modern corrections
3. History of policing and the rise of police professionalism
4. Impact of the civil rights movement and Supreme Court decisions on criminal justice policy
5. Impact of the "war on drugs" and "get-tough" sentencing and policies affected the criminal justice system
6. Significance of research and evidence-based practices in developing criminal justice system policies

Introduction

The formal criminal justice system (CJS) we know today evolved over centuries, and its transformation reflected changes in societal values and political and legal philosophies. The early system was relatively informal, with European influences, but immense change was seen after the development of

M. C. Mogavero, *Mental Health, Neurodiversity, and Criminal Justice*, https://doi.org/10.1007/978-3-031-88816-8_5

the United States (US) Constitution and the Bill of Rights. The Constitutional Amendments established fundamental principles of justice and liberty in policing, courts, and correctional systems practices. Central features of the evolution of the CJS were the reform period and the civil rights movement, which emphasized practices based on compassion, fairness, and equity. Immense changes occurred when the CJS shifted practices toward a "get-tough" stance on crime, marked by the "war on drugs" and in response to increasing crime rates. This led to an expansion of the prison population, particularly those convicted of drug offenses. These penal practices ultimately impacted racial minorities and economically and socially disadvantaged groups. Since the 2000s, the focus has shifted toward evidence-based practices and correctional reform to right-size the failings of earlier policies.

Colonial Period (1607–1775)

The colonial period covered about 170 years, from the establishment of the Virginia colony in 1607 until about 1775, when the Rebellion and Revolutionary War began. The 13 colonies underwent considerable development during this period; for example, Dutch New Netherland became English New York in the mid-1600s, and Georgia, the final colony, was established in 1733 (Preyer, 1982). The individual development of each colony resulted in a decentralized justice system that was complex and diverse. Depending on the colony, the criminal codes, policing systems, and punishments resembled those of England and other parts of Europe.

Criminal Codes

Criminal codes are society's system of **social control** in that some actions are so detrimental to the well-being of society that they must be prohibited, and those who commit such acts are punished. The criminal codes in the colonial period included English statutes with additional laws that reflected the values and customs of colonists, consisting primarily of Anglicans (Church of England), Catholics, **Quakers**, and **Puritans** (Haskins, 1960; Shelden & Vasiliev, 2017). The Quakers were members of a radical Christian sect in England in the mid-seventeenth century known as the Society of Friends (Shelden & Vasiliev, 2017). The Quakers emphasized moral conduct, but their criminal codes and punishments took a more humane approach than the Catholics or Puritans (Barnes, 1921). The Puritans were members of a reform movement known as Puritanism, which appeared in England in the late sixteenth century to "purify" the church of Roman Catholic practices. The Puritans also emphasized moral conduct, and their criminal codes reflected Old Testament biblical foundations and concepts of proportionality called **lex talionis** (i.e., "eye for an eye") (Seigel & Worrall, 2019; Shelden & Vasiliev, 2017).

Court System

The exact origin and development of the court system in Colonial America is difficult to determine because the system across the colonies was decentralized, diverse, and vague. The colonists gave little attention to creating an adequate judicial system and modeled their courts after those in England, with a magistrate (i.e., judge) and jury. Lawyers, as a profession, were not well-established or respected. There were no law schools in the colonies; some studied in Europe, but most learned through apprenticeships with already-established lawyers. Over time, the knowledge and skills of lawyers became more respected and appreciated (Shelden & Vasiliev, 2017; Surrency, 1967).

During the seventeenth century, colonial courts evolved into a three-tiered system: (1) Colonial legislatures were the first tier, who were the decision-making body; (2) Superior courts, where governors presided over criminal trials or **civil trials** (i.e., handled disputes between colonists) previously heard in lower courts; (3) Lower courts, which handled most of the trials, levied and collected taxes. Judicial authority was given to the governor of the colonies, who were under the control of the King of England (Shelden & Vasiliev, 2017). In the 1640s, Massachusetts established seven courts, and each was assigned five judges. Over the next decade, their court system evolved into a four-tiered structure with an appellate system, with (1) town courts, which conducted trials; (2) county courts, which conducted trials but also appeals from town courts; (3) assistants courts, which heard appeals from the county courts, and (4) a General Court, which was the highest appellate and trial court in the colony. Connecticut, Rhode Island, and New Haven (the western half of what is now Connecticut) formed similar court structures (Roth, 2019).

Penal System

In the colonial era, the death penalty was used as a form of punishment throughout the colonies, but the eligible crimes and the implementation varied. Executions were carried out more often in southern colonies such as

Virginia, and by the mid-1700s, hundreds of crimes commanded the death penalty, including moral offenses such as blasphemy and adultery. In Puritan New England, offenses such as blasphemy and adultery were capital offenses punishable by death but rarely enforced. However, leading up to the 1692 witch trials in Salem, Massachusetts, dozens were executed for witchcraft in New England, primarily impoverished women who were viewed as an economic drain on the community. Public shaming was a common way to handle those who committed petty crimes, where people would be forced to sit with their feet in stocks or stand with their heads and hands in pillories (Roth, 2019).

In the northern colonies, such as Pennsylvania, executions were rare, and only those who committed murder and treason were eligible (Roth, 2019). Instead, two penal institutions were used as punishments: jails and workhouses. Workhouses were mainly used for "vagrants" and "paupers" who did not own property. Jails were used to hold those who committed more serious crimes. The Quakers of West Jersey and Pennsylvania opposed corporal punishment and believed imprisonment should be the primary mode of punishment. Their ideas later favored combining the jail and workhouse, as they believed imprisoned individuals should not be idle but perform hard labor (Barnes, 1921). Jails were also used as coercion and held those who failed to pay debts, taxes, or fines (Roth, 2019). Jails were also used to detain those accused of a crime pending trial. After each court session, the jail was virtually emptied of all its imprisoned individuals and then refilled again with new individuals awaiting the next court session (Barnes, 1921). More jails were constructed as the population expanded. Massachusetts built its first jail in Boston in 1636. In 1790, Connecticut converted an abandoned copper mine into a dungeon-like jail, and Philadelphia opened its Walnut Street jail (Dale, 2011).

Policing System

Policing in the colonial period comprised sheriffs and constables, who were typically appointed by the governor and resembled the practices of England. Sheriffs were the chief law enforcement agents in the county who responded to complaints, investigated crimes, and operated the local jail but did not patrol the streets. Constables were the most common in New England and Virginia, and their duties were to keep peace and serve papers issued by the courts (Shelden & Vasiliev, 2017; Surrency, 1967). Boston, New York, and Philadelphia adopted the English **night watch system,** where men patrolled the streets at night to maintain order (Shelden & Vasiliev, 2017). The Dutch colonists of New Amsterdam adopted **the schout and rattle watch system**, who patrolled the streets but also enforced the law, served court orders, and oversaw prosecutions. Southern states had **slave patrols,** first established in 1704, and primarily consisted of impoverished White men who would apprehend and return enslaved people who ran away (Roth, 2019). The western territories used the **vigilante** system, where citizens would track down those who committed crimes to bring them to justice in exchange for payment (Seigel & Worrall, 2019).

Revolutionary Period (1775–1783) and Formation of the United States

Significant changes in the law and CJS quickly followed the American Revolution and independence in 1776 and after the signing of the Constitution. The rise of the upper social class, primarily plantation owners (south), merchants (north), and lawyers, attempted to centralize powers and control those who threatened this new social order. After the Revolution, there was a debate about whether the United States should establish a strong centralized government. This was ultimately decided after the ratification and signing of the US Constitution. A decade later, a federal court system was created after the passing of the Judiciary Act of 1789. Although every state had its own court system, and states were free to create as many courts as they desired, the Act created a separate federal district court system. The Act also created the US Supreme Court, an appellate court with nine justices that could appeal decisions from state and federal courts (Shelden & Vasiliev, 2017).

The US Constitution

The Articles of Confederation and Perpetual Union (1777) was the first written Constitution and was ratified in 1781 to give Congress authority to make treaties and alliances, maintain armed forces, and create money. However, this new central government could still not levy taxes or regulate commerce. This led to the creation of new federal laws under the Constitution, and delegates developed a strategy for a stronger centralized government. The Constitution was signed on September 17, 1787, at the Constitutional Convention held in Philadelphia at the Pennsylvania State House (currently Independence Hall) (US National Archives, n.d.).

The Constitution contains a preamble and seven Articles describing how the government should be structured. The first three Articles established the three branches of government and their powers: Legislative (Congress), Executive (Office of the President,) and Judicial (Federal Court System). They established a system of checks and balances to prevent one branch from dominating another. Articles 4–7 outlined the state's relationship to the federal government with the Constitution as the supreme law with amendment and ratification processes. In 1789, James Madison (1751–1836), then a member of the newly established US House of Representatives, introduced 19 amendments to the Constitution. On September 25, 1789, Congress adopted 12 amendments and sent them to the states for ratification. The first ten of these amendments, known collectively as the Bill of Rights, were ratified and became part of the Constitution on December 10, 1791. The Constitution established fundamental laws and basic rights for its citizens. The 14th Amendment is one of the most momentous, as Section 1 addressed citizenship rights and equal protection under the law. On July 9, 1868, Reconstruction Amendments were proposed in response to issues related to those formerly enslaved after the Civil War ended in 1865. The 14th Amendment reads,

> All persons born or naturalized in the United States and subject to the jurisdiction thereof, are citizens of the United States and of the state wherein they reside. No state shall make or enforce any law which shall abridge the privileges or immunities of citizens of the United States; nor shall any state deprive any person of life, liberty, or property, without due process of law; nor deny to any person within its jurisdiction the equal protection of the laws. (US National Archives, Amendments 11–27, n.d.)

The Fourth, Fifth, Sixth, and Eighth Amendments (*see* below), sometimes known as the criminal justice amendments, limit police and government powers when accused of or convicted of a crime.

> **Fourth Amendment**
> The right of the people to be secure in their persons, houses, papers, and effects, against unreasonable searches and seizures, shall not be violated, and no warrants shall issue, but upon probable cause, supported by oath or affirmation, and particularly describing the place to be searched, and the persons or things to be seized.
> **Fifth Amendment**
> No person shall be held to answer for a capital, or otherwise infamous crime, unless on a presentment or indictment of a grand jury, except in cases arising in the land or naval forces, or in the militia, when in actual service in time of war or public danger; nor shall any person be subject for the same offense to be twice put in jeopardy of life or limb; nor shall be compelled in any criminal

case to be a witness against himself, nor be deprived of life, liberty, or property, without due process of law; nor shall private property be taken for public use, without just compensation.

Sixth Amendment

In all criminal prosecutions, the accused shall enjoy the right to a speedy and public trial, by an impartial jury of the state and district wherein the crime shall have been committed, which district shall have been previously ascertained by law, and to be informed of the nature and cause of the accusation; to be confronted with the witnesses against him; to have compulsory process for obtaining witnesses in his favor, and to have the assistance of counsel for his defense.

Eighth Amendment

Excessive bail shall not be required, nor excessive fines imposed, nor cruel and unusual punishments inflicted. (US National Archives, Bill of Rights, n.d.)

Industrialization, Expansion, and Reforms (1800s–1960s)

During the 1800s, northern cities experienced massive population growth due to **industrialization, migration,** and **immigration**. Industrialization refers to the shift from agricultural jobs to manufacturing jobs. The increased innovation and technology led to more products being produced in factories. This increased the demand for manufacturing workers, and many migrated to the cities to fill these jobs. Migration refers to the internal movement in America (e.g., moving from rural to urban areas). There was also an increase in Black people migrating north from the southern states for greater opportunities. Many also emigrated from other countries, mostly from European countries such as Ireland, to large cities in the US. With industrialization and population growth, the cities also increased their infrastructure to support these changes, collectively called **urbanization** (Zimring, 2019).

Penitentiaries

By the 1800s, incarceration as punishment began to replace physical punishments, and most states began to build jails to hold those convicted of crimes. This marked the beginning of the **penitentiary** system (Dale, 2011). Penitentiaries (i.e., large prisons) were outside the cities, as the Quakers of West Jersey and Pennsylvania believed that those who committed crimes should be isolated from society to protect the public from being "corrupted" (Barnes,

1921). A second goal behind the isolation of penitentiaries was to allow incarcerated individuals time and solitude to repent their crimes. Pennsylvania opened two new buildings modeled after the Walnut Street Jail: Western State Penitentiary near Pittsburgh and Eastern State Penitentiary near Philadelphia. In the Pennsylvania system, incarcerated individuals were isolated, living and working in their individual cells for 23 hours per day, and required to keep silent (Dale, 2011).

The Auburn prison in central New York opened in 1805, and officials implemented a similar system where individuals were placed in isolation but were not given any work to occupy their time and were required to march in their cells and remain silent. This extreme isolation resulted in a deterioration of their mental health. After several incarcerated individuals died by suicide or survived suicide attempts, a modified system, known as the **Auburn Plan**, was implemented in 1829. In the Auburn system, individuals were still required to remain silent but worked together during the day and were confined to their individual cells at night. Federal prisons for those convicted of federal crimes were established in the late 1800s after Congress authorized their creation in 1891. The first federal prison was built in Kansas in 1895, Atlanta in 1902, and Washington State in 1904. Congress later created the Federal Bureau of Prisons in 1930; by then, there were five federal prisons, including one for women (Dale, 2011).

Formal Police Agencies

Immigrants from Germany and Ireland began settling in Boston and New York, and crimes such as public lewdness, disorderly conduct, and prostitution increased. The night watch and schout and rattle watch systems were ineffective, and cities were ill-equipped to keep order. Citizens sought a more formal approach, and modern police departments were formed. Boston created the first police department in 1838, New York City in 1844, and Philadelphia in 1854. Sheriff's roles were allocated to operating the jails and serving court orders.

These early police agencies were corrupt and inefficient, with little training, no education in the law, minimal supervision, and nearly unlimited ability to exercise **discretion** (i.e., power to make decisions to act). Their role was predominantly maintaining order and protecting private property rather than fighting crime. Police patrolled on foot and were sometimes taunted or mocked by residents, to which they responded with violence (Seigel & Worrall, 2019). Politicians dominated and largely determined the recruitment of police and the appointment and promotion of supervisors. Police used the

patronage system (known as the spoils system) in hiring, where one's political ties or wealth was used in hiring and promotions. Politicians sometimes offered police department jobs to friends and relatives, while others would reward their supporters with jobs or offer positions within the police department. Positions could also be granted in exchange for money. For example, in New York City, one was forced to pay $400 to become a police officer or pay as much as $15,000 to be promoted to police captain (Zacks, 2012).

Policing Reforms

By the late nineteenth century and early twentieth century, numerous investigations into northern city police departments took place to identify and fight corruption. In 1894, The New York Senate created the Lexow Committee (named after Senator Clarence Lexow) to investigate corruption charges in New York City's Police Department. In 1922, Nathan Roscoe Pound (1870–1964) and Felix Frankfurter (1882–1965) directed a report on criminal justice for the Cleveland Foundation in Ohio. The Illinois Association for Criminal Justice conducted a lengthy investigation and published *The Illinois Crime Survey* in 1929 (Dale, 2011). The National Commission on Unlawful Observance and Enforcement, also known as the Wickersham Commission, was organized in 1929 to study and propose changes to policing and produced a series of investigative reports with a final report published in 1931. The report contained an extensive list of concerns but focused primarily on the problem of police misconduct and police corruption, including the use of torture and abuse to induce confessions. Pound argued that police misconduct threatened the entire CJS and proposed step-by-step changes to make significant improvements (Dale, 2011; Tonrey, 2017).

Policing moved into an era of professionalism, where reformers in several states advocated ending corruption in police hiring by replacing the spoils system with a merit-based system (Dale, 2011). Reformers established a code of ethics to improve police behavior, training, hiring strategies and police management. August Vollmer (1876–1955) was one of the significant police reformers who served as town marshal and police chief of Berkeley, California, from 1905–1932. Vollmer advocated for merit in hiring and promotion, more education and training, and using technology in policing. He also advocated for police to function as social workers to intervene and promote positive change in people's lives before they become involved in the CJS, especially young people. Orlando W. Wilson (1900–1972) worked under Vollmer and, in 1925, was hired as police chief in Fullerton, California. In 1928, with Vollmer's recommendation, Wilson became the police chief for the Wichita, Kansas Police Department until he retired in 1937. Wilson focused on establishing and strengthening the relationship between the police and the community as a form of crime prevention. In 1950, he published his first edition of *Police Administration*, an influential book on managing police departments, and is still influential today (Novak et al., 2022).

Rise of the Rehabilitation Model

Significant policy changes occurred in the penal system, particularly after the Great Depression (1929–1939). Politics and cultural attitudes shifted toward a rehabilitation model called **penal welfarism**. Penal welfarism was the idea that punishments, whenever possible, should be rehabilitative interventions rather than punitive. This rehabilitative model viewed imprisonment as counterproductive and favored a model of reform and individual correction, where the term "correctional facilities" was preferred over "prisons." Proponents of the rehabilitation model believed that crime was a "symptom" of inequality and oppression, and the root cause of the crime must be understood before being sentenced (Garland, 2001).

Community Corrections

The use of community supervision, such as **probation** and **parole,** for reforming behavior increased as the use of correctional facilities fell out of favor (Garland, 2001; Seigel & Worrall, 2019). Throughout this period until the 1970s, fewer categories of crimes were considered suitable for incarceration, focusing on rehabilitation using community corrections. Probation is a sentence where individuals remain in their community instead of incarceration while adhering to a set of rules referred to as conditions. Conditions often include abstaining from crime, abstaining from drugs or alcohol, maintaining employment, and meeting regularly with their probation officer. Failure to abide by these conditions can result in revocation, in which the individual will be required to serve jail or prison time. Incarceration sentences can also be suspended or delayed in place of a probation sentence, referred to as a **suspended sentence** (Garland, 2001). Parole is another form of community supervision, but one is released before the end of the prison sentence. Like probation, one must adhere to strict conditions and meet regularly with their parole officer. Similarly, violating the parole conditions can result in revocation, where the individual must return to prison (Seigel & Worrall, 2019).

Probation and parole were not new practices and had been used since the 1800s. The development of probation has been credited to John Augustus (1785–1859), a shoemaker in Boston, Massachusetts. In 1841, he observed a man ordered to jail for public drunkenness. Shocked by the severity, he posted the man's **bail** and promised the judge he would look after him until his next court hearing. The man appeared before the judge three weeks later, having abstained from drinking, and was given a fine instead. Augustus continued this practice for the next 14 years, and the success of his efforts led the Massachusetts legislature to enact the first Probation Act in 1878. By the early 1900s, every state had passed similar probation acts (Roth, 2019). Alexander Maconochie (1787–1860) is credited for developing the early parole system in 1835 in Scotland, but this practice originated around the same time by other prison administrators in Europe: Georg Michael Von Obermaier (1842) in Germany and Colonel Manuel Montesinos (1846) in Spain. As this practice moved to the US in 1876, New York State's Elmira Reformatory was the first to establish a system to release incarcerated individuals on parole. New York already had a long-standing law to shorten prison terms to reward good behavior with the 1817 enactment of the Good Time Law. The practice of parole spread rapidly, and by 1901, 20 states had implemented parole, and today, all 50 states have a parole system (Cromwell et al., 1977).

The rehabilitation model also allowed for discretion and individualization in the handling and treating those convicted of offenses. Those with no prior criminal record and stronger connections to work and family could be granted more lenient sentences, such as probation. The use of indeterminant sentences allowed those considered violent or dangerous with a higher risk of reoffending to be incarcerated for lengthy periods (Garland, 2001). Decisions to grant early release were increasingly placed in the hands of penal experts of **parole boards** rather than judicial authorities. Parole boards are independent agencies that review cases, decide whether individuals have reached a level of rehabilitation to warrant their early release, and decide their conditions (Seigel & Worrall, 2019).

The Civil Rights Movement (1954–1968)

The end of the reform era came during civil unrest after the civil rights movement. Citizens were dissatisfied with the social and political conditions, particularly the treatment of Black Americans and segregation laws, which led to the passing of The Civil Rights Act of 1964. The country was still in turmoil, and more than 150 riots and protests broke out between 1965 and 1968, including some of the deadliest riots in Newark, New Jersey, and

Detroit, Michigan. The police responded to the riots using harsh tactics and violence to keep order, including high-pressure hoses and attack dogs. To uncover the root causes of the riots, President Lyndon Johnson (1908–1973) launched the President's National Advisory Commission on Civil Disorders. The commission consisted of 11 appointed members, known as the Kerner Commission, named after its chairperson, Otto Kerner (1908–1976). The commission members questioned police officers, politicians, social scientists, and civic leaders. The Kerner Commission report cited "deep hostility" between the police and the city community while also noting racism and insufficient police available during the riots (Roth, 2019; United States National Advisory Commission on Civil Disorders, 1968).

Efforts to address and improve race relations during the civil rights movement shed light on the pervasiveness of race and class discrimination in the US and how the arbitrary and coercive CJS was used as a tool for political oppression. The American Friends Service Committee (AFSC), a Religious Society of Friends (Quakers), founded in 1917 to assist those impacted by World War I and to improve race relations, published a 188-page report in 1971, *Struggle for Justice: A Report on Crime and Punishment in America*. The report cited the inequities and repressive practices among minorities and people who were socially and economically disadvantaged. The CJS system was also used to silence those who challenged the government and status quo (e.g., Vietnam war protesters) (American Friends Service Committee, 1971). The report declared that applying the rehabilitation model, with discretion and indeterminant sentences (under the guise of individualized treatment), was systematically discriminatory and inconsistent with some of the basic concepts of justice (Garland, 2001). The reforms outlined in the report included ending the practice of indeterminant sentences, minimizing the use of discretion, and applying criminal laws uniformly (American Friends Service Committee, 1971).

Role of the US Supreme Court

During the civil rights era, the US Supreme Court published a series of landmark decisions that strengthened individuals' civil rights and limited the investigative techniques used by police. For example, Miranda v. Arizona (1966) required police to inform suspects of their Fifth and Sixth Amendment rights before the onset of an interrogation, known as Miranda rights (*see* Chapter 8 of this book for details). Terry v. Ohio (1968) enforced the Fourth Amendment when it determined the legality of a common police practice in which officers would stop citizens on the street and search for weapons.

Case Brief: Terry v. Ohio (1968)

Facts: Cleveland Police Detective Martin McFadden (dressed in plain clothes) observed two men, John Terry and Richard Chilton, outside a store walking up to the window and then walking away; they repeated this about a dozen times. A third man, Carl Katz, approached and conversed with Terry and Chilton. McFadden suspected the men may be planning to rob the store. McFadden approached the men, identified himself as an officer, asked what they were doing, and they mumbled a response. McFadden grabbed Terry, turned him around, and patted the outside of his clothing to see if he was armed. McFadden felt a pistol in the left pocket of Terry's coat. He reached inside the pocket, but he could not remove the gun. He then removed Terry's coat and removed a 0.38 caliber revolver. McFadden patted down both Katz's and Chilton's outer clothing and found another revolver in Chilton's outer coat pocket. Terry and Chilton were charged with carrying a concealed weapon.

Terry's lawyer filed a motion to suppress the evidence of the pistol, arguing it was seized in violation of the Fourth Amendment. However, McFadden testified that he had been an officer for 39 years and a detective for 35. For 30 years of his career, he had been assigned to patrol for "shoplifters" and "pickpockets." He explained that from his observations over the years, he became familiar with the routine habits of those who commit thefts.

Issue: Whether a police officer detaining an individual on the street and conducting a limited search to find weapons without **probable cause** is unreasonable and a violation of the Fourth Amendment.

Outcome: The Court held that being stopped by police on the street constitutes a seizure, and a "pat down" of outer clothing constitutes a search under the Fourth Amendment. However, officers may conduct a limited search for weapons if they observe behavior and have **reasonable suspicion** that criminal activity is afoot, and the individual may be armed. The Court decided McFadden's search was proper and the evidentiary standard of probable cause was not necessary.

The outcome of Terry v. Ohio gave police authority to **stop and frisk,** later known as a "Terry Stop," but only under certain conditions. For a stop and frisk to be lawful and compliant with the Fourth Amendment, police must have reasonable suspicion that a crime is afoot (police must be able to articulate the suspicious behavior), and before briefly detaining and questioning, for the purpose of officer safety, police are permitted to conduct an exterior limited search of the outer clothing for weapons.

The Crime Control Era (1970s–1990s)

Throughout the 1960s, crime rates, particularly property crime, began to noticeably increase. The Federal Bureau of Investigation (FBI) tracks reported index crimes and publishes the Uniform Crime Report (UCR) annually. Drug and narcotic offenses are not counted in the index crimes, but according to the FBI's 1970 report, arrests for violations of narcotic drug laws increased by 741% from 1960 to 1970. Figure 5.1 shows UCR crime data from 1960–1970, demonstrating a 126% increase in violent crime and a 146% increase in property crime over ten years.

In 1967, President Johnson issued an executive order to establish a Commission on Law Enforcement and Administration of Justice. The 1967 report, *The Challenge of Crime in a Free Society*, presented crime trends and more than 200 specific recommendations and concrete steps to address rising crime. This report advocated for a political shift toward the **retributive** crime control model. President Johnson signed the Omnibus Crime Control and Safe Streets Act of 1968 (Omnibus Act) to assist state and local governments in increasing the effectiveness, fairness, and coordination of police and the CJS at all levels of government. The Act established the **Law Enforcement**

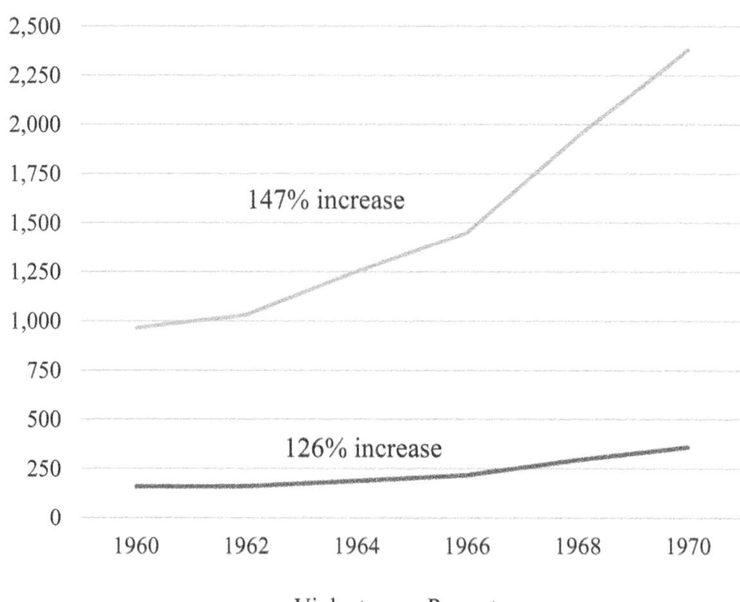

Fig. 5.1 Violent and property crime rate 1960–1970 (per 100,000 Inhabitants) (*Source* FBI. Crime Index. Crime in the United States, 1960–1970 [Violent: murder, aggravated assault, robbery, rape; Property: burglary, larceny-theft, motor vehicle theft])

Assistance Administration (LEAA), which expanded federal spending on state and local agencies, with tremendous investments in training CJS practitioners, especially police. The LEAA also motivated colleges and universities nationwide to create criminal justice programs (Tonrey, 2017).

The "War on Drugs"

The rise in recreational use of illegal substances throughout the 1960s led President Richard Nixon (1913–1994) to sign the Controlled Substances Act (CSA) in 1970. The CSA regulated certain substances and increased penalties for their possession and sale. In 1971, President Nixon declared a "war on drugs," and at a press conference on June 17, 1971, by stating that drug use was "public enemy number one." President Nixon created the Drug Enforcement Administration (DEA) in 1973, a special law enforcement agency in charge of targeting illegal drug use and drug smuggling in the US (Richard Nixon Foundation, 2016).

In 1986, Congress raised the maximum penalty for violating the Federal CSA to a sentence of 20 years to life imprisonment (P.L. 99–570, SEC. 1002). Numerous legislative acts were passed in the 1980s through the 1990s to combat the "war on drugs," mainly crack cocaine. Below are the names and brief details of the federal crime control and drug legislation.

- **Comprehensive Crime Control Act (1984)**— Established mandatory minimum sentences for some federal drug offenses, abolished federal parole, and required federal judges to use new sentencing guidelines.
- **Anti-drug Abuse Act (1986)**—Established mandatory minimums for those convicted of drug offenses, transferred sentencing power from federal judges to prosecutors, and provided $1.7 billion to states for new prison construction. The Act also established a 100-to-1 crack-to-powder-cocaine ratio in sentences for certain federal drug offenses. Under this policy, a person convicted for selling five grams of crack cocaine was treated the same as someone who sold 500 grams of powder cocaine.
- **Omnibus Anti-drug Abuse Act (1988)**—Established mandatory minimums of five years for possession of five grams of crack cocaine.
- **Violent Crime Control and Law Enforcement Act (1994)**—Provided funding for the hiring of 100,000 new police officers, $9.7 billion in funding for prisons, and $6.1 billion in funding for prevention programs. Title I: Public Safety Partnership and Community Policing Act of 1994: Amended the Omnibus Crime Control and Safe Streets Act of 1968

(Omnibus Act) and authorized $8.8 billion to fund local law enforcement agencies in the fight against crime through community policing.

- **Violent Criminal Incarceration Act of 1995**—Revised the Violent Crime Control and Law Enforcement Act of 1994 to authorize the Attorney General to provide grants to eligible states to build, expand, and operate correctional facilities to increase bed capacity for persons convicted of serious violent felonies. Title I: **Truth in Sentencing Act**: Required that persons convicted of serious violent felonies serve no less than 85% of the sentence imposed or 85% of the court-ordered maximum sentence for states that practice indeterminate sentencing.

Policing the War on Drugs

As a result of the money allocated to hire 100,000 new officers in the Violent Crime Control and Law Enforcement Act (1994), policing shifted toward the community-based proactive model. The Office of Community-Oriented Policing Services (COPS), a component of the US Department of Justice (DOJ), was formed in 1994 and handles advancing the practice of community policing. The percentage of police departments using routine foot patrols increased. This proactive policing model led to a "get tough" on crime agenda, but strategies were not limited to drug activity, and police began enforcing quality of life or "nuisance" violations such as panhandling and loitering (Roth, 2019).

Some police departments began using unethical tactics to fight the "war on drugs," For instance, the New York Police Department (NYPD) implemented Strategy 97 Goal Oriented Neighborhood Policing in 1997. As part of Strategy 97, a Street Crime Unit (SCU) of plainclothes officers was assigned to apprehend those who commit violent and drug crimes but also addressed property crimes, quality of life violations, and gun crimes. The NYPD enhanced the stop-and-frisk policy under this SCU, in which police officers stopped citizens on the street they deemed suspicious and patted them down, many engaging in **racial profiling**. According to the US Commission for Civil Rights, among the subjects in all stop-and-frisk reports registered by the SCU in one year, 65% were Black, 21% were Hispanic, and only 6% were White (Roth, 2019).[1] Similarly, Washington D.C. had a crime control patrol team, the Rapid Deploy Unit (RDU). Chambliss (1994) described the policing efforts of the RDU in D.C. during the 1990s when the "war on drugs" was considered a crisis of drugs and violence. Police engaged in racial profiling, targeting cars with young Black men inside, particularly specific models they believed to be popular among dealers, such as BMWs and Honda Accords. Officers would look for any minor violation to justify the stop, for example, going through a yellow light, not coming to a complete stop at a stop sign, or an object hanging from a review mirror. Chambliss (1994) quoted one officer, "This is the jungle…we rewrite the Constitution every day down here…. If we pull everyone over they will eventually learn that we aren't playing games anymore. We are real serious about getting the crap off the street" (p. 179).

Decline of the Rehabilitation Model

Support for the rehabilitation model waned in favor of crime control policies focused on retribution. Many began casting doubt on the effectiveness of rehabilitation efforts in the mid to late 1970s, particularly after the 1974 article by Robert Martinson titled *What Works? Questions and Answers about Prison Reform.* Martinson and colleagues reviewed 232 studies from 1945 to 1967, focusing on various efforts such as vocational programs, education achievement, community adjustment, and the effects of rehabilitative treatment on recidivism rates (e.g., returning to prison). Martinson summarized his findings with the following sentence: "With few and isolated exceptions, the rehabilitative efforts that have been reported so far have had no appreciable effect on recidivism" (Martinson, 1974, p. 25). Not long after, Martinson's findings of "what works" were viewed as conclusive empirical evidence that "nothing works" (Garland, 2001).

With the perception that "nothing works," correctional institutions were relied upon to address social problems of crime and substance use. The crime control model supports various goals of the correctional institutional system, including **retribution, incapacitation,** and **deterrence**. Advocates of retribution believe that the goal of corrections is to punish in a manner that is proportionate to the seriousness of the crime. The goal of incapacitation is to place individuals under the supervision of correctional institutions so they cannot repeat their crimes and are no longer a threat to the public. The use of punishments as a deterrent assumes individuals will be swayed from committing crimes in fear of punishment. There are two types of deterrence: general and specific. **General deterrence** is aimed at potential law violators to sway them from committing a crime when the punishment is severe (e.g., long prison sentence), and therefore, the perceived benefits of the crime are not worth the risk. **Specific deterrence** is aimed at current law violators to sway them from committing future criminal acts after enduring severe punishment (Seigel & Worrall, 2019).

Prison Population Expansion

The federal crime control policies, "get-tough" policing practices, and the "nothing works" rhetoric resulted in incarceration as the primary punishment of the legal system, which led to an exploding prison population during the end of the twentieth century. The addition of harsh sentencing policies in the Violent Criminal Incarceration Act of 1995 (e.g., mandatory minimums and truth-in-sentencing) kept individuals in prison longer, which added to the mass incarceration (Ditton & Wilson, 1999). Omnibus Anti-drug Abuse Act (1988) and Violent Criminal Incarceration Act (1995) provided federal prison construction funding to support these efforts and the growing population. As shown in Fig. 5.2, the prison population rate throughout the 1960s through the early 1970s was relatively steady. However, the last quarter of the twentieth century saw almost a 400% increase.

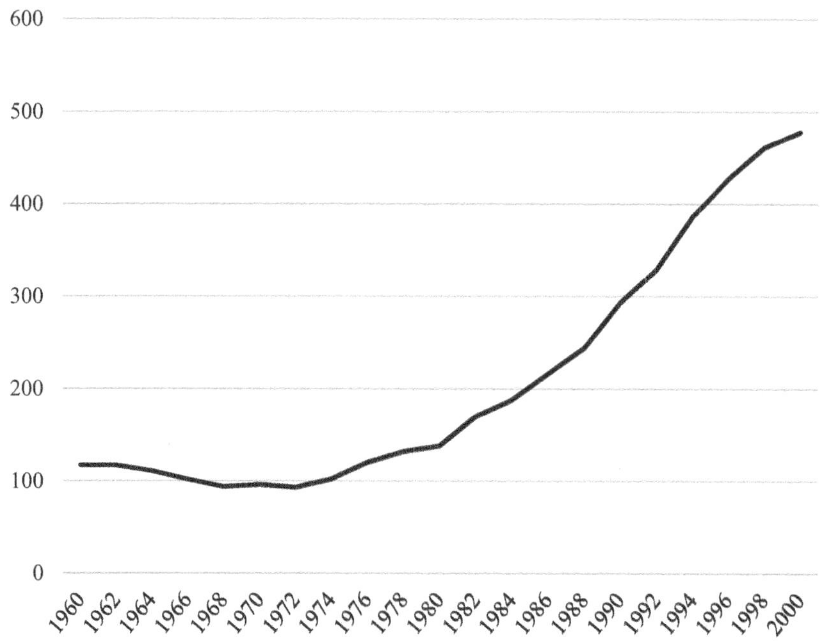

Fig. 5.2 State and federal prison incarceration rate 1960–2000 (per 100,000 inhabitants) (*Source* Carson [2021] and US DOJ [1986])

Mass Incarceration and Drug Offenses

The CJS addressed the "war on drugs" with harsh sentences for those in possession of substances (e.g., a 15-year sentence for possession of heroin or cocaine). As shown in Fig. 5.3, more than 20% of incarcerated individuals were held in state prisons, and more than 50% of those in federal prisons were for drug offenses, and those percentages decreased only slightly during the 2000s and 2010s.

The "war on drugs," including racial profiling among police and the focus on increased penalties for crack cocaine, led to a disproportionate number of Black males held in prison compared to other demographic groups. In 2013, data from the US Sentencing Commission showed that 83% of the people serving federal prison time for drug trafficking offenses involving crack cocaine were Black. As shown in Fig. 5.4, the percentage of Black males who were ever incarcerated was much higher than their counterparts across the last quarter of the twentieth century. The rate of ever being incarcerated for Black males (17%) was twice as high as for Hispanic Males (8%) and six times higher than for White males (3%) (Bonczar, 2003).

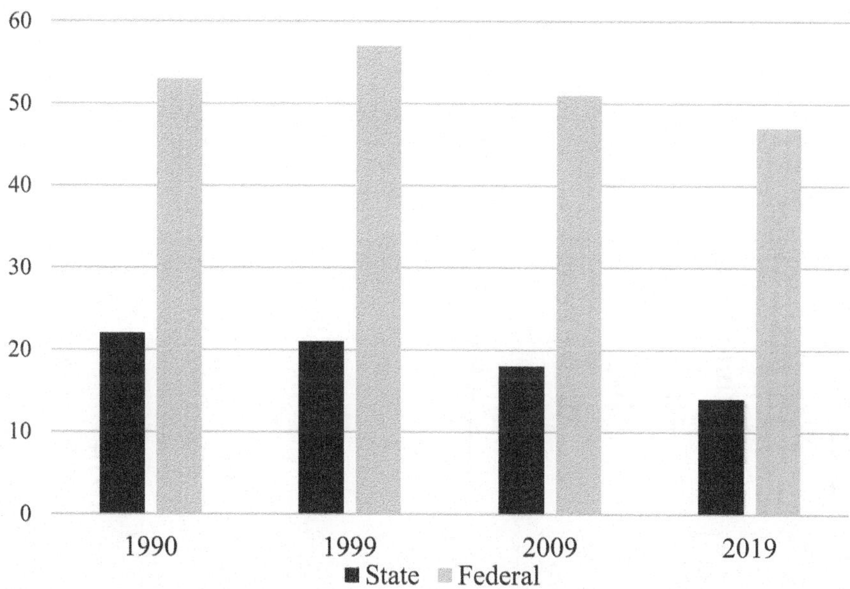

Fig. 5.3 Percentage of sentenced incarcerated individuals in state and federal prison for drug offenses (*Source* Beck and Harrison [2001], Carson [2021] and Guerino et al. [2011])

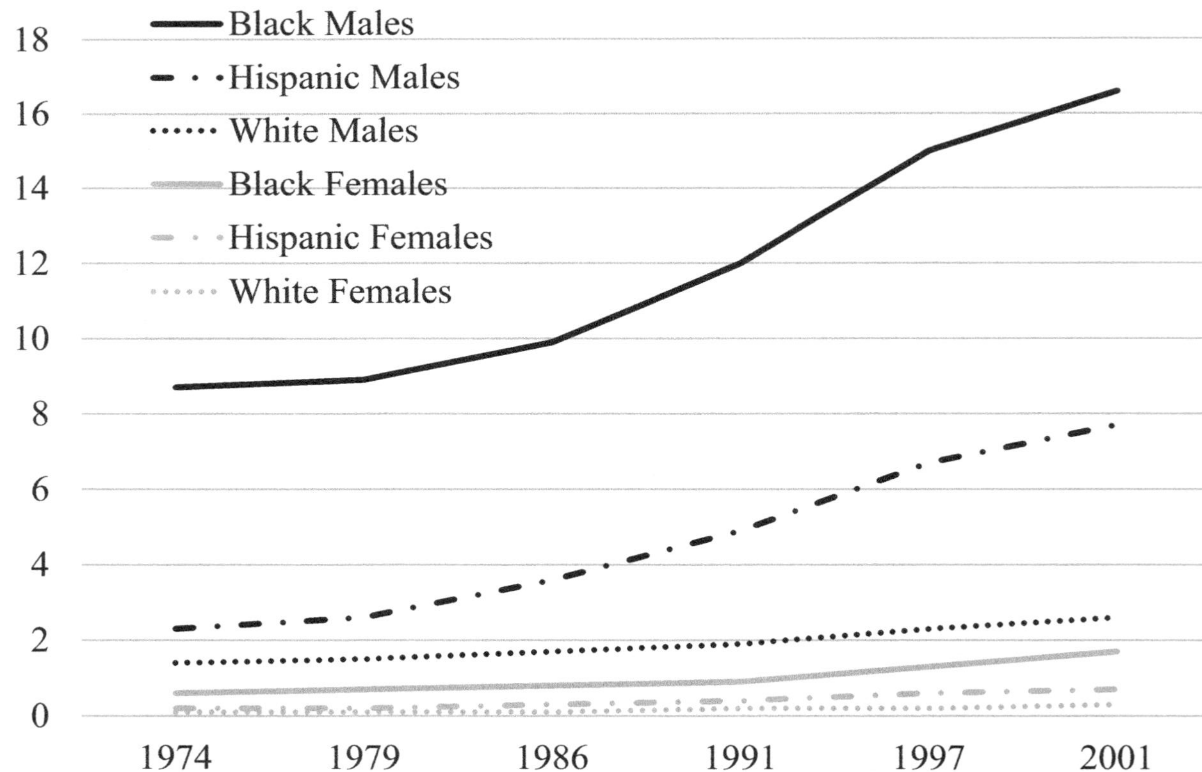

Fig. 5.4 Percentage of adults ever incarcerated by race/ethnicity and gender (1974–2001) (*Source* Bonczar [2003]. US DOJ, Bureau of Justice Statistics)

Contemporary Era (2000's–Present)

The interpretation of Martinson's (1974) paper that "nothing works" to rehabilitate justice-involved individuals and the subsequent policy response led to a decrease in CJS efforts toward rehabilitation to reduce recidivism. Instead, the crime-control policies were victim-centered and aimed at reducing future victimization. However, numerous reviews were conducted that rebutted Martinson's (1974) claims, including Gendreau (1981) and Palmer (1975). Researchers found that some programs (that Martinson reviewed) that met specific characteristics did indeed reduce recidivism. A shift toward finding "what works" led to evidence-based practices based on **research evidence**. Research evidence refers to the information gathered and generated using established scientific methods for conducting research. According to the Office of Justice Programs-Evidence-Based Practices, there are several components of evidence:

1. **Objective**: observable by others, based on facts (rather than thoughts or opinions), and free of bias or prejudice that might be caused by personal feelings.
2. **Replicable**: can be observed by others using the same methods that were used to produce the original evidence.
3. **Generalizable**: can be applied to individuals and groups other than those who were involved in producing the original evidence. (Orchowsky, 2014, p. 3)

The "get-tough" policies and policing tactics were in response to increasing crime rates that began in the 1960s and steadily increased into the 1990s. According to the UCR, property crime rates peaked in 1991, and violent crime peaked in 1994 and steadily declined thereafter. Figure 5.5 shows that by 2000, property crime decreased by 28% and violent crime by 14% since their peaks. The crime decrease, sometimes termed the "great crime decline," baffled many, including policymakers. Many researchers sought to explain this phenomenon, developing more than a dozen hypotheses (e.g., imprisonment, changing demographics) to explain the crime decrease. Others used this as an opportunity to determine "what works?" by evaluating these hypotheses to determine what is effective in reducing crime (Farrell et al., 2014).

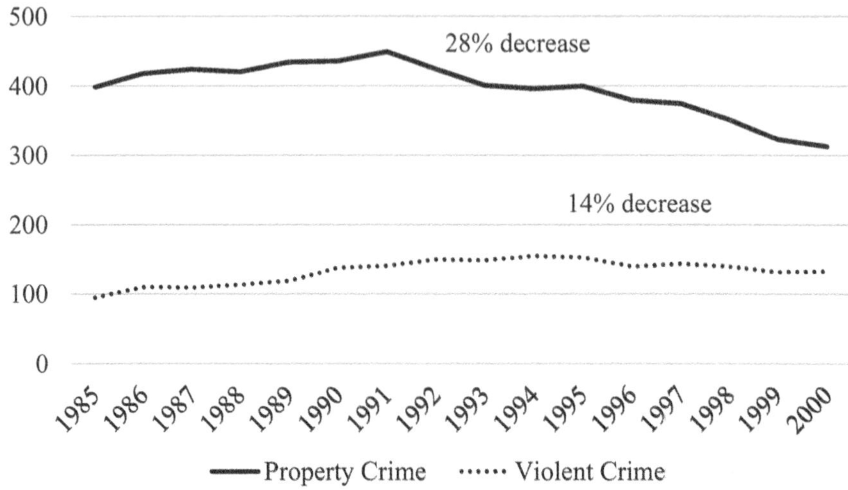

Fig. 5.5 Property and violent crime rate 1985–2000 (per 100,000 Inhabitants) (*Source* FBI. Crime in the United States crime data explorer, 1985–2000 [Violent: murder/non-negligent manslaughter, aggravated assault, robbery, rape; Property: burglary, larceny-theft, motor vehicle theft, arson])

Evidence-Based Practices in Corrections and Rehabilitation

The penal welfarism rehabilitation system was replaced by evidence-based practices based on risk level and needs. This new penology increased the use of formal assessments to identify risk and then implement social assistance to achieve the goals of recidivism prevention and public protection (Heath-Kelly & Shanaah, 2023). This evidence-based practice of rehabilitation is more person-centered, with a focus on improving self-esteem and other services deemed to reduce recidivism, such as substance use programs or anger management. Treatment and rehabilitation programs are expensive and viewed as investments and, therefore, are targeted toward those most likely to be successful (Garland, 2001). Those with only one drug offense may be considered candidates for rehabilitation treatment, while those with repeat offenses or who have failed prior treatment attempts may be perceived as more harmful to society and punished instead (Sterling, 2004).

The tremendous population growth in US prisons led to overcrowding and financial costs that were unsustainable. Community reintegration assistance programs were created to solve these problems while balancing community safety. The programs focused on improving social support for those returning to communities, employment training, and substance abuse treatment to prevent recidivism. Several federal legislative acts attempted to right-size mass incarceration created by the previous policies. Below is a list and brief details of some major federal policies that addressed jail and prison populations, alternatives to probation, and community-based recidivism reduction.

- **Community Safety Through Recidivism Prevention or the Second Chance Act of 2007**—Amended the Omnibus Crime Control and Safe Streets Act of 1968 to reauthorize, rewrite, and expand provisions for justice-involved adults and juveniles, state and local reentry projects, and expand services to individuals and their families to reenter society. Subtitle B: New and Innovative Programs to Improve Offender Reentry Services—Authorized the Attorney General to award grants of up to $500,000 to establish reentry courts to monitor individuals and provide them with access to comprehensive services and programs, including programs for drug and alcohol treatment. The Second Chance Act established The National Reentry Resource Center (NRRC). The NRRC authorized federal grants to government agencies and nonprofit organizations to provide employment assistance, substance use treatment, housing assistance, family programming, mentoring programming, victim support, and other supports to reduce recidivism (NRRC, 2023).
- **Fair Sentencing Act of 2010**—Amended the CSA and the Controlled Substances Import and Export Act to increase the amount of a controlled substance or mixture containing a cocaine base (i.e., crack cocaine) required to impose mandatory minimum prison terms for trafficking and reduced the sentencing disparity between offenses for crack and powder cocaine from 100:1 to 18:1. The Act also eliminated the five-year mandatory minimum prison term for first-time possession of crack cocaine.
- **Formerly Incarcerated Reenter Society Transformed Safely Transitioning Every Person Act or the FIRST STEP Act of 2018**—Amended the federal criminal code to direct the DOJ to establish a risk and needs assessment system to classify recidivism risk of incarcerated individuals to guide their housing and grouping, program assignments; and incentivize and reward participation and completion of recidivism reduction programs and other productive activities.

More recently, the US Sentencing Commission voted to allow for delayed retroactive application of new sentencing guidelines relating to criminal history, effective February 1, 2024, allowing certain incarcerated individuals to be eligible for reduced sentences (US Sentencing Commission, 2023).

Evidence-Based Practices in Policing

World-renowned criminologist and police educator Dr. Lawrence Sherman advocated for evidence-based practices since the 1990s. In 1998, during a lecture at the Police Foundation, Sherman advocated that scientific evidence should guide police practices about "what works" and has since continued his work for evidence-based policing (Sherman, 2013, 2015). Sherman has inspired many researchers to evaluate various targeted policing tactics for effectiveness (e.g., Piza & Welsh, 2022). In 2008, the Department of Criminology, Law and Society at George Mason University established the Center for Evidence-Based Crime Policy to provide resources related to evidence-based policing, bridging the gap between research and practice. Police receptiveness to evidence-based practices in policing has varied, and although some are knowledgeable and accepting, the implementation has been inconsistent (Telep, 2017).

The long-standing strained relationship between police and minority communities continued into the twenty-first century. On December 18, 2014, President Barack Obama signed an executive order establishing the Task Force on 21st Century Policing. The task force was formed in the aftermath of protests across the US after three high-profile deaths in 2014 involving police use of force: the shooting death of 18-year-old Michael Brown in Ferguson, Missouri (Community Relations Service, 2014), the shooting death of 12-year Tamir Rice in Cleveland, Ohio (Community Relations Service, 2020), and the death of 43-year-old Eric Garner after a takedown restraint in New York, NY (US DOJ, 2019). The task force was commissioned to identify evidence-based best practices and recommend how policing practices can promote effective crime reduction while building public trust. The 11-member task force received testimony and recommendations from various individuals, including community and faith leaders, police officers, and academics. The final report, published in 2015, focused on six areas (pillars) with many recommendations and action steps. In Pillar 1, *Building Trust and Nurturing Legitimacy*, the recommendations attempted to "undo" some of the harms caused by harsh policing strategies used decades before, including embracing a "guardian" mindset (as opposed to the "warrior" mindset) and acknowledging the past and present injustices and discrimination as a barrier to trust. This idea was also recommended in Action Item 5.1.2, which indicated that the training innovations should establish partnerships with academic institutions to develop rigorous training practices, evaluations, and curricula based on evidence-based practices (2015, p. 53). Safeguards against police violence continued in the summer of 2020 after the asphyxiation death of 46-year-old George Floyd (US DOJ, 2022). Efforts to improve police–citizen relations with minority communities are still a work in progress.

Government agencies and other organizations began developing online resources to find evidence-based practices in criminal justice. Below is a list of evidence-based practice organizations for future reference.

- **CrimeSolutions.gov**—provides information on 270 programs in numerous fields, including, but not limited to, corrections, courts, crime prevention, substance use, law enforcement, and victimization.
- **What Works in Reentry Clearinghouse**—provides information on 56 initiatives in six focus areas: brand name programs, employment, family-based programs, housing, mental health, and substance use.
- **Substance Abuse and Mental Health Services Administration's (SAMHSA) National Registry of Evidence-based Programs and Practices**—provides information on almost 300 interventions in mental health and substance use treatment, substance use prevention, and mental health promotion.

Conclusion

Colonial criminal codes were influenced by English criminal law but were more democratic and humane due to the values and influence of the Puritans and Quakers. The values of the Quakers established a more humane system of punishments with the building of penitentiaries. The Revolutionary era finally centralized the government from the fragmented practices of the colonies. The foundation of the United States of America began with the Declaration of Independence, the Articles of Confederation, and the Constitution. The Bill of Rights gave citizens, including those who committed crimes, protective rights against the government, particularly the Fourth, Fifth, Sixth, and Eight Amendments. Significant socio-cultural changes shaped how the CJS responded to crime, including urbanization and the need to create a formal police organization. The Great Depression led to a philosophical shift toward penal welfarism, which established reforms to a rehabilitative approach to crime. The civil rights movement highlighted race relations in the US and CJS inequalities. The rising crime rates and the "war on drugs" resulted in mass incarceration, particularly among racial minorities. The collateral consequences led to significant social policy changes and the shift toward procedural fairness and evidence-based practices. The future of a sound and effective CJS is dependent on policies based on evidence-based practices free of bias rather than those based on emotions or political opinions.

Key Terms

Auburn Plan
Bail
Civil trial
Community-Oriented Policing
Constables
Deterrence/Deterrent
Discretion
General deterrence
Immigration
Incapacitation
Industrialization
Jury
Lex talionis
Migration
Night watch system
Parole
Parole boards
Patronage system
Penal welfarism
Penitentiaries
Probable cause
Probation
Puritans
Quakers
Racial profiling
Reasonable suspicion
Retributive
Research Evidence
Schout and rattle watch system
Slave patrols
Social control
Specific deterrence
Stop and frisk
Suspended sentence
Urbanization

Chapter Questions

1. Which of the CJS amendments of the Bill of Rights do you believe is the most important for the administration of justice? Explain your response.
2. Summarize the characteristics and activities of the police agencies and the development of formal police departments.
3. Compare and contrast the Pennsylvania system and the Auburn Plan. Describe what their experiences would be like for those incarcerated.
4. Should evidence seized in violation of the 4th Amendment still be used at trial if there is enough evidence of their guilt? Why or why not?
5. Explain the concepts of probation and parole, their similarities and differences, and their overall purpose.
6. Describe the role of the civil rights movement and the "war on drugs" in the relationship between the police and the community, predominantly racial minority communities.
7. Describe the incarceration trends over the last 50 years. What social movements or policies do you believe contributed most to these trends?
8. Early police reformers advocated for higher education for the police. Describe the benefits of higher education with the implementation of evidence-based practices.

Suggested Readings

Camp, J. T., & Heatherton, C. (2016). *Policing the planet: Why the policing crisis led to Black Lives Matter.* Verso.

Mogavero, M. C. (2017). Teddy Roosevelt's fight against police corruption. In G. Robertello, Ed. *The use and abuse of police power in America: Historical milestones and current controversies.* Bloomsbury Publishing.

Pound, N. R. (1942). *Social control through law.* Yale University Press.

Sheridan, M. J., Rainville, R. R., King, A., Royster, B., & Fazari, G. M. (2019). *Historical dictionary of American criminal justice.* Rowman and Littlefield Publishers.

Notes

1. Such practices were ruled unconstitutional by Judge Shira A. Scheindlin in the class-action cases Ligon v. City of New York (2014) and Floyd v. City of New York (2014).

References

American Friends Service Committee. (1971). *Struggle for justice: A report on crime and punishment in America, prepared for the American Friends Service Committee.* Hill and Wang Publishers.

Anti-Drug Abuse Act, Pub. L. 99-570, Oct. 27, 100 Stat. 3207 (1986).

Barnes, H. E. (1921). The historical origin of the prison system in America. *Journal of the American Institute of Criminal Law and Criminology, 12*(1), 35–60. https://doi.org/10.2307/1133652

Beck, A. J., & Harrison, P. M. (2001). *Prisoners in 2000.* U.S. Department of Justice, Bureau of Justice Statistics.

Bonczar, T. P. (2003). *Prevalence of imprisonment in the U.S. population, 1974–2001.* U.S. Department of Justice, Office of Justice Programs, Bureau of Justice Statistics.

Carson, A. (2021). *Prisoners in 2020—Statistical tables.* U.S. Department of Justice, Office of Justice Programs, Bureau of Justice Statistics.

Chambliss, W. J. (1994). Policing the ghetto underclass: The politics of law and law enforcement. *Social Problems, 41*(2), 177–194. http://www.jstor.com/stable/3096929

Community Relations Service. (2014). *Shooting death of Michael Brown—Ferguson, MO.* U.S. Department of Justice. https://www.justice.gov/crs/timeline-event/shooting-death-michael-brown-ferguson-mo

Community Relations Service. (2020). Press Release. *Justice Department announces closing of investigation into 2014 officer-involved shooting in Cleveland, Ohio.* https://www.justice.gov/opa/pr/justice-department-announces-closing-investigation-2014-officer-involved-shooting-cleveland

Community Safety Through Recidivism Prevention or the Second Chance Act of 2007, P.L. 110-199, H.R.1593.

Cromwell, P. F., Killinger, G. G., & Kerper, H. (1977). History and concept of parole. In G. G. Killinger & P. F. Cromwell (Eds.), *Alternatives to imprisonment: Corrections in the community, selected readings* (2nd ed., pp. 233–241). West Publishing Company.

Dale, E. (2011). *Criminal justice in the United States, 1789–1939: New histories of American law.* Cambridge University Press.

Ditton, P. M., & Wilson, D. J. (1999). *Truth in sentencing in state prisons.* U.S. Department of Justice, Office of Justice Programs, Bureau of Justice Statistics.

Fair Sentencing Act, P.L. 111-220, S.1789 (2010).

Farrell, G., Tilley, N., & Tseloni, A. (2014). *Crime and justice, 43*, 421–490. https://doi.org/10.1086/678081

Federal Bureau of Investigation. *Crime in the United States, 1970.* Index of Crime, 1960–1970.

Federal Bureau of Investigation. *Crime in the United States.* Crime Data Explorer, 1985–2000.

Floyd v. City of New York, No. 13-3088 2d Cir. (2014).

Formerly Incarcerated Reenter Society Transformed Safely Transitioning Every Person Act (The First Step Act), H.R.5682, S. 756, P. L. 115-391 (2018).

Garland, D. (2001). *The culture of control: Crime and social order in contemporary society.* University of Chicago Press.

Gendreau, P. (1981). Treatment in corrections: Martinson was wrong. *Canadian Psychology, 22*, 332–338.

Guerino, P., Harrison, P. M., & Sabol, W. J. (2011). *Prisoners in 2010.* U.S. Department of Justice, Office of Justice Programs, Bureau of Justice Statistics.

Haskins, G. L. (1960). *Law and authority in early Massachusetts: A study in tradition and design.* Macmillan.

Heath-Kelly, C., & Shanaah, S. (2023). Rehabilitation within pre-crime interventions: The hybrid criminology of social crime prevention and countering violent extremism. *Theoretical Criminology, 27*(2), 183–203. https://doi.org/10.1177/13624806221108866; https://www.archives.gov/founding-docs/amendments-11-27

Ligon v. City of N.Y., 736 F.3d 118 2d Cir. (2013).

Martinson, R. (1974). What works? Questions and answers about prison reform. *The Public Interest, 35*, 22–54.

Massachusetts Act, ch. 198 (1878).

Novak, K., Cordner, G., Smith, B., & Roberg, R. (2022). *Police and society* (9th ed.). Oxford University Press.

Omnibus Anti-drug Abuse Act, P.L. 100-690 102 STAT. 4181 (1988).

Orchowsky, D. (2014). *An Introduction to evidence-based practices.* Justice Research and Statistics Association. Retrieved from https://www.ojp.gov/ncjrs/virtual-library/abstracts/introduction-evidence-based-practices

Palmer, T. (1975). Martinson revisited. *Journal of Research in Crime and Delinquency, 12*, 133–152. https://doi.org/10.1177/002242787501200206

Piza, E. L., & Welsh, B. C. (2022). *The globalization of evidence-based policing: Innovations in bridging the research-practice divide.* Routledge.

President's Task Force on 21st Century Policing. (2015). *Final report of the president's task force on 21st century policing.* Office of Community Oriented Policing Services.

President's Commission on Law Enforcement and Administration of Justice. (1967). *The challenge of crime in a free society.* U.S. Department of Justice, Office of Justice Programs. https://www.ojp.gov/ncjrs/virtual-library/abstracts/challenge-crime-free-society

Preyer, K. (1982). Penal measures in the American colonies: An overview. *The American Journal of Legal History, 26*(4), 326–353. https://www.jstor.org/stable/844940

Richard Nixon Foundation. (2016, June 29). *Public enemy number one: A pragmatic approach to America's drug problem.* https://www.nixonfoundation.org/2016/06/26404/

Roth, M. P. (2019). *A history of crime and the American criminal justice system* (3rd ed.). Taylor & Francis Group.

Seigel, L. J., & Worrall, J. L. (2019). *Essentials of criminal justice* (11th ed.). Cengage.

Shelden, R. G., & Vasiliev, P. V. (2017). *Controlling the dangerous classes: A history of criminal justice in America* (3rd ed.). Waveland Press.

Sherman, L. (1998). *Evidence-based policing: Ideas in American policing*. National Police Foundation.

Sherman, L. (2013). The rise of evidence-based policing: Targeting, testing, and tracking. *Crime and Justice, 42*(1), 377–451. https://doi.org/10.1086/670819

Sherman, L. (2015). A tipping point for "totally evidenced policing": Ten ideas for building an evidence-based police agency. *International Criminal Justice Review, 25*(1), 1–19. https://doi.org/10.1177/1057567715574372

Sterling, E. E. (2004). Drug policy: A challenge of values. In E. H. Judah & M. Byrant (Eds.), *Criminal justice: Retribution vs. restoration* (pp. 51–81). Haworth Press.

Surrency, E. C. (1967). The courts in the American colonies. *The American Journal of Legal History, 11*(4), 347–376. https://www.jstor.org/stable/844493

Telep, C. W. (2017). Police officer receptivity to research and evidence-based policing: Examining variability within and across agencies. *Crime & Delinquency, 63*(8), 976–999. https://doi.org/10.1177/0011128716642253

The Center for Evidence-Based Crime Policy. http://cebcp.org

The Civil Rights Act. Pub.L. 88-352, 78 Stat. 241 (1964).

The Comprehensive Crime Control Act, Pub. L. 98–473, S. 1762, 98 Stat. 1976 (1984).

The National Reentry Resource Center. (2023). https://nationalreentryresourcecenter.org/about-national-reentry-resource-center

The Violent Crime Control and Law Enforcement Act, 42 U.S.C. §14141 (1994).

Tonrey, M. (2017). From policing to parole: Reconfiguring American criminal justice. In M. Tonrey & D. S. Nagin (Eds.), *Reinventing American criminal justice* (pp. 1–26). The University of Chicago Press.

Tyler, T. R. (2014). What are legitimacy and procedural justice in policing? And why are they becoming key elements of police leadership? In C. Fischer (Ed.), *Legitimacy and procedural justice: A new element of police leadership* (pp. 6–32). Police Executive Research Forum.

United States Commission for Civil Rights. *Police practices and civil rights in New York City.* https://www.usccr.gov/files/pubs/nypolice/ch5.htm#_ftn105

United States Department of Justice. (1986). *State and federal prisoners, 1925–85.* Office of Justice Programs, Bureau of Justice Statistics.

United States Department of Justice. (2019). *Statement by United States Attorney Richard P. Donoghue.* United States Attorney's Office. https://www.justice.gov/usao-edny/pr/statement-united-states-attorney-richard-p-donoghue

United States Department of Justice. (2022). *Former Minneapolis police officer Derek Chauvin sentenced to more than 20 Years in prison for depriving George Floyd and a minor victim of their Constitutional Rights.* Office of Public Affairs. Press Release. https://www.justice.gov/opa/pr/former-minneapolis-police-officer-derek-chauvin-sentenced-more-20-years-prison-depriving

United States National Advisory Commission on Civil Disorders. (1968). *Report of the National Advisory Commission on Civil Disorders.* Bantam Books. https://archive.org/details/reportofnation00unit/mode/2up

United States National Archives (n.d.). *Constitution of the United States—A history.* https://www.archives.gov/founding-docs/more-perfect-union

United States National Archives. *The Bill of Rights.* https://www.archives.gov/founding-docs/bill-of-rights

United States National Archives. *The Constitution: Amendments 11–27*.

United States Sentencing Commission. (2023). *Amendment to the Sentencing Guidelines.* https://www.ussc.gov/about/news/press-releases/august-24-2023

What Works in Reentry Clearinghouse. http://whatworks.csgjusticecenter.org.

Zacks, R. (2012). *Island of vice: Theodore Roosevelt's doomed quest to clean up sin-loving New York.* Random House.

Zimring, F. E. (2019). *American juvenile justice* (2nd ed.). Oxford University Press.

6

History of the Juvenile Justice System—From Child Saving to Modern Reforms

Learning Objectives

After this chapter, readers should be able to understand the:

1) History of juveniles in the justice system and the House of Refuge
2) First juvenile court and the juvenile justice court system framework
3) Procedures and terminology applicable to juvenile courts.
4) Impact on rising crime and the hysteria over rising juvenile crime rates
5) Ways the educational system contributes to the school-to-prison pathway, especially those with disabilities.

Introduction

The juvenile justice system (JJS) has roots in the social movements of the early nineteenth century, referred to as **child saving**. Before the movement and the establishment of juvenile courts, children who violated laws were tried in adult courts and subject to the same punishments, including incarceration, whippings, and the death penalty. There were also no separate facilities for children, and they were housed in jails or prisons with adults. Social reformers intervened and established reformatories to house children separate from adults and provide education and vocational training. The reformers

M. C. Mogavero, *Mental Health, Neurodiversity, and Criminal Justice*,
https://doi.org/10.1007/978-3-031-88816-8_6

continued their mission by creating the first Juvenile Court in 1899 (Zimring, 2019). Several United States (US) Supreme Court decisions reshaped the juvenile court system and later shifted to a more punitive approach to juvenile crime. As crime rates among juveniles began to increase in the 1980s and 1990s, once again, many were treated as adults, which targeted racial minorities and those with disabilities. Recent research evidence on adolescent development led to the contemporary "children are different" era, where policies sought to "right size" the harmful effects of the past punitive approach by broadening the juvenile court jurisdiction and focusing on individualized rehabilitation and treatment.

Early Reformers: The Child Savers (1820s–1920s)

As early as 1815, concerned citizens, including Reverend John Stanford (1754–1834), pleaded for the removal of children from adult prisons and jails. Stanford's plan was to establish an institution that included work, education, and religion as a means to "cure" deviant behavior, but his plan was ignored for years. Quakers, Thomas Eddy (1758–1827) and John Griscom (1774–1852), among others concerned about the rising poverty and crime, formed the *Society for the Prevention of Pauperism and Crime.* While traveling in Europe, Griscom visited a London reform school for disadvantaged children. When he returned to the US in 1819, he presented his ideas to committee members, who expressed enthusiasm. However, it took years of advocating and convincing before the institution was approved. The organization changed its name to the *Society for the Reformation of Juvenile Delinquents*, and the **House of Refuge** reformatory finally opened in New York City in 1825. The House of Refuge not only housed children who had committed delinquent acts but also children who were neglected or impoverished and were believed to be on a path to becoming "criminals" (Pickett, 1969).

The House of Refuge operated under the **parens patriae** (Latin for "parent of the state") doctrine, a belief that society was responsible for caring for children. The term parens patriae originated in the twelfth century with the King of England (Merlo & Benekos, 2019). The state assumed the responsibility of parenting children deemed neglected, "delinquent," or "wayward" in an informal court where a judge acted as a "wise parent" (Spinak, 2023). Children were wards of the state until they exhibited positive behavioral changes or became adults, but some remained until age 21. According to the Society for the Reformation of Juvenile Delinquents 15th Annual Report, on January

1, 1840, New York City's House of Refuge housed 206 children, 156 boys and 50 girls. The report described their daily activities, noting the children spend six to seven hours per day working, with the boys performing mechanical labor and girls making, sewing, mending, and washing clothing. The children also had school instructions for three to four hours per day and religious instruction on the Sabbath. Parents whose children were removed from their care challenged the parens patriae doctrine. Below are details of two US Supreme Court cases where the first legal challenge occurred in 1838 in Pennsylvania. Pennsylvania law had established a house of refuge, modeled after the New York statute.

Case Briefs: Challenging Parens Patriae

Ex parte Crouse (1838)

Facts: Mary Ann Crouse was a 16-year-old held at a House of Refuge in Philadelphia, PA. Mary Ann's mother believed she had become unruly and unmanageable and requested she be sent to the House of Refuge. Against her father's wishes, Mary Ann was committed to the state's custody by a warrant under a justice of the peace. Mary Ann's father petitioned the Supreme Court of Pennsylvania, arguing that the commitment violated Mary Ann's Sixth Amendment right because the magistrate did not conduct a trial before placing her in the House of Refuge.

Issue: Whether a child's commitment against their parent's consent without a trial was a violation of the Sixth Amendment right to a jury trial.

Outcome: The Pennsylvania Supreme Court held that the state had an obligation and a right to assure a child's well-being. The Court agreed that parental rights were not absolute. If parents failed to exercise their rights to control their children appropriately, those rights and responsibilities were transferred to the state. The Court also disagreed that commitment violated one's constitutional rights because the House of Refuge was a place of rehabilitation, not punishment. If Mary Ann's parents could not control her behavior, educate, and protect her, then it was the state's responsibility to do so. Mary Ann's proper place was in the House of Refuge, according to parens patriae.

People ex rel. O'Connell v. Turner (1870)

Facts: After the Ex parte Crouse decision, more states opened houses of refuge. In 1863, the city of Chicago established a reform school to care for "vagrant," neglected, and "wayward" children who were found to be living in "misfortune" (i.e., economically disadvantaged) could be committed to the school without a trial. In 1870, 14-year-old Daniel O'Connell was taken into custody by the Cook County Sheriff's Office because he was in danger of engaging in delinquency. O'Connell's delinquent propensities were not clearly documented, yet the Cook County Superior Court Judge remitted O'Connell to the Cook County Reform School. His father, Michael O'Connell, sought a writ of habeas corpus (i.e., a court order to release him) to the Illinois Supreme Court, arguing that because his son committed no crime, his commitment restrained his liberty.

Issue: Whether holding a juvenile at the Cook County Reform School when they are merely in danger of engaging in delinquency and have committed no crime violated the right to due process.

Outcome: The Illinois Supreme Court held that holding juveniles when they have not committed a crime violates their personal liberties. The Court's decision focused on personal liberties and the proper supervision of minors and whether minors should be held for misfortune without committing a crime and without the conviction of an offense. The Court noted that even those who commit crimes cannot be held without a trial and due process of law. To allow children to be confined for the "good of society" was a form of tyranny and oppression. The Court decided that the laws creating the reform school were violations of due process.

First Juvenile Court: Chicago, Illinois 1899

The Turner decision demonstrated a shift in society's position regarding whether the state or the parents were better equipped to manage their children. This dilemma paved the way for the establishment of an entirely separate system. In 1899, the Illinois General Assembly created the first juvenile court in Cook County for those under 16 (Snyder & Sickmund, 1999). The mission of the juvenile court was based on the premise that juveniles were "victims" of life circumstances and, therefore, not responsible or had diminished responsibility for their behaviors. A unique feature of the juvenile court was the **indeterminate sentence,** where, instead of a specific period of time, they would remain under the juvenile court's jurisdiction until they were "cured." By 1925, most states developed juvenile courts; today, a juvenile court exists in all 50 states (Segal et al., 2019).

The main concern of juvenile court was the "best interests of the child," and the aim was to provide individualized care and not punishment. The court was paternalistic rather than adversarial, and the judge acted in **loco parentis** (Latin for "in [the] place of a parent"). The court proceedings were also civil, which has different legal standards than criminal proceedings. There was no strict adherence to legal doctrine, constitutional rights, or due process of law. Therefore, juveniles facing a potential loss of liberty were not awarded the rights of the Fifth, Sixth, and Fourteenth Amendments (Puzzanchera et al., 2022). The juvenile court also has different terminology to distinguish itself from adult courts designed for punishment. These terms also allow juveniles to avoid the classifications, burdens, and "criminal" labels that adults receive for the same actions. Box 6.1 shows the terminology used in juvenile courts and the corresponding term used in adult courts.

Box 6.1 Juvenile Court System vs. Adult Court System Terminology

Adult court terms	Juvenile court terms
Crime	**Delinquent Acts**— Acts that violate criminal law **Status Offense**- Acts considered an offense only when committed by a juvenile/minor
Arrest	**Summons**— A legal document ordering the juvenile to appear in court
Arraignment	**Initial Hearing**— when juvenile learns the accusation against them
Charge	**Intake Decision**— Whether to handle the case formally or informally **Petition**— a document filed alleging the juvenile is determined to have committed acts of delinquency or status (Non-Petition if the case is handled informally)
Trial	**Adjudication hearing**— hearing determining juveniles' guilt
Conviction	**Adjudicated delinquent**— Court decision of juveniles' guilt
Sentence	**Disposition**— Court decision on what will happen to the juvenile (e.g., placed in a residential facility or probation)

Source Siegal & Worrall (2019)

The Re-emergence of Child Saving

During the Progressive Period (1890s–1920s), the US underwent intense social and political reform aimed to improve society. Some of these improvements sought, in part, to use the power of the federal government to counteract the adverse social effects of industrialization (Levesque, 2011). During this time, cities were experiencing massive population growth (*see* Chapter 5 of this book for details). The influx of people into cities, particularly from other countries with different customs and languages, weakened the cohesiveness of communities, referred to as **collective efficacy**. There was a decreased ability and desire for families to communicate, socialize, and form a community to supervise and control their children effectively. This resulted in an increased number of neglected and dependent children (Zimring, 2019).

A re-emergence of child saving occurred to intervene and change the way society was dealing with, now primarily, immigrant children who were dependent, neglected, or committed acts of delinquency. The child savers at this time were women from middle and upper-class backgrounds, using their social status and influence to deal with children they deemed were engaging in deviant and immoral behavior (Zimring, 2019). Social worker Jane Addams (1860–1935) was one of the most influential child savers, advocating for women, children, and immigrants. During this era, child savers and social reformers established juvenile courts, developed public schools, and passed child labor laws, compulsory school attendance laws, and child protection laws (Levesque, 1995; Platt, 1977).

Due Process Period (1960s–1970s)

The juvenile court continued to operate under the civil court realm with little due process rights. The civil rights movement (1954–1968) drew greater attention to equal rights and due process. Several landmark US Supreme Court decisions in the 1960s and 1970s changed juvenile court proceedings, aligning them with many of the adult court system's constitutional and due process protections. Kent v. United States (1966) was the first US Supreme Court case that entitled juveniles facing waiver to adult court to some fundamental due process rights. A year later, In re Gault (1967), the US Supreme Court extended procedural safeguards from Kent, requiring courts to apply due process rights to juvenile proceedings. These due process requirements would introduce more order, formality, and, in some cases, aspects of the adversarial system. Critics believed that the Gault decision signaled the end of the traditional model of juvenile justice by formalizing the juvenile court and aligning it with the adult court.

The Sixth Amendment of the Constitution provides those accused of crime the right to a jury trial. Whether juveniles were allowed this same right was decided in Mckeiver v. Pennsylvania (1971). The US Supreme Court decided that a jury was not a constitutional requirement in juvenile adjudicative hearings. In re Winship (1970), the juvenile court further aligned with adult court proceedings about the burden of proof or level of standard of evidence. In adult court, one must be found guilty of a crime **beyond a reasonable**

doubt, yet in juvenile court, the standard of proof was lower with a **preponderance of the evidence** (*see* Chapter 1 of this book for details). In Breed v. Jones (1975), the US Supreme Court granted juveniles protections of the double jeopardy Clause of the Fifth Amendment, which states, "nor shall any person be subject for the same offense to be twice put in jeopardy of life or limb" (*see* Chapter 5 of this book for details). Below are case briefs of these five landmark decisions.

Case Briefs: Challenging Juvenile Court Proceedings

Kent v. United States (1966)

Facts: Washington D.C.'s Juvenile Court Act (1965) had a provision for juveniles 16 years of age who committed a felony (in the case of an adult), that after a "full investigation," could waive jurisdiction and be charged in adult court. Morris Kent was 14 years old when he first had contact with the D.C. juvenile court. He was charged with several burglaries and robberies and was placed on probation. At age 16, while still on probation, Kent was summonsed with burglary, robbery, and rape. After conducting a "full investigation," the court decided to waive Kent to the adult court for proceedings. This "full investigation" was conducted without consulting with Kent, his parents, or his lawyer, without publishing any findings or statement of the facts, and without providing a reason for the waiver. Kent was convicted on six counts and was sentenced to serve five to 15 years on each count, a 30–90-year sentence.

Issue: Whether a juvenile can be waived to adult court after conducting a "full investigation" rather than a formal hearing.

Outcome: The US Supreme Court decided that the Washington D.C. Juvenile Court Act entitled Kent to specific fundamental due process. In addition to the right to a waiver hearing, the Court held that juveniles were entitled to certain due process rights when facing possible transfer to adult court: (1) the right to be represented by counsel, (2) the right to access records considered by the juvenile court in determining waiver, and (3) the right to hear a statement of the reasons in support of waiver.

In re Gault (1967)

Facts: 15-year-old Gerald Francis Gault and his friend, Ronald Lewis, were taken into custody by the Sheriff of Gila County, Arizona. Gault was accused of making an obscene telephone call to a neighbor, Mrs. Cook. After Gault's summons, Gault was taken to the Children's Detention Home. Gault was still on probation for having been in the company of another friend who had stolen a wallet from a woman's purse. His parents were at work when

Gault was taken into custody, and neither were contacted about his placement. A hearing was held the next day; Gault, his mother, his older brother, and two Probation Officers appeared before the Juvenile Judge. Mrs. Cook, the complainant, was not present. No witness was sworn in, and no transcript, recordings, memorandum, or record of the proceedings were prepared. At a second hearing, again, Mrs. Cook was not present. After this hearing, the judge committed Gault as a "juvenile delinquent" to the State Industrial School until he was 21. An adult charged with the same offense would have received a maximum sentence of a $50 fine and two months in jail.

Issue: Whether juveniles have due process rights during the adjudication stage of a delinquency proceeding.

Outcome: The US Supreme Court held that juveniles had a right to receive fair treatment under the law and highlighted the following fundamental rights of juveniles at adjudication:

- the right to obtain legal counsel.
- the right to receive notice of the charge.
- the privilege against self-incrimination.
- the right to confront and cross-examine witnesses.

In re Winship (1970)

Facts: 12-year-old Samuel Winship broke into a locker and stole $112 from a woman's purse, which, if committed by an adult, would constitute the crime of larceny. A New York Family Court judge found that Winship had engaged in delinquent conduct and was ordered to be committed to a training school for an initial period of 18 months, subject to annual extensions of his commitment until his 18th birthday.

Issue: Whether the standard of proof beyond a reasonable doubt is required for due process and fair treatment during the adjudicatory stage when a juvenile is charged with an act that would constitute a crime if committed by an adult.

Outcome: The US Supreme Court ruled that when a juvenile is faced with a proceeding where incarceration might result, the standard of proof should be "beyond a reasonable doubt" instead of "preponderance of the evidence." The constitutional safeguard of proof beyond reasonable doubt was of utmost importance during the adjudication stage of a juvenile proceeding. The Court did not extend this level of proof to all juvenile proceedings but only to those where incarceration might be the result.

Mckeiver v. Pennsylvania (1971)

Facts: 16-year-old Joseph Mckeiver was summonsed with robbery, larceny, and receiving stolen goods. Mckeiver requested a trial by jury, but his request was denied. Mckeiver was adjudicated in the juvenile court, and the judge placed him on probation. Mckeiver argued for a right to a jury trial because they were similar to an adult court trial.

Issue: Whether the Sixth Amendment right to a jury trial applies to juveniles.

Outcome: The Court found that juveniles did not have a constitutional right to a trial by jury. The juvenile justice system had a formal system to protect juveniles, and a jury trial would end these protective proceedings for juveniles and the distinction between the adult and juvenile court systems. The decision in Mckeiver showed that the Court was not ready to "eliminate" the juvenile justice system entirely.

Breed v. Jones (1975)

Facts: 17-year-old Gary Jones was adjudicated for robbery in a California juvenile court. After the hearing and finding that he was "unfit" for treatment as a juvenile, the court determined that Jones should be tried in adult court. Jones appealed, arguing that a trial in adult court, after being adjudicated in juvenile court, for the same offense violated the double jeopardy clause. After his appeals were denied, Jones went on trial and was found guilty of robbery in the first degree.

Issue: Whether a trial in adult court following an adjudication in juvenile court for the same offense constitutes a violation of the double jeopardy clause of the Fifth Amendment.

Outcome: In a unanimous decision, The US Supreme Court agreed that this procedure violated the double jeopardy clause protected by the Fifth Amendment. The Court suggested that juvenile courts decide whether to try a juvenile as an adult at a preliminary hearing before adjudication to avoid double jeopardy violations and allow juveniles to be tried as adults when appropriate.

The Juvenile Justice and Delinquency Prevention Act

The due process protections detailed in the prior case decisions led Congress to create federal standards. The Juvenile Delinquency Prevention and Control Act (JJDPA) (1968) recommended that those who commit status offenses (those deemed "non-delinquent") be handled informally outside the court system (Snyder & Sickmund, 2006). A key feature of the JJDPA was to segregate juveniles who commit status offenses from juveniles adjudicated delinquent. Before the Act, the juveniles could be placed together in a secure institution. For example, juveniles who ran away from home or were truant from school could be housed in the same institutions that placed juveniles adjudicated for acts that would be considered crimes, such as robbery or burglary. Congress also offered financial incentives (i.e., a formula grant program) to state systems that met these standards. Funding under this formula grant program was to be allocated to states based on their relative population of those under 18, but no state was to receive less than $200,000. This money was allocated to help states improve their JJS to assist in the planning, establishing, operating, coordinating, and evaluating juvenile programs (Finklea & Hanson, 2015).

In original juvenile court legislation, status offenses (previously called noncriminal acts) justified placement in facilities for the "best interests of the child" under the parens patriae doctrine. The JJDPA was amended in 1974 and again in 1980, when the Act required the **deinstitutionalization** of juveniles who commit status offenses, recognizing the unfairness of institutional confinement for such acts. Juveniles were also to be removed from adult jails or facilities except if tried as adults for a felony or have been convicted in the adult court system. The rationale behind the separation of juveniles and adults was evidence that juveniles learned criminal behavior from older juveniles (JJDPA, 1968; 1974; 1980; Zimring, 2019).

The Crime Control Period (1980s–1990s)

Crime rates in the US steadily increased from the 1960s through the 1990s, leading Congress to action by passing several legislative acts in efforts to reduce crime (*see* Chapter 5 of this book for details). Likewise, juvenile delinquency rates steadily increased from the late 1980s and 1990s, in which minority youths were overrepresented. Figure 6.1 shows the number of juvenile delinquency cases by race from 1986–1994, and Black juveniles comprised more than double the number of cases of Whites and other races.

Black juveniles were also being detained at higher proportions than their representation in delinquency cases. As shown in Fig. 6.2, Black juveniles represented less than 30% of the overall delinquency caseload in 1988 but made up 36% of the detention cases.

In 1988, The JJDPA was amended to address this racial disparity with the disproportionate number of minorities in confinement facilities. States were required to determine the degree to which minority juveniles were confined, identify causes, and develop and implement strategies to correct

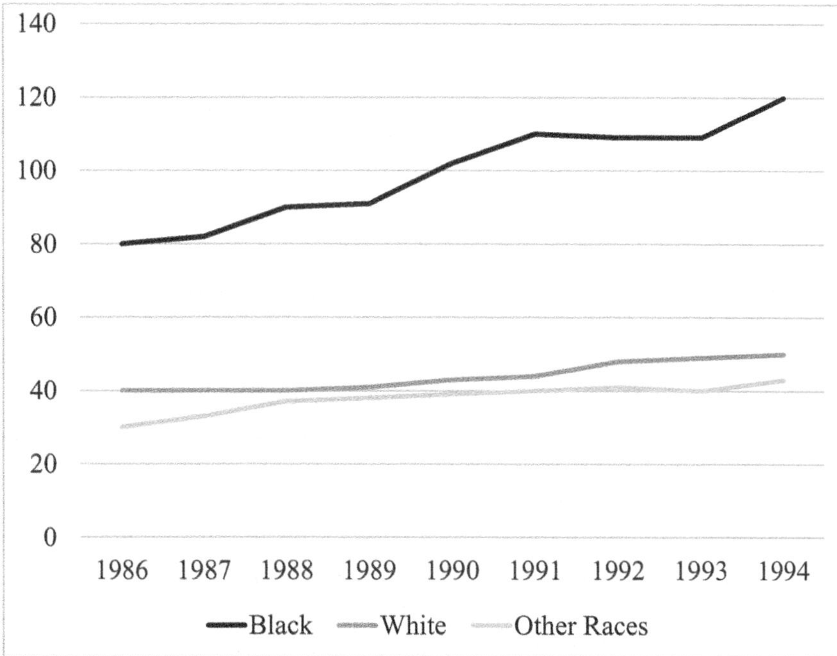

Fig. 6.1 Number of delinquency cases per 1,000 juveniles (*Source* Adapted from Stahl et al. (2005). US Department of Justice)

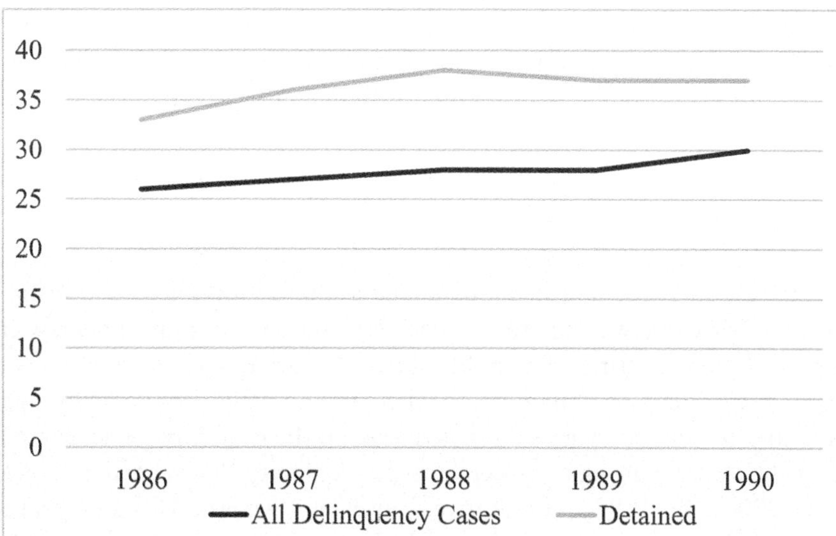

Fig. 6.2 Percentage of cases involving Black juveniles (*Source* Adapted from Stahl et al. (2005). US Department of Justice)

these imbalances. States that did not comply with this requirement (demonstrate improvements or good faith efforts) would lose 25% of the formula grant money (JJDPA). In 2002, the Act broadened the concept of disproportionate minority confinement to encompass all stages of the juvenile justice process and changed it from disproportionate minority confinement to disproportionate minority contact (Finklea & Hanson, 2015).

Transfer Waivers from Juvenile Court to Adult Court

Transfer laws address which court (juvenile or adult) has jurisdiction over certain cases involving juveniles. Depending on the offense or act, some states and jurisdictions could decide to handle cases of older juveniles (e.g., 16 years of age) in juvenile or adult court. There are several ways in which juveniles can be waived to adult court. (1) **Judicial waiver,** sometimes known as process of certification, remand, or bind over, where a juvenile court judge waives court jurisdiction. This is the most common, and nearly all states have discretionary judicial waiver provisions in which juvenile court judges have the discretion to waive jurisdiction and refer cases to adult court (Hockenberry, 2021; Snyder & Sickmund, 2006). (2) **Concurrent jurisdiction,** sometimes known as prosecutorial waiver, prosecutor discretion, or direct file, where the prosecutor has discretion to file cases in either adult or juvenile court. (3) **Statutory exclusion,** sometimes known as legislative exclusion, where a state statute excludes certain juveniles from juvenile court jurisdiction. For example, murder cases must originate in adult rather than juvenile court (Synder & Sickmund, 2006).

Increased Transfer Waivers

The increase in crime and delinquency rates among juveniles led to public perception that this was due to a lenient JJS and harsher punishments were necessary to reduce crime. The political shift to "get tough" on crime occurring in the adult CJS shifted to the JJS. In the early 1990s, many state legislatures responded by passing laws to expand the eligibility for adult court processing by lowering age requirements (Hockenberry, 2021; Snyder & Sickmund, 2006). By 1999, presumptive waiver laws were in 16 states, and at least 15 had mandatory waiver laws (Hockenberry, 2021). Many states also implemented "once an adult, always an adult" provisions, where once a juvenile is convicted in adult court, the juvenile must be charged as an adult for any subsequent offenses (Synder & Sickmund, 2006). Figure 6.3 shows the number of judicial waivers to adult courts from 1986 to 1994. Between 1986 and 1990, judicial waivers increased by about 19%, from just over 6,000 to about 8,000. Between 1990 and 1994, the waivers increased by about 68% to about 13,000, about a 100% increase in eight years.

The support for harsher laws for juveniles continued after the 1995 article by political science professor Dr. John DiLulio titled, *The coming of the super-predator*. With the increased crime rates among juveniles, DiLulio predicted these rates would increase dramatically, and his warning was clear:

> Between 1985 and 1991 the number of juveniles in custody increased from 49,000 to nearly 58,000. By my estimate, we will probably need to incarcerate at least 150,000 juvenile criminals in the years just ahead. In deference to public safety, we will have little choice but to pursue genuine get-tough law-enforcement strategies against the super-predators.

DiLulio's article was published just a few years after the 1989 "wilding" case of the Central Park Five (*see* Chapter 9 of this book for details), which continued to spread public fear of violent crime committed by juveniles.

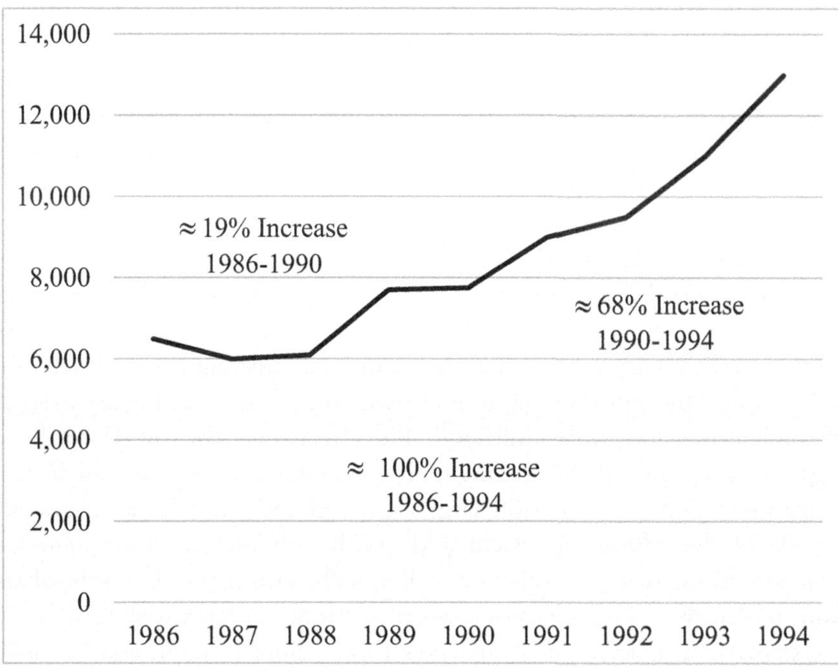

Fig. 6.3 Juvenile cases judicially waived to adult court (1986–1994) (*Source* Adapted from Hockenberry (2021) US Department of Justice)

The Collateral Consequences of "Get-Tough" Policies

By the late 1990s, the super-predator prediction had never come to fruition and had since been deemed a myth (Shust, 2014). However, the damage was done, as this moral panic of the "super-predator" led to harsher punishments, particularly for minorities, including life without parole (Muñiz, 2021). Greene et al. (2017) found that the "super-predator" stereotype continues to exist, and this stereotype is linked to increased support for transferring juveniles to adult court and harsher sentences such as life without parole.

Strict School Discipline

Waiving juveniles to adult court and the get-tough approach expanded into other facets, including schools, increasing their risk of involvement in the juvenile or adult justice systems (Fowler et al., 2010; Muñiz, 2021). In the 1990s, the height of the "get tough" on crime era, local school districts began adopting policies that included strict exclusionary school disciplines (suspensions and expulsions), which grew in popularity across the US due to fears of violence (Baker et al., 2020). One such policy was the Gun-free School Act of 1994, which mandated one-year expulsion and referral to the JJS or CJS for any student who is determined to have brought a gun to school. State legislators and local school districts began implementing zero-tolerance policies that required mandatory suspensions and expulsions to include anything that can be described as a weapon (e.g., knife), drugs, alcohol, fighting, threats, or swearing (Skibia & Knesting, 2001).

Several studies have found links between juveniles experiencing exclusionary discipline and later involvement in the CJS. Mowen and Brent (2016) note that exclusionary school discipline can be a "turning point" in the life of the juvenile and put them at an increased risk of experiencing an arrest in later adolescence and early adulthood. The effectiveness of the JJS to divert juveniles from a life of crime and their placement in a residential facility for treatment and rehabilitation largely depends on the education system. The role of the education system and youths adjudicated delinquent has drawn attention to a phenomenon colloquially known as the "**school-to-prison pathway**.[1]" The school-to-prison pathway is a term used to describe the systematic displacement of juveniles from school to confinement facilities, brought about by zero-tolerance policies, the presence of school resource officers, and stricter school discipline for disruptive behavior (Elias, 2013). However, this pathway metaphor has fallen out of favor with some, as

Waterman et al. (2018) note that the term dehumanizes the students' experience. In actuality, the link between disciplinary actions and criminal justice is not a conveyor belt or pathway but a complex "web" of various social and personal factors (Morgan, 2021; Muñiz, 2021).

Implications for Minority Students and Students with Disabilities. The harsh school policies resulted in a disproportionate effect on minorities and students with disabilities. The US Department of Education (2012) reported that students with disabilities who received special education services were twice as likely as students without disabilities to receive one or more exclusionary disciplines. A statewide study of New York schools revealed that Black students and students with disabilities were more likely to experience an exclusionary discipline, and those who experienced an exclusionary discipline had a significantly higher likelihood of involvement in the JJS (Fabelo et al., 2011). Similarly, Mowen et al. (2020) revealed that youth who experienced suspension had significantly higher levels of offending over time. Hemez et al. (2020) evaluated school records and incarceration rates among 7,623 individuals, of which 2,710 experienced at least one suspension. The results showed those experiencing a suspension during grades 7–12 increased the odds of incarceration in young adulthood by 288%, particularly for Black individuals, whose odds were 66% higher than Whites (Hemez et al., 2020).

Education Policies

Several education policies designed to improve student performance and support students with disabilities were established in the 1960s and amended in the 2000s. The Elementary and Secondary Education Act of 1965, signed by President Lyndon Johnson (1908–1973), distributed more funding to schools and school districts with a high percentage of students from low-income families. In 1969, President Richard Nixon (1913–1994) amended the Elementary and Secondary Education Act to allocate more funding for students with disabilities. The case, Mills v. the Board of Education (1972), was filed on behalf of seven children with disabilities expelled in the Washington D.C. school district due to "behavior problems." The US District Court held that students with disabilities were guaranteed access to a "free and appropriate education" in the "least restrictive environment" are entitled to due process prior to expulsion from school (Mills v. the Board of Education, 1972). Several legislative acts have been passed that specifically address the decision in the Mills case. The Education for All Handicapped Children Act of 1975, signed by President Gerald Ford (1913–2006), required the evaluation of children with disabilities and the creation of an Individualized Education Program (IEP), and the school must follow the statutory requirements in the IEP. In 1990, Education for All Handicapped Children was amended with the Individuals with Disabilities Education Act (IDEA) to require that children with disabilities be granted a free, appropriate public education in the least restrictive environment.

President George Bush reauthorized the Elementary and Secondary Education Act with the No Child Left Behind Act in 2001. The Act increased the accountability of schools (e.g., the teachers and students) via annual standardized tests. Schools were required to publish annual report cards that detailed student achievement data. The Elementary and Secondary Education Act was reauthorized in 2015 by President Barack Obama as the Every Student Succeeds Act. The Act allowed states more flexibility, so long as they implemented school accountability systems (focus on low-performing schools and those with large achievement gaps) and implemented teacher and principal evaluation systems. Students who meet the requirements for IDEA would have an IEP in place and provide the necessary accommodations.

Students with Disabilities

The above legislation education policies resulted in unintended collateral consequences for students with disabilities. One consequence was handling students with behavior problems formally rather than using informal school procedures. The IEP, as outlined in IDEA, addressed how schools could handle disruptive behaviors due to a student's disability. For example, schools could not discipline students under the school's disciplinary codes without considering their disability or mental illness. For example, the National Alliance on Mental Illness notes that behaviors such as disobedience or aggression are common among children experiencing mental illnesses, and their behaviors can be misconstrued as willful defiance. Therefore, schools may instead refer students to the JJS to address them. In a report to the US Department of Justice (DOJ), Burrell and Warboys (2000) expressed concerns about the significant proportion of students with disabilities involved in the JJS. For example, Quinn et al. (2005) reviewed a national sample of 33,831 juveniles under 21 in state correction or detention centers. Of the 27,400 juveniles enrolled in education programs, 8,613 (31%) were eligible for special education under IDEA. The most common classifications under IDEA were mental health-related (47.7%), learning disabilities (38.6%), and intellectual disability (9.7%).

Another consequence was increased suspensions to "game the system" (Figlio, 2006) in standardized test scores. These reporting practices outlined in the No Child Left Behind and Every Student Succeeds Acts increased accountability and the use of standardized test scores. According to a 2010 report by the Advancement Project and Fairtest, school districts, particularly those with higher percentages of minority students or students with disabilities, fearing a low report card rating, were more incentivized to suspend or expel low-performing students. After reviewing data of 41,803 incidents of school discipline among Florida students, Figlio (2006) found that low-performing students were more than two and a half times more likely to be suspended during the standardized testing period, and the length of suspensions was higher for Black students than White students. The zero-tolerance school discipline policies targeting those with behavioral problems (which may be associated with their disability or mental illness) was an effective method to "push out" low-performing students or students with disabilities (Figlio, 2006).

Police Presence in Schools

The decision to handle students' behavior problems formally using the JJS may result from the increased presence of police in schools. In 1986, the US DOJ published a report titled *Reducing School Crime and Student Misbehavior: A Problem-Solving Strategy*, which included a program to have schools work with local law enforcement to address truancy and other problematic behavior (Rubel et al., 1986). Police officers in schools, referred to as school resource officers (SROs), have been in place for decades and became popular in the 1980s with the **DARE program (Drug Abuse Resistance Education)**. DARE was created in 1983 in Los Angeles, CA to educate students about the dangers of drugs while creating a positive relationship with the police. DARE began and became popular during the "war on drugs" and increasing "get-tough" policies on crime, particularly drug crime. DARE programs expanded to about 75% of school districts nationwide. Despite research demonstrating the negligible effectiveness of DARE programs and some schools discontinuing DARE after these negative findings, they were still widespread (Berman & Fox, 2009).

Public fears surrounding school violence, especially after the school shooting at Columbine High School in Littleton, Colorado, in April 1999, the perception of having a police presence in schools became increasingly positive (Berman & Fox, 2009; Fowler et al., 2010). The number of SROs increased significantly in the early 2000s. A 1999 report published by The

US DOJ estimated that in 1997, there were about 9,446 SROs nationwide (Reaves & Goldberg, 1999), and a follow-up report showed 13,056 SROs in 2007, a 38% increase (Reaves, 2010). Some states demonstrated even more significant increases. According to an SRO census report published by the North Carolina Department of Juvenile Justice and Delinquency Prevention, there were 243 SROs in 1995–1996, 683 in 2001–2002 (a 164% increase), and 849 in 2007–2008 (a 249% increase). Zero-tolerance policies coupled with police presence led to more schools using the formal justice system to handle students exhibiting problematic behavior instead of handling them informally through school procedures (Baker et al., 2020). Therefore, schools may choose instead to refer students to the JJS to address the problematic behavior (Baker et al., 2020; Burrell & Warboys, 2000) or what Hirschfield (2008) referred to as the "criminalization of school discipline."

Contemporary Era (2005–Present): Children Are Different

Similar to the adult CJS, there was a pendulum shift from the harshness of the 1990s and early 2000s to "right size" many of the negative impacts of this "get-tough" era. The harsh sentencing policies for juveniles, including waivers to adult court were addressed. The new millennia saw several Landmark US Supreme Court decisions, reversing some punishment practices for juveniles. One of the first cases that considered maturity and cognitive differences between juveniles and adults was Roper v. Simmons (2005). Christopher Simmons was convicted of the murder of Shirly Crook and sentenced to death in Missouri in 1993 when he was 17. The case was appealed to the US Supreme Court, which considered whether it was a violation of the Eighth Amendment for those who commit murder as juveniles to be eligible for the death penalty. The majority opinion included, in part, that due to juveniles' lack of maturity, lack of responsibility, and vulnerability to negative influences and outside pressures (*see* Chapters 4 & 16 of this book for details), the death penalty for juveniles under 18 and was cruel and unusual punishment, protected by the Eighth Amendment.

The Supreme Court has subsequently considered similar sentencing practices for juveniles in Graham v. Florida (2010), which abolished life sentences without the possibility of parole for juveniles who were not convicted of murder. Miller v. Alabama (2012) abolished life sentences without the possibility of parole for juveniles, including those convicted of murder. In Miller v. Alabama, the sentencing judge or jury must consider "how children are different..." DiIulio, recognizing his errored prediction and the harmful unintended consequences, signed the amicus brief in support of limiting life sentences without parole for juveniles. Montgomery v. Louisiana (2016) allowed the Miller decision to be applied retroactively. The above cases cited that a juvenile's cognitive development was a critical factor in the Court's decision that juveniles must be treated differently from adults and should, therefore, not be subject to the same harsh sentences. These decisions mirrored the trend of the scientific community, particularly psychologists and neuroscientists, that juvenile brain development and cognitive decision-making processes have implications for their legal responsibility and culpability (Hanson & Lampe, 2022). However, the US Supreme Court reversed the Miller decision in Jones v. Mississippi (2021). The Court considered the vast developmental differences among adolescents and allowed states to have discretion on whether to impose a life without parole sentence for juveniles convicted of murder.

Expanding Juvenile Court

The research on juvenile brain development and cognitive decision-making processes has also led to policy changes to "right size" states' JJSs. State legislators revised their policies to expand the juvenile court's jurisdiction, colloquially referred to as "raise-the-age," to meet the developmental needs of juveniles. Since 2000, 10 states (Connecticut, Massachusetts, Illinois, New Hampshire, New York, South Carolina, North Carolina, Louisiana, Michigan, and Missouri) have passed laws raising their upper age of original juvenile court jurisdiction, as many states had ages under 17. In 2020, Vermont was the first state to expand juvenile court jurisdiction to 18 (Teigen, 2021), then in 2022, raised the age to 19 (Puzzanchera et al., 2022). This practice of treating juveniles differently reverts to the original philosophy of the juvenile court; it serves the "best interests of the child" but with an emphasis on justice that is individualized to each juvenile. In 2000, The Office of Juvenile Justice and Delinquency Prevention established the Model Programs Guide (MPG) for evidence-based practices. MPG is a resource for practitioners and communities about what programs are shown to be effective in delinquency prevention. MPG contains over 200 programs in the areas of restorative justice practices, prevention, immediate sanctions, intermediate sanctions, residential, and reentry (Model Programs Guide, n.d.).

Decreased Waivers to Adult Court

With the increased recognition that juveniles were different, there was a substantial decrease in juvenile cases judicially waived to adult court. Several states have changed their jurisdictional boundaries to keep juveniles in the JJS. Other states lessened the provisions to try juvenile cases in adult court. For example, some states added reverse waiver provisions to send cases initiated in adult court to juvenile court (Hockenberry, 2021). Adult court waivers peaked in 1994 with about 13,000 cases. Figure 6.4 demonstrates the steady decline of cases waived to adult court, showing a 73% decrease in 24 years. As shown, the 2018 numbers, just over 4,000, were lower than those in 1986, which were just over 6,000.

In December 2018, the Juvenile Justice Reform Act (JJRA) of 2018 was signed into law, reauthorizing and amending the JJDPA, and became effective in 2020. Section 223(a)(11) mirrored the progressive movement of the child savers not to treat juveniles as adults. According to the JJRA of 2018, "juveniles who are being charged and tried as adults (1) may not have sight or sound contact with adults and (2) may not be detained in a jail or lockup for adults (except as provided under the jail removal requirement)" (Harp, 2019, p. 3). The racial disparity in the JJS was also addressed in the 2018 JJRA. The Act reauthorized and amended the previous JJDPA and included

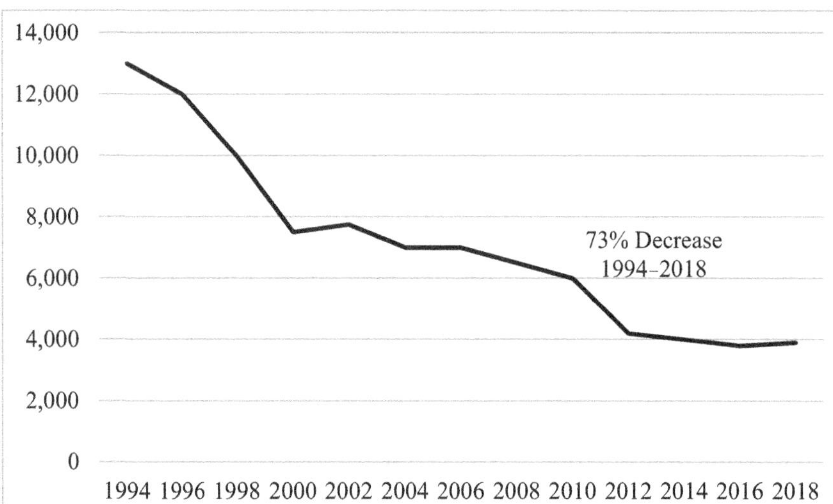

Fig. 6.4 Cases judicially waived to adult court (1994–2018) (*Source* Adapted from Hockenberry (2021). US Department of Justice)

the provision, *Reducing Racial and Ethnic Disparities*, to address the disproportionate amount of minorities confined in secure detention facilities. This new requirement emphasized the need for an action plan and outcome-based evaluation. The Act also expanded the jail removal requirement for juveniles charged as adults and provisions included mental health and substance use screening and treatment (JJRA, 2018).

Conclusion

The early reformers intended to improve the treatment and handling of juveniles. However, the policies removing children from their families under the doctrine of a parens patriae questioned their Constitutionality, which ultimately led to the establishment of a separate JJS. Over time, with the inclusion of constitutional rights, the JJS mirrored the adult system. When crime rates increased, and moral panic over the fear of increased crime committed by juveniles ensued, legislators felt pressure to address public fears by appearing "tough on crime." These get-tough attitudes filtered to other domains where the state assumes responsibility for children, such as the public school system. Zero-tolerance policies that led to expulsion ultimately led children on the "path to becoming criminals," which captured a disproportionate number of minorities and children with disabilities and mental illnesses. The scientific advances that led to a better understanding of adolescent cognitive development and decision-making and the unforeseen negative collateral consequences of policies that treated juveniles as adults led to profound changes in the justice system.

CJS practitioners, including SROs, must acquire the education and knowledge of adolescent variation and how juveniles and those with disabilities inherently understand, react, and behave. Greater recognition and background on past and current policies and practices also assist in making the best decisions on handling juveniles, particularly those with disabilities and mental illnesses. This recognition does not assert that harmful behavior should be ignored. Instead, courts, agencies, and practitioners should use this knowledge of adolescent variation to inform and modify practices. The justice system should intervene to apply appropriate punishments when necessary but also permit the system to emphasize diversion and evidence-based practices to allow juveniles opportunities to acquire the skills and resources to prevent them from engaging in delinquent acts. The unintended consequences of zero-tolerance policies, SROs, and requirements in education legislation, in essence, created the "perfect storm" for minority youths and those with disabilities or mental health conditions to become involved in the JJS, which placed them at higher risk of CJS involvement. Thus, children with disabilities or mental health conditions are often caught in the school-to-prison pathway or "web."

Key Terms

Beyond a reasonable doubt
Child saving
Collective efficacy
Concurrent jurisdiction
D.A.R.E program (Drug Abuse Resistance Education)
Deinstitutionalization
House of Refuge
Indeterminate sentence
Judicial waiver
Loco parentis
Office of Juvenile Justice and Delinquency Prevention
Parens patriae
Preponderance of the evidence
School-to-prison-pathway
Statutory exclusion

Chapter Questions

1) Describe in detail the Illinois Juvenile Justice Court Act and the formation of the Juvenile court system. Be sure to include the concept of parens patriae.
2) Discuss the major differences between the adult CJS and the JJS.
3) Why should legislators consider special application of laws for juveniles, particularly those with disabilities or mental illnesses?
4) Why should we consider juveniles apart from adults? Should there be more or less emphasis on the philosophy that juveniles and adults be treated differently? What about juveniles with disabilities or mental illnesses?
5) Describe the justification behind deinstitutionalization (removing status-offending juveniles from institutions).
6) The Eighth Amendment of the US Constitution prohibits cruel and unusual punishment. What are some punishments that courts have considered cruel and unusual for juveniles? Do you agree with these decisions? Explain your response.

Suggested Readings

Dinerstein, R., & Wakschlag, S. (2019). Using the ADA's 'integration mandate' to disrupt mass incarceration. *Denver Law Review, 917,* American University, WCL Research Paper No. 209–23. https://papers.ssrn.com/sol3/papers.cfm?abstract_id=3424085

Fox, S. J. (1996). The early history of the court. *The Juvenile Court, 6*, 29–39.

Langberg, J., & Fedders, B. (2013). How juvenile defenders can help dismantle the school-to-prison pipeline: A primer on educational advocacy and incorporating clients' education histories into delinquency representation. *Journal of Law & Education, 42*(4), 653–681. https://ssrn.com/abstract=2389405

Notes

1. The common term "prison-to-school pipeline." The term "pipleline" is offensive to some indigenous communities, and the term was replaced with "pathway."

References

Advancement Project & Fairtest. (2010, April 21). *Zero tolerance, high-stakes testing, and the school-to-prison pipeline.* https://fairtest.org/how-testing-feeds-schooltoprison-pipeline/

Baker, D. L., Drapela, L. A., & Littlefield, W. (2020). *Law and neurodiversity: Youth with autism in the juvenile justice systems in Canada and the United States.* UBC Press.

Berman, G., & Fox, A. (2009). *Lessons from D.A.R.E.: The complicated relationship between research and practice.* Center for Court Innovation. https://www.innovatingjustice.org/publications/lessons-battle-over-dare-complicated-relationship-between-research-and-practice

Breed v. Jones, 421 U.S. 519 (1975).

Burrell, S., & Warboys, L. (2000). *Special education and the juvenile justice system.* US Department of Justice, Office of Justice Programs, Office of Juvenile Justice, and Delinquency Prevention.

Dilulio, J. J. (1995, November 27). The coming of the super-predators. *Washington Examiner.* https://www.washingtonexaminer.com/magazine/1558817/the-coming-of-the-super-predators/

Education for All Handicapped Children Act. Pub. L. No. 94–142. 89 Stat. 773. (1975).

Elementary and Secondary Education Act. Pub. L. No. 89–10, 79 Stat. 27. (1965).

Every Student Succeeds Act, 20 U.S.C. §6301 (2015).

Ex parte Crouse, 4 Whart. 9 Pa. (1838).

Elias, M. (2013). The school-to-prison pipeline: Policies and practices that favor incarceration over education do us all a grave injustice. *Learning for Justice*, 39–40. https://www.learningforjustice.org/magazine/spring-2013/the-school-to-prison-pipeline

Fabelo, T., Thompson, M., Plotkin, M., Carmichael, D., Marchbanks, M. III., & Booth, E. A. (2011). *Breaking schools' rules: A statewide study of how school discipline relates to students' success and juvenile justice involvement*. Council of State Governments Justice Center and Public Policy Research Institute.

Figlio, D. N. (2006). Testing, crime, and punishment. *Journal of Public Economics, 90(*4–5), 837–851. https://www.nber.org/papers/w11194

Finklea, K., & Hanson, E. J. (2015). Juvenile Justice and Delinquency Prevention Act (2002), reauthorized by the 21st Century Department of Justice Appropriations Authorization Act, Pub. L. No. 107–273, 116 Stat. 1758.

Fowler, D., Lightsey, R., Monger, J., & Aseltime, E. (2010). *Texas' school-to-prison pipeline: Ticketing, arrest, & use of force in schools*. Texas Appleseed Report. https://dignityinschools.org/resources/texas-school-to-prison-pipeline-ticketing-arrest-use-of-force-in-schools/

Graham v. Florida, 560 U.S. 48, (2010).

Greene, E., Duke, L., & Woody, W. D. (2017). Stereotypes influence beliefs about transfer and sentencing of juvenile offenders. *Psychology, Crime & Law, 23*(9), 841–858. https://doi.org/10.1080/1068316X.2017.1332194

Gun-free School Act. 20 U.S.C. §§ 8921–23 (1994).

Hanson, E. J., & Lampe, J. R. (2022). *Juvenile life without parole: In brief.* Congressional Research Service.

Harp, C. (2019). *Key amendments to the Juvenile Justice and Delinquency Prevention Act made by the Juvenile Justice Reform Act of 2018*. US Department of Justice, Office of Justice Programs, Office of Juvenile Justice and Delinquency Prevention.

Hirschfield, P. J. (2008). Preparing for prison? The criminalization of school discipline in the USA. *Theoretical Criminology, 12*(1), 79–101. https://doi.org/10.1177/1362480607085795

Hemez, P., Brent, J. J., & Mowen, T. J. (2020). Exploring the school-to-prison pipeline: How school suspensions influence incarceration during young adulthood. *Youth Violence and Juvenile Justice, 18*(3), 235–255. https://doi.org/10.1177/1541204019880945

Hockenberry, S. (2021). *Delinquency cases waived to criminal court, 2018*. U.S. Department of Justice, Office of Justice Programs, Bureau of Justice Statistics.

In re Gault, 387 U.S. 1 (1967).

In re Winship, 397 U.S. 358 (1970).

Individuals with Disabilities Education Act, Pub. L. No. 105–17, 111 Stat. 37. (1997).

Jones v. Mississippi, 593 U.S. (2021).

Juvenile Court Act. (1899). *Illinois Laws, 131*, 131–137.

The Juvenile Justice and Delinquency Prevention Act. Pub. L. No. 93–415, 42 U.S.C. § 5601 et seq. (1968, 1974, 1980).

The Juvenile Justice Reform Act, Pub. L. No. 115–385 (2018).

Kent v. United States, 383 U.S. 541 (1966).

Levesque, R. J. R. (1995). The failures of foster care reform: Revolutionizing the most radical blueprint. *Maryland Journal of Contemporary Legal Issues, 6*, 1–35.

Levesque, R. J. R. (2011). Child savers. In R. J. R Levesque (Ed.), *Encyclopedia of adolescence*. Springer. https://doi.org/10.1007/978-1-4419-1695-2_669

Mckeiver v. Pennsylvania, 403 U.S. 528 (1971).

Merlo, A., & Benekos, P. (2019). *The juvenile justice system, Delinquency, processing, and the law* (9th ed.). Pearson.

Miller v. Alabama, 567 U.S. 460 (2012).

Mills v. Board of Education of District of Columbia, 348 F. Supp. 866 D.D.C. (1972).

Montgomery v. Louisiana, 577 U.S. 190 (2016).

Morgan, H. (2021). Restorative justice and the school-to-prison pipeline: A review of existing literature. *Education Sciences, 11*(4), 159. https://doi.org/10.3390/educsci11040159

Mowen, T. J., & Brent, J. J. (2016). School discipline as a turning point: The cumulative effect of suspension on arrest. *Journal of Research in Crime and Delinquency, 53*(5), 628–653. https://doi.org/10.1177/0022427816643135

Mowen, T. J., Brent, J. J., & Boman, J. H. (2020). The effect of school discipline on offending across time. *Justice Quarterly, 37*(4), 739–760. https://doi.org/10.1080/07418825.2019.1625428

Muñiz, J. O. (2021). Exclusionary discipline policies, school-police partnerships, surveillance technologies, and disproportionality: A review of the school to prison pipeline literature. *Urban Review, 53*, 735–760. https://doi.org/10.1007/s11256-021-00595-1

National Alliance on Mental Illness. *About mental illness. Warning signs and symptoms.* https://www.nami.org/About-Mental-Illness/Warning-Signs-and-Symptoms

National Center for Education Statistics. (2018). *Percentage of public schools with security staff.* https://nces.ed.gov/programs/digest/d18/tables/dt18_233.70.asp.

No Child Left Behind Act of 2001, P.L. 107–110, 20 U.S.C. § 6319 (2002).

North Carolina Department of Juvenile Justice and Delinquency Prevention. Center for the Prevention of School Violence. *Annual School Resource Officer Census, 2008–2009.* https://www.ncdps.gov/our-organization/juvenile-justice/datastatisticsreports/juvenile-justice-annual-report

Office of Juvenile Justice and Delinquency Prevention. *Model Programs Guide*. US Department of Justice. Office of Justice Programs. https://ojjdp.ojp.gov/model-programs-guide/home

Pickett, R. S. (1969). *House of refuge: Origins of juvenile reform in New York State, 1815–1857*. Syracuse University Press.

People Ex Rel. O'Connell v. Turner, 55 Ill. 280 (1870).

Platt, A. (1977). *The child savers: The invention of delinquency* (2nd ed.). University of Chicago Press.

Puzzanchera, C., Hockenberry, S., & Sickmund, M. (2022). *Youth and the juvenile justice system: 2022 National Report*. National Center for Juvenile Justice.

Quinn, M. M., Rutherford, R. B., Leone, P. E., Osher, D. M., & Poirier, J. M. (2005). Youth with disabilities in juvenile corrections: A national survey. *Exceptional Children, 71*(3), 339–345. https://doi.org/10.1177/001440290507100308

Reaves, B. A., & Goldberg, A. L. (1999). *Law Enforcement management and administrative statistics, 1997: Data for Individual State and Local Agencies with 100 or More Officers*. US Department of Justice, Office of Justice Programs, Bureau of Justice Statistics.

Reaves, B. A. (2010). *Local police departments, 2007*. U.S. Department of Justice Office of Justice Programs, Bureau of Justice Statistics.

Roper v. Simmons, 543 U.S. 541 (2005).

Rubel, R. J., Ames, N. L., & Zax, J. B. (1986). *Reducing school crime and student misbehavior: A problem-solving strategy*. U.S. Department of Justice, National Institute of Justice, Office of Communication and Research Utilization.

Segal, A., Winfree, T. L., & Friedman, S. (2019). *Mental health and criminal justice*. Aspen Publishers.

Shust, K. B. (2014). Extending sentencing mitigation for deserving young adults. *Journal of Criminal Law & Criminology, 104*(3) 667–704. https://scholarlycommons.law.northwestern.edu/jclc/vol104/iss3/6

Skiba, R. J., & Knesting, K. (2001). Zero tolerance, zero evidence: An analysis of school disciplinary practice. *New Directions for Youth Development, 92*, 17–43. https://doi.org/10.1002/yd.23320019204

Snyder, H. N., & Sickmund, M. (1999). *Juvenile offenders and victims: A national report*. U.S. Department of Justice, Office of Justice Programs, Office of Juvenile Justice, and Delinquency Prevention.

Snyder, H. N., & Sickmund, M. (2006). *Juvenile offenders and victims: 2006 National Report*. U.S. Department of Justice, Office of Justice Programs, Office of Juvenile Justice, and Delinquency Prevention.

Society for the Reformation of Juvenile Delinquents in the City of New York. (1840). *Annual report*. https://archive.org/details/annualreport00soci_8

Spinak, J. M. (2023). *The end of family court*. New York University Press. https://doi.org/10.18574/nyu/9781479814107.003.0004

Stahl, A. N., Puzzanchera, C., Sladky, A. Finnegan, T. A., Tierney, N., & Snyder, H. N. (2005). *Juvenile court statistics 2001–2002*. U.S. Department of Justice, Office of Justice Programs, Office of Juvenile Justice and Delinquency Prevention.

Teigen, A. (2021). *Juvenile age of jurisdiction and transfer to adult court laws*. National Conference of State Legislatures. https://www.ncsl.org/research/civil-and-criminal-justice/juvenile-age-of-jurisdiction-and-transfer-to-adult-court-laws.aspx

United States Department of Health and Human Services. (2001). *Youth violence: A report of the Surgeon General*. U.S. Department of Health and Human Services. https://pubmed.ncbi.nlm.nih.gov/20669522/

United States Department of Education. (2012). *Disability rights enforcement highlights*. Office for Civil Rights. https://www2.ed.gov/documents/news/section-504.pdf

Waterman, S., Lowe, S., & Shotton, H. (2018). *Beyond access: Indigenizing programs for Native American student success* (1st ed.). Stylus Publishing LLC.

Zimring, F. E. (2019). *American juvenile justice* (2nd ed.). Oxford University Press.

7

History of the Mental Health System—From Hospitalization to Community Care and Implications for the Criminal Justice System

Learning Objectives

After this chapter, readers should be able to understand the:

1) Ways people with mental illnesses were treated and managed in early America
2) History of the mental health system and the establishment of hospitals
3) Changes in the treatment and care for those with mental illnesses due to the efforts of Benjamin Rush and Dorothea Dix
4) The history and impact of the eugenics movement on those with mental illnesses and disabilities
5) The social impacts of the deinstitutionalization movement

Introduction

The history of the treatment of individuals with mental illnesses and disabilities in the United States (US) is quite grim. Although the beginnings of institutionalization and humane treatment seemed promising, it was not sustainable. A lack of funding led to overcrowding and poor conditions in hospitals. In the 1950s, advances in science and medicine, followed by increased civil rights for patients and economic considerations, led to

M. C. Mogavero, *Mental Health, Neurodiversity, and Criminal Justice*,
https://doi.org/10.1007/978-3-031-88816-8_7

support for the deinstitutionalization movement. The origins of this movement advocated for a shift from institutionalized care to community-based treatment. The lack of funding to support this shift meant that individuals were released into the community without adequate support. This resulted in many collateral consequences, including people experiencing homelessness and "transinstitutionalization" to jails and prisons. The criminal justice system now assumes most of the institutionalized care and treatment of those with mental illnesses (Torrey et al., 2010).

Formation of Institutionalized Care for Persons with Mental Illnesses

During the early colonial era, the laws that dictated the care for those with mental illnesses fell under the jurisdiction of the community and were based on English principles. Those with mental illnesses lived in various settings, including their families' homes, physicians' homes, workhouses, poorhouses, or wandered freely in public (Talbott, 1978). As the population grew and the colonies became more diverse and complex, this was no longer feasible, and the treatment of those with mental illnesses became increasingly inhumane (Grob, 1994). By the early 1700s, institutionalization in jails began, particularly in larger towns such as Boston. Those with mental illnesses, both men and women, were held in dark, unsanitary cells, chained in handcuffs or ankle irons to the floor or walls, and endured physical abuse (Grob, 1994; Whitaker, 2002).

The **Quakers**, whose value systems were based on humane treatment (*see* Chapter 5 of this book for details), petitioned the Pennsylvania colonial assembly in 1751 to build a hospital to care for and restore health to those in need. The Quakers hoped to bring new treatment practices from England to the colonies. Some community leaders believed society needed to be "protected" from people with mental illnesses, and the hospital could also function to segregate them from society. The first hospital opened in Philadelphia, Pennsylvania, in 1753 (Grob, 1994; Whitaker, 2002). Some members of the public did not share the same humane treatment and would visit the patients in the hospital as a spectacle for their entertainment. A fence was constructed around the hospital in 1760 to end this practice, but it was unsuccessful at keeping visitors away. In 1763, hospital staff began charging a visitor's fee of four pence (British term for penny) (Whitaker, 2002).

Significant changes occurred once Quaker Dr. Benjamin Rush (1746–1813) (*see* Fig. 7.1) arrived at the hospital in 1783. Rush was a physician who studied at the prestigious medical school at the University of Edinburgh in Scotland. Rush was also a humanitarian reformer and advocated for the abolition of slavery and prison reform and advocated for the same **moral treatment** of those with mental illnesses; they should be treated with kindness and respect. After his arrival, patients engaged in activities such as sewing and gardening. They also enjoyed living comforts such as hair mattresses and feather beds. The field of medicine as a scientific discipline was still in its infancy. Rush's views of mental health reflected the teachings of his European mentors, and he was eager to make the Pennsylvania hospital a place of modern medicine. He believed that mental illnesses were caused by irregular actions of the blood vessels in the brain. One common treatment method was bloodletting, where, for example, Rush would draw 200 ounces from one patient in less than two months. For some, he believed their symptoms were caused by too little blood circulation to the head and treated patients using a spinning therapy called a gyrator. Patients would be strapped horizontally to a board that could be spun at high speeds (Whitaker, 2002).

Fig. 7.1 Image of Dr. Benjamin Rush (Courtesy of the US National Library of Medicine)

Treatment Reforms and the Establishment of Hospitals

By the early 1800s, Rush's treatment methods began to wane, and they were perceived as abuse, and the gyrator was banished from the Pennsylvania hospital. When Rush died in 1813, his views on moral treatment took hold and remained the therapeutic ideal (Whitaker, 2002). The Philadelphia Quakers opened the first moral treatment hospital in 1817, and several others opened soon after. Members of the Congressional Church of Boston established a hospital in 1818, later known as McLean Hospital. Quaker, Thomas Eddy (1758–1827) led the establishment of Bloomingdale Hospital in New York City, which opened in 1821 and is located at the site of what is now Columbia University (Grob, 1994; Whitaker, 2002). A fundamental principle was that the care be provided in a home-like atmosphere. The standard blueprint was that the hospital should be small and have no more than 250 patients, and the buildings themselves should be architecturally beautiful. The hospital was governed by a superintendent who was expected to have meals with the patients and guide them toward a path of "reason." By 1841, there were 16 private and public hospitals in the US that provided moral treatment for those with mental illnesses (Whitaker, 2002).

The Efforts of Dorothea Dix

In the 1840s, schoolteacher and social reformer Dorothea Dix (1802–1887) (*see* Fig. 7.2) pioneered change for individuals with mental illnesses and disabilities. Jails were also used as poorhouses and would hold "paupers" and other disadvantaged people who owned depts (*see* Chapter 5 of this book for details). Dix was teaching Sunday school at the jail in Cambridge, Massachusetts (a suburb of Boston). She noticed that many people inside the jails had mental illnesses and was disturbed by the conditions and treatment. Dix began investigating the conditions in other jails in Massachusetts. She then traveled to dozens of county jails and prisons throughout New York, New Jersey, Pennsylvania, and Kentucky and documented her observations of the people and the physical conditions. Dix noted that many jails housed people who had mental illnesses or disabilities and were often held in the same rooms (men and women both) as those who committed crimes. She protested treating people with mental illnesses as "criminals," arguing that it would be better all if they were housed and humanely treated in hospitals (Dix, 1971).

Fig. 7.2 Portrait of Dorothea Dix (Courtesy of the US National Library of Medicine)

Dix wrote several Memorials to the state legislators, pleading for change. One pleaded to the legislators in Pennsylvania, where the Quakers sought change and moral treatment decades earlier.

> In Memorial: To the Honorable, the Senate, and the House of Representatives of the Commonwealth of Pennsylvania on February 3, 1845:
> I regret that I cannot refer to the jail of Fairfield County, in Uniontown, in other terms than of unqualified censure... There were no "criminal prisoners"... the only occupants of the jail apartments when I was there.... were two "mad" men, in chains... the men were chained and in separate rooms... I saw no bedstead, nor any furniture.... (Dix, 1971, p. 19, 170)

She described one man in Fairfield County Jail as... "covered with soot, and coal dust, and dirt, and was extended upon the floor, clanking his chains, and beating his head, shouting and singing" (Dix, 1971, p. 19, 170). She also noted, "Franklin County jail a young girl, very insane, had not been long removed from the jail, where she had been loaded with heavy chains and endured all exposures and sufferings... estimated number of 'insane' and 'idiotic' in the county, from 40 to 50" (Dix, 1971, pp. 14–15, 166).

Expansion of Institutionalized Care

Despite the reform efforts of the Pennsylvania Quakers to remove those with mental illnesses from jails nearly 100 years earlier, as Dix noted, this practice continued. The County Jail in Fairfield, Pennsylvania was holding dozens of people with mental illnesses and disabilities, not people who have committed crimes. Unfortunately, Dix's compassion for transitioning people with mental illnesses from jails and prisons to hospitals became too successful, which eventually led to the downfall of moral treatment (Whitaker, 2002). In response to her appeals, states, with little opposition, began constructing larger hospitals, and existing hospitals expanded to hold more patients (Grob, 1994).

Population growth due to urbanization, migration, and immigration (*see* Chapter 5 of this book for details) increased the demand for hospitals. By 1874, state hospitals had, on average, 432 patients; a third had more than 500 patients, and some had more than 1,000. By the late 1890s, there were about 74,000 patients in hospitals, compared to only 2,561 patients in 1840. However, the patients included not only those with mental illnesses but also older patients, those with diseases such as syphilis, and those with alcohol use disorders, among others. The hospitals could no longer provide personal, humane care, nor could the Superintendent provide the empathy and guidance necessary for wellness. States began cutting costs by foregoing enjoyable activities, such as day rooms, reading parlors, bathing facilities, recreational activities, education programs, and other amenities essential to moral treatment. Patients simply "existed" in hospitals and were not receiving the care and moral treatment envisioned by the Quakers, Rush, or Dix. The superintendents at the state hospitals were low-paid and turned to coercion, force, and restraints to keep order (Whitaker, 2002).

Eugenics Movement: Sterilization of Those with Mental Illnesses and Disabilities

The Progressive Era during the 1900s was a time of intense social and political reform aimed at making progress toward a better society. Unfortunately, this era was also tainted by pseudoscience aimed at improving society at the expense of those with mental illnesses and disabilities. In the early twentieth century, there was a profound shift in America's attitude toward those with mental illnesses. They were no longer viewed as human beings to be treated with respect and decency. This view was replaced by a belief, grounded in "science," that those with mental illnesses and disabilities were genetic "carriers of a defective germ plasm" (Whitaker, 2002, p. 41). Scientific articles, newspapers, and even popular books described those with mental illnesses as "degenerate strains" that not only burdened society financially with their care but "breed at alarming rates" that posed a threat to the future health of society (Whitaker, 2002, p. 42).

This new perspective of those with mental illnesses and disabilities led to the eugenics movement. The eugenics movement was arguably one of the darkest eras for those with mental illnesses and disabilities in the US. The intense discrimination justified their social isolation and maltreatment and belief that they should be eradicated from society. This view began with the work of Francis Galton (1822–1911), cousin of Charles Darwin (1809–1882). Darwin did not specifically address humankind's beginnings in his 1859 book, *On the Origin of Species*, although the implication was clear: humans evolved from animals (Whitaker, 2002). Francis Galton's 1869 book, *Studies of Heredity Genius,* showed a high proportion of prominent men in aristocratic British families, which aroused further interest in the inheritance of behavioral traits (Carlson, n.d.). Galton had a new take on understanding human evolution: that superior traits such as intelligence were nature to the person and not the result of a nurturing environment. In 1883, Galton coined the term **eugenics**, from the Greek word "well-born." Galton initially focused on **positive eugenics**, encouraging intelligent people with healthy traits to bear more children. Over time, this view shifted to **negative eugenics** to prevent those with "undesirable" traits from bearing children. With this new view of humankind, those with mental illnesses were seen as among the most unfit. They were prohibited from marrying, forcibly committed to state hospitals, and, in some states, had **sterilization** procedures performed against their will (Black, 2012; Whitaker, 2002). In 1896, Connecticut became the first state to enact eugenic legislation prohibiting marriage, and other states followed suit (Grob, 1994).

Harry Clay Sharp (1870–1940), a prison physician in Jefferson, Indiana, performed sterilization surgeries on those in prison beginning in 1899. The first eugenic sterilization law in the US was enacted in Indiana in 1907. Through the negative eugenics advocacy of Sharp and his medical colleagues, the Indiana law mandated compulsory sterilization of "degenerates." In 1913, the law expanded to include "criminals," "feeble-minded," "lunatics," and other "degenerate" persons (Grob, 1994; Whitaker, 2002). Charles Davenport (1866–1944) was a prominent American Biologist and Director of the Eugenics Record Office (est. 1910) in Cold Spring Harbor, New York. Charles Davenport and Harry Laughlin (1880–1943) ran the

Eugenics Record Office together, and both were active in the eugenics section of the American Breeders Association (Black, 2012; Carlson, n.d.). Davenport's book *Eugenics: The Science of Human Improvement through Better Breeding*, published in 1910, provided the model for negative eugenics in human populations, where he called for the sterilization of the least desirable members, leaving only the healthiest members to breed. In 1914, Laughlin published a model eugenic sterilization law, which proposed to authorize sterilization of the "socially inadequate" people who were supported by the public expense, either wholly or partially. The law included an extensive list, including, for example, people who were "feeble-minded," "insane," "blind, "deaf," "criminals," and "epileptics" (Black, 2012; Carlson, n.d.).

Justification for this compulsory sterilization law rested on the premise that mental illnesses were inherited and that those with such disorders were more promiscuous and, thus, able to pass their genes on to a more considerable number of offspring (Whitaker, 2002). Opponents of sterilization laws, which included Catholics, argued that such laws violated constitutional safeguards, due process, and equal protection. Whether or not such laws were constitutional was decided in the case Buck v. Bell (1927). At the time of this case, 8,000 eugenic sterilization surgeries were performed between 1907 and 1927 (Whitaker, 2002).

Case Brief: Buck v. Bell (1927)

Facts: Carrie Buck from Charlottesville, Virginia, was a "feeble-minded" woman committed to the State Colony of "Epileptics and Feeble Minded." Her mother, also "feeble-minded," was a resident at the same hospital. Buck also had an illegitimate daughter, Vivian, who was evaluated at six months of age and determined she may also be "feeble-minded." Buck, who was eighteen years old, was selected for sterilization under the Sterilization Act of Virginia. The Act was approved on March 20, 1924, for the sterilization of "defective persons" to promote the welfare of society. Before the procedure could be performed, a hearing was required to decide whether the surgery was necessary. Hospital Superintendent Dr. Albert Priddy testified that Carrie's mother, Emma Buck, had a record of immorality, prostitution, and syphilis, and she and her daughter Carrie shared the hereditary trait of "feeble-mindedness" and "sexual promiscuity." The judge concluded at the hearing that Carrie Buck should be sterilized to prevent the birth of other "defective" children. The Supreme Court of Appeals of Virginia affirmed a judgment ordering Buck's sterilization. Buck's case was appealed to the US Supreme Court, and Dr. John H. Bell had replaced Dr. Priddy as the superintendent of the State Colony hospital.

Issue: Whether the Virginia statute that authorized sterilization denies persons the right to due process of the law and equal protection of the Fourteenth Amendment.

Outcome: The US Supreme Court found that the Virginia statute did not violate due process or the Fourteenth Amendment of the Constitution. Justice Oliver Wendell Holmes delivered the majority opinion and stated that Buck's challenge was not the medical procedure but the process of the substantive law. Sterilization could not occur until a proper hearing was conducted and only after "months of observation," which was sufficient to satisfy the Court that there was no Constitutional violation. Citing the best interests of the state,

> it is better for all the world if, instead of waiting to execute "degenerate" offspring for crime or to let them starve for their "imbecility," society can prevent those who are manifestly unfit from continuing their kind.... three generations of "imbeciles" are enough. (Oliver Wendell Holmes, Buck v. Bell, 1927)

After the Buck decision, the number of eugenic sterilizations in the US increased, averaging more than 2,200 every year during the 1930s (Whitaker, 2002). Unfortunately, revelations later showed that Carrie Buck's sterilization was based on false information. Carrie Buck's daughter Vivian was not the result of promiscuity but of sexual abuse by a relative of her foster parents. During this time, it was common for unwed pregnant women and mothers to be institutionalized to avoid bringing shame to the family. Vivian was raised by Carrie's foster parents, and school records from her first-grade report card showed "Bs" in reading, writing, and English, contradicting the assumption that she was "feeble-minded." Unfortunately, Vivian died at eight years of age from an intestinal disease. The eugenics movement was eventually discredited as a science and arose from political and social prejudice, yet the practice of involuntary sterilization continued until the late 1970s (Health Sciences Library, n.d.).

Deteriorating Institutionalized Care

The eugenics movement encouraged the segregation and elimination of people with mental illnesses and disabilities from society. Thus, psychiatric hospitals were increasingly run as confinement facilities to segregate them from society rather than places that provided care. By 1940, there were nearly 420,000 patients in 181 hospitals. This increase was not due to admitting more patients with mental illnesses but also admitting, for example, older patients with dementia, those with various diseases, and those with alcohol use disorder (Geller, 2019; Whitaker, 2002).

Public psychiatric hospitals were created, in part, by the work of Dorothea Dix to remove people with mental illnesses from jails. The creation of large state hospitals was society's response to population growth due to urbanization and immigration, but it was also a cost-saving measure to combine resources from several smaller institutions into one. Funding for the state hospitals on a per-patient basis decreased drastically, and by the 1940s (during wartime shortages and cuts), states were spending less than a dollar per day for each patient. In comparison, adjusted for inflation, this was less than one-third of what the Pennsylvania hospital had spent on patients per day in 1860 (Whitaker, 2002). The care inside these hospitals deteriorated from the once promising moral treatment model. Due to prejudice, stigma, and a lack of concern for people with mental illnesses, support for hospitals waned over time. They rapidly developed into overcrowded, inhumane facilities with deteriorated conditions (Finch, 1985; Gilligan, 2001).

Media Exposure of Declining Care

The conditions inside hospitals gained media exposure, shocking the conscience of many Americans. On May 6, 1946, Life Magazine published *Bedlam 1946*, an exposé by journalist Albert Q. Maisel of two state hospitals: Pennsylvania's Byberry and Ohio's Cleveland State. There were photos of patients, grossly thin, naked, and huddled on the floor. He described them as "guiltless prisoners" who "spend 24 hours a day in stark and filthy nakedness" (Maisel, 1946, p. 102). In 1941, 35-year-old Mary Jane Ward was committed to a psychiatric hospital in upstate New York. In 1946, she published a fictionalized semi-autobiographical novel based on her experience, *Snake Pit* (Ward, 1946). In 1948, the book was made into an award-winning movie, *The Snake Pit,* directed by Anatole Litvak, drawing further attention to the conditions and treatment inside hospitals. Journalist and social activist Albert Deutsch toured inside more than a dozen state psychiatric hospitals, documented his observations, and took photographs of the deplorable and torturous conditions patients were experiencing. In 1948, Deutsch published *The Shame of the States,* where he described the conditions inside, for example, men sitting naked in their feces, barefoot women strapped to wooden planks, sleeping wards overcrowded with cots, and restrained patients having to lap their food from plates (Deutsch, 1948). Numerous newspapers ran scathing exposés of facilities infested with rats and cockroaches and reported that patients went weeks, months, or even years without seeing a doctor (Whitaker, 2002).

Harmful Treatments

The advances in understanding mental health treatment as a medical discipline continued since physicians regained control in the 1840s. By the 1930s, there were advances in the scientific understanding of the human brain and behavior, growing the fields of psychiatry and neuropsychology. Common procedures included **lobotomies** and **electroshock therapy**. Lobotomies, also called **leucotomies,** were introduced in Europe by Portuguese neuroscientists Dr. Antonio Egas Moniz (1874–1955) and Dr. Almeida Lima (1903–1985). They performed frontal leucotomies in the 1930s, where a thin metal rod called a leucotome was inserted into the brain through a hole in the skull (Whitaker, 2002). Dr. Walter Freeman (1895–1972) was inspired by their work and collaborated with Dr. James W. Watts (1904–1994), and "perfected" the procedure termed the prefrontal lobotomy or transorbital lobotomy (Robison et al., 2012; Whitaker, 2002). This new procedure involved a leucotome modeled after an ice pick, which entered the prefrontal cortex through the eye socket using a small hammer (Whitaker, 2002). Freeman and Watts performed the first frontal lobotomy in the US in 1936, and the procedure was marketed to hospitals to control and manage their "overpopulation problem." Unfortunately, not all patients responded well; some had uncontrollable bleeding, resulting in death. Others had neurological changes, including seizures and a condition referred to as "frontal lobe syndrome," where patients would display lethargy, inattentiveness, and socially inappropriate behavior (Robison et al., 2012).

Electroshock therapy to treat mental health conditions originated by a team of Italian physicians led by Ugo Cerletti (1877–1963) and Lucio Bini (1908–1964). They created an apparatus with electrodes to apply electric currents to the head. In 1938, they conducted their first experiment on a 39-year-old man with schizophrenia, using 110 volts of alternating current for 0.2 seconds. Electroshock therapy was considered a safe and effective treatment and rapidly spread throughout Europe and North America. However, the effects were temporary, and the electroshock therapy had to be repeated (Suleman, 2020; Whitaker, 2002). The procedure is now referred to as electroconvulsive therapy (ECT). The protocol and practice have been improved it is still used today to treat psychotic disorders (Suleman, 2020).

Deinstitutionalization

In 1955, 50% of all hospital beds in the US were for mental health patients, as documented by Mike Gorman (1956) in his book *Every Other Bed*. The deplorable conditions of the hospitals led to the social movement of **deinstitutionalization** to shift patients from hospitals to other settings. Deinstitutionalization was a complex policy that positively and negatively impacted those with mental illnesses and disabilities. The medical model heavily influenced mental health services in the field of psychiatry. The medical model stressed that a "disease" was the cause of one's symptoms, which heavily influenced treatment delivery. However, the care and treatment for those with developmental disabilities such as intellectual disability (ID) has not been the expertise of the medical profession, as ID is a lifelong "incurable" condition. Instead, services and care for those with ID have primarily been under the psychoeducational model, mainly comprised of education professionals (Finch, 1985; Koyanagi & Bazelon, 2007). Historically, individuals with mental illnesses and developmental disabilities were grouped in institutions; however, new policies surrounding services and funding were not distributed equally. Deinstitutionalization of those with developmental disabilities occurred later, mainly due to differences in services and government funding (Finch, 1985; Koyanagi & Bazelon, 2007).

The introduction of psychotropic medications was a driving factor that led to deinstitutionalizing patients from state hospitals into the community for treatment and care (Talbott, 1978). The first antipsychotic medication, chlorpromazine, sold under the trade name Thorazine®, was introduced in 1954, and two anti-depressants, imipramine and iproniazid, in 1956 (Accordino et al., 2001). There was optimism that these new medications could now effectively control or reduce psychiatric symptoms and decrease the need for inpatient treatment. States began to fund small community pilot programs for individuals who responded well to these new medications (Koyanagi & Bazelon, 2007).

Expanding Civil Rights and Restricting Eligibility for Hospitalization

The civil rights movement that began in the 1950s was another driving force that offered political support for deinstitutionalization. The Civil Rights Act of 1964 banned discrimination based on race, color, religion, sex, and national origin in schools, public accommodations, and employment. The civil rights era extended beyond striving for racial equality and brought attention to the civil and legal rights of other oppressed groups and those in need of supervision and care, including individuals with mental illnesses and disabilities. The argument of quality-of-life became central to this debate (Talbott, 1978). Landmark Supreme Court decisions restricted the eligibility standards for hospitalization throughout the 1960s–1970s, which increased civil liberties for those hospitalized under civil commitment statutes. **Civil commitment** is a legal intervention when one is court-ordered to be committed to a psychiatric hospital for a specific or indefinite period (*see* Chapter 15 of this book for details). The court cases below directly affected the civil rights of those civilly committed in psychiatric hospitals.

Case Briefs: Expanding Civil Rights for Civil Commitment

Lake v Cameron (1966)

Facts: Catherine Lake (age 60) was transported to General Hospital in Washington D.C. after a police officer found her wandering, unaware of her surroundings. She was committed to Saint Elizabeths Hospital for "chronic brain syndrome." After being hospitalized for several years, despite not showing any evidence of dangerousness to herself or anyone else, she petitioned the US District Court of the District of Columbia for release.

Issue: Whether hospitalizing someone in need of care but showing no signs of dangerousness to self or others was a violation of one's civil liberties and whether one should be released from confinement and provided with less restrictive alternative forms of care.

Outcome: The District Court decided that all patients who were not dangerous to themselves or others should not be confined if a less restrictive alternative is available. The Court concluded that depriving someone of their liberty only because they are a danger to themselves should not go beyond what is necessary for their protection.

Lessard v Schmidt (1972)

Facts: Alberta Lessard was transported by police to a Mental Health Center North Division in Milwaukee, Wisconsin, after surviving a suicide attempt. She was diagnosed with schizophrenia and detained for ten days. Lessard's detention was repeatedly extended. With no one to speak on her behalf, she sought counsel through Milwaukee Legal Services on behalf of herself and all those 18 and over who were being held involuntarily. She petitioned the US District Court for release, claiming that Wisconsin statutes violated the due process clause of the Fourteenth Amendment.

Issue: Whether Wisconsin's involuntary commitment statute violates due process guaranteed under the Fourteenth Amendment.

Outcome: The District Court held that Wisconsin's involuntary commitment statute was unconstitutional due to several reasons, including (1) inadequate notice of charges and rights, (2) detention longer than 48 hours without a probable cause hearing, (3) allowing hearsay evidence, (4) violations of privilege against self-incrimination, and (5) commitment without the proper burden of proof that the patient has a mental illness and is a danger to themselves or others. The Court decided that civil commitment can be justified in some cases if the proper burden of proof is satisfied. The determination of "danger" must be based upon the finding of a recent overt act, attempt, or threat to substantially harm oneself or another. The Court ordered that adequate due process rights be instituted, including adequate notice, the right to counsel, availability of the privilege against self-incrimination, and a speedy hearing.

O'Connor v Donaldson (1975)

Facts: Kenneth Donaldson was diagnosed with schizophrenia and was held against his will in a psychiatric hospital in Florida for 15 years. During his stay, he showed no evidence of harm to himself or others. Donaldson repeatedly petitioned for release, which was repeatedly denied by the psychiatrist in charge of his care. Donaldson petitioned the court for release. The petitioner, Dr. O'Connor, was the hospital's superintendent during most of this stay and appealed the case to the US Supreme Court.

Issue: Whether a finding of mental illness alone is justification for indefinite involuntary civil commitment when an individual is not posing a danger to self or others.

Outcome: The US Supreme Court held that if individuals are not posing a danger to themselves or others and can live independently without supervision, the state has no right to commit them to a facility against their will. Patients subject to involuntary civil commitment have the right to legal representation through the process. The party seeking civil commitment has the burden of proof that the person meets grounds for civil commitment and must respect the least restrictive alternative principle. The goal of protecting the person or the public must be carried out to minimize any infringement on the person's rights and freedoms. Once committed, patients have the right to regularly review commitment criteria, as continued confinement and treatment must be based on the least restrictive alternative.

Addington v Texas (1979)

Facts: Frank Addington had a long history of mental and emotional disorders and had many past hospitalizations. Addington's mother filed a case requesting that he be involuntarily civilly committed indefinitely because he had physically assaulted her. At the state trial, the jury was instructed to decide whether Addington had a mental illness and required hospitalization for the protection of himself and others based on "clear, unequivocal and convincing evidence." Addington was committed and appealed to the US Supreme Court, challenging that the highest standard of proof, "beyond a reasonable doubt," should have been used, not the lower standard of proof, "clear, unequivocal and convincing evidence."

Issue: Whether due process in civil commitment hearings requires states to use the highest standard of proof, beyond a reasonable doubt.

Outcome: The Court held that the beyond-the-reasonable doubt standard was not required in involuntary civil commitment hearings. Imposing such a high burden of proof may result in the state being unable to meet that burden, which may create a barrier to necessary treatment.

Legislative Acts for Individuals with Mental Illnesses and Disabilities

President John F. Kennedy (1917–1963) supported mental health and disability services. His sister, Rosemary Kennedy, had lived with mental illness and was administered a lobotomy at age 23. Her condition worsened and she had to spend most of her life in an institution (Robison et al., 2012; Stroman, 2003). The Joint Commission on Mental Illness and Health issued a report in 1961 and recommended a system to provide services for people with mental illnesses. President Kennedy enacted the Community Mental Health Act of 1963[1] (CMHA). The CMHA authorized nearly $3 billion for not only hospital care, but community-based health centers to provide mental health treatment such as halfway houses, community residences, social and recreational centers, outpatient clinics, sheltered workshops, and home-visiting mental health professionals (Koyanagi & Bazelon, 2007; Sharfstein, 2000). The Act appeared promising, as it allowed individuals to receive treatment in their community, maintain relationships with family, and be (re)integrated into their community while saving costs, as the costs for institutionalized care were much greater than community care (Sharfstein, 2000). President Kennedy also created a President's Panel on "Mental Retardation" with the mandate to prepare a "National Plan to Combat Mental Retardation" (Koyanagi & Bazelon, 2007). The 1963 report prepared by Bazelon and Boggs recommended a policy of deinstitutionalization and other guidelines on how individuals with developmental disabilities should be handled civilly, which included custody and care.

Unfortunately, only one month after the CMHA was signed into law, President Kennedy was assassinated. With no pressure from the executive branch, none of the $3 billion was appropriated to pay for mental health services. The money was diverted elsewhere, including the Vietnam War (Koyanagi & Bazelon, 2007; Sharfstein, 2000). Because the $3 billion was never appropriated, hospital conditions deteriorated. For example, Bryce State Hospital in Tuscaloosa, Alabama, had 5,200 patients living in inhumane conditions and receiving inadequate treatment. A landmark case decision, Wyatt v. Stickney (1971), ordered the Bryce State Hospital to improve its care and treatment. Alabama, which ranked last of the 50 states on funding facilities for mental illnesses and disabilities, decided to cut the state's cigarette tax in 1970. However, the proceeds from this tax were earmarked for mental health services, which would result in significant budget cuts to the state's mental health system. When this case was filed, Alabama allotted 50 cents per day per patient to fund the facility, food, and clothing. The new budget cuts eliminated nearly 100 staff, including psychologists, social workers, and occupational therapists. The fired staff members filed suits, not only for the loss of their jobs but also for diminished patient care (Carr, 2004).

Case Brief: Wyatt v. Stickney (1971)

Facts: On October 23, 1970, the fired staff members filed a lawsuit in the US District Court for the Middle District of Alabama seeking reinstatement because patients would receive inadequate care. They included 15-year-old Ricky Wyatt, a Bryce Hospital patient, as a plaintiff to strengthen their argument. The Court ordered the hospital to establish standards and implement a compliant treatment program within six months. During these six months, the conditions at Bryce Hospital were examined. The Department of Justice's Civil Rights Division, the American Psychological Association, and the American Civil Liberties Union joined in the case as **amici curiae** to assist the court by offering information and expertise.

Issue: Whether there must be minimum constitutional standards for the adequate treatment of people with mental illnesses and developmental disabilities.

Outcome: On December 10, 1971, a US District Court judge ruled and provided three basic conditions required for adequate and effective treatment programs: (1) A humane psychological and physical environment, (2) Qualified staff in numbers sufficient to administer adequate treatment, and (3) Individualized treatment plans. These conditions became known as the "Wyatt Standards." Eventually, they became national standards and set minimum constitutional standards for the adequate treatment of people with mental illnesses and developmental disabilities.

The following year, the same judge issued a court order containing 35 minimum constitutional standards for adequate treatment and appointed human rights committees at the institution to oversee their implementation (Leaf, 1977). Concerned about the costs of implementing the standards, thousands of patients were released within the first few years, and over time, the population inside Bryce Hospital held just a few hundred (Yurkanin, 2019). The state could not meet the requirements until 2003 when another US District Court judge officially approved the settlement of the original class action and dismissed the lawsuit (Wyatt ex rel Rawlins v. Sawyer, 2004).

Legislation Limiting Eligibility for Hospitalization

Deinstitutionalization was also driven by increased standards for eligibility to be hospitalized. Throughout the 1960s, states passed legislative acts to address civil commitment. The District of Columbia passed the Hospitalization of the Mentally Ill Act (Ervin Act) (1964), which established a "dangerousness standard" that required that one's mental illness will likely cause imminent harm to oneself or others to be eligible for commitment. The Ervin Act also recognized less restrictive alternatives as options. State Assemblyman Frank Lanterman and California State Senators Nicholas C. Petris and Alan Short passed the Lanterman-Petris-Short Act (LPS) (1969). The LPS Act sought to end the inappropriate, indefinite, and involuntary civil commitment of persons with mental illnesses. The Act established limited civil commitment criteria to hold for 72 hours and 14 days if one's mental illness will likely cause imminent harm to self or others or a "grave disability" if individuals are unable to meet their basic survival needs. The Act also established a right to prompt psychiatric evaluation in certain cases and set strict due process protections for mental health care. The Vocational Rehabilitation Act Amendment of 1963 expanded services and prohibited discrimination against education and employment. In 1968, the Act was amended and separated services for those with ID and those with mental illnesses but allocated less funding to serve those with mental illnesses (Finch, 1985).

Willowbrook State School

In the 1970s, there was a growing concern about the poor conditions and lack of treatment and education services in institutions for children and adults with disabilities and mental illnesses. The deplorable conditions inside institutions persisted again due to overcrowding and lack of funding. This time, media attention publicly exposed an institution caring for children, leading to shame and embarrassment, and finally, legislative action. In 1972, investigative reporter Geraldo Rivera snuck into New York's Willowbrook State School, an institution for children with ID, with a film crew for his documentary, *Willlowbrook: The Last Disgrace* (WABC-TV, 1972). Rivera shared the footage of graphic video images of children of all ages, wearing little to no clothing, sitting on floors covered in urine and feces, and being force-fed their meals quickly and hastily. He also noted that no educational instruction was provided for the children. Rivera spoke into the camera, with the horrific images and sounds behind him, "This is what it looked like. This is what it sounded like. But how can I tell you about the way it smelled? It smelled of filth. It smelled of disease. It smelled of death" (WABC-TV, 1972).

People across the country were stunned and appalled by the horrific images and mournful sounds, furthering support for the movement to shift individuals with disabilities from state institutions to community-based care. The New York Civil Liberties Union (NYCLU) responded to this exposé with a class-action lawsuit filed on behalf of the 5,400 residents of the Willowbrook State School (New York State Assoc. v. Rockefeller, 1973). The case resulted in a three-year-long legal battle that concluded in a 1975 settlement mandating significant reforms, but it took years of litigation and advocacy to force officials to improve conditions and supply the funds necessary for reform. In 1983, New York announced plans to close Willowbrook, and the last children left the school in 1987 (Office for People with Developmental Disabilities).

The nationwide publicity generated by the Willowbrook case helped pass the Civil Rights of Institutionalized Persons Act of 1980. The Act protects people's civil rights inside state-run institutions, which include prisons, jails, juvenile detention centers, nursing homes, mental healthcare facilities, and institutions for people with developmental disabilities. The Act did not create new laws; instead, it allowed the US Department of Justice to conduct investigations of conditions and enforce the existing laws that protect the rights of people in institutions.

Legislative Actions and Government Funding

The US government continued to pass legislation to fund community programs to protect the rights of children and adults with disabilities. In 1965–1966, the federal government introduced Medicaid and Medicare, but the programs did not cover inpatient costs for psychiatric institutions. Patients were forced to general hospitals, medical clinics, and community facilities for assistance and treatment. In 1972, the Supplemental Security

Income (SSI) disability benefits program was enacted to help with living costs for people with disabilities and mental illnesses and assisted people discharged from state institutions (Koyanagi & Bazelon, 2007). This was a significant step toward supporting deinstitutionalization. In 1973, the Alcohol, Drug Abuse, and Mental Health Administration (ADAMHA) of the US Department of Health and Human Services (DHHS) was established to fund community-based treatment services and research into mental illnesses, alcohol, and substance use. In 1977, The National Institute of Mental Health (NIMH), an agency of the DHHS, created the Community Support Program (CSP), a small federal program to provide contracts (not grants) between NIMH and state mental health agencies to plan comprehensive services and other supports for adults with mental illnesses and disabilities in the community (Turner & TenHoor, 1978). Several other federal acts were passed to protect the education and civil rights of those with disabilities and mental illnesses:

- **Education for Handicapped Children of 1975**—provided all children the right to free public education and required all public schools to provide education to meet the needs of children with disabilities.
- **Mental Health Systems Act of 1980**—provided grants to community mental health centers.
- **Americans with Disabilities Act of 1990**—an extension of the Civil Rights Act of 1964, which prohibits discrimination against individuals with disabilities in all areas of public life (e.g., jobs, schools, transportation).

Social Impacts of Deinstitutionalization

As hospitals were closing and discharging individuals with mental illnesses into the community, Medicaid became the most significant source of support for mental health care (Koyanagi & Bazelon, 2007). As a result, taxpayers assumed a shared fiscal responsibility for the care and treatment of mental illnesses, which questioned the cost–benefit of institutionalized care (Anfag & Appelbaum, 2009; Baillargeon et al., 2009). In 1972, Sect. 1905(a)(B) of the Social Security Act, the Institutions for Mental Disease (IMD rule) made changes in Medicaid to deny financial coverage for inpatient services for those between the ages of 21 and 65. As a result, states could no longer rely on hospitals and had to use community-based services whenever possible (Substance Abuse and Mental Health Services Administration,

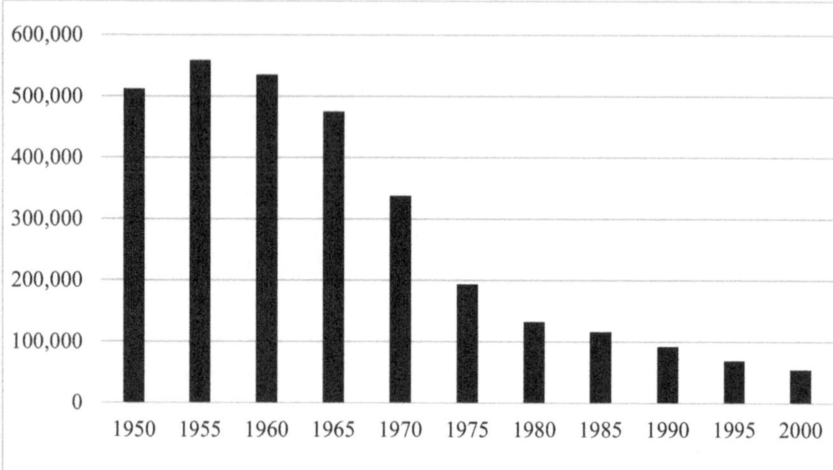

Fig. 7.3 Number of Resident Patients by End of Year: 1950–2000 (*Source* Substance Abuse and Mental Health Services Administration [2007])

2019). In the early 1980s, there was a major shift in political views toward the government having a smaller role in health care, which shifted the focus of mental health policy to the states. During this time, the US also experienced economic decline. The conservative policies of President Ronald Reagan (1911–2004) argued that for prosperity to return, the US must reduce social welfare with tax cuts and smaller government (Parsons, 2018). The Omnibus Budget Reconciliation Act (OBRA) of 1981 repealed most of the Mental Health Systems Act and shifted funding to the states. The OBRA combined ADAMHA's treatment and rehabilitation service programs into a single block grant for each state to administer and distribute the funds. This led to more budget cuts to state hospitals, and states were forced to limit the number of hospitalizations and utilize community-based services, which were lacking. Figure 7.3 shows the number of psychiatric hospital patients over 50 years. The number of patients decreased by more than 40% between 1970 and 1975 after the changes to Medicare funding and continued to decline after OBRA. In 1955, at its peak, there were 558,922 patients, and by 2000, only 54,836, about a 92% decrease (SAMSA, 2007).

Homelessness

The reduced hospital funding resulted in reduced long-term care in a secure setting. The increased reliance on community-based treatment without adequately funding such services resulted in several collateral consequences.

One such consequence was a marked increase in those with mental illnesses experiencing homelessness (Honberg et al., 2011). In the early 1980s, as many as 85% of adults experiencing homelessness had mental illnesses, substance use disorders, or both (Baum & Burnes, 1993). The number of people with mental illnesses experiencing homelessness is a problem that persists. Although the exact number of people is unknown, a 2022 report by the US Department of Housing and Urban Development estimated that 582,462 people in the US were experiencing homelessness, and an estimated 122,888 people (about 21%) experiencing homelessness have mental illnesses. Therefore, one can conclude that tens of thousands of people with mental illnesses are not receiving the treatment and care necessary.

Criminalization of Mental Illness and "Transinstutitionalization"

The "criminalization of mental illness," coined by Abramson (1972), refers to persons with mental illnesses who are arrested and prosecuted, often for minor offenses (Abramson, 1972; Lamb & Weinberger, 2005). Many individuals experiencing mental illnesses and homelessness engaged in socially disruptive behavior and quality-of-life or "nuisance" violations such as panhandling and loitering (Roth, 2019; Stroman, 2003). The "get-tough" policing policies in the 1980s and 1990s enforced quality-of-life violations (Roth, 2019), which tended to target those experiencing homelessness and mental illnesses. A 1992 study of 299 incarcerated individuals in New York City jails found that 20% were experiencing homelessness when arrested, and 50% of those who reported experiencing homelessness also reported having a mental illness (Michaels et al., 1992). For many, the criminalization of mental illness resulted in their incarceration, colloquially known as "**transinstutitionalization**." Transinstutitionalization was one of the greatest social impacts of deinstitutionalization, where patients shifted from institutionalized care in hospitals to correctional institutions.

The relationship between deinstitutionalization and transinstutitionalization was not a linear or direct process and was the result of several justice system policies that co-occurred around the same time as the changes to mental health care. During the 1970s–1980s, crime rates were rising, along with illegal substance use and violations of drug laws. With the "war on drugs" initiated in 1971, there was a political shift from the rehabilitation model to the crime control model, which used harsh sentences to address crime (Parsons, 2018). There was also a shift toward community policing, with more police patrolling on foot, increasing opportunities to encounter persons with mental illnesses. The "war on drugs" also cast a wider net and incarcerated a large number of individuals who were in possession of illegal substances, many of whom had substance use disorders and mental illnesses. Federal grants provided state governments money to expand their prisons to accommodate the growing number of incarcerated people (*see* Chapter 5 for more details).

By the late 1980s and 1990s, the impact of deinstitutionalization and criminal justice policies resulted in a massive increase in the number of people with mental illness in jails and prisons.[2] Raphael and Stoll (2013) found that early deinstitutionalization did not impact the incarceration rate; however, the deinstitutionalization of patients from hospitals between 1971 and 1996 was responsible for 4–7% of the incarcerated population growth between 1980 and 2000. Although this may appear insignificant, these estimates indicate that between 40,000 and 72,000 incarcerated individuals would have likely been treated inside psychiatric hospitals. According to a 2010 report by the Treatment Advocacy Center, three jails in the US now hold more people with mental illnesses than any psychiatric hospital: Los Angeles County Jail in California, Chicago's Cook County Jail in Illinois, Riker's Island Jail in New York City (Torrey et al., 2010). Recent estimates from the Department of Justice show that about 43% of those in state prison, 23% of those in federal prison, and 44% of those incarcerated in jails have mental illnesses (Bronson & Berzofsky, 2017; Maruschak et al., 2021).

Conclusion

Nearly 200 years ago, Dorothea Dix advocated against treating people with mental illnesses as "criminals" and housing them inside jails and prisons. Unfortunately, her social advocacy to transition people with mental illnesses to hospitals for compassionate and humane treatment never came to fruition. The hospitals were overcrowded and underfunded, and patients were living in deplorable conditions. The eugenics movement led to extreme stigma and discrimination against people with mental illnesses and disabilities, encouraging them to be segregated from society, and sterilization laws were implemented to prevent them from procreating. The deplorable conditions and many civil rights violations continued through most of the twentieth century, including children with disabilities, as exposed in the Willowbrook School scandal.

Unfortunately, the US has essentially reverted to the practices of the 1800s, having large numbers of people with mental illnesses inside jails and prisons.

The deinstitutionalization movement to reduce the number of patients in state psychiatric hospitals and serve their needs in the community with new medication gained support from those interested in fiscal spending. Those who advocated for the increased rights believed patients should be "free" and enjoy the civil rights afforded to all. Although well-intended, the plan to increase community mental health services was poorly designed and poorly funded, leading to several social failures.

As first responders, police are often considered the "gatekeepers" to the mental health and criminal justice systems. Whether police decide to arrest an individual with a mental illness depends on a variety of factors, including having more familiarity with the arrest process (as opposed to using mental health services), insufficient training in recognizing mental illnesses, mistaking mental illness symptoms for alcohol or drug intoxication, or a lack of other appropriate alternatives in the community (Lamb & Weinberger, 2005). Without massive changes and drastically increased funding for mental health, the correctional system will likely remain the primary source of treatment for those with mental illnesses. Therefore, practitioners throughout all sectors of the criminal justice system require more tools and program options to be better equipped to properly handle people with mental illnesses.

Key Terms

Amici curiae
Civil commitment
Deinstitutionalization
Electroshock therapy
Eugenics Movement
Moral treatment
Leucotomy/Lobotomy
Negative eugenics
Positive eugenics
Quakers
Sterilization
Transinstutitionalization

Chapter Questions

1) Discuss how the treatment and care of people with mental illnesses have evolved from the colonial era to the present day.
2) How has the eugenics movement aided in this mistreatment and stigma of those with mental illnesses and disabilities?

3) What do you believe contributed the most to the deplorable conditions in the hospitals and the Willowbrook School? Explain your answer.
4) Explain how the well-intentioned attempts to improve the conditions and the civil rights of those who are institutionalized eventually led to the deinstitutionalization of people with mental illnesses.
5) Discuss the major impacts of the deinstitutionalization movement to explain why jails have "replaced" psychiatric hospitals.

Suggested Readings

Deutsch, A. (2007). *The mentally ill in America: A history of their care and treatment from colonial times*. Holley Press.

Grob, G. N. (1991). *From asylum to community: Mental health policy in modern America*. Princeton University Press.

Hansen, R., & King, D. S. (2013). *Sterilized by the state: Eugenics, race, and the population scare in twentieth-century North America*. Cambridge University Press.

Miller, D., Hanson, A., & Earley, P. (2016). *Committed: The battle over involuntary psychiatric care*. John Hopkins University Press.

Sareyan, A. (1994). *The turning point: How men of conscience brought about major change in the care of America's mentally ill* (1st ed.). American Psychiatric Press.

Notes

1. Full name was the Mental Retardation Facilities and Community Mental Health Centers Construction Act.
2. In the United States, jails and prisons are not synonymous. Jails are short-term confinement facilities operated by a local law enforcement agency (county, city, or municipality). Prisons are long-term confinement facilities operated by the state or the federal government, or private organizations contracted by a government agency.

References

Abramson, M. F. (1972). The criminalization of mentally disordered behavior: Possible side-effect of a new mental health law. *Hospital & Community Psychiatry, 23*(4), 101–105.

Accordino, M. P., Porter, D. F., & Morse, T. (2001). Deinstitutionalization of persons with severe mental illness: Context and Consequences. *Journal of Rehabilitation, 67*(2), 16–21.

Addington v. Texas 441 U.S. 418 (1979).

Americans with Disabilities Act, 42 U.S.C. §1210 (1990).

Anfag, S. A., & Appelbaum, P. S. (2009). Civil commitment: The American experience. *Israeli Journal of Psychiatry and Related Sciences, 43*(3), 209–218.

Baillargeon, J., Binswanger, I. A., Penn, J. V., Williams, B. A., & Murray, O. J. (2009). Psychiatric disorders and repeat incarcerations: The revolving prison door. *The American Journal of Psychiatry, 166*(1), 103–109. https://doi.org/10.1176/appi.ajp.2008.08030416

Baum, A. S., & Burnes, D. W. (1993). *A nation in denial: The truth about homelessness.* Westview Press.

Black, E. (2012). *War against the weak: Eugenics and America's campaign to create a master race.* Dialog Press (expanded edition of the original published in 2003).

Bronson, J., & Berzofsky, M. (2017). *Indicators of mental health problems reported by prisoners and jail inmates, 2011–2012.* U.S. Department of Justice, Office of Justice Programs, Bureau of Justice Statistics.

Buck v. Bell, 274 U.S. 200 (1927).

Carlson, E. (n.d.). *Scientific origins of eugenics.* Eugenics Archive. http://www.eugenicsarchive.org/html/eugenics/essay2text.html

Carr, L. W. (2004). Wyatt v. Stickney: A landmark decision. *Alabama Disabilities Advocacy Center Program Newsletter*, 1–3. https://adap.ua.edu/ricky-wyatt.html

Carson, A., & Kluckow, R. (2023). *Correctional populations in the United States, 2021 – Statistical tables.* U.S. Department of Justice, Office of Justice Programs, Bureau of Justice Statistics.

Civil Rights Act of 1964, P.L. 88–352, 78 Stat. 241 (1964).

Civil Rights of Institutionalized Persons Act P. L. 96–247, Sec. 194 Stat. 349 (1980).

Deutsch, A. (1948). *The shame of the states.* Harcourt.

Dix, D. (1971). *On behalf of the insane poor. Selected reports.* Arno Press. Reprint Edition https://archive.org/details/onbehalfofinsane0000dixd/page/n5/mode/2up.

Education for All Handicapped Children Act PL. 94–142 (1975).

Finch, E. S. (1985). Deinstitutionalization: Mental health and mental retardation services. *Psychosocial Rehabilitation Journal, 8*(3), 36–48. https://doi.org/10.1037/h0099676

Geller, J. (2019). The rise and demise of America's psychiatric hospitals: A tale of dollars trumping decency. *Psychiatric News*. https://doi.org/10.1176/appi.pn.2019.3a36

Gilligan, J. (2001). The last mental hospital. *Psychiatric Quarterly, 72*(1), 45–77.

Gorman, M. (1956). *Every other bed*. World Publishing Company.

Grob, G. N. (1994). *The mad among us: A history of the care of America's mentally ill*. Free Press.

Health Sciences Library. (n.d.). *Eugenics*. University of Virginia. http://exhibits.hsl.virginia.edu/eugenics/5-epilogue/

Honberg, R., Kimball, A., Diehl, S. Usher, L., & Fitzpatrick, M. (2011). *State mental health cuts: The continuing crisis.* National Alliance on Mental Illness.

Hospitalization of the Mentally Ill Act (Ervin Act), D.C. Code §§ 21–501 to -592 (2011 Supp.) (1964).

Koyanagi, C., & Bazelon, D.L. (2007). Learning from history: Deinstitutionalization of people with mental illness as a precursor to long-term care reform. Kaiser Family Foundation, Kaiser Commission on Medicaid and the Uninsured. http://www.nami.org/Template.cfm?Section=About_the_Issue&Template=/ContentManagement/ContentDisplay.cfm&ContentID=137545

Lake v. Cameron, 364 F.2d 657 (1966).

Lamb, H. R., & Weinberger, L. E. (2005). The shift of psychiatric inpatient care from hospitals to jails and prisons. *Journal of the American Academy of Psychiatry and the Law, 33*, 529–534.

Lanterman-Petris-Short Act, CA Welf & Inst Code § 5000 (1969).

Leaf, P. (1977). Wyatt v. Stickney: assessing the impact in Alabama. *Hospital & Community Psychiatry, 28*(5), 351–356. https://doi.org/10.1176/ps.28.5.351

Lessard v. Schmidt, 349 F. Supp. 1078 (1972).

Litvak, A. (Director). (1948). The snake pit. [Film]. 20th Century Fox.

Maisel, A.Q. (1946, May 6). Bedlam 1946. *Life Magazine*. https://www.jerrycookearchives.com/photo-essays/bedlam-1946/ https://mn.gov/mnddc/parallels2/prologue/6a-bedlam/6a-bedlam.html

Maruschak, L. M., Bronson, J., & Alper, M. (2021). *Survey of prison inmates, 2016 alcohol and drug use and treatment reported by prisoners.* US Department of Justice, Office of Justice Programs, Bureau of Justice Statistics.

Mental Retardation Facilities and Community Mental Health Centers Construction Act, P.L. 88–164 (1963).

The Mental Health Systems Act, P.L. 88–164 (1980).

Michaels, D., Zoloth, S. R., Alcabes, P., Braslow, C. A., & Safyer, S. (1992). Homelessness and indicators of mental illness among inmates in New York City's correctional system. *Psychiatric Services, 43*(2), 150–155. https://doi.org/10.1176/ps.43.2.150

Mills v. Board of Education of District of Columbia, 348 F. Supp. 866 (D.D.C. 1972).

New York State Association for Retarded Children., Inc. v. Rockefeller, 357 F. Supp. 752 (E.D.N.Y. 1973).

O'Conner v. Donaldson, 422 U.S. 563 (1975).

Office for People with Developmental Disabilities (OPWDD). *Commemorating the Willowbrook Mile.* https://opwdd.ny.gov/willowbrook

Omnibus Budget Reconciliation Act (OBRA), PL 97–35, 95 Stat. 357–933 (1981).

Parsons, A.E. (2018). *From asylum to prison: Deinstitutionalization and the rise of mass incarceration after 1945* (Ser. Justice, power, and politics). University of North Carolina Press.

Raphael, S., & Stoll, M. A. (2013). Assessing the contribution of the deinstitutionalization of the mentally ill to growth in the U.S. incarceration rate. *The Journal of Legal Studies, 42*(1), 187–222. https://doi.org/10.1086/667773

Rivera, G. (1972). *Willowbrook: The last disgrace* (WABC-TV).

Roth, M. P. (2019). *A history of crime and the American criminal justice system* (3rd ed.). Taylor & Francis Group.

Robison, R. A., Taghva, A., Liu, C. Y., & Apuzzo, M. L. J. (2012). Surgery of the mind, mood, and conscious state: An idea in evolution. *World Neurosurgery, 77*(5–6), 662–686. https://doi.org/10.1016/j.wneu.2012.03.005

Sharfstein, S. S. (2000). Whatever happened to community mental health? *Psychiatric Services, 51*(5), 616–620. https://doi.org/10.1176/appi.ps.51.5.616

Stroman, D. (2003). *The disability rights movement: From deinstitutionalization to self-determination.* University Press of America.

Substance Abuse and Mental Health Services Administration. (2007). *Funding and characteristics of state mental health agencies, 2007.* https://www.govinfo.gov/app/details/GOVPUB-HE20-PURL-LPS123336

Substance Abuse and Mental Health Services Administration. (2019). *Civil commitment and the mental health care continuum: Historical trends and principles for law and practice.* https://digitalcommons.law.ggu.edu/federal_documents/39

Suleman, R. (2020). A brief history of electroconvulsive therapy. *American Journal of Psychiatry Residents' Journal, 16*(1), 6. https://doi.org/10.1176/appi.ajp-rj.2020.16010

Talbott, J. A. (1978). *The death of the asylum: A critical study of state hospital management, services, and care.* Grune & Stratton.

Torrey, E. F., Kennard, A. D., Eslinger, D., Lamb, R. H., & Pavie, J. (2010). *More mentally ill persons are in jails and prisons than hospitals: A survey of the states.* Treatment Advocacy Center. https://www.ojp.gov/ncjrs/virtual-library/abstracts/more-mentally-ill-persons-are-jails-and-prisons-hospitals-survey

Turner, J. C., & TenHoor, W. J. (1978). The NIMH Community Support Program: Pilot approach to a needed social reform. *Schizophrenia Bulletin, 4*(3), 319–348. https://doi.org/10.1093/schbul/4.3.319

United States Department of Housing and Urban Development. (2021). *The 2020 annual homeless assessment report (AHAR) to Congress.* https://www.huduser.gov/portal/sites/default/files/pdf/2020-AHAR-Part-1.pdf

Ward, M. J. (1946). *Snake pit.* Random House Publishers.

Whitaker, R. (2002). *Mad in America: Bad science, bad medicine, and the enduring mistreatment of the mentally ill.* Perseus Publishing.

Wyatt v. Stickney, 325 F.Supp. 781 M.D. Ala. (1971).
Wyatt ex rel Rawlins v. Sawyer, 219 F.R.D. 529, 537 M.D. Ala. (2004).
Yurkanin, A. (May 6, 2019). *The Alabama case that changed mental health care*. https://www.al.com/news/2019/05/the-alabama-case-that-changed-mental-health-care.html

Part III

Mental Health and Neurodiversity—Implications for Police

8

Police–Citizen Interactions—Challenges and Solutions for Individuals with Mental Illnesses and Neurodevelopmental Disabilities

Learning Objectives

After this chapter, readers should be able to understand the:

1) Role of police as first responders and common types of encounters
2) Extent of and effectiveness of police training on mental health and disabilities
3) De-escalation techniques and training
4) Use of risk management and lethal force
5) "Best practices" for effective and humane encounters for those with mental illnesses and disabilities.

Introduction

Nearly 100 years ago, police reformers such as August Vollmer (1876–1955) advocated for increased professionalism and education for police and encouraged them to take on more social work-type duties (Novak et al., 2022). This "de facto social worker" mindset was foresight to modern-day policing, as their current role often includes addressing the needs of those with mental illnesses or disabilities. The deinstitutionalization movement in the last quarter of the twentieth century shifted people with mental illnesses

M. C. Mogavero, *Mental Health, Neurodiversity, and Criminal Justice*,
https://doi.org/10.1007/978-3-031-88816-8_8

and disabilities from receiving supervision and care in institutions to receiving these services in their communities. The lack of services and massive budget cuts to the mental health system led to many people with untreated mental illness in the community, many of whom experienced homelessness (Honberg et al., 2011). The shift to the community policing model in the 1980s and 1990s with the enhanced enforcement of quality-of-life violations such as panhandling and loitering increased opportunities for police to interact with community members with mental illnesses and substance use disorders (SUDs) (*see* Chapter 6 of this book for more details).

As first responders, police are often tasked with identifying individuals' various mental health needs and connecting them to the appropriate mental health services, which places additional stress and consumes a tremendous amount of limited resources (Treatment Advocacy Center, TAC, 2019). Studies have shown that approximately 12–15% of those with mental illnesses use police services to access mental health care (Livingston, 2016), including having police transport people with mental illnesses to emergency rooms or psychiatric facilities. Responding to mental health calls and conducting mental health transports can comprise 10% of police agencies' annual budget (TAC, 2019). Due to their role in assisting individuals' access to the MHS, police have been labeled as "forensic gatekeepers" (Menzies, 1987).

Compared to policing roles in several other countries (e.g., Canada, United Kingdom), police in the United States (US) are more actively involved in serving the mental health community (Livingston, 2016). A review of 22 studies of police interactions revealed that between 5 and 10% of police encounters involve individuals with mental illnesses, many of whom were experiencing homelessness or a substance use disorder (SUD) (Livingston, 2016; Zhang et al., 2022). Surveys of autistic individuals[1] and caregivers revealed that as many as 16% to 19% have had contact with police (Rava et al., 2017; Tint et al., 2017). Autistic individuals encounter police for diverse reasons, including victims, suspicious persons/crime suspects, and lost or missing persons (Cooper et al., 2024; Copenhaver & Tewksbury, 2019).

Unfortunately, information about mental health and disabilities is not widely covered in standard police training (Reaves, 2016), and surveys of police have shown that many feel ill-prepared to handle individuals with mental illnesses (Tartaro et al., 2021) or autism (Gardner et al., 2019). Police lacking the skills, training, and resources to interact with these populations effectively raises concerns about **procedural justice**. Procedural justice in policing refers to four fundamental principles during citizen encounters: (1) trust (e.g., concern for citizens' well-being; willingness and motivation to help) (2) dignity and respect (e.g., professional, protecting citizens' rights and dignity, polite and courteous), (3) neutrality (e.g., absence of bias with procedures), (4) and voice (being listened to; value the public and their opinions) (Goodman-Delahunty, 2010). Therefore, it is imperative to address the possible unintended consequences of having police encounter citizens with mental illnesses or disabilities such as autism, including the use of force, and address the practical solutions to improve police–citizen encounters.

Interactions with Mental Health and Neurodiverse Populations

Most police officers encounter individuals with mental illnesses or disabilities during their duties, many on a regular basis. Tartaro et al. (2021) surveyed 167 officers from nine police departments in New Jersey and revealed that almost all (99%) reported having monthly encounters with people with mental illnesses in crisis, with about 20% reporting, on average, more than ten encounters per month. A survey of 126 officers in Indiana revealed that 75% have at least monthly encounters with people with mental illnesses, and 25% have had, on average, 3–4 encounters per month. Most (94%) police reported a problem with repeat calls regarding the same individual (Wells & Schafer, 2006). Watson et al. (2022) compared 1,524 reports on mental-health-related encounters from Chicago police agencies (428 reports) and six police agencies in Georgia (1,096 reports) and revealed that 58% involved someone with mental illnesses, 25–30% involved those with alcohol or substance use, and 7% involved those with an intellectual disability (ID) or another developmental disability (DD). Gardner and Campbell (2020) surveyed 157 officers in Florida from various-sized departments, where 60% reported interactions with autistic individuals within the last year, with 40% having three or more interactions. A similar survey of 72 officers revealed that 49% responded to a call involving an autistic individual within the last year (Gardner et al., 2019).

Despite this high volume of contact with mental health and neurodiverse populations, many officers reported they were unprepared to handle such calls. The survey of 126 officers in Indiana reported frustration with a lack of training and the inability to handle mental-health-related calls appropriately. Only 20% of police believed they were equipped to handle a mental health situation appropriately, often due to a lack of resources in the community. Specifically, 90% reported that access to mental health services was essential, and 60% believed that transporting to a mental health facility was necessary, but only 23% indicated that they commonly perform such transports (Wells & Schafer, 2006). Some police also reported feeling unprepared or encountering communication challenges when working with autistic persons, such as being able to obtain written or verbal statements when conducting interviews (Crane et al., 2016).

Context of Interactions

Considering their multiple roles, police regularly encounter mental health and neurodiverse populations for various reasons. Among the 126 officers in Indiana, most interactions involving someone with mental illnesses were for order maintenance (69%) or minor crimes (8%) (Wells & Schafer, 2006). Many instances were resolved at the scene, but 15% resulted in an arrest, and 30% were transported to a mental health facility. Autistic individuals also encounter police for diverse reasons. A survey of 285 autistic adults and 557 parents/caregivers (mainly from the US) indicated that most (71%) reported encounters for noncriminal matters (e.g., behaviors associated with autism). However, a significant minority reported contact with police in criminal matters as suspects (25%) or as crime victims (36%), with violent offenses being the most common (Cooper et al., 2024). Koffer Miller et al. (2022) surveyed 1,527 autistic adults and 6,713 parents/caregivers of autistic individuals in Pennsylvania regarding police encounters, in which 28% reported being a victim of a crime, and 22% were stopped, questioned, arrested, or charged for crimes. Another critical consideration for police is **elopement**. Elopement/eloping, sometimes referred to as wandering, is when an individual, typically a child, leaves a predetermined area without the permission or supervision of caregivers. A survey of 1,218 parents and caregivers of autistic children indicated that 49% had their child elope at some point, and police were involved in 35% of these cases. Missing children who elope are at risk of serious injury or death, including traffic-related injuries and drowning (Anderson et al., 2012).

Reported Experiences with Police

Due to the power dynamic between police and citizens, many individuals with mental illnesses have reported negative experiences during their interactions with police. In-depth interviews of 20 individuals with mental illnesses who described their experiences in 67 police encounters revealed that overall, they had negative beliefs and expectations, which included fear of police brutality and fear for their lives. Common complaints included physical or verbal abuse and outright disrespect. For example, one described an incident when he was detained by store security for shoplifting. He was already handcuffed and calm when police arrived, yet police cursed at him and struck him on the side of his head. Some reported that police were kind and treated them fairly, even when arrested, to which they expressed gratitude. Some described the encounters as "positive," simply not being "roughed up" or abused. Others believed their harsh treatment was due to stigma and that police were fearful of them (Watson et al., 2008a). Police training in how to confront, communicate, and combat the stigma of those with mental illnesses will help police become less fearful, have more confidence, and handle them appropriately and respectfully.

Autistic individuals have reported both positive and negative experiences during their interactions with police. The survey of autistic individuals and parents/caregivers by Koffer Miller et al. (2022) indicated the negative perceptions included being fearful of the police or believing the police were ineffective or unresponsive. Others described mistreatment; for instance, one parent described a situation where her autistic son was slapped, tackled, and threatened with a taser. Others described positive experiences and that police were supportive when their child exhibited behavioral problems. One parent described her satisfaction with a particular officer who later learned the officer had autism-specific training (Koffer Miller et al., 2022). In a survey of 29 autistic adults in Canada who described various interactions with police, many described encounters due to mental health where the police transported them to the hospital for a mental health assessment. Others revealed negative experiences, including 62% who reported the police treated them with disrespect, 78% feeling fearful, and more than half described their interaction with police as traumatic (Salerno & Schuller, 2019). Although training in mental health has grown considerably over the last several decades, specialized training for addressing disabilities has yet to be standardized and universal. As a result, many police are ill-equipped to handle persons with disabilities effectively, leaving many lacking a sense of procedural justice during encounters.

Use of Force

The use of force is a rare yet necessary tactic for police to gain control of a situation, an individual, or in defense of self or another. According to the most recent report by the US Department of Justice (DOJ), 21% of those aged 16 or older interacted with police during the last year, but only 2% reported that police used force during the interaction (Tapp & Davis, 2022). Police typically issue commands during their duties and expect citizens to comply. Police may use force to gain cooperation when citizens are reluctant or defiant. However, some individuals with mental illnesses, neurodevelopmental and other disabilities may be unable or unwilling to comply with commands. Characteristics of mental illness are often confused with SUD, and some may be unable to follow directions during a field sobriety test. For example, people with certain mental illnesses have been shown to exhibit less motor control, particularly with the eyes, and may be unable to keep their head still or track a moving object with their eyes (Morita et al., 2020). Some individuals may not respond to "stop" or similar commands and may walk or run away when approached out of fear. Most police departments have protocols for using force, although there is no federal standard or mandate. According to the National Institute of Justice (NIJ), police should use only the necessary force to mitigate an incident, make an arrest, or protect themselves or others from harm. Excessive force occurs when police use force beyond what is reasonable to maintain control over a person or situation. The NIJ provided **The Use of Force Continuum** (*see* below) as a guide to determine the level of force necessary for control. The continuum generally has five levels, and police are to respond with a level of force appropriate to the situation. However, police may quickly (i.e., in a matter of seconds) move from one part of the continuum to another (NIJ, n.d.).

Example of Use of force Continuum

1) Officer Presence
   - The mere presence of a police officer works to deter crime or diffuse a situation.
   - Officers' presence and attitude are professional and nonthreatening.
   - No force is used.
2) Verbalization
   - Officer issues calm, nonthreatening commands.
   - Officer may raise their voice or give more straightforward commands such as "stop" or "don't move."
   - Force is not physical.
3) Empty-Hand Control
   - Officer uses bodily force to gain control of a situation (no weapon).

- *Soft technique.* Officer grabs or holds to restrain an individual.
- *Hard technique.* Officer punches and/or kicks to restrain an individual.

4) Less-Lethal Methods

- Officer uses less-lethal weapons to gain control of a situation, such as a baton, chemical (e.g., pepper spray), or a Conducted Energy Device (e.g., taser).

5) Lethal Force

- Officer uses lethal weapons such as firearms to gain control of a situation.
- Should only be used if a suspect poses a serious threat to the officer or another individual (NIJ, n.d.).

The use of force continuum for individuals with mental illnesses requires additional training. For example, the mere presence of an officer or empty-hand control techniques may generate fear and escalate situations. Various training, techniques, and multidisciplinary terms can de-escalate volatile situations and safely handle situations for citizens and police (Watson et al., 2008b).

Persons with Mental Illnesses

Although the use of force and deadly force is highest against Black males (Gilbert & Ray, 2016), the use of force disparities among those with mental illnesses is several times higher than racial disparities. Laniyonu and Goff (2021) examined 5,978 use of force and suspect injury reports from nine US police departments and found that those with mental illnesses were overrepresented, comprising 17% of cases. The use of force rates were also nearly 12 times higher than those without a mental illness, and the risk of injury was nearly 11 times higher. These mental health disparities were four times higher than racial disparities, as Black individuals were about three times more likely to experience force than Whites. Similarly, Rossler and Terril (2017) examined 4,254 police use of force and outcome reports across three police agencies in Portland, Oregon, Colorado Springs, Colorado, and St. Petersburg, Florida. When comparing low-force tactics (e.g., soft hands, hard hands) to high-force tactics (e.g., tasers, deadly force), police were less likely to use low-force with those with mental illnesses compared to those without (12% vs. 20%). Individuals with mental illnesses also had about 1.5 times greater odds of sustaining injuries. Rossler and Terril suggest that the increased use of force may be due to the person with mental illness resisting police or the softer tactics being ineffective.

Neurodiverse Individuals

Use of force with neurodiverse individuals with ID or autism during encounters appears to be relatively rare. After reviewing 1,524 police use of force reports and comparing those with and without ID/DD, those with ID/DD were less likely to be combative (e.g., verbally abusive, damaging property, resisting), and police were less likely to perceive them as aggressive less likely to use any force (Watson et al., 2022). Among the 157 officers surveyed by Gardner and Campbell (2020), less than 14% reported using force with autistic individuals, and only 10% reported using handcuffs. However, police must use caution when using force with autistic individuals, as it may escalate encounters. Because autistic individuals often have hyper-reactivity to a sensory response (*see* Chapter 2 of this book for details), becoming physical by touching or grabbing a person's arm can evoke an adverse reaction. As Edworthy and Hylton (2010) noted, standard restraint methods used by police, such as handcuffs, may escalate to where they may become physical to prevent restraint. This response was evident in the case of Conner Leibel, an autistic boy who was injured after being stopped by Officer Grossman in Buckeye, Arizona (about 35 miles outside Phoenix). The situation quickly escalated after he attempted to restrain Connor. This high-profile case led to public outrage and embarrassment to the officer and department, placing them at risk of legal liability. The incident between Connor and the officer made national headlines, including an opinion piece in the New York Times titled *The Police Need to Understand Autism* (Silberman, 2017).

Case of Connor Leibel

Incident: On July 19, 2017, 14-year-old Connor was stimming with a piece of string in a public park in Buckeye, Arizona. Connor's caretaker, Diane C, was across the street discussing piano lessons for Connor's sister. Officer G. drove by and saw Connor's "suspicious behavior." Officer G.'s body camera footage showed him approaching Conner and asking him what he was doing, to which Connor replied, "I'm stimming." Officer G. asked him again, and Connor replied, "I stim with this," and held up his string for him to see.

Officer G. asked Connor if he had identification on him, and Connor replied, "No," and turned to walk away. Officer G. quickly grabbed Connor's arms and said, "Don't go anywhere," immediately placing Connor's hands together behind his back. As he tried to restrain him, Conner quickly turned around, screamed, and tried to pull away. Officer G. wrestled Conner to the ground and slammed him into a tree. Connor repeatedly yelled, "I'm okay." When Connor was on the ground, Officer G. ordered, "Don't you move, you understand?" After asking his name, Officer G. asks, "Why are you acting like this, Connor?" After being held on the ground for about a minute, Diane appeared, and Officer G. shouted to her, "he's fighting with me…do you know him?" Diane explained to Officer G. that Conner had autism, and he was stimming with the string. Officer G. admitted he did not know what stimming was, did not know anything about autism, and that he thought Connor was using drugs (ABC15 Arizona, 2017).

Lawsuit: As a result of this interaction, Conner had "scratches, cuts, and bruises to his face, back, and arms and a serious ankle injury that required numerous draining procedures with a heavy gauge needle as well as a surgical intervention" (Conner Leibel v. City of Buckeye, 2019). Connor's parents, Kevin and Danielle, outraged about the treatment of their son, the physical injuries and trauma he experienced, retained an attorney and sent Buckeye Police Chief Larry Hall a letter requesting an apology, for Officer G. perform community service with the autism community, and implement autism training for officers. Police ignored the request, and Kevin and Danielle filed a federal complaint on behalf of Connor against the City of Buckeye, the Buckeye Police Department, Officer G., the police chief, and the police lieutenant (Leibel v. City of Buckeye, 2019). The lawsuit sought $5 million in punitive damages on nine counts, including battery, excessive force, negligence, failure to train, and illegal arrest.

Outcome: Officer G. was trained as a drug detection expert. He claimed that because of his expertise, he believed that Conner was under the influence, and his actions were justified. After a seven-day civil trial in February 2023, the jury deliberated for about 90 minutes before issuing its verdict in favor of the Buckeye Police Department and clearing Officer G. of any wrongdoing for his actions against Connor. Although Connor's case did not prevail, this incident brought nationwide awareness of a lack of police training on disabilities and efforts to provide police with the necessary tools to be better equipped to manage and support citizens with disabilities.

Use of Force and Fatalities

Unfortunately, some use of force encounters result in fatalities, with high rates among those with mental illnesses. Mulvey and White (2014) reported that people with mental illnesses are four times more likely to be fatally shot by police than those without mental illness. A report by the Treatment Advocacy Center indicated that about 25% of police-involved shooting fatalities involved individuals with severe mental illnesses and were 16 times more likely to be killed than those without a mental illness (Fuller et al., 2015). A review of all 1,099 police-involved civilian deaths in the US in 2015 revealed that 23% of persons killed showed signs of a mental illness, a rate seven times higher than those without mental illness (Saleh et al., 2018). Baker and Pillinger (2020) interviewed 58 surviving family members of those with mental illnesses killed by police, and common themes revolved around stereotypes of violence and fear and mistaking mental health issues for drug use. One family member stated, "I think because of his disability they probably mistook him for someone who was on drugs or up to no good" (Baker & Pillinger, 2020, p. 681).

"Suicide by cop" is a colloquial term used to describe an incident in which an individual provokes police officers to shoot them. The term was first used in the early 1980s by Los Angeles police officer Karl Harris (de Similien & Okorafor, 2017). However, the concept was initially recognized by Wolfgang (1959), who referred to this as "suicide by means of victim-precipitated homicide." Wolfgang examined 588 cases of police-involved shootings in Philadelphia and found that about 26% of shootings fit these criteria. Parent (2004) identified 417 police shootings in the US between 1980 and 2002 and found that one-third of the officers responded to a lethal threat of victim-precipitated homicide. More recent estimates show they comprise about 36% of police shootings (Mohandie et al., 2009).

Police Training

In the US, each state has established training standards set by the Peace Officer Standards and Training (POST) organization. The minimum requirements to become a police officer generally include being 18 years old or older, having a high school diploma or equivalent, and graduating from an accredited police academy. POST oversees academy training for new officers and has set a minimum of about 650 hours of training, equivalent to about 16 weeks (Armstrong, 2020), although on average, most trainings are longer. A report on law enforcement training published by the DOJ reported that, on average, basic training is about 840 hours or about 21 weeks of academy training (Reaves, 2016).

Crisis Intervention Team (CIT)

Crisis Intervention Team (CIT) is a program that trains and teaches officers how to handle and de-escalate crises. CIT was developed in 1988 in Memphis, Tennessee, after an incident in which police fatally shot a man with mental illness (National Alliance on Mental Illness, NAMI, 2024). CIT was initially developed to improve officer and citizen safety. Presently, CIT is a joint community response by police, behavioral health professionals, family members, and consumers to divert individuals from the CJS and into the healthcare system or MHS. CIT International is a non-profit organization that assists police agencies in developing CIT programs (CIT International).

The CIT training curriculum includes 40 hours of classroom instruction developed by the Memphis Police Department, NAMI, the University of Tennessee, and the University of Memphis. The focus of the instruction is on mental health education, de-escalation training, and information on available community-based services where police can bring those with mental illnesses for assistance. The training can be individualized to suit the needs of the police agency based on available resources (Dupont et al., 2007; NAMI, 2019, 2024). Most 40 hour CIT training consists of:

- Active listening and de-escalation
- Legal considerations
- Mental illness basics
- Mental health conditions, including bipolar disorder, schizophrenia, depression, anxiety, and Post-traumatic stress disorder
- Suicide detection and prevention
- Local resources
- Jail diversion
- Role-playing exercises (NAMI, 2019)

De-escalation techniques and communication skills are crucial components of CIT training. De-escalation refers to a range of non-physical techniques to reduce the intensity of interactions and may be more suitable for certain situations. Police often rely on their verbal skills to prevent potentially dangerous situations from escalating into physical encounters that can result in injury or death. **Tactical repositioning** is a de-escalation technique where officers move away from the individual or to a safer location (Engel et al., 2022). Police can de-escalate situations using communication skills that include listening to what the person is saying, allowing them time to speak and respond, being mindful of one's body language and tone of voice, maintaining a calm presence, and avoiding appearing confrontational.

Effectiveness of Training and CIT

CIT is now in more than 2,700 communities nationwide (NAMI, 2024), and evaluations of CIT programs across the US have shown that it effectively reduces the use of force. Wells and Schafer (2006) surveyed 25 police officers in Indiana who underwent CIT training, and police reported an increased ability to meet individuals' needs. Specifically, 96% reported feeling confident in handling people with mental illnesses (46% increase), 93% reported being able to communicate effectively (45% increase), and 77% reported feeling more comfortable with interactions (21% increase) (Wells & Schafer, 2006). Interviews with 20 officers in Chicago, Illinois revealed that the CIT training improved their ability to recognize a possible mental illness. Officers also reported that they were less likely to respond with force and instead used more humane techniques, including verbal de-escalation, active listening, and more time talking to individuals (Canada et al., 2012). There is also evidence that CIT programs may have preventative effects. Franz and Borum (2010) compared the number of mental health-related calls to police in Florida and the number of arrests made before and after the implementation of CIT training. The number of arrests after implementing CIT declined over time. In year one, there were 296 calls and 22 arrests, while in year five, there were 307 calls and 0 arrests. A review of 12 CIT studies concluded that the effects of CIT are promising; however, with many different components to the program, it is difficult to determine what is most important when implementing CIT in diverse communities. There is wide variation in the extent to which the Core Elements are implemented (Compton et al., 2008). Some jurisdictions only implement the 40-hour training, partly due to barriers or challenges in implementing the full model (Compton et al., 2010).

Recent evaluations of similar training programs have shown positive and mixed results. Engel et al. (2022) evaluated the effectiveness of the de-escalation training program, Integrating Communications, Assessment, and Tactics (ICAT), developed by the Police Executive Research Forum. Engel et al. reviewed the number of use of force reports among police in Louisville, Kentucky, from 2018 and 2019 before and after the training. Post ICAT, there was a 28% decrease in use of force incidents, a 26% decrease in citizen injuries, and a 36% decrease in officer injuries. McLean et al. (2020) evaluated the Tact, Tactics, and Trust (T3) de-escalation program among police departments in Fayetteville, North Carolina, and Tucson, Arizona.

T3 training focused on developing decision-making, de-escalation, empathy, rapport-building, and self-control. Across both police agencies, use of force reports were compared among 114 officers who participated in T3 to 195 officers who did not participate in the training. The results showed no significant differences in the use of force among those who had the training compared to those who did not. However, the T3-trained officers prioritized procedural justice significantly more than those who did not undergo training. Thus, concluding that training emphasizing social interaction skills, focusing on procedural justice and related concepts, may be promising to improve citizen interactions (McLean et al., 2020).

Some police departments require more assistance implementing the ongoing education component of CIT (Compton et al., 2010). To address this need, the Albuquerque Police Department partnered with the Department of Psychiatry and Behavioral Sciences at the University of New Mexico to develop CIT ECHO (Extension for Community Healthcare Outcomes). CIT ECHO was designed to assist police with education about mental illness and information on community mental health resources. The program has shown positive results, and police reported having increased self-efficacy in working with and having more compassion toward individuals with mental illnesses (Crisanti et al., 2022). Steadman and Morrisette (2016) caution that CIT training alone is insufficient and should complement other police training with particular attention to mental health services. In addition to mental health training, strengthening community partnerships is essential to meeting the needs of residents with mental illnesses. Campbell et al. (2017) offer a host of similar recommendations and encourage extensive collaboration with community mental health agencies. Compton et al. (2008) noted that the adequacy of community treatment services greatly affects a CIT program's effectiveness and ability to achieve its goals.

Disability-Specific Training

The increased attention and media coverage of police interactions with autistic individuals have led stakeholders to question current practices and prompted police reform to include mental health and disability training. Throughout the US, several state-level legislative acts[2] require police officers and other first responders to undergo autism and other disabilities education awareness training, including in California, Florida, Illinois, Indiana, Massachusetts, and New Jersey. Florida is one of few states that mandated training with specific minimum standards (D. Debbaudt, personal communication on March 4, 2016).[3] Gardner and Campbell (2020) evaluated the perceptions and effectiveness of an autism-specific training program among 157 Florida officers. The training program included a minimum of a four-hour presentation on autism, with in-depth information on recognizing behaviors, signs, and characteristics and adapting their responses during crises. Those who participated in the training reported having more confidence in responding to autism-related calls, but the training did not increase feelings of preparedness (Gardner & Campbell, 2020). Love et al. (2020) evaluated the perceptions and effectiveness of an autism-specific training program among 224 police and other first responders. The training program, ENACT, was based on Police Autism Community Training (PACT), specifically designed for police. ENACT is a two-hour, in-person program comprising a lecture, video clips, and paired and group discussions. An assessment of the training showed that police knowledge of autism significantly improved. Approximately 90% of police reported that the training was valuable, productive, and informative about the difficulties autistic individuals experience and how to support them. Specifically, police indicated they were better able to recognize various accommodations they must make when interacting with autistic individuals, such as using clear communication and removing them from stressful environments (e.g., noisy areas) to meet their sensory needs. Overall, police reported feeling more confident and comfortable responding to calls involving autistic individuals after the training (Love et al., 2020).

New Jersey is another state with a statute requiring all police and other first responders to undergo autism and other disabilities training. The training can occur in various modalities with a minimum of an internet-based presentation. Kelly and Hassett-Walker (2016) surveyed 211 police and other first responders in New Jersey about their training and revealed just over half (52%) rated the training as effective, but there was vast variation in modality. Training modalities included read-and-sign, video-based, internet-based, a live speaker, or a combination. However, the read-and-sign training (6% reported) and video-based training (14% reported) are both non-compliant with the New Jersey statute (Kelly & Hassett-Walker, 2016). Love et al. (2022) conducted in-depth surveys of 317 officers about their positions and attitudes toward autism training. Not only did the officers believe autism-specific training was necessary, but a constant theme reported that such training should be mandated, not optional, and training must consist of more than a "pamphlet" or "one-time lecture" and include hands-on experiences (Love et al., 2022, p. 6). A problem with many autism training requirements is that there is often no standard for the content, length, and credentials of the person administering the training (D. Debbaudt, personal communication on March 4, 2016). However, even with minimum statutory standards, such as in New Jersey, they may not be adhered to or enforced.

Programs to Improve Community Encounters

For several decades, jurisdictions have used different training and services to respond to mental health-related encounters. **Mobile Crisis** is an interdisciplinary team of mental health professionals who respond to crises with the police. The teams can include case managers, social workers, psychiatrists, psychologists, nurses, substance use specialists, and other support specialists. In New York State (NYS), the Mobile Crisis program provides phone and in-person services to those experiencing or are at imminent risk of experiencing a mental health or substance use crisis and collaborates with police when necessary (NYS Office of Mental Health, 2019). The Arc, a national non-profit organization that has served the disability community since 1953, instated the National Center on Criminal Justice and Disability Pathways to Justice program (NCCJD). The NCCJD provides a Disability Response Team (DRT), where professionals who work with people with ID and other disabilities collaborate with police to identify barriers and act as a resource on issues related to criminal justice and disability in the community. DRT also provides in-person training for law enforcement and legal professionals on identifying, interacting with, and accommodating persons with disabilities (The Arc, 2024).

Pilot Programs

More recently, pilot programs have been implemented to address the high volume of mental health, substance use, and other social service-related calls, as such incidents use a considerable volume of police and emergency resources. In 2022, The New Jersey Senate introduced ARRIVE Together (Alternative Response to Reduce Instances of Violence and Escalation), requiring certain mental health services for police responding to specific emergencies and is active in all 21 counties (New Jersey Department of Law & Public Safety, 2024). Another joint program is On P.O.I.N.T. This program began in Ocean County, New Jersey in 2016 and provides on-site social workers from Bright Harbor Healthcare in the local police station two days per week. Social workers arrive on the scene with police to help and de-escalate situations before they erupt into crises. One example was a young autistic man who was in crisis and held a knife to his throat, threatening to take his life. Police were able to remove the knife safely, and On P.O.I.N.T staff has been working with him and his family to get him the appropriate services. The program ensures that people receive treatment and helps divert them from the CJS (Bright Harbor Healthcare, 2024).

Box 8.1 Practitioner Spotlight: Chief Mitch Little

Chief Little was a police officer for nearly 40 years, joining the Toms River, New Jersey Police Department in 1986. He spent most of his career in administration and was promoted to Sergeant in 1997, to Captain in 2008, and to Chief of Police in 2014, until he retired in August 2024. With a population of over 95,000, Toms River, NJ has a high volume of mental health-related calls. Working with community resources is critical for citizens' and officers' safety. For the last several years, the department has been working with On P.O.I.N.T. Having social workers arrive at the scene offers that delicate balance that some situations require. The social workers have the communication skills and training to assess the situation, de-escalate, and determine their needs. The police can step back when the social worker de-escalates but can step in when necessary if the situation becomes unsafe. The co-response with On P.O.I.N.T has been particularly useful for reducing the multiple service calls for the same individual by diverting them to the mental health system. The department also has a Psychiatric Emergency Screening Service counselor to handle the 100 suicide-related calls every month.

According to Little, police training in crisis intervention is essential, but above all, establishing and maintaining a relationship with the community is most important. During his tenure, Little has established 16 outreach programs to improve community relations, including Bigs in Blue, a program where officers mentor underserved youth, and "Coffee with a Cop," a monthly meet-and-greet with residents. As Chief, he was responsible for over 160 police officers. He trained his officers to be kind, respectful, and empathetic, regardless of one's exhibited behaviors or actions. This type of policing and leadership not only builds a relationship but improves the community's perception of police and allows them to gain the public's trust and respect.

Considerations and Recommendations

To ensure adherence to procedural justice and to avoid encounters such as the case of Conner Leibel, police require the tools and support to perform their professional duties effectively, efficiently, safely, and ethically. Police are often the first contact one has with the CJS and, thus, have a vital role in helping to divert individuals to the necessary services in the community. Below are several areas to consider and practical recommendations to improve police services.

Allocate Funding

Lack of funding is a significant barrier to the implementation of the services and training described above to address the issues of mental health and neurodiversity in the CJS. Ahern (2021) details how training and distributing resources have the potential to benefit all parties. Mental health programs must be adequately funded, as police cannot divert individuals from the CJS if there are no services in place to divert them. States can address this problem by passing legislative bills to allocate funds to implement essential services to serve those in need, such as NJ Bill 722/785 (2022), which allocated $2 million over three years to fund ARRIVE Together. Although this is a significant upfront investment, it has the potential to save the state and jurisdictions significant money long-term, for example, by addressing recidivism, reducing police escorts to mental health facilities, and reducing lawsuits for injuries due to excessive force, civil rights violations, and wrongful deaths.

Increase Training Standards and Content

There is little doubt that police play an essential role in keeping community members safe and helping when necessary. However, their role in today's society requires more education and training than simply the minimum, especially in jurisdictions with larger populations of people with mental illnesses, autism, and other disabilities. CIT, in addition to training on mental illness, autism, and other neurodevelopmental disabilities, are essential, but they should not be treated as an "information session" or "checked box" of completion. An assessment after the training is necessary to determine whether police met the goals of the training. Police should also be given the opportunity to provide feedback on what was effective, what was ineffective, and areas for improvement. This feedback is vital for a police-focused experience and can help instructors improve their training (Love et al., 2022).

Designate Specialized Officers

Some police have the background and disposition to work with various populations more effectively than others, and the mental health and neurodiverse populations are no different. All officers should complete the minimum training requirement outlined above, as all police officers can encounter citizens with mental illnesses, autism, and disabilities during their duties. Some officers may be better equipped to handle such situations than others and could undergo additional training and education to voluntarily become part of a specialized response team. Dispatch should be trained on what specific questions to ask and have police respond to specific calls for the best outcomes (Compton et al., 2017). Interviews of police expressed concern that crisis-intervention-trained officers would be called to higher safety risk scenarios that increase the use of force incidents. They feared this could lead to more citizen complaints and officer scrutiny, and the potential bias may be used against them (Pelfrey & Young, 2020). Therefore, a system must be in place to recognize their specialized assignments and prevent officers from being biased and "flagged" as problematic.

Establish Partnerships and Community Outreach

Establishing partnerships with the community is essential for the full implementation of CIT programs (Steadman & Morrisette, 2016). Police departments can establish partnerships and make use of the state and not-for-profit agencies in their community, including those who provide services to the autism community, those with disabilities, substance use treatment, mental health agencies, and those who serve unhoused populations. Those who work in such agencies can educate police on the scope of their services and how they can assist and provide the additional education and training officers require to communicate and handle interactions effectively. The Alabama-based KultureCity has a Becoming Sensory Inclusive™ certification that trains police and other first responders on how to approach those with mental illnesses or other "hidden" disabilities such as autism. They also provide officers with sensory items to help calm individuals and communication aids. The Pathways to Justice program of The Arc's NCCJD is a comprehensive, community-based program designed to improve the experience of those with disabilities when involved with the CJS. Part of this initiative provides full-day, in-person training for law enforcement on identifying, interacting with, and accommodating persons with ID and other disabilities.

Community partnerships can also include police "meet-and-greets" where citizens with mental illnesses and disabilities and their families/caregivers can form and develop trust-building bonds with police in their community. Police departments can partner with agencies offering psychology, social work, or related programs. Academic mental health professionals can also educate police on mental health, substance use, autism, ID, and other disabilities and how to work with and communicate with said populations effectively. Colleges and universities that offer criminal justice programs could add a course to their curriculums related to working with these populations and perhaps be required for those in practitioner-related tracks or concentrations.

Conclusion

The critical issues presented in this chapter suggest a need for increased knowledge and training about mental illness and neurodiversity among police, who, as first responders, require it the most. Wood and Watson (2017) emphasize that officers should encounter people with mental illnesses as "guardians," not "warriors," which requires additional training than what is provided in most police academies. CIT techniques, coupled with intensive education on mental illness, SUD, autism, and other developmental disabilities, can help police establish a rapport, better understand the individuals' feelings and what they are experiencing. Police can assess each situation, de-escalate, and divert individuals from the CJS as necessary.

Considering the high rates of contact with mental health and neurodiverse populations, a lack of training could result in escalating situations. The goal of police in citizen encounters is to possess and maintain control of a situation and prevent it from becoming a crisis (Steadman & Morrisette, 2016). A lack of knowledge and training to work with people with mental illnesses and neurodiverse populations creates barriers for police to work effectively and appropriately. Debbaudt (2004) warned that untrained police may mistake an autistic person for someone who is under the influence, as in the case of Conner Leibel. The absence of autism and disability training left Officer G. lacking the tools required to assess the situation accurately, and he resorted to using the tool he had—drug detection. As renowned American Psychologist Abraham H. Maslow wrote, "If the only tool you have is a hammer, everything will look like a nail" (1966, pp. 15–16). Specialized training in the academy (See Practitioner Spotlight in Chapter 10) provides future police with tools to prepare them to perform their duties and serve their communities. Specialized training, along with community outreach initiatives, allows police to gain a greater understanding of the community they serve and builds relationships and trust. Conner's parents' requests for Buckeye police to undergo training and service with the autism community are consistent with Chief Little's recommendations.

In many instances, police are the only 24-hour service provider that people contact for assistance, but a lack of resources in the community leads police to operate as a default mental health provider. Adequate resources in the community and assistance from co-response terms can allow them to work more effectively and refer those needing assistance out of the CJS. However, the above recommendations can only be implemented with adequate funding for the police and mental health services. Allocating adequate funding will not only help police obtain the skills needed to perform their duties but also help them perform them effectively, safely, and ethically, with attention to procedural justice.

Key Terms

Crisis Intervention Team
De-escalation
Elopement/eloping
Mobile Crisis
Use of Force Continuum
Procedural justice
Tactical repositioning

Chapter Questions

1) What specific challenges do police face when encountering individuals with disabilities such as autism or ID?
2) What are some potential strategies for de-escalating situations involving individuals with mental illnesses?
3) What types of training and education do police need to work effectively with individuals with mental illness and disabilities?
4) How can communities and police agencies work together to provide support and resources for individuals with mental illnesses and disabilities?
5) Of the considerations and recommendations for police when encountering individuals with mental illnesses and disabilities, which do you believe is most important and should take priority? Explain your response.

Suggested Readings

Modell, S. J., & Cropp, D. (2007). Police officers and disability: Perceptions and attitudes. *Intellectual and Developmental Disabilities, 45*(1), 60–63. https://doi.org/10.1352/1934-9556(2007)45[60:POADPA]2.0.CO;2

Shapiro, G. K., Cusi, A., Kirst, M., O'Campo, P., Nakhost, A., & Stergiopoulos, V. (2015). Co-responding police-mental health programs: A review. *Administration and Policy in Mental Health, 42*, 606–620. https://doi.org/10.1007/s10488-014-0594-9

Yu, Y., Bradley, C., Boan, A. D., Charles, J. M., & Carpenter, L. A. (2020). Young adults with autism spectrum disorder and the criminal justice system. *Journal of Autism and Developmental Disorders, 51*(10), 3624–3636. https://doi.org/10.1007/s10803-020-04805-9

Notes

1. *see A Note About Evolving Language and Term* in Chapter 1 for information on identity-first language.
2. California Senate Bill 1531, Florida Senate Bill 1352, Illinois House Bill 3454, Indiana House Bill 1242, Massachusetts House Bill 2098 and Senate Bill 1264, New Jersey Assembly Bill 1908.
3. Dennis Debbaudt is a world-renowned author and autism educator for law enforcement and emergency responders. Debbaudt also assisted in the developed standards for autism training in Florida.

References

ABC15 Arizona. (2017, July 19). Police body camera: Arizona officer detains teen with autism. [Video]. YouTube. https://www.youtube.com/watch?v=uErofKXMwq0

Ahern, M. (2021). Defunding the criminality of mental illness by funding specialized police training: How additional training and resources for dealing with mental health will be beneficial for all sides. *Journal of Law and Health, 35*(1), 181–209.

Anderson, C., Law, J. K., Daniels, A., Rice, C., Mandell, D. S., Hagopian, L., & Law, P. A. (2012). Occurrence and family impact of elopement in children with autism spectrum disorders. *Pediatrics, 130*, 870–877. https://doi.org/10.1542/peds.2012-0762

Armstrong, J. (2020, July 9). A letter to the American public: We need to increase the quantity and quality of police training. *Police 1*. https://www.police1.com/police-training/articles/a-letter-to-the-american-public-we-need-to-increase-the-quantity-and-quality-of-police-training-PEIoRJqWTIG55dqy/

Baker, D., & Pillinger, C. (2020). 'If You call 911 they are going to kill me': Families' experiences of mental health and deaths after police contact in the United States. *Policing and Society, 30*(6), 674–687. https://doi.org/10.1080/10439463.2019.1581193

Bright Harbor Healthcare. (2024). *The On P.O.I.N.T. Program*. https://brightharbor.org/on-point-program/

Canada, K. E., Angell, B., & Watson, A. C. (2012). Intervening at the entry point: Differences in how CIT-trained and non-CIT-trained officers describe responding to mental health-related calls. *Community Mental Health Journal, 48*(6), 746–755. https://doi.org/10.1007/s10597-011-9430-9

Campbell, J., Ahalt, C., Hagar, R., & Arroyo, W. (2017). Building on mental health training for law enforcement: Strengthening community partnerships. *International Journal of Prisoner Health, 13*(3–4), 207–212. https://doi.org/10.1108/IJPH-10-2016-0060

CIT International. (2012). *International Crisis Intervention Team*. http://www.citinternational.org/

Compton, M. T., Bahora, M., Watson, A. C., & Oliva, J. R. (2008). A comprehensive review of extant research on Crisis Intervention Team (CIT) programs. *The Journal of the American Academy of Psychiatry and the Law, 36*(1), 47–55. https://jaapl.org/content/36/1/47

Compton, M. T., Bakeman, R., Broussard, B., D'Orio, B., & Watson, A. C. (2017). Police officers' volunteering for (rather than being assigned to) crisis intervention team (CIT) training: Evidence for a beneficial self-selection effect. *Behavioral Science Law, 35*, 470–479. https://doi.org/10.1002/bsl.2301

Compton, M. T., Broussard, B., Hankerson-Dyson, D., Krishan, S., Stewart, T., Oliva, J. R., & Watson, A. C. (2010). System- and policy-level challenges to full implementation of the crisis intervention team (CIT) model. *Journal of Police Crisis Negotiations, 10*, 72–85. https://doi.org/10.1080/15332581003757347

Conner Leibel v. City of Buckeye, 364 F. Supp. 3d 1027, 1034 D. Ariz. (2019).

Copenhaver, A., & Tewksbury, R. (2019). Interactions between autistic individuals and law enforcement: A mixed-methods exploratory study. *American Journal of Criminal Justice, 44*, 309–333. https://doi.org/10.1007/s12103-018-9452-8

Cooper, D., Frisbie, S., Wang, S., Ventimiglia, J., Gibbs, V., Love, A. M. A., Mogavero, M., Benevides, T. W., Hyatt, J. M., Hooven, K., Basketbill, I., & Shea, L. (2024). What do we know about autism and policing globally? Preliminary findings from an international effort to examine autism and the criminal justice system. *Autism Research, 17*(10), 1957–2187. https://doi.org/10.1002/aur.3203

Crane, L., Maras, K. L., Hawken, T., Mulcahy, S., & Memon, A. (2016). Experiences of autism spectrum disorder and policing in England and Wales: Surveying police and the autism community. *Journal of Autism and Developmental Disorders, 46*(6), 2028–2041. https://doi.org/10.1007/s10803-016-2729-1

Crisanti, A. S., Fairfax-Columbo, J., Duran, D., Rosenbaum, N. A., Melendrez, B., Trujillo, I., Earheart, J. A., & Tinney, M. (2022). Evaluation of ongoing crisis intervention team (CIT) training for law enforcement using the ECHO model. *Journal of Police and Criminal Psychology, 37*(4), 863–875. https://doi.org/10.1007/s11896-022-09529-3

de Similien, R. H., & Okorafor, A. (2017). Suicide by cop: A psychiatric phenomenon. *American Journal of Psychiatry, 1*(1), 20–22. https://doi.org/10.1176/appi.ajp-rj.2017.120107

Debbaudt, D. (2004). *Beyond guilt or innocence.* Forum paper, Autism New Zealand Inc., Worcester, MA. http://autismnz.org.nz/police/Pol_BeyGuilt.pdf

Dupont, R., Cochran, S., & Pillsbury, S. (2007). *Crisis Intervention Team Core Elements.* http://cit.memphis.edu/CoreElements.pdf

Edworthy, A., & Hylton, C. (2010). Brain-injured children and the police. *Journal of Learning Disabilities and Offending Behaviour, 1*(3), 40–48. https://doi.org/10.5042/jldob.2010.0628

Engel, R. S., Corsaro, N., Isaza, G. T., & McManus, H. D. (2022). Assessing the impact of de-escalation training on police behavior: Reducing police use of force in the Louisville, KY Metro Police Department. *Criminology & Public Policy, 21*(2), 199–233. https://doi.org/10.1111/1745-9133.12574

Franz, S., & Borum, R. (2010). Crisis Intervention Teams may prevent arrests of people with mental illnesses. *Police Practice and Research, 12*(3), 265–272. https://doi.org/10.1080/15614263.2010.497664

Fuller, D. A., Lamb, H. R., Biasotti, M., & Snook, J. (2015). *Overlooked and undercounted.* Treatment Advocacy Center. http://www.tacreports.org/storage/documents/overlooked-in-the-undercounted.pdf

Gardner, L., & Campbell, J. M. (2020). Law enforcement officers' preparation for calls involving autism: Prior experiences and response to training. *Journal of Autism and Developmental Disorders, 50*(12), 4221–4229. https://doi.org/10.1007/s10803-020-04485-5

Gardner, L., Campbell, J. M., & Westdal, J. (2019). Brief report: Descriptive analysis of law enforcement officers' experiences with and knowledge of autism. *Journal of Autism and Developmental Disorders, 49*(3), 1278–1283. https://doi.org/10.1007/s10803-018-3794-4

Gilbert, K. L., & Ray, R. (2016). Why police kill Black males with impunity: Applying public health critical race praxis (PHCRP) to address the determinants of policing behaviors and "justifiable" homicides in the USA. *Journal of Urban Health, 93*(1), 122–140. https://doi.org/10.1007/s11524-015-0005-x

Goodman-Delahunty, J. (2010). Four ingredients: New recipes for procedural justice in Australian policing. *Policing-an International Journal of Police Strategies & Management, 4*(4), 403–410. https://doi.org/10.1093/police/paq041

Honberg, R., Kimball, A., Diehl, S. Usher, L., & Fitzpatrick, M. (2011). *State mental health cuts: The continuing crisis.* National Alliance on Mental Illness.

Kelly, E., & Hassett-Walker, C. (2016). The training of New Jersey emergency service first responders in autism awareness. *Police Practice and Research, 17*(6), 543–554. https://doi.org/10.1080/15614263.2015.1121390

Koffer Miller, K. H., Becker, A., Cooper, D., & Shea, L. (2022). Justice system interactions among autistic individuals: A multiple methods analysis. *Crime & Delinquency, 68*(9), 1579–1603. https://doi.org/10.1177/00111287211054733

KultureCity. *Becoming Sensory Inclusive*™. https://www.kulturecity.org/sensory-inclusive-first-responder-certification/

Laniyonu, A., & Goff, P. A. (2021). Measuring disparities in police use of force and injury among persons with serious mental illness. *BMC Psychiatry, 21*(1), 500. https://doi.org/10.1186/s12888-021-03510-w

Leibel v. City of Buckeye, 364 F. Supp. 3d 1027 (D. Ariz. 2019)

Livingston, J. D. (2016). Contact between police and people with mental disorders: A review of rates. *Psychiatric Services, 67*(8), 850–857. https://doi.org/10.1176/appi.ps.201500312

Love, A. M., Railey, K. S., Phelps, M., Campbell, J. M., Cooley-Cook, H. A., & Taylor, R. L. (2020). Preliminary evidence for training improving first responder knowledge and confidence to work with persons with autism. *Journal of Autism and Developmental Disorders, 11*(4), 211–219. https://doi.org/10.1108/JIDOB-04-2020-0007

Love, A. M., Railey, K. S., & Jones, C. P. (2022). Examining the sources of police confidence when working with autistic individuals. *Policing: An International Journal of Police Strategies and Management, 45*(3), 481–494. https://doi.org/10.1108/PIJPSM-10-2021-0152

Maslow, A. H. (1966). *The psychology of science: A reconnaissance*. Harper & Row.

Menzies, R. J. (1987). Psychiatrists in blue: Police apprehension of mental disorder and dangerousness. *Criminology, 25*(3), 429–453. https://doi.org/10.1111/j.1745-9125.1987.tb00805.x

McLean, K., Wolfe, S. E., Rojek, J., Alpert, G. P., & Smith, M. R. (2020). Randomized controlled trial of social interaction police training. *Criminology and Public Policy, 19*(2), 805–832. https://doi.org/10.1111/1745-9133.12506

Mohandie, K., Meloy, J. R., & Collins, P. I. (2009). Suicide by cop among officer-involved shooting cases. *Journal of Forensic Sciences, 54*(2), 456–462. https://doi.org/10.1111/j.1556-4029.2008.00981.x

Morita, K., Miura, K., Kasai, K., & Hashimoto, R. (2020). Eye movement characteristics in schizophrenia: A recent update with clinical implications. *Neuropsychopharmacology Reports, 40*(1), 2–9. https://doi.org/10.1002/npr2.12087

Mulvey, P., & White, M. (2014). The potential for violence in arrests of persons with mental illness. *Policing: An International Journal of Police Strategies and Management, 37*(2), 404–419. https://doi.org/10.1108/PIJPSM-07-2013-0076

National Alliance on Mental Illness. (2024). Crisis Intervention Team (CIT) Programs. https://www.nami.org/Advocacy/Crisis-Intervention/Crisis-Intervention-Team-(CIT)-Programs

National Alliance on Mental Illness. (2019, December 19). *Why Crisis Intervention team training should be the standard.* https://www.nami.org/criminal-justice-and-legal/why-crisis-intervention-team-training-should-be-the-standard/

National Institute of Justice. *The use-of-force continuum.* https://nij.ojp.gov/topics/articles/use-force-continuum

New Jersey Department of Law and Public Safety. (2024). *Arrive together program.* https://www.njoag.gov/programs/arrive-together/

New Jersey Revised Statutes. Title 26 and 52 Chapter 80. (2008).

New York State Office of Mental Health. (2019). *Mobile Crisis Program Guidance.* https://omh.ny.gov.omh.web.bho.docs.mobilecrisisprogramguidance.pdf

Novak, K., Cordner, G., Smith, B., & Roberg, R. (2022). *Police and society* (9th ed.). Oxford University Press.

Parent, R. (2004). Aspects of police use of deadly force in North America: The phenomenon of victim-precipitated homicide. Simon Fraser University (unpublished doctoral dissertation).

Pelfrey, W. V., & Young, A. (2020). Police crisis intervention teams: Understanding implementation variations and officer-level impacts. *Journal of Police and Criminal Psychology, 35*, 1–12. https://doi.org/10.1007/s11896-019-9314-4

Policy and Analytics Center at the A. J. Drexel Autism Institute. (2022). Autism and the Criminal Justice System: Policy Opportunities and Challenges (Policy brief). https://www.autism-insar.org/page/PolicyBriefs

Rava, J., Shattuck, P., Rast, J., & Roux, A. (2017). The prevalence and correlates of involvement in the criminal justice system among youth on the Autism spectrum. *Journal of Autism and Developmental Disorders, 47*(2), 340–346. https://doi.org/10.1007/s10803-016-2958-3

Reaves, B. A. (2016). *State and local law enforcement training academies, 2013.* U.S. Department of Justice, Office of Justice Programs, Bureau of Justice Statistics.

Rossler, M., & Terril, W. (2017). Mental illness, police use of force and citizen injury. *Police Quarterly, 20*(2), 189–212.

Saleh, A. Z., Appelbaum, P. S., Liu, X., Stroup, S., & Wall, M. (2018). Deaths of people with mental illness during interactions with law enforcement. *International Journal of Law and Psychiatry, 58*, 110–116. https://doi.org/10.1016/j.ijlp.2018.03.003

Silberman, S. (2017, September 19). The police need to understand autism. *New York Times.* https://www.nytimes.com/2017/09/19/opinion/police-autismunderstanding.html?partner=Bloomberg

Salerno, A. C., & Schuller, R. A. (2019). A mixed-methods study of police experiences of adults with autism spectrum disorder in Canada. *International Journal of Law and Psychiatry, 64*, 18–25. https://doi.org/10.1016/j.ijlp.2019.01.002

Steadman, H. J., & Morrissette, D. (2016). Police responses to persons with mental illness: Going beyond CIT training. *Law & Psychiatry, 67*(10), 1054–1056. https://doi.org/10.1176/appi.ps.201600348

Tapp, S. N., & Davis, E. J. (2022). *Contacts between police and the public, 2020.* U.S. Department of Justice, Office of Justice Programs, Bureau of Justice Statistics.

Tartaro, C., Bonnan-White, J., Mastrangelo, M. A., & Mulvihill, R. (2021). Police officers' attitudes toward mental health and crisis intervention: Understanding preparedness to respond to community members in crisis. *Journal of Police and Criminal Psychology, 36*, 579–591. https://doi.org/10.1007/s11896-021-09459-6

The Arc. (2024) *Pathways to Justice.* https://thearc.org/our-initiatives/criminal-justice/pathway-justice/

Tint, A., Palucka, A. M., Bradley, E., Weiss, J. A., & Lunsky, Y. (2017). Correlates of police involvement among adolescents and adults with autism spectrum disorder. *Journal of Autism and Developmental Disorders, 47*(9), 2639–2647. https://doi.org/10.1007/s10803-017-3182-5

Treatment Advocacy Center. (2019). *Road runners: The role and impact of law enforcement in transporting individuals with severe mental illness, A national survey.* https://www.treatmentadvocacycenter.org/road-runners

Watson, A. C., Angell, B., Morabito, M., & Robinson, N. (2008a). Defying negative expectations: Dimensions of fair and respectful treatment by police officers as perceived by people with mental illness. *Administration and Policy in Mental Health and Mental Health Services Research, 35*, 449–457. https://doi.org/10.1007/s10488-008-0188-5

Watson, A. C., Morabito, M. S., Draine, J., & Ottati, V. (2008b). Improving police response to persons with mental illness: A multi-level conceptualization of CIT. *International Journal of Law and Psychiatry, 31*(4), 359–368. https://doi.org/10.1016/j.ijlp.2008.06.004

Watson, A., Phan, M., & Compton, M. T. (2022). Police encounters with individuals perceived as having intellectual or developmental disabilities: An examination of encounter characteristics from two studies. *Policing, 45*(3), 393–402. https://doi.org/10.1108/PIJPSM-12-2021-0168

Wells, W., & Schafer, J. A. (2006). Officer perceptions of police responses to persons with a mental illness. *Policing: International Journal of Police Strategies and Management, 29*(4), 578–601. https://doi.org/10.1108/13639510610711556

Wolfgang, M. E. (1959). Suicide by means of victim-precipitated homicide. *Journal of Clinical & Experimental Psychopathology, 20*, 335–349. https://psycnet.apa.org/record/1960-06336-001

Wood, J. D., & Watson, A. C. (2017). Improving police interventions during mental health-related encounters: Past, present and future. *Policing & Society, 27*(3), 289–299. https://doi.org/10.1080/10439463.2016.1219734

Zhang, A., Balles, J. A., Nyland, J. E., Nguyen, T. H., White, V. M., & Zgierska, A. E. (2022). The relationship between police contacts for drug use-related crime and future arrests, incarceration, and overdoses: A retrospective observational study highlighting the need to break the vicious cycle. *Harm Reduction Journal, 19*(1), 67–77. https://doi.org/10.1186/s12954-022-00652-2

9

Interviews and Interrogations—Addressing the Needs of Suspects with Mental Illnesses, Neurodevelopmental Disabilities, and Juveniles

Learning Objectives

After this chapter, readers should be able to understand the:

1) Difference between and the purpose of interviews and interrogations
2) Miranda warning and the impact on police interrogations
3) Steps of the Reid interrogation technique
4) Types of false confessions
5) Vulnerabilities of juveniles, those with mental illness, and disabilities in police custody during interviews and interrogations
6) "Best practices" for interviewing juveniles, those with mental illness, and disabilities

Introduction

Police interviews and interrogations are critical components of crime investigations. A suspect **interview** is a relatively informal line of questioning related to a criminal matter. The questioning is non-accusatory and designed to gather information about suspects' version of events while assessing their credibility. The suspect is not in custody and is free to leave (Inbau et al., 2013; Kassin, 2005). An **interrogation**, however, is a formalized

M. C. Mogavero, *Mental Health, Neurodiversity, and Criminal Justice*,
https://doi.org/10.1007/978-3-031-88816-8_9

and accusatory manner of questioning in which the investigator attempts to elicit truthful information about the suspect's involvement in a crime (Kassin et al., 2007; Inbau et al., 2013). Most interrogations start with an interview, which helps the interrogator build rapport. During a **custodial interrogation**, the suspect is in custody and is not free to leave. Confessions typically occur during interrogations, as the aim is to obtain information to use as evidence, and confessions are compelling sources of evidence (Kassin & Sukel, 1997). The Fifth Amendment of the US Constitution provides those accused of crimes various protections against self-incrimination, and the Sixth Amendment provides them the right to have an attorney present during interrogations. However, suspects may waive these rights and agree to speak with the police without an attorney. Concerns are raised when juveniles and/or those with mental illnesses or disabilities are interviewed or interrogated, as they may have difficulty understanding their Fifth and Sixth Amendment rights, have communication limitations, and are more vulnerable to police pressure. Research has shown that juveniles, individuals with disabilities, and mental illness are at increased risk of providing false statements (Perske, 2011), and therefore, police take additional precautions, particularly when suspects are in distress. Proper interview and interrogation techniques are essential to prevent suspects from providing false or misleading statements, violations of constitutional rights, miscarriages of justice, and wrongful convictions.

Box 9.1 Practitioner Spotlight: Lieutenant Robert J. Louden

Lieutenant Louden joined the New York City Police Department (NYPD) in 1966 and was promoted to Lieutenant in 1980. In 1975, he became a hostage negotiator in the NYPD Detective Bureau Hostage Negotiation Team and Chief Hostage Negotiator in 1981. He was promoted to Commander of Detective Squad in 1983 until he retired in 1987. During an active 21-year career, he performed a wide range of patrol and investigative duties. When interacting with suspects with mental illness, situations have the potential to quickly escalate into crises. According to Louden, police must maintain a safe environment, as the end goal is to ensure everyone's safety: the subject and oneself. When the environment is safe, then the approach and interaction can be calm.

As a hostage negotiator, Louden developed impeccable communication skills, particularly when individuals were in crisis or behaving irrationally. According to Louden, during interviews, police must have an open, non-judgmental dialogue, regardless of what the suspect is accused of or threatening. An aggressive or intimidating demeanor is not the best way to gain cooperation; police must be empathic listeners and maintain a calm conversation. When initiating communication, police may first ask the person's name or how they prefer to be addressed. Then, simply begin by asking, "what's going on?" If they are in crisis or appear distressed, police must realize that they are not trying to "make sense out of nonsense" but working to "see" their point of view without "joining their distress or delusion." During the investigative process, police may also obtain information from family or friends but are sometimes given erroneous information, inadvertently or intentionally. Third-party interviewers can be helpful, but one must be vigilant to determine whether the information is useful.

After retiring from the NYPD, Louden earned his PhD in criminal justice from the City University of New York. As a Professor, Louden has spent the past several decades teaching criminal justice students and future police officers his vital communication and leadership skills.

Custodial Interrogations and Constitutional Rights

Prior to any formal police training or case law ensuring adherence to civil rights, interrogations were often brutal and consisted of hours of intense and intimidating questioning (Inbau et al., 2013), and sometimes police used violence to illicit confessions. Using violence during interrogations was found unconstitutional in Brown v. Mississippi (1936). Ed Brown, Arthur Ellington, and Henry Shields were accused of murder, in which Brown and Shields endured whippings, and Ellington was repeatedly hung from a tree until he confessed. The confessions were admitted at trial; they were found guilty and sentenced to death. On appeal, the United States (US) Supreme Court ruled that convictions based on confessions that were extracted by police using violence or torture were void under the due process clause of the Fourteenth Amendment (Brown v. Mississippi, 1936).

The Reid Technique

Many police investigators in the US are trained in the Reid Technique (referred to as "the Reid" from here on), named after Chicago police officer and polygraph expert John T. Reid (1910–1982). John Reid was a compassionate individual interested in human behavior and used the polygraph to exclude innocent suspects. He noticed better results during interrogations when exercising compassion and in the 1930s, began researching more effective interview techniques. Reid later began working with Fred Inbau (1909–1998), a legal scholar and crime laboratory director, and they developed a new strategy to gain confessions, eventually leading to the nine steps described below. In 1947, they formed the firm John T. Reid and Associates. Reid and Inbau shared their knowledge, attending conferences, and publishing their first manual, *Criminal Interrogations and Confessions* in 1962. The Reid is a multistep approach designed to increase the anxiety associated with denying while reducing the anxiety related to confessing.

Nine Steps of the Reid Method

Step 1) Positive Confrontation: The interrogator confronts the suspect with guilt by confidently stating the accusation. The interrogator then observes the suspects' reactions or responses, noting any signs of deception (e.g., nonverbal gestures). The interrogator may repeat the accusation several times.

Step 2) Theme Development: The interrogator will produce themes that justify or excuse the crime. The interrogator may display understanding and sympathy to obtain trust. For example, they may minimize the seriousness of the offense and develop rationalizations of why they may have committed the crime or blame someone else for their actions.

Step 3) Handling Denials: Most suspects deny any criminal involvement, so the interrogator will interrupt denial statements. This allows the interrogator to shift the denials and steer them toward the truth. The investigator needs to be confident in doing so and must be confident when suggesting any knowledge of the suspect's guilt.

Step 4) Overcoming Objection: This step continues, and the interrogator attempts to overcome the suspect's factual, moral, and emotional objections to their involvement in the crime. They will address reasons or excuses for the crime.

Step 5) Retaining the Suspect's Attention: The interrogator must keep the suspect's attention and prevent them from "tuning them out." The interrogator may move closer to the suspect, maintain eye contact, and gently touch them.

Step 6) Handling the Suspect's Mood: The interrogator shows sympathy and understanding and urges the suspect to tell the truth.

Step 7) Presenting an Alternative: The interrogator will give the suspect a "face-saving" alternative explanation for their crime. The interrogator may offer two possible alternatives. One face-saving and another that is callous.

Both implicate the suspect, but one is seen as a more positive explanation for the crime.

Step 8) Detailing the Offense: This follows Step 7, in which the suspect has accepted one of the alternative explanations. The interrogator will then get the suspect to recount the crime details verbally. Once this occurs, the suspect gives an oral statement.

Step 9) Elements of Oral and Written Statements: Next, the investigator will convert the oral statement into a full written confession. The suspect finally signs the confession (Inbau et al., 2013, pp. 187–191).[1]

Miranda Warnings and Police Interrogations

Police investigations were significantly impacted after the landmark US Supreme Court decisions in Escobedo v. Illinois (1964) and Miranda v. Arizona (1966). After the Miranda decision, police must issue a statement of suspects' Fifth and Sixth Amendment rights, referred to as a **Miranda Warning**. The exact wording of these rights may vary across law enforcement jurisdictions; they generally include: (a) you have the right to remain silent; (b) anything you say can be used against you in court; (c) you have the right to an attorney; and (d) if you cannot afford an attorney, one will be appointed for you. Once a suspect states they are evoking their Fifth Amendment Right against self-incrimination, the interrogation and all questioning must stop. Once a suspect explicitly requests an attorney, the interrogation and all questioning must stop, and police must allow the suspect to speak with an attorney and have the attorney present during any questioning. A suspect may agree to waive their Miranda Rights and continue to speak with the police, but to do so, they must waive them knowingly, intelligently, and voluntarily[2] (Miranda v. Arizona, 1966).

Case Brief: Miranda v. Arizona (1966)

Facts: On March 13, 1963, police arrived at the home of 24-year-old Ernesto Miranda and transported him to the police station in Phoenix, Arizona, to question him about a kidnapping and rape of an 18-year-old woman. The victim provided police with a license plate, which led them to Miranda. Police interrogated Miranda for two hours without providing him any knowledge that he had a right not to answer any questions and had the right to have an attorney present. Miranda confessed, and although he had limited reading skills and did not complete high school, he signed a written confession.

Miranda's written confession was admitted into evidence at trial. The jury found Miranda guilty, and he was sentenced to 20–30 years in prison.

Miranda appealed his conviction to the Supreme Court of Arizona, citing a prior US Supreme Court case, Escobedo v. Illinois (1964), which recognized a suspect's right to an attorney during police interrogation. The Court ruled that suspects must formally request an attorney (i.e., make a clear and unequivocal statement) (Escobedo v. Illinois, 1964). The Supreme Court of Arizona held Miranda's conviction and decided that his constitutional rights were not violated because he did not specifically ask for a lawyer. Attorney Robert Corcoran of the Phoenix chapter of the American Civil Liberties Union took an interest in Miranda's case and contacted trial lawyer John J. Flynn. Flynn contacted constitutional law expert John P. Frank. Flynn, and Frank appealed Miranda's case to the US Supreme Court.

Issue: Whether interrogating suspects without informing them of their Fifth and Sixth Amendment rights renders their statements and confessions inadmissible.

Outcome: The US Supreme Court held that the prosecution could not use suspects' statements obtained by the police while in custody unless the police had complied with several procedural safeguards to secure the Fifth Amendment privilege against self-incrimination and the Sixth Amendment right to have an attorney present. The US Supreme Court reversed Miranda's conviction and granted him a new trial.

Impact of Miranda on Police Interrogations

Failing to issue Miranda warnings could lead to the suppression of statements or confessions as evidence. The Court affirmed the Miranda decision in Dickerson v. United States (2000). Dickerson was indicted for federal robbery-related crimes and gave voluntary statements to the Federal Bureau of Investigation (FBI). He later requested his statements be suppressed because the FBI did not give him a Miranda warning. The District Court agreed with Dickerson and granted the motion to suppress his statements. Because police must now issue Miranda warnings prior to interrogations, limiting their ability to obtain information, police often use tactics to convince suspects to waive their Miranda rights and that it is in their best interest to speak with the police (Leo, 1992). Interrogations are inherently adversarial, as Step 9 of the Reid is to persuade the suspect to sign a statement to submit to the prosecutor. However, the Reid "conceals" this adversarial role and makes police appear helpful, which is a more effective approach (Kim, 2017). As shown in steps 4–7 of the Reid, interrogators appear to "help" suspects by allowing them to "morally justify" their actions.

A controversial tactic is when interrogators use deceit during interrogations to strengthen their accusation. For example, they may use the "false evidence ploy" by presenting the suspect with evidence (e.g., eyewitness identification, fingerprint) when such evidence does not exist. Deception is permitted during interrogations after the Frazier v. Cupp (1969) decision. Martin E. Frazier and his cousin, Jerry Lee Rawls, were interrogated separately about the murder of Russell Anton Marleau. Frazier denied any involvement, but police falsely told him that Rawls had implicated him. Frazier then began speaking to the police and confessed. Frazier appealed to the US Supreme Court that his Fourth, Fifth, and Sixth Amendments were violated. The Court ruled, among other decisions, that deceptive interrogation tactics did not render a confession inadmissible. However, Joseph P. Buckley, President of John E. Reid and Associates, cautions that this should only be used as a last resort, as it can result in a loss of credibility (Buckley, 2021).

The Reid manual has been updated over the years to stay consistent with legal requirements and Miranda rights and is now in its fifth edition (Inbau et al., 2013). However, the Reid is not without criticism for its psychological tactics that "deceive" suspects into confessing (e.g., Gudjonsson, 2018; Gudjonsson & Pearse, 2011; Leo, 2009). In response to such criticism, Louis C. Senese, Vice President of John E. Reid, clarified that some interrogators claim they are using the Reid, when, in fact, they have not been properly trained and are not abiding by the core principles. The core principles include: do not make promises of leniency, do not make threats of inevitable consequences, provide the opportunity to satisfy their physical needs, exercise special cautions with juveniles or those with mental or psychological impairments, and always treat individuals with dignity and respect (Senese, 2023). (*see* Chapter 2, the Case of Anthony, for an example of an interrogation of an autistic man[3] where police did not abide by these principles).

Waiving Miranda and Miranda Comprehension

Although suspects have the right not to answer any questions, many do not exercise their rights. Leo (1996) observed 182 interrogations and discovered that only 22% of suspects exercised their Miranda rights. Detectives may de-emphasize warnings; for instance, they may blend them into a conversation or read them quickly (Leo, 1996). The two most common interrogation tactics Leo found were (1) making suspects feel it is in their best interest and (2) making suspects feel their cooperation is important. In a few cases, police continued questioning after the suspect invoked their rights to learn "what really happened" (Leo, 1996, p. 276). Other reasons why people waive

Miranda rights are that people do not want to appear uncooperative or defiant, and innocent suspects want to show they have nothing to hide. Guilty suspects do not want to appear "guilty" and instead want to appear cooperative (Kassin & Norwick, 2004).

Suspects may waive their Miranda rights because they do not fully comprehend them, or the warning may be written in a manner that is beyond a suspect's reading level. Rogers et al., (2007a, 2007b) compared 560 Miranda warnings across the US and found tremendous variability among them. Specifically, some language in the Miranda warnings was simple to comprehend (2nd to 3rd-grade reading level), whereas some required a postgraduate education level to fully comprehend. Others may not fully understand them or the consequences of waiving their rights. Rogers et al. (2010) measured Miranda comprehension among 119 college students and 149 pretrial defendants by administering the Miranda Quiz. The Miranda Quiz is a self-report questionnaire of 25 true–false statements about the four components of the Miranda Warning and common misconceptions. They found little difference between college students and pretrial defendants' knowledge of Miranda except in two areas: college students had a slightly better understanding of the risks of talking, whereas pretrial defendants had a better understanding of free legal services. Overall, many believed incorrect information about Miranda. Specifically, 52% believed statements they make "off the record" cannot be used against them, 30% believed that remaining silent was incriminating, 25% believed a Miranda waiver must be signed to be valid, 13% believed they could retract past deceptive statements without consequence, and 9% believed they would be "punished" for remaining silent (Rogers et al., 2010). False assumptions about Miranda warnings and the inability to comprehend them become problematic when innocent persons naively waive their Miranda rights and are subjected to interrogations, placing them at risk of giving incriminating statements or even false statements (Leo, 1996).

Juvenile Interrogations and Perceptions of Custody. Miranda only applies when suspects are in custody, and whether juveniles can determine whether they are in "custody" remains questionable and raises ethical concerns, particularly in a school setting. This was addressed in the case of J.D.B. v. North Carolina) (2011), where the US Supreme Court recognized that children are vulnerable to custodial pressures and the coercive techniques of police interrogations. However, the US Supreme Court has yet to implement minimal safeguards and protections for children during interrogations (Jacobi & Clafton, 2024).

Case Brief: J.D.B. v. North Carolina (2011)

Facts: Thirteen-year-old J.D.B was in the seventh grade and receiving special education instruction. While in school, J.D.B. was escorted out of class to a conference room by a school resource officer, where the assistant principal, another school administrator, and police investigator Joseph DiCostanzo were waiting for him. J.D.B was questioned about two home break-ins days earlier where a digital camera was stolen. A digital camera was found at the school, and witnesses claimed they saw J.D.B with a camera. J.D.B was questioned for 30 to 45 minutes about the break-ins and a stolen camera. Prior to questioning, DiCostanzo did not give J.D.B. Miranda warnings or the opportunity to call his grandmother (his legal guardian) or tell him he was free to leave. J.D.B. first denied his involvement, but DiCostanzo pressed him for additional information and confronted him about a stolen camera. The assistant principal urged J.D.B. to tell the truth, and J.D.B. gave a statement, admitting he and his friends were involved in the break-ins.

J.D.B. was petitioned with break-in and entering and larceny. His defense attorney sought to suppress his statement and any evidence gathered from his statement because he was in police custody when he was interrogated, and the police had failed to give him a Miranda warning. The court admitted his statement and adjudicated him delinquent. The North Carolina Court of Appeals and State Supreme Court affirmed this decision and declined to find J.D.B.'s age relevant to determine whether he was in police custody. His case was appealed to the US Supreme Court.

Issue: Whether a child's age was relevant to the determination of whether one is in custody during police questioning.

Outcome: The US Supreme Court decided that police must consider a juvenile's age when determining whether the juvenile is in custody and when Miranda applied. The US Supreme Court reversed the judgment of the North Carolina Supreme Court and remanded the case to the lower court to determine whether, considering his age, J.D.B. was in custody when he was interrogated.

False Confessions

The number of suspects who provide false confessions is impossible to determine, as departments usually do not maintain records of the total number of interrogated suspects. Of those that do, they do not maintain records of the total number of true confessions, no confessions, or false confessions (National Registry of Exonerations, 2015). False confessions are typically identified after new evidence is presented that exonerated someone accused of or convicted of a crime. The National Registry of Exonerations (NRE) provides the best-known estimates of false confessions. The NRE is a joint effort of the University of California Irvine Newkirk Center for Science & Society, The University of Michigan Law School, and Michigan State University College of Law. NRE tracks cases of individuals who have been wrongfully convicted and exonerated since 1989. As of December 31, 2024, the NRE has identified 3,633 people who have been exonerated since 1989, and 458 of those reported to have allegedly[4] falsely confessed to the crime (NRE, 2024b).

Types of False Confessions

Most find it difficult to comprehend why someone would confess to a crime they did not do. Kassin (2007) documented and explained three general types of false confessions. One type is a **voluntary false confession**, where individuals confess or provide false statements without being prompted by the police. Sometimes, these individuals cover up or take the blame for the person who actually committed the crime, who may be a friend, family member, or co-defendant (Willard et al., 2016). Two other types of false confessions involve coercion resulting from a suspect's reaction to custodial pressures. One type is the **coerced-compliant** false confession, which occurs when a suspect confesses, often for short-term gains, such as ending the stress of the interrogation or gaining an implied reward (e.g., being allowed to sleep, eat, or leave) (Kassin, 2007). The stress of interrogation and confinement can lead some suspects to focus on the short-term gains of confessing (e.g., ending the interrogation or being able to go home) and not the long-term consequences (Gudjonsson, 2018).

The second type is **coerced-internalized** false confessions, which usually involve a vulnerable suspect with a malleable memory due to, for example, young age, naiveté, suggestibility, intellectual disability, fatigue, or alcohol or substance use. Kassin (2007) described the process of internalization and the five components that are often found in coerced-internalized false confessions: (1) the suspect has certain dispositions that make them suspectable to police manipulation (e.g., young, low IQ) or factors associated with custody (e.g., isolation, sleep deprivation), (2) the police present "indisputable" evidence (e.g., failed polygraph, eyewitness), (3) the suspect believes they have blocked out the memory of the crime (e.g., history of blackouts due to substance or alcohol use disorder), (4) the suspect makes a tentative admission (e.g., "I may have done it"), or (5) **confabulation.** Confabulation is a memory processing problem in which people replace memory gaps with imaginary experiences they believe to be true. Confabulations may include distortions (i.e., changes) in details of an existing memory or fabrications, a new or novel memory or element to the narrative (Gudjonsson, 2018). Confabulation may be facilitated by interrogators using imaginational exercises (e.g., "Think hard about how you would have done it") (Kassin, 2007, p. 176). It may also occur when a suspect adds more details to their statement with the help of secondhand sources (e.g., crime scene photos and overheard conversations) (Kassin, 2007, p. 176). Making accusations and using deception, coupled with the vulnerabilities of those who lack cognitive capacity, experience confusion, or disorganized thoughts, places them at greater risk of implicating themselves or giving false information (Haney-Caron et al., 2018; Redlich et al., 2010).

Age and Mental Status

Juveniles, individuals with disabilities and mental illness are overrepresented among identified false confessions (National Registry of Exonerations, 2022), particularly for serious crimes that often come with long prison sentences (Mogavero, 2020). After reviewing 2,378 cases of those exonerated for murder, rape, and child sexual abuse, 310 (13%) allegedly falsely confessed to their crime, and among those, nearly 36% had a mental or intellectual disability,[5] and more than 36% were minors under 18 (Mogavero, 2020). Figure 9.1 shows data from those who were exonerated and the percentage who provided false confessions. Those with evidence of a mental or intellectual disability and younger adolescents have significantly more false confessions in their exoneration cases than adults and those without a mental or intellectual disability.

Suspect Memory

One explanation for the high rates of false confessions among those with mental or intellectual disabilities is a phenomenon called "**memory distrust syndrome**." Gudjonsson and MacKeith (1982) coined this to explain why suspects can be persuaded to believe they might have committed a crime when police challenge their memory and create doubt of their innocence. According to Gudjonsson and MacKeith (1982), one's inability to trust one's memory is often due to a previous memory impairment. Those most vulnerable to "memory distrust syndrome" are those who lack confidence in their memory (e.g., have a disability that affects memory and cognition, or misuse

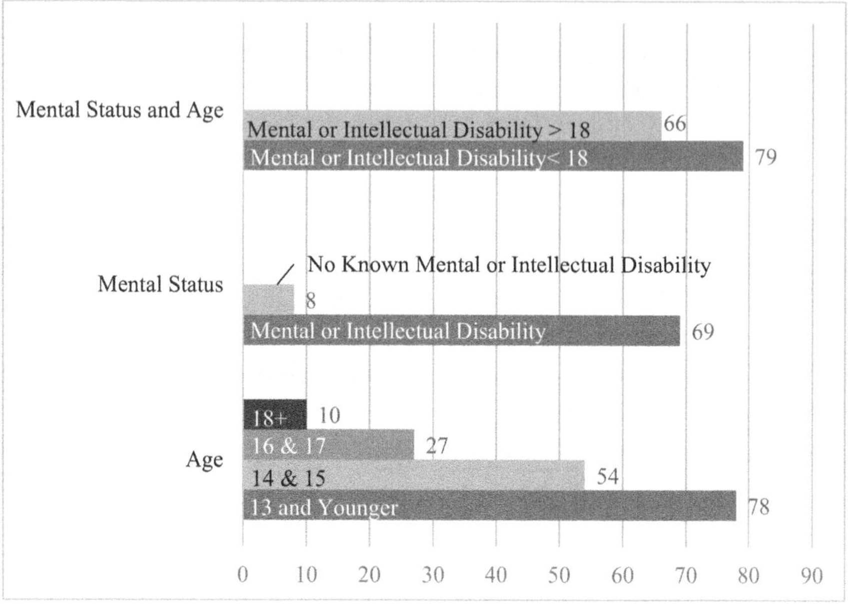

Fig. 9.1 Age and mental status of 3060 exonerees and the percentage who gave false confessions (*Source* National Registry of Exonerations [2022])

substances and experience "blackouts") or are more trustworthy of the police accounts or suggestions as to what happened (Gudjonsson, 2018).

Suggestibility

Juveniles and other populations are more susceptible to interrogative pressure during formal interviews, known as **interrogative suggestibility**, and may provide misleading information (Gudjonsson, 1984). Gudjonsson (1984) developed the Gudjonsson Suggestibility Scale (GSS1), which is a well-established forensic tool for measuring interrogative suggestibility and predicting one's likelihood of providing false or misleading statements. Another form of the GSS was developed in 1987, referred to as the GSS2. The GSS2 has a less complex narrative and is commonly used with children or adults with disabilities. The GSS1 and GSS2 consist of reading a story aloud, and then individuals are asked to freely recall as much as they can remember. After a 50-minute delay, individuals are asked again to freely recall as much as they can and then asked 20 questions, 15 of which are leading (i.e., misleading). Individuals are provided clear, firm, negative feedback on their responses (i.e., they have made several errors). Then, the questions are repeated to determine if they change their responses to be more "accurate" (Gudjonsson, 1984, 1987). There are four suggestibility scores: Yield 1, a first-round measure of all leading questions, with possible scores ranging from 0 to 15; Yield 2, a second-round measure of all leading questions after given negative feedback, with possible scores ranging from 0 to 15; and Shift, a measure of any changes in responses to all 20 questions in the second round, with possible scores ranging from 0 to 20. Total suggestibility is the sum of Yield 1 and Shift (scores range from 0–35). Gudjonsson (1989) also developed the Gudjonsson Compliance Scale (GCS), which consists of 20 true–false questions (e.g., "I give in easily to people when I am pressured," "I find it very difficult to tell people when I disagree with them" p. 540).

Juveniles have been shown to be more suggestible than adults, as evidenced by GSS measures. Frumkin et al. (2012) administered the GSS1 to 334 individuals referred by courts throughout the US (80% were in Florida) specifically to assess confession-related issues. They compared the results of 102 juveniles aged 16 and younger and 231 adults (17 and older) and assessed their vulnerability to provide false statements. The results showed that juveniles had higher GSS scores than adults (average scores of 14 vs. 12) and changed their responses more often when given negative feedback (Frumkin et al., 2012).

The GSS was also used to demonstrate interrogative suggestibility among those with neurodevelopmental disorders (NDDs). North et al. (2007) administered the GSS2 and the GCS to 26 autistic and 27 typically developed adults matched on gender and IQ scores. On the GSS2, the autistic individuals scored similarly to the typically developed individuals (average scores of 5.5 vs. 6), but their scores on the GCS were different, showing higher compliance among autistic individuals (average scores of 13 vs. 8). These results suggest that autistic individuals may be more eager to please and may change their responses to comply to avoid conflict or confrontation (North et al., 2007). Giostra and Vagni (2024) administered the GSS2 to 40 children with mild ID (average IQ of 65), 40 with borderline ID (average IQ of 78), and 40 typically developed children (average IQ of 104) between the ages of 7 and 16. The results showed that the children with mild ID had the highest number of errors and confabulations, and the children with both borderline and mild ID were equally likely to change their responses when given negative feedback. Children with both mild and borderline ID had similar GSS scores (average scores of 15.25 vs. 15.28) and were much higher than the typically developed children (average scores of 6.6). Similar to autistic individuals, those with ID may give answers they believe the interviewer wants to hear (Giostra & Vagni, 2024; North et al., 2007). Not knowing the answer to a question may also cause anxiety, and individuals may fabricate an answer rather than say, "I don't know," in fear that they might be reprimanded.

An important distinction to make with false confessions is that it is not one factor that necessarily "causes" one to falsely confess to a crime they did not commit but a cumulation of factors. Scherr et al. (2020) describe these factors in a framework they developed, which they collectively termed cumulative disadvantage. The cumulative disadvantage framework describes how once an innocent person is identified as a suspect (often coupled with a vulnerability such as young age, naivete, disability, etc.), and there is a presumption of guilt, it leads to a "domino effect." This effect may influence the gathering of evidence, forensic analysis, and pressures to enter into guilty pleas. Cumulative disadvantage can be seen in the high-profile 1989 Central Park Five case, where five teens were identified as suspects in violent sexual assault. The teens were young, ranging from 14 to 16 years of age, were racial/ethnic minorities, and were of lower socioeconomic status. The teens endured harsh and unethical police interrogation tactics, co-suspects falsely implicated one another, prosecutor misconduct, and false/misleading forensic evidence was admitted at trial, which ultimately led to their wrongful convictions. Netflix's true-crime documentary *When They See Us*, produced by DuVernay et al. (2019), covered the Central Park Five case, exposing the bias within the criminal justice system (CJS) and the vulnerability of juveniles in police custody.

The Central Park 5 Case

Offense: On the evening of April 19, 1989, a series of violent assaults (referred to as "wilding") occurred in New York City's Central Park. One man, John Loughlin was knocked to the ground, kicked, hit with a pipe, and robbed of his Walkman. Several hours later, around 1:30 am on April 20, two men walking in the park found an unconscious woman, 29-year-old Trisha Meili. Meili had been bound with her T-shirt, brutally beaten, and raped. Police immediately attributed the violent sexual assault to the earlier "wilding" incident (NRE, 2024a).

Custody and Interrogations: Officers interviewed all identifiable suspects who were in Central Park that evening and arrested them for unlawful assembly. Several teens, including 14-year-old Raymond Santana and 14-year-old Kevin Richardson, were taken to the Central Park Precinct. When Richardson was interviewed, he mentioned his friend, Antron McCray, who was later questioned with his mother. The police questioned 16-year-old Korey Wise without his parents because of his age.[6] Wise had a learning disability and hearing loss, and 15-year-old Yusef Salaam was also questioned without his parents because the police stated that Salaam claimed he was 16 years old. All five teens gave statements to police, either implicating themselves or another in the rape and attack on Meili (NRE, 2024a).

Forensic Evidence: Police searched the crime scene and found blood on a rock and hair and semen on one of Meili's socks, which was a genetic match from a cervical swab from the rape kit. The DNA of the semen was compared against the DNA samples of the five teens, and all were excluded as a match. The hair found on the sock was examined under a microscope and found to be inconsistent with the five teens. The police also examined the teens' clothing and found hairs on Richardson's clothes that were consistent with Meili's. Twelve hairs were found on Lopez's clothes, and one was said to be consistent with Meili (NRE, 2024a).

On May 4, 1989, the five teens were indicted for the assault and the rape of Meili. Before trial, all five moved to suppress their statements to the police. Wise claimed that police had slapped and threatened him while in custody. Salaam disputed that he had told police he was 15 years old and claimed that he should never have been questioned without a parent. Wise and Salaam also claimed their Miranda rights had not been adequately explained. Justice Thomas Galligan of the New York County Supreme Court denied these motions (NRE, 2024a).

Trial: McCray, Santana, and Salaam went to trial first, beginning June 25, 1990. All three were charged as juveniles for robbery, assault, and first-degree riot. They were adjudicated and sentenced to 5 and 10 years. Richardson and Wise went to trial next, beginning October 22, 1990. Richardson was charged as a juvenile, and on December 11, 1990, the jury adjudicated Richardson of attempted murder, rape, sodomy, and robbery and sentenced him to 5 to 10 years. Wise was charged as an adult and was found guilty of first-degree assault, first-degree sexual abuse, and first-degree riot and sentenced to 5 to 15 years in prison. Salaam, McCray, Wise, and Richardson all unsuccessfully appealed their convictions (Innocence Project, 2024a; b; c; d; NRE, 2024a).

Exonerations: Wise was incarcerated at Auburn Correctional Facility in New York, and in 2001, he met Matias Reyes. Reyes was serving a sentence of 33 years to life for robbery, rape, and murder. In early 2002, Reyes told a prison official that he sexually assaulted Meili, and this statement was forwarded to the New York County District Attorney's Office. Evidence from Reyes' convictions was sent to the FBI lab and compared against the DNA evidence in Meili's case. On May 8, 2002, the prosecutors in New York were informed that Reyes was a DNA match to semen found on the sock at the crime scene, and later testing revealed his DNA matched the hair found on Meili's sock. When presented with the DNA evidence, Reyes pled guilty to the sexual assault on Meili. Based on this new evidence, all five (now adults) filed motions requesting a judge to vacate their convictions. On December 19, 2002, New York County Supreme Court Justice Charles Tejada vacated the convictions and dismissed the charges; all five were officially exonerated (NRE, 2024a).

Considerations and Recommendations

Although most police officers conduct ethical interrogations (Beyer & Herndon, 2018; Kassin et al., 2007), some are not properly trained or use unethical methods (Senese, 2023). Improper methods may inadvertently lead suspects to provide inaccurate information or even a false confession. Considering the "domino effect" improper interrogations can have in the cumulative disadvantage framework (Scherr et al., 2020), greater caution must be used when questioning juveniles, those with mental illness or disabilities. Below are several considerations and recommendations for CJS practitioners and best practices for those requiring accommodations.

Training and Education on Mental Health, Disabilities, and Adolescents

Comprehensive training specific to the cognition of adolescents, those with mental illness and disabilities, including autism and ID, should be standard for all CJS professionals. Training to better understand common behaviors exhibited by neurodiverse individuals (e.g., lack of eye contact, delayed responses) can help prevent them from being misinterpreted as deception. Some with mental illness have lower stress tolerance and may confess (true or false) to escape the stressful environment of an interrogation. Those with cognitive limitations may respond "yes" to questions, regardless of whether they are true, and may require open-ended questions to receive more accurate information (Follette et al., 2018). They also require simpler questions that are not leading or misleading. A review of seven studies with a total of 1,199 individuals with ID consistently showed that they experienced confusion, had difficulty understanding information while in police custody, and required simpler language during questioning (Gulati et al., 2020). Autistic individuals may repeat statements back to police, referred to as **echolalia**, which may give police the impression that they understand what was said or could be misconstrued as disrespect (Maras, 2021). Training to better recognize signs of disabilities or mental impairments and training in communication skills can improve their ability to obtain accurate information and know what special provisions to take.

Interviewing with an Appropriate Adult

Minors and those with mental illness or disabilities may not fully understand their Miranda rights. Autistic individuals are often literal or "concrete thinkers" and may not understand "waving your rights" and may interpret it as "waving your right hand" (D. Debbaudt, personal communication, March 4, 2016). Once a disability or mental health condition that may affect comprehension is identified, police should cease all questioning until a parent or guardian (if available) and an attorney are present. However, having parents present alone may be insufficient if they, too, do not understand Miranda rights or the consequences of waiving them, as parents often encourage their children to waive their rights and confess (Viljoen et al., 2005; Woolard et al., 2008).

Assumptions of Comprehension

Many individuals with disabilities, such as ID, cannot comprehend the details of the Miranda warning or the context in which interrogation occurs (e.g., any statements can be used against them) (Cloud et al., 2002). A more comprehendible version of Miranda Warnings should be provided for juveniles and those with mental health conditions or disabilities. Many individuals with disabilities may initially present as though they understand when they do not, as they have learned to model the behaviors of others (i.e., masking) to avoid any stigma or mistreatment. They may present well and display "street smarts" because they do not want to appear unintelligent when they do not understand something (Kranendonk et al., 2019). Juveniles and those with disabilities may be able to repeat information but unable to do so in their own words. Although not required, Kranendonk et al. (2019) and Sperry et al. (2020) recommended that juveniles and those with disabilities should paraphrase statements back to the police in their own words to ensure comprehension. Similarly, for those with mental illness or other cognitive disabilities, simply asking, "Do you understand what I just said?" is not a valid way to assess comprehension, and open-ended questions (requiring the respondent to formulate their own response) are more effective (Follette et al., 2018, p. 110). If there is any question that the suspect does not adequately comprehend their Miranda Rights, questioning should resume when an attorney or an appropriate adult is present.

Reconsider School Interrogations

Questioning or interrogating children in school, regardless of age, should be avoided unless absolutely necessary. School is an environment that encourages obedience to authority and rules, and disciplinary action is evoked when a student disobeys authority or does not follow the rules. School attendance is compulsory, which, by default, puts them in "custody," as they are not free to leave school grounds. In this environment, juveniles may feel obligated to speak with police or even feel compelled to waive their Miranda rights. As in the case of J.D.B. v. North Carolina (2011), some juveniles have difficulty distinguishing what it means to be in "custody," particularly when school administrators are also present. If deemed necessary, police must exercise greater caution to ensure Miranda protections (Jacobi & Clafton, 2024; Spierer, 2017).

Avoid Misleading Tactics

When conducted properly, the Reid method complies with state and federal requirements, and Buckley (2022) and Senese (2023) detail the principles of conducting proper interviews and interrogations. Police must consider a suspect's age, mental status, and cognitive abilities associated with various conditions when determining interrogation or questioning tactics. Police should avoid using certain misleading directive interrogation tactics, such as "implying" leniency or "threatening" with consequences, which is prohibited in Reid (Reid et al., 2013; Buckley, 2022), particularly for juveniles and persons with disabilities (Spierer, 2017). Building fake trust and concealing the adversarial role to suggestible populations can be confusing and interpreted as coercive, as they may genuinely believe the interrogator is there to help them, not arrest them.

Consider Communication Barriers

When police speak with someone with autism, communication disorders, or reading difficulties, certain provisions must be implemented, beginning with the initial contact, questioning (to ensure accurate accounts of crimes are obtained), and appropriate representation. Communication provisions may include using assistive technology when necessary, eliminating or reducing distracting noise or other visual stimuli, and limiting the number of interviews or reducing their length (Edworthy & Hylton, 2010; Henry et al., 2017).

Video/Audio Recording

Although video/audio recording of interrogations has been customary practice for decades, some interrogations are not recorded for several reasons. All interviews and interrogations must be video recorded from the start of questioning until the end (not simply the confession). This way, any questions about misleading or coercive techniques can be reviewed later. Confessions from persons with mental illness or disabilities should be evaluated by experts for reliability (Gudjonsson, 2018).

Consider the Alternative Methods

Buckley (2021) cautions against using the Reid on naïve individuals, including juveniles and those with mental illness and disabilities. For interrogations of the above populations, the PEACE (Planning and preparation, Engage and explain, obtain an Account, Closure, and Evaluation) method, used in the United Kingdom since 1993 and has been adopted worldwide, should be considered instead. PEACE seeks the same goals as the Reid and preserves one's Constitutional Rights, but deception, minimizing the offense, or any coercive tactics are prohibited. Further, PEACE is more conversational, and interviewers first develop a plan and prepare questions, as the goal is to gather information for the investigation (as opposed to getting a confession). PEACE is less confrontational and accusatory and more conversational, with a focus on planning and the goal of gathering information for the investigation (as opposed to getting a confession) (Chapman, 2013; Schatz, 2018; Spierer, 2017).

Conclusion

Questioning and interrogating suspects are vital components of an investigation, which require cooperation. Suspect confessions provide powerful evidence for prosecutors and hold considerable weight in influencing jury verdicts (Costanzo et al., 2010; Leo & Davis, 2010). Police presenting themselves as aggressive or intimidating demeanor is not an effective way to obtain information. As Luitentant Dr. Louden recommends, police must be calm and empathic, regardless of what suspects are accused of. As the Central Park Five Case showed, aggressive tactics can elicit false information, which can lead to wrongful convictions. Wrongful convictions not only devastate lives but those who are a threat to the public, like Matias Reyes, are allowed to remain free to offend again.

For 60 years, preserving one's Fifth and Sixth Amendment Rights has been the policy of law. Yet, few exercise these rights, primarily due to believing one must obey authority, fear of appearing guilty or uncooperative, or simply not fully understanding these rights. For young people and others who are suggestable, these reasons are even more prevalent due to decreased assertiveness or cognitive ability to understand the long-term consequences of waving their rights. Not exercising one's rights and not having an appropriate adult present when being questioned or interrogated by police can have devastating consequences. The Reid is problematic when used with susceptible populations with "hidden disabilities," such as those with mental illness, disabilities such as autism or ID, or a combination. Interrogation techniques that include accusations or misleading questions may confuse those with mental or intellectual disabilities. Using such techniques, coupled with vulnerabilities and susceptibilities (e.g., confusion and disorganized thoughts), places them at greater risk of rendering a false confession (Haney-Caron et al., 2018; Redlich et al., 2010).

Police must take great care when interviewing suspects with limited capacity to understand their rights and the consequences of waving them. Taking the "minimal" required precautions or code of conduct is insufficient. Defense attorneys must also ensure due diligence and confirm that all statements were ethically obtained. Additional precautions and a stricter code of conduct are necessary. Defense attorneys can also challenge confession evidence by hiring mental health professionals to conduct evaluations and present such evidence to the court. These assessments can inform judgments of the voluntariness of statements and the vulnerability of the person who confessed during the interrogation (Follette et al., 2018).[7]

Key Terms

Confabulation
Voluntary false confession
Coerced-compliant false confession
Coerced-internalized false confessions

Interrogative Suggestibility
Interview
Interrogation
Memory Distrust Syndrome
Miranda Warning
PEACE Method
Reid Technique

Chapter Questions

1) Describe the difference between an interview and a custodial interrogation.
2) Describe the three types of false confessions and provide an example of each.
3) Why is it important to avoid using the Reid method on juveniles or those with disabilities?
4) Summarize each part of Miranda Warning in your own words (without looking). Then, after comparing your summary to the Miranda warning, how accurate was your summary?
5) How can police ensure that interrogations are conducted fairly and ethically?

Suggested Readings

Garrett, B. L. (2011). *Convicting the innocent*. Harvard University Press.

Rogers, R., Harrison, K. S., Hazelwood, L. L., & Sewell, K. W. (2007a). Knowing and intelligent: A study of Miranda warnings in mentally disordered defendants. *Law & Human Behavior, 31*(4), 401–418. https://doi.org/10.1007/s10979-006-9070-8

Sangero, B. (2007). Miranda is not enough: A new justification for demanding "strong corroboration" to a confession. *Cardozo Law Review, 28*(6), 101–138. https://ssrn.com/abstract=1651471

Scherr, K. C., & Madon, S. (2013). "Go ahead and sign": An experimental examination of Miranda waivers and comprehension. *Law & Human Behavior, 37*(3), 209–218. https://doi.org/10.1037/lhb0000026

Scott-Hayward, C. (2007). Explaining juvenile false confessions: Adolescent development and police interrogation. *Law & Psychology Review, 31*, 53–76. https://ssrn.com/abstract=1802884

Notes

1. Chapter 13 pp. 185–328 contains the full detail of these 9 steps.
2. Also referred to as willfully.
3. *see A Note About Evolving Language and Term i*n Chapter 1 for information on identity-first language.
4. Of the 458, 148 were exonerated by DNA evidence.
5. diagnosis of ID, developmental disability, low IQ, learning disability, traumatic brain injury, diagnosed with mental illness, history of psychiatric hospitalization.
6. In New York, at 16 one was considered an adult.
7. Some assessments, such as the GSS do not meet evidentiary standards of Frye or Daubert in some states (Willner, 2011) (s*ee* Chapter 13 of this book for more details).

References

Beyer, B. J., & Herndon, J. (2018). Interrogative specialists and false confessions: Debunking the con artist myth. *Journal of Police and Criminal Psychology, 33*(3), 233–243. https://doi.org/10.1007/s11896-018-9263-3

Brown v. Mississippi, 297 U.S. 278 (1936).

Buckley, J. P. (2021). *False confessions: The issues to be considered.* https://reid.com/resources/investigator-tips/false-confessions-the-issues-to-be-considered

Buckley, J. P. (2022). *Principles of practice: How to conduct proper investigative interviews and interrogations.* https://reid.com/resources/investigator-tips/principles-of-practice-how-to-conduct-proper-investigative-interviews-and-interrogations

Chapman, F. E. (2013). Coerced internalized false confessions and police interrogations: The power of coercion. *Law & Psychology Review, 37*(1), 159–192. https://doi.org/10.2139/ssrn.2467049

Cloud, M., Shepherd, G. B., Barkoff, A. N., & Shur, J. V. (2002). Words without meaning: The constitution, confessions, and mentally retarded suspects. *The University of Chicago Law Review, 69*(2), 495–624. https://doi.org/10.2307/1600500

Costanzo, M., Shaked-Schroer, N., & Vinson, K. (2010). Juror beliefs about police interrogations, false confessions, and expert testimony. *Journal of Empirical Legal Studies, 7*(2), 231–247. https://doi.org/10.1111/j.1740-1461.2010.01177.x

Debbaudt, D., (2004). Beyond guilt or innocence, forum paper published by Autism New Zealand Inc. https://www.autismriskmanagement.com

Dickerson v. United States, 530 U.S. 428 (2000).

DuVernay, A., Skoll, J., King, J., Rosenthal, J., De Niro, R., Welsh, B., & Winfrey, O. (Producers). (2019). When they see us. [TV series]. Netflix Films.

Edworthy, A., & Hylton, C. (2010). Brain-injured children and the police. *Journal of Learning Disabilities and Offending Behaviour, 1*(3), 40–48. https://doi.org/10.5042/jldob.2010.0628

Escobedo v. Illinois, 78 U.S. 478 (1964).

Follette, W. C., Leo, R. A., & Davis, D. (2018). False confessions. In E. Kelley (Ed.), *Representing people with mental disabilities: A criminal defense lawyer's best practices manual* (pp. 95–124). ABA Publishing.

Frazier v. Cupp, 394 U.S. 731 (1969).

Frumkin, I. B., Lally, S. J., & Sexton, J. E. (2012). A United States forensic sample for the Gudjonsson Suggestibility Scales. *Behavioral Sciences and the Law, 30*(6), 749–763. https://doi.org/10.1002/bsl.2032

Gudjonsson, G. H. (1984). A new scale of interrogative suggestibility. *Personality and Individual Differences, 5*(3), 53–58. https://doi.org/10.1016/0191-8869(84)90069-2

Gudjonsson, G. H. (1987). A parallel form of the Gudjonsson Suggestibility Scale. *British Journal of Clinical Psychology, 26*(3), 215–221. https://doi.org/10.1111/j.2044-8260.1987.tb01348.x

Gudjonsson, G. H. (1989). Compliance in an interrogative situation: A new scale. *Personality and Individual Differences, 10*(5), 535–540. https://doi.org/10.1016/0191-8869(89)90035-4

Gudjonsson, G. H. (2018). *The psychology of false confessions: Forty years of science and practice.* John Wiley & Sons.

Gudjonsson, G. H., & MacKeith, J. A. C. (1982). False confessions: Psychological effects of interrogation. A Discussion Paper. In A. Trankell (Ed.), *Reconstructing the past: The role of psychologists in criminal trials* (pp. 53–269). Kluwer.

Gudjonsson, G. H., & Pearse, J. (2011). Suspect interviews and false confessions. *Current Directions in Psychological Science, 20*(1), 33–37. https://doi.org/10.1177/0963721410396824

Gulati, G., Cusack, A., Kelly, B. D., Kilcommins, S., & Dunne, C. P. (2020). Experiences of people with intellectual disabilities encountering law enforcement officials as the suspects of crime-A narrative systematic review. *International Journal of Law and Psychiatry, 71*, Article 101609. https://doi.org/10.1016/j.ijlp.2020.101609

Haney-Caron, E., Goldstein, N. E. S., & Mesiarik, C. (2018). Self-perceived likelihood of false confession: A comparison of justice-involved juveniles and adults. *Criminal Justice and Behavior, 45*(12), 1955–1976. https://doi.org/10.1177/0093854818799806

Henry, L. A., Crane, L., Nash, G., Hobson, Z., Kirke-Smith, M., & Wilcock, R. (2017). Verbal, visual, and intermediary support for child witnesses with autism during investigative interview. *Journal of Autism and Developmental Disorders, 47*, 2348–2362. https://doi.org/10.1007/s10803-017-3142-0

Horgan, A. J., Russano, M. B., Meissner, C. A., & Evans, J. R. (2012). Minimization and maximization techniques: Assessing the perceived consequences of confessing and confession diagnosticity. *Psychology, Crime & Law, 18*(1), 65–78. https://doi.org/10.1080/1068316X.2011.561801

Inbau, F.E., Reid, J.E., Buckley, J.P., & Jayne, B.C. (2013). *Criminal interrogation and confessions* (5th ed.). Jones and Bartlett Publishers.

Innocence Project. (2024a). *Antron McCray*. https://innocenceproject.org/cases/antron-mccray/

Innocence Project. (2024b). *Korey Wise*. https://innocenceproject.org/cases/korey-wise/

Innocence Project. (2024c). *Raymond Santana*. https://innocenceproject.org/cases/raymond-santana/

Innocence Project. (2024d). *Yusef Salaam*. https://innocenceproject.org/cases/yusef-salaam/

Jacobi, T., & Clafton, R. (2024). The law of disposable children: Interrogations in schools. *Alabama Law Review, 75*, 1–51. https://doi.org/10.2139/ssrn.4394194

J.D.B. v. North Carolina, 564 U.S. 261 (2011).

Kassin, S. M. (2005). On the psychology of confessions: Does innocence put innocents at risk? *American Psychologist, 60*(3), 215–228. https://doi.org/10.1037/0003-066X.60.3.215

Kassin, S. M. (2007). Internalized false confessions. In M. P. Toglia, J. D. Read, D. Ross, &. R. C. L. Lindsay (Eds.), *The handbook of eyewitness psychology, Vol. 1. Memory for events* (pp. 169–187). Lawrence Erlbaum Associates Publisher.

Kassin, S. M., Leo, R. A., Meissner, C. A., Richman, K. D., Colwell, L. H., Leach, A. M., & La Fon, D. (2007). Police interviewing and interrogation: A self-report survey of police practices and beliefs. *Law & Human Behavior, 31*(4), 381–400. https://doi.org/10.1007/s10979-006-9073-5

Kassin, S. M., & Norwick, R. J. (2004). Why people waive their Miranda rights: The power of innocence. *Law & Human Behavior, 28*(2), 211–221. https://doi.org/10.1023/B:LAHU.0000022323.74584.f5

Kassin, S. M., & Sukel, H. (1997). Coerced confessions and the jury: An experimental test of the "harmless error" rule. *Law and Human Behavior, 21*(1), 27–46. https://doi.org/10.1023/A:1024814009769

Kim, M. (2017). When and why suspects fail to recognize the adversary role of an interrogation America: The problem and solution. *Gonzaga Law Review, 52*(3), 507–539. https://papers.ssrn.com/sol3/papers.cfm?abstract_id=3031422

Kranendonk, R., Malsch, M., de Poot, C., Teeuwen, M., & Elffers, H. (2019). Suspects with intellectual disability in police interviews: Risks of interviewing techniques for the reliability of suspects' statements [Paper Presentation]. American Society of Criminology 75th Annual Meeting, San Francisco, CA. United States, November 13–16.

Leo, R. A. (1992). From coercion to deception: The changing nature of police interrogation in America. *Crime, Law, and Social Change, 18*, 35–59. https://ssrn.com/abstract=1141388act=753084

Leo, R. A. (1996). Miranda's revenge: Police interrogation as a confidence game. *Law and Society Review, 30*(2), 259–288. https://doi.org/10.2307/3053960

Leo, R. A. (2009). False confessions: Causes, consequences, and implications. *Journal of the American Academy of Psychiatry and the Law, 37*(3), 332–343. https://pubmed.ncbi.nlm.nih.gov/19767498/

Leo, R. A., & Davis, D. (2010). From false confession to wrongful conviction: Seven psychological processes. *Journal of Psychiatry & Law, 38*(1–2), 9–56. https://doi.org/10.1177/009318531003800103

Maras, K. (2021). Obtaining testimony from autistic people. In F. R. Volkmar, R. Loftin, A. Westphal, & Woodbury M. Smith, (Eds.), *Handbook of autism spectrum disorder and the law.* Springer. https://doi.org/10.1007/978-3-030-70913-6_7

Miranda v. Arizona, 384 U.S. 436 (1966).

Mogavero, M. C. (2020). An exploratory examination of intellectual disability and mental illness associated with alleged false confessions. *Behavioral Sciences & the Law, 38*(4), 299–316. https://doi.org/10.1002/bsl.2463

National Registry of Exonerations. (2024a). *Korey Wise.* https://www.law.umich.edu/special/exoneration/Pages/casedetail.aspx?caseid=3761

National Registry of Exonerations. (2024b). *Search Exonerations.* https://www.law.umich.edu/special/exoneration/Pages/detaillist.aspx?

National Registry of Exonerations. (2015). *Guilty pleas and confessions.* https://www.law.umich.edu/special/exoneration/Documents/NRE.Guilty.Plea.Article4

National Registry of Exonerations. (2022). Age and mental status of exonerated defendant who confessed. https://www.law.umich.edu/special/exoneration/Pages/False-Confessions.aspx

North, A. S., Russell, A. J., & Gudjonsson, G. H. (2007). High functioning autism spectrum disorders: An investigation of psychological vulnerabilities during interrogative interview. *The Journal of Forensic Psychiatry & Psychology, 19*(3), 323–334. https://doi.org/10.1080/14789940701871621

Perske, R. (2011). False confessions from 53 persons with intellectual disabilities: The list keeps growing. *Intellectual and Developmental Disabilities, 46*(6), 468–479. https://doi.org/10.1352/2008.46:468-479

Redlich, A. D., Summers, A., & Hoover, S. (2010). Self-reported false confessions and guilty pleas among offenders with mental illness. *Law and Human Behavior, 34*(1), 79–90. https://doi.org/10.1007/s10979-009-9194-8

Rogers, R., Harrison, K. S., Hazelwood, L. L., & Sewell, K. W. (2007a). Knowing and intelligent: A study of Miranda warnings in mentally disordered defendants. *Law & Human Behavior, 31*(4), 401–418. https://doi.org/10.1007/s10979-006-9070-8

Rogers, R., Harrison, K. S., Shuman, D. W., Sewell, K. W., & Hazelwood, L. L. (2007b). An analysis of Miranda warnings and waivers: Comprehension and coverage. *Law & Human Behavior, 31*(2), 177–192. https://doi.org/10.1007/s10979-006-9054-8

Rogers, R., Rogstad, J. E., Gillard, N. D., Drogin, E. Y., Blackwood, H. L., & Shuman, D. W. (2010). "Everyone knows their Miranda rights": Implicit assumptions and countervailing evidence. *Psychology, Public Policy, and Law, 16*(3), 300–318. https://doi.org/10.1037/a0019316

Scherr, K. C., Redlich, A. D., & Kassin, S. M. (2020). Cumulative disadvantage: A psychological framework for understanding how innocence can lead to confession, wrongful conviction, and beyond. *Perspectives on Psychological Science: A Journal of the Association for Psychological Science, 15*(2), 353–383. https://doi.org/10.1177/1745691619896608

Senese, L. C. (2023, August 22). Setting the record straight on the Reid Technique. *Police 1.* https://www.police1.com/investigations/articles/setting-the-record-straight-on-the-reid-technique-8wlPwHfQTlk8PhBe/

Schatz, S. J. (2018). Interrogated with intellectual disabilities: The risks of false confession. *Stanford Law Review, 70*(2), 643–690. https://ssrn.com/abstract=3056103

Sperry, L., Hughes, C., & Forsee, M. J. (2020). Vulnerabilities of defendants with ASD and strategies for improving outcomes. In E. Kelley (Ed.), *Representing people autism spectrum disorders: A practical guide for criminal defense lawyer's* (pp. 175–193). ABA Publishing.

Spierer, A. (2017). The right to remain a child: The impermissibility of the Reid technique in juvenile interrogations. *New York University Law Review, 92*, 1719–1750.

Viljoen, J. L., Klaver, J., & Roesch, R. (2005). Legal decisions of preadolescent and adolescent defendants: Predictors of confessions, pleas, communication with attorneys, and appeals. *Law and Human Behavior, 29*(3), 253–277. https://doi.org/10.1007/s10979-005-3613-2

Willard, J., Guyll, M., Madon, S., & Allen, J. E. (2016). Relationship closeness and self-reported willingness to falsely take the blame. *Behavioral Sciences and the Law, 34*(6), 767–783. https://doi.org/10.1002/bsl.2270

Willner, P. (2011). Assessment of capacity to participate in court proceedings: A selective critique and some recommendations. *Psychology, Crime & Law, 17*(2), 117–131. https://doi.org/10.1080/10683160903392400

Woolard, J. L., Cleary, H. M., Harvell, S. A., & Chen, R. (2008). Examining adolescents' and their parents' conceptual and practical knowledge of police interrogation: A family dyad approach. *Journal of Youth and Adolescence, 37*(6), 685–698. https://doi.org/10.1007/s10964-008-9288-5

10

Eyewitness Identifications and Interviews—Addressing the Role of Memory and the Needs of Children and Individuals with Neurodevelopmental Disabilities

Learning Objectives

After this chapter, readers should be able to understand the:

1) Role of memory in eyewitness reports
2) Different procedures for eyewitness identifications
3) Risks of mistaken eyewitness identification and false accusations
4) Cognitive differences among juveniles and those with disabilities in identification procedures and interviews
5) Role of race in identification procedures
6) "Best practices" to safeguard against mistaken eyewitness identification or eyewitness accounts

Introduction

Identification procedures and interviews are essential to investigations but must be conducted properly for the information to be reliable and accurate. Improper procedures can bias or taint a witness' memory, leading to inaccurate accounts or mistaken eyewitness identifications (EWIDs). Interview questions that are leading, biased, or confusing can produce false or misleading information or cause witnesses to change their responses. The accuracy of one's memory can be challenged in court, particularly when

M. C. Mogavero, *Mental Health, Neurodiversity, and Criminal Justice*,
https://doi.org/10.1007/978-3-031-88816-8_10

confirming EWIDs from lineups and photospreads. Child witnesses and witnesses with disabilities are at an increased risk of providing inaccurate information with improper investigation procedures. Added safeguards must be in place for those vulnerable to providing false or misleading information to prevent mistaken EWIDs or impede investigations.

When DNA began exonerating people convicted due to mistaken EWID in the early 1990s, greater attention was drawn to identification procedures conducted by police (Smalarz & Wells, 2014). Considering these wrongful convictions, the American Psychological Association appointed a subcommittee to review the scientific research evidence of EWID. Wells and colleagues published *Eyewitness Identification Procedures: Recommendations for Lineups and Photospreads* in 1998. The same year, the National Institute of Justice (NIJ) initiated a project to instruct police on collecting and preserving eyewitness evidence and, in 2003, published *Eyewitness Evidence: A Trainer's Manual for Law Enforcement.* This 62-page document outlines procedures and best practices for preparing witnesses, conducting identifications, and minimizing errors. However, surveys of 532 police officers conducted in 2007–2009 revealed that less than 2% had implemented the NIJ procedures (Wise et al., 2011). Greenspan and Loftus (2023) further noted that larger police agencies implemented these best practice procedures more so than smaller agencies.

The failure to implement these best practices is concerning, as surveys of police officers, defense attorneys, and prosecutors during this time revealed that many were unaware of the factors that limit the accuracy and validity of EWID (Wise et al., 2009, 2011). Some police believed inaccurate information about EWID (e.g., reasons why witness statements may be inconsistent) (Krix et al., 2015). Proper procedures are essential to reduce the risk of errors and prevent wrongful convictions. The National Registry of Exonerations (NRE) has tracked wrongful convictions since 1989 and, as of December 31, 2024, has identified 3,633 people who have been exonerated, and of these, 985 were convicted based on mistaken EWID. Of these 985 individuals, 335 had DNA evidence confirming their innocence, and 30 were convicted in 2005 or later—after the NIJ published the recommendations in 2003 (NRE, 2024b).

Obtaining accurate statements and identifications from victims or witnesses with disabilities is particularly important due to potential cognitive or memory deficits but also because people with disabilities are at greater risk of violent and sexual victimization than those without disabilities. Women with intellectual disability (ID) have an estimated 1.8–2.5 times greater risk of violent victimization and a 11–17 times greater risk of sexual assault victimization (Latvala et al., 2023). A study of 678,000 individuals showed that children with ID and autism had nearly three times increased risk of violent victimization than children without disabilities (Christoffersen, 2019). Another study of more than 1.2 million people compared victimization among those with and without a neurodevelopmental disability (NDD) revealed that those with NDDs had an estimated 2–7.7 times greater risk of violent victimization than those without NDDs. A 2007 report by The Autism Society revealed that among 1,500 autistic individuals[1] and their caregivers, 17% reported physical abuse, 13% reported sexual abuse, and 8% reported a sexual assault. Weiss and Fardella (2018) found significant differences in the frequency of victimization among those with and without autism. Compared to those without a disability, a higher percentage of autistic individuals reported experiencing physical abuse in childhood (26% vs. 58%), sexual assault by someone they knew (5% vs. 27%), and physical assault (67% vs. 82%) (Weiss & Fardella, 2018). When the criminal justice system (CJS) becomes involved, victims and witnesses with disabilities may participate in interviews or make identifications of suspects. Neurodiverse individuals may have communication barriers or difficulty with memory recall, and therefore, additional safeguards and supports are necessary to allow them to participate in the judicial process.

Identification Procedures

Requesting a victim or witness to identify a suspect is a standard investigative procedure, and lineups and photospreads are the most common. A **lineup** is a live viewing, typically conducted at the police station, and a **photospread** (sometimes referred to as a photo array) is when police present witnesses with photos of suspects. In both procedures, witnesses try to identify a suspect from several other individuals, known as **fillers** or **foils,** who are innocent persons with similar physical characteristics. Witnesses sometimes feel pressure to select someone, often due to the desire to help police with their investigation and to avoid appearing unhelpful. As a result, they may be reluctant to say that the suspect is absent in a lineup or photospread and select a filler or innocent person who resembles the suspect the most. Police may first conduct a **blank lineup** of only fillers to assess witnesses' credibility or ability to resist not making an identification (Wells et al., 1998).

Whether a lineup or photospread is presented simultaneously (all at once) or sequentially (one at a time) affects the accuracy of EWIDs (Steblay et al., 2001, 2003). Wells (1984) claimed that simultaneous lineups encourage witnesses to use relative judgment processes, comparing members to one another and selecting the person who best resembles the suspect, who may be innocent. Presenting lineup members one at a time (sequential lineup) reduces one's relative judgment and can reduce false identifications (Lindsay & Wells, 1985). Researchers have continued to find evidence to support that sequential procedures improved the ability to identify suspects over simultaneous procedures, both in laboratory settings (Fitzgerald et al., 2015) and real-world settings (Wells et al., 2015; Wixted et al., 2016).

Constructing Lineups and Photospreads

A properly constructed lineup or photospread should have members or fillers who do not differ distinctly from the suspect or have characteristics that draw attention away from them or to the suspect. When they do, the lineup or photospread is considered biased, suggestive, or "stacked" (Colloff et al., 2016; Malpass & Tredoux, 2008; Wells et al., 2000). Highly dissimilar fillers (e.g., different race) are "duds" and bias the identification procedures. Biased procedures are sometimes deliberate when police want to encourage a witness to identify a specific suspect, which Gross et al. (2020) refer to as a form of **witness tampering**. However, when selecting fillers, they should not be so similar that a person acquainted with the suspect would find it too difficult to identify them (McKinley & Peterson, 2022). Having highly similar-matched foils can lead people to select one of the fillers instead, increasing the chance of identifying an innocent person (Fitzgerald et al., 2015). For photospreads, all photos should be of equal quality with similar backgrounds to avoid drawing attention to the suspect (Wells, 1998).

Sometimes, suspects have distinctive characteristics that may make them stand out (e.g., scar, birthmark). Colloff et al. (2016) examined the effects of digitally editing photos (e.g., replicating the distinctive characteristic, blurring the area) to make the photospread "fairer." Suspect-present photospreads with altered photos led to fewer identifications of suspects than those who viewed unaltered photos. In the suspect-absent photospread, they identified fewer innocent suspects than those who viewed unaltered photos. Witnesses who viewed photospreads with unaltered photos were more willing to make an identification but were less able to distinguish between a guilty and an innocent suspect, concluding that digitally editing photos may reduce the risk of MWID (Colloff et al., 2016).

Cross-racial Identifications

Cross-racial identifications where the witness is a different race than the suspect may increase mistaken EWID. Individuals tend to be more accurate in recognizing faces of one's own race than those of other races. Malpass and

Kravitz (1969) introduced this concept, known as the **other-race effect.**[2] Researchers have systematically studied other-race facial recognition for decades (Meissner & Brigham, 2001), and has even been shown to begin in infancy (Kelly et al., 2007). Pauker et al. (2009) evaluated facial recognition among 20 White and 19 Black participants by presenting them with photos of Black faces, White faces, and racially ambiguous faces (which may be the case if someone is bi-racial or multi-racial). Participants were later presented with a photo presented earlier or a filler (not presented before) and then asked if they recognized the face. White participants were better at recognizing White faces, and their memory of Black faces and ambiguous faces was similar. Similarly, Black participants were better at recognizing Black faces, and their memory of White faces and ambiguous faces were similar (Pauker et al., 2009). Ferguson et al. (2001) conducted facial recognition tests comparing 60 White and 21 Asian participants. Participants were presented with photos of White and Asian faces, then later presented with a photo and asked if they had seen the face before. White participants could recognize White faces far more accurately than Asian faces. Asian participants, however, were able to recognize the faces of both races relatively equally. Kawakami et al. (2022) compared facial recognition among a racially/ethnically diverse group of 89 participants with ethnicities other than Black (e.g., White, Asian, Middle Eastern, and South American). Participants were shown photos of 24 Black and 24 White faces and rated the face as either similar or dissimilar to theirs. They were then presented with photos and asked if they had seen the photo before. Participants were better at recognizing White faces than Black faces, and facial recognition improved the more similar the face in the photo was to their own race.

Accuracy of facial recognition appears to decrease with age. Boutet and Meinhardt-Injac (2019) found that adults in their 50s through 80s have a decreased ability to recognize unfamiliar faces than those in their 20s or 30s. Wylie et al. (2015) found evidence of more other-race bias in older adults. Younger adults (under 30 years) were more accurate in recognizing the faces of Black people than older adults (over 60). However, they suggested that this may be due to the amount of exposure, as younger adults reported having more contact with different racial/ethnic groups than older adults (Wylie et al., 2015).

Witnesses Instructions and Statements

Prior to the lineup or photospread, police must first give witnesses instructions. One necessary instruction is for police to inform witnesses that the suspect may or may not be present. Instructions are **suggestive** when police mention to the witness beforehand that they have apprehended a suspect, that another witness has identified the suspect, or that the suspect is in the lineup (Garrett, 2011). If the witness assumes the suspect is present, they will select the person who resembles the suspect most (Wells et al., 2000). Comments made by co-witnesses can also influence a witness to choose a suspect, which may lead to false identifications (Levet, 2013). After reviewing trials involving eyewitness testimony, Garrett (2011) revealed that in 27% of cases, police made suggestive comments to witnesses that biased the procedure. Studies that compared unbiased and biased instructions (e.g., participants were informed that another witness identified the suspect or the suspect was present) showed that biased instructions resulted in choosing an innocent suspect (Ask & Granhag, 2010; Charman et al., 2018). Police should also avoid prompting witnesses to re-examine the lineup, as this can lead witnesses to change their identifications (Eisen et al., 2018).

Witness Confidence and Feedback

After witnesses make an identification, police ask them to make a confidence judgment of their selection. The level of confidence they have in their selection is an indicator of their credibility as a witness. Suggestive identification procedures, such as having highly dissimilar fillers or giving biased instructions, increase witnesses' confidence in their identification. For example, 177 adult participants watched a video of a male stealing a car and were asked to point out the suspect in a lineup. Those who received biased lineup instructions (no mention that the suspect may be absent) showed greater confidence in identifying the suspect than those who received unbiased lineup instructions (Charman et al., 2018).

Police should also avoid giving any feedback after the identification (post-identification), as this can affect witness confidence (MacLean et al., 2011). Hafstad et al. (2004) had 55 adult participants watch a two-minute video of a bank robbery, and the suspect's face was in view for ten seconds. The following day, participants were presented with a six-person suspect-absent photospread. Once the participant made an identification, they were either given (1) confirming feedback ("Good. You identified the right guy!"), (2) disconfirming feedback ("Oh, you identified number..., but that was actually wrong. The correct one was number…"), or (3) no feedback (p. 904). Those who received positive confirming feedback rated their confidence level much higher than those who received either no or negative (i.e., disconfirming) feedback (Hafstad et al., 2004). Confidence levels are problematic when witnesses select an innocent person because increased confidence makes them appear more credible to juries. For this reason, **double-anonymous**[3] procedures are recommended, where neither police nor witnesses are aware if the suspect is present (Charman & Quiroz, 2016; Wells et al., 2015).

Showups

Showups are identification procedures when police present witnesses with a suspect shortly after a crime, usually on the street, at a residence, or at a police station. Showups are important for public safety because they allow police to detain a potentially dangerous suspect instead of letting the suspect go as they prepare for the lineup (Garrett, 2011). However, showups are not without controversy and have the potential to be suggestive and biased (Eisen et al., 2017; Kassin et al., 2001). Whether police station showups violated due process was decided in Neil v. Biggers (1972).

Case Brief: Neil v. Biggers (1972).

Facts: In 1965, a jury in Tennessee found Archie Biggers guilty of the rape of Margaret Beamer and was sentenced to 20 years in prison. After the assault, Beamer claimed she spent considerable time with her assailant and gave police a description. Over the next seven months, Beamer viewed several suspects, including lineups, showups at her home and police station, and photospreads of 30 to 40 individuals, but was unable to identify her assailant. Biggers, who was detained on another charge, matched Beamer's description, so police contacted her to identify him. Police tried to construct a lineup but could not find similar fillers, so they conducted a showup instead. Two detectives walked Biggers past Beamer, and Beamer requested Biggers to say, "Shut up, or I'll kill you." Beamer named Biggers as her assailant and claimed that she did not doubt her identification. Noting that a lineup is more reliable than a showup, Biggers contested that the showup procedure violated due process and appealed his case to the US Supreme Court.

Issue: Whether a police station showup procedure is so suggestive that it violates one's constitutional right to due process under the Fifth and Fourteenth Amendments.

Outcome: The US Supreme Court decided the showup was not so suggestive that it violated one's constitutional right to due process under certain circumstances. Although the station showup may have been suggestive, Beamer's identification of Biggers was considered reliable, considering the amount of time she spent with her assailant.

Memory Recall and Eyewitness Identification

Memory and cognition are complicated neurological processes that are based on several factors. Wells et al. (1999) define memory as "the mental trace of a previously experienced event" (p. 56). Many believe memories are "recordings" of life events stored in the brain and are unaware of their inaccuracy and malleability (Fenda et al., 2014; Wake et al., 2020). Memories, in fact, are not simply "recordings" but are reconstructed using information from multiple sources (Frenda et al., 2014). Memories may be incomplete, inaccurate, distorted, or changed after exposure to incorrect or misleading information or sources (Frenda et al., 2014; Lentoor, 2023). Therefore, memory processes of crime events do not necessarily encompass complete accounts (Wells et al., 1999).

Accuracy of Eyewitness Reports

EWID of suspects and witnesses' later testimony is powerful evidence for prosecutors. Elizabeth Loftus and Gary Wells are two pioneers who have conducted extensive research on memory and EWID dating back to the 1970s and have warned how standard police practices create unnecessary errors. Wells (1978) proposed two factors that can affect the accuracy of eyewitness accounts: **estimator variables** and **system variables.** Estimator variables are those that affect eyewitness accuracy but are not under the control of the CJS. These variables include the type or seriousness of the crime, the length of time that the witness was exposed to the crime or suspect, the complexity of the criminal event, how familiar the witness is to the location or the suspect, weather conditions, time of day, and characteristics of the suspect and the witness (e.g., race, age). **System variables** are those under the control of the CJS, such as the length of time between the crime and identification procedure, the type of identification procedure, or how the identification procedure is conducted (Wells, 1978). The research on EWIDs mostly deals with system variables since they are under the CJS's control and, thus, can be modified accordingly to improve accuracy. However, research has also compared differences among the characteristics of witnesses, such as age, race, or having a disability.

Interviewing witnesses to gather evidence about what happened or what they observed is essential to investigations. Police often question witnesses on multiple occasions to provide additional details, increasing the opportunity to report accurate or previously missed details. However, between interviews, witnesses can be exposed to misinformation that can alter their memories of events. The **misinformation effect** is when witnesses incorporate misinformation into their memories (Loftus, 2005; Loftus et al., 1978). Witnesses may also miss critical information due to inattention and may be unable to recall past events, referred to as **inattention blindness**. Wulff and Hyman (2022) note that people are not waiting around to witness crimes; when they occur, their attention or focus may be elsewhere. For example, 96 adult participants watched a video of a man committing a theft. When the participants were watching for the theft, they were more likely be about to point out the suspect than participants who were focused on an unrelated task in the video (Wulff & Hyman, 2022).

Witnesses may also have no memory of something they saw or may be unable to recall the event, any details, or remember accounts they previously gave, referred to as **memory blindness**. Similarly, **choice blindness** is when witnesses cannot recall or inaccurately recall previous self-reported choices. For example, 186 student participants watched a video of a woman interacting with three others, one of whom stole her wallet. After 15 minutes, the participants responded to ten questions, similar to what they would have to recall to the police as witnesses, such as the color of the suspect's clothing or height. Participants selected from a range of responses (e.g., shades of green and blue). After another 15 minutes, the experimenter showed them their responses, but the experimenter changed some of them. After another 15-minute interval, participants responded to the same ten questions, and for those exposed to changed versions of the event, some participants' memories changed to match the altered details (Cochran et al., 2016).

Memory and Recall Among Children

Sometimes, children are the only witnesses to crimes, making their statements and identifications crucial in criminal investigations. When making identifications, children can recall details and accurately identify people in certain conditions, for instance, when the suspect is present in a lineup or photospread (Parker & Carranza, 1989; Ross et al., 2006) or when there has been no change in the physical appearance of the suspect (Pozzulo & Balfour, 2006). If the suspect is absent in the lineup or photospread, children have many of the same difficulties as adults but have more difficulty when the suspect is absent (Parker & Carranza, 1989; Pozzulo & Balfour, 2006). Children have a decreased ability to resist the expectations of choosing someone and feel more pressure to make an identification (Havard, 2014).

When asked to recall details of events during interviews, children tend to have weaker memories and provide less information, particularly with

open-ended (provide their own responses) than **close-ended** (e.g., yes/no) questions. Although specific or close-ended questions may provide complete responses, they may be less accurate. **Leading questions** encourage a particular response (e.g., isn't it true that …) and are considered a coercive line of questioning. Coercive questioning strategies with children raise concerns about **confabulation, acquiescence,** and **suggestibility**. Confabulation is when one subconsciously creates an untrue story or scenario. Acquiescence is the tendency to say "yes" to every question, regardless of whether it is true. Suggestibility refers to the tendency to agree or accept others' suggestions or recollections of events and incorporate this misleading information into one's memory (Gudjonsson, 2018).

Depending on the question type, younger children could be more often misled into giving incorrect responses to questions. Wyman et al. (2018) examined children's (aged 6 to 11) willingness to give false information about a mock crime and their memory recall. While the children were sitting in a room, the experimenter took a wallet from someone's jacket and removed the money. The children were later interviewed using open-ended and direct closed-ended questions, and some were asked to lie, either make a false denial or false accusation. With open-ended questions, children aged 6–7 provided fewer details and shorter responses than those aged 8–9 and 10–11. The children who told the truth gave longer and more detailed responses than those asked to lie. The younger children provided false information when asked direct questions more often than the older children. These results highlight the limitations of open-ended questions with younger children who rely on direct closed-ended questions; thus, it is essential not to ask young children leading or biased questions when asking direct questions (Wyman et al., 2018).

Case of Gregory Kelley

Gregory Kelley of Leander, Texas, was an 18-year-old high school senior and football star planning to play for the University of Texas at San Antonio football team the following year. On August 9, 2013, his life changed forever when he was arrested for sexually abusing two four-year-old boys. His story was recounted in the 2020 Showtime Sports documentary series *Outcry*, produced by Barker et al.

Offense: Four-year-old H.M. was at an in-home daycare run by Shama McCarty, the mother of Kelley's friend, Johnathan McCarty. Kelley had stayed at the McCarty home in nearby Cedar Park, Texas, for several months during the end of his junior year because both his parents were dealing with serious medical issues. Kelley moved back home on June 11, 2013. A month later, on July 13, H.M.'s mother told police that her son said that "Greg" had put his penis in his mouth on two occasions. Police speculated the assault occurred the day before on July 12. Kelley was arrested for sexually abusing H.M., and several days later, another four-year-old boy, L.M., accused Kelley of sexual abuse. Kelley denied abusing the boys. According to cell phone data, on July 12, 2013, the day police alleged H.M. was abused, Kelley was out of town in Hutto, Texas. Police then "backtracked" the date of H.M.'s abuse from July 12, 2013, to April 15, 2013, to allow Kelley to remain their suspect (Kelley v. Cedar Park, 2020; NRE, 2024a).

Interviews: H.M. was interviewed at the Child Advocacy Center in Georgetown, Texas. H.M. gave confabulated stories about his mother walking in during the abuse and getting into a physical altercation with Kelley (both the prosecutor and defense admitted that never occurred). Detective Dailey also interviewed H.M. and asked him leading and close-ended questions (later admitting this was not best practice). H.M. had been subjected to at least eight "non-professional conversations" before his Child Advocacy Center interview. He also had four or five meetings at the prosecutor's office. During the investigation, Dailey did not visit the McCarty home to examine the layout of the room to determine if it matched H.M.'s accounts; he did not interview anyone else in the home as possible witnesses, nor did he interview Kelley (Kelley v. Cedar Park, 2020; NRE, 2024a).

L.M. was interviewed at the child advocacy center, but he never mentioned he was abused during this first interview. Detective Dailey later interviewed L.M., and only then did he accuse Kelley of abusing him. L.M. was questioned numerous times by his parents, several times at the advocacy center, once by Detective Dailey, and during four meetings at the prosecutor's office. In one of L.M.'s video-recorded statements, he mentioned Jonathan McCarty molesting him with Kelley. When L.M. first mentioned the abuse to his parents, he referred to both Jonathan McCarty and Kelley. Neither H.M. nor L.M. were shown a photospread or lineup during the investigative process (NRE, 2024a).

Trial: Kelley maintained his innocence and rejected a plea bargain to plead guilty to an indecency charge, which required a ten-year probation term and register on the state's "sex offender" registry for 20 years. In July 2014, Kelley went to trial on two counts of super-aggravated sexual assault and two counts of indecency with a child. Kelley testified in his defense and denied sexually abusing the boys. He said that whenever he was at the McCarty home, it was after school, and the daycare children were no longer there. H.M. testified via closed-circuit television (CCTV) that Kelley walked into the room wearing pajamas and sexually abused him while he was sleeping on a couch. H.M. did not identify Kelley in court. When prosecutors tried to walk H.M. near the courtroom where Kelley and the jury were located, H.M. fell to the floor and refused to move. L.M. also testified via CCTV and denied any sexual abuse; he responded "no" to every question asked about being abused. L.M. also did not identify Kelley in court (Kelley v. Cedar Park, 2020; NRE, 2024a).

Outcome: The judge dismissed one of the indecency charges involving L.M. due to lack of evidence. On July 15, 2014, the jury found Kelley guilty of two counts of super-aggravated sexual assault. Kelley faced a minimum sentence of 25 years to a maximum of life in prison without parole. Before the sentencing hearing, Kelley pleaded guilty to a 25-year prison term with no chance of parole to avoid a possible life sentence (Kelley v. Cedar Park, 2020; NRE, 2024a).

Exoneration: Kelley's defense attorney filed a motion for a new trial after new evidence was presented from two witnesses who heard Jonathan McCarty admit he had sexually abused H.M. The witnesses also said they saw pictures of nude children on Jonathan's phone. Jonathan's phone and computer were seized as evidence, and an examination revealed indecent images of children on both devices. Texas Rangers reviewed the procedures of the police investigation and concluded they failed to conduct an adequate investigation, including failing to perform basic steps. The Texas Court of Criminal Appeals vacated Kelley's convictions on November 6, 2019, and the prosecution dismissed the charges on November 27, 2019. In 2020, Kelley filed a federal civil rights lawsuit against the City of Cedar Park and several officers (Kelley v. Cedar Park, 2020; NRE, 2024a).Kelley agreed to a $500,000 settlement (Tschirhart, 2023).

Memory and Recall among Neurodiverse Individuals

Due to their increased risk of victimization, more attention has been drawn to neurodiverse individuals' memory performance when recalling events or identifying suspects. A growing body of research shows evidence of variations in memory and recall among neurodiverse children and adults.

Neurodiverse Adults. Individuals with ID tend to perform poorer than those without ID when making identifications from lineups. Wilcock and Henry (2013) compared EWID accuracy among 25 adults with ID (mean IQ of 54) and 26 adults without ID (mean IQ of 112). Participants watched a 110-second video clip of a young man and an older man breaking into a house. The participants were then presented with suspect-present and suspect-absent simultaneous lineups for both men in the video. In the suspect-present lineup, those with ID were less able to make a correct identification compared to those without ID (56% vs. 89%), selected an incorrect suspect (28% vs. 8%), or could not point out the suspect (16% vs. 4%). With the suspect-absent lineup, 75% of those with ID selected an incorrect suspect compared to 50% without ID. Other concerning findings were that those with ID were more confident in their selections (including incorrect ones), were less likely to understand the purpose of the identification procedure and were less likely to remember the non-biased instructions (Wilcock & Henry, 2013).

When recalling information during interviews, those with ID tend to be more susceptible to leading questions and misinformation effects than those without ID. Bowles and Sharman (2014) examined the impact of several types of questions among 41 adults with ID (mean IQ of 67). Participants viewed a 6.5-minute video of an electrician stealing items at a client's house. The participants were interviewed about critical information in the video (half were provided misleading information) using closed-ended non-leading questions, close-ended leading questions, and open-ended leading questions. Both types of leading questions generated significant misinformation effects, and leading open-ended questions generated the fewest correct responses. These findings emphasize that those with ID are vulnerable to leading questions, particularly those that presume incorrect information to be true.

Research has also shown differences in memory recall among autistic individuals. Maras et al. (2013) compared memory recall among 18 autistic and 18 typically developed adults without autism who participated in a mock first aid scenario on a mannequin intended to be in an auto accident. The experimenter and each participant performed various first aid tasks (e.g., checking for breathing, rolling the bandage). The participants were then interviewed using open-ended and structured **probing questions** (i.e., follow-up prompts) to elicit more information (leading questions were avoided). Autistic and typically developed adults could correctly recall the actions they performed, but the autistic adults reported more incorrect information (e.g., they performed the tasks that the experimenter performed). Thus, concluding that autistic adults can make adequate witnesses and provide investigators with accurate information with open-ended questions but may require more support and should not be subject to improper questioning techniques (Maras et al., 2013).

Neurodiverse Children. Like adults, children with ID have shown that they can recall information accurately but are suggestable to leading questions or questions with misinformation. Henry and Gudjonsson (2007) compared eyewitness memory among 34 children with ID and 40 typically developed children without ID. The children watched a three-minute video of four individuals in a car, pulling up to a gas station, filling the car up with gas, and then driving off without paying. The children were then asked open-ended questions, non-leading and misleading close-ended (yes/no) questions. The children with ID performed poorer on the open-ended questions and were more suggestible with misleading yes/no questions (i.e., more likely to agree with the incorrect account) (Henry & Gudjonsson, 2007).

Autistic children have been found to recall information similar to their typically developed peers but may require more probing questions to elicit more details. Henry et al. (2017b) compared memory and recall among 71 autistic and 201 typically developed children. The children watched a staged mock crime involving the theft of a phone or a set of keys. They were later interviewed about what they had seen using open-ended and probing questions to gain more information (e.g., what did they do?"). The autistic children could recall information with similar accuracy as the typically developed children (87% vs.89) but required more prompts to gain information. Henry et al. recommended that autistic children have more comprehensive interviews and added support.

Cognitive Interviews

Police widely use **cognitive interviews** (CI) to gather information from witnesses. Fisher and Geiselman (1992) developed the CI, which has seven phases to elicit detailed and accurate information. According to a review of 42 studies by Köhnken et al. (1999), the CI has been found to increase the recall of correct information compared to the standard interviews. However, studies of CIs have shown slight increases in errors in young children and are only recommended for those seven years and older. More recently, the CI has been tested on neurodiverse individuals to determine if it improved memory recall and communication. Gentle et al. (2013) compared the recall details and accuracy of 71 children with ID and 70 typically developed children without ID (exact IQs were unknown) between the ages of 7 and 10 years after watching a nine-minute video of a magic show in school. Both groups were later interviewed about the show, using either the CI or standard interview technique. The CI enhanced the recall of both groups of children, supporting the effectiveness of CIs, including those with ID (Gentle et al., 2013). However, these positive effects were not found in autistic individuals, and the use of CIs may actually increase the number of errors (Maras & Bowler, 2010, 2012; Mattison et al., 2015).

Because autistic individuals have difficulty with open-ended questions during interviews, researchers began exploring other methods to increase their ability to recall information. Mattison et al. (2015) compared the efficacy of a retrieval technique called Sketch reinstatement of context (Sketch-RC) to other interview techniques with 45 autistic children and 45 typically developed children. The children viewed a video of a theft at a store and were either interviewed using the Sketch-RC technique, the mental reinstatement of context technique in the CI, or with open-ended questions without support. For the Sketch-RC, children received paper and writing instruments (e.g., pencils, pens, erasers) and were instructed to draw what they saw in the video and to draw as much as they could. For the CI mental reinstatement, the children were asked to tell what they remember but were first asked to pause and think about each question (suggested closing their eyes to help). For autistic children, the Sketch-RC technique allowed them to recall correct information, make fewer errors, and have fewer confabulations than mental reinstatement and unsupported open-ended question interviews. However, Henry et al. (2017a) did not find that Sketch-RC was more beneficial than other interview methods among their sample of 71 autistic children. Therefore, interviewers should be trained in various interview interventions to accommodate individual needs and communication skills. Interviewers can use other communication aids, such as dolls and mannequins, to elicit information for those with limited verbal abilities (Pereira & Aldridge, 2023).

Box 10.1. Practitioner Spotlight: Corporal John T. Burke, Jr.

Corporal John T. Burke Jr. has worked for the Philadelphia, PA, Police Department as a police officer for the last 30 years and, since 2019, has worked as a recruit instructor at the Philadelphia Police Academy. He teaches police recruits about recognizing and responding to those with disabilities. Burke is the father of an autistic son, who has provided him with the greatest amount of knowledge and transfers that knowledge to the police recruits. His son is a routine guest at the Philadelphia Police Academy, where he assists the recruits in applying what they learned in the classroom into practice using unscripted scenarios to allow for natural responses in real-time. These scenarios help the recruits learn how to communicate and respond to someone with a disability respectfully.

Burke believes that it is important for police to know that individuals can advocate for themselves and not discount one's ability to provide information to police (including their wants and needs) simply because of a disability. Burke states, "Awareness is important, but only when we treat everyone with respect will we truly gain acceptance." Burke continues to advocate for the autism community and police interactions by attending conferences, speaking engagements, and collaborating with Drexel University's Policy and Analytics Center at the A.J. Drexel Autism Institute in Philadelphia. With Drexel University, Burke collaborated with professionals in numerous countries and co-led the 2022 International Society for Autism Research (INSAR) Policy Brief titled Autism and the Criminal Justice System: Policy Opportunities and Challenges. Collaborating on this policy brief has been a highlight of his career.

Considerations and Recommendations

Guidelines for best practices have been available to police for some time (e.g., Kassin et al., 2001; NIJ, 2013; Wells et al., 1998), although many are not adhering to them (Gross et al., 2020). When obtaining information from witnesses, police must implement added safeguards to prevent misidentifications or misinformation about event details, particularly from children and neurodiverse individuals. These safeguards include interview support and greater attention to questioning techniques. Below are some considerations and recommendations to reduce the number of investigative errors.

Adhere to Best Practice Guidelines for Identifications

Given the potential consequences of injustice resulting from mistaken EWID, police must be diligent with the witness identification process and adhere to the best practice guidelines listed below.

- Use a double-anonymous procedure.
- Only one suspect per procedure.
- Provide proper, unbiased instructions.
- Avoid bias or stacked procedures.
- Use the sequential procedure.
- Refrain from providing feedback/comments.
- Obtain a confidence statement.
- Video/audio record the entire procedure (Wells et al., 1998, pp. 627–636).

Regardless of the method, police must video/audio record all procedures to allow for an objective review of the structure, the instructions given, comments or feedback, the length of time it took the witness to identify, and their confidence level (Wells et al., 1998).

Cautions During Cross-racial Identifications

Other safeguards are needed for cross-racial identifications, particularly for Black suspects. After reviewing 1690 cases of men exonerated for violent and sexual offenses, Mogavero et al. (2022) found that Black men not only had more instances of MWID but a disproportionate amount of official misconduct by police and prosecutors, especially in sexual assault cases. Those constructing the identification procedure should be of the same race as the members and assess the suggestiveness before presenting it to the witness.

Cautions When Questioning Children and Neurodiverse Individuals

When gathering evidence, police should use caution when asking open-ended questions and use clear, specific, non-leading questions. Police should inquire and use communication aids for those with limited verbal communication skills (Pereira & Aldridge, 2023) or more intensive interview strategies with probing questions (Henry et al., 2017a). If close-ended questions are necessary, questions should be clear and specific and do not trick or lead them to answer in a particular way, as they tend to be more suggestible to such lines of questioning (Henry & Gudjonsson, 2007; Maras et al., 2018). Police should also not ask the same questions repeatedly, as this may lead them to change their responses (Henry & Gudjonsson, 2007).

Children and neurodiverse individuals may feel compelled to answer questions, even if they do not know the answer (Agnew & Powell, 2004). Police should make it clear that they should feel forced to respond to a question if they do not know and make it clear that "I don't know" is an acceptable response. Although the cognitive interview (CI) is a widely used technique to gather information from witnesses, experts have suggested avoiding it with autistic individuals until there is more research (Maras & Bowler, 2010, 2012). Interviewers can add other supports, such as the Sketch-RC method and other techniques to support an individual's cognitive or verbal skills (Henry et al., 2017b; Mattison et al., 2015). All questioning and identification procedures should be conducted in a supportive environment free from distractions, such as loud noises and bright lights (Maras et al., 2018).

Conclusion

Eyewitness accounts are crucial evidence in solving criminal cases. Obtaining the information using best practices and preserving the integrity of evidence is of utmost importance. Decades of research have shown that memory accounts are fallible, often incomplete, and prone to misinformation effects and can be altered when presented with misleading information. People can also be suggestible to respond affirmatively to leading questions, feel compelled to answer a question they do not know, or identify a suspect even when uncertain. Children, those with ID, and autistic individuals are more susceptible to these effects. To participate in the justice system as victims or witnesses, CJS practitioners must implement best practices and additional supports to assist them with more accurate and detailed recollections. As stated by Corporal Burke, autistic individuals can communicate. However, professionals must first demonstrate respect for them as individuals and respect their communication differences, which requires additional training and skills among interviewers.

Questionable or unethical practices can lead to cases of mistaken EWID. Wrongful convictions devastate lives and allow individuals to remain free to offend again. In the case of Gregory Kelley, Johnathan McCarty was not included in the original investigation. McCarty was later implicated in several sexual assaults and entered into a plea agreement (Tschirhart, 2023). Police must take great care when interviewing witnesses, and police and prosecutors should ensure that best practices are adhered to before continuing with charges. Best practices also include gathering as much corroborating evidence as possible, as one's eyewitness account, under certain circumstances, may not be sufficient evidence. Defense attorneys must also ensure due diligence and confirm that all statements and identification procedures were obtained properly.

Key Terms

Acquiescence
Confabulation
Choice blindness
Closed-ended questions
Cognitive interview
Blank lineup
Double-anonymous
Estimator variables
Foils

Inattention blindness
Leading questions
Misinformation effect
Memory blindness
Other-race effect
Open-ended questions
Probing questions
Showups
Suggestibility
System variables

Chapter Questions

1) In the case of Gregory Kelley list and describe as many identification and questioning errors you can think of.
2) Describe system variables and estimator variables concerning the memory of events. Provide examples of each.
3) Describe the specific memory problems and one's ability to recall details or identify suspects?
4) What are some specific problems for children identifying suspects as witnesses/victims?
5) Why is it important to take additional precautions when gathering information and physical descriptions from children or those with ID or autism?
6) Of the eight recommendations for best practices for identification procedures by Wells et al. (1998), which do you believe is the most important to reduce the risk of mistaken witness identification? Explain your response.

Suggested Readings

Benton, T. R., Ross, D. F., Bradshaw, E., Thomas, W. N., & Bradshaw, G. S. (2006). Eyewitness memory is still not common sense: Comparing jurors, judges, and law enforcement to eyewitness experts. *Applied Cognitive Psychology, 20*(1), 115–129.

Kaasa, S. O., Cauffman, E., Clarke-Stewart, K. A., & Loftus, E. F. (2013). False accusations in an investigative context: Differences between suggestible and non-suggestible witnesses. *Behavioral Sciences & the Law, 31*, 574–592. https://doi.org/10.1002/bsl.2075

Loftus, E. F. (2018). Eyewitness science and the legal system. *Annual Review of Law and Social Science, 14*(1), 1–10. https://doi.org/10.1146/annurev-law socsci-101317-030850

Wells, G. L., & Olson, E. A. (2001). The other-race effect in eyewitness identification: What do we do about it? *Psychology, Public Policy, & Law, 7*, 230–246. https://doi.org/10.1037/1076-8971.7.1.230

Notes

1. *See A Note About Evolving Language and Term in* Chapter 1 for information on identity-first language
2. Also known as "other-race bias" or "own-race bias," however, the terms "bias" and "own race" implies prejudice, and therefore, the neutral term, "other race effect" is used.
3. also referred to as double-blind.

References

Ask, K. & Granhag, P. A., (2010). Perception of line-up suggestiveness: Effects of identification outcome knowledge. *Journal of Investigative Psychology and Offender Profiling, 7*, 213–229. https://doi.org/10.1002/jip.123

Autism Society. (2006). Results of the victims of crime with autism survey (unpublished).

Barker, L., Espinoza, S., Germer, S., Jones, L., Kondelis, P., Malhotra, V., Rock-afellow, M., & Wingrove, J. (Producers). (2020). *Outcry*. [TV series]. Showtime.

Boutet, I., & Meinhardt-Injac, B. (2019). Age differences in face processing: The role of perceptual degradation and holistic processing. *The Journals of Gerontology. Series B, Psychological Sciences and Social Sciences, 74*(6), 933–942. https://doi.org/10.1093/geronb/gbx172

Bowles, P. V., & Sharman, S. J. (2014). A review of the impact of different types of leading interview questions on child and adult witnesses with intellectual disabilities. *Psychiatry, Psychology and Law, 21*, 205–217. https://doi.org/10.1080/13218719.2013.803276

Charman, S. D., Carol, R. N., & Schwartz, S. L. (2018). The effect of biased lineup instructions on eyewitness identification confidence. *Applied Cognitive Psychology, 32*(3), 287–297. https://doi.org/10.1002/acp.3401

Charman, S. D., & Quiroz, V. (2016). Blind sequential lineup administration reduces false identifications and confidence in those false identifications. *Law and Human Behavior, 40*, 477–487. https://doi.org/10.1037/lhb0000197

Charman, S. D., Wells, G. L., & Joy, S. W. (2011). The dud effect: Adding highly dissimilar fillers increases confidence in lineup identifications. *Law and Human Behavior, 35*(6), 479–500. https://doi.org/10.1007/s10979-010-9261-1

Cochran, K. J., Greenspan, R. L., Bogart, D. F., & Loftus, E. F. (2016). Memory blindness: Altered memory reports lead to distortion in eyewitness memory. *Memory & Cognition, 44*(5), 717–726. https://doi.org/10.3758/s13421-016-0594-y

Colloff, M. F., Wade, K. A., & Strange, D. (2016). Unfair lineups make eyewitnesses more likely to confuse innocent and guilty suspects. *Psychological Science, 27*, 1227–1239. https://doi.org/10.1177/0956797616655789

Eisen, M. L., Cedré, G. C., Williams, T. Q., & Jones, J. M. (2018). Does anyone else look familiar? Influencing identification decisions by asking witnesses to re-examine the lineup. *Law and Human Behavior, 42*(4), 306–320. https://doi.org/10.1037/lhb0000291

Eisen, M. L., Skerrit-Perta, A., Jones, J. M., Owen, J., & Cedré, G. C. (2017). Pre-admonition suggestion in live showups: When witnesses learn that the cops caught 'the' guy. *Applied Cognitive Psychology, 31*(5), 520–529. https://doi.org/10.1002/acp.3349

Frenda, S. J., Patihis, L., Loftus, E. F., Lewis, H. C., & Fenn, K. M. (2014). Sleep deprivation and false memories. *Psychological Science, 25*(9), 1674–1681. https://doi.org/10.1177/0956797614534694

Ferguson, D. P., Rhodes, G., Lee, K., & Sriram, N. (2001). "They all look alike to me": Prejudice and cross-race face recognition. *British Journal of Psychology, 92*, 567–577. https://doi.org/10.1348/000712601162347

Fisher, R. P., & Geiselman, R. E. (1992). *Memory-enhancing techniques for investigative interviewing: The cognitive interview*. Thomas.

Fitzgerald, R. J., Oriet, C., & Price, H. L. (2015). Suspect filler similarity in eyewitness lineups: A literature review and a novel methodology. *Law and Human Behavior, 39*(1), 62–74. https://doi.org/10.1037/lhb0000095

Garrett, B. L. (2011). *Convicting the innocent*. Harvard University Press. https://doi.org/10.4159/harvard.9780674060982

Gentle, M., Milne, R., Powell, M. B., & Sharman, S. J. (2013). Does the cognitive interview promote the coherence of narrative accounts in children with and without an intellectual disability? *International Journal of Disability, Development and Education, 60*(1), 30–43. https://doi.org/10.1080/1034912X.2013.757138

Christoffersen, M. N. (2019). Violent crime against children with disabilities: A nationwide prospective birth cohort study. *Child Abuse & Neglect, 98*, 104–150. https://doi.org/10.1016/j.chiabu.2019.104150

Greenspan, R. L., & Loftus, E. F. (2023). Patterns in the use of best practices for eyewitness identifications in the field. *Psychology, Crime & Law, 29*(2), 161–181. https://doi.org/10.1080/1068316X.2021.2018436

Gross, S. R., Possley, M., Roll, J. K., & Stephens, K. (2020). *Government misconduct and convicting the innocent: The role of prosecutors, police, and other law enforcement*. The National Registry of Exonerations. University of Michigan Law School.

Gudjonsson, G. H. (2018). The psychology of false confessions: Forty years of science and practice. *John Wiley & Sons.* https://doi.org/10.1002/9781119315636

Hafstad, G. S., Memon, A., & Logie, R. (2004). Post-identification feedback, confidence, and recollections of witnessing conditions in child witnesses. *Applied Cognitive Psychology, 18*(7), 901–912. https://doi.org/10.1002/acp.1037

Havard, C. (2014). Are children less reliable at making visual identifications than adults? A review. *Psychology, Crime & Law, 20*(4), 372–388. https://doi.org/10.1080/1068316X.2013.793334

Henry, L. A., & Gudjonsson, G. H. (2007). Individual and developmental differences in eyewitness recall and suggestibility in children with intellectual disabilities. *Applied Cognitive Psychology, 21*, 361–381. https://doi.org/10.1002/acp.1280

Henry, L. A., Crane, L., Nash, G., Hobson, Z., Kirke-Smith, M., & Wilcock, R. (2017a). Verbal, visual, and intermediary support for child witnesses with autism during investigative interviews. *Journal of Autism and Developmental Disorders, 47*(8), 2348–2362. https://doi.org/10.1007/s10803-017-3142-0

Henry, L. A., Messer, D. J., Wilcock, R., Nash, G., Kirke-Smith, M., Hobson, Z., & Crane, L. (2017b). Do measures of memory, language, and attention predict eyewitness memory in children with and without autism? *Autism & Developmental Language Impairments, 2*, 1–7. https://doi.org/10.1177/2396941517722139

Henry, L. A., Crane, L., Fesser, E., Harvey, A., Palmer, L., & Wilcock, R. (2020). The narrative coherence of witness transcripts in children on the autism spectrum. *Research in Developmental Disabilities, 96*, Article 103518. https://doi.org/10.1016/j.ridd.2019.103518

Kassin, S. M., Tubb, V. A., Hosch, H. M., & Memon, A. (2001). On the 'general acceptance' of eyewitness testimony research: A new survey of the experts. *American Psychologist, 56*(5), 405–416. https://doi.org/10.1037/0003-066X.56.5.405

Kawakami, K., Vingilis-Jaremko, L., Friesen, J. P., Meyers, C., & Fang, X. (2022). Impact of similarity on recognition of faces of Black and White targets. *British Journal of Psychology, 113*(4), 1079–1099. https://doi.org/10.1111/bjop.12589

Kelly, D. J., Quinn, P. C., Slater, A. M., Lee, K., Ge, L., & Pascalis, O. (2007). The other-race effect develops during infancy: Evidence of perceptual narrowing. *Psychological Science, 18*(12), 1084–1089. https://doi.org/10.1111/j.1467-9280.2007.02029.x

Kelley v. Cedar Park, USDC (W.D. Tex.), Case No. 1:20-cv-00481 (2020).

Köhnken, G., Milne, R., Memon, A., & Bull, R. (1999). The cognitive interview: A meta-analysis. *Psychology, Crime Law, 5*(1–2), 3–28. https://doi.org/10.1080/10683169908414991

Krix, A. C., Sauerland, M., Lorei, C., & Rispens, I. (2015). Consistency across repeated eyewitness interviews: Contrasting police detectives' beliefs with actual eyewitness performance. *PLoS ONE, 10*(2), Article e0118641. https://doi.org/10.1371/journal.pone.0118641

Latvala, A., Tideman, M., Søndenaa, E., Larsson, H., Butwicka, A., Fazel, S., & Lichtenstein, P. (2023). Association of intellectual disability with violent and sexual crime and victimization: A population-based cohort study. *Psychological Medicine, 53*(9), 3817–3825. https://doi.org/10.1017/S0033291722000460

Lentoor, A. G. (2023). Cognitive and neural mechanisms underlying false memories: Misinformation, distortion or erroneous configuration? *AIMS Neuroscience, 10*(3), 255–268. https://doi.org/10.3934/Neuroscience.2023020

Levet, L. M. (2013). Co-witness information influences whether a witness is likely to choose from a lineup. *Legal and Criminological Psychology, 18*(1), 168–180. https://doi.org/10.1111/j.2044-8333.2011.02033.x

Lindsay, R. C., & Wells, G. L. (1985). Improving eyewitness identifications from lineups: Simultaneous versus sequential lineup presentation. *Journal of Applied Psychology, 70*(3), 556–564. https://doi.org/10.1037/0021-9010.70.3.556

Loftus, E. F. (1984). Expert testimony on the eyewitness. In G. L. Wells & E. F. Loftus (Eds.), *Eyewitness testimony: Psychological perspectives* (pp. 273–282). Cambridge University Press.

Loftus, E. F. (2005). Planting misinformation in the human mind: A 30-year investigation of the malleability of memory. *Learning and Memory, 12*, 361–366. https://doi.org/10.1101/lm.94705

Loftus, E. F., Miller, D. G., & Burns, H. J. (1978). Semantic integration of verbal information into a visual memory. *Journal of Experimental Psychology: Human Learning and Memory, 4*, 19–31. https://doi.org/10.1037/0278-7393.4.1.19

MacLean, C. L., Brimacombe, C. A., Allison, M., Dahl, L. C., & Kadlec, H. (2011). Post-identification feedback effects: Investigators and evaluators. *Applied Cognitive Psychology, 25*, 739–752. https://doi.org/10.1002/acp.1745

Malpass, R. S., & Kravitz, J. (1969). Recognition for faces of own and other races. *Journal of Personality & Social Psychology, 13*, 330–334. https://doi.org/10.1037/h0028434

Malpass, R. S., & Tredoux, C. G. (2008). Lineup size and bias. In B. C. Cutler (Ed.), *Encyclopedia of psychology & law* (pp. 457–460). Sage.

Maras, K. L., & Bowler, D. M. (2010). The cognitive interview for eyewitnesses with autism spectrum disorder. *Journal of Autism and Developmental Disorders, 40*, 1350–1360.

Maras, K. L., & Bowler, D. M. (2012). Context reinstatement effects on eyewitness memory in autism spectrum disorder. *British Journal of Psychology, 103*(3), 330–342. https://doi.org/10.1111/j.2044-8295.2011.02077.x

Maras, K. L., Memon, A., Lambrechts, A., & Bowler, D. M. (2013). Recall of a live and personally experienced eyewitness event by adults with autism spectrum disorder. *Journal of Autism and Developmental Disorders, 43*(8), 1798–1810. https://doi.org/10.1007/s10803-012-1729-z

Maras, K. L., Mulcahy, S., Crane, L., Hawken, T., & Memon, A. (2018). Obtaining best evidence from the autistic interviewee: Police-reported challenges, legal requirements and psychological research-based recommendations. *Investigative Interviewing: Research and Practice, 9*(1), 52–60. http://www.iiirg.org/journal

Mattison, M. L., Dando, C. J., & Ormerod, T. C. (2015). Sketching to remember: Episodic free recall task support for child witnesses and victims with autism spectrum disorder. *Journal of Autism and Developmental Disorders, 45*(6), 1751–1765. https://doi.org/10.1007/s10803-014-2335-z

McKinley, G. L., & Peterson, D. J. (2022). Using objective measures to examine the effect of suspect-filler similarity on eyewitness identification performance. *Cognitive Research: Principles and Implications, 7*(1), 95. https://doi.org/10.1186/s41235-022-00442-1

Meissner, C. A., & Brigham, J. C. (2001). Thirty years of investigating the own-race bias in memory for races: A meta-analytic review. *Psychology, Public Policy, & Law, 7*, 3–35. https://doi.org/10.1037/1076-8971.7.1.3

Mogavero, M. C., Hsu, K. H., & Bolger, P. C. (2022). A conjunctive analysis of false accusations, official misconduct, and race in violent and sexual exoneration cases. *Behavioral Sciences and the Law, 40*(6), 756–786. https://doi.org/10.1002/bsl.2587

National Registry of Exonerations (2024a). *Gregory Kelley*. https://www.law.umich.edu/special/exoneration/Pages/casedetail.aspx?caseid=5645

National Registry of Exonerations (2024b). *Search exonerations*. https://www.law.umich.edu/special/exoneration/Pages/detaillist.aspx

Neil v. Biggers, 409 U.S. 188, 93 S. Ct. 375, 34 L. Ed. 2d 401 (1972).

Parker, J. F., & Carranza, L. E. (1989). Eyewitness testimony of children in target-present and target-absent lineups. *Law and Human Behavior, 13*, 133–149. https://doi.org/10.1007/BF01055920

Pauker, K., Weisbuch, M., Ambady, N., Sommers, S. R., Adams, R. B., & Ivcevic, Z. (2009). Not so black and white: Memory for ambiguous group members. *Journal of Personality and Social Psychology, 96*(4), 795–810. https://doi.org/10.1037/a0013265

Pereira, T., & Aldridge, M. (2023). 'Show me what happened': Low technology communication aids used in intermediary mediated police investigative interviews with vulnerable witnesses with an intellectual disability. *The International Journal of Evidence & Proof, 27*(1), 83–104. https://doi.org/10.1177/13657127221140469

Pozzulo, J. D., & Balfour, J. (2006). Children's and adults' eyewitness identification accuracy when a culprit changes his appearance: Comparing simultaneous and elimination lineup procedures. *Legal and Criminological Psychology, 11*(1), 25–34. https://doi.org/10.1348/135532505X52626

Ross, D. F., Marsil, D. F., Benton, T. R., Hoffman, R., Warren, A. R., Lindsay, R. C., & Metzger, R. (2006). Children's susceptibility to misidentifying a familiar bystander from a lineup: When younger is better. *Law and Human Behavior, 30*(3), 249–257. https://doi.org/10.1007/s10979-006-9034-z

Smalarz, L., & Wells, G. L. (2014). Post-identification feedback to eyewitnesses impairs evaluators' abilities to discriminate between accurate and mistaken testimony. *Law and Human Behavior, 38*(2), 194–202. https://doi.org/10.1037/lhb0000067

Steblay, N., Dysart, J., Fulero, S., & Lindsay, R. C. L. (2001). Eyewitness accuracy rates in sequential and simultaneous lineup presentations: A meta-analytic comparison. *Law and Human Behavior, 25*, 459–473. https://doi.org/10.1023/A:101288871500

Steblay, N., Dysart, J., Fulero, S., & Lindsay, R. C. L. (2003). Eyewitness accuracy rates in police showup and lineup presentations: A meta-analytic comparison. *Law and Human Behavior, 27*(5), 523–540. https://doi.org/10.1023/A:1025438223608

Tschirhart, B. (2023, July 15). $500,000 settlement for Texas man wrongly imprisoned for child sex abuse. *Prison Legal News*. https://www.prisonlegalnews.org/news/2023/jul/15/500000-settlement-texas-man-wrongly-imprisoned-child-sex-abuse/

United States National Institute of Justice. (2003). *Eyewitness evidence: A trainer's manual for law enforcement*. https://nij.ojp.gov/library/publications/eyewitness-evidence-trainers-manual-law-enforcement

United States National Institute of Justice. (2013). *A national survey of eyewitness identification procedures in law enforcement agencies*. Police Executive Research Forum. https://www.ncjrs.gov/pdffiles1/nij/grants/242617.pdf

Wake, K., Green, J. A., & Zajac, R. (2020). Laypeople's beliefs about memory: Disentangling the effects of age and time. *Memory, 28*(5), 589–597. https://doi.org/10.1080/09658211.2020.1733023

Weiss, J. A., & Fardella, M. A. (2018). Victimization and perpetration experiences of adults with autism. *Frontiers in Psychiatry, 9*, 203. https://doi.org/10.3389/fpsyt.2018.00203

Wells, G. L. (1978). Applied eyewitness testimony research: System variables and estimator variables. *Journal of Personality and Social Psychology, 36*, 1546–1557. https://doi.org/10.1037/0022-3514.36.12.1546

Wells, G. L. (1984). The psychology of lineup identifications. *Journal of Applied Social Psychology, 14*, 89–103. https://doi.org/10.1111/j.1559-1816.1984.tb02223.x

Wells, G. L., Malpass, R. S., Lindsay, R. C. L., Fisher, R. P., Turtle, J. W., & Fulero, S. M. (2000). From the lab to the police station: A successful application of eyewitness research. *American Psychologist, 55*, 581–598. https://doi.org/10.1037/0003-066X.55.6.581

Wells, G. L., Small, M., Penrod, S., Malpass, R. S., Fulero, S. M., & Brimacombe, C. A. E. (1998). Eyewitness identification procedures: Recommendations for lineups and photospreads. *Law and Human Behavior, 22*(6), 603–647. https://doi.org/10.1023/A:1025750605807

Wells, G. L., Steblay, N. K., & Dysart, J. E. (2015). Double-blind photo lineups using actual eyewitnesses: An experimental test of a sequential versus simultaneous lineup procedure. *Law and Human Behavior, 39*, 1–14. https://doi.org/10.1037/lhb0000096

Wells, G. L., Wright, E. F., & Bradfield, A. L. (1999). Witnesses to crime: Social and cognitive factors governing the validity of people's reports. In R. Roesch, S. D. Hart, & J. R. P. Ogloff (Eds.), *Psychology and law: The state of the discipline* (pp. 53–87). Kluwer Academic/Plenum Publishers.

Wilcock, R., & Henry, L. (2013). The performance of eyewitnesses with intellectual disabilities on photographic identification line-ups. *International Journal of Disability, Development and Education, 60*(1), 44–52. https://doi.org/10.1080/1034912X.2013.757141

Wise, R. A., Safer, M. A., & Maro, C. M. (2011). What US law enforcement officers know and believe about eyewitness factors, eyewitness interviews and identification procedures. *Applied Cognitive Psychology, 25*(3), 488–500. https://doi.org/10.1002/acp.1717

Wise, R. A., Pawlenko, N. B., Safer, M. A., & Meyer, D. (2009). What US prosecutors and defence attorneys know and believe about eyewitness testimony. *Applied Cognitive Psychology, 23*(9), 1266–1281. https://doi.org/10.1002/acp.1530

Wixted, J. T., Mickes, L., Dunn, J. C., Clark, S. E., & Wells, W. (2016). Estimating the reliability of eyewitness identifications from police lineups. *Proceedings of the National Academy of Sciences of the United States of America, 113*(2), 304–309. https://doi.org/10.1073/pnas.1516814112

Wogalter, M. S., Malpass, R. S., & McQuiston, D. E. (2004). A national survey of US police on preparation and conduct of identification procedures. *Psychology, Crime & Law, 10*, 69–82. https://doi.org/10.1080/10683160410001641873

Wulff, A. N., & Hyman, I. E. (2022). Crime blindness: The impact of inattentional blindness on eyewitness awareness, memory, and identification. *Applied Cognitive Psychology, 36*(1), 166–178. https://doi.org/10.1002/acp.3906

Wylie, L. E., Bergt, S., Haby, J., Brank, E. M., & Bornstein, B. H. (2015). Age and lineup type differences in the own-race bias. *Psychology, Crime & Law, 21*(5), 490–506. https://doi.org/10.1080/1068316X.2014.989173

Wyman, J., Foster, I., Crossman, A., Colwell, K., & Talwar, V. (2018). The efficacy of free-recall, cognitive load, and closed-ended questions when children are asked to falsely testify about a crime. *Applied Cognitive Psychology, 33*(4), 544–560. https://doi.org/10.1002/acp.3494

Part IV

Mental Health and Neurodiversity—Implications for the Court System

11

Competency Evaluations—Legal Precedents and Implications for Defendants with Mental Illnesses and Neurodevelopmental Disabilities

Learning Objectives

After this chapter, readers should be able to understand the:

1) Concepts of capacity and competency
2) Difference between insanity and incompetency to understand legal proceedings
3) Due process concerns when the question of incompetency to stand trial is raised
4) Competency restoration for those deemed incompetent to stand trial
5) Concept of competency to waive counsel and due process concerns
6) Concept of competency to waive Miranda rights and due process concerns

Introduction

Competency is a legal term defined as one's mental ability to participate in legal proceedings (Garner, 2019). Competency is raised when defendants' ability to make legal decisions is questioned due to a mental illness or disability. Many criminal justice system (CJS) practitioners confuse competency with insanity (i.e., legal responsibility). Competency is the defendant's current **capacity** (i.e., mental ability), while insanity addresses the defendant's mental state at the time of the offense (*see* Chapter 12 of this book

M. C. Mogavero, *Mental Health, Neurodiversity, and Criminal Justice*, https://doi.org/10.1007/978-3-031-88816-8_11

for details). Competency may be raised at any point during the entire legal system process by the defense attorney, prosecutor, judge, or other individuals involved in the case (Michaelsen & Kapoor, 2015; Wall et al., 2018). The judge ultimately decides whether to order a competency evaluation, although they rarely deny evaluations raised by defense attorneys (Callahan & Pinals, 2020).

Competent defendants are of the utmost importance not only for the protection of due process but also to preserve the dignity of the court and the entire judicial process. Competent defendants can effectively communicate and relay pertinent information to their defense attorneys. This, in turn, results in a more reliable and accurate CJS process, which serves the best interest of society (Bonnie, 1992). For defense attorneys, competency evaluations can set the trajectory for the entire case (Drogin, 2018). Although defense attorneys do not have a specific duty to provide notice that their client may be incompetent, they do have an ongoing duty to monitor and, when necessary, have a separate duty to investigate and address their client's competency (Philipsborn, 2017). Competency issues raise many concerns, and judges and attorneys often have no clinical training and limited support to meet the needs of defendants with mental illness and disabilities. A survey of 492 legal professionals found that judges were the least knowledgeable about mental illness and mental health defenses. Public defenders were the most knowledgeable compared to prosecutors and private attorneys (Frierson et al., 2015).

Defense attorneys make recommendations to their clients, but in most instances, defendants must make their own independent decisions. The defendant's decisions occur during the pretrial negotiation process involving the defense attorney and prosecutor and include entering a plea agreement, waiving the right to a jury trial and opting for a **bench trial,** or testifying on one's behalf (Bonnie, 1992). Because age, mental illnesses, and neurodevelopmental disorders (NDDs) often impact one's ability to make autonomous decisions, some may lack the ability to make autonomous decisions about their case and future, referred to as **decisional competency**. Defense attorneys without background knowledge often struggle to balance their defendants' autonomy with their specific needs (Parsons & Steadman, 2017). Mental health professionals are imperative in this pretrial process to formally assess and determine whether defendants have the capacity to understand the proceedings and determine if treatment or other interventions are necessary. Legal professionals must take a collaborative approach with the mental health system (MHS) to ensure the integrity of the court process.

Competency to Stand Trial

Competency to stand trial (CST), also known as fitness to stand trial or competency to proceed, refers to the defendant's present mental ability, measured by one's capacity to understand the charges, ability to understand the proceedings, and ability to assist in their own defense (Garner, 2019). Competency or fitness to stand trial can appear misleading, as most cases do not go to trial. The exact number of plea bargains or guilty pleas is unknown, but according to the most recent report by the National Center for State Courts, only 5% of felony cases and 8% of misdemeanor cases went to trial (Ostrom et al., 2020). A 2022 report by the United States (US) Courts estimated that about 90% of federal cases were resolved through plea bargains or guilty pleas. CST is the most common assessment for the courts. The exact number of annual evaluations is unknown, as there are no national records or precise statistics (Mossman et al., 2007), but recent annual estimates range from 25,600 to 51,500 (Gowensmith, 2019) to 94,000 (Owen et al., 2020) and may be as high as 130,000 (Kois et al., 2022).

Legal Precedent

The legal precedent for CST lies in the US Constitution's due process protections of the Fifth and Fourteenth Amendments. According to the Fifth Amendment, "no person shall be compelled in any criminal case.... be deprived of life, liberty, or property, without due process of law" (US National Archives, Bill or Rights). Section 11.1 of the Fourteenth Amendment further claims: "...nor shall any State deprive any person of life, liberty, or property, without due process of law; nor deny to any person within its jurisdiction the equal protection of the laws" (US National Archives, Amendments 11–27). One of the first federal cases that addressed CST was in 1899 in *Youtsey v. United States, which was decided by the Sixth Circuit* US Court of Appeals. The Court decided that when the issue of competency is raised, defendants have the right to have that issue considered because subjecting someone incompetent to criminal proceedings is a violation of due process (*Youtsey v. United States*, 1899).

There is no constitutional requirement that the state assume the burden of proof that a defendant is competent. Instead, if competency is questioned at any point, the state must allow defendants to demonstrate that they are incompetent to stand trial (IST). The statutory presumption is that a defendant is competent unless they can demonstrate otherwise by a **preponderance of the evidence.** One's mental health condition or cognitive deficit must be shown to affect the defendant's specific legal competencies to be found IST. The mere presence of a mental illness or condition is not sufficient. Some defendants with, for example, schizophrenia may be considered competent if their diagnosis does not legally impair their abilities (Roesch et al., 2009). *The standards for competency in federal cases were later set in Dusky* v. United States (1960) and the right to a hearing in Pate v. Robinson (1966).

Case Briefs: US Supreme Court Cases Addressing Competency to Stand Trial

Dusky v. United States (1960)

Facts: Milton Richard Dusky, who had a diagnosis of schizophrenia, was charged with assisting in the kidnapping and rape of an underage girl. After his arrest, Dusky was admitted to a hospital for a competency evaluation. Dr. Moreau conducted a brief mental status evaluation and determined that Dusky had some recollection of the offense and was "oriented to time, place, and person" (e.g., knew the day/date, where they were, their name). Dr. Sturgell also conducted an evaluation and observed that Dusky experienced hallucinations and made statements that he was framed. Dr. Sturgell confirmed his diagnosis of schizophrenia and concluded that Dusky was unable to properly understand the proceedings against him or assist counsel in his defense. Dusky was tried based on Dr. Moreau's conclusion, found guilty, and sentenced to 45 years. Dusky appealed to the US Court of Appeals for the Eighth Circuit, which affirmed his conviction, and Dusky appealed to the US Supreme Court.

Issue: Whether the right to due process encompasses the right to a competency evaluation before a defendant stands trial, as opposed to brief mental status that one is "oriented to time, place, and person."

Outcome: The US Supreme Court concluded that in criminal proceedings, there must be a finding of mental competency to stand trial, and the court cannot make that determination merely because one is "oriented to time and place" and has some recollection of events. To determine competency, the evaluation must assess whether defendants have a sufficient and present ability to consult with their attorney and have a reasonable of rational and factual understanding of the charges against them. These standards later became known as the Dusky Standards:

1. Can the defendant effectively communicate with their attorney?
2. Does the defendant have a factual understanding of the proceedings?
3. Does the defendant have a rational understanding of the proceedings?

Pate v. Robinson (1966)

Facts: Theodore Robinson had a history of mental health problems. He was previously convicted of murdering his 18-month-old son and served four years in prison. In 1959, he was convicted of murdering his common-law wife, Flossie May Ward, at a restaurant where she worked. At trial, the defense presented four witnesses who expressed their opinion that Robinson was experiencing symptoms of mental illness at the time of the murder, which raised the issue of his competency. The prosecution presented testimony from Dr. Haines that Robinson understood the nature of the charges against him and was able to cooperate with his attorney, but there was no competency hearing. Robinson was found guilty and sentenced to life in prison. Robinson appealed to the Supreme Court of Illinois, which affirmed his conviction, and Robinson appealed to the US Supreme Court.

Issue: Whether the state court's failure to conduct a competency to stand trial hearing violated the Fourteenth Amendment's constitutional right to due process.

Outcome: The US Supreme Court decided that Robinson was deprived of due process of law protected under the Fourteenth Amendment. The evidence raised at trial provided sufficient doubt as to Robinson's competence to stand trial, and he was constitutionally entitled to a competency hearing.

Assessing Competency

In most cases, the court orders the evaluation and hires an independent mental health clinician to conduct the evaluation. If the defendant currently has a treating clinician, they should not perform the evaluation to avoid bias. The typical doctor-patient confidentiality is absent, the information is not **privileged** (i.e., private), and the evaluator may be called to testify in court. Before the evaluation, evaluators must take proper measures to protect defendants against self-incrimination. This includes explaining the purpose of the evaluation, who hired them, that the information is not confidential, and explaining what confidential means. They should also explain that they may have to testify about the evaluation results and that the defendant has the right not to answer any questions (Hoge, 2016; Mossman et al., 2007).

Most of the competency evaluation focuses on assessing the defendant's ability to have a factual and rational understanding of the criminal proceedings and their ability to make legal decisions on their behalf. If found IST, court proceedings can be postponed until the defendant is able to participate in their defense (Roesch et al., 2009). Although rare, a private defense attorney may also obtain a competency evaluation of a client outside of the court system and, depending on the outcome, may remain privileged (Morris et al., 2021).

Competency evaluations typically include a validated instrument as an additional source of forensic assessment (The American Academy of Psychiatry and the Law, AAPL 2014). About a dozen instruments have been developed over the last six decades, ranging from informal checklists (e.g., Robey's Checklist, 1965) to structured criterion-based scoring instruments (e.g., Georgia Court Competency Test, Nicholson et al., 1988). Below is a list of several psychometric structured assessment tools for competency, which vary in comprehensiveness.[1]

Validated Psychometric Testing Instruments for CST

- **Robey's Checklist** (Robey, 1965)—three-option checklist (none, mental health, disability) with 22 questions that cover three areas: comprehension of court proceedings, ability to advise counsel, and susceptibility to decompensation.
- **Competency Screening Test (CST)** (Lipsitt et al., 1971)—three-point scale (0–2, higher scores = higher competency) that contains 22 sentence completion questions that cover six areas: relationship to attorney, understanding of court proceedings, affective response, judgmental qualities, trust in attorney, recognition of the seriousness of proceedings.
- **The Competence to Stand Trial Assessment Instrument** (CSTAI) (Laboratory of Community Psychiatry, 1973)—A semi-structured interview comprised of 13 open-ended questions covering areas relating to Dusky standards.
- **Georgia Court Competency Test** (GCCT) (Wildman et al., 1978)—An interview with 21 questions in three areas: knowledge of proceedings, knowledge of charges and penalties, and relationship with counsel.
- **Competence Assessment for Standing Trial for Defendants with MR** (CAST-MR) (Everington & Luckasson, 1992)—Developed for those with intellectual disability (ID), 50 questions (multiple-choice and open-ended) that cover three areas: legal concepts, assist in defense, understanding the case.

- **MacArthur Competence Assessment Tool–Criminal Adjudication** (MacCAT-CA) (Otto et al., 1998)—three-point scale (0—2, higher scores = higher competency) with 22 questions that cover three areas: understanding of proceedings, reasoning ability about specific choices, and appreciation of the meaning and consequences.
- **Evaluation of Competency to Stand Trial-Revised** (ECST-R) (Rogers et al., 2004)—18 questions covering the areas: factual understanding and rational understanding of proceedings, ability to assist counsel, overall rational ability; also contains a screening for malingering (i.e., pretending) and only used for those with IQs over 60.
- **Fitness Interview Test (FIT)**[2] (Roesch et al., 1984; 2006)—An interview with 16 questions rated on a three-point scale that covers three areas: ability to understand proceedings, ability to understand consequences of proceedings, and ability to communicate with counsel.

No one instrument is considered the "gold standard" for measuring competence (Pirelli et al., 2011). Other instruments commonly administered in competency evaluations are the Minnesota Multiphasic Personality Inventory (MMPI-2) (Tellegen & Ben-Porath, 2008, 2011) to assess different psychiatric conditions and their severity; the Wechsler Adult Intelligence Scales (WAIS-IV, 2008) to assess cognitive ability for adults, and the Brief Psychiatric Rating Scale (BPRS) (Overall & Gorham, 1988) to identify psychopathology (Pirelli et al., 2011).

The information from the instruments represents only one piece of a competency assessment and must be integrated with information from other sources (Pirelli et al., 2011). Family members and those well-acquainted with the defendant may be interviewed to speak about the defendant's current and previous mental state. The evaluation may also include reviewing prior records about the defendant's mental or intellectual ability (e.g., medical, mental health, and school records). This is especially important for juveniles, as they tend to make decisions that reflect lower psychosocial maturity (*see* Chapter 3 of this book for details), and those under 15 have been shown to perform poorly on assessments such as the MacCAT-CA (Grisso et al., 2003). If one is representing an autistic client,[3] attorneys should consider hiring an evaluator with expertise in autism, as they often have different communication needs. Autistic defendants may also present themselves as competent when they are not (Greenspan, 2020). If the mental health evaluator has no knowledge or expertise in autism, they may not be the best person to conduct a competency evaluation (Gavisk, 2020).

Once the evaluation is complete, a report will be sent to the court detailing the evaluator's opinions regarding the defendant's abilities and competency with recommendations for moving forward with the case (Hoge, 2016). The determination of competency (i.e., the ultimate decision that one is incompetent) is a legal decision made by the judge at the competency hearing. However, the judge typically agrees with the opinion of the evaluator more than 90% of the time (Zapf et al., 2004). Most defendants referred for competency evaluations are found CST, with findings of IST estimated to be about 28% (Pirelli et al., 2011).

Competency Restoration

Defendants found CST proceed with their case. For those found IST, most states have statutes that require the evaluator to provide an opinion about whether restoration of competence is likely (i.e., are restorable) within a designated time frame. For defendants with intellectual and developmental disabilities, evaluators may be unable to make an opinion on restorability, as they might not have had prior competence to restore. Therefore, the terms "attainment" and "remediation" are used (Callahan & Pinals, 2020). Restoring competence may involve civil commitment to a psychiatric facility (i.e., forensic civil commitment) (*see* Chapter 15 of this book for details) for treatment to improve defendants' mental abilities enough to where they could be considered competent (for a case example, *see* Chapter 3 of this book, Case of Alex), then released to proceed with their case and assist in their defense (Murrie et al., 2023).

Treating mental illness is often not the sole factor in restoring competency, as it also involves education in the legal concepts and procedures of the trial process so that they can perform as a criminal defendant (Callahan & Pinals, 2020). Many factors are involved in the length of restoration to competency, but most are restored within one year (Morris & Parker, 2008). Those defendants who cannot be restored to competency will generally have their charges dismissed or **nolle prosequi,** where prosecutors decide not to prosecute. In Jackson v. Indiana (1978), the issue of restorability was addressed for those who are not restorable.

Case Brief: Jackson v Indiana (1978)

Facts: Theon Jackson was a 27-year-old man who was deaf, had an intellectual disability, and his mental age was estimated to be about preschool age. He also lacked verbal communication abilities and only communicated through limited sign language. In May 1968, Jackson was charged with separate robberies of two women. In the first robbery, he stole a purse valued at $4; in the second, he stole $5 cash. The judge ordered a competency hearing, and Jackson was evaluated by two psychiatrists with the assistance of a sign language interpreter. Both psychiatrists concluded that Jackson's communication skills were extremely limited, and due to his intellectual disability and inability to hear, he was unable to understand the nature of the charges against him or participate in his defense. One psychiatrist stated it was extremely unlikely he could ever learn to read, write, or develop proficiency in sign language. The other stated that even if Jackson were not deaf, he would still be IST. The judge agreed, and Jackson was found to be IST and was committed to a psychiatric facility until he was determined to be "sane."

Jackson's attorney filed a motion, arguing that Jackson was not "insane" and he would not be able to attain a mental status that could be regarded as "sane" or CST. His attorney also argued that Jackson's commitment amounted to a "life sentence" without even being convicted of a crime, a violation of the Fourteenth Amendment. The trial court denied the motion, and on appeal, the Supreme Court of Indiana affirmed the decision. Jackson's attorney appealed his case to the US Supreme Court.

Issue: Whether a pretrial indefinite commitment violated the Fourteenth Amendment's equal protection rights by committing someone based solely on an inability to stand trial and committing someone on a more stringent standard than traditional civil commitment proceedings.

Outcome: The US Supreme Court decided those charged with a criminal offense and found IST cannot be committed for more than the reasonable period of time necessary to determine whether there is a substantial probability that they will be able to be restored to competence in the foreseeable future. If a defendant is deemed IST, the state must release the defendant. If the state believes civil commitment is necessary (due to a danger to self or others), then the state must use traditional civil commitment proceedings for indefinite commitment.

Over the last several decades, the US saw an increase in restoration orders, which has led to an increase in inpatient hospitalizations (Murrie et al., 2023). Wik et al. (2020) surveyed 27 state mental health systems between 2005 and 2014 and found, on average, a 37% increase in inpatient admissions for competency restoration on a given day. Due to the deinstitutionalization movement and the closing of hospitals (*see* Chapter 7 of this book for details), this increased demand surpassed the supply of available inpatient beds, leading to long wait lists. As a result, recent methods to restore competency include outpatient settings or alternative locations, including jails (Gowensmith et al., 2016; Heilbrun et al., 2019). Others who are ineligible for civil commitment are placed under probation supervision to determine if competency can be restored. Thus, the CJS is often tasked with handling many individuals with mental illness and disabilities awaiting competency evaluations. Below is a case of a young autistic man who was found to lack the ability to understand the proceedings and was found to be IST.

Case of Felix[4]

Background: Felix was 18 years old when he was arrested for possession of indecent images of minors. Felix has a long history of mental illnesses and other disabilities. His parents divorced shortly after he was born and was raised by his mother until his father gained custody when he was five years of age. While in his mother's care, he experienced physical and sexual abuse by a family member and witnessed his mother being physically abused by her boyfriend. He was diagnosed with autism, attention-deficit hyperactivity disorder (ADHD), post-traumatic stress disorder (PTSD) from prior abuse, major depressive disorder, epilepsy, a nonverbal learning disability, and borderline intellectual disability. He currently lives with his father, stepmother, and two stepbrothers. He graduated from public high school while receiving an individualized education program. He has no criminal record, and no history of substance use disorder.

Instant Offense: Felix was in an internet chat room on his computer when another user sent him a web address link, which led to a site of indecent images of minors. The police department in his jurisdiction received a report that someone at an IP address uploaded an indecent image of a minor. They tracked the IP address to Felix's residence. Police arrived at Felix's home and, after questioning, determined the images came from his computer. Police read Felix his Miranda warning (with his father present), and he waived his rights and agreed to speak with the officer. Felix explained that he obtained the images through a link he was sent. He initially denied uploading any images to his computer but later mentioned he had no memory of it. A search warrant was executed on Felix's computer, which revealed five indecent images of minors. Felix was arraigned and charged with five felony counts of possession of indecent images of minors.

Pretrial Supervision: At the request of his defense attorney, the judge ordered a competency evaluation and placed Felix under court supervision (pretrial probation). With his father present, he met with his assigned probation officer at his office. According to his father, the probation officer yelled at Felix while going over his probation conditions, treating him as if he were a "hardened criminal." Felix had difficulty understanding what the probation officer was saying and was confused about why he was there. Between the probation officer's yelling and his confusion, Felix became overwhelmed with anxiety; he soiled himself in the office.

Assessment Process: To assist with the competency evaluation, Felix's father obtained school and medical records, including prior evaluations and diagnoses, to present to the psychologist. Felix was interviewed and questioned about his current legal situation and understanding of the legal process, including the roles and responsibilities of various courtroom personnel. The psychologist also reviewed all the collaborating information and interviewed Felix's father. Felix was administered the WASI-III, which demonstrated a full-scale IQ of 79, which placed him in the upper limits of borderline intellectual disability.

The evaluator determined that Felix had somewhat of a factual understanding of his legal situation but not a rational understanding. He was unable to articulate the charges or their severity level and indicated he did not understand that what he did was wrong. Felix also did not understand what happens in court and was unaware of another attorney (i.e., prosecutor) or what their role might be. The evaluation concluded that due to his mental illnesses and cognitive limitations, Felix lacked the ability to rationally consult with his attorney, understand legal proceedings, or participate in his defense and was determined to be IST. Regarding his prognosis, Felix did not meet the criteria for civil commitment or any inpatient psychiatric treatment.

Outcome: The judge ordered a second competency evaluation in six months, where Felix was to remain under court supervision. The second evaluation concluded there was no change in his ability to understand the proceedings and remained IST. After more than two years under court supervision and awaiting a decision from the court, the prosecutor officially dismissed the charges against Felix "in the interest of justice" due to him being IST.

Competency to Waive Counsel

Another competency issue in court proceedings addresses defendants' Sixth Amendment right to counsel (i.e., have an attorney represent them) and the right to waive counsel. One may be deemed CST but not necessarily competent to waive their right to counsel and **proceed pro se.** Proceed pro se refers to representing oneself without the assistance of counsel, and for the waiver to be valid, it requires one to do so knowingly, intelligently, and voluntarily. The Sixth Amendment right to counsel only applied to federal prosecutions and was not applied to state prosecutions until Gideon v. Wainwright (1963). In the Gideon decision, it was deemed a violation of due process not to provide defendants with an attorney when facing a loss of civil liberties. Defendants deemed **indigent**, those who lack the financial means to hire an attorney, have the right to a court appointment attorney at no charge. Whether there should be a separate, higher standard of competence for defendants who wish to waive their right to counsel was addressed in Godinez v. Moran (1993), and what factors must be in place for one to be competent to proceed pro se was addressed in Indiana v. Edwards (2008).

Case Briefs: US Supreme Court Cases Involving Competency to Waive Counsel

Godinez v. Moran (1993)

Facts: In August 1984, Richard Allen Moran entered a tavern in Las Vegas, Nevada, and shot the bartender and a patron before stealing cash from the register. Nine days later, Moran went to his ex-wife's apartment and shot her then himself. He was hospitalized after he survived the suicide attempt. While in the hospital recovering, Moran contacted the police and admitted to the fatal shootings of three people. Moran pleaded not guilty to three counts of first-degree murder. After his competency evaluation by two psychiatrists, Moran was found CST. He then decided to discharge his attorney and plead guilty. Being CST, the court determined that Moran understood the charges and was able to assist in his own defense, and therefore, waiving his right to counsel and entering a guilty plea was done so knowingly, intelligently, and voluntarily. Moran did not want his case to go to trial, so his ability to proceed pro se was not raised. His guilty plea was accepted, and Moran was sentenced to death.

During the post-conviction appeal process, Moran claimed he was incompetent to waive counsel. The Nevada Supreme Court denied his appeal for dismissal, and a US District Court, District of Nevada, rejected his application. Moran appealed to the Federal Court of Appeals for the Ninth Circuit, who reversed the decision, concluding that the District Court should have held a hearing regarding his competence to waive counsel before accepting his guilty plea. The court decided that waiving one's right to counsel requires a higher standard of understanding than CST, citing previous state cases, *Faretta v. California* (1975), that defendants only to be "literate, competent, and understanding" and *Martinez v. Court of Appeal of California* (2000), that there is no constitutional right to proceed without counsel. Moran appealed to the US Supreme Court.

Issue: Whether waiving the right to counsel and entering a guilty plea requires a higher standard than CST.

Outcome: The US Supreme Court found that the competency standard for pleading guilty and waiving the right to counsel is the same as the test for CST. The Court upheld Moran's conviction and death sentence. Moran was executed in March 1996.

Indiana v. Edwards (2008)

Facts: In July 1999, Ahmad Edwards, armed with a gun, attempted to steal a pair of shoes from a department store and, when caught, shot at a store security officer but wounded a bystander. He was charged with attempted murder, battery with a deadly weapon, criminal recklessness, and theft. Edwards had schizophrenia, and the issue of competency was raised. The first competency hearing found him IST. Seven months later, after his condition improved, a second hearing was held, and he was found CST. Seven months later, a third hearing was held because Edwards was experiencing delusions and was found IST. Eight months later, his condition had again improved, and he was CST. Edwards requested to represent himself and proceed *pro se* and requested a **continuance** (i.e., more time to work on his case). The court refused the continuance, so he went to trial and was represented by counsel. The jury convicted Edwards of criminal recklessness and theft but was unable to reach a verdict on the attempted murder and battery. The State retried him on the attempted murder and battery charges, and Edwards, again, requested to proceed *pro se*. Although the trial court found that he was CST, he was unable to conduct a defense, as he rambled incoherently and presented irrelevant documents during the proceeding. The judge denied his request for self-representation. Edwards was represented by appointed counsel at his retrial, and the jury convicted Edwards of attempted murder and battery. Edwards appealed to Indiana's intermediate appellate court, claiming that the trial court's refusal to allow him to represent himself deprived him of his constitutional right of self-representation. The court agreed and ordered a new trial. Edwards's case was appealed to the US Supreme Court.

Issue: Whether the previous standard in *Faretta v. California* (1975), "literate, competent, and understanding" is an appropriate standard for a defendant's mental competence to proceed pro se when invoking the Sixth

Amendment right to self-representation when the defendant is otherwise unable to conduct a coherent defense.

Outcome: The US Supreme Court decided that states may use a higher competence standard for defendants wishing to proceed pro se. The Court affirmed the right to self-representation when the individual "voluntarily and intelligently elects to do so," but this does not apply when a defendant's mental competency is questioned.

Competency to Waive Miranda

Whether defendants were competent to waive their Miranda rights and speak with police during a custodial interrogation is a retroactive (past tense) competency issue, typically addressed after one is found IST. Many defendants with mental illnesses or disabilities lack comprehension of the statements in the Miranda warnings (Rogers et al., 2007) (*see* Chapter 9 of this book for details). For a Miranda waiver to be valid, one must do so "knowingly, intelligently, and voluntarily"[5] (Constitutional waivers by states & criminal defendants, 2021; Miranda v. Arizona, 1966). If one is found IST and lacks (1) the ability to understand the court process (their statements will be used in court against them), (2) lacks understanding of the role of a defense attorney (one has the right to have an attorney present while being questioned), and (3) lacks competency to make decisions on their behalf (waive their rights and speak with police), then their mental ability to "knowingly, intelligently, and voluntarily" waive their rights is questionable. However, the presence of a mental illness or disability alone may not invalidate a Miranda waiver. For a waiver to be considered voluntary, the waiver may not be the result of police coercion. The US Supreme Court ruled in Colorado v. Connelly (1986) that the presence of symptoms, such as delusions or hallucinations, do not render confessions involuntary. Evidence of additional competency factors must be presented to the court to argue that statements made to police are inadmissible.

Assessing Miranda Comprehension

Unlike CST, which is a present-tense assessment of one's current mental functioning, Miranda assessments evaluate an earlier point in time. Defense attorneys may seek an evaluation to provide relevant information to the court regarding their client's psychological characteristics that increase the risk of providing false or misleading information. If a client confessed, provided incriminating statements, or gave inaccurate statements to police, the results of this evaluation may be presented to the court to address whether the statements are admissible. Comprehension can be measured using an instrument designed to specifically evaluate various aspects of Miranda, such as vocabulary and one's rights during an interrogation. The US Supreme Court stated that Miranda warnings should be presented in "clear and unequivocal language" (Miranda v. Arizona, 1966), but each state or jurisdiction determines how its police officers issue the Miranda warning, which varies considerably. Rogers et al. (2007) reviewed 560 Miranda warnings across the US and noted that the reading level varied from about a third-grade level to a postgraduate level, and the total word count of the entire warnings ranged from 49 to 547 words. Several validated psychometric instruments are available to assess one's understanding of Miranda warnings. Grisso (1981) conceptualized the appreciation of the significance of Miranda rights in three areas:

1. the ability to recognize the interrogative and adversarial nature of police questioning.
2. the ability to recognize the defense attorney as an advocate and that information disclosed is confidential
3. the ability to recognize the right not to speak to police cannot be revoked, and statements made can be used in court.

Validated Psychometric Testing Instruments for Miranda Comprehension

Below is a list of several psychometric assessments for competency to waive Miranda.[6] As shown, some are more comprehensive than others.

- **Instruments for Assessing Understanding and Appreciation of Miranda Rights** (Grisso, 1998)—Contains four discrete instruments rated on a two or three-point scale: Comprehension of Miranda Rights (CMR): ability to paraphrase Miranda; Comprehension of Miranda Rights-Recognition (CMR-R): ability to recognize the meaning of Miranda; Comprehension of Miranda Vocabulary (CMV): ability to understand specific words; Function of Rights in Interrogation (FRI): ability to recognize significance of rights.

- **The Miranda Rights Scale (MRS)** and **The Miranda Statements Scale (MSS)** (Rogers, 2005a, b)—the MRS contains eight open-ended questions rated on a two-point scale and covers four areas: exercise-silence, exercise-counsel, waive-silence, and waive counsel). The MSS is scored by the defendants' ability to state in their own words the content of each warning.
- **Miranda Checklist Inventory (MCI)** (Greenfield et al., 2000)—A nonstandardized inventory that lists 15 guidelines (e.g., age, IQ, "street smarts," length of interrogation, prior experience with Miranda process) to retrospectively evaluate one's competency.

Neurodiverse Defendants: Challenges for Defense Attorneys

Many with disabilities, including autism and ID, have learned to "mask" to appear more competent than they are (*see* Chapter 9 of this book for details). Greenspan (2020) noted that people with autism or ID have often experienced challenges or failures, whether academically or socially. This may lead them to feel the need to maintain their self-preservation and present themselves as competent, even when it is in their best interest to do so. Some may display "street smarts" because they do not want to appear unintelligent when they do not understand something (Kranendonk et al., 2019). Brewer et al. (2016) used standardized measures of competency among those with and without autism and found that autistic individuals had a poorer understanding of the courtroom process and concluded that additional support and special measures should be implemented for autistic defendants.

Box 11.1. Practitioner Spotlight: Mark J. Mahoney, Esq

Mark J. Mahoney is a criminal defense attorney with Harrington & Mahoney in Buffalo, NY, and has practiced law for over 50 years. For over a decade, he has exclusively represented persons charged with crimes who have autism or neurological conditions with similar effects on social learning and executive functioning. For Mahoney, such cases raise human rights and justice issues that the entire criminal law system is not trained, equipped, or inclined to deal with. To justly address neurodiversity in accused persons requires reimagining each aspect of the process and the role of each participant. Although mastery of criminal law is essential, Mahoney claims that the greatest success in these cases, especially when diverting clients from the criminal process, comes from defense attorneys using every means possible to bridge the information gap between justice professionals (i.e., law enforcement, prosecutors, judges) and experts. Specifically, educating justice professionals on how these neurological conditions have rendered their clients vulnerable to engage (usually without consciousness of wrongdoing or intent to harm) in criminal conduct. This requires the defense attorney to have in-depth knowledge of the neurological differences to find the right experts to evaluate their client. With the expert evaluation, attorneys can report the condition's role in their client's conduct and culpability while using personal efforts at persuasion supported by outcomes in similar cases and empirical research articles, including data on outcomes, recidivism, victimization in custody, and available therapies.

Mahoney's efforts have resulted in a significant number of dismissals, diversions, reduced pleas, avoiding Megan's Law registration and notification, or reduced sentences. For example, to demonstrate his autistic client's severely impaired executive functioning in the criminal process, Mahoney video-recorded his 30 hours of effort to educate his client on all matters relevant to the case and, ultimately, demonstrated his client's inability to decide on his own about how to proceed. This clear demonstration of a lack of decisional competency, being recorded, would allow the judge, or possibly an appeals court, to see for themselves how his client was unable to decide for himself after accumulating a mass of rote knowledge and signed a plea agreement solely on the advice of his attorney.

Considerations and Recommendations

Considering the volume of criminal cases, it would be unreasonable and a waste of valuable resources to evaluate the mental health status of every suspect or defendant prior to arrest or arraignment. However, there are several tasks that CJS practitioners can accomplish to support and meet the needs of defendants with mental illnesses and disabilities. Below are several considerations and recommendations for CJS practitioners that may improve the efficiency and effectiveness of the court process for all parties.

Attention to Warning Signs

Experienced attorneys may be more perceptive to various signs that their client may not be competent. However, newer attorneys can also observe characteristics typically included in mental health professionals' competency evaluations. These characteristics are detailed more thoroughly in Drogin (2018) but include disheveled appearance, hyper or hypo motor activity (fidgeting, catatonic), or appear to be unable to grasp what the attorney is stating.

Cross-System Collaboration

CJS practitioners, including judges, defense attorneys, and prosecutors, should develop connections and relationships with mental health professionals and treatment providers so both systems can collaborate across systems and better understand each step in the competence process (Drogin, 2018). Understanding what resources are available in the community and the capacity of inpatient beds available in hospitals will help all parties better understand timeframes and potential backlogging (Callahan & Pinals, 2020). In some jurisdictions, mental health courts may be more appropriate for some defendants, as the judges have specialized knowledge and training to work with individuals, a therapeutic atmosphere, and a multidisciplinary team approach (*see* Chapter 14 of this book for details).

Continued Education on Mental Health and Neurodiversity

As discussed in prior chapters in Part 1 and Part 3, CJS practitioners should receive education and training on mental health and neurodevelopmental disabilities. When attorneys are not well trained in such areas or are inexperienced with these defendant populations, it is unclear how effective or efficient they may be with their cases. Philipsborn (2019) also recommends additional education in neuroscience techniques to understand learning and memory to provide explanations and corroborate evidence. Education is also important because mental health and neurodevelopmental disabilities are "non-obvious" conditions, and some defendants may mask their condition for fear of stigma. This can lead to conditions going unnoticed or even confused for behavioral, personality, or substance use problems. This may result in defense attorneys, prosecutors, or judges misinterpreting the defendant as uncooperative and may be inclined to invest less time and energy in the case (Parsons & Steadman, 2017). Training and education should include methods to better communicate with clients to maintain trust and build rapport.

Building Rapport

Building rapport and establishing relationships also assists attorneys in having a better understanding of their clients, providing them with more opportunities to examine their mental status, and raising these issues as a mitigation or defense. Defense attorneys are advocates, and the rapport and relationship with their clients are essential for them to trust the legal advice they provide. When mental health or competency issues are raised, clients may also confuse "competency" and "sanity" and react defensively or become argumentative. Knowledgeable attorneys can explain the difference in a non-judgmental manner and discuss the pros and cons. Establishing a relationship, in addition to having knowledge of mental health and disabilities, can allow attorneys to better communicate defense strategies and explain how they have their best interests in mind (Edwards & Grand, 2018).

Conclusion

Defendants have a presumption of competency, regardless of any usual behaviors or other observations. Some clients may lack the capacity to fully understand the legal process, may not be forthcoming, and may not disclose their condition for various reasons, including fear of stigma or being perceived as ignorant or unintelligent. Some may be unaware of their mental health condition or how it affects their ability to understand their rights, the court proceedings, or the role of CJS practitioners involved in their case. CJS practitioners should take steps as early as possible to protect the due process rights of suspects and the integrity of the court and the entire CJS.

Contact with the CJS typically begins with police contact. Police can identify potential issues or concerns and clearly document behaviors or any other observations in their reports, which can be used later if questions about mental health or other cognitive limitations are raised. Attention to and documenting potential competency issues ensures due process protections. As discussed in Chapter 9, police should also attempt to ensure suspects understand their Miranda rights outlined in Miranda v. Arizona (1966). Police are required to mention the rights but are not required to explain them. Interviewing suspects is essential to an investigation; however, preserving the integrity of statements provided by potentially incompetent suspects is essential. In Felix's case, due to his autism, ID, and other mental health conditions, his memory was impaired, and he gave conflicting statements to police. Considering the results of his competency evaluation, it is arguable whether he was competent to understand his Miranda rights enough to waive them and speak with police.

The stress of involvement in the CJS, including court hearings, pretrial supervision, or jail detention, can lead to further deterioration of one's mental health. The process of determining and restoring competency can be lengthy. The role of defense attorneys is crucial in such cases, where communication and rapport-building may be more difficult. Training and education for CJS practitioners is an important first step to ensuring due process and making the best decisions for defendants. As the CJS has increasingly been entrusted with the care and supervision of defendants during the pretrial process, including jails (Callahan & Pinals, 2020; Murrie et al., 2023), training and education of CJS practitioners throughout the CJS is critical to improve communications and treatment efforts for the best possible outcomes.

Key Terms

Bench trial
Capacity
Competency
Continuance
Decisional competency
Indigent
Nolle prosequi
Plea bargain agreement
Preponderance of the evidence
Privilege
Proceed pro se

Chapter Questions

1) Define the terms capacity and competency and explain how the two terms are similar but different.
2) Describe the steps involved in assessing whether a defendant is competent to stand trial
3) Describe the standards used to determine whether a defendant is competent to stand trial outlined in Dusky v. United States.
4) Describe the steps involved in restoring competence to stand trial.
5) Describe the terms Competency to Waive Miranda and Competency to Waive Counsel and Proceed Pro Se.
6) Describe the impacts of assessing and restoring competency on the CJS and MHS.

Suggested Readings

Golding, S. L. (2016). Learning forensic examinations of adjudicative competency. In R. A. Jackson & R. Roesch (Eds.), *Learning forensic assessment: Research and practice* (pp. 65–96). Routledge.

Melton, G. B., Petrila, J., Poythress, N. G., Slobogin, C., Otto, R. K., Mossman, D., & Condie, L. O. (2018). *Psychological evaluations for the courts: A handbook for mental health professionals and lawyers* (4th ed.). Guilford Press.

Redding, R. E. (2004). Why it is essential to teach about mental health issues in criminal law (And a primer on how to do it). *Villanova School of Law Working Paper Series* (3), 407–440.

Notes

1. Drogin (2018) and Roesch et al. (2009) describe these in more detail, which are helpful for attorneys representing clients in cases where competency is raised.
2. Designed for use in Canada but may be used in the United States.
3. *See A Note About Evolving Language and Term i*n Chapter 1 for information on identity-first language
4. Names and some details have been changed for anonymity.
5. Also referred to as willfully.
6. Some assessments do not meet evidentiary standards of Frye or Daubert in some states (Willner, 2011) (See Chapter 13 of this book for more details). Defense attorneys must determine what, if any, Miranda comprehension assessments meet evidentiary standards in their jurisdiction (*see* Frumkin, 2010 for more details).

References

American Academy of Psychiatry and the Law (AAPL). (2014). AAPL practice guideline for forensic psychiatric evaluation of defendants raising the insanity defense. *The Journal of the American Academy of Psychiatry and the Law, 42*, S3–S76.

Bonnie, R. J. (1992). The competence of criminal defendants: A theoretical reformulation. *Behavioral Sciences & the Law, 10*(3), 291–316. https://doi.org/10.1002/bsl.2370100303

Brewer, R. J., Davies, G. M., & Blackwood, N. J. (2016). Fitness to plead: The impact of autism spectrum disorder. *Journal of Forensic Psychology Practice, 16*(3), 182–197. https://doi.org/10.1080/15228932.2016.1177285

Callahan, L., & Pinals, D. A. (2020). Challenges to reforming the competence to stand trial and competence restoration system. *Psychiatric Services, 71*(7), 691–697. https://doi.org/10.1176/appi.ps.201900483

Colorado v. Connelly, 479 U.S. 157 (1986).

Constitutional waivers by states and criminal defendants. (2021). *Harvard Law Review, 134*(7), 2552–2573.

Drogin, E. Y. (2018). Competency to stand trial. In E. Kelley (Ed.), *Representing people with mental disabilities: A criminal defense lawyer's best practices manual* (pp. 1–15). ABA Publishing.

Dusky v. United States, 362 U.S. 402 (1960).

Edwards, W. J., & Grands, R. (2018). Working with clients. In E. Kelley (Ed.), *Representing people with mental disabilities: A criminal defense lawyer's best practices manual* (pp. 249–258). ABA Publishing.

Everington, C., & Luckasson, R. (1992). *Competence assessment to stand trial for defendants with mental retardation (CAST–MR) manual*. International Diagnostic Services.

Faretta v. California, 422 U.S. 806 (1975).

Frierson, R. L., Boyd, M. S., & Harper, A. (2015). Mental illness and mental health defenses: Perceptions of the criminal bar. *The Journal of the American Academy of Psychiatry and the Law, 43*(4), 483–491.

Frumkin, I. B. (2010). Evaluations of competency to waive Miranda rights and coerced or false confessions: Common pitfalls in expert testimony. In G. D. Lassiter & C. A. Meissner (Eds.), *Police interrogations and false confessions: Current research, practice, and policy recommendations* (pp. 191–209). American Psychological Association. https://doi.org/10.1037/12085-012

Garner, B. A. (2019). *Black's law dictionary* (11th ed.). Thomson Reuters.

Gavisk, M. (2020). Working with the expert: An attorney's perspective. In E. Kelley. (Ed.), *Representing people with autism spectrum disorders: A practical guide for criminal defense lawyers* (pp. 65–73). ABA Publishing.

Gideon v. Wainwright, 372 U.S. 335. (1963).

Godinez v. Moran, 509 U.S. 389 (1993).

Gowensmith, W. N. (2019). Resolution or resignation: The role of forensic mental health professionals amidst the competency services crisis. *Psychology, Public Policy & Law, 25*(1), 1–14. https://doi.org/10.1037/law0000190

Gowensmith, W. N., Frost, L. E., Speelman, D. W., & Therson, D. E. (2016). Lookin' for beds in all the wrong places: Outpatient competency restoration as a promising approach to modern challenges. *Psychology, Public Policy, and Law, 22*(3), 293–305. https://doi.org/10.1037/law0000088

Greenfield, D. P., Dougherty, E. J., Jackson, R. M., & Zimmerman, M. L. (2000). Retrospective evaluation of Miranda reading levels and waiver competency. *American Journal of Forensic Psychology, 19*, 75–86.

Greenspan, E. (2020). Competency. In E. Kelley (Ed.), *Representing people with autism spectrum disorders: A practical guide for criminal defense attorneys* (pp. 7–20). ABA Publishing.

Grisso, T. (1981). *Juveniles waiver of rights: Legal and psychological competence.* Plenum Press.

Grisso, T. (1998). *Instruments for assessing understanding and appreciation of Miranda rights.* Professional Resource Press/Professional Resource Exchange.

Grisso, T., Steinberg, L., Woolard, J., Cauffman, E., Scott, E., Graham, S., Lexcen, F., Reppucci, N. D., & Schwartz, R. (2003). Juveniles' competence to stand trial: A comparison of adolescents' and adults' capacities as trial defendants. *Law and Human Behavior*, *27*(4), 333–363. https://doi.org/10.1023/A:1024065015717

Heilbrun, K., Giallella, C., Wright, H. J., DeMatteo, D., Griffin, P. A., Locklair, B., & Desai, A. (2019). Treatment for restoration of competence to stand trial: Critical analysis and policy recommendations. *Psychology, Public Policy, and Law*, *25*(4), 266–283. https://doi.org/10.1037/law0000210

Hoge, S. K. (2016). Competence to stand trial: An overview. *Indian Journal of Psychiatry*, *58*(2), S187–S190. https://doi.org/10.4103/0019-5545.196830

Indiana v. Edwards, 554 U.S. 164 (2008).

Kranendonk, R., Malsch, M., de Poot, C., Teeuwen, M., & Elffers, H. (2019). Suspects with intellectual disability in police interviews: Risks of interviewing techniques for the reliability of suspects' statements [Paper Presentation]—American Society of Criminology 75th Annual Meeting, San Francisco, CA. United States, November 13–16.

Kois, L.E., Potts, H., Cox, J., & Zapf, P. (2022). Court-reported competency to proceed data across the United States: Surveying a public health crisis. [Unpublished raw data].

Laboratory of Community Psychiatry. (1973). The Competence to Stand Trial Assessment Instrument.

Lipsitt, P. D., Lelos, D., & McGarry, A. L. (1971). Competency for trial: A screening instrument. *The American Journal of Psychiatry*, *128*(1), 105–109. https://doi.org/10.1176/ajp.128.1.105

Martinez v. Court of Appeal of California, 528 U.S. 152 (2000).

Michaelsen, K., & Kapoor, R. (2015). Threshold for ordering an evaluation of competency to stand trial. *Journal of American Academy of Psychiatry and the Law*, *43*(2), 249–251. https://jaapl.org/content/43/2/249

Miranda v. Arizona, 384 U.S. 436 (1966).

Morris, N. P., McNiel, D. E., & Binder, R. L. (2021). Estimating annual numbers of competency to stand trial evaluations across the United States. *Journal of the American Academy of Psychiatry and the Law*, *49*(4), 530–539.

Morris, D. R., & Parker, G. F. (2008). Jackson's Indiana: State hospital competence restoration in Indiana. *The Journal of the American Academy of Psychiatry and the Law*, *36*(4), 522–534.

Mossman, D., Noffsinger, S. G., Ash, P., Frierson, R. L., Gerbasi, J., Hackett, M., Lewis, C. F., Pinals, D. A., Scott, C. L., Sieg, K. G., Wall, B. W., & Zonana,

H. (2007). AAPL Practice Guideline for the forensic psychiatric evaluation of competence to stand trial. *The Journal of the American Academy of Psychiatry and the Law, 35*(4 Suppl), S3–S72.

Murrie, D. C., Gowensmith, W. N., Kois, L. E., & Packer, I. K. (2023). Evaluations of competence to stand trial are evolving amid a national "competency crisis." *Behavioral Sciences & the Law, 41*(5), 310–325. https://doi.org/10.1002/bsl.2620

Ostrom, B. J., Hamblim, L. E., Schauffler, R. Y., & Raaen, N. (2020). *Timely justice in criminal cases: What the data tells us.* National Center for State Courts. The Effective Criminal Case Management Project. https://www.ncsc.org/consulting-and-research/areas-of-expertise/court-management-and-performance/caseflow-management/effective-criminal-case-management

Otto, R. K., Poythress, N. G., Nicholson, R. A., Edens, J. F., Monahan, J., Bonnie, R. J., Hoge, S. K., & Eisenberg, M. (1998). MacArthur Competence Assessment Tool-Criminal Adjudication (MacCAT-CA) [Database record]. *APA PsycTests.* https://doi.org/10.1037/t02322-000

Overall, J. E., & Gorham, D. R. (1988). The Brief Psychiatric Rating Scale (BPRS): Recent developments in ascertainment and scaling. *Psychopharmacology Bulletin, 24*(1), 97–99.

Owen, E., Perry, A., & Scher, D. P. (2020). Trauma in competency to stand trial evaluations. In R. A. Javier, E. A. Owen, & J. A. Maddux (Eds.), *Assessing trauma in forensic contexts* (pp. 65–84). Springer Nature. https://doi.org/10.1007/978-3-030-33106-1_3

Parsons, J., & Steadman, H. J. (2017). *The role of indigent defense for defendants with mental health disorders.* U.S. Department of Justice, Office of Justice Programs.

Pate v. Robinson, 383 U.S. 375, 378 (1966).

Pirelli, G., Gottdiener, W. H., & Zapf, P. A. (2011). A meta-analytic review of competency to stand trial research. *Psychology, Public Policy, and Law, 17*(1), 1–53. https://doi.org/10.1037/a0021713

Philipsborn, J. T. (2017). Competently lawyering competence: The role and duties of a lawyer in addressing competence to stand trial where the questions are focused on client communication and capacity to assist. *ABA Criminal Justice,* 34–39.

Philipsborn, J. T. (2019). Lawyering competence to stand trial with an eye on neuroscience. *The Champion, 6*. https://www.nacdl.org/Article/Nov2019-LawyeringCompetencetoStandTrialwithanEyeon

Robey, A. (1965). Checklist of criteria for competency to stand trial. *APA PsycTests.* https://doi.org/10.1037/t27252-000

Roesch, R., Webster, C. D., & Eaves, D. (1984). The Fitness Interview Test: A method for examining fitness to stand trial. Toronto, Ontario, Canada: Research Report of the Centre of Criminology, University of Toronto.

Roesch, R., Zapf, P. A., & Eaves, D. (2006). Fitness Interview Test-Revised: A structured interview for assessing competency to stand trial. Sarasota, FL: Professional Resource Press.

Roesch, R., Zapf, P. A., & Hart, S. D. (2009). *Forensic Psychology and Law.* Wiley Publishers.

Rogers, R. (2005a). *Miranda Rights Scale (MRS).* Unpublished measure.

Rogers, R. (2005b). *Miranda Statements Scale (MSS).* Unpublished measure.

Rogers, R., Harrison, K. S., Hazelwood, L. L., & Sewell, K. W. (2007). Knowing and intelligent: A study of Miranda warnings in mentally disordered defendants. *Law and Human Behavior, 31*(4), 401–418. https://doi.org/10.1007/s10979-006-9070-8

Rogers, R., Tillbrook, C. & Sewell, K. (2004). *Manual for the Evaluation of Competence to Stand Trial-Revised.* Psychological Assessment Resources.

Tellegen, A., & Ben-Porath, Y. S. (2008/2011). *MMPI-2-RF (Minnesota multiphasic personality inventory-2-restructured form): Technical manual.* University of Minnesota Press. https://www.archives.gov/founding-docs/constitution

Wall, B. W., Ash, P., Keram, E., Pinals, D. A., & Thompson, C. H. (2018). AAPL practice resource for the forensic psychiatric evaluation of competence to stand trial. *The Journal of the American Academy of Psychiatry and the Law, 46*(3), 373. https://doi.org/10.29158/JAAPL.003781-18

Wechsler, D. (2008). Wechsler Adult Intelligence Scale-Fourth Edition (WAIS-IV). *APA PsycTests.* https://doi.org/10.1037/t15169-000

Wik, A., Hollen, V., & Fisher, W. (2020). Forensic patients in state psychiatric hospitals: 1999–2016. *CNS Spectrums, 25*(2), 196–206. https://doi.org/10.1017/S1092852919001044

Wildman, R., Batchelor, E., Thompson, L., Nelson, F., Moore, J., & Patterson, M. (1978). *The Georgia Court Competency Test.* Unpublished manuscript, Milledgeville, Georgia.

Willner, P. (2011). Assessment of capacity to participate in court proceedings: A selective critique and some recommendations. *Psychology, Crime & Law, 17*(2), 117–131. https://doi.org/10.1080/10683160903392400

United States National Archives. *The Bill of Rights.* https://www.archives.gov/founding-docs/bill-of-rights

United States National Archives. *The Constitution: Amendments 11–27.* https://www.archives.gov/founding-docs/amendments-11-27

Youtsey v. United States, 97 F. 937, 941, 6th Cir. (1899).

Zapf, P. A., Hubbard, K. L., Cooper, V. G., Wheeles, M. C., & Ronan, K. A. (2004). Have the courts abdicated their responsibility for determination of competency to stand trial to clinicians? *Journal of Forensic Psychology Practice, 4*(1), 27–44. https://doi.org/10.1300/J158v04n01_02

12

Legal Responsibility and the Insanity Defense—Legal Standards and Implications for Defendants with Mental Illnesses and Neurodevelopmental Disabilities

Learning Objectives

After this chapter, readers should be able to understand the:

(1) Role of actus rea and mens rea in determining legal responsibility
(2) Difference between the insanity defense and competence to stand trial.
(3) Due process concerns when the question of legal responsibility is raised
(4) Various legal standards used across the United States when determining legal responsibility
(5) Role of the mental health system in determining legal responsibility
(6) Common misconceptions about the insanity defense

Introduction

The insanity defense or defense of legal responsibility[1] is often misunderstood, even by criminal justice system (CJS) professionals. Unlike the lay use of the term, insanity is not synonymous with mental illness or psychosis (*see* Chapters 1 & 3 of this book for details), nor does having a mental illness automatically qualify defendants to meet the legal definition of insanity. Insanity is a legal construct, not a moral or psychological term, and the legal definition is determined legislatively, not by clinicians. The specific construct

M. C. Mogavero, *Mental Health, Neurodiversity, and Criminal Justice*,
https://doi.org/10.1007/978-3-031-88816-8_12

of insanity, who has the burden of proof (prosecution or defense), and the required degree of certainty vary by state and jurisdiction (Sanabria, 2023b).

The question of one's legal responsibility may be raised when one has a mental illness or other condition that affects decision-making. When the insanity defense is raised, mental health professionals are hired to conduct evaluations of the defendant's mental state at the time of the offense. Unlike competency to stand trial, which focuses on one's current mental state, assessment of legal responsibility is **retrospective**, as it focuses on the defendant's mental state at an earlier time. The decision of a defendant's sanity or legal responsibility is ultimately decided by the court (i.e., a jury or judge).

Crime Elements: Actus Rea and Mens Rea

For most crimes, except for **strict liability offenses** (i.e., crimes where intent is not required), the prosecutor has the burden of proof to demonstrate two elements of a crime: the physical and mental. **Actus rea** (Latin for "guilty act") refers to the physical element of the crime, which is the voluntary act.[2]**Mens rea** (Latin for "guilty mind ") refers to the mental element of the crime or the intent of the act. Defendants must possess a state of mind where they are aware of their actions or behavior. The insanity defense is one of more than a dozen types of defenses and falls under the category of **excuse defenses,** as they address the mental element, not the physical act. When determining mens rea, one questions whether, due to mental illness or mental disorder, the defendant lacked the mental capacity to form intent.

Mens rea does not require the defendant to know that their actions or behavior were illegal to be guilty of a criminal offense. Simply lacking knowledge of wrongdoing (i.e., not knowing their behavior was a crime) is not a legal defense. This presents a particular set of legal challenges for attorneys when assessing legal responsibility for some clients.

Neurodevelopmental disorders (NDDs) such as autism and intellectual disability (ID) are not mental illnesses, which, in practice, makes it challenging to establish the level of intent and motive to determine the extent of one's legal responsibility (Varelius, 2021). Clients with ID, autism, or other disabilities that impair the ability to grasp cultural and social norms during social interactions may be more susceptible to engage in illegal behavior. Although the details of this legal construct described in this chapter focus on verdicts of not guilty by reason insanity (NGRI) (i.e., not legally responsible), elements of this legal construct are also used to mitigate an element of mens rea (i.e., diminished capacity) to reduce the charges or the sentence.

The Insanity Defense

The handling of individuals with mental illnesses who committed crimes is based on British common law. In the early sixteenth century, British law considered insanity grounds for acquittal. Specific procedures for handling those deemed too dangerous to be at large (i.e., set free) were established when the British Parliament passed the Criminal Lunatics Act of 1800. This Act was passed after James Hadfield was charged with high treason for the assassination attempt of King George III at the Drury Lange Theatre in 1800 (Moran, 1985). Hadfield claimed insanity and was acquitted. King George and the public were displeased with this decision, which led Parliament to act. Hadfield was imprisoned while Parliament drafted and passed the Criminal Lunatics Act. The Act required that a person who committed acts such as high treason or murder and was of "unsound mind" at the time shall be acquitted but held in a psychiatric hospital "until his Majesty's pleasure shall be known," which was the legal term for an indeterminate period (Criminal Lunatics Act, 1800).

M'Naghten Rule

The first formal legal standard for determining the criteria for insanity was established after Daniel M'Naghten[3] was acquitted of murder (R v. M'Naghten, 1843). In Queen v. M'Naghten (1843), the House of Lords (the British Supreme Court), which consisted of a panel of 15 judges, developed specific standards that later became known as the M'Naghten rule.

Case Brief: Queen v. M'Naghten (1843)

Facts: On January 20, 1843, 30-year-old Daniel M'Naghten, armed with two pistols, pointed one and fired at Tory Prime Minister Sir Robert Peel. Standing next to Sir Peel was his secretary, Edward Drummond, who was shot instead. M'Naghten was arrested and later charged with murder when Drummond succumbed to his gunshot wound to his diaphragm five days later.[4] M'Naghten was tried on February 27, 1843. Police Inspector John Matthew Tierney testified at his trial that when questioning M'Naghten about the shooting, M'Naghten believed he shot Sir Robert Peel. M'Naghten's counsel introduced witnesses who testified about M'Naghten's delusional thoughts. Mr. Solicitor General testified and read aloud M'Naghten's statement he gave on January 21st, "The **Tories** in my native city have driven me to this, and have followed me to France, Scotland, and other parts; I can get no sleep from the system they pursue towards me; I believe I am driven into a consumption by them; they wish to murder me" (R. v. M'Naghten, 1843b, p. 725).

The judge instructed the jury regarding M'Naghten's lack of understanding upon commission of the act, and they reached a verdict of not guilty (R. v. M'Naghten, 1843a). Queen Victoria and the public were displeased with this verdict and requested that the House of Lords review the verdict and determine the standards for the insanity defense.

Issue: The House of Lords addressed several issues, including the proper instruction for the jury and standards for when a person under an "insane delusion" commits an offense and, consequently, is excused.

Outcome: The House of Lords decided that jurors should be instructed that everyone is presumed sane and possesses a sufficient degree of reason to be responsible for their crimes. Therefore, to establish an insanity defense, it must be clearly proven that

> At the time of the act, the accused was under such a defect of reason from disease of the mind that he did not know the nature and quality of the act he was committing; or if he did know, he did not know what he was doing was wrong. (Queen v. M'Naghten, 1843)

Criticisms of the M'Naghten Rule

The M'Naghten rule, referred to as the moral standard, has been criticized for being too rigid. Not all mental illnesses or conditions cause one to experience hallucinations or delusional thoughts (as in M'Naghten's case), where they do not understand right from wrong. Another criticism of M'Naghten is that one may have a psychiatric condition and have moral reasoning. Isaac Ray (1807–1881), one of the founders of the American Psychiatric Association, believed that the ability to distinguish right from wrong as a standard of insanity was misleading. Ray argued that having a psychiatric condition does not mean one lacks moral standards or reasoning. Ray noted in his book titled, *A Treatise on the Medical Jurisprudence of Insanity* (1838),

> The insane mind is not entirely deprived of this power of moral discernment, but on many subjects is perfectly rational and displays the exercise of a sound and well-balanced mind, is one of those facts now so well established that to question it would only betray the height of ignorance and presumption. The first result, therefore, to which the doctrine leads is that no man can ever successfully plead insanity in defence of crime, because it can be said of no one who would have occasion for such a defence, that he was unable in any case to distinguish right from wrong. (p. 32)

In 2001, the M'Naghten rule was used in Texas and was criticized for being too narrow and strict in the Andrea Yates case. Thirty-six-year-old Andrea Yates drowned all five of her children while experiencing delusions that she must kill her children to save them from Satan (Denno, 2003). Texas's M'Naghten standard did not define the meaning of "wrong" (i.e., whether the defendant knew it was legally wrong or morally wrong) (McLellan, 2006).

Case of Andrea Yates

Background: Andrea Yates was raised Roman Catholic and worked as a nurse for about eight years. She met her husband, Rusty, and they married four years later, in 1993, when they were both 28. Rusty was raised a Methodist and worked as a NASA engineer at the Johnson Space Center. Their first son, Noah, was born in 1994, and Andrea became a stay-at-home mother. The couple had four more children over the next seven years: John, Paul, Luke, and Mary. Over time, the couple became profoundly religious but were not members of a local church. Instead, they hosted a fundamental Christian bible study group in their home three nights a week (Denno, 2003; McLellan, 2006).

Mental Health History and Diagnoses: Andrea had four prior hospitalizations and received several diagnoses, including major depressive disorder, schizophrenia, bipolar disorder, and postnatal psychosis. She began to experience hallucinations shortly after having Noah and experienced depression after the birth of each child. After the birth of her fourth child, Luke, she survived a suicide attempt by overdosing on sedatives. She was hospitalized, prescribed an anti-depressant medication, and discharged despite persistent symptoms. She was hospitalized again after another suicide attempt when she held a knife to her throat. Her psychiatrist warned against having any more children, but they had a fifth child, Mary, on November 30, 2000 (Denno, 2003; McLellan, 2006).

In early 2001, her mental health began deteriorating; she stopped speaking and drinking and began pulling out her hair. She experienced delusions that there were cameras throughout their home watching her, and television characters were talking to her, telling her she was a "bad mother." She was hospitalized for a third time, and a new psychiatrist placed her on antipsychotic medications. She was discharged after only ten days, even though she was still experiencing symptoms and not speaking. She was hospitalized a fourth time, and her psychiatrist began to wean her off the antipsychotic medication. When her mental health continued to decline, Rusty asked her psychiatrist to restart her medication, but he declined, stating that the medication was only for those with severe mental illness (McLellan, 2006).

Delusions on the Day of the Offense: Andrea experienced delusional thoughts that she had not been a good mother to her children and had been "marked" by Satan. She believed the only way to save her children was to kill them and send them to heaven. Then, when she was arrested and punished, Satan would be destroyed. On the morning of June 20, 2001, Andrea filled the bathtub and, one by one, drowned all five of her young children: 6-month-old Mary, 2-year-old Luke, 3-year-old Paul, 5-year-old John, and 7-year-old Noah. Afterward, she left Noah in the tub but placed the other four children on the bed, wrapping the boy's arms around baby Mary. Andrea called 911, then called Rusty at work and told him to come home. When the police arrived, an officer asked Andrea what was wrong; she said, "I killed my kids." Andrea was arrested and charged with capital murder (Denno, 2003; McLellan, 2006).

First Trial and Conviction: Both the prosecution and defense agreed that Andrea had a mental illness but presented different opinions: one that was ill and one that was evil. Several psychiatrists testified for the defense, including Dr. Phillip Resnick, who described Andrea as a loving mother and concluded that although she knew her actions were illegal (legally wrong), she believed it was the right thing to do (not morally wrong), as she was sending her children to heaven. Her subsequent punishment for killing her children would destroy Satan. Another psychiatrist, Dr. George Ringholz, explained that at the time of the offense, she was incapable of knowing right from wrong because she was not in contact with reality (Denno, 2003).

The prosecution hired psychiatrist Dr. Park Dietz to conduct the evaluation. Dr. Dietz was a well-known evaluator who had been hired by the prosecution in many high-profile cases, including Jeffrey Dahmer, who murdered and dismembered 15 men (FBI, 2014). He was not a practicing physician and had not treated patients in over two decades. The last patient with postnatal depression he treated was in 1977, and he never treated a case of postnatal depression with psychosis. Dr. Dietz concluded that Andrea knew what she was doing was wrong because it was Satan, not God, who told her to kill the children. Dr. Dietz worked as a consultant for the television show Law and Order.[5] He testified that shortly before Andrea drowned her children, an episode aired where the plot was a mother with postnatal depression who drowned her children and was found not guilty by reason of insanity (NGRI), implying Andrea had got the idea from watching this episode. Andrea was found guilty and sentenced to life in prison (Denno, 2003; McLellan, 2006).

Retrial and Verdict: Andrea's guilty verdict largely rested on Dr. Dietz's testimony. However, upon appellate review, it was revealed that no such episode of Law and Order aired. Dr. Dietz acknowledged his mistake and false testimony, Andrea's conviction was overturned, and she was granted a new trial. On July 26, 2006, she was found NGRI and committed to a state psychiatric hospital (McLellan, 2006).

Other Legal Standards

The insanity defense is defined by several legal standards. The standards are based on prior case law, and each state adopted its own version or abolished the defense entirely. In 1982, John Hinkley Jr. was found NGRI after attempting to assassinate President Ronald Regan (1911–2004). The public outrage led many states to revise their insanity defense laws, shifting the burden of proof to the defendant. Most states and federal courts set the burden of proof on the defendant with the standard of clear and convincing evidence (Sanabria, 2023b). Some states, such as New Jersey, use the lower standard of proof, preponderance of the evidence. The various legal standards and supported cases are described in detail below.

The Irresistible Impulse Test

The Irresistible Impulse Test for legal insanity refers to one's **volitional control** (the ability to control one's impulses) or ability to conform one's behavior or conduct to the law. This test focuses on whether a "mental disease or defect" prevents individuals from controlling their behavior at the time of the offense. This test was first used in the United States (US) in the Alabama case, Parsons v. State (1886). Parsons was convicted of murdering his wife. On appeal, the Alabama Supreme Court decided that one can be not responsible if, due to a mental illness, they had an irresistible impulse to commit a crime even if they knew their actions were morally wrong. Parsons v. State (1886) indicates

> . . . he may nevertheless not be legally responsible if the following conditions occur: (i) if by reason of the duress of such mental disease, he had so far lost the power to choose between the right and the wrong and to avoid doing the act in question, as that his free agency was at the time destroyed, (ii) and if, at the same time, the alleged crime was so connected with such mental disease, in the relation of cause and effect, as to have been a product of it solely.

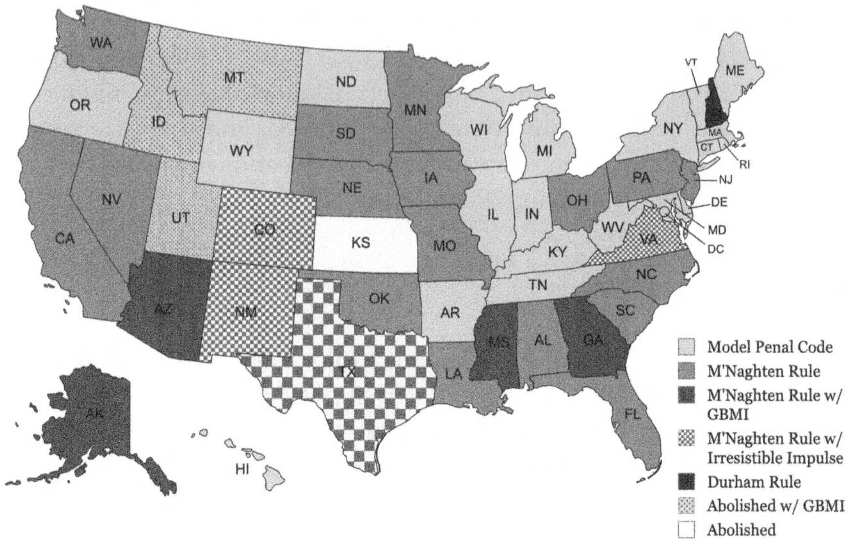

Fig. 12.1 US map of standards for legal responsibility (*Source* Adapted from Sanabria [2023a], created with mapchart.net)

No state uses irresistible impulse as its sole insanity defense, yet four states combine it with the M'Naghten standard (see Fig. 12.1).

Model Penal Code

In 1955, the American Law Institute (ALI) formulated the **Model Penal Code**, which contained a second model insanity test. The test, which is described in Section 4.01 of the Model Penal Code titled Mental Disease or Defect Excluding Responsibility, states:

(1) A person is not responsible for criminal conduct if, at the time of such conduct, because of mental disease or defect, he lacks substantial capacity either to appreciate the criminality [wrongfulness] of his conduct or to conform his conduct to the requirements of law
(2) As used in this article, the terms "mental disease or defect" do not include an abnormality manifested only by repeated criminal or otherwise anti-social conduct (MPC, 2017).

This section does not define mental disease or defect, nor does the standard require a total lack of capacity. Repeated wrongful conduct does not suffice to establish mental disease or defect (MPC, 2017). John's case below is an example of the application of the MPC.

Case of John[6]

Background: John was 50 years old when he was arrested and charged with attempted murder. He has an extensive history of mental illness and substance use, with diagnoses of schizophrenia and alcohol and cocaine use disorder. John is the youngest of five children, with two sisters and two brothers. He was raised by his mother and stepfather; both were physically and verbally abusive toward John and his siblings. John's mental health problems began around the age of 14 when he claimed he began experiencing auditory hallucinations in the form of voices. He claimed the voices were "nice" and did not mind them. John graduated high school and joined the Marines immediately after. He began abusing alcohol and got into several physical altercations that led to his discharge after only two years. John's hallucinations persisted, and he continued to misuse alcohol. By the time he was in his early 20s, the voices became "mean" and told him to harm others. He began using crack cocaine and alcohol to manage his symptoms.

For most of John's adult life, he "cycled" in and out of jail, prison, and psychiatric hospitals, each time discharged with little access to mental health care and unable to fill his prescription medications. John's criminal history consisted of five misdemeanor assaults and three violent felonies. In his mid-20s, he struck a store clerk in the head with a liquor bottle after an argument. He was convicted of aggravated assault and served a three-year prison term. In his late 30s, he was charged with attempted murder for stabbing a bar patron during an argument. He pleaded guilty to aggravated assault and served ten years in prison. During this sentence, John experienced the same "mean voices" along with grandiose delusions, believing he had superpowers. He was "back and forth" between prison and a secure psychiatric facility his entire sentence. Upon release, he continued to experience hallucinations. Once, he heard voices throughout his apartment (e.g., the walls, the toilet). They tormented him to the point where he destroyed the walls and removed the toilet.

Instant Offense: At the time of the offense, John was residing in a motel used to house people experiencing homelessness. He was standing in the middle of the road outside the motel, yelling at cars and waving his arms in the air while holding a knife. Traffic had stopped, and a crowd began forming. The motel clerk, who noticed the crowd, went outside and slowly approached John, attempting to calm him down. John ran toward him and plunged the knife into his chest, repeatedly screaming, "You're not going to take me!" Police arrived shortly after the stabbing, restrained John, and placed him in the vehicle. While in police transport, his delusions continued as he claimed that the government was trying to take him to a laboratory to conduct experiments on his brain because of his superpowers.

Outcome: The motel clerk survived the attack, and John was formally charged with attempted murder. Because of the bizarre statements made shortly after the offense, extensive mental health history, records of psychiatric treatment, and hospitalizations, John's defense attorney entered a plea of not guilty due to mental disease or defect, as the state standard followed the Model Penal Code. His mental health evaluation confirmed his diagnoses. In a jury trial, the psychiatrist for the defense testified that due to his alcohol and cocaine use, his mental health deteriorated. At the time of the stabbing, the psychologist testified he was in an "active psychotic state" and, with a high degree of certainty, was unable to appreciate the consequences of his actions. John was found not guilty due to mental disease or defect and involuntarily civilly committed to a state psychiatric hospital indefinitely. While committed, John participated in treatment and was compliant with his medications. In treatment, he learned the role of his alcohol and substance use and how it led to not only his violent outbursts but also exacerbated his symptoms. He also expressed great remorse for his crimes, particularly for stabbing the motel clerk, because "he was a nice man." He remained hospitalized and understood that he was not ready to be released and stated, "I don't want to hurt anyone."

The Durham Rule

Another standard is the Durham rule, also known as the product test. This rule states that defendants are not legally responsible if their actions were the product of a mental disease or defect. The Circuit Court of Appeals for the District of Columbia adopted this standard in Durham v. United States (1954).

Case Brief: Durham v. United States (1954)

Facts: On July 13, 1951, 23-year-old Monte Durham was arrested and charged with housebreaking in Washington, D.C. Durham had a long history of mental illness and criminal behavior. He had three prior hospitalizations; the most recent discharge was just two months before the housebreaking. After his arrest, he was found to be of unsound mind, was committed for a fourth time, and treated for 16 months. Upon discharge, he was released to the custody of the district jail and was determined to be competent to stand trial. At trial, psychiatrist Dr. Gilbert testified for the defense that he was of unsound mind at the time of the crime. The trial court convicted Durham using the M'Naghten rule because there was no evidence of Durham's inability to understand right from wrong. On appeal, Durham sought to reverse the conviction, claiming the M'Naghten rule of knowledge of right and wrong is an inadequate test of responsibility.

Issue: Whether the presumption of one's sanity using the "right and wrong test" is adequate and justified.

Outcome: The US Circuit Court of Appeals held that a finding of sanity only using the "right and wrong test" is inadequate. There was sufficient testimony provided at trial to overcome the presumption of sanity. The Court concluded that a broader test should be adopted where the accused is not legally responsible if the crime was the product of mental disease or mental defect.

Each state has established a standard for legal responsibility (*see* Fig. 12.1). The New Hampshire Supreme Court viewed the M'Naghten standard as too rigid and is currently the only state that uses the Durham rule. Some states allow for one or more legal standards. Currently, the two most common insanity defense standards in the US are the ALI's modified version of the traditional M'Naghten rule (25 states) and the ALI's Model Penal Code (21 states). Four states added another option, Guilty but "Mentally Ill" / Insane (GBMI), to the M'Naghten standard, which allows a guilty verdict but a reduced sentence due to the mitigating factor of one's mental illness. Montana, Idaho, and Utah do not provide defendants with a "not guilty" insanity defense but allow a GBMI verdict (Sanabria, 2023a). Below are brief definitions of these standards.

- **M'Naghten Rule**—The defendant was experiencing a disease of the mind (i.e., a mental disorder), which causes impairment in terms of either (a) not understanding the nature and quality of their actions or (b) not knowing that those actions were wrong.
- **Model Penal Code**—The defendant has a professional diagnosis of a mental defect and was unable to either appreciate the criminality of their conduct (did not know right from wrong) or conform their conduct to the requirements of the law (i.e., unable to control the impulse to commit the criminal act).
- **Irresistible Impulse Test**—Includes a volitional component (added to M'Naghten rule) the defendant knew what they were doing, and knew it

was wrong, but were unable to control their behavior to avoid committing the crime.

- **Durham Rule**—Also known as the product rule and is currently only used in New Hampshire when the defendant's actions were the product of a mental disease or defect.
- **Guilty but "Mentally Ill"/Insane**—GBMI is an alternative that allows for a finding of guilt but a reduction in either the seriousness of the charge or the severity of the punishment if one's mental illness was determined to have influenced the criminal act. Defendants found guilty may be sentenced to prison or a psychiatric facility.

Kansas is the only state that does not have some type of insanity defense or the GBMI verdict. The Kansas legislature enacted K.S.A. 22–3220 Defense of Lack of Mental State (effective January 1, 1996), which abandoned the M'Naghten rule and adopted what is known as the "mens rea approach." The Act allows evidence of mental disease or defect but does not allow a lack of ability to know right from wrong as a defense. In the case Kahler v. Kansas (2020), Kahler challenged the constitutionality of K.S.A. 22–3220 after being convicted of capital murder and sentenced to death.

Case Brief: Kahler v. Kansas (2020)

Facts: James Kahler was convicted of capital murder for the 2009 shooting deaths of his estranged wife Karen, two teenage daughters, Emily (18 years) and Lauren (16 years), and his wife's grandmother, Dorothy Wight. James and his wife were in the process of a divorce, and Karen, Emily, Lauren, and their 12-year-old son Sean were spending Thanksgiving at Wight's home. Kahler's mental health began deteriorating after his marriage ended, and he lost his job. He entered Wight's home and shot and killed all five, but his son Sean was not harmed. Kahler's defense argued that because of his major depressive disorder, he was incapable of forming the intent and did not possess the premeditation required for the crime of capital murder. The defense presented testimony from Dr. Stephen Peterson that Kahler was experiencing symptoms of major depressive disorder at the time of the shooting, and his capacity to control his behavior was so degraded that he was unable to refrain from committing the acts. Kahler was convicted and sentenced to death. His case was appealed to the US Supreme Court to decide whether an insanity defense is required for due process.

Issue: Whether the due process clause of the Fourteenth Amendment requires states to adopt a moral capacity test from the M'Naghten rule.

Outcome: The US Supreme Court declined to require that Kansas adopt an insanity test to determine defendants' ability to recognize that their crime was morally wrong. The due process clause does not require states to provide an insanity defense that acquits defendants who could not distinguish right from wrong or require states to adopt a moral incapacity test from the M'Naghten rule. If defendants manifest mental illness, Kansas could consider this later to mitigate culpability and lessen the punishment.

Assessment of Legal Responsibility

Determining responsibility for criminal behavior is a legal construct, and mental health evaluators must gather evidence to describe the presence, nature, and behavioral impact of a defendant's mental condition. The evaluation of responsibility is retrospective and often conducted weeks to months after the fact. Therefore, the evaluator must gather evidence from multiple sources, including medical and mental health history, psychiatric assessments, and collateral sources of information (e.g., police reports). Below are various guidelines and sources used for a comprehensive evaluation.

Guidelines for Assessment

The Council of the American Academy of Psychiatry and the Law (AAPL) has developed 74-page best practice guidelines for insanity defense evaluations. The Statement of Intent indicated that the guidelines were determined by a consensus among members and experts, and the guidelines do not present all acceptable or current ways of performing these forensic evaluations (AAPL, 2014). As with the competency assessment (*see* Chapter 11 of this book for details), the mental health evaluators should be independent and objective. The typical doctor-patient confidentiality is absent as the evaluator testifies their findings in court.

As shown in Fig. 12.1, the legal standards for responsibility vary between states, as do the laws on expert testimony (*see* Chapter 13 of this book for details). Some jurisdictions cannot explicitly state their opinion on the defendant's sanity and, for example, may only state their opinion in terms of likelihood or degree of certainty. According to the AAPL, evaluators must answer three basic questions:

1. Did the defendant have a mental disorder at the time of the alleged crime?
2. Was there a relationship between the mental disorder and the criminal behavior?

3. If so, were the criteria met for the jurisdiction's legal test for being found not criminally responsible? (AAPL, 2014, p. S22).

Evaluators should have prior experience testifying in court and be aware of the jurisdiction restrictions, especially when conducting out-of-state evaluations (AAPL, 2014). Evaluators have a wide range of discretion regarding how they conduct evaluations to determine legal responsibility. However, ethically, they should not provide an opinion without evaluating the defendant in person (or at least make attempts to). Ideally, the in-person interviews should occur on multiple occasions to establish a **rapport**. This is particularly important for those who may be uncomfortable or experience anxiety with strangers, including those with disabilities such as autism (Kaser-Boyd, 2020).

Collateral Information

In addition to forensic interviewing, evaluations should include a thorough review of any collateral information relevant to the legal responsibility standards. Because the evaluation is retrospective, the extent of their mental health history, cognitive history, and history of any other problematic behaviors helps to determine and formulate a more objective opinion about the defendant's mental state at the time of the offense. Below are a few essential collateral sources relevant to legal responsibility evaluations (see AAPL, 2014) for the full scope of sources).

Validated Psychometric Testing Instruments

Validated psychometric testing instruments are beneficial as additional sources for providing forensic opinions (AAPL, 2014). Below is a list of several psychometric structured assessments for legal responsibility, some more comprehensive than others. Drogin (2018) describes these in more detail in the chapter for attorneys representing clients in cases where legal responsibility is raised.

- **The Mental State at the Time of the Offense Screening Evaluation** (MSE) (Slobogin et al., 1984)—A brief interview with items that cover three areas: defendant's psychological history, offense information, and mental status. This brief assessment is designed to "screen out" those who do not require further evaluation.

- **The Rogers Criminal Responsibility Assessment Scales** (R-CRAS) (Rogers et al., 1984)—25 items rated on a five-point scale (none, slight, moderate, severe, extreme) that cover five areas: reliability (including malingering, i.e., pretending), organic (e.g., medical) factors, psychopathology, cognitive control, and behavioral control.
- **The Rating Scale of Criminal Responsibility for Mentally Disordered Offenders** (RSCRs) (Cai et al., 2014)—18 items that cover two dimensions: capacity of cognition (presence of realistic motivation, inducement of crime, understanding the nature of behavior); capacity of control (time of crime, place of crime, responsibility after the offense, and concealing the truth).
- **The Criminal Responsibility Scale (CRS)** (Meyer et al., 2020)—Uses vignettes that describe an offense, with a brief history of an offense with 12 items and 19 questions rated on a three-point scale that covers two areas: capacity for understanding and capacity for self-determination.
- **The Defendant's Insanity Assessment Support Scale** (DIASS) (Parmigiani et al., 2022)—Eight items rated on a two-point scale that cover four areas: knowledge/understanding of crime, appreciation of crime, reasoning, and control of voluntary motor activity.

If defense attorneys or evaluators suspect defendants may have autism, they should obtain a comprehensive developmental history and consider administering the Autism Diagnostic Observation Schedule–Second Edition (ADOS-2) (Lord et al., 2012). The ADOS-2 measures social behavior and social communication. The Autism Diagnostic Interview-Revised (ADI-R) (Le Coureur et al., 2003) is another assessment tool. Many common behaviors exhibited by autistic individuals when they are younger decrease in adulthood, which makes the ADI-R helpful in detecting autism in adults (Kaser-Boyd, 2020).

Mental Health and Medical Records

To better understand one's full scope of mental health symptoms, interviews with family members are helpful to gain more information about their childhood experiences and family history of mental health conditions or substance use (AAPL, 2014). Evaluators should obtain consent to review all records, including any hospitalization records, to gain a comprehensive understanding of the defendant's psychiatric, substance use, and medical history to strengthen one's case. For example, Dirks-Linhorst and Kondrat (2012) reviewed 27 years of insanity defenses in Missouri and found that the number of prior hospitalizations was associated with successful defenses in murder cases. The scientific field of neuropsychiatry has been recently used to address the debate about one's psychopathological impairments in their decision-making process (Kalis & Meynen, 2014; Kalis et al., 2008). The evaluator should obtain consent to review any past brain imaging, functional MRI (fMRI), positron emission tomography (PET), and single-photon emission computed tomography (SPECT). Attorneys may request diffusion tensor imaging (DTI) to demonstrate evidence of a brain abnormality (AAPL, 2014).

Education Records

Education records are vital in cases involving legal responsibility. A review of any disciplinary reports or referrals, symptoms that impaired their academic functioning, individualized education programs (IEPs), standardized achievement tests, cognitive tests (e.g., IQ tests), and any counseling records can support claims of one's mental health history. They can also provide the evaluator with a baseline of prior cognitive functioning or a timeline of when mental health symptoms developed. Although cognitive style and functioning remain relatively stable, the evaluator may administer cognitive tests for current mental functioning (AAPL, 2014).

Police Records and Reports

Police officers have a pivotal role in defendant's cases. Police reports that are well-written and detailed and include observations made by the officers (particularly when made shortly after the offense) can provide the prosecution and defense insight into the defendant's mental state. Reports that include the defendant's demeanor (if at the crime scene), descriptions of the defendant's interactions with police or others afterward, and any statements made during these interactions are beneficial for forensic evaluations. Interviews and interrogations should be audio–video recorded, and the evaluator should review the recording to note the defendant's behavior and responses to questions. This information can assist the evaluator in accurately determining the defendant's mental state at the time of the offense (AAPL, 2014).

Box 12.2 Practitioner Spotlight: Elizabeth Kelley, Esq

Elizabeth Kelley has been a criminal defense attorney since 1994. She has worked on cases in approximately 50 state and federal jurisdictions nationwide and has vast experience defending clients with various mental illnesses and disabilities. According to Kelley, what is most important to know when working with clients is to recognize the complexity of their mental health. Clients may have a primary mental health diagnosis but often have one or more co-occurring mental disabilities. Each condition affects one's behavior, cognition, mental capacity, and ability to understand the wrongfulness of their actions.

Kelley works with forensic mental health experts to conduct thorough evaluations to assess legal responsibility, assess for competency, sanity, to negate an element of the statute such as mens rea, and/or mitigation. An essential aspect of these evaluations is allowing the evaluator to explore other conditions rather than only focusing on self-reported or documented diagnoses. For example, the evaluator may uncover a head injury, and Kelley would hire another expert, such as a neurologist. Insanity defenses are extremely difficult because clients must meet the statutory requirements and the high burden of proof. For such cases to be successful, the (retrospective) evaluations should be as close to the crime event as possible—when the client is still experiencing symptoms and has not had interventions such as psychotropic medications. Unfortunately, this is rarely done. Most often, evaluation reports are used to negotiate a plea deal for a reduced charge. If there is a mandatory sentence and probation is not an option, she will negotiate for the lowest sentence length, best prison placement, or prison accommodations. For example, a client who had schizencephaly (a malformation of the brain), a traumatic brain injury, and endured childhood trauma was charged with attempted murder. He was evaluated by a psychologist and neuropsychologist and used the information from both reports to negotiate a lesser charge to avoid prison. After a lengthy hearing, which included testimony from forensic mental health experts, he was sentenced to probation.

Dispelling Misconceptions of the Insanity Defense

Because the insanity defense is complex and often misunderstood, many myths and misconceptions surround its use. Perlin (1985, 2017) identified several myths of the insanity defense, with empirical data debunking such myths. Below is a list of some common misconceptions among the lay public and some CJS professionals surrounding this defense. Debunking such myths and acquiring a factual understanding of this defense not only upholds the integrity of the judicial system but also respects the rights and dignity of defendants who have mental health conditions that impact their ability to conform to the law.

(1) "They Are Faking it"

Reality: Pretending or exaggerating one's psychological or physical symptoms is a concept known as **malingering**. The Diagnostic and Statistical Manual of Mental Disorders (DSM-5-TR, 2022) defines malingering as "the intentional production of false or grossly exaggerated physical or psychological symptoms, motivated by external incentives such as... evading criminal prosecution" (APA, 2022, p. 369). Although malingering occurs in a small subset of those who commit crimes, studies have shown that it is not pervasive. Malingering a mental illness in criminal forensic cases is estimated to be about 20% (Miller, 2001). Among a sample of 35 defendants charged with homicide, only six (17%) were determined to be malingering. Mental health evaluators rule out malingering during assessments and have many methods to detect this (Rogers, 2008). Evaluators must also rule out malingering in competency assessments (*see* Chapter 11 of this book for details).

The collateral information detailed above (e.g., past mental health records, education records) validate and substantiate the findings of one's mental health status at the time of the offense while detecting the possibility of malingering. Evaluators may also use validated instruments for psychiatric impairment, including the Structured Interview of Reported Symptoms (SIRS) (Rogers et al., 1992) and the Miller Forensic Assessment of Symptoms Test (M-FAST) (Miller, 2001). The Test of Memory Malingering (TOMM) (Tombaugh, 1996) and the Validity Indicator Profile (VIP) (Frederick, 1997) have been developed to evaluate the malingering of a cognitive impairment. Another standard instrument used is the Minnesota Multiphasic Personality Inventory-3 (MMPI-3) (2020). The MMPI-3 has several validity scales designed to evaluate test items' accuracy, including scales to detect the underreporting or over reporting of symptoms (Ben-Porath & Tellegen, 2020).

Defense attorneys may also use the polygraph exam to detect deception (*see* Chapter 13 of this book for details). The polygraph is a scientific instrument that continuously records autonomic nervous system responses, including heart rate, blood pressure, respiration rate, and skin conductivity or electrodermal activity, which measures continuous variation in the electrical characteristics of the skin. The polygraph is used with the Control Question Technique (CQT), where examiners will ask irrelevant questions such as "What is your age?" along with control questions such as "Have you ever stolen anything?" (Vrij & Mann, 2001; Walczyk et al., 2018).

(2) **The Insanity Defense is Overused**

Reality: Public perceptions of the insanity defense are that it is used often and is frequently successful. Because of the strict standards and high burden of proof, in reality, this defense is rarely used. Comprehensive studies have shown that the insanity plea rate is extremely low (less than 2% of cases). Cirincione et al. (1995) examined the use and success rates in seven states: California, Georgia, New Jersey, New York, Ohio, Washington, and Wisconsin from July 1979 through December 1983. The results showed that New York had the lowest rate of 0.29%, whereas Georgia had the highest use rate (1.73% of cases). The success rate varied per state; Georgia had the lowest success rate, with only 13% of cases where the defendant was found not guilty. Less than 1% of cases in Washington state (0.6%) used the insanity plea but had the highest success rate of 87.4%. Overall, the use among these seven states averaged about 0.85%, and the success rate averaged about 28%. Furthermore, evaluators for the prosecutor and defense sometimes have differing opinions about legal responsibility. For example, Gowensmith et al. (2013) examined 483 evaluation reports of 165 defendants, where two or three mental health evaluators offered independent opinions on a defendant's legal responsibility, and evaluators reached a unanimous agreement in 55% of the cases.

(3) **Those Who Plead Insanity Get Off "Scot-Free"**

Reality: A common misconception is that pleading insanity is used as a loophole to evade punishment. When one is found not legally responsible, they are rarely released into the community without some conditional release (Dirks-Linhorst & Kondrat, 2012; Silver, 1995). Individuals are typically confined to psychiatric hospitals indefinitely or until they are no longer deemed a danger to themselves or others (i.e., continue to meet the criteria for civil commitment—*see* Chapter 15 of this book for details). In some cases, those found not legally responsible are subjected to longer lengths of confinement than those found or plead guilty. Silver (1995) examined the same insanity defense data of the seven states collected by Cirincione et al. (1995) and compared the length of confinement using the number of days between admission and release from a prison or psychiatric hospital). In two states, Georgia and Ohio, those found not legally responsible spend less time confined than persons found guilty. In contrast, in California and New York, those found not legally responsible spent more time confined than those found guilty. However, in all seven states, the lengths of hospital confinement were positively related to the seriousness of the offense (Silver, 1995).

(4) **Only Those Who Commit Murder Plea Insanity**

Reality: Those who commit both misdemeanors and various felonies can raise an insanity defense. A two-decade study in North Carolina found that less than 28% of those who plead insanity were charged with murder, and about half were charged with other serious felonies (Haroon et al., 2023). This myth is reinforced by a small number of high-profile cases such as Jeffrey Dahmer (FBI, 2014) or James Holmes, who, on July 20, 2012, shot and killed 12 people and wounded dozens of others in a Colorado movie theater (Allely, 2020). Such extreme cases do not depict reality and undermine the merit, as both Dahmer and Holmes were found guilty and sentenced to prison (Allely, 2020; FBI, 2014). As discussed in Chapters 1 and 3, such extreme cases have led to the public perception that people with mental illnesses are violent.

Considerations and Recommendations

Defense attorneys, prosecutors, and judges must balance seeking justice and protecting society from future harm while protecting defendants' due process rights. To ensure that balance, the CJS and the MHS must work in tandem. The more accurate and comprehensive the documentation provided to the court, the better equipped the system will be to make the best decision for all parties. Below are several considerations and recommendations to ensure the best outcomes for individual liberty and public safety.

Continued Education on Mental Health and Neurodiversity

As discussed in Chapter 11 and prior chapters in Part 1 and Part 3, CJS practitioners should receive education and training on mental health and NDDs including autism and ID. The education and application of knowledge will assist prosecutors and judges in exercising their discretion in cases where defendants, due to their cognitive, social, and communication difficulties, have a diminished ability to understand the wrongfulness of the behavior. Defense attorneys with training and experience with mental health populations can become more effective and efficient in ensuring the best outcomes for their clients and saving the court time and resources. Education and training on mental health and NDDs can also help defense attorneys to be more in tune with conditions that may affect the direction and outcome of their cases. Similar to the assessment of competence, attorneys who suspect their client does not understand the court process, their role in their case, if they suspect a cognitive disability, autism, or mental illness should consider a mental health evaluation for legal responsibility (Mathis, 2020). Attorneys may also consider obtaining medical records early on to foresee any mental health conditions, as clients may not disclose them (Fabian, 2018).

Build a Rapport Over Time

Rapport-building is an essential component of the attorney-client relationship, but building rapport with clients with mental illnesses or disabilities that affect communication can make this process more difficult or may take longer. When discussing the possibility of mental health or disabilities, attorneys should be aware of the possible stigma and fears and ascertain whether their client is reluctant to pursue that path (Drogin, 2018). Due to various stigmas surrounding disabilities and mental illnesses, clients may be reluctant to disclose such conditions and may make attempts to hide or "mask" them (Fabian, 2018).

Cross-System Collaboration

Assessing responsibility requires much collaboration across the CJS and MHS. The defense attorney and evaluator should know legal statutes and jurisdiction restrictions regarding expert testimony. The US has no national or uniform standard for the definition or approach to assessing legal responsibility. The attorney's approach and the retained evaluator must comply with the rules ascribed in one's jurisdiction. During this collaboration, attorneys should become familiar with the assessment tools for measuring legal responsibility. Some testing instruments have not been validated on individuals with ID, and attorneys should consult with a mental health expert to ensure their clients have the requisite cognitive skills, academic skills, and reading or oral vocabulary levels to comprehend test questions and complete a particular assessment tool (Drogin, 2018).

No case can be successful without a psychological assessment of a scientifically and legally accepted mental health condition or disability confirmed by a mental health expert. Evaluators, both for the prosecutor and defense, should have knowledge, expertise, and experience in the mental health condition(s) the defendant presents. This information can also determine whether there is diminished mens rea and address one's moral blameworthiness. Moral blameworthiness is a complex philosophical concept rooted in moral responsibility. Defense attorneys can address the underlying causes of one's criminal behavior. With the mental health assessment information, defense attorneys can argue a level of moral blameworthiness to mitigate responsibility for a reduced sentence (Mahoney, 2021).

Police Officer's Role

The reports provided by police can have a pivotal role in the evaluation process. Police observations and interviews, shortly after the offense, can provide valuable information for evaluators' insight into one's mental status at the time of the offense (AAPL, 2014). Police should provide well-written, clear, and comprehensive reports that explain the abovementioned details. Police should not assume that suspect's statements or behaviors that appear minor at the time will not be valuable later in the case.

Conclusion

Although controversial, the practice of not holding people legally responsible for crimes when experiencing mental illness symptoms such as delusional thoughts is not a new concept. This was common practice for centuries, and in 1843, the M'Naghten case established clear standards. Across the US, nearly all states have implemented some standard to handle cases where people with mental illnesses commit crimes. States implemented systems where defendants can be handled and diverted from the CJS to the MHS for care and treatment. This process can be more effective and just when CJS and MHS practitioners work together. Both defense attorneys and prosecutors should be more versed in the evaluation process, including the various psychometric testing instruments, to ensure a thorough and appropriate evaluation of a specific defendant's needs.

The standards for the insanity defense do not take into consideration one's moral blameworthiness or other barriers related to the legality or wrongfulness of one's actions. Blame is often an emotional response to another's act of wrongdoing or the failure to act morally responsible (Graham, 2014). Failing to acknowledge one's condition and how it relates to one's blameworthiness could lead to more severe punishments than warranted. Autistic individuals may have deficits in cognitive empathy and higher-order moral reasoning, intrinsic factors when determining the extent of one's legal responsibility. One may not understand morally responsible behavior due to social and communication difficulties. Thus, one's disability should be considered when assessing the extent of legal responsibility (Grant et al., 2018). Addressing mental health and its role in responsibility reduces the burden on the CJS while maintaining one's due process and human rights.

Key Terms

Actus rea
Durham Rule or Product Test
Excuse defenses
Guilty but "Mentally Ill"/Insane
The Irresistible Impulse Test
M'Naghten Rule
Malingering
Mens rea
Model Penal Code
Volitional control

Chapter Questions

(1) Review the concept of competency in Chapter 11. Compare and contrast incompetency and insanity (not legally responsible). What are the similarities and differences between these two concepts?
(2) Describe the history and evolution of the insanity defense, including the M'Naghten case.
(3) How is the insanity defense of not legally responsible demonstrated in court? What steps are involved when an insanity defense is raised?
(4) Compare and contrast the two most common standards used in the United States: the M'Naghten Rule and the Model Penal Code.
(5) Review Fig. 12.1. What legal responsibility standard (if any) is being used in the state in which you reside? Provide your position as to why

you agree with the standard in your state or if you would prefer another standard.

(6) Andrea Yates was committed to a psychiatric hospital indefinitely and will likely remain there for decades. Provide your position as to why you agree or disagree with the jury's decision.

Suggested Readings

Crehan, E. T., & Ury, F. S. (2021). Legal defense in criminal cases. In F. R. Volkmar, R. Loftin, A. Westphal & M. Woodbury-Smith (Eds.), *Handbook of autism spectrum disorder and the law* (pp. 501–522). Springer. https://doi.org/10.1007/978-3-030-70913-6_6

Diamond, B. L. (1956). Isaac Ray and the trial of Daniel M'Naghten. *American Journal of Psychiatry, 112*(8), 651–656. https://doi.org/10.1176/ajp.112.8.651

Linhorst, D. M., Ann Dirks-Linhorst, P., McGraugh, S., Choate, L., & Riley, S. (2018). A comparison of defendants with mental illness represented by public defenders and private attorneys: An analysis of court-ordered pretrial psychiatric evaluations. *American Journal of Criminal Justice, 43*, 810–830. https://doi.org/10.1007/s12103-017-9430-6

Siegel, D. M., & Kinscherff, R. (2018). Recording routine forensic mental health evaluations should be a standard of practice in the 21st century. *Behavioral Sciences & the Law, 36*(3), 373–389. https://doi.org/10.1002/bsl.2349

Notes

1. Also known as "criminal responsibility" or whether one is legally criminally responsible for their actions.
2. May also include the failure to act when one has a legal duty, as required by the criminal statute.
3. The spelling of M'Naghten is questionable, as it has been spelled at least nine other ways in the medical and legal literature (AAPL, 2014).
4. The event occurred on Friday, January 20, 1843. Surgeon Richard Jackson testified at trial that Drummond suffered a wound to his diaphragm and "died on the Wednesday morning following" which would be five days later on Wednesday January 25. However, some published case briefs mention his date of death as April 25th·

5. TV Series (1990–) created by Wolf, D. & Eid, R. (see https://www.imdb.com/title/tt0098844/).
6. Name and some details have been changed for anonymity.

References

Allely, C. S. (2020). The contributory role of psychopathology and inhibitory control in the case of mass shooter James Holmes. *Aggression and Violent Behavior, 51,* 101382, 1–10. https://doi.org/10.1016/j.avb.2020.101382

American Academy of Psychiatry and the Law (AAPL). (2014). AAPL practice guideline for forensic psychiatric evaluation of defendants raising the insanity defense. *The Journal of the American Academy of Psychiatry and the Law, 42,* S3–S76.

American Psychiatric Association. (2022). *Diagnostic and statistical manual of mental disorders* (5th ed. Text Revision). https://doi.org/10.1176/appi.books.9780890425787

Ben-Porath, Y. S., & Tellegen A. (2020). *MMPI-3: Manual for administration, scoring, and interpretation.* Pearson.

Cai, W., Zhang, Q., Huang, F., Guan, W., Tang, T., & Liu, C. (2014). The reliability and validity of the rating scale of criminal responsibility for mentally disordered offenders. *Forensic Science International, 236*, 146–150. https://doi.org/10.1016/j.forsciint.2013.12.018

Cirincione, C., Steadman, H. J., & McGreevy, M. A. (1995). Rates of insanity acquittals and the factors associated with successful insanity pleas. *The Bulletin of the American Academy of Psychiatry and the Law, 23*(3), 399–409.

Denno, D. W. (2003). Who is Andrea Yates? A short story about insanity. *Duke Journal of Gender, Law & Policy, 10*(1), 1–60. https://doi.org/10.2139/ssrn.452040

Dirks-Linhorst, P. A., & Kondrat, D. (2012). Tough on crime or beating the system: An evaluation of Missouri Department of Mental Health's not guilty by reason of insanity murder acquittees. *Homicide Studies, 16*(2), 129–150. https://doi.org/10.1177/1088767912438711

Drogin, E. Y. (2018). Criminal responsibility. In E. Kelley (Ed.), *Representing people with mental disabilities: A criminal defense lawyer's best practices manual* (pp. 17–31). ABA Publishing.

Durham v. United States, 214 F.2d 862 (D.C. Cir. 1954).

Fabian, J. M. (2018). Malingering. In E. Kelley (Ed.), *Representing people mental disabilities: A criminal defense lawyer's best practices manual* (pp. 57–78). ABA Publishing.

Federal Bureau of Investigation (FBI). (2014). News stories, serial killers part 7: The FBI and Jeffrey Dahmer. https://www.fbi.gov/news/stories/serial-killers-part-7-jeffrey-dahmer

Frederick, R. I. (1997). Validity indicator profile manual. NCS Assessments.

Gowensmith, W. N., Murrie, D. C., & Boccaccini, M. T. (2013). How reliable are forensic evaluations of legal sanity? *Law and Human Behavior, 37*(2), 98–106. https://doi.org/10.1037/lhb0000001

Graham, P. A. (2014). A sketch of a theory of moral blameworthiness. *Philosophy and Phenomenological Research, 88*(2), 388–409. https://doi.org/10.1111/j.1933-1592.2012.00608.x

Grant, T., Furlano, R., Hall, L., & Kelley, E. (2018). Criminal responsibility in autism spectrum disorder: A critical review examining empathy and moral reasoning. *Canadian Psychology, 59*(1), 65–75. https://doi.org/10.1037/cap0000124

Haroon, H., Wolfe, N., Feizi, S., & Barboriak, P. (2023). Assessing two decades of insanity acquittees release from the North Carolina forensic program. *The Journal of the American Academy of Psychiatry and the Law, 51*(3), 342–352. https://doi.org/10.29158/JAAPL.230024-23

Kahler v. Kansas, 589 U.S. (2020).

Kalis, A., & Meynen, G. (2014). Mental disorder and legal responsibility: The relevance of stages of decision making. *International Journal of Law and Psychiatry, 37*(6), 601–608. https://doi.org/10.1016/j.ijlp.2014.02.034

Kalis, A., Mojzisch, A., Schweizer, T. S., & Kaiser, S. (2008). Weakness of will, akrasia, and the neuropsychiatry of decision making: An interdisciplinary perspective. *Cognitive, Affective & Behavioral Neuroscience, 8*(4), 402–417. https://doi.org/10.3758/CABN.8.4.402

Kaser-Boyd, E. (2020). Criminal responsibility. In E. Kelley (Ed.), *Representing people with autism spectrum disorders: A practical guide for criminal defense attorneys* (pp. 21–32). ABA Publishing.

Le Couteur, A., Lord, C., & Rutter, M. (2003). *Autism diagnostic interview-revised*. Western Psychological Services.

Lord, C., Rutter, M., DiLavore, P. C., Risi, S., Gotham, K., & Bishop, S. (2012). *Autism diagnostic observation schedule, second edition: ADOS-2*. Western Psychological Services.

Mathis, A. J. (2020). Creative Mitigation. In E. Kelley (Ed.), *Representing people with autism spectrum disorders: A practical guide for criminal defense lawyers,* (pp. 121–136). ABA Publishing.

Meyer, L. F., Leal, C. C. S., Omena, A. A. S., Mecler, K., & Valenca, A. M. (2020). Criminal responsibility scale: Development and validation of a psychometric tool structured in clinical vignettes for criminal responsibility assessments in Brazil. *Frontiers in Psychiatry, 11*, Article 579243. https://doi.org/10.3389/fpsyt.2020.579243

McLellan, F. (2006). Mental health and justice: The case of Andrea Yates. *The Lancet, 368*(9551), 1951–1954. https://doi.org/10.1016/s0140-6736(06)69789-4

Minnesota Multiphasic Personality Inventory-3 (MMPI-3). (2020). Pearson.

Model Penal Code, § 4.01(1) (2017).

Mahoney, M.J. (2021). Defending men with autism accused of online sexual offenses. In F. R. Volkmar, R. Loftin, A. Westphal & M. Woodbury-Smith (Eds.), *Handbook of autism spectrum disorder and the law* (pp. 269–306). Springer. https://doi.org/10.1007/978-3-030-70913-6_6

Moran, R. (1985). The origin of insanity as a special verdict: The trial for treason of James Hadfield (1800). *Law & Society Review, 19*(3), 487–519. https://doi.org/10.2307/3053574

Miller, H.A. (2001). Miller Forensic Assessment of Symptoms Test (M-FAST): Professional manual. Psychological Assessment Resources.

Parsons v. State, 81 Ala. 577, 2 So. 854 (1886).

Perlin, M.L. (1985). After Hinckley: Old myths, new realities, and the future of the insanity defense. *Directions in Psychiatry, 5,* Lesson 22.

Perlin, M. L. (2017). The insanity defense: Nine myths that will not go away. In M. D. White (Ed.), *The insanity defense: Multidisciplinary views on its history, trends, and controversies* (pp. 3–22). Praeger/ABC-CLIO.

Queen v. M'Naghten, 10 Cl. & Fin. 200, 8 Eng. Rep. 718 H. L. (1843).

Ray, I. (1838). *Treatise on the medical jurisprudence of insanity.* Little Brown Publisher. Retrieved from https://archive.org/details/28430960R.nlm.nih.gov

R v M'Naghten 8 E.R. 718; (1843) 10 Cl. & F. 200, (1843a).

R v M'Naghten. (1843b). February 1843. Trial of Daniel M'Naghten (t18430227–874). *Old bailey proceedings online.* Retrieved from https://www.oldbaileyonline.org/record/t18430227-874

Rogers, R., Bagby, R. M., & Dickens, S. E. (1992). *Structured interview of reported symptoms (SIRS) and professional manual*. Psychological Assessment Resources.

Rogers, R. (2008). *Clinical assessment of malingering and deception* (3rd ed.). Guilford Press.

Rogers, R., Wasyliw, O. E., & Cavanaugh, J. L. (1984). Evaluating insanity. A study of construct validity. *Law and Human Behavior, 8*(3/4), 293–303. https://doi.org/10.1007/BF01044697

Sanabria, L. (2023a). *The insanity defense among the states.* https://www.findlaw.com/criminal/criminal-procedure/the-insanity-defense-among-the-states.html

Sanabria, L. (2023b). *What is the insanity defense?* https://www.findlaw.com/criminal/criminal-procedure/insanity-defense.html

Silver, E. (1995). Punishment or treatment? Comparing the lengths of confinement of successful and unsuccessful insanity defendants. *Law and Human Behavior, 19*(4), 375–388. https://doi.org/10.1007/BF01499138

Slobogin, C., Melton, G. B., & Showalter, C. R. (1984). The feasibility of a brief evaluation of mental state at the time of the offense. *Law and Human Behavior, 8*(3/4), 305–320. https://doi.org/10.1007/BF01044698

The Criminal Lunatics Act 1800 (39 & 40 Geo. 3.c. 94).

Tombaugh, T. N. (1996). Test of Memory Malingering (TOMM). Multi-Health Systems, Inc.

Varelius, J. (2021). Autism spectrum condition, good and bad motives of offending, and sentencing. *Neuroethics, 14*, 143–153. https://doi.org/10.1007/s12152-020-09432-w

Vrij, A., & Mann, S. (2001). Who killed my relative? Police officers' ability to detect real-life high-stake lies. *Psychology, Crime & Law, 7*(2), 119–132. https://doi.org/10.1080/10683160108401791

Walczyk, J. J., Sewell, N., & DiBenedetto, M. B. (2018). A review of approaches to detecting malingering in forensic contexts and promising cognitive load-inducing lie detection techniques. *Frontiers in Psychiatry, 9*, 700. https://doi.org/10.3389/fpsyt.2018.00700

13

Witness Testimony and Evidentiary Standards—Accommodations and Support Strategies for Children and Individuals with Mental Illnesses and Neurodevelopmental Disabilities

Learning Objectives

After this chapter, readers should be able to understand the:

(1) Legal standards to determine whether one is competent to testify
(2) Accommodations provided to victims and witnesses when providing testimony
(3) Various roles of expert witnesses to educate the court
(4) Legal standards for the admissibility of evidence and expert witness testimony
(5) Questioning strategies used by attorneys
(6) Role of psychology research as evidence for determining legal responsibility

Introduction

The United States (US) court system uses an adversarial model with two opposing parties, the defense and the prosecution, and a judge who acts as an impartial referee between them. The **confrontation clause** of the Sixth Amendment of the US Constitution allows those accused of a crime to confront their accusers and any witnesses in court. This process aims to

M. C. Mogavero, *Mental Health, Neurodiversity, and Criminal Justice*,
https://doi.org/10.1007/978-3-031-88816-8_13

uncover the truth by questioning victims, witnesses, and sometimes defendants through **direct examination** and **cross-examination.** Direct examination is the initial questioning by the attorney who calls their witness to testify to provide evidence and facts supporting their case. Cross-examination is the questioning of a witness called to testify by the opposing attorney, and questions are usually limited to matters raised during direct examination. The aims of cross-examination are to uncover facts and truths but also to invalidate, discredit, or cause doubt about the witness' credibility or truthfulness of their knowledge about the case or matter (American Bar Association, 2019).

There are additional considerations for victims/witnesses who are children or have disabilities such as autism or intellectual disability (ID). Witnesses must be considered competent to testify, meaning they must demonstrate an understanding of the court process, what it means to speak the truth, and standard terms used in court proceedings. Witnesses must be able to communicate their testimony to participate in the court process. Some may lack adequate verbal communication skills, and accommodations are required to help them provide their testimony, including using interpreters. Testifying in court can be frightening, stressful, and traumatic, particularly during cross-examination (Beckene et al., 2020). Children and those with mental illnesses or disabilities may require an accommodation to provide out-of-court testimony. There are also concerns regarding witnesses' credibility or believability of their testimony, as children and those with disabilities often experience bias from attorneys and juries (Crane et al., 2020; Nathanson & Platt, 2005). Attorneys may call upon mental health professionals as expert witnesses (EWs) to provide testimony affirming a witness' competency to testify and attest to their credibility and believability. For defendants, mental health professionals are often called upon to provide expert testimony in competency hearings and insanity defenses of legal responsibility (*see* Chapters 11 & 12 of this book for details).

Witness Competence and Credibility

Witnesses must be competent to testify, meaning they must have the capacity (i.e., mental ability) to remember and accurately recall past events, communicate them to the court, and take an **oath** that their testimony is truthful (i.e., agree to tell the truth). Competency is determined by one's capacity and level of intelligence. In federal courts, witness testimony must adhere to the **Federal Rules of Evidence** standards (enacted in 1975). Article VI.

Rules 601–606 address determining the admissibility of evidence, including competency to testify.

Relevant Federal Rules of Evidence Article VI. Witness

Rule 601. Competency to Testify in General—Every person is competent to be a witness unless these rules provide otherwise
Rule 602. Need for Personal Knowledge—Witnesses must have personal knowledge of the matter
Rule 603. Oath or Affirmation to Testify Truthfully—Witnesses must give an oath or affirmation to testify truthfully
Rule 604. Interpreter—Interpreters must be qualified and must give an oath or affirmation to make a true translation (Legal Information Institute, 2023)

Child Witnesses

Questions of competency are often raised for witnesses who are young children. Although some states have a presumptive age threshold, no precise age determines competency. For example, a child is presumed competent in New York State at age nine. If the child is under nine, a hearing is mandated to assess the child's competency (N.Y. Crim. Proc. Law §60.20[2]) (2014). Competency is usually ascertained during a **voir dire**, where potential witnesses are questioned to determine if they have sufficient mental ability and are able to answer questions truthfully (Garner, 2019). The judge often asks various questions to assess witnesses' ability to give a proficient account of the facts and assess their oath obligations. The judge will then make a ruling as to whether a witness is competent to testify. The standards for children's competency were first decided in Wheeler v. United States (1895).

Case Brief: Wheeler v. United States (1895)

Facts: On December 21, 1894, George L. Wheeler was on trial in a Texas court for murder that occurred six months earlier on June 12, 1894. The victim's five-and-a-half-year-old son witnessed the murder and testified against Wheeler. Prior to testifying, the victim's son was questioned in a voir dire whether he knew the difference between the truth and a lie. His responses showed that he did, such as if he told a lie, the bad man would get him, or they would put him in jail. He also stated that his mother told him that morning to "Tell no lie." He was also able to answer a question by repeating what the court clerk said. He was also able to correctly answer questions about where he lived, his relationship with the murder victim, and if he ever went to school. The judge decided that the victim's son was competent to testify. On January 2, 1895, Wheeler was found guilty of murder and was sentenced to death. Wheeler later filed a **writ of error** (petition for an appellate court to review the proceeding), claiming the court erred in admitting the testimony of the victim's young son, and appealed his case to the United States (US) Supreme Court.

Issue: Whether the trial court erred when allowing the five-year-old boy to testify as a witness, as his youth should have disqualified him.

Outcome: The US Supreme Court held that the trial court did not err in allowing the victim's son to testify. After reviewing his statements during the voir dire, the Court concluded that the boy was competent to testify because he was intelligent, understood the difference between truth and a lie, the consequences of telling a lie, and what was required in taking an oath. The Court decided that no precise age determines competency; it depends on one's capacity and intelligence, ability to appreciate between truth and a lie, and their duty to tell the truth.

Witness Credibility

Witness **credibility** differs from witness competence, as credibility is a perception and refers to the qualities that make a witness worthy of belief. Competency only refers to the knowledge that enables them to testify. As demonstrated in Chapter 10, children, those with ID, and autistic individuals[1] can be competent witnesses and provide accurate witness statements and eyewitness identifications. However, when testifying in court, others may doubt their credibility.

Children

Research has demonstrated that potential jurors often question the credibility of child witnesses and their statements, including factors such as **suggestibility**. Suggestibility refers to the tendency to agree or accept others' suggestions or recollections of events. A survey of 30 criminal defense attorneys and nine prosecutors revealed that compared to adults, most (88%) believed children were more suggestible than adults, 74% perceived them as being able to recall less information, and 59% believed they were less able to accurately identify an assailant (59%) (Nathanson & Platt, 2005). To assess the effects of witness age on their credibility, Wright et al. (2010) had 612 adult participants read vignettes that described scenarios of a physical abuse case in the home or a sexual abuse case at school. Participants were told the witnesses in the scenario were either children or adults (ages ranged from 3–18). Their perceptions of honesty and credibility increased with the witness's age, but this was not linear, as their perceptions increased rapidly at age 5 to 6 and then leveled off when they reached 18 years (Wright et al., 2010).

Neurodiversity

Perceptions of the credibility of children with neurodevelopmental disabilities (NDDs) are often lower than typically developed children without disabilities. Henry et al. (2011) evaluated the effects of a child's disability and their credibility as a witness among 31 children with ID and 29 without ID. The children viewed a three-minute video that portrayed a minor, nonviolent crime and were later interviewed about what happened, and the interviews were transcribed into text. Then, 130 adult participants read a random sample of six transcripts (three from the group with ID and three from the group without ID). The participants were not made aware of any diagnoses, and each transcript was rated based on eight credibility-related factors (e.g., believability, honesty, perceived convincingness, and completeness). They rated the transcripts of the children with ID significantly lower on all eight factors than those without ID. Similar results were found when participants viewed a video-recorded interview of a child with ID. Brown and Lewis (2013) showed 71 participants a four-minute video of an interview with a young boy with ID describing a health and safety event at school. The participants were told that the boy was either a seven-year-old with ID or a five-year-old or a seven-year-old with no mention of ID. They then rated the child's interview on 18 factors related to witness credibility (e.g., reliability, suggestibility, confidence, consistency, **acquiescence**). Acquiescence is the tendency to say "yes" to every question, regardless of whether it is true. The participants rated the seven-year-old with ID as less credible on every measure than both the seven-year-old and five-year-old, except for acquiescence, where the five-year-old was rated to acquiesce more (Brown & Lewis, 2013).

Potential jurors' awareness of a child's autism diagnosis may affect perceptions of credibility. Crane et al. (2020) showed 120 adult participants video interviews of children after they watched an event at school that involved a mock cell phone theft. The videos were of two autistic boys, similar in age, IQ scores, and cognitive and language abilities. However, the two boys' interview statements differed; one was ten minutes with 43 details, and the second was seven minutes with 27 details. The participants were told that the child in the video had autism or were not given a diagnosis. They then rated the credibility of the statements on 11 different factors (e.g., convincing, confident, honest, complete). The autism diagnosis did not impact the perceptions of credibility for the longer interview that provided more details. For the child who provided a shorter interview, those who were told the child had autism found him to be less credible. Although awareness of one's autism may affect credibility, the amount of information the child can recall can influence their confidence in the child's abilities, thereby affecting perceptions of credibility (Crane et al., 2020).

Box 13.2 Practitioner Spotlight: Cristina Russo, MA

Cristina Russo worked as a Victim Witness advocate for the Monmouth County, New Jersey, Prosecutor's Office for over eight years. The prosecutor's office handles a wide range of offenses, including homicides, vehicular homicides, robberies, burglaries, assaults, sexual assaults, and sexual abuse cases. As an advocate in the Victim Witness Unit, Russo worked directly with the prosecutor and the detectives and became actively involved in victims' cases to gain their trust. What is most important for advocates to possess is patience, empathy, and communication skills. These skills are essential not only to support victims but also to give them autonomy. Victims have the right to attend all hearings except for the grand jury hearing. The unit would contact victims to inform them of every hearing and give them the opportunity to attend, but it must be their decision. Russo would also attend hearings with victims as a supportive figure. Her ongoing support builds trust and empowers victims to testify against the defendant at trials.

Victims come from a wide range of socioeconomic statuses, and some require more support than others. Some have physical disabilities and require wheelchairs. She has worked and assisted with cases of victims with various disabilities, including autism, learning disabilities, and intellectual disabilities. Working with such victims requires more patience and communication. Victim credibility is another matter, and unfortunately, some victims, including autistic children, were unable to testify due to a lack of communication skills. Other times, victims with disabilities did not testify because the defense believed they were not credible. Some victims are not proficient in English, which is an added communication barrier that requires an interpreter. Some interpreters are more difficult to acquire. For example, a victim of aggravated assault only spoke Mandarin. Neither the prosecutor nor Russo was able to communicate in his language, but they did their best to ensure the victim was getting all the correct information and supported him to the best of their ability.

Courtroom Procedures

An unfamiliarity with court procedures can lead to increased stress and anxiety for witnesses. Steps should be taken to increase familiarity, including visiting the courtroom and explaining the various processes and standard terms. Courtroom procedures can be modified, and accommodations can be implemented to reduce stress and anxiety so witnesses can testify while still adhering to the standard rules of evidence. Attorneys should also adhere to best practices concerning questioning strategies, particularly during cross-examination. As mentioned, one of the aims of cross-examination is to invalidate, discredit, or cause doubt about the witness' credibility (American Bar Association, 2019). For children and those with disabilities, where bias toward their credibility already exists, improper questioning may further impact their ability to provide accurate testimony.

Questioning Strategies

When children or those with disabilities are questioned in court, questioning strategies can influence the accuracy and completeness of responses. Attorneys generally may not ask **leading questions** (i.e., questions that persuade a particular response) during direct examination, as this is more common during cross-examination (ABA, 2019). Such coercive questioning raises concerns about suggestibility and acquiescence. Similarly, confusing questions such as **double-negative questions** (e.g., did you not want to not go…?) or **double-barreled questions** (i.e., asking two questions but only allowing one response) may confuse witnesses and provide inaccurate information.

Children are more susceptible to coercive questioning strategies and may change their responses when encouraged to. Zajac and Hayne (2003) examined the effects of questioning strategies on the accuracy of children's responses and whether they changed their responses when given misinformation. Forty-six children (ages 5 and 6) experienced a live event at a police station (e.g., fingerprinted and picture taken). The children were questioned two weeks and four weeks after the event, and 30 (65%) were given misinformation during the questioning. Nine months after the police station visit, children were questioned again, with **leading questions** (e.g., "…didn't you?") or questions that expressed disbelief of the original answer (e.g., "Are you sure?"). Despite only 65% receiving misinformation, 85% of the children changed at least one of their original responses, and 33% changed all their original responses. The children exposed to misinformation made the largest number of errors, showing that young children are more suggestible and change their responses with coercive questioning styles (Zajac Hayne, 2003).

There is also evidence that the cross-examination process may be biased toward those with ID and may influence the accuracy of their responses. Kebbell et al. (2004) compared 32 actual trial transcripts (26 cases of rape, 6 cases of sexual abuse) among trial witnesses with or without ID. After carefully reviewing the transcripts, the researchers noticed that the witnesses with ID were asked significantly more repetitive, yes/no, leading, negative, and double-barreled questions than those without ID. The witnesses with ID were significantly more likely to **acquiesce** to leading questions than those without ID. Thus, Kebbell et al. advised against attorneys using such questioning techniques and to use more appropriate ways of obtaining testimony, as the goal of direct and cross-examination is to ascertain the truth.

Accommodations

Children and people with disabilities often present a range of difficulties with cognition and communication, which makes testifying in court more difficult. According to Title II of the **Americans with Disabilities Ac**t (ADA) of 1990, courts are required to provide accommodations. The US Supreme Court held in Tennessee v. Lane (2004) that the ADA applies to all state courts, defendants, and witnesses. Mental illnesses that substantially limit one or more major life activities, such as post-traumatic stress disorder (PTSD), bipolar disorder, and schizophrenia, are also recognized disabilities under the ADA (42 U.S.C. § 12102(1)(A)). Because the ADA is a federal law, it entitles witnesses to participate in legal proceedings and testify with accommodations regardless of state law, so long as they are necessary, reasonable, and available.

Alternate Forms of Communication

Courts have granted special communication accommodations to children and adults with disabilities or other additional needs with alternative methods to give their testimony in court. Among a survey of 39 attorneys, 41% reported using anatomically correct dolls and other props that aid a child victim of sexual abuse in giving testimony, and 6% reported using other alternative forms of communication, such as an interpreter or a communication board (Nathanson & Platt, 2005). Several court cases have challenged the admissibility of alternative forms of communication. Below is a list and brief description of cases that permitted alternate forms of communication for testimony.

- **People v. Spencer** (1983)—Permitted a victim of sexual assault who was deaf and unable to speak to testify at trial by pointing to numbers, letters, colors, and picture symbols on a blackboard and using an anatomically correct doll.
- **United States v. Bell** (2004) —Allowed a victim of sexual assault who was deaf and unable to speak to use an interpreter to testify on his behalf.
- **Commonwealth v. Brown** (2008)—Permitted a victim of assault who indicated he stuttered when nervous to use non-verbal responses to the defense attorney's questions by nodding or shaking his head.

Out of Court Testimony

Testifying in court can be traumatic, especially for victims having to face their assailant and for those who experience stress-related mental illnesses, such as PTSD. Courts may allow accommodations for witnesses to testify outside the courtroom via **closed-circuit television (CCTV)**. With CCTV, one can testify at the courthouse in another room or a remote location, and the witness is displayed on a large television or monitor in the actual courtroom. Whether CCTV violated the Sixth Amendment Confrontation Clause was decided in Maryland v. Craig (1990), which involved a child sexual abuse victim. The Court decided this was not a violation of the confrontation clause and children may testify via CCTV if testifying in court would be traumatic. In Blackhouse v. Doe (2011), the Maine Supreme Court allowed a man with PTSD to testify outside the courtroom due to his intense startle response, particularly in the presence of uniformed officers.

Hearsay Rule Exceptions

Hearsay refers to secondhand evidence in which witnesses state what others have said to them and not what they personally have seen or heard (Garner, 2019). Such evidence is inadmissible under Rule 802 of the Federal Rules of Evidence (see below). For some victims or witnesses, this rule can be waived and allows testimony by a second party. Some common second-party witnesses include physicians, parents, and psychologists (Nathanson & Platt, 2005). The **tender-years hearsay exception** allows for an out-of-court statement by a child ten years of age and younger describing an act of physical or sexual abuse (Garner, 2019). Another person can take the stand and repeat the out-of-court statements made by the child, sparing the child from having to testify in court. Courts have weighed the rights provided by the confrontation clause to the risk of psychological harm or trauma that might occur for a witness, and at least 38 states allow an exception to the hearsay rule for a child victim (Rowe, 2022).

Relevant Federal Rules of Evidence for Article VIII. Hearsay

Rule 801. Definitions That Apply to This Article: Exclusions from Hearsay
Rule 802. The Rule Against Hearsay—Hearsay is not admissible unless a federal statute; these rules, the Supreme Court provides otherwise
Rule 803. Exceptions to the Rule Against Hearsay—Provides exceptions to hearsay, regardless of whether the one is available as a witness, including medical diagnosis or treatment
Rule 804. Hearsay Exceptions; Declarant Unavailable—Provides exceptions to hearsay, when one is unavailable as a witness, including physical illness or mental illness
Rule 805. Hearsay Within Hearsay—Hearsay within hearsay is not excluded if each part of the combined statements conforms with an exception to the rule.
Rule 806. Attacking and Supporting the Declarant's Credibility—Credibility may be attacked, and then supported, by any evidence that would be admissible (Legal Information Institute, 2023)

Hearsay exceptions are not without controversy, and various procedural safeguards must be in place for the hearsay statements to be admissible (e.g., audio-video, proper questioning). The case Idaho v. Wright (1990) ensured these procedural safeguards for exceptions to the hearsay rule. Laura Lee Wright was convicted of lewd conduct on her five-year-old and two-year-old daughters. Her two-year-old daughter was incompetent to testify, so hearsay evidence was admitted by a physician who examined and interviewed her. Wright challenged the hearsay evidence because the physician knew beforehand what the child would disclose, asked leading questions, and did not audio–video record the interview. The US Supreme Court ruled that the physician's hearsay testimony was untrustworthy, violated the confrontation clause, and reversed Wright's conviction (Idaho v. Wright, 1990).

Although child witnesses are often deemed less credible than adults, there is evidence that hearsay testimony may be less influential than in-person testimony. Goodman et al. (2006) had 370 participants view testimony in a sexual abuse case given by a child either live in court, on video, or by a social worker testifying on behalf of the child. The participants then rated the credibility of the testimony (e.g., accuracy to direct questions, inconsistencies). Participants exposed to the live testimony perceived the child victim as more credible and expressed greater empathy. The social worker's testimony was considered the least credible. Thus, attorneys must weigh the risks and benefits of live versus hearsay testimony (Goodman et al., 2006).

Expert Witness Testimony

Expert witnesses (EWs), particularly mental health professionals, have a vital role in the adversarial court process. Prosecutors and defense attorneys hire EWs to inform and educate attorneys, judges, or citizens of the jury about scientific and other specialized knowledge and expertise beyond what they possess. Although hired by either party, their intended role is to be impartial and independent educators of the court about the case and subject at hand (Auxier, 1989). EWs can also testify on findings from psychological research (e.g., eyewitness testimony, long-term effects of abuse), behaviors and symp toms they commonly see in their clinical practice, and to correct misbeliefs and misassumptions among those with mental illnesses, substance use disorders, or disabilities. For instance, Stobbs and Kebbell (2003) found that EWs offering their opinion and assurance about the competence and capabilities of witnesses with ID to provide testimony under oath can debunk potential jurors' negative perceptions of their creditability.

Standards for Expert Testimony

Mental health professionals, including psychologists, are not automatically deemed qualified experts, as this is determined by meeting specific legal criteria. The earliest standard for the admissibility of expert testimony was established in Frye v. United States (1923), referred to as the "Frye Test," or general acceptance test. The Frye test is why polygraph exams to detect deception are inadmissible in court.

Case Brief: Frye v. United States (1923)

Facts: In July 1922, James Alphonzo Frye was convicted of the murder of Dr. Robert W. Brown. On November 27, 1920, Dr. Brown was shot and killed in Washington, D.C. Several police officers interviewed Frye, and he confessed. The officers testified at trial and read Frye's statement to the jury. Officer Jones testified that during a conversation shortly after his arrest on

August 16, 1921, Frye initially stated that he did not know Dr. Brown and did not know anything about his murder. Officers Jones and Officer Jackson testified about a later conversation in August 1921 where Frye confessed to killing Dr. Brown. Officer Jackson testified that Frye's statements were voluntary.

Frye later recanted his confession and testified in his defense that he confessed to the killing of Dr. Brown so he could have pending forgery and robbery charges against him dropped. To prove he was truthful, Frye's attorneys sought to enter the results of the systolic blood pressure test as evidence, a precursor polygraph exam or "lie detector" test. Dr. Marston conducted the test, and Frye also offered to have Dr. Marston administer the systolic blood pressure test while on the witness stand. The judge refused to allow the results of a systolic blood pressure deception test, as there has not been sufficient scientific evidence developed to demonstrate that it is a valid instrument. The judge also refused expert testimony from Dr. Marston regarding the test results. Frye appealed to the Court of Appeals of the District of Columbia.

Issue: Whether the court erred in refusing evidence from a systolic blood pressure test due to a lack of scientific evidence.

Outcome: The Court agreed that the systolic blood pressure deception test has not been "sufficiently established to have gained general acceptance in the particular field in which it belongs." The test had not gained enough "standing and scientific recognition among physiological and psychological authorities" to justify its admission as evidence in courts of law. The Court decided that the exclusion of the test was proper, and Frye's conviction was affirmed.

The Federal Rules of Evidence established new standards for the admissibility of evidence and expert witness testimony. Under Rule 702, the judge is the "gatekeeper" of evidence and determines or assures that scientific expert testimony indeed proceeds from "scientific knowledge." Whether the Frye standard of "general acceptance" of the scientific community should apply in federal court was determined in Daubert et al. v. Merrell Dow Pharmaceuticals (1993). As a result of this case, the use of the Federal Rules of Evidence in state courts is referred to as the Daubert Standard.

Relevant Federal Rules of Evidence Article VII. Opinions and Expert Testimony

Rule 701. Opinion Testimony by Lay Witnesses—Limited to one based on the witness's perception, helpful to understand the testimony or determine a fact, and not based on scientific, technical, or other specialized knowledge

Rule 702. Testimony by Expert Witnesses—Qualified as an expert by knowledge, skill, experience, training, or education
Rule 703. Bases of an Expert's Opinion Testimony—May base an opinion on facts or data in the case that the expert has been made aware of or personally observed
Rule 704. Opinion on an Ultimate Issue—In a criminal case, an expert witness must not state an opinion about whether the defendant did or did not have a mental state or condition that constitutes an element of the crime charged or of a defense. Those matters are for the trier of fact alone. (Legal Information Institute, 2023)

Case Brief: Daubert et al. v. Merrell Dow Pharmaceuticals (1993)

Facts: Two minors, Jason Daubert and Eric Schuller, were born with severe congenital disabilities. Daubert, Schuller, and their parents sued Merrell Dow Pharmaceuticals in a California state court, alleging their congenital disabilities were caused by their mother's ingestion of Bendectin in utero. Bendectin was a prescription anti-nausea medication developed by Merrell Dow. Merrell Dow denied this claim and submitted an **affidavit** (i.e., sworn statement) from a physician and epidemiologist, who concluded that using Bendectin during the first trimester of pregnancy was not a risk factor for congenital disabilities in humans. In their lawsuit, Daubert et al. provided testimony of eight experts who concluded that Bendectin can cause congenital disabilities. The experts based their conclusions on their unpublished reanalysis of previously published human statistical studies. The court determined that this evidence did not meet the applicable "general acceptance" of the Frye standard for admitting expert testimony as reliable in the relevant scientific community. The case was appealed to the US Court of Appeals for the Ninth Circuit.

Issue: Whether the Frye Standard of "general acceptance" or the Federal Rules of Evidence be the standard for admitting expert scientific testimony in a federal trial.

Outcome: The Court decided that in Federal Courts, the Federal Rules of Evidence, not the Frye standard, are the standards for admitting expert scientific testimony.

The Federal Rules of Evidence (Daubert standard) are required in federal courts. The Frye test has been replaced in most states by the test established in the Daubert Standard. Some states have adopted Daubert, other states still use the Frye standard, while others have adopted their own standards of admissibility or have a hybrid model of two or more standards (Matthiesen et al., 2023; Roesch et al., 2009), as shown in Fig. 13.1.

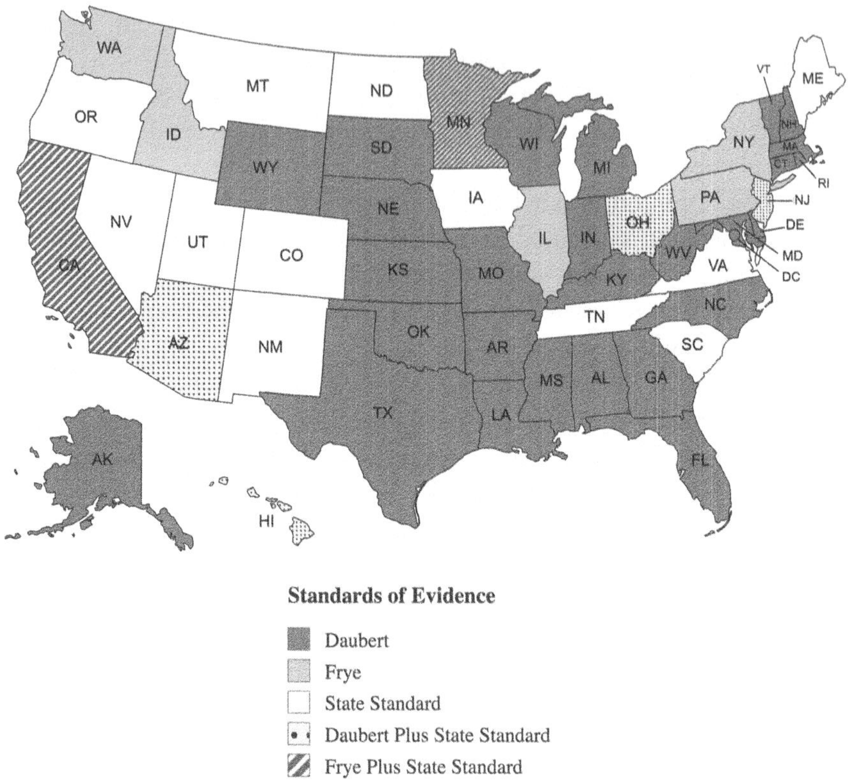

Fig. 13.1 US map of evidence standards for expert witnesses and evidence (Adapted from Matthiesen et al. [2023], created with mapchart.net)

Defendants

Mental health evaluations and subsequent EW testimony are vital for a variety of legal issues, including competency to stand trial (*see* Chapter 11), legal responsibility/insanity defense or diminished capacity (*see* Chapter 12), civil commitment (*see* Chapter 15), and sentencing mitigation (*see* Chapter 16 of this book for details). EWs can also educate the court by explaining the behavior of autistic defendants. Berryessa (2016) interviewed 19 mental health professionals who served as EWs in cases involving autism and reported that their testimony and expertise mainly aimed to communicate information about autism to the court. Specifically, in criminal cases, they explained how the defendants' behavior may have been related to the characteristics of autism, including social impairments, and how misreading social cues can lead to offending behavior (e.g., stalking, assaults, and sexual offenses) (Berryessa, 2016).

Potential jurors may change their perceptions once made aware of someone's condition and common characteristics. Blackhurst et al. (2022) investigated whether one's awareness of a defendant's autism diagnosis influenced their judgments. Three-hundred-twenty-eight participants read a case summary and court transcript of a defendant's testimony and behavior in court (e.g., avoided eye contact on the stand and displayed little emotion). Participants rated the defendant's honesty and blameworthiness before being informed of the autism diagnosis. Once informed of the diagnosis, participants reevaluated the defendant, where they judged the defendant to be significantly more honest and less blameworthy and were more empathic toward the defendant (Blackhurst et al., 2022). For autistic defendants, mental health professionals can educate the court to explain also explain certain behaviors to reduce stigma. As Debbaudt (2004) noted, in court, autistic individuals may laugh, speak loudly, or present "aloof" body language, which may leave defense attorneys, prosecutors, judges, and jurors perceiving them as abhorrent or disrespectful.

Insanity Defense and Legal Responsibility

When defendants plead not guilty by reason of insanity (NGRI), the court appoints mental health evaluators to examine defendants and investigate their mental status at the time of the offense. Separate from insanity defense cases, EWs can also provide evidence of defendants' mental state to mitigate mens rea (i.e., criminal intent), showing diminished capacity to counter the prosecution's evidence. However, a controversial question is whether EWs can provide an ultimate opinion (opinion of absolute certainty) on whether one was insane at the time of committing the offense. Mental health experts largely disagree on whether they should provide an ultimate opinion. In state courts, this permissibility varies (Geary & Law, 2015) depending on the standard used. In federal courts, where the Federal Rules of Evidence apply, or state courts that use the Daubert standard, EWs may only present their opinion in terms of likelihood/probability or degree of certainty. Then, the judge or jury must decide the ultimate opinion (*see* Rule 704 above) (Legal Information Institute, 2023).

Post-Traumatic Stress Disorder

When the American Psychiatric Association (APA) added PTSD to the third edition of the Diagnostic and Statistical Manual of Mental Disorders (DSM-III) in 1980 (APA, 1980), it was used in criminal defense cases and met both the Frye and Daubert standards. Berger et al. (2012) conducted an extensive case review of dozens of cases in the United States where PTSD was used as a defense. For example, in State of New Jersey v. Cocuzza (1981), Cocuzza was arrested for assaulting a police officer and was found to be NGRI. At the time of the attack on the officer, Cocuzza, a Vietnam veteran, was experiencing flashbacks and holding a stick like a riffle, believing he was back in Vietnam combating enemy soldiers.

Battered partner syndrome[2] (BPS), formally referred to as battered woman syndrome (BWS) and battered spouse syndrome, is considered a "subset" of PTSD. BPS/BWS has been used to mitigate legal responsibility or as an insanity defense. Psychologist Dr. Lenore Walker developed BPS/BWS in 1979 after years of researching women who experienced repeated **Intimate partner violence** (IPV). IPV refers to the physical, sexual, or psychological violence between romantic partners (Centers for Disease Control and Prevention, 2024).

BPS/BWS was also based on the **Theory of Learned Helplessness.** Seligman and Maier (1967) coined this theory after studying the behavior of dogs harnessed in cages and exposed to repeated electric shocks. Initially, the dogs tried to escape, but over time, they stopped trying to escape after being exposed to repeated shocks they could not control. The dogs learned they had no control over their situation from prior unsuccessful attempts and stopped taking action to change it. Walker's research on BPS/BWS was based on findings from interviews with 400 women who experienced IVP and noticed these same patterns of learned helplessness (Walker, 2017). Due to the stigma associated with the term "helpless," it has since been renamed **learned optimism** (Walker, 2017). BPS/BWS is not a recognized mental disorder in any edition of the DSM but is recognized by the World Health Organization, International Classification of Diseases (World Health Organization, 2018).

Walker (2017) identified seven factors of BWS/BPS:

> (1) Re-experiencing the trauma events, (2) High levels of arousal and anxiety, (3) High levels of avoidance and numbing of emotions, (4) Cognitive difficulties, (5) Disruption in interpersonal relationships, (6) Physical health and body image problems, (7) Sexual and intimacy issues (p. 3).

Factors 1–4 are the categories under PTSD diagnostic criteria (*see* Chapter 3 of this book for details), and 5–7 were derived from women's responses in Walker's prior research, which makes BPS/BWS a subcategory of PTSD (Walker, 2017). According to Walker, IVP follows a predictable pattern and identifies three phases, sometimes referred to as the cycle of violence, shown in Fig. 13.2 and described in more detail below.

- **Phase 1: Tension Building**—The couple argues, the abusive partner withholds affection or engages in less severe forms of abuse. In attempts to prevent the violence from escalating to more severe forms, the victim tries to placate and act as complacent as possible.
- **Phase 2: Acute Battering**—The abusive partner releases the built-up tension and inflicts severe physical injury upon the victim.
- **Phase 3: Loving Contriction**—The abusive partner profusely apologizes, tries to help, shows kindness and remorse, gives gifts, and promises they will never do it again. The victim wants to believe the abusive partner and remains hopeful. This period eventually ends and returns to Phase 1 (arguing, name-calling) and the cycle begins again (Walker, 2017).

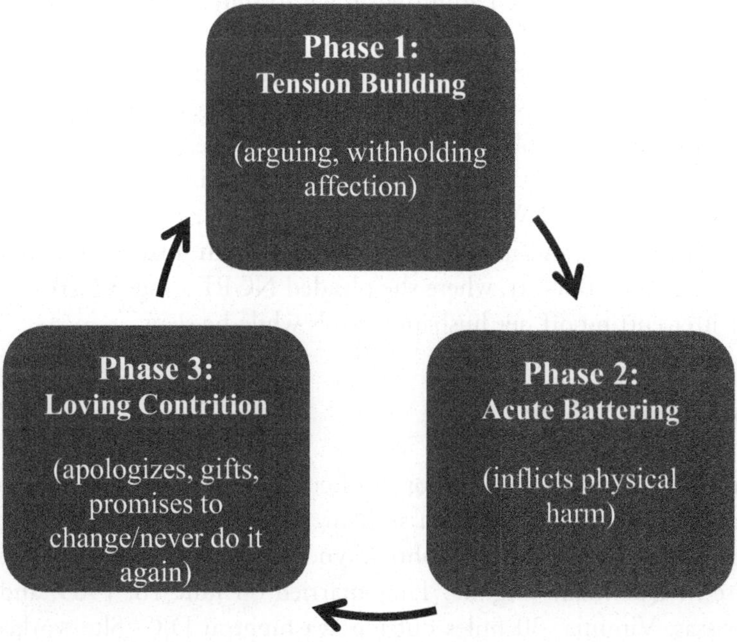

Fig. 13.2 Walker's three phases of interpersonal violence (Adapted from Walker [1979, 2017])

EW testimony is also essential in cases when victims have a disability or mental illness that limits their ability to effectively communicate their abuse experience to jurors. The testimony of EWs can help victims get the entire story before the court (Walker, 2017). Walker has testified as an EW in over 400 spousal homicide cases where she explained how, after enduring years of abuse, sometimes victims will have a mental "breakdown" and become violent toward their abusive partner. In court, the defense attorney can present an EW to explain this violence as a mitigation of mens rea or criminal intent. EWs can help the triers of fact (i.e., judges, jurors) understand that even when violence is not actively occurring, the anticipation of future abuse due to the repetitive pattern is present in the victims' minds. When the abusive partner begins their pattern of escalating behavior, this can trigger memories from past experiences, as if they were happening in the moment, similar to the flashbacks those with PTSD experience (Walker, 2017).

After reviewing the research on BPS/BWS, the US Department of Justice (DOJ) Department of Health and Human Services (DHHS) released a report in May 1996, noting that Walker's three phases were not universally replicable throughout IPV relationships. The three phases should not be used *as* a defense but to *support* a defense. The DOJ DHHS noted that expert testimony on battering has been admitted in all 50 states and Washington D.C. Regarding the validity of the defense, the DOJ DHHS (2006) concluded from their research review that "testimony on battering and its effects can be supported by an extensive body of scientific and clinical knowledge about the dynamics of domestic violence and traumatic stress reactions." (p. ii).

Holliday et al. (2022) conducted an extensive case review of dozens of cases in the US where EW testimony on BPS/BWS and PTSD was used as a defense in the US, and its success in cases has been mixed. One successful case was of Lorena Bobbitt, where she pleaded NGRI using BPS/BWS in her defense after cutting off her husband's penis while he slept.

Case of Lorena Bobbitt

Background: Lorena Gallo was born in Ecuador, raised in Venezuela, and in 1987, at age 18, immigrated on a student visa to the US to attend college. She met 20-year-old US Marine John Wayne Bobbitt at a dance near the military base in Quantico, Virginia. They married on June 18, 1989, and lived in Manassas, Virginia, 30 miles outside Washington D.C. She worked as a nail technician at a salon owned by Janna Bisutti. According to Lorena, John repeatedly physically, sexually, and emotionally abused her during their four-year marriage. They separated several times and had already agreed to separate again the night of the attack (Anolik, 2018; Chozick, 2019; Margolick, 1994).

Instant Offense: According to reports, on the evening of June 23, 1993, John came home intoxicated and raped Lorena before falling asleep. Later, between 3:30 and 4:30 A.M., Lorena went into the kitchen to get a glass of water and became overwhelmed with fear, having recurrent thoughts of all the past traumatic abuse. She saw a knife on the counter, grabbed it, went into the bedroom, and used it to cut off John's penis. She then panicked and drove to Janna's house, tossing the severed penis out the window on the way. Janna called the police and gave them the address and an approximate location to look for the penis. John was rushed to the hospital, and police searched a grassy field that was on the way to Janna's home. Police found John's penis, put it on ice, then rushed it to the hospital, where doctors surgically reattached it. Lorena was charged with malicious wounding and faced a 20-year prison sentence (Anolik, 2018; Chozick, 2019; Sorrentino et al., 2019).

Testimony: At trial, several witnesses testified to John's anger that he beat and humiliated Lorena and saw bruises on her arms, legs, and head. Lorena testified in her own defense and described the years of abuse that occurred in her marriage, including being forced to have an abortion. She claimed that when she saw the knife, she was overcome by years of abuse and feared for her life (Anolik, 2018; Margolick, 1994). Both the defense and prosecution offered EW testimony from psychiatrists, who agreed that Lorena was experiencing a mental illness but offered conflicting opinions regarding her legal responsibility. Dr. Susan Fiester, who testified for Lorena, diagnosed her with major depressive disorder, PTSD, and panic disorder. She described Lorena's behavior as consistent with BPS/BWS. At the time of the offense, Dr. Fiester testified that her mental state had deteriorated; she was in a psychotic state, and due to an irresistible impulse, she had no control over her actions. Dr. Miller Ryans also evaluated Lorena, testified for the prosecution, and claimed there was no evidence that she was not in touch with reality or experienced any delusions and that her actions were not due to an irresistible impulse (Sorrentino et al., 2019).

Outcome: The jury deliberated on whether Lorena met Virginia's criteria for an NGRI defense, which combined the M'Naghten standard with the irresistible impulse test (*see* Chapter 12 of this book for details). On January 21, 1994, the jury found Lorena NGRI, and she was committed to Central State Hospital for evaluation and treatment (Sorrentino et al., 2019).

Considerations and Recommendations

There are several ways in which CJS practitioners can support and prepare children, those with disabilities, and those with mental illnesses when providing testimony. As discussed in chapters 11 and 12 in this book, defense attorneys, prosecutors, and judges with more knowledge about mental illnesses, neurodevelopmental disorders such as autism and ID, and child development can help improve communication while reducing misconceptions. Education and training can assist with being more effective and efficient, supporting individuals during the court process, and improving the credibility of statements in court.

Build a Rapport and Explain the Court Process Over Time

Rapport-building is essential to building trust; however, for children, those with disabilities such as autism, or those with mental illnesses, this process can take longer. Attorneys should build a rapport of trust over time, explain the terms they may hear in court, and introduce them to the courtroom (Grant et al., nd). Attorneys should also practice the direct and cross-examination questioning process (Rainville, 2013). This is particularly important for victims, as cross-examination can make victims feel re-victimized or blameworthy (Walker, 2017). As Beckene et al. (2020) explained, most are unfamiliar with the legal process, and fearing the unknown can increase anxiety, making them feel as if they lack control over the process. Victims must rely on and place trust in the prosecuting attorney handling their case, and attorneys should guide them in decision-making to help them feel they have more control (Mathis, 2020). Victim advocates like Russo, who work with the prosecutor and police, can help bridge the gap to increase victims' trust, communicate the process, and provide victims more autonomy, increasing their sense of control.

Inquire About Diverse Communication Methods

During the rapport process, attorneys can inquire about and establish the best communication methods, whether writing, typing, or pointing to pictures or letters. If family members are present, defense attorneys and prosecutors should notice and follow the family members' communication methods. What may be effective for one individual or family may not be for others (Grant et al., nd). During conversations, some individuals may not be as forthright as others and, therefore, may require more probing questions to get them to elaborate (Mathis, 2020).

Obtain Evaluations for Defendants

Due to the stigma related to mental illnesses and disabilities, not all defendants voluntarily disclose their diagnoses. During the initial meeting, attorneys should ask about any diagnosis or other concerns. If unnoticed or undocumented, behaviors associated with a disability can be misinterpreted as being disinterested, flippant, or disrespectful (Mathis, 2020), which may negatively affect the ability to establish rapport. Attorneys should pay attention to any behaviors suggesting overstimulation, such as stimming or other repetitive movements, and ask if they need a break. In general, attorneys should consider keeping meetings shorter and more frequent (Mathis, 2020). Lastly, defense attorneys and prosecutors should adhere to the sensitive language and terms outlined in Chapter 1 of this book in the section titled, *A Note About Evolving Language and Terms*, while communicating and establishing rapport. For example, using outdated terms or functioning labels can have a negative connotation and make establishing rapport and trust more difficult (Grant et al., nd).

If the defendant denies having a disability or mental illness or does not have a formal diagnosis, attorneys can explain the value of having an evaluation. This can better determine whether their mental status can be used to mitigate mens rea to justify a reduced sentence. The defendant may refuse, but attorneys can have ongoing conversations about the potential consequences during the rapport process. Attorneys should also document their efforts for post-conviction reviews (Shein, 2018). If not requesting an insanity defense or competency hearing (*see* Chapters 11 and 12 of this book for details), the evaluation cannot be court-ordered. Public defenders and private defense attorneys sometimes have clients with different or limited funding resources for experts. If one's jurisdiction requires attorneys to file a petition to request funding to secure an expert, they can file the motion for the request **ex parte** (i.e., without the presence or participation of the opposing party) and **under seal** (kept confidential) (Mathis, 2020).

Work with Family Members

Family members can offer continued support during the court process. Working with family members is also vital for obtaining information, especially for those with communication challenges. For defendants, family members can also assist with providing mitigating evidence, including school records and medical records. School records can provide evidence of any education needs under the Individuals with Disabilities Education Act of 1997, any accommodation in their Individualized Education Program (IEP), and assessment results (e.g., IQ tests) (*see* Chapter 6 of this book for details). As with evaluations for competency and the insanity defense (*see* Chapters 11 and 12 of this book for details), information about one's life, including school and mental health history, is helpful, as the information "humanizes" the defendant to the prosecutor and minimizes preconceived negative perceptions. Communication with family can become challenging due to attorney-client privilege, and therefore, this confidentiality must be explained to family members who would like to be involved in the processes (Shein, 2018).

Request Accommodations

Prosecutors and defense attorneys can request accommodations through the ADA. After building rapport, specific needs can be identified. For some autistic individuals, bright lights or excessive noise can produce sensory overload; dimming the lights and reducing excess noise can help them communicate better. Some may require sensory stimulation to communicate effectively, such as holding something in their hand, having an object to stim with, or standing or walking around the room (Rainville, 2013).

Another accommodation is to provide testimony via CCTV or out-of-court testimony. For children and those with mental illnesses, especially PTSD, the court experience can be traumatic, and they may request out-of-court testimony or utilize the hearsay rule exception and allow another to testify on their behalf. Additional accommodations may also include a later start time, as some with mental illness require medications, which can make early court appearances more difficult. Attorneys can also request that the judge take more frequent breaks (Nemens & Ruttenberg, 2018). Due to the problems with leading questions described above, attorneys can also request accommodation of no leading questions (Rainville, 2012), which should be filed before the trial to raise these concerns with the trial judge (Rainville, 2013).

Secure Expert Witnesses

Various directories and databases are available to identify potential EWs (see Berryessa, 2016, p. 580). Securing an EW is one of the most critical steps for defense attorneys and prosecutors, particularly mental health experts. Attorneys should ensure that the experts adhere to the standard criteria for obtaining mental health evidence, as failing to do so could discredit them from being qualified to provide expert testimony, and their creditability could be challenged during cross-examination. Adhering to these standards also helps to reduce EW bias (Kelley, 2018).

Conclusion

Individuals with mental illnesses and neurodevelopmental disorders such as autism and ID can become involved in the criminal justice system for various reasons, including crime victims or defendants. As discussed in Chapter 10 of this book, the victim or witness identification of perpetrators, recollection of events, and their subsequent testimony are essential and integral components of the legal system. However, younger age, mental illnesses, and disabilities can present various barriers in court. Some experience communication difficulties, are suggestible to confusing or leading questions, and experience stigma and misconceptions of their credibility. The necessary accommodations must be in place to allow them meaningfully to participate in the court process to ensure fairness or to seek justice. The defense of insanity is a legal construct, and the defense uses psychology research and EW testimony to explain behaviors, whether self-defense or diminished capacity. The role of EW testimony is invaluable, as they can be educators of the court and describe various conditions to explain behavior, dispel any myths or other misconceptions about the credibility of testimony, and testify to their assessment results regarding legal responsibility/insanity defense or sentence mitigation.

Key Terms

Acquiescence/Acquiesce
Affidavit
Battered partner syndrome
Confrontation Clause
Credibility
Cross examination

Cycle of violence
Direct examination
Double negative questions
Double-barreled questions
Hearsay
Intimate partner violence
Theory of Learned Helplessness
Learned optimism
Oath
Sensory stimulation
Suggestibility
Tender-years hearsay exception
Ultimate opinion
Voir dire

Chapter Questions

(1) Compare and contrast the Frye Standard and Rule 702 of the Federal Rules of Evidence: Testimony by Expert Witnesses.
(2) Review Fig. 13.1. What standard is being used in the state where you live: Frye, Daubert, or another? Provide your position on why you agree with the standard in your state or if you would prefer another standard.
(3) What are the major differences in the perceived credibility of child witness testimony provided by children versus adults? Describe the differences between witnesses with ID versus those without ID.
(4) The Sixth Amendment to the Constitution allows defendants to confront their accusers and cross-examine them in court. What problems does this pose for child victims testifying in court? Describe the accommodations given to children asked to testify.
(5) List and describe as many accommodations as possible you can think of that can be provided to witnesses with disabilities who have difficulties communicating.
(6) What is meant by expert opinion on the ultimate issue, and what are the pros and cons of giving expert testimony to answer the ultimate question? What is your position on whether experts should give an opinion?

Suggested Readings

The Arc, National Alliance on Mental Illness, Prosecutors" Center for Excellence. (2020, Feb). Victims, witnesses, and defendants with mental illness or intellectual and developmental disabilities: A guide for prosecutors. https://pceinc.org/victims-witnesses-and-defendants-with-mental-illness-or-intellectual-and-developmental-disabilities-arc-nami-pce/

Dicker, S., & Marion, R. (2012). Judicial spectrum primer: What judges need to know about children with autism spectrum disorders. *Juvenile & Family Court Journal, 63*(2), 1–19. https://doi.org/10.1111/j.1755-6988.2012.01074.x

Freckelton, I. (2021). Expert evidence about autism spectrum disorder. In F. R. Volkmar, R. Loftin, A. Westphal & M. Woodbury-Smith (Eds.), *Handbook of autism spectrum disorder and the law* (pp. 39–69). Springer. https://doi.org/10.1007/978-3-030-70913-6_3

Maras, K. (2021). Obtaining testimony from autistic people. In F. R Volkmar, R. Loftin, A. Westphal & M. Woodbury-Smith (Eds.), *Handbook of autism spectrum disorder and the law* (pp. 145–183). Springer. https://doi.org/10.1007/978-3-030-70913-6_7

Maras, K. L., Crane, L., Mulcahy, S., Hawken, T., Cooper, P., Wurtzel, D., & Memon, A. (2017). Brief report: Autism in the courtroom: Experiences of legal professionals and the autism community. *Journal of Autism and Developmental Disorders, 47*(8), 2610–2620. https://doi.org/10.1007/s10803-017-3162-9

Notes

1. *see A Note About Evolving Language and Term i*n Chapter 1 for information on identity-first language
2. Due to citing Walker (1979, 2017) battered women syndrome (BWS), BWS is used throughout instead of exclusively using the gender-neutral, battered partner syndrome.

References

American Bar Association. (2019, September 9). *How courts work.* https://www.americanbar.org/groups/public_education/resources/law_related_education_network/how_courts_work/crossexam/

American Psychiatric Association. (1980). *Diagnostic and statistical manual of mental disorders* (3rd ed.). Americans with Disabilities Act (ADA), 42 U.S.C. §12132.

Anolik, L. (2018, June 28). Lorena Bobbitt's American dream. *Vanity Fair.* https://www.vanityfair.com/style/2018/06/lorena-bobbitt-john-wayne-bobbitt-25-years

Auxier, J. A. (1989). The role of the expert witness. *Radiation Research, 117*(2), 178–180.

Beckene, T., Forrester-Jones, R., & Murphy, G. H. (2020). Experiences of going to court: Witnesses with intellectual disabilities and their carers speak up. *Journal of Applied Research in Intellectual Disabilities, 33*(1), 67–78. https://doi.org/10.1111/jar.12334

Berger, O., McNiel, D. E., & Binder, R. L. (2012). PTSD as a criminal defense: A review of case law. *The Journal of the American Academy of Psychiatry and the Law, 40*(4), 509–521. https://jaapl.org/content/40/4/509

Berryessa, C. M. (2016). Brief report: Judicial attitudes regarding the sentencing of offenders with high-functioning autism. *Journal of Autism and Developmental Disorders, 46*(8), 2770–2773. https://doi.org/10.1007/s10803-016-2798-1

Blackhouse v. Doe, 24 A.3d 72. (Me. 2011).

Blackhurst, T., Hartley, C., Turner, P., & Warmelink, L. (2022). Jurors' judgments of an autistic defendant are influenced by awareness of autism, knowledge of psychological conditions and trait-empathy. *Journal of Intellectual Disabilities and Offending Behaviour, 13*(3/4), 90–101.

Brown, D. A., & Lewis, C. N. (2013). Competence is in the eye of the beholder: Perceptions of intellectually disabled child witnesses. *International Journal of Disability, Development and Education, 60*(1), 3–17. https://doi.org/10.1080/1034912X.2013.757132

Centers for Disease Control and Prevention. (2024). *Preventing intimate partner violence.* https://www.cdc.gov/violenceprevention/intimatepartnerviolence/fastfact.html

Chozick, A. (2019, Jan). You know the Lorena Bobbitt story. But not all of it. *The New York Times.* https://www.nytimes.com/2019/01/30/arts/television/lorena-bobbitt-documentary-jordan-peele.html

Commonwealth v. Brown, 884 N.E.2d 488 Mass. (2008).

Crane, L., Wilcock, R., Maras, K. L., Chui, W., Marti-Sanchez, C., & Henry, L. A. (2020). Mock juror perceptions of child witnesses on the autism spectrum: The impact of providing diagnostic labels and information about autism. *Journal of Autism and Developmental Disorders, 50*(5), 1509–1519. https://doi.org/10.1007/s10803-018-3700-0

Debbaudt, D. (2004). Beyond guilt or innocence. *Forum paper, Autism New Zealand Inc.* http://autismnz.org.nz/police/Pol_BeyGuilt.pdf

Daubert et al. v. Merrell Dow Pharmaceuticals, Inc., 509 U.S. 579 (1993).

Frye v. United States, 293 F. 1013 D.C. Cir. (1923).

Garner, B. A. (2019). *Black's law dictionary* (11th ed.). Tomson Reuters.

Geary, R. C., & Law, K. -B. (2015). Conflicting expert witness testimony in insanity defense. *Journal of the American Academy of Psychiatry and the Law, 43*(4), 511–512. https://jaapl.org/content/43/4/511

Goodman, G. S., Myers, J. E., Qin, J., Quas, J. A., Castelli, P., Redlich, A. D., & Rogers, L. (2006). Hearsay versus children's testimony: Effects of truthful and deceptive statements on jurors' decisions. *Law and Human Behavior, 30*(3), 363–401. https://doi.org/10.1007/s10979-006-9009-0

Grant, C., Munday, L., Nolan, K., Peters, R., Vieth, V., Johnson, R., & Farrell, R. (nd). *Zero abuse project. Child victims with disabilities: A guide for prosecutors.* https://www.zeroabuseproject.org/child-victims-with-disabilities-a-guide-for-prosecutors/

Henry, L., Ridley, A., Perry, J., & Crane, L. (2011). Perceived credibility and eyewitness testimony of children with intellectual disabilities. *Journal of Intellectual Disability Research, 55*(4), 385–391. https://doi.org/10.1111/j.1365-2788.2011.01383.x

Holliday, J. R., McNiel, D. E., Morris, N. P., Faigman, D. L., & Binder, R. L. (2022). The use of battered woman syndrome in U.S. Criminal courts. *The Journal of the American Academy of Psychiatry and the Law, 50*(3), 373–380. https://doi.org/10.29158/jaapl.210105-21

Idaho v. Wright, 497 U.S. 805. (1990).

Individuals with Disabilities Education Act, Pub. L. No. 105–17, 111 Stat. 37. (1997).

Kebbell, M. R., Hatton, C., & Johnson, S. D. (2004). Witnesses with intellectual disabilities in court: What questions are asked and what influence do they have? *Legal and Criminological Psychology, 9*(1), 23–35. https://doi.org/10.1348/135532504322776834

Kelley, E. (2018). Working with families. In E. Kelley (Ed.), *Representing people with mental disabilities: A criminal defense lawyer's best practices manual* (pp. 259–262). ABA Publishing.

Legal Information Institute. (2023). Federal rules of evidence. http://www.law.cornell.edu/rules/fre/.

Margolick, D. (1994, January 12). Witnesses say mutilated man often hit wife. *New York Times.* https://www.nytimes.com/1994/01/12/us/witnesses-say-mutilated-man-often-hit-wife.html

Maryland v. Craig, 497 U.S. 836. (1990).

Mathis, A. J. (2020). Creative mitigation. In E. Kelley (Ed.), *Representing people with autism spectrum disorders: A practical guide for criminal defense lawyers* (pp. 121–136). ABA Publishing.

Matthiesen, B. W., Wickert, L. R. & Lehrer, D. W. (2023). Admissibility of expert testimony is all 50 states. Retrieved from https://www.mwl-law.com/helpful-resources/subrogation-reference-charts/

Nemens, K., & Ruttenberg, M. (2018, September 26–29). Reasonable modifications in court for persons with psychiatric disabilities. Paper Presented at the National Association for Rights Protection and Advocacy Conference, Baltimore, MD. https://www.narpa.org/conferences/2018/reasonable-modifications-in-court

Nathanson, R., & Platt, M. D. (2005). Attorneys' perceptions of child witnesses with mental retardation. *The Journal of Psychiatry & Law, 33*(1), 5–42. https://doi.org/10.1177/009318530503300102

N.Y. Crim. Proc. Law §60.20(2). Criminal procedure (2014). https://newyork.public.law/laws/n.y._criminal_procedure_law_section_60.20

People v. Spencer, 457 N.E.2d 473 Ill. App. Ct. (1983).

Rainville, C. (2012). Prosecuting cases for children with intellectual disabilities. *American Bar Association.* https://www.americanbar.org/groups/public_interest/child_law/resources/child_law_practiceonline/child_law_practice/vol_31/december_2012/prosecuting_casesforchildrenwithintellectualdisabilities/

Rainville, C. (2013). Prosecuting cases for children on the autism spectrum. *American Bar Association.* https://www.americanbar.org/groups/public_interest/child_law/resources/child_law_practiceonline/child_law_practice/vol_32/april-2013/prosecuting-cases-for-children-on-the-autism-spectrum/

Roesch, R., Zapf, P. A., & Hart, S. D. (2009). *Forensic Psychology and Law.* Wiley Publishers.

Rowe, M. (2022). Babe in the woods: Why the federal rules of evidence should adopt a new hearsay exception to protect children. *Arkansas Law Notes*, 1–17. https://scholarworks.uark.edu/arlnlaw/11/

Seligman, M. E., & Maier, S. F. (1967). Failure to escape traumatic shock. *Journal of Experimental Psychology, 74*(1), 1–9. https://doi.org/10.1037/h0024514

Shein, M. G. (2018). Mitigation: Mental health and sentencing. In E. Kelley (Ed.), *Representing people with mental disabilities: A criminal defense lawyer's best practices manual* (pp. 33–44). ABA Publishing.

Sorrentino, R., Musselman, M., & Broderick, L. (2019). Battered woman syndrome: Is it enough for a not guilty by reason of insanity plea? *Psychiatric Times, 36*(7). https://www.psychiatrictimes.com/view/battered-woman-syndrome-it-enough-not-guilty-reason-insanity-plea

State v. Cocuzza, No. 1484–79 N.J. Super. Ct. (1981).

Stobbs, G., & Kebbell, M. R. (2003). Jurors' perception of witnesses with intellectual disabilities and the influence of expert evidence. *Journal of Applied Research in Intellectual Disabilities, 16*, 107–114. https://doi.org/10.1046/j.1468-3148.2003.00151.x

Tennessee v. Lane, 541 U.S. 509, 532. (2004).

United States Code Title 42, The Public Health and Welfare, Chapter 126, Equal Opportunity for Individuals with Disabilities, Sec. 12102(1)(A)—Definition of disability.

United States Department of Justice, Department of Health, and Human Services. (2006). *The validity and use of evidence concerning battering and its effects in criminal trials: Report responding to section 40507 of the Violence Against Women Act.* https://www.ojp.gov/pdffiles/batter.pdf

United States v. Bell, 367 F.3d 452 5th Cir. (2004).

United States v. Wheeler, 159 U.S. 523, 524. (1895).

Walker, L. E. (1979). *The battered woman syndrome.* Springer.

Walker, L. E. (2017). *The battered woman syndrome* (4th ed.). Springer.

World Health Organization. (2018). *International classification of diseases and related health problems* (11th ed.). https://idc.who.int/

Wright, D. B., Hanoteau, F., Parkinson, C., & Tatham, S. (2010). Perceptions about memory reliability and honesty for children of 3 to 18 years old. *Legal and Criminological Psychology, 15*(2), 195–207. https://doi.org/10.1348/135532508X400347

Zajac, R., & Hayne, H. (2003). I don't think that's what really happened: The effect of cross-examination on the accuracy of children's reports. *Journal of Experimental Psychology Applied, 9*(3), 187–195. https://doi.org/10.1037/1076-898X.9.3.187

Part V

Mental Health and Neurodiversity—Implications for the Correctional and Mental Health Systems

14

Community-Based Corrections—Probation and Specialty Court Interventions for Individuals with Mental Illnesses and Substance Use Disorders

Learning Objectives

After this chapter, readers should be able to understand the:

(1) Practice of alternative sanctions, including probation and specialized probation
(2) Effectiveness of probation on recidivism reduction
(3) Alternative models for those with mental illness and comorbid substance use disorder
(4) Development and structure of drug court and mental health court programs
(5) Risk-need-approach to supervision for recidivism prevention

Introduction

The shift to the crime control model in sentencing, coupled with the "war on drugs" during the last quarter of the twentieth century, resulted in the increased reliance on jails and prisons to address increasing crime rates with incapacitation and deterrence. This increased reliance on harsh sentences to control crime resulted in overcrowded jails and prisons, with many incarcerated for drug offenses (*see* Chapter 5 of this book for details). Mass

M. C. Mogavero, *Mental Health, Neurodiversity, and Criminal Justice*,
https://doi.org/10.1007/978-3-031-88816-8_14

incarceration cast a wide net that resulted in the imprisonment of many individuals with mental illnesses, substance use disorders (SUDs), and disabilities. These same crime control policies negatively changed the landscape for juveniles engaging in crime and delinquency. The number of juveniles diverted from the juvenile justice system (JJS) and processed in the adult court system increased because states passed laws supporting harsher penalties. The percentage of juveniles waived from juvenile court (designed for rehabilitation) to adult court increased by 100% in only eight years (1986–1994) (Hockenberry, 2021) (*see* Chapter 6 of this book for details).

The negative collateral consequences resulting from mass incarceration led criminal justice system (CJS) professionals to pursue effective community sanctions. Many jurisdictions increased the use of probation and established other community-based diversion programs to address overcrowded jails and prisons. Unfortunately, existing probation programs were unprepared to serve those with mental illnesses and SUDs. Veysey (1994) authored a report for the United States (US) Department of Justice (DOJ), highlighting the ineffectiveness of community supervision for those with mental illness due to an inability to effectively respond to their unique needs. By the late 1990s, there was a shift to the person-centered rehabilitation focus to reduce **recidivism** (e.g., reoffending) to protect the public while reducing costs. Since then, specialized interventions for justice-involved persons with mental illnesses and SUDs have grown, including specialized probation units with smaller and exclusive caseloads and separate court systems. Some public defender offices employ social workers to assess defendants' needs and collaborate with defense attorneys (in agreement with the prosecutor and the judge) to determine appropriate alternatives to incarceration (Reamer, 2004). Alternatives to incarceration grew across the US, with greater attention to evidence-based practices.

Probation

Probation is a type of community sanction where defendants are placed under the control and supervision of the court and must follow the court-ordered conditions (i.e., rules). Judges may sentence adult or juvenile defendants to probation for first-time offenses, minor offenses, or an alternative to institutional confinement for more severe offenses (Torbet, 1996). Most adults[1] on probation are sentenced for nonviolent offenses, with only 15% for violent offenses (Kaeble, 2021). About 34% of juvenile probation clients were sentenced for violent offenses and 10% for drug offenses (Hockenberry &

Puzzanchera, 2023). A jail or prison sentence can also be suspended in place of probation, or the defendant may receive a **split sentence**, where they serve part of their sentence in jail or prison and part on probation. Defendants may also be placed on **Intensive Probation Supervision**, which requires more frequent meetings and may require home confinement. According to the most recent reports by the DOJ and the National Center for Juvenile Justice, an estimated three million adults (Kaeble, 2021) and a quarter of a million juveniles are on probation in a given year (Puzzanchera et al., 2018, 2022). Probation should not be confused with **parole**. Parole is when individuals are either discretionary or mandatorily released into the community after serving a prison term. Those on parole must also adhere to conditions and be supervised by the state/county agency for the rest of their sentence.

Probation clients are assigned and supervised by a probation officer (PO), who assesses and decides their conditions, schedules regular meetings to ensure adherence to conditions, and provides case management and other support services (Reamer, 2004). General conditions typically include refraining from further crime, reporting regularly to their PO, abstaining from illicit substances or alcohol, and maintaining consistent work or school attendance. Specific conditions are customized to one's individual rehabilitative needs, such as mental health or substance use counseling or abiding by curfews. For probation clients on a suspended sentence, not adhering to their conditions can result in **revocation**, where their probation is rescinded, and they serve the rest of their sentence in jail or prison.

Effectiveness of Probation

According to a DOJ report, in 2020, most (66%) completed their probation term successfully, and only 14% were incarcerated (Kaeble, 2021). The effectiveness of probation in reducing recidivism is more nuanced and depends on several factors, but those sentenced to probation do not appear to reoffend more than those sentenced to jail or prison. Cochran et al. (2014) evaluated the recidivism rates among a large sample of justice-involved individuals in Florida, comparing those convicted of similar crimes and were placed either on probation, intensive probation, or in jail or prison. After three years, 31% of those on probation reoffended compared to 34% on intensive probation, 35% of those sentenced to jail, and 47% of those sentenced to prison. Unlike incarceration, community sanctions allow for individuals to receive rehabilitation services and family and community support, factors shown to be effective in reducing recidivism (Cochran et al., 2014).

The working relationship between the PO and the client also appears to influence recidivism. Beck and McGinnis (2022) reviewed 18 studies on the effectiveness of probation in discontinuing criminal behavior and noted that the supportive caseworker relationship (as opposed to non-supportive and surveillance-focused) was overwhelmingly more conducive to crime reduction. Over-focusing on conditions interferes with building a therapeutic relationship and, thus, may lead to an increased risk of reoffending (Bonta et al., 2011). Bonta et al. acknowledge the importance of discussing and enforcing conditions, but POs must balance their "dual role" of enforcing supervision conditions while acting as supportive figures and addressing the factors that led to criminal behavior in the first place. Using feedback from POs and other stakeholders, Epperson et al. (2020) developed and published *Brief Intervention to Promote Service Engagement,* a manual to guide POs to establish therapeutic relationships with their clients that can be aligned and structured with standard probation practices.

Evidence-Based Approach to Probation

Evidence-based practices in the CJS gained traction in the 2000s (*see* Chapter 5 of this book for details), and one approach used by CJS practitioners is the **Risk-Need and Responsivity Model** (RNR) (Andrews & Bonta, 2010). These RNR factors became the standard for probation (Crime & Justice Institute, 2009), as they align conditions and services to one's specific needs, unlike previous approaches that focused on monitoring compliance with court-ordered conditions. The RNR model is based on an individual's recidivism risk and treatment needs that guide professionals in developing plans for recidivism prevention and changing their behavior.

The **risk principle** is the framework's first application, where one's risk level for recidivism is assessed to identify the appropriate intervention and treatment level. Andrews and Bonta warn that overservicing individuals with low to moderate risk and underservicing those with higher risk can increase recidivism. Because risk level assessment is the foundation for determining the extent of supervision and monitoring needs, POs should receive training on properly administering risk assessment tools. One such tool is the Level of Service Inventory-Revised (LSI-R; Andrews & Bonta, 1995). The LSI-R is a comprehensive assessment that consists of 54 items ranging across ten domains. If resources are limited or there are time constraints, POs can use the Level of Service Inventory: Screening Version (LSI-SV, Andrews & Bonta, 1998) or a combination of the LSI-R and LSI-SV (Austin et al., 2003; Lowenkamp et al., 2009). Another common tool is the Ohio Risk Assessment

System (ORAS) (Latessa et al., 2010). The ORAS has multiple assessments to determine the risk and needs of those in different stages in the CJS. The LSI and ORAS are for use with adults, but the Oregon Juvenile Crime Prevention Risk Assessment (JCP) (2006) is a validated instrument to assess risk in juveniles.

POs should also be trained and aware of potential bias in risk assessment, as there is elevated risk bias against racial and ethnic minorities (Whiteacre, 2006). The LSI-SV has been validated with individuals with mental illnesses, but caution should be used when assessing risk among those with a co-occurring SUD (Ferguson et al., 2009). POs should also use caution when administering risk assessment with those with ID. For example, risk ratings using age may be positively skewed, as those with ID tend to be younger or report a younger age at first offense (Lindsay et al., 2006). Ho et al. (2018) further cautioned the possibility of bias using risk assessments for juveniles to determine their risk level and community supervision needs, especially when information is missing in their files, as POs tend to select the "less intrusive" option, which may underestimate risk level, resulting in fewer interventions for recidivism prevention.

The **needs principle** addresses the specific interventions that focus on an individual's criminogenic needs (i.e., the risk factors for engaging in crime) (Wilson & Yates, 2009). A common criminogenic risk factor is substance use. If an individual uses substances to cope with negative emotions, then intervention goals should emphasize addressing alternative coping mechanisms (Bonta & Andrews, 2007). The **responsivity principle** considers the individual's skills and cognitive needs. Responsivity has two subprinciples: general and specific. General responsivity bases the program's structure on a relevant model that affects change in the individual (e.g., cognitive behavioral therapy intervention). Specific responsivity modifies the program to meet the needs of the individual based on their characteristics (e.g., group therapy or individual one-on-one therapy) (Andrews & Bonta, 2010).

Effectiveness of RNR with Probation

Research has supported the effectiveness of the RNR with probation clients when applied as recommended. Taxman (2008) evaluated Maryland's Proactive Community Supervision (PCS), one of the first programs to implement the RNR approach. Taxman compared 274 adult probation clients supervised by POs in the PCS model to 274 probation clients receiving traditional probation, considering the length of time on probation and prior criminal history. Clients of POs who applied the PCS supervision model were less likely to be rearrested (30% vs. 42%) and had fewer probation violations (35% vs. 40%) than those on traditional probation.

Some supervision skills and methods are more effective in helping clients desist from crime. Bonta et al. (2011) evaluated supervision practices among 33 POs after receiving an RNR training program to 19 who did not and compared their clients' recidivism. The RNR-trained POs spent more supervision sessions discussing the criminogenic needs (and had lower recidivism rates), while the untrained officers focused more on probation conditions (and had higher recidivism rates). Smith et al. (2012) compared the practices of RNR-trained POs to untrained POs by evaluating recorded probation meetings with 272 probation clients. The RNR-trained officers were more likely to spend more time focusing on their clients' criminogenic needs during the first meeting (96% vs. 18%), reinforce pro-social behaviors (80% vs. 40%), and use more encouraging words or praises (92% vs. 33%) than the untrained officers.

Clients with Mental Health and Substance Use Disorders

High rates of individuals on probation were identified as having a mental illness or SUD. A survey of 179 POs across the US revealed that about 24% of clients had a mental illness (Van Deinse et al., 2023). Rossheim et al. (2018) interviewed 313 adults on probation who reported recent substance use and found that about 38% also had a mental illness (e.g., schizophrenia, bipolar disorder). Givens and Cuddeback (2021) evaluated the types of mental illnesses among 207 probation clients and found more than half a diagnosis of post-traumatic stress disorder (PTSD), making it the most common mental illness reported. Probation clients with mental illnesses and SUDs need a variety of services in their community, as they reported more negative consequences resulting from their substance use (e.g., physical, interpersonal, and legal problems), which leads to additional risks and needs for POs to address. Services that POs commonly refer their clients include outpatient programs, substance use programs, psychiatric hospitals, behavioral health crisis services, employment services, shelters, and intimate partner violence (IPV) programs (Van Deinse et al., 2022). Access to community outreach services and programs is important for probation clients with mental illnesses, as they tend to have fewer social support systems (e.g., family and friends). Having a more positive and trusting relationship with one's PO is also essential for those with mental illnesses; not only improved service engagement, but those with fewer social support systems also tend to have poorer relationships with their POs (Longmate et al., 2021).

Identifying mental illnesses among probation clients, particularly those who have not yet been diagnosed, is essential to meeting their specific needs. Van Deinse et al. (2023) surveyed 179 POs to determine what strategies they used to identify and address mental illnesses among their probation clients. Most (67%) relied on clients self-reporting, and only 27% reported using any mental health screening tool. Agency tracking of mental illnesses among probation clients was also lacking, with only 40% reporting that their agency tracks and 28% having any electronic management system to identify those with a mental illness (Van Deinse et al., 2023). The lack of screening using formal assessments likely leads to underreporting or misidentifying mental illnesses. This can result in POs confusing any related behavioral problems, such as defiance or noncompliance, possibly increasing their risk of revocation.

Specialized Mental Health Probation

Probation clients with mental illness experience additional challenges and barriers to remaining compliant with their probation conditions. Clients who lack transportation may be unable to access treatment, which may lead to deterioration of their mental health, increasing their risk of rearrest for disorderly or violent behavior (Lurigio et al., 2012). To address their specific needs, community corrections professionals developed specialized probation programs (Lurigio et al., 2012; Veysey, 1996). The specialized POs typically receive substantial training on mental health, SUDs, and supportive supervision strategies (Prins & Osher, 2009; Skeem et al., 2006). Specialized POs, with their advanced training, can also work closely with the treatment providers and sometimes assist in treatment decisions instead of simply making referrals (Eno Louden et al., 2012). Specialized POs also tend to have caring and supportive relationships with probation clients instead of the supervision-focused authoritative style (Skeem et al., 2003, 2017). Specialized POs not only have homogenous caseloads composed solely of people with mental illnesses but also have smaller caseloads (typically less than 50) than traditional probation services, which are often more than 100 (Manchak et al., 2014; Skeem et al., 2006). Smaller caseloads allow POs to meet with their clients more often and for longer. Manchak et al. (2014) interviewed 176 clients with mental illnesses on traditional probation and 183 on specialty mental health probation. Those on specialty probation, on average, met more often (twice a month vs. once a month), and meetings were longer (26 minutes vs. 18 mins) than those on traditional probation. Those on specialty mental health probation also had their mental health needs met and were significantly more likely to receive treatment than those on traditional probation (Manchak et al., 2014).

Effectiveness of Specialized Mental Health Probation. Evidence to date shows that specialized mental health probation seems promising in producing better outcomes for clients. Jesse et al. (2008) reviewed the probation and arrest records of 241 clients on specialized probation three years after their probation was terminated and reported that 67% had no felony arrests and 50% had no misdemeanor arrests. Skeem et al. (2017) also compared rearrest rates among 183 clients on specialized probation to 176 on traditional probation, and those in the specialty probation program had fewer rearrests (29% vs. 52%) than those on traditional probation. Wolff et al. (2014) examined the effectiveness of a new specialized probation program with even smaller caseloads. They compared the outcomes of 1,367 clients in the new probation program (caseload of no more than 30), 495 clients in a previously established probation program (average caseloads of 50), and 5,453 clients in traditional probation (average caseloads of 130). After six months of supervision, rearrests decreased by 20% for the clients in the new probation program compared to those in the established program and on traditional probation, which remained relatively stable with only 2% and 4% decreases (Wolff et al., 2014).

Box 14.1 Practitioner Spotlight: Joshua Wolarik

Joshua Wolarik has worked as a probation officer in Ocean County, New Jersey, since 2018, first working with juveniles and then adults since December 2021. He manages a caseload of about 50 clients of various risk levels and needs. Over the last several years, probation has shifted from a "punishment-focused" approach to a needs-based approach focusing on success and recidivism prevention. Using formal risk assessment tools, Wolarik determines clients' risk levels and specific needs and then develops a success plan. Many of his clients have mental health needs, including bipolar disorder, anxiety, and substance use disorders. Many also have various disabilities, mostly with limitations in learning and literacy.

According to Wolarik, probation officers must have interpersonal skills to communicate and work effectively with clients "from all walks of life." His clients have different mental abilities and attitudes towards their probation or the criminal justice system in general. Therefore, developing a rapport with clients and building relationships based on trust is essential. He also recognizes that some officers may go into the profession with stereotypes. However, once you see the different reasons clients become involved in the justice system and meet their families, those stereotypes dissipate, and you see the client as an individual and not simply a "criminal." When meeting with clients with mental health disorders and disabilities, one must demonstrate empathy and understanding. If a client is in distress, one must be able to pivot, address how they are feeling, provide them with mental health resources, and shorten meetings to address only essential matters. Some clients may have memory difficulties or difficulty grasping information and may require more reminders or flexibility if they forget specific tasks. Strong interpersonal skills and the ability to adapt communication styles to individual clients are essential to being an effective probation officer.

Specialty Courts

In the late 1980s and early 1990s, CJS practitioners expressed dissatisfaction with the effectiveness of the "get tough on crime" methods of handling those convicted of offenses, noting the "revolving door" of individuals with SUD cycling through the CJS. Specialty courts were developed to address the specific needs of justice-involved adults and juveniles, to reduce the dependence on jails and prisons, and the financial burden on the CJS. Specialty court programs are collaborative efforts between the CJS or JJS and various mental health and social services to provide individualized plans addressing one's unique needs and allow individuals to avoid jail or prison (Contrino et al., 2016). Due to their integrated approach, other terms to describe specialty courts include "problem-solving courts" and "treatment courts." Upon successfully completing the program, graduates may be rewarded by having their charges dismissed (DeVall et al., 2022a).

The practices and ideology of specialty courts are rooted in the concept of **sociological jurisprudence.** Sociological jurisprudence was described by legal scholar and criminal justice reformer Roscoe Pound (1870–1964) in a 1911 Harvard Law Review article where he argued that laws should adjust to social change to benefit the best interests of society. Drawing from this concept, psychology professor Dr. David Wexler published *Therapeutic Jurisprudence: The Law as a Therapeutic Agent* in (1990). This concept established the theory of therapeutic jurisprudence, which involves an interdisciplinary approach to the law and mental health (Wexler & Winick, 1991). Therapeutic jurisprudence supports a problem-solving approach for justice-involved individuals that is proactive, results-oriented, and responsive to one's emotional and social problems (Lurigio & Snowden, 2009). With the increase of evidence-based practices, specialty courts were well-researched, improved, and rapidly spread throughout the US. According to the most recent report on specialty courts, as of December 31, 2019, there were 3856 specialty court programs in the US, with 91% serving adults and 9% serving juveniles (DeVall et al., 2022a).

Adult Drug Courts

Greater efforts to divert justice-involved individuals with SUDs from the CJS began with the development of drug courts (DCs). The first DC opened in Miami, Florida, in 1989 in response to their widespread substance use problem. These specialized programs offered a new way to combat rising crime and the cycle of substance use—crime—incarceration. DC programs are collaborative efforts with a multidisciplinary team consisting of the presiding judge, prosecutor, defense attorney, treatment professional, PO, and case manager. In 1997, the non-profit organization National Association of Drug Court Professionals (NADCP),[2] since renamed All Rise, developed *Ten Key Components of Drug Courts*, defining the roles and responsibilities. Services typically involve intensive treatment, random substance/alcohol testing, community supervision, case management services, and regularly scheduled court appearances before the judge. Case managers connect participants to support services based on their needs, for example, employment, educational, and peer recovery support (e.g., Alcoholics Anonymous®) (DeVall et al., 2022a).

Each participant is considered for admittance into the program on a case-by-case basis, as program requirements may vary from one jurisdiction to another. Participants may be admitted into DC as a pre-trial or pre-plea diversion program (i.e., before a trial or entering a guilty plea). They may also enter the program after pleading guilty to their charges (post-plea diversion) or as a condition of a sentence (post-sentence/adjudication) (DeVall et al., 2022a). Considering this wide variation among DCs, Longshore et al. (2001) provided a conceptual framework of five items for best practices for DCs, which include (1) Leverage (rewards and sanctions), (2) Population Severity (evaluating severity for eligibility), (3) Program Intensity (based on need and risk) (4) Program Predictability (rewards and sanctions applied consistently) and (5) Rehabilitation (emphasize rehabilitation as opposed to punishment). Contrino et al. (2016) surveyed 600 graduates of a DC program, who reported that although incentives such as avoiding jail and having their charges reduced were important reasons for entering the program, the top reported reasons they remained in the program were the positive improvements it made on various social factors and the quality of the treatment the program offered.

Effectiveness of Adult Drug Courts

The success of DCs depends on several factors, including the extent of the participant's criminal and substance use history (Longshore et al., 2001), but research measuring the overall effectiveness of adult DCs in reducing substance use and crime recidivism has been positive. A review of 55 studies by Wilson et al. (2006) concluded that those participating in a DC were less likely to reoffend than those sentenced to traditional probation. An analysis of 92 adult DCs revealed that crime recidivism was about 38% and drug-related recidivism was 37%, both below a control average of 50% but were generally more effective in reducing recidivism for those with less severe SUD (Mitchell et al., 2012). Latimer et al.'s (2006) analysis of 66 adult DCs revealed that 57% of those who participated in drug treatment courts were not charged with a new criminal offense during the follow-up period, compared to 43% of those involved in other justice system responses, showing a 14% reduction in recidivism. Successfully completing the DC also has a positive effect on reducing recidivism. Gibbs and Lytle (2020) compared crime recidivism among 733 DC participants and revealed that those who did not complete the program had more than a 50% increased likelihood of reoffending than those who successfully completed it.

Juvenile Drug Courts

DCs for juveniles were developed in 1995 in Wilmington, Delaware, and Visalia, California (DeVall et al., 2022a) and modeled after adult DCs. To qualify, juveniles within the required age range must be referred by a juvenile court judge and be at risk for crime recidivism (DeVall et al., 2022b). Adolescents have varying levels of psychosocial maturity development that affect decision-making, judgment, and susceptibility to peer influences (*see* Chapter 3 of this book for details). Thus, juvenile DCs address these needs by recognizing these cognitive differences and following the same reform practices in the JJS (Office of Juvenile Justice and Delinquency Prevention, 2016). In 2003, the DOJ published a report prepared by the National Drug Court Institute and the National Council of Juvenile and Family Court Judges detailing 16 strategies to serve as a framework for planning, implementing, and operating juvenile DCs. The strategies aim to provide appropriate, individualized substance use treatment to juveniles, which include establishing eligibility criteria, appropriate treatment to their developmental needs (DOJ, 2003, p. 10), and an emphasis on family, as family involvement has been shown to improve outcomes (Dakof et al., 2015). The collaborative team also includes the educational systems via a school liaison who reports on their school progress (DeVall et al., 2022b).

Effectiveness of Juvenile Drug Courts

Like adult DCs, the effectiveness of juvenile DCs is nuanced and dependent on several factors. Chernoff et al. (2022) compared 737 juvenile DC participants to 461 juveniles in traditional juvenile courts and found that those receiving DC services were less likely to recidivate. However, juveniles who did not have a history of substance use but still received DC services had higher recidivism rates than those who received traditional court services. Their results highlight the importance of not "over-treating," as this can increase risk, which is consistent with RNR principles. Konecky et al. (2016) found that juveniles with a prior criminal history were less likely to be successful in the program than those without, but a history of substance use was a major factor. Although some effectiveness results have been mixed, Mitchell et al.'s (2012) analyses of 34 juvenile DCs revealed that some are mildly effective at reducing general recidivism but seem to have no statistically significant effect on drug offense recidivism or substance use.

Juveniles' ability to succeed in DC programs may depend upon addressing their needs, recognizing that juveniles are developmentally different from adults and their reasons for substance use vary. For example, juveniles may use substances because they have an undiagnosed mental illness or to address mental health symptoms resulting from physical or sexual abuse (Fletcher, 2021; Konecky et al., 2016). Taylor (2016) evaluated whether general responsivity techniques (as opposed to specific responsivity) of the RNR model were effective in decreasing substance use among juveniles in a DC program. In contrast to predictions, the general responsivity approach in treatment interventions actually increased substance use among juveniles. This suggests that the general responsivity approach may not work well with juveniles, and they may require specific approaches tailored to their needs.

Mental Health Courts

Many justice-involved individuals referred to DCs had co-occurring mental illnesses. A 1997 report showed that 60% of the DC programs surveyed had participants who reported experiencing depression, bipolar disorder, anxiety disorders, or psychosis (Cooper, 1997). Devall et al. (2022a) noted that individuals with co-occurring mental illness had difficulty engaging in the DC process, including the inability to understand and follow rules, and, unfortunately, had fewer completion rates. As a result, several jurisdictions developed separate mental health tracks within their DCs, eventually leading to separate mental health courts (MHCs).

The first MHC was established in Ft. Lauderdale, Florida in 1997 (Goldkamp & Irons-Guynn, 2000). Modeled after DCs, MHCs also involve a multidisciplinary team of CJS professionals and clinicians that connect participants with community-based mental health treatment and other needed supports (DeVall et al., 2022d). MHCs have multiple goals in addressing one's mental health recovery and crime recidivism. They are similar to specialized mental health probation, except that MHCs have a specialized jurisdiction and are overseen by a judge with mental health training. POs in MHC programs also tend to have a more therapeutic relationship with their clients (Epperson et al., 2017). Similar to DCs, adults may enter an MHC program as a pre-trial or pre-plea diversion program, post-plea diversion, or post-sentence/adjudication for misdemeanor or felony offenses. The mental illness aspect for eligibility varies; some have broad criteria (any mental illness), some require documentation or formal assessment and diagnosis, while others allow participants to self-report their mental illnesses (DeVall et al., 2022d). MHCs have since expanded to 39 states and the District of Columbia. As of December 31, 2019, there were 490 adult MHCs in the US (DeVall et al., 2022d).

The first juvenile MHC was developed in San Jose, California in 2001. Juvenile MHCs address the needs of juveniles with mental illnesses but also those with developmental disabilities, including autism and intellectual disability (ID) (Gardner, 2011). Juvenile MHCs provide early intervention to address mental health and substance use to prevent them from continuing to engage in crime as they age into adulthood. In collaboration with the justice system, mental health agencies, families, and other community partners, they provide treatment services, individual and family counseling, and substance use treatment if necessary. MHC eligibility varies considerably for juveniles, including age, offense severity (i.e., misdemeanor or felony offenses), or certain mental illnesses or disabilities. As of December 31, 2019, there were 46 juvenile MHCs in the US (DeVall et al., 2022c).

Effectiveness of Mental Health Courts

The overall effectiveness of MHCs in reducing recidivism appears promising, particularly when the RNR model is adhered to (Campbell et al., 2015). A review of 20 studies of adult MHCs by Loong et al. (2019) revealed that those who complete MHC programs were less likely to be rearrested. An analysis of 34 adult and four juvenile studies of MHCs by Fox et al. (2021) indicated that MHC participation reduced the odds of recidivism by 74%, and the effect was similar for adults and juveniles. Like DCs, completing the program has a greater effect on recidivism than simply participating. Ray (2014) followed 449 MHC participants between five and ten years and found that those who completed the program were significantly less likely to be rearrested than those who did not (40% vs. 75%). Ray also reported that those who completed the MHC program remained crime-free for longer than those who did not, averaging 17 months before a rearrest versus 12 months. Studies that compared the effectiveness of MHC programs to traditional supervision services in reducing recidivism have consistently found them to be more effective. Lowder et al. (2016) compared 57 MHC participants to 40 individuals who received traditional probation supervision and found that only those who completed the MHC program had significant reductions in arrests and convictions. After one year, those receiving traditional community supervision incurred nearly twice the number of charges and more than 2.5 times more convictions than those who completed the MHC program. Hiday et al. (2013) compared 408 MHC participants to 687 who received traditional probation supervision and found that those who participated in the MHC had a significantly lower average number of arrests (0.21 vs. 0.60). Below is a case that describes the therapeutic effects of a MHC program.

Case of Eric[3]

Background: Eric was 23 years old when he was arrested for burglary in the second degree and endangering the welfare of a child. He was the youngest of five children raised in a working-class family with both parents. His family was devoutly religious, and he was raised strictly in the church's tradition. According to Eric, when he was young, his family dismissed him when he mentioned career aspirations (i.e., what he wants to be when he grows up) and told him, "God will lead you to your path." He exhibited no behavioral problems in childhood and earned high grades in school. When he was about 16 years old, he began rebelling by using alcohol and marijuana and engaging in petty crimes, such as theft. He graduated high school and had several jobs working in the food service industry but continued to use alcohol and marijuana and commit minor thefts. His formal criminal record includes three misdemeanor larceny offenses, all of which he committed with others.

Mental Health History: At around 18 years of age, he experienced symptoms of major depressive disorder and was formally diagnosed after he attempted suicide by overdosing on Tylenol® (acetaminophen). After a brief hospitalization, he was discharged and prescribed anti-depressant medications. At age 22, he began using crack cocaine and stopped taking his medication, and his depressive symptoms returned. He attempted suicide a second time by overdosing on his anti-depressant medications. After a two-week hospitalization, he was discharged and prescribed anti-depressant medications.

Instant Offense: Eric was under the influence of alcohol and crack cocaine when, at approximately 7 PM, he and a friend, also 23 years of age, barged through the front door of the home of a 26 year old single mother and demanded money. The woman was sitting on the couch with her two-year-old son on her lap. She grabbed her son and got up to run, but Eric's friend pulled her son from her arms and demanded money again. She gave him about $50 cash and said that was all she had, and Eric and his friend fled. The woman called the police and provided a physical description. Minutes later, police found Eric and his friend walking down the street. The women later positively identified the two men, and they were arrested.

Evaluation: Eric was detained in the country jail after his arrest, pending his initial hearing. Because of the seriousness of the charges, Eric was facing a prison sentence. However, because this was his first felony, he was under the influence of alcohol and crack cocaine, and his mental health history, his defense attorney requested an evaluation to determine if he was a candidate for the MHC program. The mental health evaluator confirmed his diagnosis of major depressive disorder, and he was also diagnosed with alcohol use disorder and polysubstance use disorder. His cognitive evaluation demonstrated an IQ of 110, demonstrating above-average cognition. His evaluator noted he presented with a passive and dependent personality, with a vague self-concept of who he is and what he wants in life.

Outcome: Eric was accepted into the MHC program, and the judge court-ordered him to attend mental health counseling sessions and a substance use treatment program, meet with his supervision officer, refrain from alcohol and illegal substances, comply with his medication, and agree to random testing. Through his counseling session, he developed greater insight into his mental health and the extent and role of his alcohol and substance use. Eric began drawing connections from his strict religious upbringing and being coddled as the youngest of five children. His upbringing resulted in him being overly dependent on others and lacking assertiveness and independence, negatively impacting his self-esteem. His frustration with the lack of control he felt led him to rebel and eventually associate with crime-involved peers. Eric learned that his alcohol and substance use and criminal activities were indicative of his passivity, a lack of independent judgment, and giving into peer pressure rather than malicious intent. He later enrolled in a program to improve his self-image, which also addresses healthy lifestyles. He expressed interest in enrolling in a vocational culinary program and continuing a career in the restaurant industry. He successfully graduated from the MHC program with no rearrests or substance or alcohol use.

Considerations and Recommendations

The shift toward community sanctions in place of incarceration has shown to be an effective alternative to incarceration for many justice-involved individuals. There are several ways in which CJS practitioners can support those with mental illnesses, disabilities, and SUDs under community correction programs. Below are several areas to consider and practical recommendations to improve services to support justice-involved individuals in the community to reduce further or repeat involvement in the CJS.

Provide Adequate Training in the RNR Model

Whether working with MHCs, traditional probation, or specialized MHP, POs should receive adequate training in the RNR model and training in the specific risk assessment instruments used. The needs of each client must be individualized and based on valid needs and risk assessments and their response to treatment (James, 2015). Training is typically determined by jurisdiction, and instruments used to assess risk may vary. Once risk has been established, conditions, supervision level, and services should reflect one's individual needs and avoid "over" or "under" servicing. While overservicing low-risk individuals may appear to err on the side of caution, Bonta and Andrews (2007) warn that this leads to destabilization, which can increase recidivism risk.

Establish Effective Relationships with Clients

The relationship between PO and their clients has been identified as essential in achieving successful probation outcomes, where an over-authoritative role is ineffective and hinders the relationship (Epperson et al., 2020; Longmate et al., 2021). Whether a PO handles cases in traditional probation, specialized MHP, or specialty courts, evidence-based approaches include establishing "firm but fair" client relationships (Fabelo et al., 2011). Research has demonstrated that authoritative yet caring relationships with a problem-solving focus have clients with lower recidivism (Bonta et al., 2011; Epperson et al., 2020; Longmate et al., 2021). Fabelo et al. (2011) noted that some POs may have to undergo training to "unlearn" outdated practices, such as over-focusing on identifying and sanctioning violations, particularly those in probation departments who provided POs incentives to do so. POs rely on effective communication with their clients to determine their current and ongoing needs. Thus, a PO that is perceived as caring and trustworthy will allow clients to communicate their needs, particularly among those with mental illnesses or SUDs, as there often a barrier of stigma and shame.

Designating Specialized Officers

Some POs will have the background and disposition to work with various populations more effectively than others, and those with mental illnesses, SUDs, and disabilities such as autism or ID are no different. All POs should complete the minimum training requirements outlined in best practices. Clients with mental illnesses may have unmet needs, supporting that POs should have education or training in mental health. Van Deinse et al. (2023) revealed that only 36% of the POs had any standardized training in mental health, and Longmate et al. (2021) revealed that only half of clients with mental illnesses were receiving mental health services. Little is known about the specified needs of probation clients with autism and other developmental disabilities; however, different communication skills and strategies are necessary for those with social and communication deficits or limited cognitive skills (*see* Chapters 8, 9, and 11 of this book for details). Treatment needs are also different for some populations. For example, referrals to treatment in group formats are common due to their cost-effectiveness. However, such referrals should be applied judiciously with juveniles and those with NDDs as some may be more vulnerable to anti-social peers, and others may find group therapy sessions stressful and may require individual sessions (Dishion et al., 1999; Mogavero et al., 2025).

Adhere to Best Practice Guidelines

Government and non-profit agencies have published recommendations compiled by diverse experts who, over many years, reviewed scientific evidence-based research on best practices in specialty courts and other community correction programs. These best practice guidelines provide measurable and achievable recommendations for probation and specialty courts.

Drug Courts

(1) What Works? The Ten Key Components of Drug Court: Research-Based Best Practices, by Carey et al. (2012) of the National Center of Substance Abuse and Child Welfare
(2) Best Practice Standards for Adult Treatment Courts, Allrise.org (formally the National Association of Drug Court Professionals) Professionals (Allrise, 2024).
(3) Juvenile Drug Treatment Court Guidelines (Office of Juvenile Justice and Delinquency Prevention, OJJDP, 2016).

Mental Health Courts

(1) State Standards: Building Better Mental Health Courts by the National Center for State Courts and the Council of State Governments (CSG, 2016). They also published and offered a free online multimedia curriculum with a companion Handbook for Facilitators.
(2) Ten Essential Elements for Mental Health Courts, by Thompson et al. (2007) of the Council of State Governments

Probation

(1) A Ten-Step Guide to Transforming Probation Departments to Reduce Recidivism, by Fabelo et al. (2011) of the Council of State Governments Justice Center.

Conclusion

Although some believe that the use of community supervision is "soft on crime" and that people who commit crimes deserve imprisonment, imprisonment is not necessary for individuals to experience the consequences of crime and prevent reoffending. The use of probation, specialized probation, and specialty courts are alternative approaches to address the influx of people with mental illnesses and SUDs into the CJS as a result of the wide net cast by the "tough on crime" efforts. These alternative approaches require a shift in mindset from one that believes those who commit crimes "deserve" incarceration and that incarceration is necessary for public safety to the evidence-based "what works" mindset. These programs also promote a humane approach toward those involved in crime, which supports providing appropriate treatment for those with mental illnesses and SUDs so they are not cycling in and out of jail or prison.

Evidence has shown that, for some individuals, alternative sanctions are effective at reducing crime and promoting public safety. In the case of Eric, the MHC program allowed him to not only seek substance use treatment, but the mental health treatment allowed him to self-reflect and gain insight into his substance use and offense patterns and improve his self-esteem. Alternatives to incarcerations and specialty programs that address mental health and substance use also require support and participation by stakeholders at the local and state levels, as funding must be allocated to support not only the programs but also to ensure the availability of community services for mental illnesses and SUDs, particularly in rural areas (Van Deinse et al., 2023). One must not overlook these options, particularly when there is a need to alleviate jail and prison overcrowding. For traditional probation, specialized probation, and specialty courts to thrive and be effective, POs also require additional education and training to develop the knowledge and skills to provide adequate care and supervision to clients with mental health and other conditions requiring varying needs. This is particularly important for POs assigned to handle specialized caseloads, as specialized MHP services appear to be the most promising.

Key Terms

Drug court
Mental health court
Parole
Probation
Recidivism

Revocation
Risk-Need and Responsivity Model
Risk assessment
Responsivity
Sociological jurisprudence
Split sentence
Suspended sentence

Chapter Questions

(1) Define and discuss probation as a standalone sentence and an alternative to incarceration.
(2) Describe the key features of specialty mental health probation programs and how they differ from traditional probation.
(3) Define and discuss the Risk-Need and Responsivity Model. Why is this model important for services such as probation to be effective?
(4) Is SUD a public health crisis, criminal justice challenge, or both? How could our understanding of the problem influence the response to it?
(5) What are the advantages of specialty courts for those with mental illnesses and SUDs over handling such cases in the traditional criminal justice court system?
(6) Should all probation and community corrections administrators be legally required to screen all clients for mental illnesses or SUDs? Explain your position.

Suggested Readings

Epperson, M. W., Canada, K. E., Thompson, J. G., & Lurigio, A. (2014). Walking the line: Specialized and standard probation officer perspectives on supervising probationers with serious mental illnesses. *International Journal of Law & Psychiatry, 37*, 473–483. https://doi.org/10.1016/j.ijlp.2014.02.020

Festinger, D. S., Dugosh, K. L., & Marlowe, D. (2015). Improving outcomes for low-risk/low-need drug court clients: Life in the fast lane. *Drug & Alcohol Dependence, 146,* e276. https://doi.org/10.1016/j.drugalcdep.2014.09.217

Johnson, J. (2018). Mental Health Courts. In E. Kelley (Ed.), *Representing people with mental disabilities: A criminal defense lawyer's best practices manual* (pp. 171–193). ABA Publishing.

Trotter, C. (2013). Reducing recidivism through probation supervision: What we know and don't know from four decades of research. *Federal Probation, 77*(2), 43–48.

Notes

1. Includes those under the age of 18 sentenced as adults.
2. All Rise, see https://allrise.org/.
3. Name and some details have been changed for anonymity.

References

Allrise. (2024). *Adult treatment court best practice standards* (2nd ed.). https://allrise.org/publications/standards/

Andrews, D. A., & Bonta, J. (1995). *LSI-R: The Level of Service Inventory manual*. Multi-Health Systems.

Andrews, D. A., & Bonta, J. (1998). *Level of service inventory-revised: Screening version*. Multi-Health systems.

Andrews, D. A., & Bonta, J. (2010). Rehabilitating criminal justice policy and practice. *Psychology, Public Policy, and Law, 16*(1), 39–55. https://doi.org/10.1037/a0018362

Austin, J., Coleman, D., Peyton, J., & Johnson, K. (2003). *Reliability and validity study of the LSI-R risk assessment instrument* (Final Report: Submitted to The Pennsylvania Board of Probation and Parole, 1–25).

Beck, P., & McGinnis, E. (2022). An exploration of the relationship between probation supervision and desistance: A systematic narrative review. *Irish Probation Journal, 19*, 97–118.

Bonta, J., & Andrews, D. A. (2007). *Risk-need-responsivity model for offender assessment and rehabilitation*. Public Safety Canada. https://www.publicsafety.gc.ca/cnt/rsrcs/pblctns/rsk-nd-rspnsvty/rsk-nd-rspnsvty-eng.pdf

Bonta, J., Bourgon, G., Rugge, T., Scott, T. -L., Yessine, A. K., Gutierrez, L., & Li, J. (2011). An experimental demonstration of training probation officers in evidence-based community supervision. *Criminal Justice and Behavior, 38*(11), 1127–1148. https://doi.org/10.1177/0093854811420678

Campbell, M. A., Canales, D. D., Wei, R., Totten, A. E., Macaulay, W. A., & Wershler, J. L. (2015). Multidimensional evaluation of a mental health court: Adherence to the risk-need-responsivity model. *Law and Human Behavior, 39*(5), 489–502. https://doi.org/10.1037/lhb0000135

Carey, S. M., Mackin, J. R., & Finigan, M. W. (2012). What works? The ten key components of drug court: Research-based best practices. *Drug Court Review, 8*(1), 6–42. http://npcresearch.com/publication/what-works-the-ten-key-components-of-drug-court-research-based-best-practices-3/

Chernoff, W. A., Olson, L. M., Rodriguez, T., O'Krepki, M., & Bisciglia, M. G. (2022). Resolving the paradox of juvenile drug courts: How matching substance abuse needs with juvenile court services reduces recidivism. *Juvenile and Family Court Journal, 73*(3), 5–19. https://doi.org/10.1111/jfcj.12223

Cochran, J. C., Mears, D. P., & Bales, W. D. (2014). Assessing the effectiveness of correctional sanctions. *Journal of Quantitative Criminology, 30*(2), 317–347. https://doi.org/10.1007/s10940-013-9205-2

Cooper, C. S. (1997). *1997 Drug court survey report*. U.S. Department of justice, office of justice programs, Bureau of Justice Statistics.

Council of State Governments Justice Center Staff. (2016). *State standards: Building better mental health courts.* https://csgjusticecenter.org/2016/04/28/state-standards-building-better-mental-health-courts/

Contrino, K. M., Nochajski, T., Farrell, M. G., & Logsdon, E. (2016). Factors of success: Drug court graduate exit interviews. *American Journal of Criminal Justice, 41*, 136–150. https://doi.org/10.1007/s12103-015-9333-3

Crime and Justice Institute at Community Resources for Justice (2009). *Implementing Evidence-Based Policy and Practice in Community Corrections*, 2nd ed. Washington, DC: National Institute of Corrections.

Dakof, G. A., Henderson, C. E., Rowe, C. L., Boustani, M., Greenbaum, P. E., Wang, W., Hawes, S., Linares, C., & Liddle, H. A. (2015). A randomized clinical trial of family therapy in juvenile drug court. *Journal of Family Psychology, 29*(2), 232–241. https://doi.org/10.1037/fam0000053

DeVall, K., Lanier, C., & Baker, L. (2022a). Painting the current picture: A national report on treatment courts in the United States. Adult drug courts brief. National drug court resource center.

DeVall, K., Lanier, C., & Baker, L. (2022b). Painting the current picture: A national report on treatment courts in the United States. Juvenile drug treatment courts brief. National drug court resource center.

DeVall, K., Lanier, C., & Baker, L. (2022c). Painting the current picture: A national report on treatment courts in the United States. Juvenile mental health courts brief. National drug court resource center.

DeVall, K., Lanier, C., & Baker, L. (2022d). Painting the Current picture: A national report on treatment courts in the United States. Mental health courts brief. National drug court resource center.

Dishion, T. J., McCord, J., & Poulin, F. (1999). When interventions harm: Peer groups and problem behavior. *American Psychologist, 54*(9), 755–764. https://doi.org/10.1037/0003-066X.54.9.755

Eno Louden, J., Skeem, J. L., Camp, J., Vidal, S., & Peterson, J. (2012). Supervision practices in specialty mental health probation: What happens in officer-probationer meetings? *Law and Human Behavior, 36*(2), 109–119. https://doi.org/10.1037/h0093961

Epperson, M. W., Sawh, L., & Sarantakos, S. P. (2020). Building a therapeutic relationship between probation officers and probationers with serious mental illnesses. *CNS Spectrums, 25*(5), 723–733. https://doi.org/10.1017/S1092852919001871

Epperson, M. W., Thompson, J. G., Lurigio, A. J., & Kim, S. (2017). Unpacking the relationship between probationers with serious mental illnesses and probation officers: A mixed-methods examination. *Journal of Offender Rehabilitation, 56*(3), 188–216. https://doi.org/10.1080/10509674.2017.1290005

Fabelo, T., Nagy, G., & Prins, S. (2011). *A ten-step guide to transforming probation departments to reduce recidivism.* Council of State Governments Justice Center. https://www.ojp.gov/ncjrs/virtual-library/abstracts/ten-step-guide-transforming-probation-departments-reduce-recidivism

Ferguson, A. M., Ogloff, J. R. P., & Thomson, L. (2009). Predicting recidivism by mentally disordered offenders using the LSI-R:SV. *Criminal Justice and Behavior, 36*(1), 5–20. https://doi.org/10.1177/0093854808326525

Fletcher, K. (2021). A systematic review of the relationship between child sexual abuse and substance use issues. *Journal of Child Sexual Abuse, 30*(3), 258–277. https://doi.org/10.1080/10538712.2020.1801937

Fox, B., Miley, L. N., Kortright, K. E., & Westman, R. J. (2021). Assessing the effect of mental health courts on adult and juvenile recidivism: A meta-analysis. *American Journal of Criminal Justice, 46*(4), 644–664. https://doi.org/10.1007/s12103-021-09629-6

Gardner, P. (2011). *An overview of juvenile mental health courts.* ABA. https://www.americanbar.org/groups/public_interest/child_law/resources/child_law_practiceonline/child_law_practice/vol30/september_2011/an_overview_of_juvenilementalhealthcourts/

Gibbs, B. R., & Lytle, R. (2020). Drug court participation and time to failure: An Examination of recidivism across program outcome. *American Journal of Criminal Justice, 45*(2), 215–235. https://doi.org/10.1007/s12103-019-09498-0

Givens, A., & Cuddeback, G. S. (2021). Traumatic experiences among individuals with severe mental illnesses on probation. *Criminal Behaviour and Mental Health, 31*(5), 310–320. https://doi.org/10.1002/cbm.2212

Goldkamp, J. D., & Irons-Guynn, C. (2000). Emerging judicial strategies for the mentally ill in the criminal caseload: Mental health courts in Fort Lauderdale, Seattle, San Bernardino, and Anchorage (pub no NCJ 182504). U.S. Department of justice, office of justice programs, Bureau of Justice Assistance.

Hiday, V. A., Wales, H. W., & Ray, B. (2013). Effectiveness of a short-term mental health court: Criminal recidivism one year postexit. *Law and Human Behavior, 37*(6), 401–411. https://doi.org/10.1037/lhb0000030

Ho, A., Lesneskie, E., & Hsu, K. -H. (2018). What we don't know may hurt us: An examination of systematic bias in offender risk assessments. *Deviant Behavior, 39*(12), 1566–1577. https://doi.org/10.1080/01639625.2017.1410620

Hockenberry, S. (2021). *Delinquency cases waived to criminal court, 2018.* U.S. Department of justice, office of justice programs, Bureau of Justice Statistics.

Hockenberry, S. & Puzzanchera C. (2023). *Juvenile Court Statistics 2020.* Pittsburgh, PA: National Center for Juvenile Justice.

James, N. (2015). *Risk and needs assessment in the criminal justice system.* Congressional Research Service. https://crsreports.congress.gov.product.R44087.10.pdf

Jesse, K., Bishop, D., Thomas, J., & Dudish-Poulsen, J. (2008). Adult probation department mental health unit: An outcomes investigation. *Professional Issues in Criminal Justice, 3*, 1–17.

Kaeble, D. (2021). *Probation and parole in the United States, 2020*. U.S. Department of justice office of justice programs, Bureau of Justice Statistics. https://bjs.ojp.gov/library/publications/probation-and-parole-united-states-2020

Konecky, B., Cellucci, T., & Mochrie, K. (2016). Predictors of program failure in a juvenile drug court program. *Addictive Behaviors, 59*, 80–83. https://doi.org/10.1016/j.addbeh.2016.03.025

Latessa, E. J., Lemke, R., Makarios, M., Smith, P., & Lowenkamp, C. T. (2010). The creation and validation of the Ohio risk assessment system. *Federal Probation, 74*(1), 16–22.

Latimer, J., Morton-Bourgon, K., & Chrétien, J. (2006). *A meta-analytic examination of drug treatment courts: Do they reduce recidivism?* Department of Justice Canada. http://herzog-evans.com/wp-content/uploads/2014/10/A-meta-analytic-examination-of-DTC-Latimer-et-al.pdf

Lindsay, W. R., Steele, L., Smith, A. H., Quinn, K., & Allan, R. (2006). A community forensic intellectual disability service: Twelve year follow up of referrals analysis of referral patterns and assessment of harm reduction. *Legal and Criminological Psychology, 11*(1), 113–130. https://doi.org/10.1348/135532505X55669

Longmate, C., Lowder, E., Givens, A., Van Deinse, T. B., Ghezzi, M., Burgin, S., & Cuddeback, G. S. (2021). Social support among people with mental illnesses on probation. *Psychiatric Rehabilitation Journal, 44*(1), 70–76. https://doi.org/10.1037/prj0000428

Longshore, D., Turner, S. W., Morral, A., Harrell, A., McBride, D., Deschenes, E., & Iguchi, M. (2001). Drug courts: A conceptual framework. *Journal of Drug Issues, 31*(1), 7–26. https://doi.org/10.1177/002204260103100103

Loong, D., Bonato, S., Barnsley, J., & Dewa, C. S. (2019). The effectiveness of mental health courts in reducing recidivism and police contact: A systematic review. *Community Mental Health Journal, 55*(7), 1073–1098. https://doi.org/10.1007/s10597-019-00421-9

Lowder, E. M., Desmarais, S. L., & Baucom, D. J. (2016). Recidivism following mental health court exit: Between and within-group comparisons. *Law and Human Behavior, 40*(2), 118–127. https://doi.org/10.1037/lhb0000168

Lowenkamp, C. T., Lovins, B., & Latessa, E. J. (2009). Validating the Level of Service Inventory-Revised and the Level of Service Inventory: Screening Version with a sample of probationers. *The Prison Journal, 89*(2), 192–204. https://doi.org/10.1177/0032885509334755

Lurigio, A. J., Epperson, M. W., Canada, K. E., & Babchuk, L. C. (2012). Specialized probation programs for people with mental illnesses: A review of practices and research. *Journal of Crime and Justice, 35*(2), 317–326. https://doi.org/10.1080/0735648x.2012.682845

Lurigio, A. J., & Snowden, J. (2009). Putting therapeutic jurisprudence into practice: The growth, operations, and effectiveness of mental health court. *The Justice System Journal, 30*(2), 196–218. http://www.jstor.org/stable/27977444

Manchak, S. M., Sullivan, C. C., Schweitzer, M., & Sullivan, C. J. (2014). The influence of co-occurring mental health and substance use problems on the effectiveness of juvenile drug courts. *Criminal Justice Policy Review, 27*(3), 247–264. https://doi.org/10.1177%2F0887403414564464

Mitchell, O., Wilson, D. B., Eggers, A., & MacKenzie, D. L. (2012). Assessing the effectiveness of drug courts on recidivism: A meta-analytic review of traditional and non-traditional drug courts. *Journal of Criminal Justice, 40*(1), 60–71. https://doi.org/10.1016/j.jcrimjus.2011.11.009

Mogavero, M. C., Fenrich, A., Patel, R., & Etzi, S. (2025). Neurodevelopmental disorders and sexual offending. In R. Tully, G. Bohall, & D. S. Prescott (Eds.), *Best practices in sexual offender assessment and management* (pp. 541–84). Springer Publishers.

National Association of Drug Court Professionals. (1997). *Defining drug courts: The key components.* U.S. Department of Justice, Office of Justice Programs, Drug Court Programs Office.

Office of Juvenile Justice and Delinquency Prevention. (2016). *Juvenile drug treatment court guidelines.* U.S. Department of Justice, Office of Justice Programs. https://ojjdp.ojp.gov/programs/juvenile-drug-treatment-court-guidelines

Oregon Juvenile Department Directors Association. (2006). *JCP assessment 2006.* https://www.ojdda.org/default.asp?pg=risk

Prins, S. J., & Osher, F. C. (2009). *Improving responses to people with mental illnesses: The essential elements of specialized probation initiatives.* Council of State Governments Justice Center. https://csgjusticecenter.org/publications/improving-responses-to-people-with-mental-illnesses-the-essential-elements-of-specialized-probation-initiatives/

Puzzanchera, C. (2018). *Juveniles on formal probation, 2012.* Office of juvenile justice and delinquency prevention. National Center for Juvenile Justice. https://www.ojp.gov/ncjrs/virtual-library/abstracts/juveniles-formal-probation-2012

Puzzanchera, C., Hockenberry, S., & Sickmund, M. (2022). *Youth and the juvenile justice system: 2022 National report.* National Center for Juvenile Justice.

Ray, B. (2014). Long-term recidivism of mental health court defendants. *International Journal of Law and Psychiatry, 37*(5), 448–454. https://doi.org/10.1016/j.ijlp.2014.02.017

Reamer, F. G. (2004). Social work and criminal justice: The uneasy alliance. In E. H. Judah & M. Byrant (Eds.), *Criminal justice: Retribution vs. restoration* (pp. 213–231). Haworth Press.

Rossheim, M. E., Livingston, M. D., Lerch, J. A., Taxman, F. S., & Walters, S. T. (2018). Serious mental illness and negative substance use consequences among adults on probation. *Health & Justice, 6*(1), 6. https://doi.org/10.1186/s40352-018-0064-7

Skeem, J. L., Encandela, J., & Eno Louden, J. (2003). Perspectives on probation and mandated mental health treatment in specialized and traditional probation departments. *Behavioral Sciences and the Law, 21*(4), 429–458. https://doi.org/10.1002/bsl.547

Skeem, J. L., Emke-Francis, P., & Eno Louden, J. (2006). Probation, mental health, and mandated treatment: A national survey. *Criminal Justice and Behavior, 33*(2), 158–184. https://doi.org/10.1177/0093854805284420

Skeem, J. L., Manchak, S., & Montoya, L. (2017). Comparing public safety outcomes for traditional probation vs specialty mental health probation. *JAMA Psychiatry, 74*(9), 942–948. https://doi.org/10.1001/jamapsychiatry.2017.1384

Smith, P., Schweitzer, M., Labrecque, R. M., & Latessa, E. J. (2012). Improving probation officers' supervision skills: An evaluation of the EPICS model. *Journal of Crime & Justice, 35*(2), 89–199. https://doi.org/10.1080/0735648X.2012.674826

Taxman, F. (2008). No illusions: Offender and organizational change in Maryland's proactive community supervision efforts. *Criminology & Public Policy, 7*(2), 275–302. https://doi.org/10.1111/j.1745-9133.2008.00508.x

Taylor, L. R. (2016). General responsivity adherence in juvenile drug treatment court: Examining the impact on substance-use outcome. *Journal of Drug Issues, 46*(1), 24–40. https://doi.org/10.1177/0022042615610618

Thompson, M., Osher, F., & Tomasini-Joshi, D. (2007). *Improving responses to people with mental illnesses: The essential elements of a mental health court.* https://www.bja.gov/publications/mhc_essential_elements.pdf

Torbet, P.M. (1996). *Juvenile probation: The workhorse of the juvenile justice system.* U.S. Department of Justice Office of Justice Programs. https://ojjdp.ojp.gov/library/publications/juvenile-probation-workhorse-juvenile-justice-system

United States Department of Justice. (2003). *Juvenile drug courts: Strategies in practice.* Office of Justice Programs, Bureau of Justice Assistance. https://www.ojp.gov/ncjrs/virtual-library/abstracts/juvenile-drug-courts-strategies-practice

Van Deinse, T. B., Givens, A., Frey, J. J., Cowell, M., & Cuddeback, G. S. (2022). Size and attributes of probation officers' service provider networks: Connecting individuals with mental illnesses to community-based supports. *Journal of Offender Rehabilitation, 61*(5), 245–262. https://doi-org.library.georgian.edu/10.1080/10509674.2022.2082623

Van Deinse, T. B., Mercier, M. C., Waters, A. K., Disbennett, M., Cuddeback, G. S., Velázquez, T., Lichtman, A. M., & Taxman, F. (2023). Strategies for supervising people with mental illnesses on probation caseloads: Results from a nationwide study. *Health & Justice, 11*(1), 41. https://doi.org/10.1186/s40352-023-00241-w

Veysey, B.M. (1994). *Challenges for the future. Topics in community corrections.* US Department of Justice, National Institute of Corrections, 1994 Annual Report, 3–10.

Veysey, B. M. (1996). Effective strategies to provide mental health services to probationers with mental illnesses. In A. J. Lurigio (Ed.), *Responding to the mental and substance abuse health care needs for persons on probation* (pp. 146–159). National coalition for mental and substance abuse health care in the justice system.

Wexler, D. B. (1990). *Therapeutic jurisprudence: The law as a therapeutic agent*. Carolina Academic Press.

Wexler, D. B., & Winick, B. J. (1991). *Essays in therapeutic jurisprudence*. Carolina Academic Press.

Whiteacre, K. (2006). Testing the Level of Service Inventory-Revised (LSI-R) for racial/ethnic bias. *Criminal Justice Policy Review, 17*(3), 330–342. https://doi.org/10.1177/0887403405284 76

Wilson, D. B., Mitchell, O., & MacKenzie, D. L. (2006). A systematic review of drug court effects on recidivism. *Journal of Experimental Criminology, 2*(4), 459–487. https://doi.org/10.1007/s11292-006-9019-4

Wilson, R. J., & Yates, P. M. (2009). Effective interventions and the good lives model: Maximizing treatment gains for sexual offenders. *Aggression and Violent Behavior, 14*(3), 157–161. https://doi.org/10.1016/j.avb.2009.01.007

Wolff, N., Epperson, M., Shi, J., Huening, J., Schumann, B. E., & Sullivan, I. R. (2014). Mental health specialized probation caseloads: Are they effective? *International Journal of Law & Psychiatry, 37*(5), 464–472. https://doi.org/10.1016/j.ijlp.2014.02.019

15

Involuntary Civil and Outpatient Commitment—Legal Criteria, Processes, and the Intersection of Mental Health and Criminal Justice Systems

Learning Objectives

After this chapter, readers should be able to understand the:

(1) Process and requirements for traditional civil commitment.
(2) Various case law supporting civil rights for those civilly committed.
(3) Difference between traditional civil commitment and forensic civil commitment.
(4) Process and requirements for outpatient civil commitment.
(5) Process and requirements for civil commitment of those convicted of sexual offenses.

Introduction

Involuntary civil commitment (CC) for those who engage in violent or other criminal behaviors is a substantial intersection and collaboration between the criminal justice system (CJS) and the mental health system (MHS). With CC, a judge may order an individual experiencing symptoms of mental illness and considered a danger to themselves or others to be confined to a psychiatric hospital or receive outpatient treatment (Lessard v. Schmidt, 1972; Substance Abuse and Mental Health Services Administration, SAMSA, 2019). Various case law determined the legal standards for CC: Lessard v

M. C. Mogavero, *Mental Health, Neurodiversity, and Criminal Justice*,
https://doi.org/10.1007/978-3-031-88816-8_15

Schmidt (1972) established the "serious danger" requirement, which typically means that the harm has the potential to result in severe injury or death, and Humphrey v. Cady (1972) required that the danger must be imminent. The definition of dangerousness also included the inability to provide for one's basic needs for survival (Lanterman-Petris-Short Act, 1967) (*see* Chapter 7 of this book for details). The legal justifications for CC include the powers of **parens patriae** (Latin for "parent of the state"), which grant the government legal authority to act as guardians for individuals with mental illnesses and make decisions about their welfare, and **police powers**, which grant the police to control those who threaten public order or the health and safety of others.

Forensic civil commitment occurs after one has committed a criminal offense and can take several forms. Individuals found incompetent to stand trial may be civilly committed (CC'd) for treatment to restore competence (*see* Chapter 11 of this book for details). Individuals who plead not guilty by reason of insanity and are acquitted may also be CC'd for treatment (*see* Chapter 12 of this book for details). A more controversial form of involuntary CC is when one is committed after they have completed their prison sentence but meet the state's criteria for CC based on the presence of a mental disorder and risk of danger to others. These statutes assess the "dangerousness" requirement based on the risk of committing a future offense. Similarly, outpatient civil commitment laws require individuals with mental illnesses who have committed criminal offenses or are at risk of committing acts of violence to participate in court-ordered treatment in the community or risk involuntary CC. These inpatient and outpatient commitment laws were based on the traditional civil commitment process.

Traditional Civil Commitment

All states and Washington D.C. have statutes allowing involuntary CC to a psychiatric facility for treatment, observation, and stabilization. Involuntary CC and treatment infringe on one's rights and freedoms; therefore, every state's statute must conform to the due process protection provided in the United States (US) Constitution. Throughout the 1970s, landmark Federal District Court and US Supreme Court Cases provided greater due process protections and civil rights for those with mental illnesses facing involuntary CC. By the late 1970s, nearly every state's civil commit laws were in accordance with the Lanterman-Petris-Short Act (1967), which was California's statute that set out strict due process protections. Below is a list and brief description of landmark Court cases whose decisions changed the landscape of involuntary CC (*see* Chapter 7 for full case briefs).

- **Lake v. Cameron (1966)**—US District Court decision that required CC based on dangerousness cannot go beyond what is necessary for their protection and should not be confined if a less restrictive alternative is available.
- **Lessard v. Schmidt (1972)**—US District Court decision that narrowly defined the dangerousness standard to immediate harm to oneself or others and required a right to counsel, the right to remain silent, and the exclusion of hearsay evidence.
- **O'Connor v. Donaldson (1975)**—US Supreme Court decision that, once committed, patients have the right to regular reviews of commitment criteria, as continued confinement and treatment must be based on the least restrictive alternative.
- **Addington v. Texas (1979)**—US Supreme Court decision that allowed courts to use the burden of proof for CC based on "clear, unequivocal and convincing evidence" as opposed to "beyond a reasonable doubt."

Civil Commitment Process

Although the specific CC processes may vary from one state to another, most CC proceedings generally follow a five-step process:

Step 1: One must first apply for a mental health warrant with information about the mental illness and the risk of harm.

Step 2: Based on the application, a judge can order a police officer to transport one to a psychiatric facility. On an emergency basis, police can detain and transport one to an inpatient mental health facility without a court order or a warrant if the danger is imminent. Imminent typically means that the harm will likely occur in the immediate future, and there is not enough time to obtain a warrant or court order. However, "imminent" is not a psychiatric or medical term, and most states have relaxed this requirement so that it is not too restrictive to prevent necessary intervention (Simon, 2006; Treatment Advocacy Center, TAC, 2020).

Step 3: A physician examines the individual as soon as possible or within 12 hours of arriving at the psychiatric facility. An individual may not be detained for more than a designated period (e.g., 48 hours) after arrival at

the facility unless a judge signs an Order of Protective Custody or Order of Commitment.
Step 4: If an order is issued, a probable cause hearing must be held within 72 hours. Prior to this hearing, two Physician Certificates are required to be on file; one must be by a psychiatrist.
Step 5: At the probable cause hearing, the judge decides whether the individual will be held at a psychiatric facility or released (Hedman et al., 2016; SAMSA, 2019) (Fig. 15.1).

Specific state CC laws' requirements vary depending on the reason, whether a judicial review of the emergency hold is required, the maximum length of the hold, and the rights to which one is entitled. Some states include mental health deterioration or a clinical worsening of mental health symptoms, either as a separate and distinct (but not exclusive) criterion. Some include a "grave disability" as part of the definition, which is the inability to meet their basic needs for survival (SAMSA, 2019). The most common maximum length of time permitted for the emergency hold is 72 hours (Hedman et al., 2016).

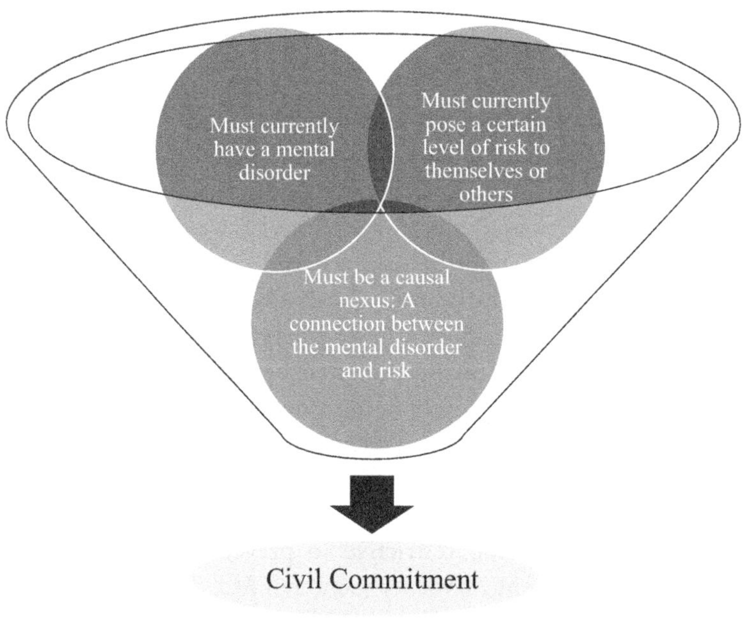

Fig. 15.1 Three Standard Requirements for Traditional Civil Commitment

Forensic Civil Commitment

The MHS overlaps with the CJS when those with mental illnesses commit criminal offenses and go through the criminal court process. For defendants found not legally responsible after pleading the insanity defense (*see* Chapter 12 of this book for details), depending on the severity of their offense and perceived dangerousness, they are either released into the community under supervision or are CC'd to a secure psychiatric facility for an indefinite period (Dirks-Linhorst & Kondrat, 2012). As outlined in O'Connor v Donaldson (1975), their cases will be reviewed to determine whether they continue to meet CC requirements.

Box 15.1 Practitioner Spotlight: Samantha Etzi, LSW

Samantha Etzi has worked as a licensed forensic social worker for several years, including at a forensic state hospital in Pennsylvania from 2020–2022. Etzi saw patients who were involuntarily civilly committed for both restoration of competency and those who had been deemed a danger to themselves or others. With 25–30 patients in the unit, she provided various treatment services, including therapy, psychoeducational group programming, education on legal matters (i.e., plea bargains, courtroom personnel, legal jargon), education on psychological disorders, and general well-being. Patients also have various backgrounds, abilities, and functioning levels, and their needs and treatment goals vary.

According to Etzi, while treating patients, it is important to listen to them (without judgment) and to allow them to have as much autonomy as possible. Involvement in the criminal justice system is often incredibly demeaning and constricting, and they have had their liberties taken away. These individuals have almost nothing in their control, so it is important to encourage them to make decisions about what they can, and then respect those decisions. There is a humanizing aspect as well. Recognizing patients as autonomous humans who are the "experts" on their own lives allows practitioners to meet them where they are and make progress. For example, a patient was admitted after committing a criminal offense and experienced delusions and paranoia related to his offense. While hospitalized, his sister passed away. Etzi approached him to discuss the grieving process, but he refused to meet with her. She respected his autonomy and space, said she would return later, and left. Upon her return, he was initially reluctant, but she was patient, allowed him to speak first, and did not pressure him. He slowly began opening up, sharing memories and stories of his sister. After an hour, his demeanor changed, and he appeared to have a different mindset. Allowing patients to have autonomy when they can and providing active listening and support can be enough to get someone through a difficult time.

Civil Commitment of Those with Substance Use Disorders

Forensic civil commitment legislation was enacted for those with an SUD. In 1961, California passed the Civil Addict Program, which used its traditional involuntary CC procedures to provide inpatient treatment for those with a narcotic (e.g., opiates, opioids, heroin) SUD who were arrested for a drug-related crime. In 1962, New York State passed the Metcalf-Volker Act (sponsored by State Senator George Metcalf and Assemblyman Julius Volker). The Act allowed those with SUDs who were arrested for minor offenses or drug use/possession to opt for treatment and rehabilitation at a state hospital in lieu of a prison sentence.

In 1966, Congress passed the federal Narcotic Addict Rehabilitation Act (NARA). Under NARA, specific individuals with a narcotic SUD charged with or convicted of violating federal laws were eligible for CC. Those excluded from CC under NARA were (1) those charged with violent crimes, (2) drug trafficking, (3) those with two or more prior felony convictions, (4) those who have undergone CC twice before, and (5) those with a pending felony charge. Treatment would be provided in pretrial CC instead of prosecuting those with SUD charged with specific crimes. The Act was intended to provide care to eligible individuals who were screened and deemed amendable to treatment (Lindblad, 1988). Whether individuals are legally entitled to treatment for SUDs was decided in Marshall v. United States (1974).

Case Brief: Marshall v. United States (1974)

Facts: Robert Edward Marshall pleaded guilty to entering a bank with the intent to commit a felony. Marshall, who had a SUD, requested at his sentencing hearing to be considered for treatment under NARA. The sentencing judge denied his request, finding him ineligible due to him having more than two prior felony convictions: burglary, forgery, and possession of a firearm. He was sentenced to ten years in prison, but the judge recommended that he receive treatment while incarcerated. Marshall filed to vacate his sentence, stating that the "two prior felony" rule under NARA violated due process.

Issue: Whether individuals with SUDs have a constitutional right to treatment and whether the "two prior felonies" exclusion of NARA violated equal protection under the due process clause of the Fifth Amendment.

Outcome: The US Supreme Court determined that individuals with SUDs do not have a constitutional right to treatment. Therefore, by excluding someone with two or more prior felony convictions, NARA does not violate due process or equal protection.

There was controversy surrounding NARA, specifically disagreements about eligibility, who was determined to be amenable to receiving a "second chance," and high rejection rates due to limited capacity (Lindblad, 1988; Marlowe et al., 2003). NARA was short-lived and ceased in 1978 (Friedman et al., 1982). Other legislation specific to handling SUDs and drug-related offenses was passed, including the Comprehensive Drug Abuse Prevention and Control Act of 1970 (*see* Chapter 5 of this book for details) (Lindblad, 1988). However, NARA and the subsequent Marshall v. United States decision set precedents and standards as to whether those with SUDs who commit criminal offenses are entitled to treatment. There is presently no federal statute outlining a CC program for those with SUDs; however, to date, 37 states and Washington D.C. have CC programs for those with SUDs (Hazelton Betty Ford Foundation, 2017).

Outpatient Civil Commitment

The deinstitutionalization movement and the closing of psychiatric hospitals (*see* Chapter 7 of this book for details) decreased the availability of inpatient beds. As hospital capacity diminished and the increased need for "least restricted alternatives," programs involving involuntary outpatient commitment (OC) began to develop. Legally mandated involuntary OC is known by a variety of names, including assisted outpatient treatment (AOT) and compulsory community treatment (Heyman-Kantor & Dinwiddie, 2024). The first OC program was developed in North Carolina in 1973 (Lietzan, 1995), and by 1999, they were implemented in all but one state, New York. New York State did not have an OC statute and, instead, specifically required involuntary care and treatment in a hospital, and only after hospitalization may one be court-ordered for conditional release into the community (Allbright et al., 2002; Keilitz & Hall, 1985). This changed after the high-profile death of Kendra Webdale by Andrew Goldstein, which led New York State to quickly address mental health care. Presently, all but three states, Connecticut, Maryland, and Massachusetts continue to offer OC as an option (TAC, 2020), although it is not widely used in many states (Heyman-Kantor & Dinwiddie, 2024).

Case of Andrew Goldstein

On January 3, 1999, 29-year-old Andrew Goldstein stood near the subway platform at 23rd Street and Broadway. Standing in front of him was 32-year-old Kendra Webdale. She had just left her job where she worked as a receptionist and was on her way home. She had moved to New York City just three years earlier from a town outside of Buffalo, NY, hoping to land a job in the music industry. At 5:06 P.M., her life came to a tragic end when Andrew Goldstein, a 29-year-old man with schizophrenia, pushed her off the platform in the path of an oncoming train (Winerip, 1999a).

Background: Goldstein grew up in Queens, NY and attended the elite Bronx High School of Science (Lennon & Keller, 2018; Winerip, 1999a). His psychiatric symptoms began when he was 16 years old, but did well in school, graduated and attended two semesters of college at Stony Brook before his symptoms worsened. He experienced his first psychotic episode at 19 while on vacation with his family. He ran out of the hotel room and flipped a table over where two women were sitting (Lennon & Keller, 2018).

Mental Health History: According to Goldstein's 3,500-page psychiatric file, in the two years before Kendra Webdale's death, Goldstein physically attacked at least 13 other people. For example, on November 14, 1997, he assaulted a psychiatrist at a Queens clinic; on March 2, 1998, he attacked two male strangers at a Burger King restaurant; and on June 20, 1998, he attacked a female stranger on a New York subway. Goldstein's hospital record also had notes showing a propensity for violence. An example included a note made on May 6, 1998, that mentioned he was at "high risk" for violence, and on July 31, 1998, a note stated that he had been aggressively and impulsively striking others, unprovoked. Goldstein knew he needed help and requested long-term treatment at a state facility at Creedmoor Group Home, a hospital in Queens Village, NY. Goldstein's file notes contained repeated pleas for long-term care, but there were no vacancies. On November 20, 1998, Goldstein went to Jamaica Hospital in Queens, requesting to be hospitalized. His last hospitalization was at North General on November 24, 1998, but he was released on December 15 because he could only receive short-term care due to cost-saving measures. He did not follow up with the outpatient services and stopped taking his psychotropic medication. The clinic where he was supposed to attend appointments mailed Goldstein a letter that if he did not contact the clinic by January 6, 1999, his case would be closed (Winerip, 1999a).

Day of the Offense: According to Goldstein, shortly before he pushed Kendra Webdale, he felt a "sensation" and had an overwhelming urge to push her in front of the train. He first distracted her by asking her the time, then he waited until he heard the train, then shoved her onto the tracks (Winerip, 1999a). She was killed instantly. Goldstein was arrested and charged with first degree murder (Hartocolis, 2006).

Trials: A mental health evaluation determined that Goldstein was competent to stand trial (Lennon & Keller, 2018). Goldstein's defense team pleaded Not Guilty by Reason of Mental Disease or Defect (Winerip, 1999a), as NY used the Model Penal Code standard (*see* Chapter 12 of this book for details). His trial was held in March 2000. His 20-minute videotaped confession was played for the jury, showing Goldstein alert and able to answer questions correctly and calmly, with no apparent evidence of psychosis (Winerip, 1999b). The first trial ended in a hung jury and the judge declared a mistrial.

At his second trial, Dr. Spencer Eth testified for the defense, stating that at the time he pushed Webdale, he experienced an acute exacerbation of his psychotic symptoms because he was not taking his psychotropic medication. His actions were not planned or premeditated, and he did not know what he was doing was wrong. Dr. Angela Hegarty testified for the prosecution and claimed that although she agreed with his diagnosis of schizophrenia, his symptoms were mild and in remission. She testified that Goldstein resented women due to feelings of rejection and sexual frustration and was using his schizophrenia as an excuse for his actions. She reached this conclusion after interviewing people who personally knew Goldstein. In May 2001, 12 new jurors determined Goldstein was not insane at the time of his crime and found him guilty, and he was sentenced to life in prison (Lennon & Keller, 2018; People v. Goldstein, 2005).

Goldstein's attorneys appealed his conviction to the New York State Court of Appeals, People v. Goldstein (2005). The appeal was based on Dr. Hegarty's testimony that her statements from interviews were inadmissible hearsay and violated his Sixth Amendment right to confront the witnesses. The Court overturned his conviction, agreeing the prosecution expert's testimony had been hearsay (People v. Goldstein, 2005). Instead of a third trial, Goldstein's attorney recommended he plead guilty to manslaughter, as opposed to another not guilty plea, which would result in indefinite CC with no limit. Andrew agreed and pleaded guilty and was sentenced to 23 years (Lennon & Keller, 2018).

Kendra's Law

Within months of Kendra Webdale's death, NY Governor George Pataki allocated $125 million in funding for the care of persons with mental illnesses. He also signed Kendra's Law on August 9, 1999, named after Kendra Webdale. Kendra's Law Assisted Outpatient Treatment (AOT) legislation established a stringent outpatient treatment regimen for those with severe mental illnesses who have a history of treatment noncompliance and violent behavior. For those under Kendra's Law, a court-ordered treatment plan is developed and monitored by a case manager or community team, and noncompliance can result in CC to a hospital (Lennon & Keller, 2018). Kendra's Law initially stipulated that the maximum duration of the court-ordered treatment was six months. However, evaluations showed that participants experienced better outcomes when receiving treatment for longer periods, and in 2013, Kendra's Law was amended to increase the maximum to 12 months (SAMSA, 2019). The constitutionality of Kendra's Law was challenged in the Matter of K.L. (2004), but New York's Court of Appeals upheld its practice. Since the implementation on November 8, 1999, as of December 31, 2024, there have been 36,497 petitions for Kendra's Law in New York State, and 96% (34,892) have been granted (NYS Office of Mental Health).

The guidelines for eligibility for involuntary OC are nearly identical to hospital CC. The court must find, using the evidentiary standard of "clear and convincing evidence," that individuals have a mental illness that requires treatment to prevent them from becoming a danger to themselves or others, including a grave disability, and will unlikely comply with treatment without a court order. Individuals under OC must comply with their prescribed treatment plan, including engaging with their treatment team and physician. Those under OC may not be forced to take prescribed medications without an additional legal process to determine capacity. Those who fail to comply with their treatment plan requirement may face hospitalization for observation (Anfang & Appelbaum, 2006; Heyman-Kantor & Dinwiddie, 2024).

Specific involuntary OC laws vary widely from state to state (Heyman-Kantor & Dinwiddie, 2024; Meldrum et al., 2016); however, research has found them to be generally effective in their intended goals. An early evaluation of involuntary OC of 262 individuals revealed that six months or more of services effectively reduced violence. To significantly reduce violence, researchers noted that frequent mental health service visits of three or more a month (on average) were necessary (Swanson et al., 2000). Segal (2022) reviewed 74 studies that evaluated the effectiveness of OC and found they were associated with increased access to medical care and reduced risks of violence and victimization. Overall, the availability and utilization of services in the community reduce the risk of violence among those with mental illnesses, and possibly not necessarily the court order requiring them.

Civil Commitment of Those Convicted of Sexual Offenses

Another form of forensic CC is legislation specific to those convicted of sexual offenses, referred to as "Sexually Violent Predator[1]" (SVP) or "Sexually Dangerous Person" Acts. SVP Acts allow those convicted of sexual offenses who meet the statutory criteria to be involuntary CC'd upon completing their custodial sentence. The present CC laws for those who have committed sexual offenses were modeled after the same procedures as traditional CC but are referred for an evaluation through the correctional system.

Legislation to hospitalize those convicted of sexual offenses via the MHS has been in operation for nearly a century. Michigan enacted a "Sexual Psychopath" law in 1937, which confined those deemed "sexual psychopaths" considered a danger to the public to be eligible for CC to a psychiatric facility. By 1949, 12 states and the District of Columbia had enacted similar laws (Sutherland, 1950). Present SVP laws are modeled after the updated CC procedures that adhere to the decisions in landmark Federal District Court and US Supreme Court decisions that addressed traditional involuntary CC and decisions that specifically addressed SVP laws (see case briefs below). Washington was the first state to enact a modern SVP CC law in 1990, and to date, 20 states have SVP laws (Association for the Treatment & Prevention of Sexual Abuse, 2021). The criteria used to determine if an individual is eligible for CC vary by state but generally include the presence of a mental illness or mental disorder that predisposes the individual to commit sexual offenses. A significant difference between SVP laws and traditional CC is that the "danger to themselves or others" criteria were replaced with the designation of at high risk or long-term risk for committing another sexual offense. Not all those convicted of sexual offenses are eligible or meet the criteria for CC. For example, under Florida's SVP act, the Jimmy Ryce Act, named after nine-year-old Jimmy Ryce, as of July 2023, 89,564 individuals were referred for consideration for CC. Of those, 5,321 underwent an evaluation (6% of referrals) and 530 were CC'd (about 5% of evaluations and 0.6% of referrals) (Florida Legislature, Office of Economic and Demographic Research, 2023).

Criteria for SVP Laws

Although some who commit sexual offenses have co-occurring mental illnesses, there is no diagnosis of "sexual offender." However, some may be diagnosed with paraphilic disorders, which are atypical sexual interests in objects, situations, or individuals. The Diagnostic and Statistical Manual of Mental Disorders, Fifth Edition Text Revision (DSM-5-TR), published by the American Psychiatric Association (APA) (2022) contains paraphilic disorders, defined as "recurrent, intense" behaviors that cause distress, impairment, or harm to oneself or others. They consist of sexually arousing fantasies, sexual urges, or behaviors generally involving (1) nonhuman objects, (2) the suffering or humiliation of oneself or one's partner, or (3) children or other non-consenting persons, which occur over at least six months (APA, 2022, p. 779). The DSM-5-TR lists eight paraphilic disorders but notes that clinicians have identified and named dozens of other paraphiliac disorders and have an "Other Specified Paraphilic Disorder" category. One may or may not act on their urges, but those who do may have contact with the CJS. Many paraphilic disorders are diagnosed after an arrest for a sexual offense (First, 2014). Pedophilic disorder (involving prepubescent children, generally age 13 and younger), exhibitionistic disorder (exposure of one's genitals to an unsuspecting person), and voyeuristic disorder (spying on unsuspecting others during private activities) account for most individuals with paraphilic disorders involved in the CJS who have committed sexual offenses (APA, 2022).

Although some neurodiverse individuals display behaviors consistent with paraphilic disorders, clinicians use caution when diagnosing individuals with NDDs, such as autism or ID, to rule out **counterfeit deviance** (Griffiths et al., 2013). First used by Hingsburger et al. (1991), counterfeit deviance differentiates clinical assessments of individuals with developmental disabilities whose behaviors meet the DSM diagnostic criteria of paraphilic disorders. The primary concept involved in counterfeit deviance is that people with NDDs may engage in inappropriate sexual behavior for reasons other than malice or deviance. The DSM does not include a "counterfeit deviance" classification, nor does counterfeit deviance deny that paraphilia exists among persons with NDDs.

Constitutional Challenges of Civil Commitment

The controversy surrounding SVP laws focused on civil rights violations, violations of due process, and equal protection under the law. Some argued that SVP laws are punishment or preventative detention under the guise of treatment. Those who support SVP laws emphasize risk to public safety and the need for treatment. Federal District Court and the US Supreme have affirmed the constitutionality of these statutes.

Case Briefs: Cases Challenging Civil Commitment

Humphrey v. Cady (1972)

Facts: Donald Gilbert Humphrey was convicted of a sexually motivated misdemeanor, contributing to the delinquency of a minor. Humphrey was subject to the Wisconsin Sex Crimes Act, which transfers those convicted of sexually motivated offenses to the Department of Health and Social Services for an examination and CC. Humphrey was not represented by counsel at the hearing and was CC'd to a facility for those convicted of sexual offenses for an indefinite period of time. He challenged that the commitment procedures under the Sex Crimes Act were equivalent to CC under Wisconsin's Mental Health Act, which provides a jury. Humphrey argued that his commitment without a jury deprived him of his Fourteenth Amendment protections of due process and equal protection of the law. He appealed his case to the US Court of Appeals for the Seventh Circuit.

Issue: Whether the commitment procedures of the Wisconsin Sex Crimes Act lack the procedural safeguards to protect one's Fourteenth Amendment right to due process and equal protection.

Outcome: The Court concluded that an evidentiary hearing was necessary to resolve Humphrey's constitutional claims. When CC involves a significant loss of liberty, safeguards and due process must be in place. The Court reversed and remanded the case to the District Court for a hearing.

Kansas v Hendricks (1997)

Facts: Kansas enacted its SVP Act in 1994, which established procedures for the CC of persons with a mental disorder that makes it "difficult, if not impossible," to control their behavior. Kansas exercised the SVP Act for the first time when attempting to commit Leroy Hendricks before his release from prison. Hendricks had an extensive history of sexual offending at least a dozen children spanning nearly two decades. On August 19, 1994, Hendricks and his counsel appeared before the court to dismiss the petition, stating the Act violated federal constitutional due process provisions, including the Fifth Amendment protections against **double jeopardy** and the **ex post facto** clause in Article 1 of the US Constitution. Double jeopardy prohibits being punished twice for the same offense, and ex post facto prohibits the application of new punishments that were not in place when the crime was originally committed. Hendricks appealed the decision to the US Supreme Court.

Issue: Whether the Kansas SVP Act violated the Fifth Amendment protections against double jeopardy and whether the retroactive application was a violation of the ex post facto clause.

Outcome: The US Supreme Court decided that the Kansas statute was civil, not criminal, and was not in violation of the ex post facto clause. The Act did not criminalize Hendricks' behavior before its enactment nor deprive him of any defense that was available to him at the time of his crimes. Therefore, the Constitutional protections of the ex post facto and double jeopardy clauses did not apply.

Kansas v. Crane (2002)

Facts: Michael Crane was convicted of aggravated sexual battery of a woman working at a tanning salon in 1993. According to video footage inside the salon, Crane waited until he was the only customer and then grabbed the woman from behind. With his genitals exposed, Crane lifted her and squeezed her neck with his hands. Crane ordered her to perform oral sex and threatened to rape her. The assault ended when Crane suddenly stopped and ran out of the salon. Crane pleaded guilty and was evaluated for CC under the Kansas SVP Act. He was diagnosed with exhibitionistic disorder and antisocial personality disorder[2] and was CC'd. Crane questioned the constitutionality of the SVP Act and claimed he was ineligible for CC because his mental disorders did not impair his volitional control (i.e., did not make it "difficult, if not impossible," to control his behavior).

Issue: Whether the dangerousness requirement under the Kansas SVP Act, "difficult, if not impossible, to control one's behavior," required a complete lack of volitional control.

Outcome: The US Supreme Court decided the term; "difficult" did not establish a requirement for a total or complete lack of control. In other words, "lack of control" was not given a particularly narrow or technical meaning and upheld the constitutionality of the Kansas SVP Act. This decision clarified the language and terms used in Kansas v. Hendricks to define the criteria for CC. The Court allowed states to retain considerable discretion in defining the mental disorders that make an individual eligible for CC.

Westerheide v. State (2000)

Facts: In 1995, Mitchell Westerheide was convicted and sentenced for aggravated assault, lewd and lascivious behavior on a child, and sexual performance by a child by a Florida court. Westerheide sexually tortured a 15-year-old girl for over six months. In 1999, he underwent a CC hearing under the Jimmy Ryce Act. He was diagnosed with the paraphilic disorder, sexual sadism, and antisocial personality disorder. At his CC trial in March 1999, he was found to have met the criteria for the Jimmy Ryce Act. Westerheide challenged that the Jimmy Ryce Act violated the ex post facto and double jeopardy clauses because the commitment was a punishment for an offense before the law took effect and extended the punishment offense. Westerheide also challenged the equal protection clause of the Fourteenth Amendment, partly because "sexually violent predators" were treated differently from other civilly committed individuals, as the Jimmy Ryce Act does not offer a least restrictive alternative to total confinement. Westerheide appealed to the Florida Supreme Court, who confirmed the decision at his CC trial. He then appealed to the US District Court.

Issue: Whether the Jimmy Ryce SVP Act violated federal constitutional due process provisions, including the Fifth Amendment protections against double jeopardy, ex post facto, and the equal protection clause of the Fourteenth Amendment.

Outcome: The District Court agreed with the Florida Supreme Court, and similar to Kansas v. Hendricks, the Court found that the Jimmy Ryce Act was civil, not criminal, and the intention was to treat, not punish. The Court decided that "sexually violent predators" are not a class protected under the equal protection clause and found no merit to Westerheide's constitutional challenges.

Case of Robert[3]

Background: Robert was 41 years old when he was arrested for aggravated sexual assault. Robert had an extensive history of using alcohol beginning in his early teens and had been diagnosed with bipolar disorder and alcohol use disorder. He grew up with both parents and was the youngest of three, with one older brother and sister. His father had misused alcohol and was physically abusive toward him and his siblings, but Robert denied any sexual abuse. Robert completed high school and maintained a steady work history. He served seven years in the military and was honorably discharged. He has one other prior sexual offense, where he was convicted of sexual assault of a 12-year-old boy who was the son of his ex-girlfriend. He served six years in prison and was released on parole. Prior to his sexual offenses, his criminal history consisted of two DWIs (driving while intoxicated).

Instant Offense: Robert approached a ten-year-old girl in a park, threatened her with a knife, then demanded she follow him into a nearby wooded area. Robert sexually assaulted the girl, threatened to kill her if she told anyone, and left her in the woods. The girl was later found stumbling out of the woods and treated at a nearby hospital. The girl was able to provide a detailed description to the police. Along with other witnesses' descriptions, police were able to identify Robert as the suspect and arrested him for aggravated sexual assault.

Outcome: The victim testified as a witness at trial and identified Robert as her assailant. He was convicted and sentenced to nine years in prison. While incarcerated, he repeatedly denied the offense and claimed he was innocent. However, he was overheard by correctional officers making statements about how he planned to kidnap more children for sex, and next time, he would "kill them" so there would be no witnesses.

Civil Commitment: When his sentence was about to end, Robert was evaluated for involuntary CC under the state's SVP law. It was determined at the hearing that Robert met the criteria for an SVP because of his past sexual offenses, one of which included a weapon, and his diagnoses of bipolar disorder and alcohol use disorder. He was deemed a danger to others due to his high risk of sexually reoffending and the overheard statements from correctional officers, who testified at the hearing. Robert was involuntarily CC'd indefinitely. His psychological evaluation confirmed his diagnosis of bipolar disorder and alcohol use disorder, and there was no clinical indication of pedophilia or any other paraphilic disorders.

While committed, he initially refused to participate in treatment, repeatedly denied his offenses, and repeatedly demanded to be released. The hospital staff explained the steps to release, which would not be initiated until he began to participate in treatment, which included admitting to the sexual assaults. Robert began participating in treatment and finally admitted his sexual assault on his ten-year-old victim but continued to deny sexually abusing his ex-girlfriend's son. He also began making the connection between his alcohol use to manage bipolar depression and feelings of anger from his childhood, which led to his violent sexual acts against children. He continued to participate in treatment and made progress but remained hospitalized for continued treatment.

Treatment Interventions

As renowned sociologist Edwin Sutherland (1950) recognized decades ago, legislation that requires those convicted of sexual offenses to undergo treatment creates a general assumption that they must be "fiends" and creates an assumption that sexual offending is an illness. Others may deny the effectiveness of treatment for those convicted of sexual offenses because they are not "curable." This belief was reinforced by the outdated study by Furby et al. (1989), who concluded that there was no evidence that clinical treatment reduced sexual offending. However, several researchers have since debunked this conclusion (Hanson & Bussière, 1998; Hanson & Morton-Bourgon, 2004; Zgoba & Simon, 2005). This myth is inaccurate and misleading because although there is no disease or illness to be cured, sexual offenses are crimes (i.e., criminal acts), and like any other criminal act or behavior, people can and do have the ability to control their actions and behaviors with interventions. Those seeking treatment undergo **rehabilitation** to address their mental health and any SUDs but also undergo **habilitation** to address their offense patterns. Rehabilitation treatment is the term used in the medical community for treating, curing, or helping others regain skills lost due to illness or injury (i.e., restoring one to a prior state). However, some may have never had said skills, so rehabilitation (i.e., returning them to a prior state) is not the goal, and a more accurate term is habilitation. Habilitation efforts provide individuals with new skills to better control their behavior and develop new and effective ways to manage their emotions and impulses (Holmes & Holmes, 2009).

Once released, one must continue treatment to maintain the skills to avoid offending behavior and control their impulses. For some, a barrier to community treatment for those convicted of sexual offenses is registration and notification laws, also known as Megan's Law. These laws apply to those on probation, parole, or after being released from prison or jail after serving their entire sentence. Megan's Law was enacted in New Jersey in 1996 in response to the 1994 murder of seven-year-old Megan Kanka from Hamilton, New Jersey, by a neighbor with prior sexual offense convictions against children. On May 7, 1996, the US House of Representatives amended the Violent Crime Control and Law Enforcement Act of 1994 and added Megan's Law, which required all 50 states to establish a public registry by risk level (level 1 = low, level 2 = moderate, level 3 = high). By 1999, all states had implemented their version of Megan's Law, with significant variability among them. Some registries make all risk levels public, whereas some only make public moderate risk and high risk.

Public registration has resulted in stigma, such as losing a job, being denied housing, and being threatened or harassed (Tewksbury, 2005; Tewksbury & Lees, 2006). Some states and jurisdictions have residence restrictions for those subject to Megan's Law, making securing housing difficult. Zgoba (2011) explained how the added stress of being unable to secure stable housing could result in destabilization, which can hinder treatment efforts. Therefore, CJS professionals who work with those on probation or parole subject to Megan's

Law must consider the impact on their supervision plans. Not all individuals listed on the registry require the same treatment, interventions, or probation supervision level to desist from further offending.

Considerations and Recommendations

Involuntary CC, both inpatient and outpatient, remains a controversial approach to the treatment of people with mental illnesses who decline to participate in treatment or are court-ordered based on their risk of dangerousness to the community. Nonetheless, there are several factors to consider and practical recommendations to bridge the MHS and CJS and improve outcomes for justice-involved individuals with mental illnesses.

Strengthen Mental Health Case Systems

As commitment laws and policies have evolved, public healthcare systems face new challenges in delivering mental health services for CC and OC under fiscal and budget constraints. There is little question that the MHS has logistical and resource limitations when implementing community programming. For too long, the MHS lacked funding to support those in need of mental health services, leaving jails and prisons as backup systems. Meldrum et al. (2016) noted that the MHS and OC programs across the country vary widely and have many shortcomings. States must establish a well-developed and functioning MHS with adequate coverage for counseling and other psychiatric services, services to treat co-occurring SUDs, and resources to support MHS staff, including education and training (Meldrum et al., 2016; SAMSA, 2019).

Community Supervision and Support Services

Those receiving OC and those released from a psychiatric facility will require adequate community-based supervision and treatment strategies. Excessively harsh restrictions/conditions may hinder successful integration and treatment as they disallow or remove essential support systems, which could lead to destabilization and increase recidivism risk. Clinicians can also advocate for appropriate supervision conditions and treatment efforts to address risk management strategies and ongoing community support and services. Judges and supervision officers should also use caution when mandating treatment, particularly in the group setting. Group treatment settings are inappropriate for some but may not be therapeutic environments for those with autism or intellectual disability and may worsen underlying conditions (Mogavero et al., 2025).

Consider the Effects of Registration Laws

Public registration for those convicted of sexual offenses has resulted in stigma, with negative consequences that may hinder treatment efforts. Legislation named after victims murdered by strangers often influences public perceptions of dangerousness when such cases are rare, and 84% to 95% of sexual offenses are committed by someone known to the victim (Danni & Hampe, 2000; Mogavero & Kennedy, 2017; Zgoba et al., 2010). Assessing risk levels is more difficult for neurodiverse individuals, as many risk assessment instruments have not been validated (Craig, 2010). Defense attorneys must collaborate with prosecutors and others in charge of assigning risk levels, whether that risk level is made public, and be mindful of how such legislation affects one's treatment and recidivism risk (Mogavero et al., 2025).

Conclusion

People with mental illnesses encounter the CJS, often due to untreated symptoms. Although most with mental illnesses are not violent, those who have a history of acts of violence may be eligible for Involuntary CC and OC. The availability of community services is linked to OC's effectiveness. The MHS requires funding and resources to support these programs, particularly for those in need of SUD care and treatment. Unfortunately, it took the murder of Kendra Webdale for New York State to allocate funding for mental health services and to establish legislation to court-order treatment for those who are non-compliant. Such high-profile cases lead to misconceptions about those with mental illnesses, including that people with mental illnesses are violent and need to be contained, which often justifies harsh sentences. However, most are not violent and, with access to adequate and appropriate systems, can successfully integrate into the community and live productive and fulfilling lives.

SVP Acts for those who have served their prison sentence are a controversial use of involuntary CC. Those who commit sexual offenses are often viewed with disdain, particularly those who commit violent offenses against children. Such cases often justify indefinite involuntary CC to prevent those deemed at high risk from being released back into the community, as in the case of Robert. Inpatient hospitalization is necessary for those in acute need of long-term care for stabilization, especially when other interventions have been ineffective. Therefore, it is imperative that the laws appropriately target the small percentage of those who require them. Casting too wide a net, under the goal of "preventative detention," occupies limited beds in hospitals for those indeed in need of mental health care under traditional CC or those found incompetent to stand trial awaiting inpatient treatment.

Key Terms

Civil Commitment
Counterfeit Deviance
Double Jeopardy
Ex Post Facto
Habilitation
Involuntary Medication
Outpatient Commitment
Parens Patriae
Police Powers
Rehabilitation

Chapter Questions

(1) List and describe the three requirements for involuntary civil commitment.
(2) Describe the similarities and differences between inpatient and outpatient civil commitment.
(3) Explain the constitutionality concerns with involuntary civil commitment.
(4) What is your position on involuntary civil commitment for those who commit sexual offenses?
(5) Should those with opiate use disorder have the right to medication treatment, which was not guaranteed with the Marshall v. United States (1974) decision?
(6) What more do you think should be done to support and assist those with mental illnesses to prevent them from self-harming or harming others and having contact with the CJS?

Suggested Readings

Lamb, H. R., & Weinberger, L. E. (2017). Understanding and treating offenders with serious mental illness in public sector mental health. *Behavioral Sciences & the Law, 35*(4), 303–318. https://doi.org/10.1002/bsl.2292

Lave, T. R. (2011). Inevitable recidivism: The origin and centrality of an urban legend. *International Journal of Law and Psychiatry, 34*, 186–194.

Stone, D. (2016). There are cracks in the civil commitment process: A practitioner's recommendations to patch the system. *Fordham Urban Law Journal, 43*(3), 789–845.

Notes

1. The terms "sex offender," "sexual offender," "sexual predator," and "sexually violent predator" are common terms of laws and statutes and are used only when referring to such and are placed in quotations.
2. A DSM-5-TR diagnosis that describes individuals who habitually violate rules, norms, laws, or socially acceptable behavior, disregarding the rights and considerations of others, often lacking feelings of guilt or remorse.
3. Name and some details have been changed for anonymity.

References

Addington v. Texas, 441 U.S. 418 .(1979).

Allbright, A., Levy, F., & Wagle, N. C. (2002). Outpatient civil commitment laws: An overview. *Mental and Physical Disability Law Reporter, 26*(2), 179–182. https://www.jstor.org/stable/20785940

Anfang, S. A., & Appelbaum, P. S. (2006). Civil commitment: The American experience. *The Israel Journal of Psychiatry and Related Sciences, 43*(3), 209–218.

American Psychiatric Association. (2022). *Diagnostic and statistical manual of mental disorders* (5th ed. Text Revision). https://doi.org/10.1176/appi.books.9780890425787

Association for the Treatment & Prevention of Sexual Abuse. (2021). *Civil commitment: Best practice informed recommendations.* https://members.atsa.com/learn/Details/report-summary-civil-commitment-best-practice-informed-recommendations-194322

Civil Addict Program. (1961). *Cal. Code Regs. Tit, 15*, 5005.

Craig, L. A. (2010). Controversies in assessing risk and deviancy in sex offenders with intellectual disabilities. *Psychology, Crime & Law, 16*(1–2), 75–101. https://doi.org/10.1080/10683160802621982

Danni, K. A., & Hampe, G. D. (2000). An analysis of predictors of child sex offender types using presentence investigation reports. *International Journal of Offender Therapy and Comparative Criminology, 44*(4), 490–504. https://doi.org/10.1177/0306624X00444007

Dirks-Linhorst, P. A., & Kondrat, D. (2012). Tough on crime or beating the system: An evaluation of Missouri department of mental health's not guilty by reason of insanity murder acquittees. *Homicide Studies, 16*(2), 129–150. https://doi.org/10.1177/1088767912438711

Friedman, S. B., Horvat, G. L., & Levinson, R. B. (1982). Narcotic Addict Rehabilitation Act—Its impact on federal prisons. *Contemporary Drug Problems, 11*(1), 101–111.

First, M. B. (2014). DSM-5 and paraphilic disorders. *Journal of the American Academy of Psychiatry and the Law, 42*(2), 191–201.

Florida Legislature (2023). *Sexually violent predator program reports.* Office of Economic and Demographic Research. http://edr.state.fl.us/Content/resource-demand/criminal-justice/reports/sexually-violent-predators/index.cfm

Furby, L., Weinrott, M. R., & Blackshaw, L. (1989). Sex offender recidivism: A review. *Psychological Bulletin, 105*(1), 3–30. https://doi.org/10.1037/0033-2909.105.1.3

Griffiths, D., Hingsburger, D., Hoath, J., & Ioannou, S. (2013). Counterfeit deviance revisited. *Journal of Applied Research in Intellectual Disabilities, 26*(5), 471–480. https://doi.org/10.1111/jar.12034

Hanson, R. K., & Bussière, M. T. (1998). Predicting relapse: A meta-analysis of sexual offender recidivism studies. *Journal of Consulting and Clinical Psychology, 66*(2), 348–62. https://doi.org/10.1037/0022-006X.66.2.348

Hanson, R. K., & Morton-Bourgon, K. (2004). *Predictors of sexual recidivism: An updated meta-analysis.* Public Works and Government Services. https://www.publicsafety.gc.ca/cnt/rsrcs/pblctns/2004-02-prdctrs-sxl-rcdvsm-pdtd/index-en.aspx

Hazelden Betty Ford Foundation. (2017). *Involuntary commitment for substance use disorders: Emerging drug trends.* https://www.hazeldenbettyford.org/research-studies/addiction-research/involuntary-commitment

Hedman, L. C., Petrila, J., Fisher, W. H., Swanson, J. W., Dingman, D. A., & Burris, S. (2016). State laws on emergency holds for mental health stabilization. *Psychiatric Services, 67*(5), 529–535. https://doi.org/10.1176/appi.ps.201500205

Hartocolis, A. (2006, May 23). A subway nightmare will be the focus of yet a third trial. *The New York Times.* https://www.nytimes.com/2006/05/23/nyregion/a-subway-nightmare-will-be-the-focus-of-yet-a-third-trial.html

Heyman-Kantor, R., & Dinwiddie, S. H. (2024). Outpatient commitment in the United States: Utilization, benefits, and patient perspectives. *Psychiatric Annals, 54*(5), e141–e145. https://doi.org/10.3928/00485713-20240507-01

Hingsburger, D., Griffiths, D., & Quinsey, V. (1991). Detecting counterfeit deviance: Differentiating sexual deviance from sexual inappropriateness. *The Habilitative Mental Healthcare Newsletter, 10*, 51–54.

Holmes, S. T., & Holmes, R. M. (2009). *Sex crimes: Patterns and behavior* (3 Eds). Sage Publications.

Humphrey v. Cady, 405 U.S. 504, 509. (1972).

Kansas v. Crane, 534 U.S. 407. (2002).

Kansas v. Hendricks, 521 U.S. 346, 353. (1997).

Keilitz, I., & Hall, T. (1985). State statutes governing involuntary outpatient civil commitment. *Mental & Physical Disability Law Reporter, 9*(5), 378–397.

Kendra's Law, New York Mental Hygiene Law 9.60. (1999).

In the Matter of K.L., 1 NY3d 362. (2004).

Lanterman-Petris-Short Act, California Welfare and Institutions Code, Sec. 5150ff. (1967). https://doi.org/10.1016/j.ijlp.2011.04.005

Lennon, J. J., & Keller, B. (2018, September 3). A turbulent mind. *The Marshall Project*. https://www.themarshallproject.org/2018/09/03/a-turbulent-mind

Lessard v Schmidt, 349 F. Supp. 1078 E.D. Wis. (1972).

Lietzan, E. (1995). Outpatient civil commitment in North Carolina: Constitutional and policy concerns. *Law and Contemporary Problems, 58*(2), 251–281. https://ssrn.com/abstract=2221465

Lindblad, R. (1988). Civil commitment under the Federal Narcotic Addict Rehabilitation Act. *Journal of Drug Issues, 18*(4), 595–624. https://doi.org/10.1177/002204268801800407

Marlowe, D. B., Patapis, N. S., & DeMatteo, D. (2003). Amenability to treatment of drug offenders. *Federal Probation, 67*(2), 40–46. https://ssrn.com/abstract=3593786

Marshall v. United States, 414 U.S. 417. (1974).

Megan's Law, 42 U.S.C. (1996).

Meldrum, M. L., Kelly, E. L., Calderon, R., Brekke, J. S., & Braslow, J. T. (2016). Implementation status of assisted outpatient treatment programs: A national survey. *Psychiatric Services, 67*(6), 630–635. https://doi.org/10.1176/appi.ps.201500073. PMID:26828396.

Mogavero, M. C., & Kennedy, L. W. (2017). The social and geographic patterns of sexual offending: Is sex offender residence restriction legislation practical? *Victims & Offenders, 12*(3), 401–433. https://doi.org/10.1080/15564886.2015.1084962

Mogavero, M. C., Fenrich, A., Patel, R., & Etzi, S. (2025). Neurodevelopmental disorders and sexual offending. In R. Tully, G. Bohall, & D. S. Prescott (Eds.), *Best practices in sexual offender assessment and management* (pp. 541–584). Springer Publishers.

NYS Office of Mental Health. AOT Reports. *Program statistics: Petitions filed*. https://omh.ny.gov/omhweb/statistics/index.htm

O'Connor v. Donaldson, 422 U.S. 563. (1975).

People v. Goldstein, 6 N.Y.3d 119, 843 N.E.2d 727. (2005).

Segal, S. P. (2022). Protecting health and safety with needed treatment: The effectiveness of outpatient commitment. *The Psychiatric Quarterly, 93*(1), 55–79. https://doi.org/10.1007/s11126-020-09876-6

Substance Abuse and Mental Health Services Administration (SAMSA). (2019). *Civil commitment and the mental health care continuum: Historical trends and principles for law and practice.* https://www.samhsa.gov/sites/default/files/civil-commitment-continuum-of-care.pdf

Simon, S. I. (2006). The myth of "imminent" violence in psychiatry and the law. *University of Cincinnati Law Review, 75*(2), 631–643.

Sutherland, E. (1950). The diffusion of sexual psychopath laws. *The American Journal of Sociology, 56*(2), 142–148. https://doi.org/10.1086/220695

Swanson, J. W., Swartz, M. S., Borum, R., Hiday, V. A., Wagner, H. R., & Burns, B. J. (2000). Involuntary out-patient commitment and reduction of violent behaviour in persons with severe mental illness. *The British Journal of Psychiatry, 176*, 324–331. https://doi.org/10.1192/bjp.176.4.324

Treatment Advocacy Center. (2020). *Grading the states: An analysis of involuntary psychiatric treatment laws 2020.* https://www.treatmentadvocacycenter.org/reports_publications/grading-the-states-an-analysis-of-involuntary-psychiatric-treatment-laws-2020/

Tewksbury, R. (2005). Collateral consequences of sex offender registration. *Journal of Contemporary Criminal Justice, 21*(1), 67–81. https://doi.org/10.1177/1043986204271704

Tewksbury, R., & Lees, M. (2006). Perceptions of sex offender registration: Collateral consequences and community experiences. *Sociological Spectrum, 26*(3), 309–334. https://doi.org/10.1080/02732170500524246

The Violent Crime Control and Law Enforcement Act, 42 U.S.C. 14141. (1994).

Westerheide v. State, 767 So. 2d 637, 642, Fla. Dist. Ct. App. (2000).

Winerip, M. (1999a, May 23). Bedlam on the streets. *The New York Times Magazine.* https://www.nytimes.com/1999/05/23/magazine/bedlam-on-the-streets.html

Winerip, M. (1999b, October 18). Oddity and normality vie in subway killer's confession. *The New York Times.* https://www.nytimes.com/1999/10/18/nyregion/oddity-and-normality-vie-in-subway-killer-s-confession.html

Zgoba, K. M. (2011). Residence restriction buffer zones and the banishment of sex offenders: Have we gone one step too far? *Criminology & Public Policy, 10*(2), 391–400. https://doi.org/10.1111/capp.2011.10.issue-2

Zgoba, K. M., & Simon, L. M. J. (2005). Recidivism rates of sexual offenders up to 7 years later: Does treatment matter? *Criminal Justice Review, 30*(2), 155–173. https://doi.org/10.1177/0734016805284146

Zgoba, K. M., Veysey, B. M., & Dalessandro, M. (2010). An analysis of the effectiveness of community notification and registration: Do the best intentions predict the best practices? *Justice Quarterly, 27*(5), 667–691. https://doi.org/10.1080/07418820903357673

16

Correctional Facilities and Capital Punishment—Addressing Civil and Human Rights Among Individuals with Mental Illnesses, Substance Use Disorders, and Neurodevelopmental Disabilities

Learning Objectives

After this chapter, readers should be able to understand the:

(1) Prevalence of those with mental illnesses, substance use disorders, and disabilities in correctional institutions.
(2) Vulnerabilities and victimization risks for those with disabilities and mental illnesses.
(3) Available mental health and substance use treatment services.
(4) Extent of protective custody use and concerns for those with disabilities and mental illnesses.
(5) History of case law covering the eligibility and application of capital punishment for those with mental illnesses, intellectual disability, and juveniles.

Introduction

The correctional system is responsible for overseeing the well-being and supervision of those who have been arrested for, charged with, or convicted of criminal offenses. High percentages of incarcerated individuals have mental illnesses, substance use disorders (SUDs), or disabilities, creating various challenges for correctional professionals in meeting their health and supervision

M. C. Mogavero, *Mental Health, Neurodiversity, and Criminal Justice*, https://doi.org/10.1007/978-3-031-88816-8_16

needs. Nearly 200 years ago, social reformer Dorothea Dix pleaded for those with mental illnesses to be removed from jails or prisons after documenting her observations of inhumane treatment. Her efforts resulted in the establishment of psychiatric hospitals throughout the United States (US). With the advancements in medical treatment, policy changes, and increased civil rights for those with mental illnesses and disabilities, hospitals began closing in favor of community-based services. Unfortunately, the community mental health care system was unable to meet their needs, resulting in many individuals with mental illnesses experiencing homelessness, misusing illegal substances, and encountering the CJS (*see* Chapter 7 of this book for details).

The number of individuals with mental illnesses in the CJS began to increase, and by the late 1990s, the US Department of Justice (DOJ) reported that about 16% of incarcerated individuals in prison and jail had a mental illness (Ditton, 1999). By 2010, three jails held more people with mental illnesses than any psychiatric hospital: (1) Los Angeles County Jail in California, (2) Rikers Island Jail in New York, NY, and (3) Cook County Jail in Chicago, Illinois (Torrey et al., 2010). Advocates warned that correctional facilities have essentially replaced hospitals for institutionalized care and treatment, and the situation was only getting worse (Torrey et al., 2014). According to the most recent estimates by the DOJ, 43% incarcerated in state prisons, 23% in federal prisons, and 44% in jails have a mental illness (Bronson & Berzofsky, 2017; Maruschak et al., 2021). The rate of incarcerated individuals with SUDs is also alarmingly high, with an estimated 58% in state prisons and 63% in jails (Bronson et al., 2017).

No comprehensive research to date has been published on the prevalence of neurodiverse individuals incarcerated in the US. However, according to the most recent report published by the DOJ, high rates of incarcerated individuals have reported a cognitive disability.[2] Approximately 20% of those in prisons and 20%–30% in jails have reported a cognitive disability, compared to an estimated 5% of the general population. Those with cognitive disabilities also reported experiencing co-occurring mental health symptoms, where 33% of those in prison and 47% of those in jail reported experiencing severe psychological distress within the last month (Bronson & Berzofsky, 2015).

History of Institution Conditions and Treatment Reforms

For most of US history, the judicial system focused on protecting the rights of persons accused of a crime rather than those convicted. They were viewed as "outlaws" without legally protected constitutional rights where the government followed a "hands-off doctrine" and did not intervene with correctional administration (Vogelman, 1968). This changed in the 1960s after increased attention to civil rights and rising crime rates. President Lyndon Johnson (1908–1973) initiated a Commission on Law Enforcement and Administration of Justice. The Commission addressed various areas, including correctional reform and rehabilitation. The 342-page report published in 1967, *The Challenge of Crime in a Free Society*, noted the conditions inside correctional facilities were "unspeakably brutal and degrading" (p. 159), and the lack of programming left individuals "aimless loitering in corridors or yards" (p. 164). The Commission recommended increasing resources to alternatives to incarceration (e.g., probation and parole), improving facility conditions, and improving screening and treatment for those with mental illnesses or SUDs to address their individual programming needs (President's Commission on Law Enforcement and Administration of Justice, 1967).

Unfortunately, the recommendations were not fully implemented, and the poor treatment and conditions inside correctional facilities continued. In the 1970s, formal investigations were launched, which exposed the deplorable conditions inside some facilities. In 1972, the American Civil Liberties Union investigated the intake procedures, living conditions, and disciplinary practices in a Washington, D.C., jail. The 52 page report noted inadequate screening process, delayed medical care, lack of due process in disciplinary hearings, and overcrowded and unsanitary living conditions (Powledge, 1972). In 1973, The American Medical Association (AMA) surveyed 1,159 county sheriffs to assess areas needing improvement and reported that overall healthcare was lacking; most jails only had first aid facilities, and most did not have regularly scheduled on-call physicians (Steinwald & Alevizon, 1973). In 1982, The National Institute of Corrections (NIC) surveyed 2,664 jail administrators and sheriffs and reported that many jails were overcrowded, lacked security, and lacked medical and mental health care. The NIC also noted that many jails were in such poor condition that they could not even maintain minimal fire, health, and sanitation standards (Kerle & Ford, 1982).

Federal courts began hearing cases filed by incarcerated individuals claiming abuse, neglect, and a lack of medical and mental health care. The cases claimed the conditions and treatment amounted to violations of Eighth Amendment protections against cruel and unusual punishments and the Fourteenth Amendment's equal protection by depriving a class of citizens (i.e., incarcerated individuals) of minimal standards of care. In Newman v. Alabama (1972), those incarcerated within the Alabama Correctional System claimed they were deprived of adequate medical treatment and basic medical needs. Complaints included understaffed medical facilities, correctional staff denying exams and treatment, and refusing to administer prescribed medications. The US District Court decided in favor of the incarcerated individuals that the inadequate medical care and treatment violated the Eighth and Fourteenth Amendments and ordered the Board of Corrections to undertake extensive changes.

Although the US Constitution does not guarantee the right to health care, the US Supreme Court decision in Estelle v. Gamble (1976) held that states must provide basic human needs to incarcerated individuals. While incarcerated in a Texas prison, J.W. Gamble was injured after a 600-lb bale of cotton fell on him while he was unloading a truck. When he was forced to return to work duty while he was still in pain, Gamble filed a civil rights violation against Estelle, the Director of the Department of Corrections, and other staff. The Court ruled that a "deliberate indifference" to one's serious medical needs is a violation of the Eighth Amendment. Despite the ruling in Estelle v. Gamble, many more cases were filed in Federal Courts, citing similar grievances, including unsanitary conditions, lack of medical care, and physical abuse.

In response to the increase in litigations, President William J. Clinton signed the Prison Litigation Reform Act (PLRA) on April 26, 1996. PLRA requires incarcerated individuals to allow correction officials to remedy grievances with procedural steps that individuals must strictly follow. Incarcerated individuals must first exhaust all the administrative remedies available before filing a lawsuit. In practice, the PLRA made it more difficult for individuals to challenge conditions or treatment in court. Nonetheless, lawsuits continued, including the New Jersey case, D.M v. Terhune (1999), which drastically changed how the New Jersey Department of Corrections (DOC) handles incarcerated individuals with mental illnesses. On April 11, 1996, D.M. and four other incarcerated individuals filed a lawsuit in the US District Court, District of New Jersey, claiming violations of the **Americans with Disabilities Act** (ADA) (1990) for unlawfully denying treatment and medication. The settlement appropriated $16 million to fund mental health treatment and implement dozens of requirements, including the DOC maintaining rosters of those with mental health conditions or taking psychotropic medications, having specialized treatment units, implementing treatment plans, and providing mental health training for correctional officers. They were also required to institute policies for disciplinary procedures, including the use of force for those on the roster and medication administration procedures (D.M. v. Terhune, 1999).

Box 16.1: Practitioner Spotlight: Major Luis R. Soto

Major Luis Soto worked in corrections for more than 25 years and spent most of his career in the administration at Northern State Prison, a medium-security facility outside Newark, New Jersey. He worked as a correctional officer for eight years before being promoted to sergeant, lieutenant, and then the highest position, Security and Administrative Major. As Major, Soto oversaw 700 staff members and ensured they were trained under the guidelines in the D.M. v. Terhune settlement. Soto also supervised the specialized units that housed those with mental illnesses. According to Soto, what is most important for those working in corrections to know is that being strict and authoritative is not the best way to manage those with mental illnesses.

Soto saw firsthand the way those with mental illnesses were treated before the DOC was forced to implement the strategic changes outlined in Terhune. Before the settlement, when incarcerated individuals with mental illnesses engaged in behavioral infractions, they were treated as any other, including force or chemical sprays, which worsened their condition. Those with mental illnesses have more difficulty coping in the demanding prison environment, so it is important to take a collaborative approach by working closely with mental health professionals. In one case, a man with schizophrenia refused to take his prescribed medications, his mental health deteriorated, and he became aggressive toward correctional staff. Instead of immediately resorting to force, the trained staff spoke to him calmly and de-escalated the situation by offering him a seat and a drink of water. He was then escorted to a stabilization unit and met with the psychiatrist, who was able to successfully administer medication. If it had not been for the highly skilled and attentive correctional staff, adequate availability of mental health services, and their collaborative efforts, this situation could have been met with vastly different results.

Treatment and Support Services

With the growing number of individuals with mental illnesses in need of treatment in correctional facilities, on October 30, 2004, President George W. Bush signed the Mentally Ill Offender Treatment and Crime Reduction Act. The Act authorized the Justice and Mental Health Collaboration Program (JMHCP), which allocated funding to various programs, including training for law enforcement and other CJS practitioners, treatment programs for incarcerated individuals, and reentry programs to transition back into society. With correction-based programming, treatment goals typically empower individuals to manage their symptoms and improve their psychosocial adjustment. Options include but are not limited to, individual or group psychotherapy or counseling, SUD programs, peer-support programs, and prescription medications. According to the most recent report by the DOJ, among those receiving mental health services, 52% in federal and 42% in state prisons were prescribed medication, 46% in federal and 41% in state prisons received counseling, and 21% in federal and 19% in state prisons participated in self-help or peer groups (Reingle Gonzalez & Connell, 2014).

Although the availability of correction-based treatment programming has increased, participation varies on several factors, including eligibility, screening procedures, co-occurring mental illness and SUD, and the availability of resources and staff (Meyer et al., 2014; van Wormer & Persson, 2010). All incarcerated individuals with mental illnesses and disabilities are protected under the ADA and Sect. 504 of the Rehabilitation Act of 1973. However, this does not guarantee the right to programming, but those with disabilities or mental illness cannot be excluded from or denied from programming based on discrimination (Dlugacz, 2018). Others may refuse to participate in treatment for various reasons. Some may hide or deny their condition due to the stigma associated with mental illnesses or disabilities. Some may refuse treatment services for fear of being portrayed as weak or vulnerable to other incarcerated individuals (Haney, 2006). However, prescription medications can be involuntarily administered if considered medically necessary and individuals are deemed a danger to themselves or others.

Substance Use Treatment

Considering the high percentage of incarcerated individuals with SUDs, small percentages receive treatment, with 26% of those in state and 19% in federal prisons reporting participating in a program. Of those who received treatment, self-help groups or peer counseling was most common, reported by 16% of those in state prisons and 10% of those in jails (Bronson et al., 2017). Effective medications to treat opiate use disorder (OUD) withdrawal symptoms, referred to as **opioid antagonists,** include naloxone, naltrexone, buprenorphine, and methadone (Lim et al., 2023; Schwartzapfel, 2017). Heroin/opiates are highly addictive substances with severe withdrawal effects (*see* Chapter 3 of this book for details). Unfortunately, most jails in the US do not provide opioid antagonists such as methadone and buprenorphine (Lim et al., 2023). A DOJ report noted that few received **detoxification** (1%) or opioid antagonists (0.4%–0.6%) for OUD (Bronson et al., 2017).

Untreated withdrawal symptoms for those with OUD can have dangerous consequences for newly incarcerated individuals (Fiscella et al., 2004). Individuals are also at increased risk of fatal overdose upon release (Scavone, 2022). However, methadone and buprenorphine treatment during incarceration has been shown to be associated with an 80% reduction in fatal overdose risk during the first month post-release (Lim et al., 2023). Although there may be challenges with implementing methadone and buprenorphine treatment programs in US jails and prisons, evaluations have shown they can be implemented successfully (Bandara et al., 2021).

Benefits of Treatment

Correctional institutions were designed to segregate, supervise, and control incarcerated individuals and were not designed nor intended to be therapeutic environments conducive to clinical care and treatment. Correction-based mental health programs have shown, in general, to have little effect on recidivism reduction post-release, but results vary depending on one's psychological and social functioning, motivation level, and time in treatment (Beaudry et al., 2021). Correction-based SUD treatment programs, on the other hand, have demonstrated more positive impacts. Welsh (2010) examined SUD treatment outcomes among 347 individuals who participated in a prison-based program over 12 months. On average, the participants reported significant reductions in attitudes toward risk-taking, external pressures (e.g., peer pressure), and increases in treatment motivation and engagement.

Participating in prison-based SUD treatment has also been shown to reduce disciplinary infractions. Taylor et al. (2019) reviewed Department of Corrections data on 4,622 individuals, comparing correction-based SUD treatment participation and the number of misconduct reports, and showed that participation resulted in an 18%–23% decrease in misconduct. Participation in correction-based SUD treatment has also been shown to reduce recidivism. However, results may vary by treatment modality, individual characteristics (Welsh et al., 2014), and treatment climate (e.g., program structure, counselor rapport, counselor competence) (Kelly & Welsh, 2016). Kelly et al. (2019) examined 618 participants in 12 different treatment groups within a Pennsylvania prison and compared reincarceration rates within three years post-release. Their results showed that participating in SUD treatment significantly reduced the odds of reincarceration, with similar results among the different treatment modalities (e.g., group treatment vs. treatment in a separate housing unit) (Kelly et al., 2019).

Additional Problems and Considerations

Jails and prisons were by no means intended to be pleasant or comfortable, and all incarcerated individuals are vulnerable to the harsh conditions. However, some individuals with mental illnesses and disabilities are particularly vulnerable, which raises additional problems to address. With correctional officers significantly outnumbered, maintaining order is a priority, and correctional facilities typically require all incarcerated individuals to follow and adhere to the same rules and strict regimens. However, some may be unable to understand or adhere to rules due to their cognitive limitations or exhibit uncontrollable behaviors due to their condition. Although incarcerated individuals with and without mental illnesses engage in rule violations and other behavioral problems, a DOJ report showed higher percentages of those with mental illnesses violating facility rules in state prisons (58% vs. 43%) and in jails (19% vs. 9%). The report also showed higher rates of physical or verbal assaults exhibited by those with mental illnesses compared to those without, both in state prisons (24% vs. 14%) and in jails (8% vs. 2%) (James & Glaze, 2006).

Increased Risk of Self-injury and Suicide

Those with mental illnesses and SUDs are at increased risk of **self-injury behavior** (SIB), suicide attempts, or death by suicide, placing additional strains on already limited resources in correctional institutions (Smith & Kaminski, 2010). SIB is the deliberate destruction or alteration of the body tissue without suicide intent (e.g., cutting, scratching, or burning the skin) (Favazza & Rosenthal, 1993). A nationwide survey of mental health directors in 39 state and federal prisons showed that among those who engaged in SIB, 16% had a mental illness that affected mood, such as major depressive disorder, 8% had a psychotic disorder, and 3% had an intellectual disability (ID) or autism (Appelbaum et al., 2011). Little is known about the SIB and risks among incarcerated individuals with neurodevelopmental disabilities (NDDs) in the US. However, Chaplin et al. (2017) compared incarcerated individuals with ID and other learning disabilities to those without an NDD in a London prison and noted that those with ID had higher rates of SIB (3% vs. 1%) or survived suicide attempts (3% vs. 0%).

Correctional staff may misinterpret SIB as attention-seeking or manipulation. A survey of 54 correctional mental health staff revealed that 91% perceived the SIB was to receive special treatment or move to another facility, and 28% believed it was to intimidate others (DeHart et al., 2009). For some,

SIB was the result of prior requests for mental health assistance being ignored (Dlugacz, 2018). Those who engage in SIB and those who attempt suicide are not always mutually exclusive, as those who engage in SIB may also be at risk for death by suicide (Dear et al., 2000). DeHart et al. (2009) noted as many as one-third of those who engaged in SIBs survived suicide attempts. Risk factors for suicide differ by condition; alcohol use disorder has been shown to double the risk, and a psychiatric diagnosis increases the risk of suicide by more than six times (Zhong et al., 2021).

Increased Physical and Sexual Violence Victimization Risk

Violent and sexual victimization among incarcerated individuals have been persistent problems inside jails and prisons. A survey of 18,185 incarcerated individuals in state and federal prisons shows that about 13% reported victimization, and 4% of them were severely injured (e.g., stab wounds, broken bones) (Pare & Logan, 2011). According to the most recent DOJ report, there were 36,264 allegations of sexual victimization in prisons, jails, and other adult correctional facilities in 2020, with 6.5% of them substantiated (Buehler & Kottke-Weaver, 2024). Physical and sexual victimization risk is higher among those with mental illnesses. A DOJ report indicated that a higher percentage of those with a mental illness compared to those without have been injured by physical violence in prison (20% vs. 10%) (James & Glaze, 2006). Wolff et al. (2007) surveyed incarcerated individuals (6.964 men, 564 women) in 13 New Jersey prisons about experiencing sexual victimization within the last six months. They reported that sexual victimization by other incarcerated individuals was more common among those with mental illnesses than those without, both among men (15% vs. 9%) and women (27% vs. 21%).

To address the ongoing problem of sexual violence, on September 4, 2003, President George W. Bush signed the Prison Rape Elimination Act (PREA). A product of the PREA was the Protecting Inmates and Safeguarding Communities Discretionary Grant Program (2004), which allocated $20 million to states to address sexual abuse in correctional facilities. The PREA also included a Commission that undertook a five-year study, and the national report indicated that those with mental illnesses and other disabilities were at increased risk for sexual assault (National PREA Commission Report, 2009). The Commission made specific recommendations to protect individuals at risk, improved the procedures for individuals to report sexual assaults, for facilities to document the assaults, and required the DOJ to publish annual reports. Despite these efforts, sexual victimization continues, with an increase in allegations since 2013 and the rates of substantiated cases remaining stable (Buehler & Kottke-Weaver, 2024).

Physical and sexual victimization can also lead to post-traumatic stress disorder (PTSD). Schappell et al. (2016) surveyed 100 formerly incarcerated men and found that among those with no prior mental illness, many who experienced victimization had PTSD. Experiencing or exposure to violence in correctional facilities generates a state of constant fear, which can create mental health problems or worsen existing conditions. The chronic and prolonged stress one endures while incarcerated can lead to depression, apathy, and a sense of hopelessness (Haney, 2006).

Use of Segregation Units

Segregation involves separating individuals from the general prison population. Three forms of segregation are used for various reasons: disciplinary, administrative, and protective custody (PC). Segregation can also include solitary confinement (SC), which is one of the most controversial practices. The sole use of SC and sensory isolation was customary practice in the eighteenth and early nineteenth centuries until the extreme isolation resulted in mental health deterioration and suicide (*see* Chapter 5 of this book for details). Although SC conditions vary across jurisdictions and institutions, they generally refer to individuals confined to their cells for 22–24 hours a day, with little or no contact with others (McLeod & Martin, 2020). Correctional staff may use SC as a punishment or disciplinary segregation, viewed as a "prison within a prison" (Miller & McCoy, 2013).

Incarcerated individuals may also be placed in restricted environments of PC or a special housing unit (SHU), usually when they are at risk of harm by other incarcerated individuals or are being threatened. Incarcerated individuals may also request placement in PC or SHU if they fear they may be harmed in the general population, which is usually granted if they are indeed at risk. Incarcerated individuals convicted of sexual offenses are often placed in PC for their protection (Miller & McCoy, 2013). According to Holmes and Holmes (2009), those who commit sexual offenses, particularly against children, are deemed to be lowest in the prison status hierarchy and are vulnerable to physical attacks by other incarcerated individuals. Others placed in PC include those with mental illnesses or disabilities, as they are more susceptible to abuse. Incarcerated individuals may also be placed in segregation for administrative purposes, for instance, while they investigate a situation or whether they pose a serious threat to the order of operation or security of the facility (e.g., threat to property or other individuals) (Miller & McCoy, 2013). Below is a case of an individual who was at high victimization risk and was placed in PC after his attack, which later led to mental health problems.

Case of Charlie[3]

Background: Charlie was 18 years old when he was charged with two counts of aggravated sexual assault and endangering the welfare of a child. He was raised with both parents and had one brother, who was ten years older and no longer lived at home. In grade school, he was academically behind his classmates, was assessed and diagnosed with ID. Recent cognitive evaluations have validated this diagnosis, with an IQ of 68. He had no criminal history, no history of SUD, and no evidence of any past physical or sexual abuse. At the time of his arrest, he was still attending public high school and receiving an individualized education program.

Instant Offense: Charlie was left alone briefly to watch his seven-year-old female cousin who was there visiting. The eight-year-old daughter of his neighbors was also at the house, as she often came to the home when his cousin visited. According to Charlie, he was curious about what the girls were like "down there." Charlie told them to undress, and he touched their genital areas, penetrating them. Immediately afterward, his young neighbor went home and told her mother what happened because she felt pain in her genital area; her mother called the police.

Outcome: Charlie's parents were home when police arrived to investigate the complaint. The police read Charlie the Miranda warning, and he waived his rights and agreed to speak with the officer. During questioning, Charlie admitted to the police what he had done and explained he wanted to know what the girls' "were like." When police explained that his actions were against the law, he became confused and did not understand why it was wrong. Charlie believed that because he was at home (i.e., not in public), he was free to do what he wanted.

Charlie was charged with two counts of sexual assault and felony endangering the welfare of a child. At the request of his defense attorney, the judge ordered a competency evaluation, and Charlie was found competent to stand trial. Because of the nature of the offense, the age of the victims, and appearing to have no "remorse" for his actions, the prosecutor would not accept a plea deal that would not include a prison sentence. In consultation with Charlie's parents, his defense attorney recommended that he accept the plea deal, as he would potentially face a longer prison sentence with a trial. Charlie accepted the plea, and the judge sentenced him to 16 months in prison and five years of probation.

Prison Experience: Charlie's cognitive disabilities and his sexual offense conviction made him particularly vulnerable to torment and abuse by others. While using the restroom, he was sexually assaulted by two incarcerated individuals with the end of a mop handle, which caused considerable damage to his rectum and required emergency medical care and surgery. After this incident, Charlie was placed in protective custody to prevent future victimization. Shortly after, he developed symptoms of depression and anxiety and would break down crying whenever he saw someone with a mop, a broom, or an object that resembled either. Charlie's symptoms persisted, and he was later diagnosed with PTSD.

Concerns with the Use of Segregation Units

The use of strict SC in prisons has raised civil and human rights concerns. *The United Nations Standard Minimum Rules of the Treatment of Prisoners,* referred to as the Nelson Mandela Rules (2015), prohibit prolonged SC exceeding 15 consecutive days (rule 43.1b). Similarly, the National Commission on Correctional Health Care (2016) issued a series of principles concerning the ethical use of SC and included a statement that any longer than 15 days is cruel, inhumane, and degrading, particularly for those with mental illnesses. Unfortunately, this practice continues in some states. A 2022 report titled *Punishment of People with Serious Mental Illness in New York State Prisons* analyzed disciplinary data from 2017–2019. The results showed that those receiving mental health treatment were sanctioned with SC periods exceeding 15 days and punished for conduct that was related to their underlying condition, citing Black and Latino individuals were overrepresented (Punishment of People with Serious Mental Illness in New York State Prisons, 2022).

The use of SC has also been linked to mental health deterioration among those with and without preexisting mental illnesses (Haney, 2006). Haney (2003) warned that long-term social isolation often leads to social withdrawal and apathy, and Haney (2006) later cautioned that those placed in long-term SC are at increased risk for developing symptoms of mental illness. Adverse effects of SC may also result from restrictions in treatment and program participation. In a review of research evaluating the psychological effects of SC, Arrigo and Bullock (2008) suggested that those with a current or a history of mental illness be excluded from punitive segregation and those exhibiting disruptive behaviors stemming from a mental illness be managed in a secure unit designed to provide treatment.

Experience for Autistic Individuals

Autistic individuals[4] have various difficulties in the prison environment, which are compounded when they have co-occurring mental illnesses. Young et al. (2018) reported that among the 33 autistic individuals incarcerated in a Scotland prison, high percentages experienced mental health symptoms such as anxiety (74%) and paranoia (73%). The limitations of social and communication skills can also make navigating the social environment in prison exceedingly problematic. Robertson and McGillivray (2015) reviewed the research regarding incarcerated autistic individuals and noted problems with adapting to the physical and social environment, including increased risk of victimization, social isolation, and behavioral problems. A review of 14 studies of autistic individuals in hospitals or prisons (outside the US) noted higher rates of SIB, disruptive, and violent behavior (Peraire et al., 2023). Newman et al. (2015) interviewed eight autistic individuals incarcerated in an Australian prison, and one stated he experienced anxiety because he was aware he was different from others, which made him a target for abuse. Another reported he was consistently physically abused and explained, "(prison is) real hard (because of) prisoners standing over me and bashing me up all the time" (Newman et al., 2015, p. 636). Vinter et al. (2023) interviewed seven autistic incarcerated individuals in a United Kingdom (UK) prison and noted that social interactions, sometimes due to misunderstanding social cues, can escalate into physical altercations. One described a situation with another incarcerated individual resulting from miscommunication. "… I misread a situation, and he was, kind of, angry and, kind of, frustrated… he elbowed me in the eye, and cut all my eye open, …" (Vinter et al., 2023, p. 251).

Some incarcerated autistic individuals choose to remain isolated in their cells to avoid social interaction, to protect themselves from others, or to cope with social rejection (Newman et al., 2015). Allely and Wood (2020) described a case of an incarcerated autistic man named C.T. in a UK prison. When he was first incarcerated, he reported that he experienced "several attacks, threats of violence, and psychological intimidation" (p. 62). Ten years into his sentence, he spent most of his time isolated in his cell and claimed, "The best way to do your time here is to mind your own business and have as little to do with other prisoners as possible" (p. 62). Patterson (2008) detailed the experiences of two young autistic men, "Michael" and "Paul," incarcerated in a UK prison. Michael had several mental illnesses, including depression, psychosis, and SIB. He reported difficult interactions with others that resulted in disciplinary actions, and therefore, he remains in his cell during the daytime. On the other hand, Paul reported that he interacted well with others and had many "friends." According to staff, these "friendships" were superficial, and Paul appeared oblivious when others ridiculed him. Staff also reported having to intervene several times to prevent him from being bullied (Paterson, 2008).

Considering incarcerated individuals have little to no control over their physical environment, exposure to excessive amounts of stimuli (e.g., hypersensitivity to light, smells, sounds, and touch) can cause sensory overload for autistic individuals, increasing anxiety and behavioral problems. C.T., the autistic man incarcerated in the UK, reported that many of the common daily sensory stimuli in prison would trigger his anxiety, including the loud banging of unlocking/locking cell doors, jangling keys, high-pitched smoke and cell emergency alarms, and the constant smells of aftershave, cologne/perfume (Allely & Wood, 2020). Eisner (2020) authored an article for the Marshal Project titled *Prison Is Even Worse When You Have a Disability Like Autism*. Eisner described the sensory overload experiences of an autistic man, Drew. The common daily sensory stimuli in prison were so unbearable that he would cover the fluorescent bulbs with toothpaste or paper and wrap his uniform around his head to mask overwhelming odors. For some autistic individuals, the sensory overload in the prison environment amounts to one that is borderline torturous.

Capital Punishment

Capital punishment (i.e., the death penalty) is arguably one of the most controversial practices. The Federal Government still uses the death penalty, but it is banned in 23 states and the District of Columbia, and five states have an executive pause on all executions. The reasons for banning include Eighth Amendment violations against cruel and unusual punishments, concerns of potential innocence, and the high financial costs (Death Penalty Information Center, [DPIC], 2024; Kaplan et al., 2016). For example, in Oregon, a cost analysis revealed that death sentence cases ranged between $800,000 and $1,000,000 more per case compared to similar non-death sentence cases (Kaplan et al., 2016). Oregon currently has a moratorium on executions. Death sentences make up a minority of incarcerated individuals in prisons. With approximately 1,190,000 incarcerated in prisons and approximately 2,300 awaiting a death sentence, they comprise about 0.19% of the prison population (DPIC, 2024).

According to the most recent data from the DPIC, most (98%) of those awaiting execution are men. Black individuals are also overrepresented, comprising 32% of all sentenced individuals in state and federal prisons (Carson & Kluckow, 2023) but 41% of those awaiting execution (DPIC, 2024; Snell, 2021). Carrying out the sentences is also relatively rare, and the number of individuals executed has declined by 71% since 2000. Recent data shows 21 individuals were executed in 2022 and 2023, and 25 in 2024 (DPIC, 2024).

Mental Status and Eligibility

While incarcerated individuals are awaiting their death sentence, they are often isolated from the general population, excluded from various prison programs, and may spend as much as 23 hours a day in their cells. Many spend more than a decade awaiting their sentence to be carried out, and currently, more than half have been waiting nearly two decades. The isolation and uncertainty can lead to the deterioration of one's mental health or exacerbate one's mental illness (DPIC, 2024). The US has no categorical ban on capital punishment for people with mental illnesses, although several states have laws that exempt those with severe mental illnesses (DPIC, 2024; Equal Justice Initiative, 2024). In the Ford v. Wainwright (1986) decision, the US Supreme Court limited carrying out executions among those with mental illness who are considered incompetent to understand the nature and reason for the execution.

Case Brief: Ford v. Wainwright (1986)

Facts: Alvin Bernard Ford was convicted and sentenced to death for the murder of a Florida police officer in 1974. No issues of insanity or competency were raised during pretrial hearings, at trial, or the sentencing hearing. In 1982, Ford experienced delusions of working with the Ku Klux Klan, a White supremacist hate group and believed he had become a target of a conspiracy involving the Klan. Ford also began referring to himself as Pope John Paul III. He was evaluated and treated by Dr. Jamal Amim, who concluded that Ford had delusions consistent with schizophrenia. Ford's attorney claimed that because he no longer understood why he was being executed, the sentence should not be carried out. After a brief evaluation, the Florida governor signed Ford's death warrant. His attorney petitioned the Federal District Court to stay the execution, and the court declined to hear the case. His attorney petitioned Ford's case to the US Supreme Court.

Issue: Whether executing individuals with mental illness who do not understand why they are being executed violates the Eighth Amendment and the due process clause of the Fourteenth Amendment.

Outcome: The US Supreme Court ruled that carrying out the death penalty upon one who no longer understands why they are being executed was a violation of the Eighth and Fourteenth Amendments. Justice Marshall added that executing a person who is mentally incompetent was "savage and inhumane." The Court held that one must undergo a mental competency evaluation and hearing, as executing someone incompetent would not serve any punishment goals.

Competency to be executed raises many ethical and human rights concerns for courts to address. One issue is whether one can be involuntarily medicated to restore competency. This practice was permitted in the Federal Court case in Arizona, Singleton v. Norris (2003). The AMA Code of Ethics opinion permits court-initiated medication so long as it is "therapeutically efficacious" (AMA, 2017). The interpretation of competency to be executed in the Ford decision was that only a factual understanding was required, a lesser standard than competency to stand trial, which requires both a factual and rational understanding (*see* Chapter 11 of this book for details). The issue of whether one requires a rational understanding was raised in Panetti v. Quarterman (2007). The US Supreme Court ruled that a rational understanding of the execution was not required, but one must be aware of it. The US Supreme Court later decided in Madison v. Alabama (2019) that competency required a rational understanding. Vernon Madison was convicted and sentenced to death for the murder of an Alabama police officer in 1985. While incarcerated for nearly 30 years, he experienced several strokes, was diagnosed with a major vascular neurological disorder, and had no memory of the murder. In 2016, a stay of execution was petitioned because he became incompetent. The Court decided that having no memory of the crime does not necessarily make one incompetent but ruled one must rationally understand the reason for the execution.

Intellectual Disability

The US Supreme Court placed a categorical ban on the eligibility of capital punishment for those with ID, which was decided in the US Supreme Court case Atkins v. Virginia (2002). However, ID is a social construct (Rapley, 2004), and a diagnosis is determined using a variety of clinical assessments and judgments (*see* Chapter 2 of this book for details). Accurately diagnosing ID among incarcerated adults can be challenging because of difficulties gathering past records, discrepancies over the timeline when ID characteristics first occurred, and difficulties assessing abnormal behavior in restricted prison environments. To further complicate matters, the US Supreme Court did not define what constitutes ID in the Atkins ruling, only noting a definition where there is a national consensus. Therefore, states are free to adopt definitions that may vary in wording and, thus, eligibility to be executed (Everingon & Olley, 2008).

In earlier versions of the Diagnostic and Statistical Manual of Mental Disorders, an IQ of 70 was the cut-off for an ID diagnosis (*see* Chapter 2 of this book for details). However, the sole and arbitrary use of an IQ score to determine eligibility for the death penalty was decided by the US Supreme Court case Hall v. Florida (2014). In 1978, Freddie Lee Hall was convicted of rape in Florida and sentenced to death. After the Atkins decision, Hall, with an IQ of 71, appealed his sentence. Florida's statute mandated that one must have an IQ of 70 or below to present evidence of ID. Due to a **margin of error** with IQ tests (i.e., the statistical range where actual IQ may fall), the US Supreme Court decided Florida's mandatory 70 IQ cutoff violated the Eighth Amendment, and states must use other evidence when IQ scores range between 70 and 75. Unfortunately, due to several factors, including poor legal representation and errors in evidentiary requirements, those with ID are still sentenced to death and executed (Death Penalty Information Center, 2024).

Juveniles

Some juveniles are handled in the adult court system and sentenced as adults (*see* Chapter 6 of this book for details). In Stanford v. Kentucky (1989), the US Supreme Court decided capital punishment for those convicted of murder who were 16 or 17 years of age at the time did not violate the Eighth Amendment. This decision was challenged in Roper v. Simmons (2005). In 1993, 17-year-old Christopher Simmons was convicted of the murder of Shirly Crook and sentenced to death in Missouri. After the Atkins decision, his sentence was appealed to the US Supreme Court. The American Psychological Association and the Missouri Psychological Association submitted a **writ of certiorari** (i.e., petition) on behalf of Simmons, detailing recent research on adolescent behavior and neuropsychology, providing established scientific evidence that adolescents lack full mental capacity. The Court decided that executing those who were 17 years or younger at the time of the offense was a violation of the Eighth Amendment. This decision was partly due to research advancements in neuroscience and adolescent brain development (*see* Chapter 4 of this book for details).

Considerations and Recommendations

To ensure fair and just treatment of those with mental illnesses, SUDs, and disabilities, correctional staff require several resources to perform their professional duties effectively and ethically. Correctional institutions are stressful environments for those incarcerated and staff. Below are several areas to consider and practical recommendations to improve services for all those involved, leaving incarcerated individuals better prepared to reenter the community.

Training for Correctional Officers

Overcrowding and the influx of people with disabilities, mental illnesses, and SUDs, especially when experiencing symptoms, can be challenging for officers to manage. Most (81%) of correctional officers reported that having to deal with those with mental illnesses added more stress to their jobs (Lavoie et al., 2006). Added stress can not only lead to negative perceptions of those with mental illnesses and SUDs but can also lead to burnout, which involves emotional exhaustion and **depersonalization** (i.e., disconnection from others or environment) (Lavoie et al., 2006). Lavoie et al. revealed that mental health training among officers improved perceptions of people with mental illnesses. Providing correctional officers with additional knowledge and training can allow them to be better able to detect signs of mental distress so they can intervene before their condition deteriorates. Trained staff have the skills to not only identify when one's condition is deteriorating but also when one, with no history of mental health problems, begins to develop them. Major Soto acknowledges that the harsh prison environment can lead individuals to develop mental health problems among those with no prior history (personal communication, November 18, 2024). Correctional officers should also receive interactive training to better understand autism and ID and prevent misidentifying associated behaviors with defiance. Training may also help improve communication and support individuals throughout their incarceration (Allely & Wood, 2022; Chaplin, 2017).

Improve Correctional Mental Health Screening and Services

Some incarcerated individuals require rehabilitation and treatment to stabilize their mental health or to prevent their condition from worsening. Although the JMHCP allocated funding for treatment programs, only a small fraction was allocated specifically for programming for incarcerated individuals, particularly mental health treatment. Correctional institutions require more assistance and collaboration with their local or state mental health system to implement evidence-based treatment programs to address the specific needs of incarcerated individuals. Most correctional institutions require screening for preexisting mental or medical conditions at the point of intake (Lurigio & Swartz, 2006). However, there is currently no routine, standardized screening for autism or ID. Such instruments can be included at intake (Michna & Trestman, 2016). Follow-up screenings should also take place to ensure screening reliability and detect future mental health conditions.

Consider Alternate Housing

Although most facilities have separate units for mental health populations, such units should be as therapeutic as possible and adequately staffed with mental health professionals. Such units provide safety for all parties. If a facility has several incarcerated individuals with NDDs or sensory issues, if feasible, separate housing or wings for those with similar conditions or needs could help improve the environment for both incarcerated individuals and correctional staff. Housing those with NDDs with others who are behaving violently or exhibiting destructive behaviors can increase the risk of victimization or escalate volatile situations. Those with autism or ID may not be able to fully understand their victimization risk, which, in turn, requires continuous supervision among officers, adding to their occupational stress level (Michna & Trestman, 2016; Minick, 2020). Separate housing environments can also be modified to reduce lighting or other stimuli to decrease sensory overload and potential behavioral problems.

Conclusion

By incarcerating high percentages of individuals with mental illnesses, SUDs, and other disabilities, particularly for nonviolent offenses, without providing adequate treatment and care, the US risks reverting to practices that Dorthea Dix protested. Correctional institutions without specialized units staffed with adequate mental health professionals are not suitable environments for individuals with mental illnesses. Those with disabilities require specialized units to protect them from victimization. In the case of Charlie, he was exposed to other violent individuals, and he was sexually victimized, leading to a subsequent mental illness because of the trauma he endured. The Standard Minimum Rules or the Treatment of Prisoners (Nelson Mandela Rules) (2015) supports the human rights of those incarcerated and respects their dignity as human beings. As MacDonald and Stöver (2005) affirmed, "People go to prison as punishment, not for punishment" (p. 1).

Incarceration is often necessary for public safety, but those with mental illnesses or SUDs require additional care and treatment. A proactive approach avoids waiting for litigation due to civil rights violations to compel correctional facilities to implement proper procedures and program changes. Adequate mental health care promotes the humane treatment that Dix advocated for nearly 200 years ago by not allowing individuals to languish in jail or prison with mental health or withdrawal systems. People with mental illnesses and SUDs can also be diverted with the use of specialized probation and specialty courts, as outlined in Chapter 14. These alternative approaches require a shift from a strict retribution mindset to a rehabilitation perspective. The cognitive and mental health differences that affected the eligibility of capital punishment demonstrate that specific populations of justice-involved individuals are different and should be handled/treated differently by the CJS to protect civil and human rights.

Key Terms

Detoxification
Margin of Error
Opioid Antagonist
Segregation.
Protective Custody
Solitary Confinement
Writ of Certiorari

Chapter Questions

(1) Should all jails and prisons adopt a mandatory policy for screening for mental illnesses, SUDs, and NDDs such as autism? Explain your response.
(2) Should states and prison administrators be legally required to treat incarcerated people with SUDs? What about those who experience withdrawal symptoms? Explain your response.
(3) Describe the legal, medical, and behavioral concerns associated with incarcerated people with mental illnesses. Which of these concerns alarmed you most and why?

(4) What future work do you feel needs to be done to protect those with mental illnesses and NDDs, such as autism and ID, from experiencing victimization in prisons?
(5) How do you feel about executing those with severe mental illnesses? Should individuals be forced to take medications to make them eligible? Explain your response.

Suggested Readings

Eldridge, T. E. (2017, September 20). *When a mental health emergency lands you in jail.* The Marshall Project. https://www.themarshallproject.org/2017/09/20/when-a-mental-health-emergency-lands-you-in-jail
McAdam, P. (2012). Knowledge and understanding of the autism spectrum among prison staff. *Prison Service Journal, 202*, 26–30.
Preston, A. G., Rosenberg, A., Schlesinger, P., & Blankenship, K. M. (2022). I was reaching out for help and they did not help me: Mental healthcare in the carceral state. *Health & Justice, 10*(1), 23. https://doi.org/10.1186/s40352-022-00183-9
Walsh, J. P., & Cwick, J. M. (2018). Victimization within prison and jail facilities. In C. M. Hilinshi-Rosick & D. R. Lee (Eds.), *Contemporary issues in victimology: Identifying patterns and trends.* Lexington Books.

Notes

1. Measured with the question: "Because of a physical, mental, or emotional problem, do you have serious difficulty concentrating, remembering, or making decisions?" (Bronson et al., 2015, p. 2).
2. Name and some details have been changed for anonymity.
3. *see A Note About Evolving Language and Term* in Chapter 1 for information on identity-first language

References

Allely, C. S., & Wood, T. (2022). "Cardboard gangsters", "in crowd" and "no control": A case study of autism spectrum disorder in the prison environment.

Journal of Intellectual Disabilities and Offending Behaviour, 13(2), 57–76. https://doi.org/10.1108/JIDOB-02-2022-0002

American Medical Association. (2017). *Court-initiated medical treatment in criminal cases.* https://code-medical-ethics.ama-assn.org/ethics-opinions/court-initiated-medical-treatment-criminal-cases

Americans With Disabilities Act, 42 U.S.C. § 12101 et seq. (1990).

Arrigo, B. A., & Bullock, J. L. (2008). The psychological effects of solitary confinement on prisoners in supermax units: Reviewing what we know and recommending what we should change. *International Journal of Offender Therapy and Comparative Criminology, 52*(6), 622–640.

Appelbaum, K. L., Savageau, J. A., Trestman, R. L., Metzner, J., & Baillargeon, J. (2011). A national survey of self-injurious behavior in American prisons. *Psychiatric Services, 62*, 285–290. https://doi.org/10.1176/appi.ps.62.3.285

Atkins v. Virginia, 536 U.S. 304. (2002).

Bandara, S., Kennedy-Hendricks, A., Merritt, S., Barry, C. L., & Saloner, B. (2021). Methadone and buprenorphine treatment in United States jails and prisons: Lessons from early adopters. *Addiction, 116*(12), 3473–3481. https://doi.org/10.1111/add.15565

Beaudry, G., Yu, R., Perry, A. E., & Fazel, S. (2021). Effectiveness of psychological interventions in prison to reduce recidivism: A systematic review and meta-analysis of randomised controlled trials. *The Lancet Psychiatry, 8*(9), 759–773. https://doi.org/10.1016/S2215-0366(21)00170-X

Bronson, J., & Berzofsky, L. M. (2015). *Disabilities among prison and jail inmates, 2011–12.* U.S. Department of Justice, Office of Justice Programs, Bureau of Justice Statistics.

Bronson, J., & Berzofsky, L. M. (2017). *Indicators of mental health problems reported by prisoners and jail inmates, 2011–12.* U.S. Department of Justice, Office of Justice Programs, Bureau of Justice Statistics.

Bronson, J., Stroop, J., Zimmer, S., & Berzofsky, L. M. (2017). *Drug use, dependence, and abuse among state prisoners and jail inmates, 2007–2009.* Department of Justice, Office of Justice Programs, Bureau of Justice Statistics.

Buehler, E. D., & Kottke-Weaver, S. (2024). *Sexual victimization reported by adult correctional authorities, 2019–2020—Statistical tables.* U.S. Department of Justice, Office of Justice Programs, Bureau of Justice Statistics.

Carson, A., & Kluckow, R. (2023). *Correctional populations in the United States, 2021—Statistical tables.* Department of Justice. Office of Justice Programs, Bureau of Justice Statistics.

Chaplin, E., McCarthy, J., Underwood, L., Forrester, A., Hayward, H., Sabet, J., Mills, R., Young, S., Asherson, P., & Murphy, D. (2017). Characteristics of prisoners with intellectual disabilities. *Journal of Intellectual Disability, 61*(12), 1185–1195. https://doi.org/10.1111/jir.12441

Dear, G. E., Thomson, D. M., & Hills, A. M. (2000). Self-harm in prison: Manipulators can also be suicide attempters. *Criminal Justice and Behavior, 27*(2), 160–175. https://doi.org/10.1177/0093854800027002002

Death Penalty Information Center. (2024). https://deathpenaltyinfo.org/

DeHart, D. D., Smith, H. P., & Kaminski, R. J. (2009). Institutional responses to self-injurious behavior among inmates. *Journal of Correctional Health Care, 15*(2), 129–160. https://doi.org/10.1177/1078345809331444

Ditton, P. M. (1999). *Mental health and treatment of inmates and probationers.* U.S. Department of Justice, Office of Justice Programs, Bureau of Justice Statistics.

Dlugacz, H. (2018). Jail and prison conditions. In E. Kelley (Ed.), *Representing people with mental disabilities: A criminal defense lawyer's best practices manual* (pp. 225–247). ABA Publishing.

D.M. v. Terhune, 67 F. Supp. 2d 401. (D.N.J. 1999).

Equal Justice Initiative. (2024). *Recent rulings in some states bar death penalty for people with serious mental illness.* https://eji.org/news/recent-rulings-in-some-states-bar-death-penalty-for-people-with-serious-mental-illness/

Eisner, C. (2020, November 2). Prison is even worse when you have a disability like autism. *The Marshall Project.* https://www.themarshallproject.org/2020/11/02/prison-is-even-worse-when-you-have-a-disability-like-autism

Estelle v. Gamble, 429 U.S. 97. (1976).

Everington, C., & Olley, J. G. (2008). Implications of Atkins v. Virginia: Issues in defining and diagnosing mental retardation. *Journal of Forensic Psychology Practice, 8*(1), 1–23. https://doi-org.library.georgian.edu/10.1080/15228930801947278

Favazza, A. R., & Rosenthal, R. J. (1993). Diagnostic issues in self-mutilation. *Hospital & Community Psychiatry, 44*(2), 134–140. https://doi.org/10.1176/ps.44.2.134

Fiscella, K., Pless, N., Meldrum, S., & Fiscella, P. (2004). Alcohol and opiate withdrawal in US jails. *American Journal of Public Health, 94*(9), 1522–1524. https://doi.org/10.2105/ajph.94.9.1522

Ford v. Wainwright, 477 U.S. 399. (1986).

Hall v. Florida, 572 U.S. 701. (2014).

Haney, C. (2003). Mental health issues in long-term solitary and "supermax" confinement. *Crime & Delinquency, 49*(1), 124–156. https://doi.org/10.1177/0011128702239239

Haney, C. (2006). *Reforming punishment: Psychological limitations to the pains of imprisonment.* American Psychological Association.

Holmes, S. T., & Holmes, R. M. (2009). *Sex crimes: Patterns and behavior* (3rd Ed). Sage Publications.

James, D. J., & Glaze, L. E. (2006). *Mental health problems of prison and jail inmates.* U.S. Department of Justice, Office of Justice Programs, Bureau of Justice Statistics.

Kaplan, A. B., Collins, P. A., & Mayhew, V. L. (2016). *Oregon's death penalty: A cost analysis.* https://doi.org/10.2139/ssrn.2926131

Kelly, C. E., & Welsh, W. N. (2016). Examining treatment climate across prison-based substance abuse treatment groups. *Substance Use & Misuse, 51*(7), 902–911. https://doi.org/10.3109/10826084.2016.1155621

Kelly, C. E., Welsh, W. N., & Stanley, J. N. (2019). The treatment group and recidivism: A multilevel analysis of prison-based substance abuse treatment. *The Prison Journal, 99*(5), 515–534.https://doi.org/10.1177/0032885519875002

Kerle, K. E., & Ford, F. R. (1982). *The state of our nation's jails.* National Sheriffs Association.

Lavoie, J. A., Connolly, D. A., & Roesch, R. (2006). Correctional officers' perceptions of inmates with mental illness: The role of training and burnout syndrome. *International Journal of Forensic Mental Health, 5*(2), 151–166. https://doi.org/10.1080/14999013.2006.10471239

Lim, S., Cherian, T., Katyal, M., Goldfeld, K. S., McDonald, R., Wiewel, E., Khan, M., Krawczyk, N., Braunstein, S., Murphy, S. M., Jalali, A., Jeng, P. J., MacDonald, R., & Lee, J. D. (2023). Association between jail-based methadone or buprenorphine treatment for opioid use disorder and overdose mortality after release from New York city jails 2011–17. *Addiction, 118*(3), 459–467. https://doi.org/10.1111/add.16071

Lurigio, A. J., & Swartz, J. A. (2006). Mental illness in correctional populations: The use of standardized screening tools for further evaluation or treatment. *Federal Probation, 70*(2), 29–35.

MacDonald, M., & Stöver, H. (2005). Editorial. *International Journal of Prisoner Health, 1*(2–4), 99–101. https://doi.org/10.1080/17449200600552821

Madison v. Alabama, 586 U.S. (2019).

Maruschak, L. M., Bronson, J., & Alper, M. (2021). *Survey of prison inmates, 2016 alcohol and drug use and treatment reported by prisoners.* U.S. Department of Justice, Office of Justice Programs, Bureau of Justice Statistics.

Mentally Ill Offender Treatment and Crime Reduction Act (S. 1194). (2004).

Meyer, C. L., Tangney, J. P., Stuewig, J., & Moore, K. E. (2014). Why do some jail inmates not engage in treatment and services? *International Journal of Offender Therapy and Comparative Criminology, 58*(8), 914–930. https://doi.org/10.1177/0306624X13489828

McLeod, K. E., & Martin, R. E. (2020). Solitary confinement, post-release health, and the urgent need for further research. *The Lancet Public Health, 5*(2), e74–e75. https://doi.org/10.1016/S2468-2667(20)30009-8

Michna, I., & Trestman, R. (2016). Correctional management and treatment of autism spectrum disorder. *The Journal of the American Academy of Psychiatry and the Law, 44*(2), 253–258. https://jaapl.org/content/44/2/253

Miller, H. A., & McCoy, L. (2013). Inmates under protective custody. In L. Gideon (Ed.), *Special needs offenders in correctional institutions* (pp. 259–283). Sage Publications.

Minick, D. (2020). Note, intellectually or developmentally disabled in jail: The need for reform in Texas jails. *Thomas Jefferson Law Review, 86*, 85–123.

National Commission on Correctional Health Care. (2016). *Solitary Confinement.* https://www.ncchc.org/position-statements/solitary-confinement-isolation-2016/

National Prison Rape Elimination Commission Report. (2009). https://www.prearesourcecenter.org/resource/national-prison-rape-elimination-commission-report

Newman, C., Cashin, A., & Waters, C. (2015). A hermeneutic phenomenological examination of the lived experience of incarceration for those with autism. *Issues in Mental Health Nursing, 36*(8), 632–640. https://doi.org/10.3109/01612840.2015.1014587

Newman v. State of Alabama, 349 F. Supp. 278 (M.D. Ala.). (1972).

Panetti v. Quarterman, 551 U.S. 930. (2007).

Pare, P. P., & Logan, M. W. (2011). Risks of minor and serious violent victimization in prison: The impact of inmates' mental disorders, physical disabilities, and physical size. *Society and Mental Health, 1*(2), 106–123. https://doi.org/10.1177/2156869311416828

Peraire, M., Cantos, P., Sampedro-Vidal, M., Bonet-Mora, L., & Arnau-Peiró, F. (2023). Characterization of autism spectrum disorder inside prison. *Revista espanola de sanidad penitenciaria, 25*(1), 30–39. https://doi.org/10.18176/resp.00064

Paterson, P. (2008). How well do young offenders with Asperger syndrome cope in custody? Two prison case studies. *British Journal of Learning Disability, 36*, 54–58.

Powledge, F. (1972). *The seeds of anguish: An ACLU study of the D.C. jail*. American Civil Liberties Union.

President's Commission on Law Enforcement and Administration of Justice. (1967). *The challenge of crime in a free society*. U.S. Department of Justice, Office of Justice Programs. https://www.ojp.gov/ncjrs/virtual-library/abstracts/challenge-crime-free-society

Prison Litigation Reform Act, 42 U.S.C.§. (1997).

Prison Rape Elimination Act, P.L. 108–79. (2003).

Protecting Inmates and Safeguarding Communities Discretionary Grant Program. (2004). U.S. Department of Justice.

Rapley, M. (2004). The social construction of intellectual disability. *Cambridge University Press*. https://doi.org/10.1017/CBO9780511489884

Rehabilitation Act, Pub. L. 93–112. (1973).

Reingle Gonzalez, J. M., & Connell, N. M. (2014). Mental health of prisoners: Identifying barriers to mental health treatment and medication continuity. *American Journal of Public Health, 104*(12), 2328–2333. https://doi.org/10.2105/AJPH.2014.302043

Robertson, C. E., & McGillivray, J. A. (2015). Autism behind bars: A review of the research literature and discussion of key issues. *The Journal of Forensic Psychiatry & Psychology, 26*(6), 719–736. https://doi.org/10.1080/14789949.2015.1062994

Roper v. Simmons, 543 U.S. 551. (2005).

Punishment of people with serious mental illness in New York state Prisons. (2022, May). *An analysis of 2017–19 disciplinary data in prison residential mental health treatment units*. https://drive.google.com/file/d/16yzZ-LJ8-JwVBvG3ptPlfu6kUfJw01CL/view?pli=1

Scavone, C. E. (2022). Battleground of the opioid crisis: The eighth amendment right to medication-assisted treatment in prisons and jails, and upon release.

Emory Law Journal, 71(6), 1273–1319. https://scholarlycommons.law.emory.edu/elj/vol71/iss6/4

Schappell, A., Docherty, M., & Boxer, P. (2016). Violence and victimization during incarceration: Relations to psychosocial adjustment during reentry to the community. *Violence and Victims, 31*(2), 361–378. https://doi.org/10.1891/0886-6708.VV-D-13-00188

Schwartzapfel, B. (2017, March 1). A better way to treat addiction in jail. *The Marshall Project.* https://www.themarshallproject.org/2017/03/01/a-better-way-to-treat-addiction-in-jail

Singleton v. Norris, 319 F.3d 1018. (8th Cir. 2003).

Smith, H. P., & Kaminski, R. J. (2010). Inmate self-injurious behaviors: Distinguishing characteristics within a retrospective study. *Criminal Justice and Behavior, 37*(1), 81–96. https://doi.org/10.1177/0093854809348474

Snell, T. N. (2021). *Capital punishment, 2020—Statistical tables.* U.S. Department of Justice, Office of Justice Programs, Bureau of Justice Statistics.

Stanford v. Kentucky, 492 U.S. 361. (1989).

Steinwald, C., & Alevizon, G. (1973). *Medical care in U.S. jails—A 1972 AMA survey*. American Medical Association.

Taylor, L. R., Lee, J., & Taxman, F. S. (2019). Participant and program characteristics: Correlates of substance abuse treatment participation and prison misconducts. *The Prison Journal, 99*(1), 3–25. https://doi.org/10.1177/0032885518814704

Torrey, E. F., Kennard, A. D., Eslinger, D., Lamb, R. H., & Pavie, J. (2010). *More mentally ill persons are in jails and prisons than hospitals: A survey of the states.* Treatment Advocacy Center. https://www.ojp.gov/ncjrs/virtual-library/abstracts/more-mentally-ill-persons-are-jails-and-prisons-hospitals-survey

Torrey, E. F., Zdanowicz, M. T., Kennard, A. D., Lamb, R. H., Eslinger, D., Biasotti, M. C., & Fuller, D. A. (2014). *The treatment of persons with mental illness in prisons and jails: A state survey.* Treatment Advocacy Center. https://www.treatmentadvocacycenter.org/reports_publications/the-treatment-of-persons-with-mental-ilnnes-in-prisons-and-jails-a-state-survey/

van Wormer, K. S., & Persson, L. (2010). Drug treatment within the U.S. federal prison system: Are treatment needs being met? *Journal of Offender Rehabilitation, 49*, 363–375. https://doi.org/10.1080/10509674.2010.489472

Vinter, L. P., Dillon, G., & Winder, B. (2023). 'People don't like you when you're different': Exploring the prison experiences of autistic individuals. *Psychology, Crime & Law, 29*(3), 243–262. https://doi.org/10.1080/1068316X.2020.1781119

Vogelman, R. P. (1968). Prison restrictions—Prisoner rights. *The Journal of Criminal Law, Criminology, and Police Science, 59*(3), 386–396. https://doi.org/10.2307/1141762

Welsh, W. N. (2010). Inmate responses to prison-based drug treatment: A repeated measures analysis. *Drug and Alcohol Dependence, 109*(1–3), 37–44. https://doi.org/10.1016/j.drugalcdep.2009.11.024

Welsh, W. N., Zajac, G., & Bucklen, K. B. (2014). For whom does prison-based drug treatment work? Results from a randomized experiment. *Journal of Experimental Criminology, 10*, 151–177. https://doi.org/10.1007/s11292-013-9194-z

Wolff, N., Shi, J., Blitz, C. L., & Siegel, J. (2007). Understanding sexual victimization inside prisons: Factors that predict risk. *Criminology & Public Policy, 6*, 535–564.

Young, S., González, R. A., Mullens, H., Mutch, L., Malet-Lambert, I., & Gudjonsson, G. H. (2018). Neurodevelopmental disorders in prison inmates: Comorbidity and combined associations with psychiatric symptoms and behavioural disturbance. *Psychiatry Research, 261*, 109–115. https://doi.org/10.1016/j.psychres.2017.12.036

Zhong, S., Senior, M., Yu, R., Perry, A., Hawton, K., Shaw, J., & Fazel, S. (2021). Risk factors for suicide in prisons: A systematic review and meta-analysis. *The Lancet Public Health, 6*(3), e164–e174. https://doi.org/10.1016/S2468-2667(20)30233-4

Glossary

Ableism Discrimination or prejudice against people with disabilities in favor of persons without any disabilities.

Acquiescence/Acquiesce Tendency to say agree or say "yes" to every question, regardless of whether it is true.

Actus rea Latin for "guilty act," which refers to the act or omission that forms the physical element of a crime.

Addiction Non-clinical or diagnostic term to describe compulsive or habitual use of a substance.

Adjudication hearing Juvenile court hearing where the factfinder (judge) determines the juvenile's guilt.

Adolescent-limited Those who exhibit delinquency or antisocial behavior only during adolescence.

Affidavit Sworn statement to the court.

Alcoholics Anonymous® A peer-led fellowship group founded in 1935 that is dedicated to abstinence-based recovery from alcohol use disorder, through spirituality and a twelve-step program to achieve and maintain sobriety.

Amici curiae Latin for "friend of the court." An individual or organization assists the court by offering information, expertise, or insight on the issues in the case for the plaintiff, prosecutor, or defense.

Antisocial personality disorder DSM-5 diagnosis describes individuals who habitually violate rules, norms, laws, or socially acceptable behavior, disregarding the rights and considerations of others, often lacking feelings of guilt or remorse.

Aphasia Language disorder that affects both spoken and written communication, usually caused by a brain injury due to stroke or head trauma.

M. C. Mogavero, *Mental Health, Neurodiversity, and Criminal Justice*, https://doi.org/10.1007/978-3-031-88816-8

Appellate court Also called a court of appeal(s), empowered to review a case upon appeal from a trial court. In criminal cases, they can grant the defendant a new trial or order their release.

Arraignment First court appearance after an arrest; defendant is provided the charges against them and the defendant enters a plea to the charges (e.g., guilty or not guilty).

Asperger's syndrome Formerly used diagnosis for someone with a neurodevelopmental disorder for one who exhibits deficits in communication, socialization, and the presence of restricted and repetitive patterns of behavior but often has typical cognitive development, age-appropriate self-help skills, and often had average or above-average intelligence.

Asylum Term formally used to describe a mental or psychiatric hospital that provides shelter and support for people with mental health disorders, disabilities, and conditions such as epilepsy and dementia.

Attention deficit/hyperactivity disorder (ADHD) Neurodevelopmental disability disorder is characterized by having difficulty paying attention, excessive activity, and poor impulse control.

Auburn plan Prison model designed to keep those incarcerated separate and unable to communicate with each other and were forced to labor during the day.

Autism spectrum disorder Neurodevelopmental disability disorder that is characterized by deficits in communication, socialization, and the presence of restricted and repetitive patterns of behavior.

Bail Security or collateral, usually in the form of money or other assets, is exchanged for the release of a detained person as a guarantee they appear in court.

Battered partner syndrome Formally referred to as battered woman syndrome and battered spouse syndrome; the pattern of signs and symptoms displayed by one who has experienced persistent intimate partner violence and a form of posttraumatic stress disorder (PTSD)

Bench trial Trial where the determination of a verdict of guilty or not guilty is by a judge, as opposed to a trial by jury.

Bipolar disorder Mental disorder diagnosis characterized by periods of depression and an abnormally elevated mood, which may last from days to weeks.

Capacity Possessing the mental ability to make autonomous choices.

Catatonic Decrease in reactivity to the environment, which may include resistance to instructions, maintaining a rigid, inappropriate, or bizarre posture; a complete lack of verbal responses (mutism), or a complete lack of motor responses (stupor).

Child saving Social movement of the early nineteenth century that influenced the development of the juvenile justice system. The movement intervened in the form of redemption with children who were dependent, neglected, or engage in deviant behavior.

Choice blindness When one can cannot remember or can be misled about one's own memories or self-reported choices

Civil trial Legal process in court before a judge or jury to resolve disputes between private parties, such as individuals or organizations.

Closed-circuit television (CCTV) Also known as video surveillance, where video cameras transmit a signal to a specific place on a monitor or TV screen.

Closed-ended questions Respondents are provided a list of responses to questions to choose from

Cocaine Illegal stimulant (powdered) substance derived from coca leaves that can be snorted, injected, or smoked. Mainly used as a recreational substance and causes feelings of euphoria.

Coerced-compliant false confession Confesses to a crime one did not commit to escape from the stress of the interrogation to avoid a perceived threat of harm or punishment or to gain a reward, such as being allowed to sleep or eat.

Coerced-internalized false confessions Confesses to a crime they did not commit, usually one with a malleable memory due to youth, interpersonal trust, naiveté, suggestibility, low intelligence, fatigue, and alcohol or substance use.

Cognitive interview Seven-phase technique of interviewing witnesses and victims about what they remember about an event.

Collective efficacy Form social control where cohesive communities communicate and socialize together, effectively supervise children, and control crime and delinquency.

Community oriented policing Policing strategy that emphasizes developing relationships with community members.

Competency Legal term that refers to one's mental ability to participate in legal proceedings or transactions.

Concurrent jurisdiction Prosecutor has discretion to file cases in either criminal or juvenile court.

Confabulation Someone subconsciously creates an untrue story or scenario in response to a specific question because they do not know the answer, to conceal the truth, or to fill in the gaps in their memory.

Confrontation Clause Clause in the Sixth Amendment of the US Constitution; allows defendants the right to confront their accusers and witnesses and to cross-examine them in court.

Constables One of the earliest peace officer roles created, and their duty was to keep the peace and serve papers issued by the courts.

Continuance Postponement of a hearing or trial, typically requested by the defendant/defense attorney for more time to prepare for a defense.

Counterfeit deviance Concept that suggests that inappropriate or criminal sexual behavior by those with disabilities may be the result of factors other than sexual urges, fantasies, or paraphilias.

Crack cocaine Rock crystal form of cocaine that is less expensive than the powdered form.

Credibility Characteristics or qualities that make someone worthy of believing (e.g., statements or accusations).

Crisis Intervention Team Partnership program between police, mental health professionals, substance use professionals, and other partners to improve community responses to mental health crises.

Cross-examination Questioning of a witness called to testify by the opposing attorney.

Custodial interrogation Suspect is questioned while "in custody" and is not free to leave.

Cycle of violence Pattern in abusive relationships, where phases of tension, battering incident, and reconciliation repeat

Decisional competency Mental ability to make one's own autonomous decisions in their case, including whether to enter a plea agreement, have a jury trial, a bench trial, or testify on their own behalf.

De-escalation Process or system of techniques police use to calm the situation before it becomes worse.

Deinstitutionalization Policy that began after the Civil Rights Movement, where the care and treatment for those with mental disorders or developmental disabilities in psychiatric hospitals were replaced with community mental health services. For juveniles, the removal of those who commit status offenses or non-noncriminal acts from detention facilities.

Delayed gratification Ability to resist an impulse for an immediate reward, with the intent to obtaining a higher-valued reward in the future.

Delusional disorder Mental disorder diagnosis and a type of psychotic disorder where an individual displays one or more delusions for one month or longer

Delusions False beliefs that are not amenable to change, even when presented with conflicting evidence, and there are generally several types, including Persecutory, Erotomania, Grandiose, Referential, Nihilistic, and Somatic

Dementia Group of diseases and illnesses that occur with age that affect thinking, memory, reasoning, personality, mood, and behavior.

Depersonalization Condition or phenomenon where one feels disconnected from oneself and one's environment.

Depression/Major depressive disorder Metal disorder that affects mood and is characterized by symptoms that include overwhelming sadness, poor appetite or overeating, insomnia or hypersomnia, low energy, fatigue, poor concentration, and feelings of hopelessness.

Deterrence/Deterrent Discouraging or preventing crime or delinquency by instilling fear of punishment or other negative consequences to discourage, prevent, or inhibit criminal behavior.

Detoxification Also referred to as withdrawal treatment, the first stage of treatment for those with substance use disorders and is a process of clearing substances from the body.

Diagnostic and Statistical Manual of Mental Disorders Diagnostic Reference book for epidemiology, health management, and clinical purposes on mental health and brain-related conditions and disorders, published by the American Psychiatric Association (APA).

Direct examination Initial questioning by the attorney who calls the witness to testify to provide evidence and facts in support of their case.

Disability rights movement Social movement that began after the Civil Rights Movement to seek equal rights and opportunities for people with disabilities.

Discretion Latitude or freedom to make legal decisions; examples include police deciding to stop, arrest, or pursue a suspect or the prosecutor deciding to pursue a case.

Disposition Juvenile court term of the court's decision on what sanction or treatment will be court-ordered.

Double jeopardy Clause in the Fifth Amendment to the US Constitution; prohibits individuals from being prosecuted twice for th same offense.

Double negative questions Two negative forms of questions by adding a negation to a verb and a modifier to the noun.

Double-barreled questions Two questions in one question but only allowing one response.

Double-anonymous/blind When neither the witness or the person conducting the lineup or photospread is aware the suspect is present.

Drug Substance (other than food) that affects the body or mind.

Durham rule or Product test Standard of legal responsibility where defendants are considered not criminally responsible because the criminal act was the product of a mental disease.

Elopement/Eloping Sometimes referred to as wandering, is when an individual, typically a child or someone with a disability, leaves a predetermined area without the permission or supervision of caregivers.

Estimator variables Factors that affect eyewitness accuracy that are not under the control of the criminal justice system, such as time of day or the amount of time the witness viewed the suspect.

Eugenics From the Greek word, "well-born." Belief system based on genetics, aimed to improve genetic quality of a human population by limiting marriage or procreation among those believed to be of lower genetic quality, typically those with mental illnesses and disabilities.

Eugenics movement Social and political movement that began in the late 1800s rooted in the biological determinist ideas of Sir Francis Galton, to improve the genetic quality of a human population using the concept of being "well-born."

Ex parte Without the presence or participation of the opposing party

Ex post-facto Latin for "a thing done afterward." Article 1 of the US Constitution, Sect. 9 (U.S. Government) and Sect. 10 (States) prohibit criminal statutes that punish acts retroactively which criminalizes acts that were legal when originally committed.

Excuse defenses Category of legal defenses where defendants do not deny they committed the offense but claim they should not be held legally responsible or less responsible because of an excuse, such as they lacked the mental capacity.

Executive functions Higher-level mental skills and processes that develop in the brain's medial prefrontal cortex (mPFC), and are responsible for functions such as planning, decision-making, problem-solving, and impulse control.

False confession Suspect confesses to a crime they did not commit.

Flashbacks Intense and involuntary memories where individuals feel they are reliving a traumatic event. The memories can involve visually seeing the event in their mind and may also experience other physical sensations that they experienced during the event (e.g., smells, sounds).

Foils/Fillers The known innocent persons present in the lineup or photospread.

Forensic Relating to or used in the law, often when applying scientific principles and practices to the judicial process.

Forensic psychology Application of psychological science and the psychology profession to the law and the legal system.

Free will Ability to choose between different possible actions or behaviors.

Functional magnetic resonance imaging or fMRI Radiology tool used to detect changes in magnetic properties associated with blood flow in the brain, brain activity, or the degree of functional connectivity between brain regions.

General deterrence Using punishments to instill fear so that individuals will avoid committing crimes in the future.

Good time Earned time off a sentence or period of incarceration for participation in productive activities, programs, following prison rules, and participating in required activities.

Grand jury hearing Formal preceding where a jury of citizens hears the state's evidence and decides whether there is enough evidence to charge the defendant and require the defendant to stand trial.

Guilty But Insane/ "Mentally Ill" Alternative to the defense of not criminally responsible that allows for a finding of guilt but a reduction in either the seriousness of the charge or the severity of the punishment if one's mental disorder was determined to have influenced the criminal act.

Habilitation Treatment that involves the developement of new skills and abilities that have not yet developed to better control behavior, including new and effective ways to manage their emotions and impulses.

Hallucinations Involuntary experiences that involve one's sensory perceptions that occur without an external stimulus. They can occur among any of the five senses, but auditory and visual are the most common.

Hearsay Secondhand evidence where one does not state what they personally know or have seen or heard, but what others have said to them.

Identity-first language Stating a person's condition first with the idea that the condition is an integral part of a person's identity and should be emphasized rather than minimized.

Immigration Traveling from one country to another for permanent residence.

Incapacitation Restricting individuals' freedoms so they are incapable of committing future crimes.

Indeterminate sentence Sentence that is not a fixed amount of time but a range of years, and the release date is open.

Indigent Individuals arrested for a crime and cannot afford the fees associated with a defense lawyer.

Industrialization Economy transformation from agriculture to manufacturing resulting from improved technology and increased trade.

Informal social controls Sanctions from individuals or social groups, such as peers, family, or community members, which ensure compliance with social norms and do not generally involve the justice system.

Intelligence Quotient (IQ) Score obtained by administering an intelligence test to determine how an individual performs intellectually at a specific age (years/months), referred to as their "mental age." The score was obtained by dividing a person's mental age score by the person's chronological age (years/months), then the fraction (quotient) was multiplied by 100.

International Classification of Diseases Globally used diagnostic tool for epidemiology, health management, and clinical purposes maintained by the World Health Organization

Interrogation Formal and accusatory manner of questioning in which the investigator attempts to elicit truthful information about the suspect's involvement in a crime.

Interrogative suggestibility Accepts messages communicated during formal questioning (e.g., accused of participating in a crime), and this acceptance affects subsequent behavioral responses.

Intersectionality Sociological construct to describe how the complexities of one's identity combine, overlap, and intersect, which can lead to experiencing multiple forms of discrimination among marginalized individuals or groups (e.g., racism, sexism, classism, ableism).

Interview Informal line of questioning of a suspect related to a criminal matter.

Intimate partner violence Physical, sexual, or psychological violence/abuse between romantic or sexual partners

Intoxication Temporary changes in the body, including physiological responses behavior, emotion, or thoughts caused by ingesting substances.

Involuntary civil commitment Contested judicial process by which a person, due to acute mental health disorder, disease, or disability, poses a danger to self or others and is directed by a court order to remain in a secure treatment facility for a specified time.

Involuntary medication Judicial process in which a judge decides if medication is necessary for a patients safety or and should be ordered to restore the defendant's mental competency to proceed with a criminal prosecution.

Irresistible impulse test Standard of legal responsibility where the defendants know what they were doing, knew it was wrong, but could not control their behavior to avoid committing the crime.

Judicial waiver Formal procedure where a juvenile court judge waives court jurisdiction from the juvenile court to criminal court.

Jurisdiction Legal authority of a local, state or federal government.

Juror Someone who sits on a jury.

Jury Group of citizens convened to make a legal decision by findings of facts and rendering an impartial verdict.

Justification defenses Category of legal defenses where defendants do not argue whether they committed the act but claim their actions were justified and should not be held legally responsible (e.g., self-defense).

Ku Klux Klan Commonly shortened to the KKK, a White supremacist group founded by Confederate veterans in the late 1860s who assaulted and murdered Black people and their allies.

Landmark decision The majority decision of a Supreme Court case, the rule or decision becomes president and is considered a landmark decision that must now be followed in all lower courts (state and federal) in that jurisdiction.

Leading questions Questions that encourage someone to answer in a particular way.

Learned optimism Formally referred to as learned helplessness, but the focus is on a positive state of mind where one believes they are capable of changing their circumstances after repeatedly experiencing a stressful event.

Leucotomy/Lobotomy Surgical procedure used to treat mental health disorders by cutting brain tissue in the frontal lobe.

Lex talionis Latin for "the law of retaliation." A legal concept that the severity of a punishment for a crime should be proportional to the severity of the crime.

Life-course persistent Those who begin antisocial behaviors and delinquency in childhood or adolescence and continue criminal behavior into adulthood.

Loco parentis Latin for "in [the] place of a parent" where the judge or court acts in place of the child's parent for the "best interests of the child"

M'Naghten rule Standard of legal responsibility where the defendants are considered not responsible if they were experiencing a disease of the mind (i.e., a mental disorder), which causes impairment in terms of either (a) not understanding the nature and quality of their actions or (b) not knowing that those actions were wrong

Malingering Pretending or exaggerating one's psychological or physical symptoms, usually motivated by some incentives.

Mania State of abnormally elevated mood or arousal, affect, and energy levels.

Margin of error Statistical term that quantifies the amount of error in measure and provides a range of numbers where the true measure is expected to fall.

Masking Techniques, strategies, and processes of hiding or suppressing one's disability or mental illness.

Maturity gap Difference or disconnection between an adolescent's biological and social maturity.

Medial forebrain bundle Structure of the brain comprised of the ventral segmental area, nucleus accumbens, ventral segmental, locus coeruleus, and the amygdala.

Medial prefrontal cortex Part of the brain responsible for executive functions such as planning, decision-making, and impulse control.

Memory blindness Having no memory of something they witness and are unable to recall the event or any details of the event.

Memory distrust syndrome Individual doubts or does not trust the accuracy of one's own memory, including the content or context of events and often depend on outside sources of information to fill in the gaps.

Mens rea Latin for "guilty mind," refers to the mental element or the intent of the act or behavior.

Mental disorder Syndrome that causes dysfunction in the psychological, biological, or developmental processes characterized by clinically significant disturbance in an individual's cognition, emotion regulation, or behavior.

Methamphetamine Potent central nervous system stimulant substance with a high potential for misuse; mainly used as a recreational substance that can cause euphoria.

Migration Broad term for traveling from one location to another for permanent residence, but typically used to describe travel within a country or crossing a border into another country.

Miranda warning Required per Miranda v. Arizona (1966); a statement where police must inform suspects of their Fifth and Sixth Amendment Constitutional rights before the onset of an interrogation. (a) you have the right to remain silent; (b) anything you say can be used against you in court; (c) you have the right to an attorney; and (d) if you cannot afford an attorney, one will be appointed for you.

Mobile crisis Community response team for those who are experiencing a mental health emergency, often work with police and other first responders.

Model Penal Code Standard of criminal responsibility where the defendant has a professional diagnosis of a mental defect and was unable to either appreciate the criminality of their conduct (did not know right from wrong) or conform their conduct to the requirements of the law (i.e., unable to control the impulse to commit the criminal act)

Needs principle Part of the Risk-Need-Responsivity model (RNR), where one's specific needs are identified, and the specific interventions address the individual's criminogenic needs because one's needs to reduce recidivism varies.

Negative eugenics Prohibiting marriage and breeding (often with sterilization) between those with "defective" genes, mainly those with disabilities, mental illness, or other illnesses or diseases, to improve the genetic quality of a human population.

Neurodevelopmental disability disorder Class of disorders that affect neurological development, causing difficulties in social, cognitive, and emotional functioning.

Neurodiversity Idea that people are neurologically different from others and simply experience and interact differently in the world around them. These differences are not viewed as deficits.

Night watch system Group of citizens who patrolled the cities at night to maintain order; e.g., watched for fires, crimes, or riots.

Nolle prosequi Latin for "to be unwilling to pursue," decision made by the prosecutor, declining to pursue the case against the defendant.

Oath Sworn promise that witnesses give in court, affirming that they will provide truthful testimony.

Open-ended questions Questions where the responder provides their own response.

Opioid antagonist Prescription medications that block the effects of opioids and support the recovery of opioid dependence and withdrawal.

Order of commitment Judicial directive (court order) specifying why a person is detained in a psychiatric medical facility for a specified period to undergo medication regime, counseling, and interventions.

Other-race effect Concept where individuals tend to have better accuracy in recognizing the faces of one's own race compared to other races.

Outpatient commitment Also known as assisted outpatient treatment, a civil court procedure where an individual with a mental illness is court-ordered to adhere to a treatment plan in the community to prevent further mental health deterioration or recurrence of behavior that is harmful to themselves or others.

Paraphrase Rephrasing or giving the same text in different words without losing the meaning of the phrase itself.

Parens patriae Latin for "parent of the state" where the government/state has the power to act as guardians or caretakers for individuals who are unable to make decisions about their own health and welfare because they are physically unable to or have a mental illness. Also where the state intervenes and acts in place of the parent to care for children when deemed necessary.

Parole board Panel of individuals who decide whether incarcerated individuals, after serving their minimum sentence, should be released from prison and serve the rest of their sentence in the community on parole.

Parole Also known as provisional release or supervised release. A type of community supervision sanction where a formerly incarcerated individuals are released from prison early and serves the rest of their sentence in the community. They must agree to abide by behavioral conditions, including checking in with their parole officers, or else they may be rearrested and returned to prison.

Patronage system Practice in which politicians (after winning an election) give government jobs to their supporters, friends, and relatives as a reward for working their victory (also known as a spoils system)

PEACE method Planning and preparation, Engage and explain, Obtain an Account, Closure, and Evaluation. An interrogation technique that is more focused on gathering information for the investigation and less confrontational, accusatory, and deceptive.

Penal welfarism Idea that criminal punishments should be rehabilitative interventions rather than negative or punitive.

Penitentiaries Large institutions that hold those who violate the law and are confined for detention, punishment, in hopes to reform individuals.

Person-first language Stating that a person has a condition, rather than a person "is" their condition. The person-first language emphasizes the person, rather than their condition, to avoid using labels or adjectives to describe someone.

Perspective Aspect of psycho-social maturity; ability to acknowledge both short-term and long-term consequences of one's actions and how those actions might affect others.

Plea bargain Formal legal agreement between the defendant and prosecutor, which must be approved by the judge where the defendant agrees to plead guilty to a reduced charge, some or all the charges against them, usually in exchange for a reduced sentence, and avoid a trial.

Pleasure center Also referred to as the "reward center" of the brain that contributes to the reinforcement of behaviors and the production of memories and is activated when an individual engages in a pleasurable activity.

Police powers Power the government has provided to police to control those who threaten public order and for the health, safety, and welfare of others.

Polygraph exam Scientific instrument used to detect deception; continuously records autonomic nervous system responses, including heart rate, blood pressure, respiration rate, and skin conductivity or electrodermal activity.

Positive eugenics Encouraging intelligent people with healthy traits to bear more children to improve the genetic quality of the human population.

Posthumous Occurring or continuing after one's death.

Post-traumatic stress disorder (PTSD) Mental disorder that may occur one month or later among those who have experienced or witnessed a traumatic event, or series of traumatic events. Symptoms include intrusive and recurrent recollections of the event, dissociative episodes of reliving the traumatic event ("flashbacks"), and nightmares. The symptoms last for more than a month after the event or experience.

Preliminary hearing Formal preceding where a judge hears the state's evidence and decides whether there is enough evidence to charge the defendant and require the defendant to stand trial.

Preponderance of the evidence Type of evidentiary standard, where the burden of proof is met when the party demonstrates the claim is true more likely than not or greater than 50%.

Privilege Protected confidential communications between an attorney and their client, and only the client has the authority to waive or invoke it.

Probable cause Type of evidentiary standard where there is enough information to warrant a reasonable belief of criminal activity to allow searches and arrests by police.

Probation Court-ordered sanction that requires defendants to be supervised in the community as an alternative to incarceration or following a period of incarceration. Defendants must agree to follow rules or conditions for the entire length of their sentence.

Procedural justice Criminal justice officials emphasizing four key principles while engaging with citizens: trust, dignity, respect, neutrality, and voice.

Proceed pro se Latin for "for self," where a defendant proceeds with their case without legal counsel or legal representation.

Protective custody Form of segregation or solitary confinement where incarcerated individuals are removed from the general prison population and placed in a solitary cell for their own protection.

Psychosocial maturity Individual's general level of adaptive functioning and socioemotional competence, attitudes, and dispositions.

Puritans Members of a reform movement known as Puritanism that emerged in England in the late sixteenth century to "purify" the church of Roman Catholic practices. They emphasized moral conduct but harsh punishments.

Quakers Members of a radical Christian sect in England in the mid-seventeenth century known as the Society of Friends, who emphasized moral conduct and humane punishment.

Racial profiling When race is the sole factor in an officer's decision to stop or investigate a citizen, particularly with traffic stops or stop and frisks.

Reasonable suspicion Type of evidentiary standard based on specific facts or circumstances that indicate criminal activity. It is a less stringent standard than probable cause.

Recidivism Broad term that refers to one who relapses or repeats criminal behavior after contact with the criminal justice system for a previously engaging in the behavior, including re-arrests, re-convictions, re-incarceration, or self-reported criminal behavior.

Rehabilitation Treatment that focuses on restoring skills that have been lost to better control their behavior and manage their emotions and impulses.

Reid technique Psychologically based interrogation techniques designed to increase the anxiety associated with denying while reducing the anxiety related to confessing.

Research evidence Information gathered and generated using established scientific methods for conducting research.

Responsibility Part of psychosocial maturation in adolescents, where individuals develop a coherent sense of identity.

Responsivity principle Part of the Risk-Need-Responsivity model (RNR), where treatment, programs, and services are tailored to meet the needs of the individual based on their characteristics (e.g., individual skills and cognitive needs) because one's ability to participate in programming varies.

Restitution Court order requiring defendants to make amends monetarily or perform acts or services that benefit the victim to restore the harm the defendant has caused.

Retributive Concept involving retaliation and punishing someone for their crimes as a form of justice.

Revocation When a probation client violates a term or condition of their probationary sentence. They may have their probationary sentence repealed and then must serve the rest of the sentence in jail or prison. This decision is made by a judge at the probation violation hearing, sometimes called the probation revocation hearing.

Risk principle Part of the Risk-Need-Responsivity model (RNR). Because one's level of recidivism risk varies, a risk assessment is conducted to identify and determine the appropriate intervention and treatment.

Risk-Need-Responsivity model Evidence-based model that develops individualized plans for justice-involved individuals, which includes how they are assessed based on the risk they present, programs or treatment, types of environments, and resources they require to reduce recidivism.

Rockefeller drug laws Statutes regarding the sale and possession of illegal drugs in the New York State Penal Law, named after Nelson Rockefeller, who was the governor at the time the laws were enacted.

Schizophrenia Mental disorder and type of psychotic disorder, characterized by reoccurring episodes of symptoms of a general misperception of reality, and often include hallucinations, delusions, and disorganized thinking and behavior.

School-to-prison pathway/pipeline Systematic displacement of juveniles from school to confinement facilities due to suspensions and expulsions brought about by zero-tolerance policies and stricter school discipline for disruptive behavior.

Schout and rattle watch system Informal system to maintain order before formal police agencies were created. Schout was a watchman whose duty was to protect private citizens, watch for infractions of laws and ordinances, and carried rattles to warn others of their presence.

Segregation unit Sometimes referred to as solitary confinement or restricted housing, where incarcerated individuals are placed in a solitary cell, sometimes for administrative reasons, behavioral problems, or they are at risk of harm.

Self-control Ability to exercise restraint over one's behavior, including impulses, emotions, or desires.

Sequential Intercept Model Framework that details how individuals with mental health and substance use disorders encounter and process through the criminal justice system with intercept points where services can intervene to support or divert.

Showups Identification procedures where victims or witnesses are presented with a suspect, either on the street or at police stations

Slave patrols Organized group of armed men who monitored and enforced discipline upon enslaved people in the southern states. Their function was to police enslaved people, especially those who escaped.

Social capital Total value individuals derive from their social network, for example, friends, parents, other family members, and coworkers.

Social control Means for a society to regulate the behavior of others through norms, rules, laws, and structures. It can be informal through the public, peers, family ensuring compliance or formal through government agencies using laws and penalties.

Socioemotional competence Ability to recognize and manage one's emotions by expressing emotions in socially appropriate ways.

Sociological jurisprudence Perspective from the sociological school of jurisprudence. A legal theory that emphasizes societal context, social-cultural values, and the effect of societal forces in developing and applying the law.

Solitary confinement Sometimes referred to as segregation or restricted housing, where incarcerated individuals are placed in a solitary cell, sometimes for administrative reasons, behavioral problems, or they are at risk of harm.

Specific deterrence Using punishments to prevent an individual from committing the same crime or any crime again in the future.

Split sentence Sentence where the defendant serves a proportion of their term of imprisonment in jail or prison and the remaining term of their sentence under community supervision probation.

Stare decisis Latin for "to stand by things decided." A doctrine that precedent cases should determine future legal decision-making in a case involving similar facts.

Status Offense Acts, based on one's age or status as a juvenile that when committed, may initiate juvenile proceedings, and include drinking alcohol, using tobacco, truancy (skipping school), running away.

Statutory exclusion Also known as legislative exclusion, a state statute that excludes certain juveniles from the juvenile court when accused of specific offenses (e.g., murder)

Sterilization Surgery performed on the reproductive organs (fallopian tubes in females and vas deferens in men) to render one incapable of reproduction.

Stimming Also known as self-stimulation, repetitive physical movements of the body, which may include the hands, moving physical objects, making sounds, or other repetitive behaviors. Stimming is common among those with neurodevelopmental disabilities such as ADHD and autism. Stimming is often a protective response to overstimulation, where those can reduce environmental stimuli to relieve anxiety and other negative or heightened emotions.

Stop and frisk Temporary seizure of an individual for a pat-down search of the outer clothing by police if they have a reasonable suspicion that the individual engaged in, or about to be involved in criminal conduct and may be armed.

Stressor Any event, situation, or occurrence that causes a stress response in the body.

Strict liability offenses Crimes in which defendants are legally liable for their actions, regardless of their intent or mental state.

Substance Term used to describe a drug, either illegal or prescribed, that affects the body or mind.

Substance-medication-induced psychotic disorder Type of psychotic disorder that is caused by using a substance or medication, characterized by the presence of one (or more) of the symptoms associated with psychotic disorder (delusions, hallucinations, disorganized speech, negative symptoms)

Suggestibility Tendency to agree or accept others' suggestions or recollection of events and may incorporate this misleading information in their memory.

Suicide by cop Term used to describe a situation when an individual who wishes to die by suicide provokes police officers to shoot them.

Suspended sentence When a jail or prison sentence is partially or entirely delayed. Defendants perform a probation period instead and must adhere to certain conditions. If the conditions are violated, the judge revokes the suspended sentence and reimposes the original term of incarceration at a hearing.

System variables Factors affecting eyewitness accuracy, such as the amount of time between the crime and identification procedure, the type of identification procedure, or how the identification procedure is conducted.

Tactical repositioning De-escalation technique where one moves away from the individual or moves to another location believed safer or lessening the level of danger to avoid or delay the use of force.

Temperance Part of psychosocial maturity in adolescents, refers to the ability to limit impulsivity and evaluate situations (short-term and long-term consequences) before acting.

Theory of learned helplessness State where one accepts their powerlessness and lack of control after enduring repeated abuse, and discontinue attempts to escape the abusive relationship, and previous attempts to escape have failed. Has since been renamed to Learned Optimism.

Theory of mind Ability to attribute mental states (beliefs, intents, desires, emotions, and knowledge) to others; allows individuals to understand that others have unique mental states that are different from their own.

Thorazine® Brand name for the drug Chlorpromazine, the first anti-psychotic drug to come to the market in the early 1950s and used primarily to treat psychotic disorders such as schizophrenia.

Tolerance When one requires an increased dose of the substance to achieve the same or desired effect or experiences a reduced effect when the usual dose is consumed.

Tory Someone who supports a political philosophy known as Toryism, based on a British version of traditionalist conservatism.

Transinstutitionalization Term used to describe the increase of individuals with mental health disorders incarcerated in jail and prisons after state hospitals closed.

Typically developed Individuals with no known disabilities or developmental delays

Ultimate opinion Judge or jury's opinion on the defendant's mental state; expert witness during testimony provides their opinion on the defendant's mental state, sometimes in terms of probability.

Under seal Information is kept confidential.

Urbanization Population shifts from rural to urban areas, leading to increasing population and infrastructure.

Use-of-force continuum Provides police officers with guidelines as to how much force may be used against a resisting individual in each situation.

Utilitarianism Idea that individuals evaluate their actions based upon their consequences to bring "pleasure" and reduce "pain."

Vaping Also known as vaporing, a method to inhale substances such as tobacco or marijuana; involves heating the plant without burning it to release psychoactive chemicals.

Voir dire French for "speak the truth," A preliminary examination of prospective jurors by a judge or attorney to decide whether they are qualified to serve.

Volitional control Ability to control one's impulses or ability to conform one's behavior or conduct to the law.

Voluntary false confession Confess to crimes they did not commit without being prompted by the police.

Withdrawal Set of physical symptoms such as nausea or vomiting, agitation, sleep difficulties (e.g., insomnia) that occur when an individual who has maintained prolonged heavy use of a substance ceases or decreases its use.

Word salad Term for incoherent or meaningless speech that lacks logical structure.

Writ of certiorari Latin for "to be more fully informed," a petition for a formal court process where a higher appellate court is requested to review the decision of a lower court.

Index of Cases

M. C. Mogavero, *Mental Health, Neurodiversity, and Criminal Justice*, https://doi.org/10.1007/978-3-031-88816-8

Index of Legislation

M. C. Mogavero, *Mental Health, Neurodiversity, and Criminal Justice*, https://doi.org/10.1007/978-3-031-88816-8

Index of People

M. C. Mogavero, *Mental Health, Neurodiversity, and Criminal Justice*, https://doi.org/10.1007/978-3-031-88816-8

Index of Terms and Topics

M. C. Mogavero, *Mental Health, Neurodiversity, and Criminal Justice*,
https://doi.org/10.1007/978-3-031-88816-8

I

J

L

T

The manufacturer's authorised representative in the EU is Springer Nature Customer Service Centre GmbH, Europaplatz 3, 69115 Heidelberg, Germany. If you have any concerns regarding our products, please contact ProductSafety@springernature.com

Printed and bound by CPI Group (UK) Ltd, Croydon, CR0 4YY

02/06/2026

02125508-0010